International Business

THE CHALLENGES OF GLOBALIZATION

SEVENTH EDITION

John J. Wild
University of Wisconsin, Madison

Kenneth L. Wild
University of London, England

PEARSON

Boston   Columbus   Indianapolis   New York   San Francisco   Upper Saddle River
Amsterdam   Cape Town   Dubai   London   Madrid   Milan   Munich   Paris   Montréal   Toronto
Delhi   Mexico City   São Paulo   Sydney   Hong Kong   Seoul   Singapore   Taipei   Tokyo

Editor in Chief: Stephanie Wall
Senior Acquisitions Editor: Kris Ellis-Levy
Editorial Project Manager: Sarah Holle
Editorial Assistant: Bernard Ollila IV
Director of Marketing: Maggie Moylan
Senior Marketing Manager: Erin Gardner
Senior Managing Editor: Judy Leale
Senior Production Project Manager: Ann Pulido
Operations Specialist: Cathleen Petersen
Creative Art Director: Blair Brown

Art Director: Steve Frim
Interior and Cover Designer: Jill Lehan
Media Project Manager, Editorial: Denise Vaughn
Media Project Manager, Production: Lisa Rinaldi
Composition/Full-Service Project Management: Haylee
  Schwenk, PreMedia Global USA, Inc.
Printer/Binder: Von Hoff. dba RRD/Jefferson City
Cover Printer: Lehigh-Phoenix Color/Hagerstown
Text Font: Times

Credits and acknowledgments borrowed from other sources and reproduced, with
permission, in this textbook appear on the appropriate page within text.

Many of the designations by manufacturers and sellers to distinguish their products are
claimed as trademarks. Where those designations appear in this book, and the publisher was
aware of a trademark claim, the designations have been printed in initial caps or all caps.

Library of Congress Cataloging-in-Publication Data
Wild, John J.
  International business : the challenges of globalization / John J. Wild, UNIVERSITY OF
WISCONSIN, MADISON, Kenneth L. Wild, UNIVERSITY OF LONDON, ENGLAND.
— seventh edition.
      pages cm
Includes bibliographical references and index.
ISBN-13: 978-0-13-306300-4 (alk. paper)
ISBN-10: 0-13-306300-3 (alk. paper)
  1. International business enterprises—Management.   2. International trade.   I. Wild,
Kenneth L.   II. Title.
  HD62.4.W586 2012b
  658'.049—dc23

                                                          2012039708

10 9 8 7 6 5 4 3 2

ISBN 10: 0-13-306300-3
ISBN 13: 978-0-13-306300-4

Brief Contents

Contents

Dear Friends and Colleagues,

As we roll out the new edition of *International Business: The Challenges of Globalization*, we thank each of you who provided suggestions to enrich this textbook. This seventh edition reflects the advice and wisdom of many dedicated reviewers and instructors. Together, we have created the most readable, concise, and innovative international business book available today.

As teachers, we know how important it is to select the right book for your course. Instructors say that this book's clear and lively writing style helps students to learn international business. And this book's streamlined and clutter-free design is a competitive advantage that will never be sacrificed.

This book's leading-edge technology package also helps students to better understand international business. MyManagementLab is an innovative set of course-management tools for delivering all or part of your course online. MyManagementLab makes it easier for you to add meaningful assessment to your course. Whether you're interested in testing your students on simple recall of concepts and theories or you'd like to gauge how well your students can apply their newly minted knowledge to real-world scenarios, MyManagementLab offers a variety of assessment questions to fit your needs. You and your students will find these and other components of this book's learning system fun and easy to use.

We owe the success of this book to our colleagues and our students who keep us focused on their changing educational needs. In this time of rapid global change, we must continue to instill in our students a passion for international business and to equip them with the skills and knowledge they need to compete. Please accept our heartfelt thanks and know that your input is reflected in everything we write.

John J. Wild

Kenneth L. Wild

Preface

Welcome to the seventh edition of *International Business: The Challenges of Globalization*. As in previous editions, this book resulted from extensive market surveys, chapter reviews, and correspondence with scores of instructors and students. We are delighted that an overwhelming number of instructors and students agree with our fresh approach to international business. The reception of this textbook in the United States and across the world has exceeded all expectations.

This book presents international business in a comprehensive yet concise framework. Real-world examples and engaging features bring the concepts of international business to life and make international business accessible for all students. A main goal in this seventh edition is to continue to deliver the most readable, current, and concise international business textbook available. And this book's paperback format ensures that its price matches a student's budget.

This book is our means of traveling on an exciting tour through the study of international business. It motivates the reader by making international business challenging yet fun. It also embraces the central role of people and their cultures in international business. Each chapter is infused with real-world discussion, while underlying theory appears in the background where it belongs. Terminology is used consistently, and theories are explained in direct and concise terms. This book's visual style is innovative yet subtle and uses photos, illustrations, and features sparingly. The result is an easy-to-read and clutter-free design.

What's New in This Edition

- This seventh edition of *International Business* updates the influence of the global credit crisis and recent recession on international business. For example, Chapter 7 presents data showing that businesses continue to shift their foreign investments away from slow-growth developed nations and toward emerging markets, such as China and India.
- A completely upgraded and redesigned Marketing Entry Strategy Project (MESP) is now integrated into and available only through MyManagementLab. The MESP asks students to work as a team to research a country market and recommend a course of action to MES-Sim Corporation.
- This edition more fully embraces the crucial role that sustainability plays in the global economy and international business. For example, the Global Sustainability feature box in Chapter 1, titled "Three Markets, Three Strategies," discusses how companies tailor their product offerings and strategies to the sustainability needs of particular markets.
- Balance of payments coverage in Chapter 7 has been simplified to improve understanding. The numbers are removed from Table 7.1 showing the balance of each U.S. Balance of Payments account. The table now shows only positive (+) or negative (−) signs depending on whether changes in an account increase or decrease its balance.
- Coverage of foreign exchange in Chapter 9 is further streamlined and made less complicated. Instructors and students appreciated the removal of extended cross rate calculations and of discounts and premiums from the last edition. We again listened to feedback and moved the section on calculating percentage change in exchange rates to an end-of-chapter appendix.
- All chapters contain the latest available data and reference sources as of the date of printing. For example, Table 5.1 in Chapter 5 presents the latest ranking of the world's top merchandise and service exporters, and Table 5.2 provides updated figures on the amount of trade that flows between different world regions.
- This edition keeps pace with current events around the world. Wherever possible, we integrate recent events into chapter-opening company profiles, tables and figures, feature boxes, in-text examples, and end-of-chapter mini cases.

Hallmark Features of International Business

Culture Early and Often

Culture is a fundamental element of all international business activity. This book's presentation of culture sensitizes students to the lives of people in other nations. Culture appears early (Chapter 2) and is integrated throughout the text using culture-rich chapter openers and lively examples of how culture affects international business. Covering culture in this way gets students interested in chapter material because it illustrates how concepts relate to the real world.

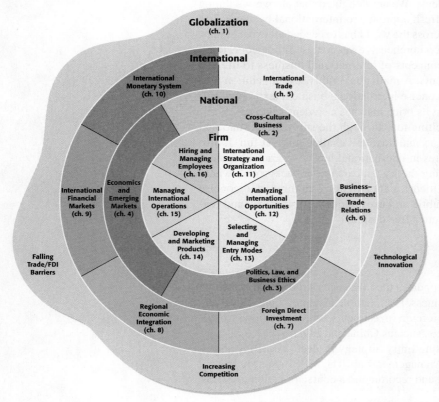

Highly Readable

A successful book for the first course in international business must be accessible to students. We describe conceptual material and specialized business activities in concrete, straightforward terms and illustrate them appropriately. For example, we introduce the concepts of absolute and comparative advantage in Chapter 5 by discussing whether a highly paid CEO should install her own hot tub or let a professional installer perform the job. This approach—presenting complex material in an accessible manner—helps students to better master the material.

Uniquely Integrative

International business is not simply a collection of separate business functions and environmental forces. The model shown here (and detailed in Chapter 1) is a unique organizing framework that helps students to understand how the elements of international business are related. It depicts a dynamic, integrated system that weaves together national business environments, the international business environment, and international business management. It also shows that characteristics of globalization (new technologies and falling barriers to trade and investment) are causing greater competition.

Market Entry Strategy Project

Completely upgraded and redesigned, this interactive simulation is now available through MyManagementLab. The MESP simulation asks students to research a country as a future market for a new video game system, the M-Box. Working as part of a team, students research and analyze a country, and then recommend a course of action to the producer of the M-Box, MES-Sim Corporation. Four activities that build on one another give instructors flexibility in the time and intensity that they wish to devote to it:

* *Market Intelligence Report (MIR)* asks students to gather market data on a nation's people, economy, government, and technological status from online sources over a one- to two-week period.
* *Business Environment Analysis Report (BEAR)* gives students the opportunity to analyze a selected country as a potential market over a four- to six-week period.
* *Report on Opportunities for Market Entry (ROME)* asks students to identify potential import and export prospects for a firm in the chosen national market over a six- to eight-week period.
* *Market Entry Strategy Assignment (MESA)* is a course-long, critical- and creative-thinking exercise that allows students to develop a market-entry strategy for launching a new product in a selected country.

Innovative Pedagogy

This book's pedagogy stands apart from the competition:

- *NEW Global Sustainability* boxes present special topics related to economic, social, and environmental sustainability. Today, businesses know that flourishing markets rely on strong economies, thriving societies, and healthy environments. Topics include the factors that contribute to sustainable development, ending civil wars that destroy fragile societies, and how companies make their supply chains more environmentally friendly.

- *Chapter-opening company profiles* are brief, easy-to-read introductions to each chapter's content filtered through the lens of a real-world example. Instructors say these profiles of high-interest firms motivate students to turn the page and get reading the chapters. Companies profiled are on the leading edge of their industries and are inherently interesting to students, including Apple, PepsiCo, Infosys, Nintendo, Ryanair, Marvel, and Red Bull.

- *Manager's Briefcase* boxes address issues facing companies active in international business. Issues presented can be relevant to entrepreneurs and small businesses or to the world's largest global companies. Topics include obtaining capital to finance international activities, getting paid for exports, and how to be mindful of personal security while abroad on business.

- *Culture Matters* boxes present the relation between culture and a key chapter topic. For example, Chapter 2 presents the importance of businesspeople developing a global mindset and avoiding cultural bias. Another chapter presents the debate over globalization's influence on culture, and still another box shows how entrepreneurs succeed by exploiting their knowledge of local cultures.

- *Bottom Line for Business* sections conclude chapters and explain the impact of the chapter's topics on managers and their firms' policies, strategies, and activities abroad.

- *Quick Study* concept checks help students to verify that they have learned the section's key terms and important concepts before moving on.

- *Full-Color World Atlas*, which appears as an appendix to Chapter 1, is a primer for students to test their knowledge of world geography and acts as a reference tool throughout the course.

CULTURE MATTERS   Creating a Global Mindset

In this era of globalization, companies need employees who function without the blinders of ethnocentricity. Here are some ways managers can develop a *global mindset*:

- **Cultural Adaptability.** Managers need the ability to alter their behavior when working with people from other cultures. The first step in doing this is to develop one's knowledge of unfamiliar cultures. The second step is to act on that knowledge to alter behavior to suit cultural expectations. The manager with a global mindset can evaluate others in a culturally unbiased way and can motivate and lead multicultural teams.

- **Bridging the Gap.** A large gap can emerge between theory and practice when Western management ideas are applied in Eastern cultures. Whereas U.S. management principles are not accepted at face value in businesses throughout the world, U.S. business customs are not. In Asia, for example, Western managers might try implementing "collective leadership" practices more in line with Asian management styles.

- **Building Global Mentality.** Companies can apply personality-testing techniques to measure the global aptitude of managers. A global-mindset test evaluates an individual's openness and flexibility, understanding of global principles, and strategic implementation abilities. It can also identify areas in which training is needed and generate a list of recommended programs.

- **Flexibility Is Key.** The more behavioral the issues, the greater the influence of local cultures. Japanese and Korean managers are more likely than U.S. managers to wait for directions and consult peers on decisions. Western managers posted in the Middle East must learn to work within a rigid hierarchy in order to be successful. And although showing respect for others is universally valued, respect is defined differently from country to country.

- **Want to Know More?** Visit the Center for Creative Leadership (www.ccl.org), The Globalist (www.theglobalist.com), and Transnational Management Associated (www.tmaworld.com).

- *Learning Objectives* focus on the main lessons students should take away from the material and are summarized in bullet-point format at the end of the chapter.
- *Beacons* provide students with a "road map" of how chapters relate to one another. These beacons appear at the start of each chapter and are appropriately titled, "A Look Back," "A Look at This Chapter," and "A Look Ahead."
- *PowerPoint slides* for instructors contain both written and verbal teaching notes and include question slides to use as in-class comprehension checks. Updated student PowerPoint slides contain written study notes.
- *Videos* are available to accompany this text and cover topics such as globalization, culture's impact on business, international business ethics, foreign direct investment, emerging markets, and entry modes.

Tools for Active Learning

Feedback on previous editions shows that this book has more—and more useful—end-of-chapter assignment material than any other international business book. Well-planned assignment materials span the full range of complexity in order to test students' knowledge and ability to apply key principles. Assignment materials are often experiential in nature to help students develop international business skills and make business decisions. Assignment materials include the following:

- *Talk It Over* questions can be used for in-class discussion or as homework assignments. These exercises raise important issues currently confronting entrepreneurs, international managers, policy makers, consumers, and others.
- *Teaming Up* projects go beyond the text and require students to collaborate in teams to conduct interviews, research other countries, or hold in-class debates and role-playing exercises. Projects expose students to different perspectives when they bring together students who have different cultural backgrounds.
- *Take It to the Web* assignments ask students to conduct research using the Internet. *Website Report* exercises send students to specific websites to research a single company or ask students to locate information using the Web.
- *Video Report* exercises ask students to view and report on brief YouTube videos on a channel maintained by the authors (www.youtube.com/myibvideos). Videos are kept up to date with a variety of international business videos gathered from other YouTube users' videos that may or may not always be available.
- *Ethical Challenges* exercises (in a "You are the ..." format) ask students to assume the role of a manager, government official, or someone else and to make a decision based on the facts presented to them.
- *Practicing International Management* cases ask students to analyze the responses of real-world companies to the issues, problems, and opportunities discussed in each chapter.

Practicing International Management Case

A Tale of Two Cultures

Many cultures in Asia are in the midst of an identity crisis. In effect, they are being torn between two worlds. Pulling in one direction is a traditional value system derived from agriculture-based communities and extended families—that is, elements of a culture in which relatives take care of one another and state-run welfare systems are unnecessary. Pulling from the opposite direction is a new set of values emerging from manufacturing- and finance-based economies—elements of a culture in which workers must often move to faraway cities to find work, sometimes leaving family members to fend for themselves.

For decades, Western multinational corporations set up factories across Southeast Asia to take advantage of relatively low-cost labor. Later, local companies sprang up and became competitive global players in their own right. Spectacular rates of economic growth in a few short decades elevated living standards beyond what was thought possible. Young people in Malaysia and Thailand felt the lure of "Western" brands. Gucci handbags (www.gucci.com), Harley-Davidson motorcycles (www.harley-davidson.com), and other global brands became common symbols of success. Many parents felt that brand-consciousness among their teenage children signaled familywide success.

Despite the growing consumer society, polls of young people show them holding steadfast to traditional values such as respect for family and group harmony. Youth in Hong Kong, for example, overwhelmingly believe that parents should have a say in how hard they study, in how they treat family members and elders, and in their choice of friends.

Now globalization is washing over India. An explosion in outsourcing jobs is causing a social revolution among India's graduates of technical colleges and universities. Unlike in India's traditional high-tech service jobs, young call-center staffers are in direct contact with Western consumers, answering inquiries on items such as tummy crunchers and diet pills. For these young, mostly female staffers, the work means money, independence, and freedom—sometimes far away from home in big cities such as Bangalore and Mumbai. But in addition to the training in American accents and geography, these workers are learning new ideas about family, materialism, and relationships.

Parents are suspicious of call-center work because it must typically be performed at night in India, when consumers are awake in Canada, Europe, or the United States. When her parents objected, Binitha Venugopal quit her call-center job in favor of a "regular" daytime job. Binitha says her former coworkers' values are changing and that dating and live-in relationships among them are common. Indian tradition dictates that young adults live with their parents at least until they get married (typically to someone their parents choose). Perhaps facilitating shifting values in India is an

influx of Western professionals, such as lawyers, who accepted good-paying jobs there that could not be found back home during the global recession.

Roopa Murthy works for an Indian company that offers call-center and back-office services. Roopa moved to Bangalore from her native Mysore in 2002 armed with an accounting degree. She now earns $400 per month, which is several times what her father earned before he retired from his government job. Roopa cut her hair short and tossed aside her *salwar kameez*, the traditional loose-fitting clothing she wore back home, in favor of designer-labeled Western attire.

Although she once shunned drinking and her curfew at home was 9 p.m., Roopa now frequents a pub called Geoffrey's, where she enjoys dry martinis and rum, and The Club, a suburban disco. Roopa confesses that she is "seeing someone" but that her parents would disapprove, adding, "It is difficult to talk to Indian parents about things like boyfriends." She said she sometimes envies her callers' lives but that she hopes her job will help her succeed. "I may be a small-town girl, but there is no way I'm going back to Mysore after this," she said. Many observers wonder whether Asia can embrace modernization and yet retain traditional values.

Thinking Globally

1. If your international firm were doing business in Asia, is there anything that your company could do to ease the tensions these cultures are experiencing? Be specific.
2. In your opinion, is globalization among the causes of the increasing incidence of divorce, crime, and drug abuse in Asia? Why or why not?
3. Broadly defined, Asia comprises more than 60 percent of the world's population—a population that practices Buddhism, Confucianism, Hinduism, Islam, and numerous other religions. Thus, do you think it is possible to carry on a valid discussion of "Asian" values? Why or why not?
4. Consider the following statement: "Economic development and capitalism require a certain style of doing business in the twenty-first century. The sooner Asian cultures adapt the better." Do you agree or disagree? Explain.

Source: Heather Timmons, "Outsourcing to India Draws Western Lawyers," *New York Times* (www.nytimes.com), August 4, 2010; Lisa Tsering, "NBC Picks up Series 'Outsourced' for Fall 2010," *Indiawest.com* website (www.indiawest.com), May 27, 2010; Saritha Rai, "India Outsourcing Workers Stressed to The Limit," *Silicon.com* website (www.silicon.com; now www.techrepublic.com), August 26, 2009; Sol E. Solomon, "Vietnam's IT Way to Social Progress," *Bloomberg Businessweek* (www.businessweek.com), May 19, 2008.

Faculty Resources

Instructor's Resource Center

At www.pearsonhighered.com/irc, instructors can access a variety of print, digital, and presentation resources available with this text in downloadable format. Registration is simple and gives you immediate access to new titles and new editions. As a registered faculty member, you can download resource files and receive immediate access and instructions for installing course management content on your campus server.

This textbook's extensive array of supplements includes test-generating software containing thousands of multiple-choice, true/false, fill-in, and essay questions. The book's instructor's resource manual is a complete instruction toolkit containing a wealth of teaching aids.

If you ever need assistance, our dedicated technical support team is ready to help with media supplements that accompany this text. Visit http://247.pearsoned.com for answers to frequently asked questions.

The following supplements are available to adopting instructors (for detailed descriptions and to download the supplements, please visit www.pearsonhighered.com/irc):

- **Instructor's Manual**
- **Test Item File**
- **TestGen: Test Generating Software**
- **PowerPoint Slides**
- **Video Library:**
  Videos illustrating the most important subject topics are available in two formats:
  DVD – available for in classroom use by instructors, includes videos mapped to Pearson textbooks.
  MyLab – available for instructors and students, provides round the clock instant access to videos and corresponding assessment and simulations for Pearson textbooks.
  Contact your local Pearson representative to request access to either format.
- **BlackBoard/WebCT Course Cartridges:** These standard course cartridges contain the Instructor's Manual, TestGen, Instructor PowerPoints, and Student Powerpoints.

Student Resources

Market Entry Strategy Project

Originally designed by David C. Wyld of Southeastern Louisiana University, this online, interactive project is available only through www.MyManagementLab.com.

CourseSmart

CourseSmart is an exciting new choice for students looking to save money. As an alternative to purchasing the print textbook, students can purchase an electronic version of the same content and save up to 50 percent off the suggested list price of the print text. With a CourseSmart e-textbook, students can search the text, make notes online, print out reading assignments that incorporate lecture notes, and bookmark important passages for later review. For more information, or to purchase access to the CourseSmart e-textbook version of this text, visit www.coursesmart.com.

Acknowledgments

We are grateful for the encouragement and suggestions provided by many instructors, professionals, and students in preparing this seventh edition of *International Business*. We especially thank the following instructors who provided valuable feedback to improve this and previous editions:

Reviewers for the 7th edition:

Ogugua Anunoby	*Lincoln University*
Robert Armstrong	*University of North Alabama*
Thierry Brusselle	*Chaffey College*
Bruce Keillor	*Youngstown State University*
Ki Hee Kim	*William Paterson University*
Tomasz Lenartowicz	*Florida Atlantic University*
Tim Muth	*Florida Institute of Technology*
Hui Pate	*Skyline College*
Krishnan Ramaya	*Pacific University of Oregon*

James Reinnoldt	*University of Washington–Bothell*
William Walker	*University of Houston*
Bashar A. Zakaria	*California State University, Sacramento*

Reviewers for previous editions:

Rob Abernathy	*University of North Carolina, Greensboro*
Hadi S. Alhorr	*Drake University*
Gary Anders	*Arizona State University West*
Madan Annavarjula	*Northern Illinois University*
Wendell Armstrong	*Central Virginia Community College*
Mernoush Banton	*Florida International University*
George Barnes	*University of Texas at Dallas*
Constance Bates	*Florida International University*
Marca Marie Bear	*University of Tampa*
Tope A. Bello	*East Carolina University*
Robert Blanchard	*Salem State College*
David Boggs	*Eastern Illinois University*
Chuck Bohleke	*Owens Community College*
Erin Boyer	*Central Piedmont CC*
Richard Brisebois	*Everglades University*
Bill Brunsen	*Eastern New Mexico at Portales*
Mikelle Calhoun	*Ohio State University*
Martin Calkins	*Santa Clara University*
Kenichiro Chinen	*California State University at Sacramento*
Joy Clark	*Auburn University–Montgomery*
Randy Cray	*University of Wisconsin at Stevens Point*
Tim Cunha	*Eastern New Mexico University at Portales*
Robert Engle	*Quinnipiac University*
Herbert B. Epstein	*University of Texas at Tyler*
Blair Farr	*Jarvis Christian College*
Stanley Flax	*St. Thomas University*
Ronelle Genser	*Devry University*
Carolina Gomez	*University of Houston*
Jorge A. Gonzalez	*University of Wisconsin at Milwaukee*
Andre Graves	*SUNY Buffalo*
Kenneth R. Gray	*Florida A&M University*
James Gunn	*Berkeley College*
James Halteman	*Wheaton College*
Alan Hamlin	*Southern Utah University*
Charles Harvey	*University of the West of England, UK*
M. Anaam Hashmi	*Minnesota State University at Mankato*
Les Jankovich	*San Jose State University*
R. Sitki Karahan	*Montana State University*
Ken Kim	*University of Toledo*
Ki Hee Kim	*William Paterson University*

Anthony Koh	*University of Toledo*
Donald Kopka	*Towson University*
James S. Lawson Jr.	*Mississippi State University*
Ian Lee	*Carleton University*
Tomasz Lenartowicz	*Florida Atlantic University*
Joseph W. Leonard	*Miami University (Ohio)*
Antoinette Lloyd	*Virginia Union University*
Carol Lopilato	*California State University at Dominguez Hills*
Jennifer Malarski	*North Hennepin Community College*
Donna Weaver McCloskey	*Widener University*
James McFillen	*Bowling Green State University*
Mantha Mehallis	*Florida Atlantic University*
John L. Moore	*Oregon Institute of Technology*
David Mosby	*University of Texas, Arlington*
Rod Oglesby	*Southwest Baptist University*
Patrick O'Leary	*St. Ambrose University*
Yongson Paik	*Loyola Marymount University*
Clifford Perry	*Florida International University*
Susan Peterson	*Scottsdale Community College*
Janis Petronis	*Tarleton State University*
William Piper	*William Piedmont College*
Abe Qastin	*Lakeland College*
Nadine Russell	*Central Piedmont Community College*
C. Richard Scott	*Metropolitan State College of Denver*
Deepak Sethi	*Old Dominion University*
Charlie Shi	*Diablo Valley College*
Coral R. Snodgrass	*Canisius College*
Rajeev Sooreea	*Penn State—University Park*
John Stanbury	*George Mason University*
William A. Stoever	*Seton Hall University*
Kenneth R. Tillery	*Middle Tennessee State University*
William Walker	*University of Houston*
Paula Weber	*St. Cloud State University*
James E. Welch	*Kentucky Wesleyan College*
Steve Werner	*University of Houston*
David C. Wyld	*Southeastern Louisiana University*
Robert Yamaguchi	*Fullerton College*

It takes a dedicated group of individuals to take a textbook from first draft to final manuscript. We thank our partners at Pearson for their tireless efforts in bringing the seventh edition of this book to fruition. Special thanks on this project go to Stephanie Wall, Editor-in-Chief; Kris Ellis-Levy, Senior Acquisitions Editor; Ashley Santora, Director of Editorial Services; Ann Pulido, Senior Production Project Manager; Maggie Moylan, Director of Marketing; and Erin Gardner, Senior Marketing Manager.

About the Authors

John J. Wild and Kenneth L. Wild provide a blend of skills uniquely suited to writing an international business textbook. They combine award-winning teaching and research with a global view of business gained through years of living and working in cultures around the world. Their writing makes the topic of international business practical, accessible, and enjoyable.

John J. Wild John J. Wild is a distinguished Professor of Business at the University of Wisconsin at Madison. He previously held appointments at the University of Manchester in England and at Michigan State University. He received his B.B.A., M.S., and Ph.D. from the University of Wisconsin at Madison.

Teaching business courses at both the undergraduate and graduate levels, Professor Wild has received several teaching honors, including the Mabel W. Chipman Excellence-in-Teaching Award, the Teaching Excellence Award from the 2003 and 2005 business graduates from the University of Wisconsin, and a departmental Excellence-in-Teaching Award from Michigan State University. He is a prior recipient of national research fellowships from KPMG Peat Marwick and the Ernst and Young Foundation. Professor Wild is also a frequent speaker at universities and at national and international conferences.

The author of more than 60 publications, in addition to 5 best-selling textbooks, Professor Wild conducts research on a wide range of topics, including corporate governance, capital markets, and financial analysis and forecasting. He is an active member of several national and international organizations, including the Academy of International Business, and has served as associate editor and editorial board member for several prestigious journals.

Kenneth L. Wild Kenneth L. Wild is affiliated with the University of London, England. He previously taught at Pennsylvania State University. He received his Ph.D. from the University of Manchester (UMIST) in England and his B.S. and M.S. degrees from the University of Wisconsin. Dr. Wild also undertook postgraduate work at École des Affairs Internationale in Marseilles, France.

Having taught students of international business, marketing, and management at both the undergraduate and graduate levels, Dr. Wild is a dedicated contributor to international business education. An active member of several national and international organizations, including the Academy of International Business, Dr. Wild has spoken at major universities and at national and international conferences.

Dr. Wild's research covers a range of international business topics, including market entry modes, country risk in emerging markets, international growth strategies, and globalization of the world economy.

International Business

THE CHALLENGES OF GLOBALIZATION

Globalization

LEARNING OBJECTIVES

After studying this chapter, you should be able to

1. Identify the types of companies that participate in international business.

2. Describe the process of globalization and how it affects markets and production.

3. Describe the two forces causing globalization to increase.

4. Summarize the evidence for each main argument in the globalization debate.

5. Describe the global business environment and identify its four main elements.

A Look at This Chapter

This chapter defines the scope of international business and introduces us to some of its most important topics. We begin by identifying the key players in international business today. We then present globalization, describing its influence on markets and production and the forces behind its growth. Next, we analyze each main argument in the debate over globalization in detail. This chapter closes with a model that depicts international business as occurring within an integrated global business environment.

A Look Ahead

Part 2, encompassing Chapters 2, 3, and 4, introduces us to different national business environments. Chapter 2 describes important cultural differences among nations. Chapter 3 examines different political and legal systems. And Chapter 4 presents the world's various economic systems and issues surrounding economic development.

APPLE'S GLOBAL iMPACT

CUPERTINO, California—The Apple (www.apple.com) iPhone excites style lovers the world over and changed how all sorts of items are designed. With its focus on beauty and simplicity, the iPhone is making "user-centered design" a catch phrase in business.

The daily launch of new applications (or "apps") is constantly expanding the capabilities of the iPhone and its sibling, the iPad. The App Store boasts more than 725,000 diverse offerings, including apps for games and entertainment, data processing, and even health monitoring. And the iCloud allows customers to access personal content and data that instantly reflects changes made on any Apple device, be it an iPhone, iPad, or Mac computer.

Globalization allows Apple to produce and sell many of the same models worldwide, with little or no modification. This approach reduces Apple's pro-

Source: APPLE INC./UPI/Newscom

duction and marketing costs while supporting its global brand strategy. It also forces Apple to monitor its supply chain carefully. Apple outsources some production to a firm called Foxconn (www.foxconn.com) in China. Despite Apple having a code of conduct for its suppliers, critics have accused Foxconn of mistreating workers.

So Apple asked the Fair Labor Association (www.fairlabor.org) to investigate. The FLA found ethical issues at Foxconn's plants in China, although it admitted conditions were better than expected. To demonstrate its corporate social responsibility, Apple promised to resolve the issues that included excessive overtime hours and matters related to worker health and safety.

iTunes U is a free hosting service that Apple offers to colleges and universities that provides 24/7 access to educational materials. Students download lectures and other content to their mobile devices and watch or listen on the go. So if you see a backpack-toting student listening to her iPod, she might be listening to her favorite playlist or her favorite instructor. As you read this chapter, consider how globalization is reshaping our lives and altering the activities of international companies.[1]

By knitting the world more tightly together, globalization is altering our private lives and transforming the way companies do business. We are increasingly exposed to the traits and practices of other cultures as technology drives down the cost of global communication and travel. Globalization is forcing industries to grow more competitive as countries reduce barriers to trade and investment. And competition is intensifying as large firms from advanced countries and emerging markets seek out new customers on a global scale.

As we saw in this chapter's opening company profile, Apple (www.apple.com) is an undisputed global success story. Its spectacular rise illustrates the opportunities that globalization creates for entrepreneurs and businesses everywhere. In addition, technology products like Apple's iPhone and other smartphones are changing how we interact through social media. Many of these changes are positive and generate all sorts of efficiencies. For example, people anywhere in the world can tune in to what is happening in their Facebook friends' lives in real time.

But are all the changes positive ones? Larry Rosen, a psychologist and professor, says the desire to stay connected and following through on persistent urges to check for messages on smartphones delivers little satisfaction. "The relief is not pleasurable," he says. "That's the sign of an obsession." Rosen says the best and worst thing about a smartphone today "is that we carry it with us all day long."[2] Yet, this is the world in which we now live and work. The more we embrace technology, the faster paced our lives seem to grow.

International Business Involves Us All

Each of us experiences the results of international business transactions as we go about our daily routines. The General Electric (www.ge.com) alarm clock/radio that woke you this morning was likely made in *China*. The breaking news buzzing in your ears was produced by *Britain's* BBC radio (www.bbc.co.uk). You slip on your Adidas sandals (www.adidas.com) that were made in *Indonesia*, an Abercrombie & Fitch T-shirt (www.abercrombie.com) made in the *Northern Mariana Islands*, and American Eagle jeans (www.ae.com) made in *Mexico*. As you head out the door, you pull the battery charger off your Apple iPhone (www.apple.com), which was designed in the *United States* and assembled in *China* with parts from *Japan, South Korea, Taiwan*, and several other nations. You hop into your *Korean* Hyundai (www.hmmausa.com) that was made in *Alabama*, grab your iPod, and play a song by the *English* band Coldplay (www.coldplay.com). You drive into the local Starbucks (www.starbucks.com) to charge your own batteries with coffee brewed from beans harvested in *Colombia* and *Ethiopia*. Your day is just one hour old, but in a way, you've already taken a virtual trip around the world. A quick glance at the "Made in" tags on your jacket, backpack, watch, wallet, or other items with you right now will demonstrate the pervasiveness of international business transactions.

International business is any commercial transaction that crosses the borders of two or more nations. You don't have to set foot outside a small town to find evidence of international business. No matter where you live, you'll be surrounded by **imports**—goods and services purchased abroad and brought into a country. Your counterparts around the world will undoubtedly spend some part of their day using your nation's **exports**—goods and services sold abroad and sent out of a country. Every year, all the nations of the world export goods and services worth $18 trillion. This figure is around 40 times the annual global revenue of Walmart Stores (www.walmart.com).[3]

Technology Makes It Possible

Technology is a primary driver of societal and commercial change today. Consumers use technology to reach out to the world on the Internet—gathering and sending information and purchasing all kinds of goods and services. Companies use technology to acquire materials and products from distant lands and to sell goods and services abroad.

When businesses or consumers use technology to conduct transactions, they engage in **e-business (e-commerce)**—the use of computer networks to purchase, sell, or exchange products; to service customers; and to collaborate with partners. E-business is making it easier for companies to make their products abroad, not simply to import and export finished goods.

Consider how Hewlett-Packard (HP; www.hp.com) designed and built a computer server for small businesses. Once HP identified the need for a new low-cost computer server, it seized the rewards of globalization. HP dispersed its design and production activities throughout a specialized

international business
Commercial transaction that crosses the borders of two or more nations.

imports
Goods and services purchased abroad and brought into a country.

exports
Goods and services sold abroad and sent out of a country.

e-business (e-commerce)
Use of computer networks to purchase, sell, or exchange products; to service customers; and to collaborate with partners.

We see the result of embracing globalization in this photo of skyscrapers in the Lujiazui Financial and Trade Zone of the Pudong New Area in Shanghai, China. After years of stunning economic growth and expansion, Shanghai has emerged as a key city for companies entering China's marketplace. Pudong was developed to reinvigorate Shanghai as an international trade and financial center. Pudong is now a modern, cosmopolitan district. How has globalization changed the economic landscape of your city and state?

Source: Amanda Hall/Robert Harding/Newscom

manufacturing system across five Pacific Rim nations and India. This helped the company minimize labor costs, taxes, and shipping delays yet maximize productivity when designing, building, and distributing its new product. Companies use such innovative production and distribution techniques to squeeze inefficiencies out of their international operations and boost their competitiveness.

Global Talent Makes It Happen

Firms can tap a global pool of talent in preparing their products for distribution. For example, Fox and NBC Universal created Hulu (www.hulu.com) as a cool venue for fans to watch movies and TV shows online. Hulu engages in a global relay race by employing two technical teams—one in the United States and one in China—to manage its website. Members of the team in Santa Monica, California, work late into the night detailing code specifications that they send to the team in Beijing, China. The Chinese team then writes the code and sends it back to Santa Monica before the U.S. team gets to work in the morning.

Some innovative companies use online competitions to attract innovative ideas worldwide. InnoCentive (www.innocentive.com) connects companies and institutions seeking solutions to difficult problems by using a global network of 250,000 creative thinkers. These engineers, scientists, inventors, and businesspeople with expertise in life sciences, engineering, chemistry, math, computer science, and entrepreneurship compete to solve some of the world's toughest problems in return for significant financial awards. InnoCentive is open to anyone, is available in seven languages, and pays cash awards that range from as little as $500 to more than $1 million.[4]

This chapter begins by examining the key players in international business. Then, we describe globalization's powerful influence on markets and production and explain the forces behind its expansion. Next, we cover each main point in the debate over globalization. We also explain why international business is special by presenting the dynamic, integrated global business environment. Finally, the appendix at the end of this chapter contains a world atlas to be used as a primer for this chapter's discussion and as a reference throughout the remainder of the book.

Key Players in International Business

Companies of all types and sizes and in all sorts of industries become involved in international business, yet they vary in the extent of their involvement. A small shop owner might only import supplies from abroad, whereas a large company may have dozens of factories located around the world. Large companies from the wealthiest nations still dominate international business. But firms from emerging markets (such as Brazil, China, India, and South Africa) now vigorously compete for global market share. Small and medium-sized companies are also increasingly active in international business largely because of advances in technology.

Multinational Corporations

multinational corporation (MNC)
Business that has direct investments abroad in multiple countries.

A **multinational corporation (MNC)** is a business that has direct investments (in the form of marketing or manufacturing subsidiaries) abroad in multiple countries. Multinationals generate significant jobs, investment, and tax revenue for the regions and nations they enter. Likewise, they can leave thousands of people out of work when they close or scale back operations. Mergers and acquisitions between multinationals are commonly worth billions of dollars and increasingly involve companies based in emerging markets.

Some companies have more employees than many of the smallest countries and island nations have citizens. Walmart, for example, has 2.2 million employees. We see the enormous economic clout of multinational corporations when we compare the revenues of the Global 500 ranking of companies with the value of goods and services that countries generate. Figure 1.1 shows the world's 10 largest companies (measured in revenue) inserted into a ranking of nations according to their national output (measured in GDP). If Walmart (www.walmart.com) were a country, it would weigh in as a rich nation and rank just three places behind Norway. Even the $22 billion in revenue generated by the 500th largest firm in the world, Manpower Group (www.manpowergroup.com), exceeds the output of many countries.[5]

Entrepreneurs and Small Businesses

born global firm
Company that adopts a global perspective and engages in international business from or near its inception.

International business competition has given rise to a new entity, the **born global firm**—a company that adopts a global perspective and engages in international business from or near its inception. Many of these companies become international competitors in less than three years'

FIGURE 1.1

Comparing the World's Largest Companies with Selected Countries

Source: Based on data obtained from "Fortune Gll 500: The World's Largest Corporations," *Fortune*, July 23, 2012, pp. F1–F7; World Bank data set available at data.worldbank.org.

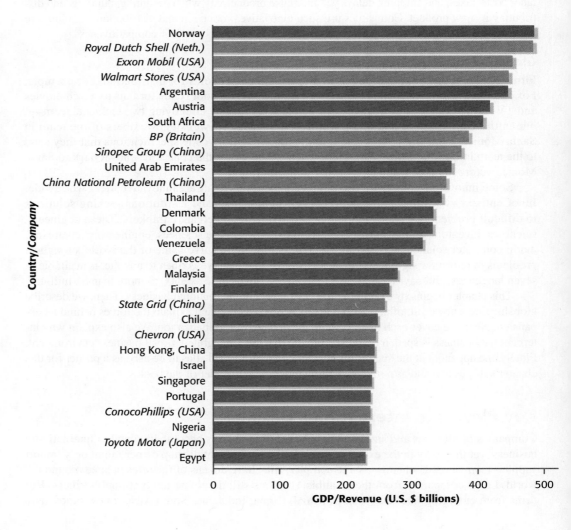

time. Born global firms tend to have *innovative* cultures and *knowledge-based* organizational capabilities. And in this age of globalization, companies are exporting earlier and growing faster, often with help from technology.

Small firms selling traditional products benefit from technology that lowers the costs and difficulties of global communication. Vellus Products (www.vellus.com) of Columbus, Ohio, makes and sells pet-grooming products. Around 20 years ago, a dog breeder in Spain became Vellus's first distributor after the breeder received a request for more information on Vellus's products from a man in Bahrain. "The way this [business transaction] transpired just blew me away," says Sharon Kay Doherty, president of Vellus. The company now has distributors in 31 countries. Vellus resembles a global company in that it earned more than half its revenues from international sales soon after going international.[6]

Electronic distribution for firms that sell digitized products is an effective alternative to traditional distribution channels. Alessandro Naldi's Weekend in Italy website (en.firenze.waf.it) offers visitors more authentic Florentine products than they'll find in the scores of overpriced tourist shops in downtown Florence. A Florentine himself, Naldi established his site to sell high-quality, authentic Italian merchandise made only in the small factories of Tuscany. Weekend in Italy averages 200,000 visitors each month from places as far away as Australia, Canada, Japan, Mexico, and the United States.[7]

QUICK STUDY 1

1. Define the term *international business,* and explain how it involves us all.
2. Explain how *e-business* (*e-commerce*) affects international business.
3. What types of companies are involved in international business?

Globalization

Nations historically retained absolute control over the products, people, and capital crossing their borders. But today, economies are becoming increasingly intertwined. This greater interdependence means an increasingly freer flow of goods, services, money, people, and ideas across national borders. **Globalization** is the name we give to this trend toward greater economic, cultural, political, and technological interdependence among national institutions and economies. Globalization is characterized by *denationalization* (national boundaries becoming less relevant) and is different from *internationalization* (entities cooperating across national boundaries).

As its definition implies, globalization involves much more than the expansion of trade and investment among nations. Globalization embraces concepts and theories from political science, sociology, anthropology, and philosophy as well as economics. As such, it is not a term exclusively reserved for multinational corporations and international financial institutions. Nor is globalization the exclusive domain of those with only altruistic or moral intentions. In fact, globalization has been described as going "well beyond the links that bind corporations, traders, financiers, and central bankers. It provides a conduit not only for ideas but also for processes of coordination and cooperation used by terrorists, politicians, religious leaders, anti-globalization activists, and bureaucrats alike."[8]

For our purposes, this discussion focuses on the business implications of globalization. Two areas of business in which globalization is having profound effects are the globalization of *markets* and *production*.

globalization
Trend toward greater economic, cultural, political, and technological interdependence among national institutions and economies.

Globalization of Markets

Globalization of markets refers to the convergence in buyer preferences in markets around the world. This trend is occurring in many product categories, including consumer goods, industrial products, and business services. Clothing retailer L.L. Bean (www.llbean.com), shoe producer Nike (www.nike.com), and electronics maker Vizio (www.vizio.com) are just a few companies that sell *global products*—products marketed in all countries essentially without any changes. For example, the iPad qualifies as a global product because of its highly standardized features and Apple's global marketing strategy and globally recognized brand.

Global products and global competition characterize many industries and markets, including semiconductors (Intel, Philips), aircraft (Airbus, Boeing), construction equipment (Caterpillar, Mitsubishi), automobiles (Toyota, Volkswagen), financial services (Citicorp, HSBC), air travel (Lufthansa, Singapore Airlines), accounting services (Ernst & Young, KPMG), consumer goods (Procter & Gamble, Unilever), and fast food (KFC, McDonald's). The globalization of markets is important to international business because of the benefits it offers companies. Let's now look briefly at each of those benefits.

REDUCES MARKETING COSTS   Companies that sell global products can reduce costs by *standardizing* certain marketing activities. A company selling a global consumer good, such as shampoo, can make an identical product for the global market and then simply design different packaging to account for the language spoken in each market. Companies can achieve further cost savings by keeping an ad's visual component the same for all markets but dubbing TV ads and translating print ads into local languages.

CREATES NEW MARKET OPPORTUNITIES   A company that sells a global product can explore opportunities abroad if its home market is small or becomes saturated. China holds enormous potential for e-business with more than 500 million Internet users, which is greater than the population of the entire United States. But while more than 70 percent of people in the United States actively surf the web, only around 38 percent of people in China do.[9] So as time goes on, more and more Chinese citizens will go online to research and purchase products. The appeal of reaching such a vast audience drives firms from relatively small countries to explore doing business in the Chinese market.

LEVELS UNEVEN INCOME STREAMS   A company that sells a product with universal, but seasonal, appeal can use international sales to level its income stream. By supplementing domestic sales with international sales, the company can reduce or eliminate wide variations in sales between seasons and steady its cash flow. For example, a firm that produces suntan and sunblock lotions can match product distribution with the summer seasons in the northern and southern hemispheres in alternating fashion—thereby steadying its income from these global, yet highly seasonal, products.

LOCAL BUYERS' NEEDS   Despite the potential benefits of global markets, managers must constantly monitor the match between the firm's products and markets in order not to overlook the needs of buyers. The benefit of serving customers with an adapted product may outweigh the benefit of a standardized one. For instance, soft drinks, fast food, and other consumer goods are global products that continue to penetrate markets around the world. But sometimes these products require small modifications to better suit local tastes. In southern Japan, Coca-Cola (www.cocacola.com) sweetens its traditional formula to compete with the sweeter-tasting Pepsi (www.pepsi.com). In India, where cows are sacred and the consumption of beef is taboo, McDonald's (www.mcdonalds.com) markets the "Maharaja Mac"—two all-mutton patties on a sesame-seed bun with all the usual toppings.

sustainability
Development that meets the needs of the present without compromising the ability of future generations to meet their own needs.

GLOBAL SUSTAINABILITY   Another need that multinationals must consider is the need among all the world's citizens for **sustainability**—development that meets the needs of the present without compromising the ability of future generations to meet their own needs.[10] Most companies today operate in an environment of increased transparency and scrutiny regarding their business activities. The rise of social media is partly responsible for this trend. Concerned individuals and nongovernmental organizations will very quickly use Internet media to call out any firm caught harming the environment or society.

For years, forward-looking businesses have employed the motto, "reduce, reuse, and recycle." The idea is to *reduce* the use of resources and waste, *reuse* resources with more than a single-use lifespan, and *recycle* what cannot be reduced or reused. The most dedicated managers and firms promote sustainable communities by adding to the motto, "redesign and reimagine." This means *redesigning* products and processes for sustainability and *reimagining* how a product is designed and used to lessen its environmental impact.[11] To read more about the call for more sustainable business practices, see this chapter's Global Sustainability feature, titled "Three Markets, Three Strategies."

Globalization of Production

Globalization of production refers to the dispersal of production activities to locations that help a company achieve its cost-minimization or quality-maximization objectives for a good or service. This includes the sourcing of key production inputs (such as raw materials or products for

GLOBAL SUSTAINABILITY   Three Markets, Three Strategies

A company adapts its business strategy to the nuances of the market it enters. The world's population of 7 billion people lives in three different types of markets:

- **Developed Markets.** These include the world's established consumer markets, around *one billion* people. The population is solidly middle class, and people can consume almost any product desired. The infrastructure is highly developed and efficient.
- **Emerging Markets.** These markets, around *two billion* people, are racing to catch up to developed nations. The population is migrating to cities for better pay and is overloading cities' infrastructures. Rising incomes are increasing global demand for resources and basic products.
- **Traditional Markets.** Globalization has bypassed these markets, nearly *four billion* people. The population is mostly rural, the infrastructure is very poor, and there is little credit or collateral. People have almost no legal protections, and corruption prevails.

Like business strategy, sustainability strategies reflect local conditions. Examples of businesses working toward sustainability in these three markets include the following:

- **Toyota** focused on the environment in its *developed markets*. After extensively researching gas-electric hybrid technologies, Toyota launched the Prius. As *Motor Trend's* Car of the Year, the Prius drove Toyota's profits to record highs and gave it a "green" image.
- **Shree Cement** faced limited access to low-cost energy in India's *emerging market*. So it developed the world's most energy-efficient process for making its products. The world's leading cement companies now visit Shree to learn from its innovations in energy usage.
- **Blommer Chocolate** of the United States works closely with cocoa farmers in *traditional markets*. Blommer received the Rainforest Alliance's "Sustainable Standard-Setter" award for training farmers in safe farming practices, environmental stewardship, and HIV awareness.

Source: Jeremy Jurgens and Knut Haanæs, "Companies from Emerging Markets Are the New Sustainability Champions," *The Guardian* (www.guardian.co.uk), October 12, 2011; Stuart L. Hart, *Capitalism at the Crossroads, Third Edition* (Upper Saddle River, NJ: Wharton School Publishing, 2010); Daniel C. Esty and Andrew S. Winston, *Green to Gold* (New Haven, CT: Yale University Press, 2006).

assembly) as well as the international outsourcing of services. Let's now explore the benefits that companies obtain from the globalization of production.

ACCESS LOWER-COST WORKERS Global production activities allow companies to reduce overall production costs through access to low-cost labor. For decades, companies located their factories in low-wage nations in order to churn out all kinds of goods, including toys, small appliances, inexpensive electronics, and textiles. Yet whereas moving production to low-cost locales traditionally meant *production of goods* almost exclusively, it increasingly applies to the *production of services* such as accounting and research. Although most services must be produced where they are consumed, some services can be performed at remote locations where labor costs are lower. Many European and U.S. businesses have moved their customer service and other nonessential operations to places as far away as India to slash costs by as much as 60 percent.

ACCESS TECHNICAL EXPERTISE Companies also produce goods and services abroad to benefit from technical know-how. Film Roman (www.filmroman.com) produces the TV series *The Simpsons*, but it provides key poses and step-by-step frame directions to AKOM Production Company (www.akomkorea.com) in Seoul, South Korea. AKOM then fills in the remaining poses and links them into an animated whole. But there are bumps along the way, says animation director Mark Kirkland. In one middle-of-the-night phone call, Kirkland was explaining to the Koreans how to draw a shooting gun. "They don't allow guns in Korea; it's against the law," says Kirkland. "So they were calling me [asking]: 'How does a gun work?'" Kirkland and others put up with such cultural differences and phone calls at odd hours to tap a highly qualified pool of South Korean animators.[12]

ACCESS PRODUCTION INPUTS Globalization of production allows companies to access resources that are unavailable or more costly at home. The quest for natural resources draws many companies into international markets. Japan, for example, is a small, densely populated island nation with very few natural resources of its own—especially forests. But Japan's largest paper company, Nippon Seishi, does more than simply import wood pulp. The company owns huge forests and corresponding processing facilities in Australia, Canada, and the United States. This gives the firm not only access to an essential resource but also control over earlier stages in the papermaking process. As a result, the company is guaranteed a steady flow of its key ingredient (wood pulp) that is less subject to the swings in prices and supply associated with buying pulp on the open market. Likewise, to access cheaper energy resources used in manufacturing, a variety of Japanese firms are relocating production to China and Vietnam, where energy costs are lower than in Japan.

QUICK STUDY 2

1. Define *globalization*. How does denationalization differ from internationalization?
2. List each benefit a company might obtain from the globalization of markets.
3. How might a company benefit from the globalization of production?

Forces Driving Globalization

Two main forces underlie the globalization of markets and production: *falling barriers to trade and investment* and *technological innovation*. These two features, more than anything else, are increasing competition among nations by leveling the global business playing field. Greater competition is driving companies worldwide into more direct confrontation *and* cooperation. Local industries once isolated by time and distance are increasingly accessible to large international companies based many thousands of miles away. Some small and medium-sized local firms are compelled to cooperate with one another or with larger international firms to remain competitive. Other local businesses revitalize themselves in a bold attempt to survive the competitive onslaught. And on a global scale, consolidation is occurring as former competitors in many industries link up to challenge others on a worldwide basis. Let's now explore the pivotal roles of two forces driving globalization.

Falling Barriers to Trade and Investment

General Agreement on Tariffs and Trade (GATT)
Treaty designed to promote free trade by reducing both tariffs and nontariff barriers to international trade.

In 1947, political leaders of 23 nations (12 developed and 11 developing economies) made history when they created the **General Agreement on Tariffs and Trade (GATT)**—a treaty designed to promote free trade by reducing tariffs and nontariff barriers to international trade. *Tariffs* are essentially taxes levied on traded goods, and *nontariff barriers* are limits on the quantity of an imported product. The treaty was successful in its early years. After four decades, world merchandise trade had grown 20 times larger, and average tariffs had fallen from 40 percent to 5 percent.

Workers at a factory in Indonesia inspect electronic parts bound for global markets. Today, companies can go almost anywhere in the world to tap local expertise and favorable business climates. For example, U.S. businesses exploit technology by subcontracting work to Chinese companies that write computer software code and then e-mail their end product to the U.S. clients. In this way, companies can lower costs, increase efficiency, and grow more competitive. In what other ways might technology and global talent facilitate international business activity?

Source: BOB LOW/AFP/Newscom

Significant progress occurred again with a 1994 revision of the GATT treaty. Nations that had signed on to the treaty further reduced average tariffs on merchandise trade and lowered subsidies (government financial support) for agricultural products. The treaty's revision also clearly defined *intellectual property rights*. This gave protection to copyrights (including computer programs, databases, sound recordings, and films), trademarks and service marks, and patents (including trade secrets and know-how). A major flaw of the original GATT was that it lacked the power to enforce world trade rules. Thus, the creation of the *World Trade Organization* was likely the greatest accomplishment of the GATT revision.

THE WORLD TRADE ORGANIZATION The **World Trade Organization (WTO)** is the international organization that enforces the rules of international trade. The three main goals of the WTO (www.wto.org) are to help the free flow of trade, help negotiate the further opening of markets, and settle trade disputes among its members. It is the power of the WTO to settle trade disputes that sets it apart from its predecessor, the GATT. The various WTO agreements are essentially contracts between member nations that commit them to maintaining fair and open trade policies. Offenders must realign their trade policies according to WTO guidelines or face fines and, perhaps, trade sanctions (penalties). Because of its ability to penalize offending nations, the WTO's dispute-settlement system truly is the spine of the global trading system. The WTO replaced the *institution* of GATT but absorbed all of the former GATT *agreements*. Thus, the GATT institution no longer officially exists. Today, the WTO recognizes 157 members and 27 "observers."

The WTO launched a new round of negotiations in Doha, Qatar, in late 2001. The renewed negotiations were designed to lower trade barriers further and to help poor nations in particular. Agricultural subsidies that rich countries pay to their own farmers are worth $1 billion per day—more than six times the value of their combined aid budgets to poor nations. Because 70 percent of poor nations' exports are agricultural products and textiles, wealthy nations had intended to further open these and other labor-intensive industries. Poor nations were encouraged to reduce tariffs among themselves and were supposed to receive help in integrating themselves into the global trading system. Although the Doha round was to conclude by the end of 2004, negotiations are proceeding more slowly than anticipated.[13]

REGIONAL TRADE AGREEMENTS In addition to the WTO, smaller groups of nations are integrating their economies by fostering trade and boosting cross-border investment. For example, the *North American Free Trade Agreement (NAFTA)* gathers three nations (Canada, Mexico, and the United States) into a free-trade bloc. The more ambitious *European Union (EU)* combines 27 countries. The *Asia Pacific Economic Cooperation (APEC)* consists of 21 member economies committed to creating a free-trade zone around the Pacific. The aims of each of these smaller trade pacts are similar to those of the WTO but are regional in nature. Moreover, some nations encourage regional pacts because of recent resistance to worldwide trade agreements.

TRADE AND NATIONAL OUTPUT Together, the WTO agreements and regional pacts have boosted world trade and cross-border investment significantly. Trade theory tells us that openness to trade helps a nation produce a greater amount of output. Map 1.1 illustrates that growth in national output over a recent 10-year period has been significantly positive. Economic growth has been greater in nations that have recently become more open to trade, such as China, India, and Russia, than it has been in many other countries. Much of South America is also growing rapidly, whereas Africa's experience is mixed. This relation between trade and output has persisted despite a drop in nations' economic growth rates due to the global financial crises of recent years.

Let's take a moment in our discussion to define a few terms that we will encounter time and again throughout this book. **Gross domestic product (GDP)** is the value of all goods and services produced by a domestic economy over a one-year period. GDP excludes a nation's income generated from exports, imports, and the international operations of its companies. We can speak in terms of world GDP when we sum all individual nations' GDP figures. GDP is a somewhat narrower figure than **gross national product (GNP)**—the value of all goods and services produced by a country's domestic and international activities over a one-year period. A country's **GDP or GNP per capita** is simply its GDP or GNP divided by its population.

World Trade Organization (WTO)
International organization that enforces the rules of international trade.

gross domestic product (GDP)
Value of all goods and services produced by a domestic economy over a one-year period.

gross national product (GNP)
Value of all goods and services produced by a country's domestic and international activities over a one-year period.

GDP or GNP per capita
Nation's GDP or GNP divided by its population.

MAP 1.1
Growth in National
Output

Average annual GDP growth
rate, 1998-2007, (%)

negative
less than -2.5
-2.5 to 0
no data available

positive
0 to 1
1 to 2
2 to 3
3 to 4
4 to 5
over 5

Technological Innovation

Although falling barriers to trade and investment encourage globalization, technological innovation is accelerating its pace. Significant advancements in information technology and transportation methods are making it easier, faster, and less costly to move data, goods, and equipment around the world. Let's examine several innovations that have had a considerable impact on globalization.

E-MAIL AND VIDEOCONFERENCING Operating across borders and time zones complicates the job of coordinating and controlling business activities. But technology can speed the flow of information and ease the tasks of coordination and control. E-mail is an indispensable tool that managers use to stay in contact with international operations and to respond quickly to important matters.

Videoconferencing allows managers in different locations to meet in virtual face-to-face meetings. Primary reasons for 25 to 30 percent annual growth in videoconferencing include the lower cost of bandwidth (communication channels) used to transmit information, the lower cost of equipment, and the rising cost of travel for businesses. Videoconferencing equipment can cost as little as $5,000 and as much as $340,000. A company that does not require ongoing video-conferencing can pay even less by renting the facilities and equipment of a local conference center.[14] And for those willing to videoconference on a desktop, laptop, tablet computer, or mobile device (which includes most people) there is iMeet (www.imeet.com). This service provider charges less than $70 per month for unlimited video meetings.[15]

THE INTERNET Companies use the Internet to quickly and cheaply contact managers in distant locations—for example, to inquire about production runs, revise sales strategies, and check on distribution bottlenecks. They also use the Internet to achieve longer-term goals, such as sharpen their forecasting, lower their inventories, and improve communication with suppliers. The lower cost of reaching an international customer base especially benefits small firms, which were among the first to use the Internet as a global marketing tool. Additional gains arise from the ability of the Internet to cut postproduction costs by decreasing the number of intermediaries a product passes through on its way to the customer. Eliminating intermediaries greatly benefits online sellers of books, music, and travel services, among others.

COMPANY INTRANETS AND EXTRANETS Internal company websites and information networks (*intranets*) give employees access to company data using personal computers. A particularly effective marketing tool on Volvo Car Corporation's (www.volvocars.com) intranet is a quarter-by-quarter database of marketing and sales information. The cycle begins when headquarters submits its corporate-wide marketing plan to Volvo's intranet. Marketing managers at each subsidiary worldwide then select those activities that apply to their own market, develop their marketing plan, and submit it to the database. This allows managers in every market to view every other subsidiary's marketing plan and to adapt relevant aspects to their own plan. In essence, the entire system acts as a tool for the sharing of best practices across all of Volvo's markets.

Extranets give distributors and suppliers access to a company's database so they can place orders or restock inventories electronically and automatically. These networks permit international companies (along with their suppliers and buyers) to respond to internal and external conditions more quickly and more appropriately.

ADVANCEMENTS IN TRANSPORTATION TECHNOLOGIES Retailers worldwide rely on imports to stock their storerooms with finished goods and to supply factories with raw materials and intermediate products. Innovation in the shipping industry is helping globalize markets and production by making shipping more efficient and dependable. In the past, a cargo ship would sit in port up to 10 days while it was unloaded one pallet at a time. But because cargo today is loaded onto a ship in 20- and 40-foot containers that are quickly unloaded onto railcars or truck chassis at the final destination, a 700-foot cargo ship is routinely unloaded in just 15 hours.

Operation of cargo ships is now simpler and safer due to computerized charts that pinpoint a ship's movements on the high seas using Global Positioning System (GPS) satellites. Combining GPS with radio frequency identification (RFID) technology allows continuous monitoring of individual containers from port of departure to destination. RFID can tell whether a container's doors are opened and closed on its journey and can send an alert if a container deviates from its planned route.

TABLE 1.1 Globalization's Top 10

| | Rank | | | |
Country	Overall	Economic	Social	Political
Belgium	1	5	5	3
Ireland	2	3	2	28
Netherlands	3	6	8	14
Austria	4	14	4	4
Singapore	5	1	3	74
Sweden	6	8	17	7
Denmark	7	13	9	15
Hungary	8	7	22	21
Portugal	9	17	12	9
Switzerland	10	25	6	11

Source: Based on the 2012 KOF Index of Globalization (www.globalization.kof.ethz.ch), March 16, 2012.

Measuring Globalization

Although we intuitively feel that our world is becoming smaller, researchers have created ways to measure the extent of globalization scientifically. One index of globalization is the one created by the KOF Swiss Economic Institute (www.kof.ethz.ch). This index ranks nations on 23 variables within three dimensions: economic globalization (trade and investment volumes, trade and capital restrictions), social globalization (dissemination of information and ideas), and political globalization (political cooperation with other countries).[16]

By incorporating a wide variety of variables, the globalization index attempts to cut through cycles occurring in any single category and capture the broad nature of globalization. Table 1.1 shows the 10 highest-ranking nations according to the KOF Index of Globalization. European nations occupy 9 of the top 10 positions, with smaller nations clearly dominating the rankings. The city-state of Singapore is the only Asian nation listed in the top 10. The United States appears in 35th place overall, and ranks 79th in economic globalization, 29th in social globalization, and 22nd in political globalization. Large nations often do not make it into the higher ranks of globalization indices because a large home market means they tend to depend less on external trade and investment.

The world's least-globalized nations account for around half the world's population and are found in Africa, East Asia, South Asia, Latin America, and the Middle East. Some of the least-globalized nations are characterized by never-ending political unrest and corruption (Bangladesh, Indonesia, and Venezuela). Other nations with large agricultural sectors face trade barriers in developed countries and are subject to highly volatile prices on commodity markets (Brazil, China, and India). Still others are heavily dependent on oil exports but are plagued by erratic prices in energy markets (Iran and Venezuela). Kenya has suffered from recurring droughts, terrorism, and burdensome visa regulations that hurt tourism. Finally, Turkey and Egypt, along with the entire Middle East, suffer from continued concerns over violence and social unrest, high barriers to trade and investment, and heavy government involvement in the economy. To deepen their global links, these nations will need to make great strides forward in their economic, social, and political environments.

QUICK STUDY 3

1. How have global and regional efforts to promote trade and investment advanced globalization?
2. How does technological innovation propel globalization?
3. What factors make some countries more globalized than others?

Untangling the Globalization Debate

Globalization means different things to different people. A businessperson may see globalization as an opportunity to source goods and services from lower-cost locations and to pry open new markets. An economist may see it as an opportunity to examine the impact of globalization on jobs and standards of living. An environmentalist may be concerned with how globalization affects our ecology. An anthropologist may want to examine the influence of globalization on the culture of a group of people. A political scientist may be concerned with the impact of globalization on the power of governments relative to that of multinational companies. And an employee may view globalization either as an opportunity for new work or as a threat to his or her current job.

It is because of the different lenses through which we view events around us that the globalization debate is so complex. Entrepreneurs, small business owners, and globetrotting managers need to understand globalization and the arguments of those who oppose it. In the pages that follow, we explain the main arguments of those opposed to globalization and the responses of those in favor of it. But before we address the intricacies of the debate, it is helpful to put today's globalization into its proper context.

Today's Globalization in Context

Many people forget that there was a first age of globalization that extended from the mid-1800s to the 1920s.[17] In those days, labor was highly mobile, with 300,000 people leaving Europe each year in the 1800s and 1 million people leaving each year after 1900.[18] Other than in wartime, nations did not even require passports for international travel before 1914. And like today, workers in wealthy nations back then feared competition for jobs from high- and low-wage countries.

Trade and capital flowed more freely than ever during that first age of globalization. Huge companies from wealthy nations built facilities in distant lands to extract raw materials and produce all sorts of goods. Large cargo ships plied the seas to deliver their manufactures to distant markets. The transatlantic cable (completed in 1866) allowed news between Europe and the United States to travel faster than ever before. The drivers of that first age of globalization included the steamship, telegraph, railroad, and, later, the telephone and airplane.

That first age of globalization was abruptly halted by the arrival of the First World War, the Russian Revolution, and the Great Depression. A backlash to fierce competition in trade and unfettered immigration in the early 1900s helped usher in high tariffs and barriers to immigration. The great flows of goods, capital, and people common before the First World War became a mere trickle. For 75 years from the start of the First World War to the end of the Cold War, the world remained divided. There was a geographic divide between East and West and an ideological divide between communism and capitalism. After the Second World War, the West experienced steady economic gains, but international flows of goods, capital, and people were confined to their respective capitalist and communist systems and geographies.

Fast-forward to 1989 and the collapse of the wall separating East and West Berlin. One by one, central and eastern European nations rejected communism and began marching toward democratic institutions and free-market economic systems. Although it took until the 1990s for international capital flows, in absolute terms, to recover to levels seen prior to the First World War, the global economy had finally been *reborn*. The drivers of this second age of globalization include communication satellites, fiber optics, microchips, and the Internet.

Introduction to the Debate

World Bank
Agency created to provide financing for national economic development efforts.

International Monetary Fund
Agency created to regulate fixed exchange rates and to enforce the rules of the international monetary system.

In addition to the WTO presented earlier, several other supranational institutions play leading roles in fostering globalization. The **World Bank** is an agency created to provide financing for national economic development efforts. The initial purpose of the World Bank (www.worldbank.org) was to finance European reconstruction following the Second World War. The World Bank later shifted its focus to the general financial needs of developing countries, and today it finances many economic development projects in Africa, South America, and Southeast Asia. The **International Monetary Fund (IMF)** is an agency created to regulate fixed exchange rates and to enforce the rules of the international monetary system. Today, the IMF (www.imf.org) has 185 member countries. Some of the purposes of the IMF include promoting international monetary cooperation, facilitating the expansion and balanced growth of international trade,

Employees cheerfully celebrate at Volkswagen's (www.vw.com) automobile plant in Anchieta, Brazil. Factory employees are celebrating the production of more than 15 million vehicles in Volkswagen's 50-plus years in Brazil. The country is one of the strongest emerging markets in the world and one that benefited tremendously by embracing the opportunities offered by globalization. Can you identify other emerging markets in which globalization helped create good jobs and rising incomes for people?

Source: Agentur/Newscom

avoiding competitive exchange devaluation, and making financial resources temporarily available to members.

At this point, we should note one caveat. Each side in the debate over globalization tends to hold up results of social and economic studies that it says show "definitive" support for its arguments. Yet many organizations that publish studies on globalization have political agendas, such as decreasing government regulation or expanding government programs. This can make objective consideration of a group's claims and findings difficult. A group's aims may influence the selection of the data to analyze, the time period to study, the nations to examine, and so forth. It is essential to take into account such factors anytime we hear a group arguing the beneficial or harmful effects of globalization.

Let's now engage the debate over globalization by examining its effects on (1) jobs and wages, (2) labor and environmental regulation, (3) income inequality, (4) cultures, (5) and national sovereignty.

QUICK STUDY 4

1. How does this current period of globalization compare with the first age of globalization?
2. Explain the original purpose of the *World Bank* and its mandate today.
3. What are the main purposes of the *International Monetary Fund*?

Globalization's Impact on Jobs and Wages

We open our coverage of the globalization debate with an important topic for both developed and developing countries—the effect of globalization on jobs and wages. We begin with the arguments of those against globalization and then turn our attention to how supporters of globalization respond.

AGAINST GLOBALIZATION   Groups opposed to globalization blame it for eroding standards of living and ruining ways of life. Specifically, they say globalization *eliminates jobs* and *lowers wages* in developed nations and *exploits workers* in developing countries. Let's explore each of these arguments.

Eliminates Jobs in Developed Nations   Some groups claim that *globalization eliminates manufacturing jobs in developed nations*. They criticize the practice of sending good-paying manufacturing jobs abroad to developing countries where wages are a fraction of the cost for international firms. They argue that a label reading "Made in China" translates to "Not Made Here." Although critics admit that importing products from China (or another low-wage nation) lowers consumer prices for televisions, sporting goods, and so on, they say this is little consolation for workers who lose their jobs.

To illustrate their argument, globalization critics point to the activities of big-box retailers such as Costco (www.costco.com) and Walmart (www.walmart.com). It is difficult to overstate the power of these retail giants and symbols of globalization. Some say that by relentlessly pursuing low-cost goods, these retailers force their suppliers to move to China and other low-wage nations.

Lowers Wages in Developed Nations Opposition groups say *globalization causes worker dislocation that gradually lowers wages*. They allege that, when a manufacturing job is lost in a wealthy nation, the new job (assuming new work is found) pays less than the previous one. Those opposed to globalization say this decreases employee loyalty, employee morale, and job security. They say this causes people to fear globalization and any additional lowering of trade barriers.

Big-box retailers also come under fire in this discussion. Globalization critics say powerful retailers continually force manufacturers in low-wage nations to accept lower profits so that the retailers can slash prices to consumers. As a result of these business practices, critics charge, powerful retailers force down wages and working conditions worldwide.

Exploits Workers in Developing Nations Critics charge that *globalization and international outsourcing exploit workers in low-wage nations*. One notable critic of globalization, Naomi Klein, vehemently opposes the outsourced call center jobs of Western companies. Klein says such jobs force young Asians to disguise their nationality, adopt fake Midwestern accents, and work nights when their U.S. customers are awake halfway around the world. Klein maintains that free trade policies are "a highly efficient engine of dispossession, pushing small farmers off their land and laying off public-sector workers."[19]

FOR GLOBALIZATION Supporters of globalization credit it with improving standards of living and making possible new ways of life. They argue that globalization *increases wealth and efficiency in all nations, generates labor market flexibility in developed nations*, and *advances the economies of developing nations*. Let's examine each of these arguments.

Increases Wealth and Efficiency in All Nations Some economists believe *globalization increases wealth and efficiency in both developed and developing nations*. Globalization supporters argue that openness to international trade increases national production (by increasing efficiency) and raises per capita income (by passing savings on to consumers). For instance, by squeezing inefficiencies out of the retail supply chain, powerful global retailers help restrain inflation and boost productivity. Some economists predict that removing all remaining barriers to free trade would significantly boost worldwide income and greatly benefit developing nations.

Generates Labor Market Flexibility in Developed Nations Globalization supporters believe *globalization creates positive benefits by generating labor market flexibility in developed nations*. Some claim that there are benefits from worker dislocation, or "churning" as it is called when there is widespread job turnover throughout an economy. Flexible labor markets allow workers to be redeployed rapidly to sectors of the economy where they are highly valued and in demand. This also allows employees, particularly young workers, to change jobs easily with few negative effects. For instance, a young person can gain experience and skills with an initial employer and then move to a different job that provides a better match between employee and employer.

Advances the Economies of Developing Nations Those in favor of globalization argue that *globalization and international outsourcing help to advance developing nations' economies*. India initially became attractive as a location for software-writing operations because of its low-cost, well-trained, English-speaking technicians. Later, young graduates who would not become doctors and lawyers found bright futures in telephone call centers that provide all sorts of customer services. More recently, jobs in business-process outsourcing (including financial, accounting, payroll, and benefits services) is significantly elevating living standards in India. Western corporations can outsource such work to Indian firms for a fraction of what they pay at home.

Today, the relentless march of globalization is bringing call center jobs to the Philippines. Young Filipinos possess an excellent education, a solid grasp of the English language and

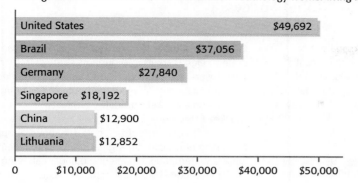

Average annual net income of an Information Technology worker living in:

United States	$49,692
Brazil	$37,056
Germany	$27,840
Singapore	$18,192
China	$12,900
Lithuania	$12,852

0    $10,000 $20,000 $30,000 $40,000 $50,000

FIGURE 1.2

Comparing Salaries of Information Technology Workers

Source: Based on data obtained from the *International Average Salary Income Database* (www.worldsalaries.org).

U.S. culture, and a neutral accent. Top Indian firms, such as Wipro (www.wipro.com), now have substantial operations in the Philippines and happily pay more, not less, than what they would need to pay workers in India. The work is not considered low-paying by any means, and instead represents a solid, middle-class job.[20]

Figure 1.2 illustrates why companies in industrialized nations choose to outsource jobs to emerging markets. The figure shows the average net annual salary of a computer programmer living in each country. The salary of a programmer in the United States is nearly four times that of one in some eastern European nations, including Lithuania. So long as such economic disparities exist, international outsourcing will continue to be popular.

Summary of the Jobs and Wages Debate All parties appear to agree that globalization eliminates some jobs in a nation but creates jobs in other sectors of the nation's economy. Yet, although some people lose their jobs and find new employment, it can be very difficult for others to find new work. The real point of difference between the two sides in the debate, it seems, is whether overall gains that (may or may not) accrue to *national economies* are worth the lost livelihoods that *individuals* (may or may not) suffer. Those in favor of globalization say individual pain is worth the collective gain, whereas those against globalization say it is not.

Globalization's Impact on Labor, the Environment, and Markets

Critics of globalization say companies locate operations to where labor and environmental regulations are least restrictive and, therefore, least costly. They argue this puts downward pressure on labor and environmental protection laws in all countries as nations compete to attract international firms. Let's examine these claims and the responses of globalization supporters.

LABOR STANDARDS Trade unions claim globalization reduces labor's bargaining power and lowers global labor standards when international firms are permitted to continually move to nations with lower labor standards. One place to test this assertion is in developing nations' *export-processing zones (EPZs)*—special areas in which companies engage in tariff-free importing and exporting. More than 850 EPZs employ 27 million people worldwide. Yet a study by the International Labor Organization (www.ilo.org), hardly a pro-business group, found no evidence to support the claim that nations with a strong union presence suffered any loss of investment in their EPZs. In fact, another study by the World Bank found that the higher occupational safety and health conditions an EPZ had in place, the greater foreign investment it attracted.[21] The evidence fails to support critics' allegations that economic openness and foreign investment contribute to lower labor standards.

ENVIRONMENTAL PROTECTION Some environmental groups say globalization causes a "race to the bottom" in environmental conditions and regulations. Yet studies show that pollution-intensive U.S. firms tend to invest in countries with stricter environmental standards. Many developing nations, including Argentina, Brazil, Malaysia, and Thailand, liberalized their foreign investment environment while simultaneously enacting *stricter* environmental legislation. If large international companies were eager to relocate to nations having poor environmental protection laws, they would not have invested in these countries for decades. Additional evidence that closed, protectionist economies are worse than open ones at protecting the environment includes Mexico

MANAGER'S BRIEFCASE   The Keys to Global Success

Making everything from 99-cent hamburgers (McDonald's) to $150 million jumbo jets (Boeing), managers of global companies must overcome obstacles when competing in unfamiliar markets. Global managers acknowledge certain common threads in their approaches to management and offer the following advice:

- *Communicate Effectively.* Cultural differences in business relationships and etiquette are central to global business and require cross-cultural competency. Effective global managers welcome uniqueness and ambiguity while demonstrating flexibility, respect, and empathy.
- *Know the Customer.* Successful managers understand how a company's different products serve the needs of international customers. Then, they ensure that the company remains flexible and capable enough to customize products that meet those needs.

- *Emphasize Global Awareness.* Good global managers integrate foreign markets into business strategy from the outset. They ensure that products and services are designed and built with global markets in mind, and not used as dumping grounds for the home market's outdated products.
- *Market Effectively.* The world will beat a path to your door to buy your "better mousetrap" only if it knows about it. A poor marketing effort can cause great products to fade into obscurity while an international marketing blunder can bring unwanted media attention. Top global managers match quality products with excellent marketing.
- *Monitor Global Markets.* Successful managers keep a watchful eye on business environments for shifting political, legal, and socioeconomic conditions. They make obtaining accurate information a top priority.

before NAFTA, Brazil under military rule, and the former Warsaw Pact of communist nations—all of which had extremely poor environmental records. Again, the evidence does not support claims of lower environmental standards being the result of economic openness and globalization.

FUTURE MARKETS Opponents to globalization claim that international firms exploit local labor markets and the environment to produce goods that are then exported back to the home countries. Such claims may not only perpetuate a false image of corporations but may also have no factual basis. Most international firms today support reasonable labor and environmental laws because (if for no other reason) they want to expand future local markets for their goods and services. They recognize that healthy future markets will require a sustainable approach to business expansion. When analyzing a country prior to investing, companies today often examine a location for its potential as a future market as well as a production base. Less than 5 percent of U.S. firms invest in developing countries to obtain low-cost resources and then export finished products back to the United States. For additional insights into how managers today succeed by respecting unfamiliar markets, see the Manager's Briefcase, titled, "The Keys to Global Success."

QUICK STUDY 5

1. What are the claims of those who say globalization eliminates jobs, lowers wages, and exploits workers?
2. Identify the arguments of those who say globalization creates jobs and boosts wages.
3. Why do critics say globalization adversely affects labor standards, environmental regulations, and future markets?
4. How do supporters of globalization argue that it does not harm labor standards, environmental regulations, and future markets?

Globalization and Income Inequality

Perhaps no controversy swirling around globalization is more complex than the debate over its effect on income inequality. Here, we focus on three main aspects of the debate: inequality within nations, inequality between nations, and global inequality.

INEQUALITY WITHIN NATIONS The first aspect of the inequality debate is whether globalization is increasing income inequality among people *within* nations. Opponents of globalization argue that freer trade and investment allows international companies to close factories in high-wage, developed nations and to move them to low-wage, developing nations. They argue that this increases the wage gap between white-collar and blue-collar occupations in rich nations.

Two studies of *developed and developing nations* find contradictory evidence on this argument. The first study, of 38 countries over almost 30 years, supports the increasing inequality argument. The study found that as a nation increases its openness to trade, income growth among the poorest 40 percent of a nation's population declines, whereas income growth among other groups increases.[22] The second study, of 80 countries over 40 years, failed to support the increasing inequality argument. It found that incomes of the poor rise one-for-one with overall economic growth and concluded that the poor benefit from international trade along with the rest of a nation.[23] The mixed findings of these two studies are typical of a large set of research examining inequality between developed *and* developing nations.

Two studies of *developing nations only* are more consistent in their findings. One study found that an increase in the ratio of trade to national output of 1 percent raised average income levels by 0.5 to 2 percent. Another study showed that incomes of the poor kept pace with growth in average incomes in economies (and periods) of fast trade integration, but that the poor fell behind during periods of declining openness.[24] Results of these two studies suggest that, by integrating their economies into the global economy, developing nations (by far the nations with the most to gain) can boost the incomes of their poorest citizens.

A new approach being developed takes a multidimensional view of poverty and deprivation. Proponents of this approach say that the problem with focusing on income alone is that higher income does not necessarily translate into better health or nutrition. The new approach examines 10 basic factors, including whether the family home has a decent toilet and electricity service; whether children are enrolled in school; and whether family members are malnourished or must walk more than 30 minutes to obtain clean drinking water. A household is considered poor if it is deprived on over 30 percent of the indicators. This new approach reveals important differences among poor regions. For example, whereas material measures contribute more to poverty in sub-Saharan Africa, malnutrition is a bigger factor in South Asia.[25]

INEQUALITY BETWEEN NATIONS The second aspect of the inequality debate is whether globalization is widening the gap in average incomes *between* rich and poor nations. If we compare average incomes in high-income countries with average incomes in middle- and low-income nations, we do find a widening gap. But *averages* conceal differences between nations.

On closer inspection, it appears the gap between rich and poor nations is not occurring everywhere: *One group of poor nations is closing the gap with rich economies, while a second group of poor countries is falling further behind.* For example, China is narrowing the income

A man dismantles the carcass of a car for recycling in the "Cité Soleil" slum of Port-au-Prince, Haiti. Haiti is a "traditional" market that has not benefited as much from globalization as have other nations. The plight of people like the man shown here incites calls for a wider distribution of the benefits of economic progress. What, if anything, do you think businesses and governments can do to improve the lives of people enduring such harsh living conditions?

Source: THONY BELIZAIRE/Newscom

gap between itself and the United States as measured by GDP per capita, but the gap between Africa and the United States is widening. China's progress is no doubt a result of its integration with the world economy and annual economic growth rates of between 7 and 9 percent. Another emerging market, India, is also narrowing its income gap with the United States by embracing globalization.[26]

Developing countries that embrace globalization are increasing personal incomes, extending life expectancies, and improving education systems. In addition, post-communist countries that welcomed world trade and investment experienced high growth rates in GDP per capita. But nations that remain closed off from the world economy have performed far worse.

GLOBAL INEQUALITY The third aspect of the inequality debate is whether globalization is increasing *global inequality*—widening income inequality between all people of the world, no matter where they live. A recent study paints a promising picture of declining poverty. This study found that the percentage of the world's population living on less than a dollar a day (a common poverty gauge) fell from 17 percent to just 7 percent over a 30-year period, which reduced the number of people in poverty by roughly 200 million.[27] Yet, a widely cited study by the World Bank finds that the percent of world population living on less than a dollar a day fell from 33 percent to 18 percent over a 20-year period, which reduced the number of people in poverty from 1.5 billion to 1.1 billion.[28]

For a variety of reasons, the real picture likely lies somewhere in between these two studies' estimates. For example, whereas the World Bank study used population figures for developing countries only, the first study used global population in its analyses, which lowered poverty estimates, all else being equal. What is important is that most experts agree that global inequality has fallen, although they disagree on the extent of the fall.

What it is like to live on less than a dollar a day in sub-Saharan Africa, South Asia, or elsewhere is too difficult for most of us to comprehend. The continent of Africa presents the most pressing problem. Home to 13 percent of the world's population, Africa accounts for just 3 percent of world GDP. Rich nations realize they cannot sit idly by while so many of the world's people live under such conditions.

What can be done to help the world's poor? First of all, rich nations could increase the amount of foreign aid they give to poor nations—foreign aid as a share of donor country GDP is at historically low levels. Second, rich nations can accelerate the process of forgiving some of the debt burdens of the most heavily indebted poor countries (HIPCs). The HIPC initiative is committed to reducing the debt burdens of the world's poorest countries. This initiative would enable these countries to spend money on social services and greater integration with the global economy instead of on interest payments on debt.[29]

Summary of the Income Inequality Debate For the debate over inequality *within nations*, studies suggest that developing nations can boost incomes of their poorest citizens by embracing globalization and integrating themselves into the global economy. In the debate over inequality *between nations*, nations open to world trade and investment appear to grow faster than rich nations do. Meanwhile, economies that remain sheltered from the global economy tend to be worse off. Finally, regarding the debate over *global inequality*, although experts agree inequality has fallen in recent decades, they disagree on the extent of the drop.

Globalization's Influence on Cultures

National culture is a strong shaper of a people's values, attitudes, customs, beliefs, and communication. Whether globalization eradicates cultural differences between groups of people or reinforces cultural uniqueness is a hotly debated topic.

Protesters complain that globalization is homogenizing our world and destroying its rich diversity of cultures. Critics say that in some drab, new world we all will wear the same clothes bought at the same brand-name shops, eat the same foods at the same brand-name restaurants, and watch the same movies made by the same production companies.

But supporters argue that globalization allows us all to profit from our differing circumstances and skills. Trade allows countries to specialize in producing the goods and services they can produce most efficiently. Nations can then trade with each other to obtain goods and services they desire but do not produce. In this way, France still produces many of the world's finest wines, South Africa yields much of the world's diamonds, and Japan continues to design some

CULTURE MATTERS   The Culture Debate

The debate over globalization's influence on culture evokes strong opinions. Here are a few main arguments in this debate:

- **Material Desire.** Critics say globalization fosters the "Coca-Colanization" of nations through advertising campaigns that promote material desire. They also argue that global consumer-goods companies destroy cultural diversity (especially in developing nations) by putting local companies out of business.
- **Artistic Influence.** Evidence suggests, however, that the cultures of developing nations are thriving and that the influence of their music, art, and literature has grown (not shrunk) throughout the past century. African cultures, for example, have influenced the works of artists including Picasso, the Beatles, and Sting.
- **Western Values.** International businesses reach far and wide through the Internet, global media, increased business travel, and local marketing. Critics say local values and traditions are being replaced by U.S. companies promoting "Western" values.

- **A Force for Good.** On the positive side, globalization tends to foster two important values: tolerance and diversity. Advocates say nations should be more tolerant of opposing viewpoints and should welcome diversity among their peoples. This view interprets globalization as a potent force for good in the world.
- **Deeper Values.** Globalization can cause consumer purchases and economic ideologies to converge, but these are rather superficial aspects of culture. Deeper values that embody the essence of cultures may be more resistant to a global consumer culture.
- **Want to Know More?** Visit the globalization page of the Global Policy Forum (www.globalpolicy.org), Globalization 101 (www.globalization101.org), or The Globalist (www.theglobalist.com).

Source: "Economic Globalization and Culture: A Discussion with Dr. Francis Fukuyama," Merrill Lynch Forum website (www.ml.com); "Globalization Issues," The Globalization website (www.sociology.emory.edu/globalization); Cultural Diversity in the Era of Globalization," UNESCO Culture Sector website (www.unesco.org/culture).

of the world's finest-engineered automobiles. Other nations then trade their goods and services with these countries to enjoy the wines, diamonds, and automobiles that they do not, or cannot, produce. To learn more about the interplay between culture and globalization, see this chapter's Culture Matters feature, titled, "The Culture Debate."

Globalization and National Sovereignty

National sovereignty generally involves the idea that a nation-state (1) is autonomous, (2) can freely select its government, (3) cannot intervene in the affairs of other nations, (4) can control movements across its borders, and (5) can enter into binding international agreements. Opposition groups allege that globalization erodes national sovereignty and encroaches on the authority of local and state governments. Supporters disagree, saying that globalization spreads democracy worldwide and that national sovereignty must be viewed from a long-term perspective.

GLOBALIZATION: MENACE TO DEMOCRACY? A main argument leveled against globalization is that it empowers supranational institutions at the expense of national governments. It is not in dispute that the WTO, the IMF, and the United Nations are led by appointed, not democratically elected, representatives. What is debatable, however, is whether these organizations unduly impose their will on the citizens of sovereign nations. Critics argue that, by undercutting the political and legal authority of national, regional, and local governments, such organizations undercut democracy and individual liberty.

Opponents of globalization also take issue with the right of national political authorities to enter into binding international agreements on behalf of citizens. Critics charge that such agreements violate the rights of subfederal (local and state) governments. For example, state and local governments in the United States had no role in creating the NAFTA. Yet WTO rules require the U.S. federal government to take all available actions (including enacting preemptive legislation or withdrawing funding) to force subfederal compliance with WTO terms. Protesters say that such requirements directly attack the rights and authority of subfederal governments.[30]

GLOBALIZATION: GUARDIAN OF DEMOCRACY? Globalization supporters argue that an amazing consequence of globalization has been the spread of democracy worldwide. In recent decades, the people of many nations have become better educated, better informed, and more empowered. Supporters say globalization has not sent democracy spiraling into decline but instead has been instrumental in spreading democracy to the world.

Backers of globalization also contend that it is instructive to take a long-term view on the issue of national sovereignty. Witnessing a sovereign state's scope of authority altered is nothing new, as governments have long given up trying to control issues they could not resolve. In the mid-1600s, governments in Europe surrendered their authority over religion because attempts to control it undermined overall political stability. Also, Greece in 1832, Albania in 1913, and the former Yugoslavian states in the 1990s had to protect minorities in exchange for international recognition. And over the past 50 years, the United Nations has made significant progress on worthy issues such as genocide, torture, slavery, refugees, women's rights, children's rights, forced labor, and racial discrimination. Like the loss of sovereignty over these issues, globalization supporters say lost sovereignty over some economic issues may actually enhance the greater good.[31]

QUICK STUDY 6

1. What does the evidence suggest for each aspect of the debate over globalization and income inequality?
2. Summarize the claims of each side in the debate over globalization's influence on cultures.
3. What are the arguments on each side of the debate over globalization's impact on national sovereignty?

Why International Business Is Special

As we've already seen in this chapter, international business differs greatly from business in a purely domestic context. The most obvious contrast is that different nations can have entirely different societies and commercial environments. Let's take a moment to examine what makes international business special by introducing a model unique to this book—a model we call the *global business environment*.

The Global Business Environment

International business is special because it occurs within a dynamic, integrated system that weaves together four distinct elements:

1. The forces of *globalization*
2. The *international* business environment
3. Many *national* business environments
4. International *firm* management

The model in Figure 1.3 identifies each of these elements and their subparts that together comprise the *global business environment*. Thinking about international business as occurring within this global system helps us understand the complexities of international business and the interrelations between its distinct elements. Let's preview each of the four main components in the global business environment.

Globalization is a potent force transforming our societies and commercial activities in countless ways. Globalization, and the pressures it creates, forces its way into each element shown in Figure 1.3. In this way, the drivers of globalization (technological innovation and falling trade and investment barriers) influence every aspect of the global business environment. The dynamic nature of globalization also creates increasing competition for all firms everywhere, as managers begin to see the entire world as an opportunity. At home and abroad, firms must remain vigilant to the fundamental societal and commercial changes that globalization is causing.

The *international business environment* influences how firms conduct their operations in both subtle and not-so-subtle ways. No business is entirely immune to events in the international business environment, as evidenced by the long-term trend toward more porous national borders. The drivers of globalization are causing the flows of trade, investment, and capital to grow and to become more entwined—often causing firms to search simultaneously for production bases *and* new markets. Companies today must keep their fingers on the pulse of the international business environment to see how it may affect their business activities.

Each *national business environment* is composed of unique cultural, political, legal, and economic characteristics that define business activity within that nation's borders. This set of national characteristics can differ greatly from country to country. But as nations open up and embrace globalization, their business environments are being transformed. Globalization can cause powerful synergies and enormous tensions to arise within and across various elements of

FIGURE 1.3

The Global Business Environment

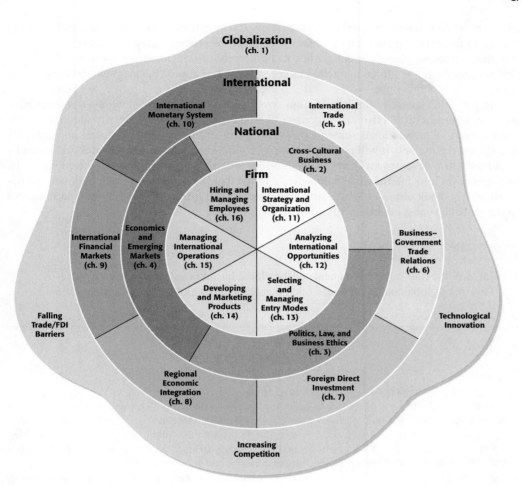

Globalization (ch. 1)

International

International Monetary System (ch. 10)

International Trade (ch. 5)

National

Cross-Cultural Business (ch. 2)

Firm

Hiring and Managing Employees (ch. 16)

International Strategy and Organization (ch. 11)

Economics and Emerging Markets (ch. 4)

International Financial Markets (ch. 9)

Managing International Operations (ch. 15)

Analyzing International Opportunities (ch. 12)

Business–Government Trade Relations (ch. 6)

Developing and Marketing Products (ch. 14)

Selecting and Managing Entry Modes (ch. 13)

Falling Trade/FDI Barriers

Politics, Law, and Business Ethics (ch. 3)

Technological Innovation

Regional Economic Integration (ch. 8)

Foreign Direct Investment (ch. 7)

Increasing Competition

a society. Company managers must be attentive to such nuances, adapting their products and practices as needed.

International firm management is vastly different from the management of a purely domestic business. Companies must abide by the rules in every market in which they choose to operate. Therefore, the context of international business management is defined by the characteristics of national business environments. Because of widely dispersed production and marketing activities today, firms commonly interact with people in distant locations within the international business environment. Finally, managers and their firms are compelled to be knowledgeable about the nations in which they operate because of the integrating power of globalization. Businesses should try to anticipate events and forces that can affect their operations by closely monitoring globalization, national business environments, and the international business environment.

The Road Ahead for International Business

The coverage of international business in this book follows the model of the global business environment displayed in Figure 1.3. In this chapter, we learned how *globalization* is transforming our world and how elements of the global business environment are becoming increasingly intertwined. As globalization penetrates deeper into the national context, every aspect of international business management is being affected.

In Part 2 (Chapters 2 through 4), we explore how *national business environments* differ from one nation to another. We examine how people's attitudes, values, beliefs, and institutions differ from one culture to another and how this affects business. This part also covers how nations differ in their political, legal, and economic systems. This material is placed early in the text because such differences between countries help frame subsequent topics and discussions, such as how companies modify business practices and strategies abroad.

We describe major components of the *international business environment* in Part 3 (Chapters 5 through 8) and Part 4 (Chapters 9 and 10). Our coverage begins with an examination of trade and investment theories and a discussion of why governments encourage or discourage these two forms of international business. We explore the process of regional economic integration that is sweeping the globe and outline its implications for international business. Finally, we discuss how events in global financial markets affect international business and how the global monetary system functions.

In Part 5 (Chapters 11 through 16), our coverage turns to ways in which *international business management* differs from management of a purely domestic firm. We explain how a company creates an international strategy, organizes itself for international business, and analyzes and selects the markets it will pursue. We explore different potential entry modes and then discuss how a firm develops and markets products for specific nations, regions, or the entire world. We then cover how international companies manage their sometimes far-flung international operations. The book closes by discussing how international firms manage their human resources in the global business environment.

QUICK STUDY 7

1. Identify the four main components of the global business environment.
2. How does globalization influence other elements in the global business environment?

BOTTOM LINE FOR BUSINESS

The main theme of this chapter is that the world's national economies are becoming increasingly intertwined through the process of globalization. Cultural, political, legal, and economic events in one country increasingly affect the lives of people in other countries. Companies must pay attention to how changes in nations where they do business can affect operations. In this section, we briefly examine several important business implications of globalization.

Harnessing Globalization's Benefits

People opposed to globalization say it negatively affects wages and environmental protection, reduces political freedom, increases corruption, and inequitably rewards various groups. Yet there is evidence that the most globalized nations have the strongest records on equality, the most robust protection of natural resources, the most inclusive political systems, and the lowest levels of corruption. People in the most globalized nations also live the healthiest and longest lives, and women there have achieved the most social, educational, and economic progress.

One thing the debate over globalization has achieved is a dialogue on the merits and demerits of globalization. What has emerged is a more sober, less naïve notion of globalization. Those on each side of the debate understand that globalization can have positive effects on people's lives, but globalization cannot, by itself, alleviate the misery of the world's poor. Both sides in the debate are now working together to harness the benefits of globalization while minimizing its costs.

Intensified Competition

The two driving forces of globalization (lower trade and investment barriers and increased technological innovation) are taking companies into previously isolated markets and increasing competitive pressures worldwide. And innovation is unlikely to slow any time soon.

As the cost of computing power continues to fall and new technologies are developed, companies will find it easier and less costly to manage widely dispersed marketing activities and production facilities. Technological developments may even strengthen the case for outsourcing more professional jobs to low-cost locations. As competition intensifies, international companies will increase their cooperation with suppliers and customers.

Wages and Jobs

Some labor groups in wealthy nations contend that globalization is forcing companies to join the "race to the bottom" in terms of wages and benefits. But to attract investment, a location must offer low-cost, adequately skilled workers in an environment with acceptable levels of social, political, and economic stability.

Rapid globalization of markets and production is making delivery a complex engineering task. And as companies cut costs by outsourcing activities, supply and distribution channels grow longer and more complex. Corporate logistics departments and logistics specialist firms are helping international companies untangle lengthy supply chains, monitor shipping lanes, and forecast weather patterns. High-wage logistics jobs represent the kind of high-value-added employment that results from the "churning" in labor markets caused by globalization.

The Policy Agenda

Countless actions could be taken by developed and developing nations to lessen the negative effects of globalization. The World Bank calls on rich countries to (1) open their markets to exports from developing countries, (2) slash their agricultural subsidies that hurt poor-country exports, and (3) increase development aid, particularly in education and health. It calls on poor countries to improve their investment climates and improve social protection for poor people in a changing economic environment.

The Peterson Institute for International Economics (www.iie.com) proposed a policy agenda for rich nations on two fronts. On the *domestic front,* it proposes (1) establishing on-the-job training to help workers cope with globalization, (2) offering "wage insurance" to workers forced by globalization to take a lower-paying job, (3) subsidizing health insurance costs in case of lost work, and (4) improving education and lifetime learning. On the *international front,* it proposes (1) better enforcing labor standards, (2) clarifying the relation between international trade and environmental agreements, and (3) reviewing the environmental implications of trade agreements.

This chapter has only introduced you to the study of international business—we hope you enjoy the rest of your journey!

Chapter Summary

MyManagementLab

Go to **mymanagementlab.com** to complete the problem marked with this icon .

1. **Identify the types of companies that participate in international business.**
   - Large *multinational corporations (MNCs)* conduct most international business transactions.
   - MNCs have great economic and political muscle, and their deals are often worth billions of dollars.
   - Globalization has given rise to the *born global firm*—a company that adopts a global perspective and engages in international business from or near its inception.
   - Born global firms tend to have an innovative culture, knowledge-based capabilities, and the status of international competitor in less than three years.
   - Entrepreneurs and small firms benefit from the Internet and other technologies that help them overcome high advertising and distribution costs.

2. **Describe the process of globalization and how it affects markets and production.**
   - *Globalization* is the trend toward greater economic, cultural, political, and technological interdependence among national institutions and economies.
   - Globalization is marked by denationalization, in which national borders become somewhat less relevant.
   - The globalization of *markets* helps a company to (1) reduce costs by standardizing marketing activities, (2) explore international markets if the home market is small or saturated, and (3) level income streams, especially for makers of seasonal products.
   - The globalization of *production* helps a company to (1) access low-cost labor and become more price competitive and (2) access technical know-how or natural resources nonexistent or too expensive at home.

3. **Describe the two forces causing globalization to increase.**
   - *Falling barriers to trade and investment* is one major force behind globalization.
   - Trade barriers have been drastically reduced through institutions such as the *General Agreement on Tariffs and Trade* and the *World Trade Organization.*
   - Groups of several or more nations are reducing trade barriers by creating regional trade agreements.
   - *Technological innovation* is a second main force driving globalization.
   - Companies can manage global business activities through the use of e-mail, videoconferencing, intranets, and extranets.
   - Technology increases the speed and ease with which companies can manage far-flung operations.
   - Innovations in transportation technologies are making the shipment of goods between nations more efficient and dependable.

4. **Summarize the evidence for each main argument in the globalization debate.**
   - Regarding *jobs and wages,* both sides agree that globalization causes dislocation in labor markets: Those supporting globalization believe overall gains of national economies are worth lost jobs for individuals; but critics of globalization do not.
   - Labor unions argue that globalization causes a "race to the bottom" in *labor and environmental regulation,* though they lack supporting evidence.
   - Regarding inequality *within nations,* developing nations can boost the incomes of their poorest citizens by integrating themselves into the global economy.
   - In the debate over *inequality between nations,* nations that embrace world trade and investment grow faster than rich nations, whereas sheltered economies become worse off.
   - Groups agree that *global inequality* has fallen in recent decades but differ on the extent of the drop.
   - Evidence suggests that the *cultures* of developing nations are thriving in an age of globalization and that deeper elements of culture are not easily abandoned.
   - In terms of *national sovereignty,* globalization has helped spread democracy worldwide and has aided progress on many global issues.

5. **Describe the global business environment and identify its four main elements.**
   - International business occurs within an integrated, *global business environment* consisting of four elements.

- *Globalization* is transforming business and society and increasing competition for all firms.
- The *international business environment* influences how firms conduct operations, while globalization further entwines the flows of trade, investment, and capital.
- Separate *national business environments* comprise unique cultural, political, legal, and economic characteristics that define business activity within a nation.
- *International business management* differs from management of a purely domestic firm in nearly all respects.

Talk It Over

1. Today, international businesspeople must think globally about production and sales opportunities. Many global managers will eventually find themselves living and working in cultures altogether different from their own. Many entrepreneurs will find themselves booking flights to places they had previously never heard of. What do you think companies can do now to prepare their managers for these new markets? What can entrepreneurs and small businesses with limited resources do?
2. In the past, national governments greatly affected the pace of globalization through agreements to lower barriers to international trade and investment. Is the pace of change now outpacing the capability of governments to manage the global economy? Will national governments become more or less important to international business in the future? Explain your answer.
3. Information technologies are developing at a faster rate than ever before. How have these technologies influenced globalization? Give specific examples. Do you think globalization will continue until we all live in one "global village"? Why or why not?
⭐4. Consider the following statement: "Globalization and the resulting increase in competition harm people, as international companies play one government against another to get the best deal possible. Meanwhile, governments continually ask for greater concessions from their citizens, demanding that they work harder and longer for less pay." Do you agree? Why or why not?

Teaming Up

1. **Research Project.** Imagine that you and a group of your fellow classmates own a company that manufactures cheap sunglasses. To lower production costs, you want to move your factory from your developed country to a more cost-effective nation. Choose a prospective country to which you will move production. What elements of the national business environment might affect your move? Are there obstacles to overcome in the international business environment? How will managing your company be different when you undertake international activities? What challenges will you face in managing your new employees?
2. **Market Entry Strategy Project.** This exercise corresponds to the *MESP* online simulation. With a group of classmates, select a country that interests you. Describe its national flag: What do its colors and any symbols on it represent? Identify neighbors with which it shares borders. Give some important facts about the country, including its population, population density, land area, topography, climate, and natural resources and the locations of its main industries. What does the nation produce? Do any aspects of the natural environment help explain why it produces what it does? Integrate your findings into your completed *MESP* report.

Key Terms

born global firm (p. 6)
e-business (e-commerce) (p. 4)
exports (p. 4)
GDP or GNP per capita (p. 11)
General Agreement on Tariffs and Trade (GATT) (p. 10)
globalization (p. 7)

gross domestic product (GDP) (p. 11)
gross national product (GNP) (p. 11)
imports (p. 4)
international business (p. 4)

International Monetary Fund (IMF) (p. 16)
multinational corporation (MNC) (p. 6)
sustainability (p. 8)
World Bank (p. 16)
World Trade Organization (WTO) (p. 11)

Take It to the Web

1. **Video Report.** Visit this book's channel on YouTube (www.YouTube.com/MyIBvideos). Click on "Videos" near the top of the page, and click on the set of videos labeled "Ch 01: Globalization." Watch one video from the list, and then summarize it in a half-page report. Reflecting on the contents of this chapter, which aspects of globalization can you identify in the video? How might a company engaged in international business act on the information contained in the video?

2. **Website Report.** In this chapter, we've seen how globalization is fundamentally changing business and society. Managers can be more effective if they know what drives globalization and are familiar with its positive and negative aspects.

    Select a controversial globalization topic that interests you, and visit the Websites of two organizations that have opposing views on this topic. (Hint: You might begin by visiting an organization noted in this chapter.) For the topic you've chosen, report on (1) the specific argument(s) of each side, (2) the evidence each side uses to support its position(s), and (3) the policy agenda, if any, each side promotes.

    Which argument(s) do you agree with most? Have your views on this topic changed as a result of your research? If yes, explain how. Which types of firms/industries do you think this topic affects most? Explain. Write a short summary of your findings and include key websites you found helpful.

Ethical Challenges

1. You are a U.S. citizen recently assigned as the manager of distribution in a European country where bribery is relatively accepted. Your job description includes responsibility for accepting shipments as they enter the local port authority. On your first trip down to the docks to sign for a shipment, the customs agent in charge asks for a "tip" to clear the goods for pickup. The value of the incoming shipment is around $150,000. Knowing that the government has recently launched an initiative to reduce corruption, how do you react? If additional information would be helpful to you, what would it be?

2. You are the CEO of a major U.S. apparel company that contracts work to garment manufacturers abroad. Employees of the contractors report 20-hour workdays, pay below the minimum wage, overcrowded living conditions, physically abusive supervisors, and confiscation of their passports. Contractors and government officials say local labor laws are adhered to and enforced, though abuses appear widespread. You send inspectors to the factories abroad, but they uncover no labor violations. A labor-advocacy group claims that supervisors coached workers to lie to your inspectors about conditions and threatened workers with time in makeshift jails without food if they talked. How do you handle this situation? Do you implement some type of monitoring system? Do you help the factories improve conditions, withdraw your business, or do nothing? How might your actions affect your relations with the factory owners and your ability to do business in the country?

3. You are the mayor of a midsized U.S. town on the Colorado River between Mexico and Arizona. Pollution from factories on both sides of the U.S.–Mexico border has contaminated your community and the Colorado River. The North American Free Trade Agreement (NAFTA) requires the U.S. government to pay for environmental cleanup in the United States. Yet critics accuse both the U.S. and Mexican governments of not doing enough to safeguard the environment along the border. As mayor, what can you do to persuade business leaders and government officials to adhere to environmental standards? Which body do you think presents your biggest challenge: the Arizona state legislature, the U.S. government, or the Mexican government? What can business leaders do if governments ignore their environmental responsibilities?

MyManagementLab

Go to **mymanagementlab.com** for Auto-graded writing questions as well as the following Assisted-graded writing questions:

1-1. Some say globalization is homogenizing the attitudes and spending habits of young consumers worldwide. Do you agree or disagree? Why or why not?

1-2. Advances in technology often spur evolution in the entertainment industry. How might new products and services affect entertainment in years to come?

1-3. Mymanagementlab Only – comprehensive writing assignment for this chapter.

Practicing International Management Case

MTV Goes Global with a Local Beat

As asked by the Buggles song, did "video kill the radio star"? Well, perhaps not, but no company has been more successful at getting teenagers around the world to tune in to music television than MTV Networks (www.mtv.com). Applying the maxim "Think globally, act locally," the company beams its irreverent mix of music, news, and entertainment to 640 million homes in more than 162 countries in 34 languages. Although style and format are largely driven by the U.S. youth culture, content is tailored to suit local markets. MTV has never grown old with its audience and has remained true to young people between the ages of 18 and 24.

In 1987, MTV commanded an audience of 61 million in the United States. But to counteract slowing demand, the company took the music revolution global by starting MTV Europe (www.mtv.tv) and MTV Australia (www.mtv.com.au). Through its experiences in Europe, MTV refined its mix of programming to become a "global national brand with local variations." At first, it took a pan-European approach, marketing the same product to all European countries. MTV broadcast primarily British and U.S. music (both of which were topping the charts throughout Europe) and used European "veejays" who spoke English. The European network was a huge overnight success.

Seven years later, however, MTV had become the victim of its own success. It suddenly had to compete with a new crop of upstart rivals that tailored content to language, culture, and current events in specific countries. One successful competitor was Germany's VIVA (www.viva.tv), launched in 1993 and featuring German veejays and more German artists than MTV Europe. Managers at MTV Networks were not overly concerned because MTV was still extremely popular. But they did realize they were losing their edge (and some customers) to the new national networks. So, the company's top managers had to reassess the company's strategy.

Because they had spent almost two decades building a global brand identity, MTV executives initially rejected the idea of splitting MTV into national stations. But the company gradually decided to go ahead with a national strategy because a new technology made it possible for MTV to think globally and act locally at little cost. The breakthrough was digital compression technology, which allows multiple services to be offered on a single satellite feed. "Where there were three or four services," explained one MTV official, "now we can broadcast six or eight."

Today, teens all over the world can have their MTV cake and eat it, too. German teens see German-language programs that are created and produced in Germany and shown on MTV Germany (www.mtv.de)—along with the usual generous helpings of U.S., British, and international music and the ever-popular cartoon duo of Beavis and Butthead. European nations that still share an MTV channel are those that share cultural similarities—such as the Nordic nations (www.mtve.com). Likewise, whereas much of Latin America receives MTV Latin America (www.mtvla.com), Brazilian teens see Portuguese-language programs that are created in Brazil and shown on MTV Brazil (www.mtv.uol.com.br). National advertisers who shunned MTV during its pan-European days can now beam their targeted ads to teenage consumers.

In 2012, MTV launched a new website (www.artists.mtv.com). Both famous and not-so-famous musicians can sell music and merchandise on their own page and even book a gig. Fans can "tip" performers using virtual tip jars. Shannon Connolly, V.P. of Digital Music Strategy for MTV, says, "Creating ways for artists to afford to keep doing what they do is a huge challenge in the music business today. Technology has really interrupted a lot of the traditional methods through which artists sold product and built their careers."

Now, nearly three decades after MTV planted its flag on the pop-culture moon in 1981, the beat goes on for the MTV generation. As Robert Thompson, professor of media and popular culture at Syracuse University, says, "It's the only television entity of any kind that ever had a generation named after it."

Thinking Globally

1. Some people outside the United States say teens exposed to large doses of U.S. culture on MTV will identify less with their own societies and will desire Western goods they cannot afford. MTV's response: "It's just fun, it's only TV." What do you think? Are there dangers in broadcasting U.S.–style programs and ads to developing countries?

2. Digital compression technology made it possible for MTV to program across a global network. What other technological innovations have helped companies to think globally and act locally?

Source: Sabrina Ford, "MTV Unveils New Website for Fans to Reach Artists," *Reuters* (www.reuters.com), March 15, 2012; "Madrid Rocks!! MTV Selects Madrid as Host City for 2010 MTV EMAs," *PR Newswire* (www.prnewswire.com), March 16, 2010; Marcus Dowling, "The Day the 'Music' Died," *The Couch Sessions* (www.thecouchsessions.com), February 12, 2010; George Winslow, "Q&A with MTV Networks International Managing Director Bhavneet Singh," *Multichannel News* (www.multichannel.com), January 2, 2008.

Appendix World Atlas

As globalization marches across the globe, international business managers can make more-informed decisions if they know the locations of countries and the distances between them. This atlas presents the world in a series of maps and is designed to assist you in understanding the global landscape of business. We encourage you to return to this atlas frequently to refresh your memory, especially when you encounter the name of an unfamiliar city or country.

Familiarize yourself with each of the maps in this appendix, and then try to answer the following 20 questions. For each question, select all answers that apply.

Map Exercises

1. Which of the following countries border the Atlantic Ocean?
   a. Bolivia   d. Japan
   b. Australia   e. United States
   c. South Africa

2. Which of the following countries are found in Africa?
   a. Guyana   d. Pakistan
   b. Morocco   e. Niger
   c. Egypt

3. Which one of the following countries does not border the Pacific Ocean?
   a. Australia   d. Mexico
   b. Venezuela   e. Peru
   c. Japan

4. Prague is the capital city of:
   a. Uruguay   d. Tunisia
   b. Czech Republic   e. Hungary
   c. Portugal

5. If transportation costs for getting your product from your market to Japan are high, which of the following countries might be good places to locate a manufacturing facility?
   a. Thailand   d. Indonesia
   b. Philippines   e. Portugal
   c. South Africa

6. Seoul is the capital city of (capitals are designated with red dots):
   a. Vietnam   d. China
   b. Cambodia   e. South Korea
   c. Malaysia

7. Turkey, Romania, Ukraine, and Russia border the body of water called the
   _____ Sea.

8. Thailand shares borders with:
   a. Cambodia   d. Malaysia
   b. Pakistan   e. Indonesia
   c. Singapore

9. Which of the following countries border no major ocean or sea?
   a. Austria   d. Niger
   b. Paraguay   e. all of the above
   c. Switzerland

10. Oslo is the capital city of:
    a. Germany   d. Australia
    b. Canada   e. Norway
    c. Brazil

11. Chile is located in:
    a. Africa   d. South America
    b. Asia   e. Central Europe
    c. the Northern Hemisphere

12. Saudi Arabia shares borders with:
    a. Jordan   d. United Arab Emirates
    b. Kuwait   e. all of the above
    c. Iraq

13. The body of water located between Sweden and Estonia is the _____ Sea.

14. Which of the following countries are located on the Mediterranean Sea?
    a. Italy   d. France
    b. Croatia   e. Portugal
    c. Turkey

15. The distance between Sydney (Australia) and Tokyo (Japan) is shorter than that between:
    a. Tokyo and Cape Town (South Africa)
    b. Sydney and Hong Kong (China, SAR)
    c. Tokyo and London (England)
    d. Sydney and Jakarta (Indonesia)
    e. all of the above

16. Madrid is the capital city of:
    a. Madagascar   d. Spain
    b. Italy   e. United States
    c. Mexico

17. Which of the following countries is not located in central Asia?
    a. Afghanistan   d. Kazakhstan
    b. Uzbekistan   e. Suriname
    c. Turkmenistan

18. If you were shipping your products from your production facility in Pakistan to market in Australia, they would likely cross the _____ Ocean.

19. Papua New Guinea, Guinea-Bissau, and Guinea are alternative names for the same country.
    a. true
    b. false

20. Which of the following countries are island nations?
    a. New Zealand
    b. Madagascar
    c. Japan
    d. Australia
    e. all of the above

Answers

(1) c. South Africa, e. United States; (2) b. Morocco, c. Egypt, e. Niger; (3) b. Venezuela; (4) b. Czech Republic; (5) a. Thailand, b. Philippines, d. Indonesia; (6) e. South Korea; (7) Black; (8) a. Cambodia, d. Malaysia; (9) e. all of the above; (10) e. Norway; (11) d. South America; (12) e. all of the above; (13) Baltic; (14) a. Italy, c. Turkey, d. France; (15) a. Tokyo and Cape Town (South Africa), c. Tokyo and London (England); (16) d. Spain; (17) e. Suriname; (18) Indian; (19) b. false; (20) e. all of the above.

Self-Assessment

If you scored 15 correct answers or more, well done! You seem well prepared for your international business journey. If you scored fewer than 8 correct answers, you may wish to review this atlas before moving on to Chapter 2.

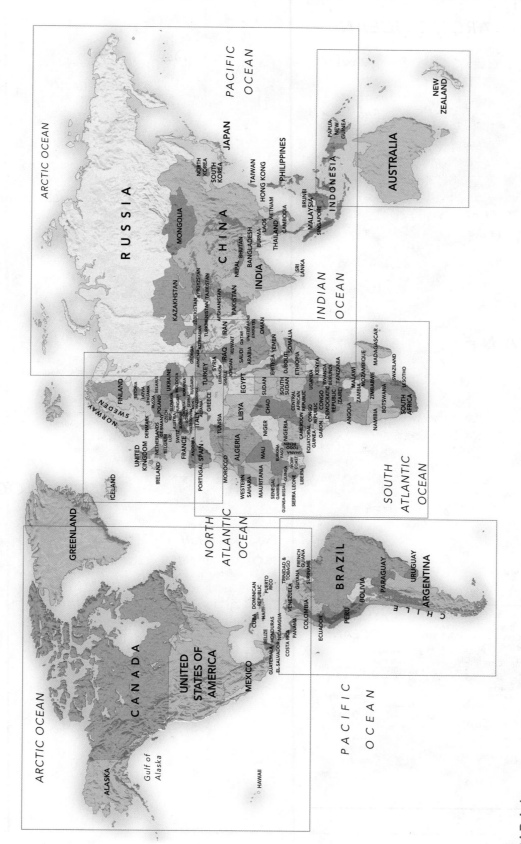

MAP A.I
The World

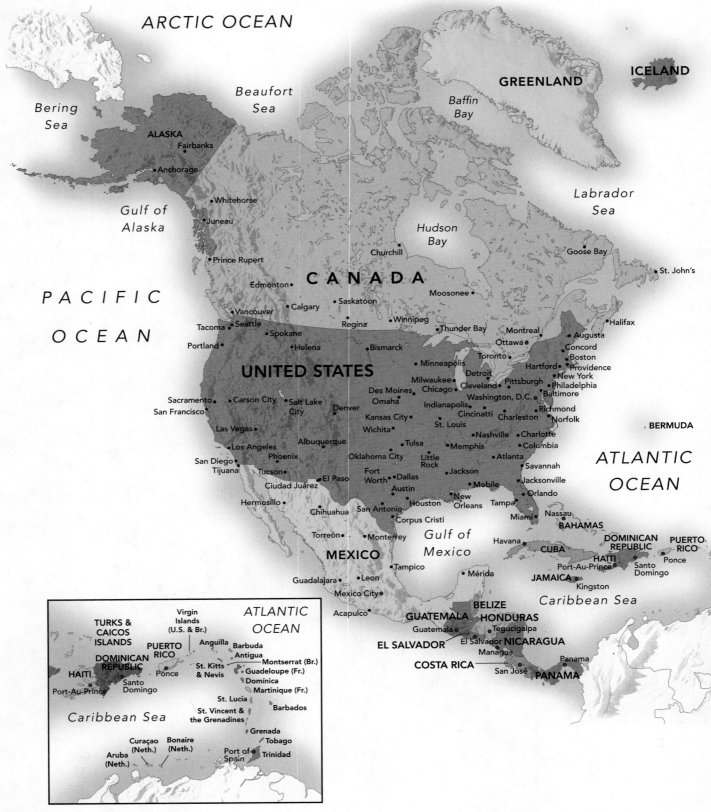

MAP A.2

North America

Caribbean Sea

CURAÇAO
(Neth.)

Barranquilla
Cartagena
Maracaibo
Barquisimeto
Caracas
Valencia
Port of Spain
Cumaná
Maturín
**TRINIDAD &
TOBAGO**

NORTH
ATLANTIC
OCEAN

Montería
Cúcuta
San Cristóbal
Bucaramanga
Ciudad
Bolívar
Ciudad Guayana
Georgetown
Paramaribo

Medellín
Manizales
Ibagué
Bogotá
Neiva
VENEZUELA
GUYANA
Mackenzie
SURINAME
Cayenne

Buenaventura
Cali
Popoyán
Pasto
COLOMBIA
**FRENCH
GUIANA**

ECUADOR Quito
Guayaquil Ambato

Manaus
Belém
São Luís
Fortaleza

Iquitos
Teresina

Chiclayo
Trujillo
B R A Z I L
Campina Grande Natal
Caruaru Recife

P E R U

Callao Lima
Salvador
Itabuna

Cuzco **B O L I V I A**
Brasília
Goiânia

Arequipa La Paz
Arica Santa Cruz
Sucre
Iquique Potosí
Campo
Grande
Uberlândia
Uberaba
Belo Horizonte

Araraquara
Bauru
Campinas Juiz de Fora
PARAGUAY
São Paulo Niterói
Santos Rio de Janeiro

**PACIFIC
OCEAN**
Antofagasta
Asunción
Ponta
Grossa
Curitiba

Salta
San Miguel
de Tucumán
Posadas
CHILE
Santiago
del Estero
Corrientes
Santa
Maria
Pôrto Alegre

Córdoba
Santa Fe
Pelotas
San Juan
Río Cuarto Paraná
Rosario
Rio Grande

Viña del Mar
Valparaíso
Mendoza
Santiago
URUGUAY
Rancagua
Buenos Aires
La Plata
Montevideo
**SOUTH
ATLANTIC
OCEAN**

Talcahuano
Concepción
Bahía Blanca
Temuco
Valdivia **ARGENTINA**

**FALKLAND/MALVINAS
ISLANDS (UK)**
Port Stanley

Tierra del Fuego

MAP A.3

South America

MAP A.4

Europe

MAP A.5

Asia

MAP A.6

Africa

MAP A.7

Oceania

Cross-Cultural Business

LEARNING OBJECTIVES

After studying this chapter, you should be able to

1. Describe culture and explain the significance of both national culture and subcultures.

2. Identify the components of culture and describe their impact on international business.

3. Describe cultural change and explain how companies and culture affect each other.

4. Explain how the physical environment and technology influence culture.

5. Describe the two main frameworks used to classify cultures and explain their practical use.

A Look Back

Chapter 1 introduced us to international business. We examined the impact of globalization on markets and production, the forces behind globalization's expansion, and each main argument in the debate over globalization. We also profiled the kinds of companies engaged in international business.

A Look at This Chapter

This chapter introduces the important role of culture in international business. We explore the main elements of culture and how they affect business policies and practices. We learn different methods of classifying cultures and how these methods can be applied to business.

A Look Ahead

Chapter 3 describes the political and legal systems of nations. We will learn how different national systems affect international businesses and how managers can reduce political risk. We also will discover how ethics and social responsibility affect international business.

HOLD THE PORK, PLEASE!

BONN, Germany—"Kids and grownups love it so, the happy world of Haribo!" So goes the phrase that drives sales of Haribo gummi candies worldwide. In operation since the 1920s, Germany-based Haribo (www.haribo.com) gets its name from that of the company's founder, **Ha**ns **Ri**egel **Bo**nn.

Haribo candies, with names such as Gold Bears and Horror Mix, are available in 46 shapes, including soda bottles and glowworms. Haribo supplies 105 countries from its 18 factories at home and abroad, producing over 100 million gummi candies a day. But despite its success, Haribo was not meeting the needs of a globally dispersed subculture potentially worth $2 billion annually. The culprit: the pork-based substance that gives the candy its sticky, rubbery feel makes the candy off-limits to Muslims and Jews who adhere to a strict religious diet.

So the company embarked on a four-year mission to create a gummi candy free of the pork-based gelatin. "The first time we made it, we got a marmalade you could spread on bread," reported Neville Finlay, the British exporter who ships the new product under his own brand. "And at the other extreme was something you could fill a swimming pool with and drive a truck across," he added. Haribo found success eventually with a bacteria-based compound already common in salad dressings and sauces.

Later, a local supplier committed a language blunder—a common occurrence in international business. The printing on the first packages of candies destined for Hebrew communities was backward—Hebrew is read from right to left, not left to right like English. But today production is going smoothly. Haribo even has a Jewish rabbi (for *kosher* candies) or a Muslim cleric (for *halal* candies) inspect ingredients and oversee production to ensure that it adheres to religious customs.

As you read this chapter, consider all the ways culture affects international business and how companies affect cultures around the world.[1]

Source: Roy McMahon/Corbis

This chapter is the first of three that describe the links between international business activity and a nation's business environment. We discuss these topics early because they help determine how commerce is conducted in different countries. Success in international business can often be traced directly to a deep understanding of some aspect of a people's commercial environment. This chapter explores the influence of *culture* on international business activity. Chapter 3 presents the roles of *political and legal systems*, and Chapter 4 examines the impact of *economic systems and emerging markets* on international business.

Assessment of a nation's overall business climate is typically the first step in analyzing its potential as a host for international commercial activity. This means addressing some important questions, such as the following: What language(s) do the people speak? What is the climate like? Are the local people open to new ideas and new ways of doing business? Do government officials and the people want our business? Is the political situation stable enough so that our assets and employees are not placed at unacceptable levels of risk? Answers to these kinds of questions—plus statistical data on items such as income level and labor costs—allow companies to evaluate the attractiveness of a location as a place for doing business.

We address culture first in our discussion of national business environments because of its pivotal role in all international commercial activity. Whether we are discussing an entrepreneur running a small import/export business or a huge global firm directly involved in more than 100 countries, *people* are at the center of all business activity. When people from around the world come together to conduct business, they bring with them different backgrounds, assumptions, expectations, and ways of communicating—in other words, *culture*.

We begin this chapter by exploring the influence of nation-states and subcultures on a people's overall cultural image. Next, we learn the importance of values, attitudes, manners, and customs in any given culture. We then examine ways in which social institutions, religion, language, and other key elements of culture affect business practices and national competitiveness. We close this chapter with a look at two alternative methods for classifying cultures.

What Is Culture?

When traveling in other countries, we often perceive differences in the way people live and work. In the United States, dinner is commonly eaten around 6:00 p.m.; in Spain, it's not served until 8:00 or 9:00 p.m. In the United States, most people shop in large supermarkets once or twice a week; Italians tend to shop in smaller local grocery stores nearly every day. Essentially, we are experiencing differences in **culture**—the set of values, beliefs, rules, and institutions held by a specific group of people. Culture is a highly complex portrait of a people. It includes everything from high tea in England to the tropical climate of Barbados, to Mardi Gras in Brazil.

Before we learn about the individual components of culture, let's look at two important concepts: one that should be discouraged and one that should be fostered.

AVOIDING ETHNOCENTRICITY **Ethnocentricity** is the belief that one's own ethnic group or culture is superior to that of others. Ethnocentricity can seriously undermine international business projects. It causes people to view other cultures in terms of their own and, therefore, disregard the beneficial characteristics of other cultures. Ethnocentricity played a role in many stories, some retold in this chapter, of companies that failed when they tried to implement a new business practice in a subsidiary abroad. Failure can occur when managers ignore a fundamental aspect of the local culture. This can provoke a backlash from the local population, its government, or nongovernmental groups. As suppliers and buyers increasingly treat the world as a single, interconnected marketplace, managers should eliminate the biases inherent in ethnocentric thinking. To read about how companies can foster a nonethnocentric perspective, see this chapter's Culture Matters feature, titled "Creating a Global Mindset ."

DEVELOPING CULTURAL LITERACY As globalization continues, people directly involved in international business increasingly benefit from a certain degree of **cultural literacy**—detailed knowledge about a culture that enables a person to work happily and effectively within it. Cultural literacy improves people's ability to manage employees, market products, and conduct negotiations in other countries. Global brands such as Procter & Gamble (www.pg.com) and Apple (www.apple.com) have a competitive advantage because consumers know and respect

culture
Set of values, beliefs, rules, and institutions held by a specific group of people.

ethnocentricity
Belief that one's own ethnic group or culture is superior to that of others.

cultural literacy
Detailed knowledge about a culture that enables a person to work happily and effectively within it.

CULTURE MATTERS   Creating a Global Mindset

In this era of globalization, companies need employees who function without the blinders of ethnocentricity. Here are some ways managers can develop a *global mindset*:

- **Cultural Adaptability.** Managers need the ability to alter their behavior when working with people from other cultures. The first step in doing this is to develop one's knowledge of unfamiliar cultures. The second step is to act on that knowledge to alter behavior to suit cultural expectations. The manager with a global mindset can evaluate others in a culturally unbiased way and can motivate and lead multicultural teams.
- **Bridging the Gap.** A large gap can emerge between theory and practice when Western management ideas are applied in Eastern cultures. Whereas U.S. management principles are often accepted at face value in businesses throughout the world, U.S. business customs are not. In Asia, for example, Western managers might try implementing "collective leadership" practices more in line with Asian management styles.

- **Building Global Mentality.** Companies can apply personality-testing techniques to measure the global aptitude of managers. A global-mindset test evaluates an individual's openness and flexibility, understanding of global principles, and strategic implementation abilities. It can also identify areas in which training is needed and generate a list of recommended programs.
- **Flexibility Is Key.** The more behavioral the issues, the greater the influence of local cultures. Japanese and Korean managers are more likely than U.S. managers to wait for directions and consult peers on decisions. Western managers posted in the Middle East must learn to work within a rigid hierarchy in order to be successful. And although showing respect for others is universally valued, respect is defined differently from country to country.
- **Want to Know More?** Visit the Center for Creative Leadership (www.ccl.org), The Globalist (www.theglobalist.com), and Transnational Management Associated (www.tmaworld.com).

these highly recognizable names. Yet, cultural differences often dictate alterations in some aspect of a business in order to suit local tastes and preferences. The culturally literate manager who compensates for local needs and desires brings his or her company closer to customers and improves the firm's competitiveness.

As you read through the concepts and examples in this chapter, try to avoid reacting with *ethnocentricity* while developing your own *cultural literacy*. Because these two concepts are central to the discussion of many international business topics, you will encounter them throughout this book. In the book's final chapter (Chapter 16), we explore specific types of cultural training that companies use to develop their employees' cultural literacy.

National Culture and Subcultures

Rightly or wrongly, we tend to invoke the concept of the *nation-state* when speaking of culture. In other words, we usually refer to British and Indonesian cultures as if all Britons and all Indonesians are culturally identical. We do this because we are conditioned to think in terms of *national culture*. But this is at best a generalization. For example, the British population consists of the English as well as the Scottish and Welsh peoples. And people in remote parts of Indonesia build homes in treetops even as people in the nation's developed regions pursue ambitious economic development projects. Let's take a closer look at the diversity that lies beneath the veneer of national culture.

NATIONAL CULTURE Nation-states *support* and *promote* the concept of national culture by building museums and monuments to preserve the legacies of important events and people. Nation-states also intervene in business to preserve other treasures of national culture. Most nations, for example, regulate culturally sensitive sectors of the economy, such as filmmaking and broadcasting. France continues to voice fears that its language is being tainted with English and its media with U.S. programming. To stem the English invasion, French laws limit the use of English in product packaging and storefront signs. At peak listening times, at least 40 percent of all radio station programming is reserved for French artists. Similar laws apply to television broadcasting. The French government even fined the local branch of a U.S. university for failing to provide a French translation on its English-language website.

Cities, too, get involved in enhancing national cultural attractions, often for economic reasons. Lifestyle enhancements to a city can help it attract companies, which benefit by having

Subculture members define themselves by their style (such as clothing, hair, tattoos) and may rebel against mass consumerism. London, England's Camden district is famous for its historic markets and as a gathering place for alternative subcultures such as goth, punk, and emo. Businesses like Facebook help subcultures to spread quickly worldwide. Can you think of a company that targets an international subculture with its products?

Source: Nik Wheeler Danita Delimont Photography/Newscom

an easier task retaining top employees. The Guggenheim Museum in Bilbao, Spain (www. guggenheim-bilbao.es), designed by Frank Gehry, revived that old Basque industrial city. And Hong Kong's government enhanced its cultural attractions by building a Hong Kong Disney to lure businesses that may otherwise locate elsewhere in Asia.

subculture
A group of people who share a unique way of life within a larger, dominant culture.

SUBCULTURES A group of people who share a unique way of life within a larger, dominant culture is called a **subculture**. A subculture can differ from the dominant culture in language, race, lifestyle, values, attitudes, or other characteristics.

Although subcultures exist in all nations, they are often glossed over by our *impressions* of national cultures. For example, the customary portrait of Chinese culture often ignores the fact that China's population includes more than 50 distinct ethnic groups. Decisions regarding product design, packaging, and advertising should consider each group's distinct culture. Marketing campaigns also need to recognize that Chinese dialects in the Shanghai and Canton regions differ from those in the country's interior; not everyone is fluent in the official Mandarin dialect.

A multitude of subcultures also exists within the United States. Of 300 million U.S. residents, around 80 million are black, Latino, or Asian. Initially, Frito Lay (www.fritolay.com) had trouble convincing 46 million U.S. Latinos to try its Latin-flavored versions of Lay's and Doritos chips. But then Frito Lay brought four popular brands into the U.S. market from its Mexican subsidiary, Sabritas. The gamble paid off. Sales of the Sabritas brand doubled to more than $100 million over a two-year period.

Cultural boundaries do not always correspond to political boundaries. In other words, subcultures sometimes exist across national borders. People who live in different nations but who share the same subculture can have more in common with one another than with their fellow nationals. These subcultures may share purchasing behaviors rooted in lifestyle or values that allow them to be marketed to with a single worldwide campaign.

QUICK STUDY 1

1. Define *culture*. How does ethnocentricity distort one's view of other cultures?
2. What is *cultural literacy*? Why should businesspeople understand other cultures?
3. How do nation-states and *subcultures* influence a people's overall cultural image?

Components of Culture

A culture is defined by more than the actions of nation-states and the presence of subcultures. A people's culture also includes what they consider beautiful and tasteful, their underlying beliefs, their traditional habits, and the ways in which they relate to one another and their surroundings. These elements of culture are the building blocks of society on which all else rests. Let's take a detailed look at each main component of culture (see Figure 2.1): *aesthetics*, *values* and *attitudes*, *manners* and *customs*, *social structure*, *religion*, *personal communication*, *education*, and *physical* and *material environments*.

Aesthetics

What a culture considers "good taste" in the arts (including music, painting, dance, drama, and architecture), the imagery evoked by certain expressions, and the symbolism of certain colors is called **aesthetics**.

Aesthetics are important when a company does business in another culture. The selection of appropriate colors for advertising, product packaging, and even work uniforms can improve the odds of success. For example, green is a favorable color in Islam and adorns the national flags of most nations of the Middle East. Companies take advantage of the emotional attachment to the color green in these countries by incorporating it into a product, its packaging, or its promotion. Across much of Asia, on the other hand, green is associated with sickness. In Europe, Mexico, and the United States, the color of death and mourning is black; in Japan and most of Asia, it's white.

Music is deeply embedded in culture and, when used correctly, can be a clever and creative addition to a promotion; if used incorrectly, it can offend the local population. The architecture of buildings and other structures should also be researched to avoid making cultural blunders attributable to the symbolism of certain shapes and forms.

The importance of aesthetics is just as great when going international using the Internet. Many companies exist that teach corporations how to globalize their Internet presence. These companies often provide professional guidance on how to adapt websites to account for cultural preferences such as color scheme, imagery, and slogans. The advice of specialist firms can be particularly helpful for entrepreneurs and small businesses because they rarely have in-house employees well versed in other cultures.

Values and Attitudes

Ideas, beliefs, and customs to which people are emotionally attached are called **values**. Values include concepts such as honesty, freedom, and responsibility. Values are important to business because they affect a people's work ethic and desire for material possessions. For example, whereas people in Singapore value hard work and material success, people in Greece value leisure and a modest lifestyle. The United Kingdom and the United States value individual freedom; Japan and South Korea value group consensus.

aesthetics
What a culture considers "good taste" in the arts, the imagery evoked by certain expressions, and the symbolism of certain colors.

values
Ideas, beliefs, and customs to which people are emotionally attached.

FIGURE 2.1

Components of Culture

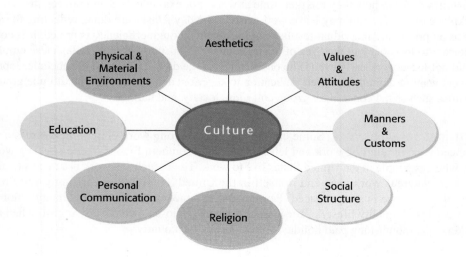

The influx of values from other cultures can be fiercely resisted. Many Muslims believe drugs, alcohol, and certain kinds of music and literature will undermine conservative values. This is why the Arab world's reality TV programs tend to be short-lived. In Bahrain, the local version of *Big Brother* was canceled after people objected to the program's format, which involved young unmarried adults of both sexes living under the same roof. The Lebanon-based program *Hawa Sawa* (*On Air Together*) was shut down because its "elimidate" format (a young man gradually eliminates women to finally select a date) was perceived as too Western. And Indonesia's National Police denied Lady Gaga a permit to perform despite her concert being sold out. She is the first foreign artist ever to be denied a permit by authorities there. Conservative religious groups accused Gaga of "being vulgar, corrupting the morals of the country's youth, and worshiping Satan."[2]

Attitudes are positive or negative evaluations, feelings, and tendencies that individuals harbor toward objects or concepts. Attitudes reflect underlying values. For example, a Westerner would be expressing an attitude if he or she were to say, "I do not like the Japanese purification ritual because it involves being naked in a communal bath." The Westerner quoted here might hold conservative beliefs regarding exposure of the body.

Similar to values, attitudes are learned from role models, including parents, teachers, and religious leaders. Attitudes also differ from one country to another because they are formed within a cultural context. But unlike values (which generally concern only important matters), people hold attitudes toward both important and unimportant aspects of life. And whereas values remain quite rigid over time, attitudes are more flexible.

A "European" *attitude* has sunk into the psyche of young people across Europe as companies from different countries merge, industries consolidate, and nations grow closer together in the European Union. Many young people in Europe today consider themselves to be "European" as much as they identify with their individual national identities. Still, the underlying *values* of young Europeans tend to remain similar to those of their parents. Such cultural knowledge can help managers decide whether to adapt promotions to local attitudes for maximum effectiveness.

Let's now look at how people's attitudes differ toward three important aspects of life that directly affect business activities: time, work, and cultural change.

ATTITUDES TOWARD TIME People in many Latin American and Mediterranean cultures are casual about their use of time. They maintain flexible schedules and would rather enjoy their time than sacrifice it to unbending efficiency. Businesspeople, for example, may arrive after the scheduled meeting time and prefer to build personal trust before discussing business. Not surprisingly, it usually takes longer to conduct business in these parts of the world than in the United States or northern Europe.

By contrast, people in Japan and the United States typically arrive promptly for meetings, keep tight schedules, and work long hours. The emphasis on using time efficiently reflects the underlying value of hard work in both these countries. Yet people in Japan and the United States sometimes differ in how they use their time at work. For example, U.S. employees strive toward workplace efficiency and may leave work early if the day's tasks are done, reflecting the value placed on producing individual results. But in Japan, although efficiency is prized, it is equally important to look busy in the eyes of others even when business is slow. A Japanese employee would not leave work early even if he or she finished the day's task ahead of schedule. Japanese workers want to demonstrate their dedication to superiors and coworkers—an attitude grounded in values such as the concern for group cohesion, loyalty, and harmony.

ATTITUDES TOWARD WORK Some cultures display a strong work ethic; others stress a more balanced pace in juggling work and leisure. People in southern France like to say they work to live, whereas people in the United States live to work. The French say work is a means to an end for them, whereas work is an end in itself in the United States. Not surprisingly, the lifestyle in southern France is slower-paced. People tend to concentrate on earning enough money to enjoy a relaxed, quality lifestyle. Businesses practically close down during August, when many workers take month-long paid holidays, often outside the country.

attitudes
Positive or negative evaluations, feelings, and tendencies that individuals harbor toward objects or concepts.

People tend to launch their own businesses when capital is available for new business start-ups and when the cultural stigma of entrepreneurial failure is low. In European countries, start-ups are considered quite risky, and capital for entrepreneurial ventures can be scarce. Moreover, if an entrepreneur's venture goes bust, he or she can find it very hard to obtain financing for future projects because of the stigma of failure. This remains true despite some progress recently. The opposite attitude tends to prevail in the United States. A prior bankruptcy is sometimes considered a valuable learning experience (assuming lessons were learned) when referenced in a business plan. As long as U.S. bankers or venture capitalists see promising business plans, they are generally willing to loan money. Today, many European nations are working to foster an entrepreneurial spirit similar to that of the United States.

ATTITUDES TOWARD CULTURAL CHANGE A **cultural trait** is anything that represents a culture's way of life, including gestures, material objects, traditions, and concepts. Such traits include bowing to show respect in Japan (gesture), a Buddhist temple in Thailand (material object), celebrating the Day of the Dead in Mexico (tradition), and practicing democracy in the United States (concept). Let's look more closely at the role of cultural traits in causing cultural change over time and the relation between international companies and cultural change.

cultural trait
Anything that represents a culture's way of life, including gestures, material objects, traditions, and concepts.

Cultural Diffusion The process whereby cultural traits spread from one culture to another is called **cultural diffusion**. As new traits are accepted and absorbed into a culture, *cultural change* occurs naturally and, as a rule, gradually. Globalization and technological advances are increasing the pace of both cultural diffusion and cultural change. The global spread of media today along with the expanding reach of the Internet and services like YouTube play a role in cultural diffusion. These forces expose people of different (sometimes isolated) nations to the cultural traits and ideas of other cultures.

cultural diffusion
Process whereby cultural traits spread from one culture to another.

When Companies Change Cultures International companies are often agents of cultural change. As trade and investment barriers fall, for example, U.S. consumer-goods and entertainment companies are moving into untapped markets. Critics in some of these places charge that, in exporting the products of such firms, the United States is practicing **cultural imperialism**—the replacement of one culture's traditions, folk heroes, and artifacts with substitutes from another.

cultural imperialism
Replacement of one culture's traditions, folk heroes, and artifacts with substitutes from another.

Cultural diffusion is a powerful force of cultural change. Traditional cultures are especially vulnerable when introduced to the lifestyles of people in wealthy, industrialized nations. Satellite TV and the Internet are highly effective at exposing people to the cultural traits of other societies. Do you think people in this village in northern Namibia view the world any differently since they acquired satellite TV?

Source: Thomas Schulze/Newscom

Fears of cultural imperialism still drive some French to oppose the products of the Walt Disney Company (www.disney.com) and its Disneyland Paris theme park. They fear "Mickey and Friends" could replace traditional characters rooted in French culture. McDonald's (www. mcdonalds.com) is also sometimes charged with cultural imperialism. It is reported that the average Japanese child thinks McDonald's was invented in Japan and exported to the United States. Chinese children consider "Uncle" McDonald to be "funny, gentle, kind, and understanding." Meanwhile, politicians in Russia decry the "Snickerization" of their culture—a snide term that refers to the popularity of the Snickers candy bar made by Mars Incorporated (www.mars.com). And when the Miss World Pageant was held in India, conservative groups criticized Western corporate sponsors for spreading the message of consumerism and portraying women as sex objects.

Sensitivity to the cultures in which they operate can help companies avoid charges of cultural imperialism. Firms must focus not only on meeting people's product needs but also on how their activities and products affect people's traditional ways and habits. Rather than view their influence on culture as the inevitable consequence of doing business, companies can take several steps to soften those effects. For example, policies and practices that are at odds with deeply held beliefs can be introduced gradually. Managers could also seek the advice of highly respected local individuals such as elders, who fulfill key societal roles in many developing countries. And businesses should always make clear to local workers the benefits of any proposed changes that are closely linked to cultural traits.

An area in which U.S. companies may be changing the workplace in other cultures is fairness in the workplace. Just a few years ago, sexual harassment lawsuits were a peculiar phenomenon of U.S. culture. Increased awareness of this issue in other nations coincides with the international outsourcing of jobs. As U.S. companies outsource jobs to other nations, they are being held accountable for how these subcontractors treat their employees. In the process, U.S. companies export the values of the U.S. workplace, such as what constitutes sexual harassment.

When Cultures Change Companies Culture often forces companies to adjust their business policies and practices. Managers from the United States, for example, often encounter cultural differences that force changes in how they motivate employees in other countries. Managers sometimes use *situational management*—a system in which a supervisor walks an employee through every step of an assignment or task and monitors the results at each stage. Although time-consuming, this technique helps employees fully understand the scope of their jobs and clarifies the boundaries of their responsibilities.

Other types of changes might also be needed to suit local culture. Vietnam's traditional, agriculture-based economy means that people's concept of time revolves around the seasons. The local "timepiece" is the monsoon, not the clock. Western managers, therefore, modify their approach and take a more patient, long-term view of business by modifying employee evaluation and reward systems. For example, individual criticism should be delivered privately to save employees from "losing face" among coworkers. Individual praise for good performance can be delivered either in private or in public, if done carefully. The Vietnamese place great value on group harmony, so an individual can be embarrassed if singled out publicly as being superior to the rest of the work unit.

Is a Global Culture Emerging? What does the rapid pace of cultural change worldwide mean for international business? Are we witnessing the emergence of a new, truly global culture in which all people share similar lifestyles, values, and attitudes? The rapid pace of cultural diffusion today is causing cultures to converge to some extent. The successful TV show *American Idol*, where aspiring singers compete for a chance to become a celebrity, is one example of global pop culture. The U.S. show is one of 39 clones around the world based on the original British show, *Pop Idol*. The same company helped develop and market *The Apprentice,* another successful global TV platform.[3]

It might be true that people in different cultures are developing similar perspectives on certain issues. But it seems that just as often as we see signs of an emerging global culture, we discover some new habit unique to one culture. When that happens, we are reminded of the roles of history and tradition in defining culture. Though values and attitudes are under continually greater pressure from globalization, their transformation will be gradual rather than abrupt because they are deeply ingrained in culture. This is why the managers of tomorrow must work to develop their knowledge and understanding of other cultures.

QUICK STUDY 2

1. What is meant by a culture's *aesthetics*? Give several examples.
2. Compare and contrast *values* and *attitudes*. How do cultures differ in their attitudes toward time, work, and cultural change?
3. Describe the process of *cultural diffusion*. Why should international businesses be sensitive to charges of *cultural imperialism*?

Manners and Customs

When doing business in another culture, it is important to understand a people's manners and customs. At a minimum, understanding manners and customs helps managers avoid making embarrassing mistakes or offending people. In-depth knowledge, meanwhile, improves the ability to negotiate in other cultures, market products effectively, and manage international operations. Let's explore some important differences in manners and customs around the world.

MANNERS Appropriate ways of behaving, speaking, and dressing in a culture are called **manners**. Jack Ma founded Alibaba (www.alibaba.com) as a way for suppliers and buyers to increase efficiency by cutting through layers of intermediaries and trading companies. But he realized early that his Chinese clients needed training in business etiquette to cross the cultural divide and do business with people from Western cultures. So Alibaba offers seminars on business manners that instruct clients to spend more time chitchatting with clients and conversing more casually.[4]

> **manners**
> Appropriate ways of behaving, speaking, and dressing in a culture.

Conducting business during meals is common practice in the United States. In Mexico, however, it is poor manners to bring up business at mealtime unless the host does so first. Business discussions in Mexico typically begin when coffee and brandy arrive. Likewise, toasts in the United States tend to be casual and sprinkled with lighthearted humor. In Mexico, where a toast should be philosophical and full of passion, a lighthearted toast would be offensive.

CUSTOMS When habits or ways of behaving in specific circumstances are passed down through generations, they become **customs**. Customs differ from manners in that they define appropriate habits or behaviors in *specific situations*. For example, the Japanese tradition of throwing special parties for young women and men who turn age 20 is a custom. Let's examine two types of customs and see how instances of each vary around the world.

> **customs**
> Habits or ways of behaving in specific circumstances that are passed down through generations in a culture.

Folk and Popular Customs A **folk custom** is behavior, often dating back several generations, that is practiced by a homogeneous group of people. Celebrating the Dragon Boat Festival in China and the art of belly dancing in Turkey are both folk customs. A **popular custom** is behavior shared by a heterogeneous group or by several groups. Popular customs can exist in just one culture or in two or more cultures at once. Wearing blue jeans and playing golf are both popular customs across the globe. Folk customs that spread by cultural diffusion to other regions develop into popular customs.

> **folk custom**
> Behavior, often dating back several generations, that is practiced by a homogeneous group of people.

> **popular custom**
> Behavior shared by a heterogeneous group or by several groups.

Despite their appeal, popular customs can be seen as a threat by some members of a culture. Authorities in a strict religious district of Indonesia's Aceh province banned Muslim women from wearing tight clothing, short skirts, and blue jeans. Religious police set up raids to distribute long skirts to women found violating the ban and to confiscate their offending garments. Violators were released from custody after they provided their identities to police and received religious advice.[5]

We can also distinguish between folk and popular food. Popular Western-style fast food, for instance, is rapidly replacing folk food around the world. Widespread acceptance of "burgers 'n' fries" (born in the United States) and "fish 'n' chips" (born in Britain) is altering deep-seated

MANAGER'S BRIEFCASE   A Globetrotter's Guide to Meetings

Large multinationals need top managers who are comfortable living, working, and traveling worldwide. Here are a few guidelines for a manager to follow when meeting colleagues from other cultures:

- *Familiarity.* Avoid the temptation to get too familiar too quickly. Use titles such as "doctor" and "mister." Switch to a first-name basis only when invited to do so, and do not shorten people's names from, say, Catherine to Cathy.
- *Personal Space.* Culture dictates what is considered the appropriate distance between two people. Middle Eastern and Latin American nations close the gap significantly. And in Latin America the man-to-man embrace can occur regularly in business.
- *Religious Values.* Be cautious so that your manners do not offend people. Former Secretary of State Madeline Albright acquired the nickname "The Kissing Ambassador" for

kissing the Israeli and Palestinian leaders of those two religious peoples.
- *Business Cards.* In Asia, business cards are considered an extension of the individual. Business cards in Japan are typically exchanged after a bow, with two hands extended, and the wording facing the recipient. Leave the card on the table for the entire meeting—don't quickly stuff it in your wallet or toss it into your briefcase.
- *Comedy.* Use humor cautiously because it often does not translate well. Avoid jokes that rely on wordplay and puns or events in your country, of which local people might have little or no knowledge.
- *Body Language.* Do not "spread out" by hanging your arms over the backs of chairs, but don't be too stiff either. Look people in the eye lest they deem you untrustworthy, but don't stare too intently in a challenging manner.

dietary traditions in many Asian countries, especially among young people. In Japan and South Korea today, these popular foods are even becoming a part of home-cooked meals.

The Business Custom of Gift Giving Although giving token gifts to business and government associates is customary in many countries, the proper type of gift varies. A knife, for example, should not be offered to associates in Russia, France, or Germany, where it signals the severing of a relationship. In Japan, gifts must be wrapped in such a delicate way that it is wise to ask someone trained in the practice to do the honors. It is also Japanese custom for the giver to protest that the gift is small and unworthy of the recipient and for the recipient to not open the gift in front of the giver. This tradition does not endorse trivial gifts but is simply a custom.

Cultures differ in their legal and ethical rules against giving or accepting bribes. Large gifts to business associates are particularly suspicious. The U.S. Foreign Corrupt Practices Act, which prohibits companies from giving large gifts to government officials in order to win business favors, applies to U.S. firms operating at home *and* abroad. Yet in many cultures, bribery is woven into a social fabric that has worn well for centuries. In Germany, bribe payments may even qualify for tax deductions. Though many governments worldwide are adopting stricter measures to control bribery, in some cultures large gifts are still an effective way to obtain contracts, enter markets, and secure protection from competitors. See the Manager's Briefcase, titled "A Globetrotter's Guide to Meetings," for additional pointers on manners and customs when abroad on business.

Social Structure

social structure
A culture's fundamental organization, including its groups and institutions, its system of social positions and their relationships, and the process by which its resources are distributed.

Social structure embodies a culture's fundamental organization, including its groups and institutions, its system of social positions and their relationships, and the process by which its resources are distributed. Social structure plays a role in many business decisions, including production-site selection, advertising methods, and the costs of doing business in a country. Three important elements of social structure that differ across cultures are social group associations, social status, and social mobility.

social group
Collection of two or more people who identify and interact with each other.

SOCIAL GROUP ASSOCIATIONS People in all cultures associate themselves with a variety of **social groups**—collections of two or more people who identify and interact with each other. Social groups contribute to each individual's identity and self-image. Two groups that play especially important roles in affecting business activity everywhere are family and gender.*

---

*We put these two "groups" together for the sake of convenience. Strictly speaking, a gender is not a group. Sociologists regard it as a category—people who share some sort of status. A key to group membership is mutual interaction. Individuals in categories know that they are not alone in holding a particular status, but the vast majority remain strangers to one another.

Family There are two different types of family groups:

- The *nuclear family* consists of a person's immediate relatives, including parents, brothers, and sisters. This concept of family prevails in Australia, Canada, the United States, and much of Europe.
- The *extended family* broadens the nuclear family and adds grandparents, aunts and uncles, cousins, and relatives through marriage. It is an important social group in much of Asia, the Middle East, North Africa, and Latin America.

Extended families can present some interesting situations for businesspeople unfamiliar with the concept. In some cultures, owners and managers obtain supplies and materials from another company at which someone from the extended family works. Gaining entry into such family arrangements can be difficult because quality and price are not sufficient motives to ignore family ties.

In extended-family cultures, managers and other employees often try to find jobs for relatives inside their own companies. This practice (called nepotism) can present a challenge to the human resource operations of a Western company, which typically must establish explicit policies on the practice.

Gender *Gender* refers to socially learned traits associated with, and expected of, men or women. It includes behaviors and attitudes such as styles of dress and activity preferences. It is not the same thing as sex, which refers to the biological fact that a person is either male or female.

Though many countries have made great strides toward gender equality in the workplace, others have not. In countries where women are denied equal opportunity in the workplace, their unemployment rate can easily be double that for men and their pay half that for men in the same occupation. Women's salaries can be so low and the cost of childcare so high that it simply makes more sense for mothers to stay home with their children. Caring for children and performing household duties are also likely considered women's work and not the responsibility of the entire family.

SOCIAL STATUS Another important aspect of social structure is the way a culture divides its population according to *status*—that is, according to positions within the structure. Although some cultures have only a few categories, others have many. The process of ranking people into social layers or classes is called **social stratification**.

social stratification
Process of ranking people into social layers or classes.

Three factors that normally determine social status are family heritage, income, and occupation. In most industrialized countries royalty, government officials, and top business leaders occupy the highest social layer. Scientists, medical doctors, and others with a university education occupy the middle layer. Below are those with vocational training or a secondary-school education, who dominate the manual and clerical occupations. Although rankings are fairly stable, they can and do change over time. For example, because Confucianism (a major Chinese religion) stresses a life of learning, not commerce, Chinese culture frowned on businesspeople for centuries. In modern China, however, people who have obtained wealth and power through business are now considered important role models for younger generations.

SOCIAL MOBILITY Moving to a higher social class is easy in some cultures but difficult or impossible in others. **Social mobility** is the ease with which individuals can move up or down a culture's "social ladder." For much of the world's population today, one of two systems regulates social mobility: a *caste system* or a *class system*.

social mobility
Ease with which individuals can move up or down a culture's "social ladder."

Caste System A **caste system** is a system of social stratification in which people are born into a social ranking, or *caste*, with no opportunity for social mobility. India is the classic example of a caste culture. Although the Indian constitution officially bans discrimination by caste, its influence persists. Little social interaction occurs between castes, and marrying out of one's caste is taboo. Opportunities for work and advancement are defined within the system, and certain occupations are reserved for the members of each caste. For example, a member of a lower caste cannot supervise someone of a higher caste because personal clashes would be inevitable.

caste system
System of social stratification in which people are born into a social ranking, or caste, with no opportunity for social mobility.

The caste system forces Western companies to make some hard ethical decisions when entering the Indian marketplace. They must decide whether to adapt to local human resource policies in India or to import their own from the home country. As globalization penetrates deeper into Indian culture, the nation's social system and international companies will face many challenges.

class system
System of social stratification in which personal ability and actions determine social status and mobility.

Class System A **class system** is a system of social stratification in which personal ability and actions determine social status and mobility. It is the most common form of social stratification in the world today. But class systems vary in the amount of mobility they allow. Highly class-conscious cultures offer less mobility and, not surprisingly, experience greater class conflict. Across Western Europe, for example, wealthy families have retained power for generations by restricting social mobility. Countries there must sometimes deal with class conflict in the form of labor–management disputes that can increase the cost of doing business.

Conversely, lower levels of class consciousness encourage mobility and lessen conflict. A more cooperative atmosphere in the workplace tends to prevail when people feel that a higher social standing is within their reach. Most U.S. citizens share the belief that hard work can improve their standard of living and social status. People attribute higher status to greater income or wealth but often with little regard for family background.

QUICK STUDY 3

1. How do *manners* and *customs* differ? Give examples of each.
2. List several manners to consider when doing business abroad.
3. Define *folk* and *popular* customs. How can a folk custom become a popular custom?
4. Define *social structure*. How do social rank and *social mobility* affect business?

Religion

Human values often originate from religious beliefs. Different religions take different views of work, savings, and material goods. Identifying why they do so may help us understand business practices in other cultures. Knowing how religion affects business is especially important in countries with religious governments.

Map 2.1 (on pages 54–55) shows where the world's major religions are practiced. Religion is not confined to national political boundaries but can exist in different regions of the world simultaneously. It is also common for several or more religions to be practiced within a single nation. In the following sections, we explore Christianity, Islam, Hinduism, Buddhism, Confucianism, Judaism, and Shinto. We examine their potential effects, both positive and negative, on international business activity.

CHRISTIANITY Christianity was born in Palestine around 2,000 years ago among Jews who believed that God sent Jesus of Nazareth to be their savior. Although Christianity boasts more than 300 denominations, most Christians belong to the Roman Catholic, Protestant, or Eastern Orthodox churches. With 2 billion followers, Christianity is the world's single largest religion. The Roman Catholic faith asks its followers to refrain from placing material possessions above God and others. Protestants believe that salvation comes from faith in God and that hard work gives glory to God—a tenet known widely as the "Protestant work ethic." Many historians believe this conviction to be a main factor in the development of capitalism and free enterprise in nineteenth-century Europe.

Christian organizations sometimes get involved in social causes that affect business policy. For example, some conservative Christian groups have boycotted the Walt Disney Company (www.disney.com), charging that, in portraying young people as rejecting parental guidance, Disney films impede the moral development of young viewers worldwide.

The Catholic Church itself has been involved in some highly publicized controversies. Ireland-based Ryanair (www.ryanair.com), Europe's leading low-fare airline, ruffled the feathers of the Roman Catholic Church with an ad campaign. The ad depicted the pope (the head of the Catholic Church) claiming that the fourth secret of Fatima was Ryanair's low fares. The Church sent out a worldwide press release accusing the airline of blaspheming the pope. But much to the Church's dismay, the press release generated an enormous amount of free publicity for Ryanair.

Hyundai (www.hyundai.com) offended the Catholic Church when it ran a TV commercial during World Cup soccer matches. The spot showed a "church" in Argentina with a stained glass window of a soccer ball, a soccer ball topped with a crown of thorns, and parishioners receiving slices of pizza instead of communion hosts. The Catholic Church took offense at the images of people worshipping soccer and at the mocking of its practice of receiving Holy Communion. Hyundai put a stop to the ad two days after it began airing, saying that upon review it found the ad to be unintentionally insensitive.[6]

ISLAM With 1.3 billion adherents, Islam is the world's second-largest religion. The prophet Muhammad founded Islam around A.D. 600 in Mecca, the holy city of Islam located in Saudi Arabia. Islam thrives in north Africa, the Middle East, Central Asia, Pakistan, and some Southeast Asian nations, including Indonesia. Muslim concentrations are also found in most European and U.S. cities. *Islam* means "submission to Allah," and *Muslim* means "one who submits to Allah." Islam revolves around the "five pillars": (1) reciting the *Shahada* (profession of faith), (2) giving to the poor, (3) praying five times daily, (4) fasting during the holy month of *Ramadan*, and (5) making the *Hajj* (pilgrimage) to the Saudi Arabian city of Mecca at least once in one's lifetime.

Religion strongly affects the kinds of goods and services acceptable to Muslim consumers. Islam, for example, prohibits the consumption of alcohol and pork. Popular alcohol substitutes are soft drinks, coffee, and tea. Substitutes for pork include lamb, beef, and poultry (all of which must be slaughtered in a prescribed way so as to meet *halal* requirements). Because hot coffee and tea often play ceremonial roles in Muslim nations, the markets for them are quite large. And because usury (charging interest for money lent) violates the laws of Islam, credit card companies collect management fees rather than interest, and each cardholder's credit line is limited to an amount held on deposit.

Nations governed by Islamic law (see Chapter 3) sometimes segregate the sexes at certain activities and in locations such as schools. In Saudi Arabia, women cannot drive cars on public streets. In orthodox Islamic nations, men cannot conduct market research surveys with women at their homes unless they are family members. Women visiting Islamic cultures need to be especially sensitive to Islamic beliefs and customs. In Iran, for example, the Ministry of Islamic Guidance and Culture posts this reminder to visiting female journalists: "The body is a tool for the spirit and the spirit is a divine song. The holy tool should not be used for sexual intentions." Although the issue of *hejab* (Islamic dress) is hotly debated, both Iranian and non-Iranian women are officially expected to wear body-concealing garments. They are also expected to wear scarves over their hair because hair is considered enticing.

HINDUISM Hinduism formed around 4,000 years ago in present-day India, where more than 90 percent of Hinduism's 900 million adherents live. It is also the majority religion of Nepal and a secondary religion in Bangladesh, Bhutan, and Sri Lanka. Considered by some to be a way of life rather than a religion, Hinduism recalls no founder and recognizes no central authority or spiritual leader. Integral to the Hindu faith is the caste system described earlier in this chapter.

Hindus believe in reincarnation—the rebirth of the human soul at the time of death. For many Hindus the highest goal of life is *moksha*—escaping from the cycle of reincarnation and entering a state of eternal happiness called *nirvana*. Hindus tend to disdain materialism. Strict Hindus do not eat or willfully harm any living creature because it may be a reincarnated human soul. Because Hindus consider cows to be sacred animals, they do not eat beef. Yet, consuming cow's milk is considered a means of religious purification. Firms such as McDonald's (www.mcdonalds.com) must work closely with government and religious officials in India in order to respect Hindu beliefs. In many regions, McDonald's has removed all beef products from its menu and prepares vegetable and fish products in separate kitchen areas. And for those Indians who do eat red meat (but not cows because of their sacred status), the company sells the Maharaja Mac, made of lamb, in place of the Big Mac.

In India, there have been attacks on Western consumer-goods companies in the name of preserving Indian culture and Hindu beliefs. Some companies such as Pepsi-Cola (www.pepsi.com) have been vandalized, and local officials even shut down a KFC restaurant (www.kfc.com) for a time. Although it currently operates in India, Coca-Cola (www.cocacola.com) once left the market completely rather than succumb to demands that it reveal its secret formula to authorities. India's investment environment has improved greatly in recent years. Yet labor–management relations sometimes deteriorate to such a degree that strikes cut deeply into productivity.

MAP 2.1
World Religions

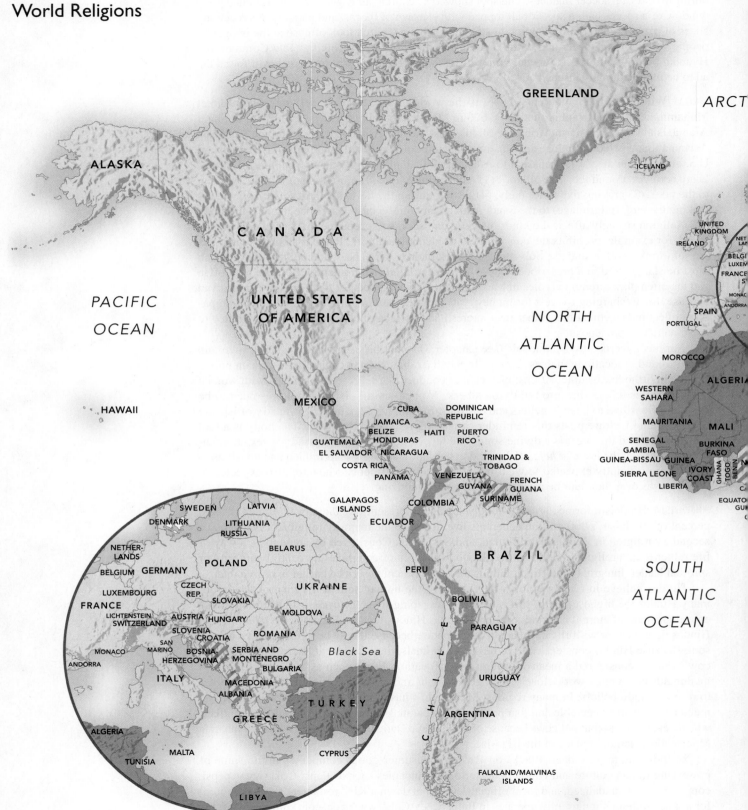

Christianity

Judaism

Hinduism

Islam

Buddhism

Nature religion

Chinese religion

Other groups

BUDDHISM Buddhism was founded about 2,600 years ago in India by a Hindu prince named Siddhartha Gautama, who later became the Buddha. Today, Buddhism has around 380 million followers, mostly in China, Tibet, Korea, Japan, Vietnam, and Thailand, and there are pockets of Buddhists in Europe and the Americas. Although founded in India, Buddhism has relatively few adherents there. Unlike Hinduism, Buddhism rejects the caste system of Indian society. But like Hinduism, Buddhism promotes a life centered on spiritual rather than worldly matters. Buddhism also teaches that seeking pleasure for the human senses causes suffering. In a formal ceremony, Buddhists take refuge in the "three jewels": the Buddha, the *dharma* (his teachings), and the *sangha* (community of enlightened beings). They seek *nirvana* (escape from reincarnation) through charity, modesty, compassion for others, restraint from violence, and general self-control.

Although monks at many temples are devoted to lives of solitary meditation and discipline, many other Buddhist priests are dedicated to lessening the burden of human suffering. They finance schools and hospitals across Asia and are active in worldwide peace movements. In Tibet, most people still acknowledge the exiled Dalai Lama as the spiritual and political head of the Buddhist culture. In the United States, a coalition of religious groups and human rights advocates continue to press the U.S. Congress to apply economic sanctions against countries that are seen as practicing religious persecution.

CONFUCIANISM An exiled politician and philosopher named Kung-fu-dz (pronounced "Confucius" in English) began teaching his ideas in China nearly 2,500 years ago. Today, China is home to most of Confucianism's 225 million followers. Confucian thought is also ingrained in the cultures of Japan, South Korea, and nations with large numbers of ethnic Chinese, such as Singapore.

South Korean business practice reflects Confucian thought in its rigid organizational structure and unswerving reverence for authority. Whereas Korean employees do not question strict chains of command, non-Korean managers and workers often feel differently. Efforts to apply Korean-style management in overseas subsidiaries have caused some high-profile disputes with U.S. executives and confrontations with factory workers in Vietnam.

Some observers contend that the Confucian work ethic and a commitment to education helped spur East Asia's phenomenal economic growth. But others respond that the link between culture and economic growth is weak. They argue that economic, historical, and international factors are at least as important as culture. They say that Chinese leaders distrusted Confucianism for centuries because they believed that it stunted economic growth. Likewise, many

Buddhism instructs its followers to live a simple life void of materialistic ambitions. But as globalization pries open Asia's markets, the products of Western multinational corporations are streaming in. Here, young Buddhist monks in Bhutan gather around a laptop computer. Do you think Asian cultures can modernize while retaining their traditional values and beliefs?

Source: Timothy Allen/Newscom

Chinese despised merchants and traders because their main objective (earning money) violated Confucian beliefs. As a result, many Chinese businesspeople moved to Indonesia, Malaysia, Singapore, and Thailand, where they launched successful businesses. Today, overseas Chinese people in these countries (and Taiwan) are helping finance China's rapid economic growth.

JUDAISM More than 3,000 years old, Judaism was the first religion to preach belief in a single God. Nowadays, Judaism has roughly 18 million followers worldwide. In Israel, Orthodox ("fully observant") Jews make up 12 percent of the population and constitute an increasingly important economic segment. In Jerusalem, there is even a modeling agency that specializes in casting Orthodox Jews in ads aimed both inside and outside the Orthodox community. Models include scholars and one rabbi. In keeping with Orthodox principles, women model only modest clothing and never appear in ads alongside men.

Employers and human resource managers must be aware of important days in the Jewish faith. Because the Sabbath lasts from sundown on Friday to sundown on Saturday, work schedules might need adjustment. Devout Jews want to be home before sundown on Fridays. On the Sabbath itself, they do not work, travel, or carry money. Several other important observances are Rosh Ha-Shanah (the two-day Jewish New Year, in September or October), Yom Kippur (the Day of Atonement, 10 days after New Year), Passover (which celebrates the Exodus from Egypt, in March or April each year), and Hanukkah (which celebrates an ancient victory over the Syrians, usually in December).

Marketers must take into account foods that are banned among strict Jews. Pork and shellfish (such as lobster and crab) are prohibited. Meat is stored and served separately from milk. Other meats must be slaughtered according to a practice called *shehitah*. Meals prepared according to Jewish dietary traditions are called *kosher*. Most airlines offer *kosher* meals for Jewish passengers on their flights.

SHINTO Shinto (meaning "way of the gods") arose as the native religion of the Japanese. But today, Shinto can claim only about 4 million strict adherents in Japan. Because modern Shinto preaches patriotism, it is sometimes said that Japan's real religion is nationalism. Shinto teaches sincere and ethical behavior, loyalty and respect toward others, and enjoyment of life.

Shinto beliefs are reflected in the workplace through the traditional practice of lifetime employment (although this is waning today) and through the traditional trust extended between firms and customers. Japanese competitiveness in world markets has benefited from loyal workforces, low employee turnover, and good labor–management cooperation. The phenomenal success of many Japanese companies in recent decades gave rise to the concept of a Shinto work ethic, certain aspects of which have been emulated by Western managers.

QUICK STUDY 4

1. What are the main beliefs of each of the seven religions presented in the previous sections?
2. In what ways does religion affect international business activities?
3. Identify the dominant religion in each of the following countries: (a) Brazil, (b) China, (c) India, (d) Ireland, (e) Mexico, (f) Russia, and (g) Thailand.

Personal Communication

People in every culture have a **communication** system to convey thoughts, feelings, knowledge, and information through speech, writing, and actions. Understanding a culture's spoken language gives us great insight into why people think and act the way they do. Understanding a culture's body language helps us avoid sending unintended or embarrassing messages. Let's examine each of these forms of communication more closely.

communication
System of conveying thoughts, feelings, knowledge, and information through speech, writing, and actions.

SPOKEN AND WRITTEN LANGUAGE Spoken and written language is the most obvious difference we notice when traveling in another country. We overhear and engage in a number of conversations and read many signs and documents to find our way. Knowledge of a people's language is the key to deeply understanding a culture.

Linguistically different segments of a population are often culturally, socially, and politically distinct. Malaysia's population is composed of Malay (60 percent), Chinese (30 percent), and

GLOBAL SUSTAINABILITY   Speaking in Fewer Tongues

One day this year, somewhere in the world, an old man or woman will die and with them will go their language. Dozens of languages have just one native speaker still living, and some blame globalization. Here are the facts, the consequences, and what can be done.

- **Some Are Losing.** Of the world's roughly 6,000 languages, about 90 percent have fewer than 100,000 speakers. By the end of this century, more than half of the world's languages may be lost; perhaps fewer than 1,000 will survive. One endangered language is Aramaic, a 2,500-year-old Semitic language that was once the major language in the Middle East.
- **Some Are Gaining.** Even as minority languages die out, three languages continue to grow in popularity: Mandarin, Spanish, and English. English has emerged as the universal language of business, higher education, diplomacy, science, popular music, entertainment, and international travel. More than 70 nations give special status to English, and roughly one-quarter of the world's population is fluent or competent in it.

- **The Consequences.** The loss of a language can diminish the richness of a people's cultural, spiritual, and intellectual life. What is lost includes prayers, myths, humor, poetry, ceremonies, conversational styles, and terms for emotions, behaviors, and habits. When a language dies, all these must be expressed in a new language with different words, sounds, and grammar.
- **What Can Be Done?** Linguists are concerned that such a valuable part of human culture could vanish. So, they are busily creating videotapes, audiotapes, and written records of endangered tongues before they disappear. Communities are also taking action. In New Zealand, Maori communities set up nursery schools called *kohanga reo,* or "language nests," that are staffed by elders and conducted entirely in Maori.
- **Want to Know More?** Visit Enduring Voices (http://travel.nationalgeographic.com/travel/enduring-voices), Living Tongues (www.livingtongues.org), and the Foundation For Endangered Languages (www.ogmios.org).

Indian (10 percent) peoples. Although Malay is the official national language, each ethnic group speaks its own language and continues its traditions. The United Kingdom includes England, Northern Ireland, Scotland, and Wales. The native languages of Ireland and Scotland are dialects of *Gaelic,* and the speaking of *Welsh* in Wales predates the use of English in Britain. After decades of decline, Gaelic and Welsh are staging comebacks on radio and television and in school curricula.

The global reach of media today and increased travel for tourism and business mean that some cultures face the possibility of losing their native languages. Read the Global Sustainability feature, titled "Speaking in Fewer Tongues," to see how a lack of social sustainability can endanger languages around the world.

Implications for Managers The importance of understanding local languages is becoming increasingly apparent on the Internet. Roughly two-thirds of all web pages are in English, but around three-fourths of all Internet users are nonnative English speakers. Software-solutions providers are assisting companies from English-speaking countries in adapting their websites for global e-business. Web surfers from cultures across the globe bring their own specific tastes, preferences, and buying habits online with them. The company that can provide its customer in Mexico City, Paris, or Tokyo with a quality buying experience in his or her native language will have an edge on the competition.

Language proficiency is crucial in production facilities where nonnative managers are supervising local employees. One U.S. manager in Mexico was confused when his seemingly relaxed and untroubled workers went on strike. The problem lay in different cultural perspectives. Mexican workers generally do not take the initiative in problem solving and workplace complaints. Workers concluded the plant manager knew, but did not care, about their concerns because he did not question employees about working conditions.

American-born Thomas Kwan, who works for a health products company in Shanghai, China, says similar scenarios occur there. "Whereas Americans are encouraged to challenge their boss to explain things, I have to ask Chinese staff what they think and encourage them to speak up. A lot of [expatriate] managers fail in China because they don't understand that Chinese don't tell you what they think," he says.[7]

Marketers prize insights into the interests, values, attitudes, and habits of teenagers. Habbo (www.habbo.com), the world's largest virtual hangout for teens, surveyed more than 50,000 teenagers in 31 countries to learn how they communicate with each other. The study found that, although 72 percent of teens have active e-mail accounts, 76 percent communicate with friends primarily through instant messaging. Teens reserve e-mail for nonpersonal needs such as school, work, and correspondence with family members. And, of course, teens keep in touch on Facebook (www.facebook.com). Knowledge of these habits help marketers to better target promotions.[8]

Language Blunders Advertising slogans and company documents must be translated carefully so that messages are received precisely as intended. If they are not carefully translated, a company can make a language blunder in its international business dealings. In Sweden, Kellogg (www.kellogg.com) had to rename its Bran Buds cereal because the Swedish translation came out roughly as "burned farmer." And then there's the entrepreneur in Miami who tried to make the most of a visit to the United States by the Pope of the Roman Catholic Church. He quickly began printing T-Shirts for Spanish-speaking Catholics that should have read, "I saw the Pope (el Papa)." But a gender error on the noun resulted in T-Shirts proclaiming, "I saw the Potato (la Papa)"![9] Other translation blunders include:

- An English-language sign in a Moscow hotel read, "You are welcome to visit the cemetery where famous Russian composers, artists, and writers are buried daily except Thursday."
- A sign for English-speaking guests in a Tokyo hotel read, "You are respectfully requested to take advantage of the chambermaids."
- An airline ticket office in Copenhagen read in English, "We take your bags and send them in all directions."
- A Japanese knife manufacturer labeled its exports to the United States with "Caution: Blade extremely sharp! Keep out of children."
- Braniff Airlines' English-language slogan "Fly in Leather" was translated into "Fly Naked" in Spanish.

Such blunders are not the exclusive domain of humans. The use of machine translation—computer software used to translate one language into another—is booming along with the explosion in the number of nonnative English speakers using the Internet. One search engine allows its users to search the Internet in English and Asian languages, translate web pages, and compose an e-mail in one language and send it in another. The computers attempted a translation of the following: "The Chinese Communist Party is debating whether to drop its ban on private-enterprise owners being allowed to join the party." And it came up with this in Chinese: "The Chinese Communist Party is debating whether to deny its ban in join the Party is allowed soldier enterprise owners on." Various other machine translators turned the French version of "I don't care" ("*Je m'en fou*") into "I myself in crazy," "I of insane," and "Me me in madman."

Lingua Franca A **lingua franca** is a third or "link" language understood by two parties who speak different native languages. The original *lingua franca* arose to support ancient trading activities and contained a mixture of Italian and French, along with Arabic, Greek, and Turkish. Although only 5 percent of the world's population speaks English as a first language, it is the most common *lingua franca* used in international business, followed closely by French and Spanish.

The Cantonese dialect of Chinese spoken in Hong Kong and the Mandarin dialect spoken in Taiwan and on the Chinese mainland are so different that a *lingua franca* is often preferred. And, although India's official language is Hindi, its *lingua franca* among the multitude of dialects is English because it was once a British colony. Yet many young people speak what is referred to as "Hinglish"—a combination of Hindi, Tamil, and English words mixed within a single sentence. Multinational corporations also sometimes choose a *lingua franca* for official internal communications because they operate in many nations, each with its own language.

Companies that use English for internal correspondence include Philips (www.philips.com; a Dutch electronics firm), Asea Brown Boveri (www.abb.com; a Swiss industrial giant), and Alcatel-Lucent (www.alcatel-lucent.com; a French telecommunications firm). Japan's number-one Internet shopping site, Rakuten (www.rakuten.co.jp), officially adopted English because of its pervasiveness on the Internet. All executive meetings are held in English, and all internal documents will eventually be written in English.[10]

BODY LANGUAGE **Body language** communicates through unspoken cues, including hand gestures, facial expressions, physical greetings, eye contact, and the manipulation of personal space. Similar to spoken language, body language communicates both information and feelings

lingua franca
Third or "link" language understood by two parties who speak different native languages.

body language
Language communicated through unspoken cues, including hand gestures, facial expressions, physical greetings, eye contact, and the manipulation of personal space.

Forming the thumb-and-index circle in most of Europe and in the United States means "okay"; in Germany it's a rude gesture. Tapping one's nose in England and Scotland means "You and I are in on the secret"; in Wales it means "You're very nosy." Tapping one's temple in much of Western Europe means "You're crazy"; in the Netherlands it means "You're very clever."

Sources: oto.fritz/ Shutterstock; Stephen Orsillo/ Shutterstock; ostill /Shutterstock

and differs greatly from one culture to another. Italians, French, Arabs, and Venezuelans, for example, tend to animate conversations with lively hand gestures and other body motions. Japanese and Koreans, although more reserved, can communicate just as much information through their own body languages; a look of the eye can carry as much or more meaning as two flailing arms.

Most body language is subtle and takes time to recognize and interpret. For example, navigating the all-important handshake in international business can be tricky. In the United States, a firm grip and several pumps of the arm is usually the standard. But in the Middle East and Latin America, a softer clasp of the hand with little or no arm pump is the custom. And in some countries, such as Japan, people do not shake hands at all but bow to one another. Bows of respect carry different meanings, usually depending on the recipient. Associates of equal standing bow about 15 degrees toward one another. But proper respect for an elder requires a bow of about 30 degrees. Bows of remorse or apology should be about 45 degrees.

Proximity is an extremely important element of body language to consider when meeting someone from another culture. If you stand or sit too close to your counterpart (from their perspective), you may invade their personal space and appear aggressive. If you remain too far away, you risk appearing untrustworthy. For North Americans, a distance of about 19 inches is about right between two speakers. For Western Europeans, 14 to 16 inches seems appropriate, but someone from the United Kingdom might prefer about 24 inches. Koreans and Chinese are likely to be comfortable about 36 inches apart; people from the Middle East will close the distance to about 8 to 12 inches.

Physical gestures often cause the most misunderstanding between people of different cultures because they can convey very different meanings. For example, the thumbs-up sign is vulgar in Italy and Greece but means "all right" or even "great" in the United States.

QUICK STUDY 5

1. Define *communication*. Why is knowledge of a culture's spoken language important for international business?
2. Describe the importance of a *lingua franca* to conducting international business.
3. Why is *body language* influential for international business? Give several examples.

Education

Education is crucial for passing on traditions, customs, and values. Each culture educates its young people through schooling, parenting, religious teachings, and group memberships. Families and other groups provide informal instruction about customs and how to socialize with others. In most cultures, intellectual skills such as reading and mathematics are taught in formal educational settings. Two important topics in education are education level and brain drain.

EDUCATION LEVEL Data that a government provides on its people's education level must be taken with a grain of salt. Comparisons from country to country can be difficult because many nations rely on literacy tests of their own design. Although some countries administer standardized tests, others require only a signature as proof of literacy. Yet searching for untapped markets or new factory locations can force managers to rely on such undependable benchmarks. As you can see from Table 2.1, some countries have further to go than others to increase national

TABLE 2.1 Illiteracy Rates of Selected Countries

Country	Adult Illiteracy Rate (% of People Age 15 and Up)
Burkina Faso	71
Pakistan	44
Morocco	44
Nigeria	39
Egypt	29
Cambodia	22
Saudi Arabia	14
Peru	10
Brazil	10
Zimbabwe	8
Jordan	8
Mexico	7
Colombia	7
Philippines	5
Portugal	5

Source: Based on *World Development Indicators 2012*, World Bank website (www.worldbank.org).

literacy rates. Around 800 million adults remain illiterate globally. And although global illiteracy rates are higher for women, the gap with men is closing.[11]

Countries with poorly educated populations attract the lowest-paying manufacturing jobs. Nations with excellent programs for basic education tend to attract relatively good-paying industries. Those that invest in worker training are usually repaid in productivity increases and rising incomes. Meanwhile, countries with skilled, highly educated workforces attract all sorts of high-paying jobs.

Emerging economies in Asia owe much of their rapid economic development to solid education systems. They focus on rigorous mathematical training in primary and secondary schooling. University education concentrates on the hard sciences and aims to train engineers, scientists, and managers.[12]

THE "BRAIN DRAIN" PHENOMENON The quality of a nation's education system is related to its level of economic development. **Brain drain** is the departure of highly educated people from one profession, geographic region, or nation to another. Over the years, political unrest and economic hardship has forced many Indonesians to flee their homeland for other nations, particularly Hong Kong, Singapore, and the United States. Most of Indonesia's brain drain has occurred among Western-educated professionals in finance and technology—exactly the people needed for economic development.

brain drain
Departure of highly educated people from one profession, geographic region, or nation to another.

Many countries in Eastern Europe experienced high levels of brain drain early in their transition to market economies. Economists, engineers, scientists, and researchers in all fields fled westward to escape poverty. But as these nations continue their long transition from communism, some of them are luring professionals back to their homelands—a process known as *reverse brain drain*.

Physical and Material Environments

The physical environment and material surroundings of a culture heavily influence its development and pace of change. In this section, we first look at how physical environment and culture are related, and then we explore the effect of material culture on business.

PHYSICAL ENVIRONMENT Although the physical environment affects a people's culture, it does not directly determine it. Two aspects of the physical environment that heavily influence a people's culture are topography and climate.

topography
All the physical features that characterize the surface of a geographic region.

Topography   All the physical features that characterize the surface of a geographic region constitute its **topography**. Some surface features such as navigable rivers and flat plains facilitate travel and contact with others. By contrast, treacherous mountain ranges and large bodies of water can discourage contact. Cultures isolated by topographical features can find themselves less exposed to the cultural traits of other peoples, which can mean slower cultural change.

Topography can affect consumers' product needs. For example, there is little market for Honda scooters (www.honda.com) in most mountainous regions because their engines are too small. These are better markets for the company's more rugged, maneuverable motorcycles with larger engines.

Topography can have a profound impact on personal communication in a culture. For example, mountain ranges and the formidable Gobi Desert consume two-thirds of China's land surface. Groups living in the valleys of these mountain ranges hold on to their own ways of life and speak their own languages. Although the Mandarin dialect was decreed the national language many years ago, the mountains, desert, and vast expanse of China still impair personal communication and, therefore, the proliferation of Mandarin.

Climate   Climate affects where people settle and helps direct systems of distribution. In Australia, for example, intensely hot and dry conditions in two large deserts and jungle conditions in the northeast pushed settlement to coastal areas. These climatic conditions combined with the higher cost of land transport means coastal waters are still used to distribute products between distant cities.

Climate plays a large role in lifestyle and work habits. The heat of the summer sun grows intense in the early afternoon hours in the countries of southern Europe, northern Africa, and the Middle East. For this reason, people often take afternoon breaks of one or two hours in July and August. People use this time to perform errands, such as shopping, or even to take short naps before returning to work until about 7 or 8 p.m. Companies doing business in these regions must adapt to this local tradition.

Climate also affects customs such as the type of clothing people wear. People in many tropical areas wear little clothing and wear it loosely because of the warm, humid climate. In the desert areas of the Middle East and North Africa, people also wear loose clothing, but they wear long robes to protect themselves from intense sunshine and blowing sand.

Members of the "Chinese Root-Seeking Tour" pose for photos under an old tree at the Temple of Heaven in Beijing, China. The summer camp program attracts more than 6,000 overseas Chinese youths from 51 countries and regions each year. It is designed to educate young people in the cultural traditions of their Chinese ancestors. Organizers hope that by gaining a better understanding of Chinese history and culture, these youths will grow to become good cross-cultural communicators between China and other nations.

Source: Wang Yongji/Newscom

MATERIAL CULTURE All the technology used in a culture to manufacture goods and provide services is called its **material culture**. Material culture is often used to measure the technological advancement of a nation's markets or industries. Generally, a firm enters a new market under one of two conditions: Demand for its products has developed or the infrastructure is capable of supporting production operations.

Many regions and nations lack the most basic elements of a modern society's material culture. Yet technology is helping some nations at the bottom of the global economic pyramid break down barriers that keep their people mired in poverty.

Uneven Material Culture Material culture often displays uneven development across a nation's geography, markets, and industries. For example, much of China's recent economic progress is occurring in coastal cities. Shanghai has long played an important role in China's international trade because of its strategic location and its superb harbor on the East China Sea. Although it is home to only 1 percent of the total population, Shanghai accounts for about 5 percent of China's total output—including about 12 percent of both its industrial production and its financial-services output.

Likewise, Bangkok, the capital city of Thailand, houses only 10 percent of the nation's population but accounts for about 40 percent of its economic output. Meanwhile, the northern parts of the country remain rural, consisting mostly of farms, forests, and mountains.

material culture
All the technology used in a culture to manufacture goods and provide services.

QUICK STUDY 6

1. Why is the education level of a country's people important to international companies?
2. What is meant by the terms *brain drain* and *reverse brain drain*?
3. How are a people's culture and physical environment related?
4. What is the significance of *material culture* for international business?

Classifying Cultures

Throughout this chapter, you've seen how cultures can differ greatly from one another. People living in broadly different cultures tend to respond differently in similar business situations. There are two widely accepted ways to classify cultures based on differences in characteristics such as values, attitudes, social structures, and so on. Let's now take a detailed look at each of these tools: the Kluckhohn–Strodtbeck and Hofstede frameworks.

Kluckhohn–Strodtbeck Framework

The **Kluckhohn–Strodtbeck framework** compares cultures along six dimensions. It studies a given culture by asking each of the following questions:[13]

* Do people believe that their environment controls them, that they control the environment, or that they are part of nature?
* Do people focus on past events, on the present, or on the future implications of their actions?
* Are people easily controlled and not to be trusted, or can they be trusted to act freely and responsibly?
* Do people desire accomplishments in life, carefree lives, or spiritual and contemplative lives?
* Do people believe that individuals or groups are responsible for each person's welfare?
* Do people prefer to conduct most activities in private or in public?

Kluckhohn–Strodtbeck framework
Framework for studying cultural differences along six dimensions, such as focus on past or future events and belief in individual or group responsibility for personal well-being.

CASE: DIMENSIONS OF JAPANESE CULTURE By providing answers to each of these six questions, we can apply the Kluckhohn–Strodtbeck framework to Japanese culture:

1. *Japanese believe in a delicate balance between people and environment that must be maintained.* Suppose an undetected flaw in a company's product harms customers using it. In many countries, a high-stakes class-action lawsuit would be filed against the manufacturer on behalf of the victims' families. This scenario rarely plays out in Japan.

Japanese culture does not feel that individuals can possibly control every situation but that accidents happen. Japanese victims would receive heartfelt apologies, a promise it won't happen again, and a relatively small damage award.

2. *Japanese culture emphasizes the future.* Because Japanese culture emphasizes strong ties between people and groups, including companies, forming long-term relationships with people is essential when doing business there. Throughout the business relationship, Japanese companies remain in close, continuous contact with buyers to ensure that their needs are being met. This relationship also forms the basis of a communication channel by which suppliers learn about the types of products and services buyers would like to see in the future.

3. *Japanese culture treats people as quite trustworthy.* Business dealings among Japanese companies are based heavily on trust. After an agreement to conduct business is entered into, it is difficult to break unless there are extreme, uncontrollable factors at work. This is due to the fear of "losing face" if one cannot keep a business commitment. In addition to business applications, society at large reflects the Japanese concern for trustworthiness. Crime rates are quite low, and the streets of Japan's largest cities are very safe to walk at night.

4. *Japanese are accomplishment-oriented—not necessarily for themselves, but for their employers and work units.* Japanese children learn the importance of groups early by contributing to the upkeep of their schools. They share duties such as mopping floors, washing windows, cleaning chalkboards, and arranging desks and chairs. They carry such habits learned in school into the adult workplace, where management and labor tend to work together toward company goals. Japanese managers make decisions only after considering input from subordinates. Also, materials buyers, engineers, designers, factory floor supervisors, and marketers cooperate closely throughout each stage of a product's development.

5. *Japanese culture emphasizes individual responsibility to the group and group responsibility to the individual.* This trait has long been a hallmark of Japanese corporations. Traditionally, subordinates promise hard work and loyalty, and top managers provide job security. But to remain competitive internationally, Japanese companies have eliminated jobs and moved production to low-wage nations like China and Vietnam. As the tradition of job security falls by the wayside, more Japanese workers now consider working for non-Japanese companies, whereas others find work as temporary employees. Although this trait of loyalty is diminishing somewhat in business, it remains a very prominent feature in other aspects of Japanese society, especially family.

6. *The culture of Japan tends to be public.* You will often find top Japanese managers located in the center of a large, open-space office surrounded by the desks of many employees. In comparison, Western executives are often secluded in walled offices located on the perimeter of workspaces. This characteristic reaches deep into Japanese society—consider, for example, Japan's tradition of bathing in public bathhouses.

Hofstede Framework

Hofstede framework
Framework for studying cultural differences along five dimensions, such as individualism versus collectivism and equality versus inequality.

The **Hofstede framework** compares cultures along five dimensions.[14] Dutch psychologist Geert Hofstede developed the framework from a study of more than 110,000 people working in IBM subsidiaries (www.ibm.com) in 40 countries and from a follow-up study of students in 23 countries. Let's examine each of these dimensions in detail:[15]

1. *Individualism versus collectivism.* This dimension identifies the extent to which a culture emphasizes the individual versus the group. Individualist cultures (those scoring high on this dimension) value hard work and promote entrepreneurial risk taking, thereby fostering invention and innovation. Although people are given freedom to focus on personal goals, they are held responsible for their actions. That is why responsibility for poor business decisions is placed squarely on the shoulders of the individual in charge. At the same time, higher individualism may be responsible for higher rates of employee turnover.

On the contrary, people in collectivist cultures (those scoring low on this dimension) feel a strong association to groups, including family and work units. The goal of maintaining group harmony is probably most evident in the family structure. People in collectivist cultures tend to work toward collective rather than personal goals and are responsible to the group for their actions. In turn, the group shares responsibility for the well-being of each of its members. Thus, in collectivist cultures, success or failure tends to be shared among the work unit, rather than any particular individual receiving all the praise or blame. All social, political, economic, and legal institutions reflect the group's critical role.

2. *Power distance.*   This dimension conveys the degree to which a culture accepts social inequality among its people. A culture with large power distance tends to be characterized by much inequality between superiors and subordinates. Organizations tend also to be more hierarchical, with power deriving from prestige, force, and inheritance. This is why executives and upper management in cultures with large power distance often enjoy special recognition and privileges. On the other hand, cultures with small power distance display a greater degree of equality, with prestige and rewards more equally shared between superiors and subordinates. Power in these cultures (relative to cultures with large power distance) is seen to derive more from hard work and entrepreneurial drive and is therefore often considered more legitimate.

Figure 2.2 shows how various countries rank according to these first two dimensions: power distance and individualism versus collectivism. What is striking about this figure is the tight grouping of nations within the five clusters (plus Costa Rica). You can see the concentration of mostly African, Asian, Central and South American, and Middle Eastern nations in Quadrant 1 (cultures with relatively larger power distance and lower individualism). By contrast, Quadrants 3 and 2 comprise mostly the cultures of Australia and the nations of North America and Western Europe. These nations had the highest individualism scores, and many had relatively smaller power distance scores.

3. *Uncertainty avoidance.*   This dimension identifies the extent to which a culture avoids uncertainty and ambiguity. A culture with large uncertainty avoidance values security and places its faith in strong systems of rules and procedures in society. It is perhaps not surprising then that cultures with large uncertainty avoidance normally have lower employee turnover, more formal rules for regulating employee behavior, and more difficulty implementing change. Cultures scoring low on uncertainty avoidance tend to

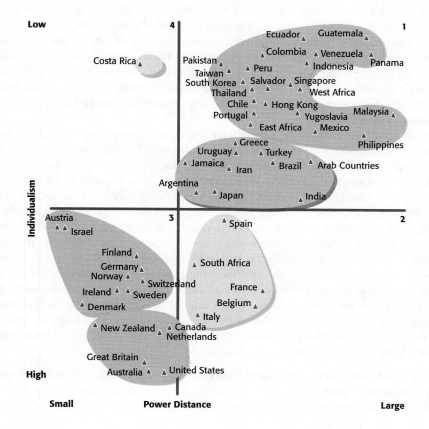

FIGURE 2.2

Power Distance and Individualism versus Collectivism

Source: Geert Hofstede, "The Cultural Relativity of Organizational Practices and Theories," *Journal of International Business Studies*, Fall 1983, p. 82.

FIGURE 2.3

Power Distance and Uncertainty Avoidance

Source: Geert Hofstede, "The Cultural Relativity of Organizational Practices and Theories," *Journal of International Business Studies*, Fall 1983, p. 84.

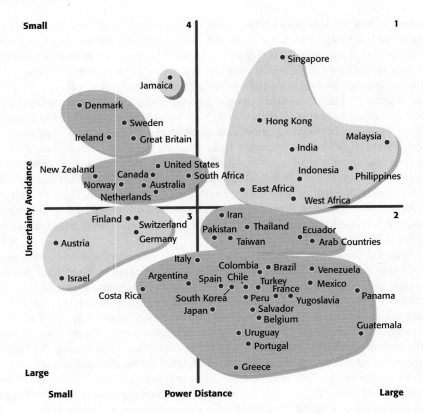

be more open to change and new ideas. This helps explain why individuals in this type of culture tend to be entrepreneurial and organizations tend to welcome the best business practices from other cultures. Because people tend to be less fearful of change, however, these cultures can also suffer from higher levels of employee turnover.

Figure 2.3 plots countries according to the second and third dimensions: power distance and uncertainty avoidance. Although the lines of demarcation are somewhat less obvious in this figure, patterns do emerge, forming six clusters (plus Jamaica). Quadrant 4 contains nations characterized by small uncertainty avoidance and small power distance, including Australia, Canada, Jamaica, the United States, and several Western European nations. Meanwhile, Quadrant 2 contains many Asian, Central American, South American, and Middle Eastern nations—nations having large power distance and large uncertainty avoidance indexes.

4. ***Masculinity versus femininity.*** This dimension captures the extent to which a culture emphasizes masculinity versus femininity. According to Hofstede, cultures scoring high on masculinity tend to be characterized more by personal assertiveness and the accumulation of wealth, typically translating into an entrepreneurial drive. Cultures scoring low on this dimension (greater tendency toward femininity) generally have more relaxed lifestyles, wherein people are more concerned about caring for others as opposed to material gain.

5. ***Long-term orientation.*** This dimension indicates a society's perspective on time and attitudes about overcoming obstacles with time, if not with will and strength. It attempts to capture the differences between Eastern and Western cultures. A high-scoring culture (strong long-term orientation) values respect for tradition, thrift, perseverance, and a sense of personal shame. These cultures tend to have a strong work ethic because people expect long-term rewards from today's hard work. A low-scoring culture is characterized by individual stability and reputation, fulfillment of social obligations, and reciprocation of greetings and gifts. These cultures can change more rapidly because tradition and commitment are not impediments to change.

Locate your country in Figure 2.2 and Figure 2.3. In your personal experience, do you agree with the placement of your nation in these figures? Do you believe managers in your country display the types of behaviors depicted on each dimension just described?

QUICK STUDY 7

1. What six dimensions comprise the *Kluckhohn–Strodtbeck framework* for classifying cultures?
2. What are the five dimensions of the *Hofstede framework* for classifying cultures?
3. Briefly explain how each framework can be used to analyze a culture.

BOTTOM LINE FOR BUSINESS

As globalization continues to draw companies into the international arena, understanding local culture can give a company an advantage over rivals. By avoiding ethnocentric thinking, managers can avoid mistakenly disregarding the beneficial aspects of other cultures. By contrast, culturally literate managers who understand local needs and desires bring their companies closer to customers and, therefore, increase their competitiveness. They can become more-effective marketers, negotiators, and production managers. Let's explore several areas in which culture has a direct impact on international business activity.

Marketing and Cultural Literacy

Many international companies operating in local markets abroad take advantage of the public relations value of supporting national culture. Some of India's most precious historical monuments and sites are crumbling due to a lack of government funds for upkeep. Companies are helping the government to maintain key sites and are earning the goodwill of the people.

This chapter introduced the Kluckhohn–Strodtbeck and Hofstede frameworks for classifying cultures. Local culture is important for a company exploring international markets for its products. We can see the significance of power distance in the export of luxury items. A nation with a large power distance accepts greater inequality among its people and tends to have a wealthy upper class that can afford luxury goods. Thus, companies marketing products such as expensive jewelry, high-priced cars, and even yachts could find wealthy market segments within relatively poor nations.

Work Attitudes and Cultural Literacy

National differences in work attitudes are complex and involve other factors in addition to culture. Perceived opportunity for financial reward is no doubt a strong element in attitudes toward work in any culture. Research suggests both U.S. and German employees work longer hours when there is a greater likelihood that good performance will lead to promotion and increased pay. Yet this appears relatively less true in Germany, where wages are less variable and job security and jobless benefits (such as free national health care) are greater. Thus, other aspects of German society are at least as important as culture in determining work attitudes. The culturally literate manager understands the complexity of national workplace attitudes and incorporates this knowledge into reward systems.

Expatriates and Cultural Literacy

As stated in our discussion of classifying cultures, people living in broadly different cultures tend to respond differently in similar business situations. This is why companies that send personnel abroad to unfamiliar cultures are concerned with cultural differences. For example, a Norwegian manager working in Japan for a European car manufacturer, but whose colleagues were mostly Japanese, soon became frustrated with the time needed to make decisions and take action. The main cause for his frustration was that the uncertainty avoidance index for Japan is much larger than that in his native Norway (see Figure 2.3). In Japan, a greater aversion to uncertainty led to the need for a greater number of consultations than would have been needed in the home market. The frustrated manager eventually left Japan to return to Europe.

Gender and Cultural Literacy

In Japan, men have traditionally held nearly all positions of responsibility. Women have generally served as office clerks and administrative assistants until their mid- to late 20s, when they were expected to marry and then focus on tending to family needs. Although this is still largely true today, progress is being made in expanding the role of women in Japan's business community. Women own nearly a quarter of all businesses in Japan, but many of these businesses are very small and have little economic influence. Greater gender equality prevails in Australia, Canada, Germany, and the United States, but women in these countries still tend to earn less money than men in similar positions.

Chapter Summary

MyManagementLab
Go to **mymanagementlab.com** to complete the problem marked with this icon .

1. **Describe culture and explain the significance of both national culture and subcultures.**
   - *Culture* is the set of values, beliefs, rules, and institutions held by a specific group of people.
   - Managers should try to avoid *ethnocentricity* (the tendency to view one's own culture as superior to others) and to develop *cultural literacy* (detailed knowledge necessary to function effectively in another culture).
   - We are conditioned to think in terms of national culture—that is, to equate a nation-state and its people with a single culture.

- Governments promote national culture and intervene in business to protect it from the influence of other cultures.
- Most nations are also home to numerous *subcultures*—groups of people who share a unique way of life within a larger, dominant culture.
- Subcultures contribute greatly to national culture and must be considered in marketing and production decisions.

2. Identify the components of culture and describe their impact on international business.
   - *Aesthetics* help determine which colors and symbols will be effective in promotions and advertising.
   - *Values* influence a people's *attitudes* toward time, work, and cultural change.
   - Knowledge of *manners* and *customs* is necessary for negotiating, marketing products, and managing operations in other cultures.
   - *Social structure* affects business decisions, including production-site selection, advertising methods, and the costs of doing business in a country.
   - Different *religions* take different views of work, savings, and material goods.
   - Understanding a people's system of *personal communication* provides insight into their values and behavior.
   - A culture's *education* level affects the quality of the workforce and a people's standard of living.
   - *Physical* and *material environments* influence work habits and preferences for products such as clothing and food.

3. Describe cultural change and explain how companies and culture affect each other.
   - *Cultural change* occurs when people integrate the gestures, material objects, traditions, or concepts of another culture through *cultural diffusion*.
   - Globalization and technology are increasing the pace of cultural change around the world.
   - Companies influence culture when they import new products, policies, and business practices into a host country.
   - Companies should try to avoid *cultural imperialism*—the replacement of one culture's traditions, folk heroes, and artifacts with substitutes from another.
   - Cultures affect management styles, work scheduling, and reward systems.
   - Adapting to local cultures around the world means heeding the maxim "Think globally, act locally."

4. Explain how the physical environment and technology influence culture.
   - A people's *physical environment* includes *topography* and climate and how people relate to their surroundings.
   - Cultures isolated by topographical barriers, such as mountains or seas, normally change relatively slowly, and their languages are often distinct.
   - Climate affects a people's work hours, clothing, and food.
   - *Material culture* refers to all the technology a culture uses to manufacture goods and provide services, and it can be uneven within a nation.
   - Businesspeople measure material culture to determine whether a market has developed adequate demand for a company's products and whether it can support production activities.

5. Describe the two main frameworks used to classify cultures and explain their practical use.
   - The *Kluckhohn–Strodtbeck framework* compares cultures along six dimensions by seeking answers to questions on six topics, including a people's (1) relation to the environment; (2) focus on past, present, or future; (3) trustworthiness; (4) desire for accomplishment; (5) group–individual responsibility; and (6) public versus private nature.
   - The *Hofstede framework* compares cultures along five dimensions, including a people's (1) individualism versus collectivism, (2) power distance, (3) uncertainty avoidance, (4) masculinity versus femininity, and (5) long-term orientation.
   - Taken together, these frameworks help companies understand many aspects of a culture, including risk taking, innovation, job mobility, team cooperation, pay levels, and hiring practices.

Talk It Over

1. Two students are discussing the various reasons why they are not studying international business. "International business doesn't affect me," declares the first student. "I'm going to stay here, not work in some foreign country." "Yeah, me neither," agrees the second. "Besides, some cultures are really strange. The sooner other countries start doing business our way, the better." What counterarguments can you present to these students' perceptions?
2. In this exercise, two groups of four students each will debate the benefits and drawbacks of individualist versus collectivist cultures. After the first student from each side has spoken, the second student questions the opponent's arguments, looking for holes and inconsistencies. The third student attempts to reply to these counterarguments. Then, the fourth student summarizes each side's arguments. Finally, the class votes on which team presented the more compelling case.

Teaming Up

1. **Research Project.** Select a company in your city or town that does business internationally and make an appointment to interview the owner or a senior manager. Your team's goal is to learn how cultural differences affect the decisions of this business as it pursues international opportunities. How does the company balance the need for global efficiency and local responsiveness in a cultural sense? Has local culture ever required the company to alter its personnel or corporate practices? Be sure to ask your interviewee for specific examples. Present a brief talk or paper on your group's interview findings.
2. **Market Entry Strategy Project.** This exercise corresponds to the *MESP* online simulation. For the nation you are studying, list several of its people's manners and customs. What values do people hold dear? Describe their attitude toward time, work, and cultural change. What religions are practiced there? What language(s) are spoken? What ethnicities reside in the nation, and do they form distinct subcultures? Describe the nation's social structure and its education system. Turn to Figures 2.2 and 2.3, and either (a) explain why you think the nation appears where it does in the figures, or (b) identify where you think it belongs on the figure and explain why. Integrate your findings into your completed *MESP* report.

Key Terms

aesthetics (p. 45)	cultural trait (p. 47)	material culture (p. 63)
attitudes (p. 46)	culture (p. 42)	popular custom (p. 49)
body language (p. 59)	customs (p. 49)	social group (p. 50)
brain drain (p. 61)	ethnocentricity (p. 42)	social mobility (p. 51)
caste system (p. 51)	folk custom (p. 49)	social stratification (p. 51)
class system (p. 52)	Hofstede framework (p. 64)	social structure (p. 50)
communication (p. 57)	Kluckhohn–Strodtbeck framework	subculture (p. 44)
cultural diffusion (p. 47)	(p. 63)	topography (p. 62)
cultural imperialism (p. 47)	lingua franca (p. 59)	values (p. 45)
cultural literacy (p. 42)	manners (p. 49)	

Take It to the Web

1. **Video Report.** Visit this book's channel on YouTube (www.YouTube.com/MyIBvideos). Click on "Videos" near the top of the page, and click on the set of videos labeled "Ch 02: Cross-Cultural Business." Watch one video from the list and then summarize it in a half-page report. Reflecting on the contents of this chapter, which components of culture can you identify in the video? How might a company engaged in international business act on the information contained in the video?
2. **Website Report.** Culture affects the product a company sells in a market or region, how it markets the product, its human resource practices, and so on. It is increasingly important that managers have cultural understanding of their markets in this age of globalization.

    Select a well-known multinational company and visit its website. Locate the section of the website that tells about the company's activities (usually titled "About Us"). Report on

(1) the main products or services the company offers; (2) the extent to which the company pursues international business operations (often expressed as percentage of sales or assets); (3) ways that the company has adapted to cultures around the world; and (4) the general policies it follows in doing business internationally.

Regarding its online presence, does the company offer its website in another widely spoken language? Find and click on several of the company's other national websites. What kinds of products are advertised on the home pages of the different sites? Can you identify how the company adapts its website to suit cultural preferences?

Ethical Challenges

⭐**1.** You are the vice president of operations for a U.S.–based software firm. Your firm's board of directors wants you to explore building a software-design operation in India. Typically, when international firms enter the Indian market, they quickly learn about the various ways in which a rigid caste system can affect business activities. Do you think it will be possible to uphold a U.S. management style in India? Or should your company be prepared to adjust to the local Indian managerial style and human resource practices?

2. You are the public relations director for a company that recently announced its decision to close its factory in the United States and outsource the work to manufacturers in Asia and Latin America. Your firm is doing what many other companies have already done, reducing labor costs by shifting work to low-wage countries such as China, India, Mexico, and Central American nations. Yet the media and disgruntled workers are lambasting your firm's decision. Is there a reasonable response to charges that the companies you will hire frequently exploit child labor, force workers—often women—to work 75-hour weeks, and destroy family units?

MyManagementLab

Go to **mymanagementlab.com** for Auto-graded writing questions as well as the following Assisted-graded writing questions:

2-1. You are the vice president of international operations for a large pharmaceutical firm that manufactures an anti-malarial drug. Your firm is considering opening up a factory in a small Central American nation where malaria is common. The operation will be a cooperative venture between your firm and the local government. The majority of the people in that country cannot afford the medicine because of the high import tariffs. Yet if your plan goes through, more than 200 jobs will be created and the drug's international price will drop by more than 50 percent. In a final meeting with a senior government official, the gentleman informs you that, if you pay him $500,000 cash, the deal will go through. What issues must you consider? What do you do?

2-2. Mymanagementlab Only – comprehensive writing assignment for this chapter.

Practicing International Management Case

A Tale of Two Cultures

Many cultures in Asia are in the midst of an identity crisis. In effect, they are being torn between two worlds. Pulling in one direction is a traditional value system derived from agriculture-based communities and extended families—that is, elements of a culture in which relatives take care of one another and state-run welfare systems are unnecessary. Pulling from the opposite direction is a new set of values emerging from manufacturing- and finance-based economies—elements of a culture in which workers must often move to faraway cities to find work, sometimes leaving family members to fend for themselves.

For decades, Western multinational corporations set up factories across Southeast Asia to take advantage of relatively low-cost labor. Later, local companies sprang up and became competitive global players in their own right. Spectacular rates of economic growth in a few short decades elevated living standards beyond what was thought possible. Young people in Malaysia and Thailand felt the lure of "Western" brands. Gucci handbags (www.gucci.com), Harley-Davidson motorcycles (www.harley-davidson.com), and other global brands became common symbols of success. Many parents felt that brand-consciousness among their teenage children signaled familywide success.

Despite the growing consumer society, polls of young people show them holding steadfast to traditional values such as respect for family and group harmony. Youth in Hong Kong, for example, overwhelmingly believe that parents should have a say in how hard they study, in how they treat family members and elders, and in their choice of friends.

Now globalization is washing over India. An explosion in outsourcing jobs is causing a social revolution among India's graduates of technical colleges and universities. Unlike in India's traditional high-tech service jobs, young call-center staffers are in direct contact with Western consumers, answering inquiries on items such as tummy crunchers and diet pills. For these young, mostly female staffers, the work means money, independence, and freedom—sometimes far away from home in big cities such as Bangalore and Mumbai. But in addition to the training in American accents and geography, these workers are learning new ideas about family, materialism, and relationships.

Parents are suspicious of call-center work because it must typically be performed at night in India, when consumers are awake in Canada, Europe, or the United States. When her parents objected, Binitha Venugopal quit her call-center job in favor of a "regular" daytime job. Binitha says her former coworkers' values are changing and that dating and live-in relationships among them are common. Indian tradition dictates that young adults live with their parents at least until they get married (typically to someone their parents choose). Perhaps facilitating shifting values in India is an influx of Western professionals, such as lawyers, who accepted good-paying jobs there that could not be found back home during the global recession.

Roopa Murthy works for an Indian company that offers call-center and back-office services. Roopa moved to Bangalore from her native Mysore in 2002 armed with an accounting degree. She now earns $400 per month, which is several times what her father earned before he retired from his government job. Roopa cut her hair short and tossed aside her *salwar kameez,* the traditional loose-fitting clothing she wore back home, in favor of designer-labeled Western attire.

Although she once shunned drinking and her curfew at home was 9 p.m., Roopa now frequents a pub called Geoffrey's, where she enjoys dry martinis and rum, and The Club, a suburban disco. Roopa confesses that she is "seeing someone" but that her parents would disapprove, adding, "It is difficult to talk to Indian parents about things like boyfriends." She said she sometimes envies her callers' lives but that she hopes her job will help her succeed. "I may be a small-town girl, but there is no way I'm going back to Mysore after this," she said. Many observers wonder whether Asia can embrace modernization and yet retain traditional values.

Thinking Globally

1. If your international firm were doing business in Asia, is there anything that your company could do to ease the tensions these cultures are experiencing? Be specific.
2. In your opinion, is globalization among the causes of the increasing incidence of divorce, crime, and drug abuse in Asia? Why or why not?
3. Broadly defined, Asia comprises more than 60 percent of the world's population—a population that practices Buddhism, Confucianism, Hinduism, Islam, and numerous other religions. Thus, do you think it is possible to carry on a valid discussion of "Asian" values? Why or why not?
4. Consider the following statement: "Economic development and capitalism require a certain style of doing business in the twenty-first century. The sooner Asian cultures adapt the better." Do you agree or disagree? Explain.

Source: Heather Timmons, "Outsourcing to India Draws Western Lawyers," *New York Times* (www.nytimes.com), August 4, 2010; Lisa Tsering, "NBC Picks up Series 'Outsourced' for Fall 2010," *Indiawest.com* website (www.indiawest.com), May 27, 2010; Saritha Rai, "India Outsourcing Workers Stressed to The Limit," *Silicon.com* website (www.silicon.com; now www.techrepublic.com), August 26, 2009; Sol E. Solomon, "Vietnam's IT Way to Social Progress," *Bloomberg Businessweek* (www.businessweek.com), May 19, 2008.

Politics, Law, and Business Ethics

LEARNING OBJECTIVES

After studying this chapter, you should be able to

1. Describe each main type of political system.

2. Identify the origins of political risk and how managers can reduce its effects.

3. Describe each main type of legal system and some important global legal issues.

4. Explain ethics and social responsibility and key issues facing international companies.

5. Explain how international relations affect international business activities.

A Look Back

Chapter 2 explored the main elements of culture and showed how they affect business practices. We learned about different methods used to classify cultures and how these methods can be applied to business.

A Look at This Chapter

This chapter explores the roles of politics and law in international business. We begin by explaining different types of political systems and how managers cope with political risk. We then examine several kinds of legal systems, ethics, social responsibility, and how international relations affect business.

A Look Ahead

Chapter 4 discusses the world's different economic systems. We learn about emerging markets and development and explore challenges facing countries that are transforming their economies into free markets.

PEPSICO'S GLOBAL CHALLENGE

PURCHASE, New York—Entrepreneurial despite its enormity, PepsiCo's (www.pepsico.com) sales have grown an amazing 13 percent annually for nearly half a century. To keep sales bubbling, PepsiCo is targeting international sales, which comprise 40 percent of total revenue, and is investing aggressively in India, which ranks among PepsiCo's top 10 markets and its three fastest-growing countries. PepsiCo needed the approval of India's government in order to increase its investment there by nearly a third in an effort to triple its revenue in the country by 2015.

Like all companies operating internationally, PepsiCo must carefully navigate unfamiliar political and legal systems. If PepsiCo's bottling operations in India were to drain the water table to unacceptable levels, it would face the wrath of India's regulators and its people. And British regulators, for example, would pull PepsiCo's Baked Lays brand of chips off store shelves if it fails to live up to its health claims. PepsiCo knows that today companies are expected to be model citizens wherever they operate.

PepsiCo's CEO, Indra Nooyi, is moving the company's product line in healthier directions. She introduced the motto "Performance with Purpose" to reflect how the company is transforming its global businesses. She wants the company to balance its drive for profits with making healthier snacks, decreasing its impact on the environment, and taking care of its workforce. Born and raised in India, Nooyi believes it is essential that "we use corporations as a productive player in addressing some of the big issues facing the world."

Source: TPG Top Photo Group/Newscom

Nooyi also helped spark "green" initiatives at PepsiCo. She has proved that investments in water- and heat-related conservation projects can be worthy endeavors. In addition to their environmental benefits, those projects now save the company $55 million annually. Nooyi says, "Companies today are bigger than many economies. We are little republics. We are engines of efficiency. If companies don't do [responsible] things, who is going to?" As you read this chapter, consider how companies adapt to political and legal systems worldwide while fulfilling their ethical and social responsibilities.[1]

hapter 2 explained that an understanding of culture contributes to success in the international marketplace. Another crucial element of success is political and legal savvy. Businesses involved internationally need to overcome some tricky political and legal situations in other countries. This is true for both brick-and-mortar and online companies. Although the web shrinks the distance between two points, it still matters where those two points are located. The Internet community consists of about 250 country domains and dozens of political and legal environments.

Just as brick-and-mortar companies have always adapted to local politics and laws in the global marketplace, so too do Internet companies. Yahoo! (www.yahoo.com) held back certain news stories from its website in China, though the stories appeared on the company's U.S. site. Rupert Murdoch's News Corp. (www.newscorp.com) removed BBC news (www.bbc.co.uk) from its Asian television broadcasts because it occasionally criticized China. Barnes & Noble (www.barnesandnoble.com) and Amazon (www.amazon.com) stopped selling the English-language version of *Mein Kampf* to Germans when the German government complained—although it's illegal only to sell the German-language version. A statement by Barnes & Noble read, "Our policy with regard to censorship remains unchanged. But as responsible corporate citizens, we respect the laws of the countries where we do business." And a broad spectrum of German politicians and citizens decried Google's (www.google.com) plan to introduce its mapping service called Street View there. Memories of secret police prying into personal lives under past dictatorial and fascist regimes make Germans fearful of allowing the entire world to see photos of their homes and gardens on the Internet.[2]

Understanding the nature of politics and laws in other countries lessens the risks of conducting international business. In this chapter, we present the basic differences between political and legal systems around the world. We explain how disputes arising from political and legal matters affect business activities and how companies can manage the associated risks. We also discuss key ethical issues for international managers and how companies fulfill their social responsibilities. We close this chapter by briefly discussing the interaction between business and international relations.

Political Systems

political system
Structures, processes, and activities by which a nation governs itself.

A **political system** includes the structures, processes, and activities by which a nation governs itself. Japan's political system, for instance, features a *Diet* (Parliament) that chooses a prime minister who will carry out the operations of government with the help of Cabinet ministers. The *Diet* consists of two houses of elected representatives who enact the nation's laws. These laws affect the personal lives of people living in and visiting Japan, as well as the activities of companies doing business there.

Politics and Culture

Politics and *culture* are closely related. A country's political system is rooted in the history and culture of its people. Factors such as population, age and race composition, and per capita income influence a country's political system.

Consider the case of Switzerland, where the political system actively encourages all eligible members of society to vote. By means of *public referendums,* Swiss citizens vote directly on many national issues. The Swiss system works because Switzerland consists of a relatively small population living in a small geographic area. Contrast this practice with that of most other democracies, in which representatives of the people, not the people themselves, vote on specific issues.

Political Participation

We can characterize political systems by *who* participates in them and *to what extent* they participate. *Participation* occurs when people voice their opinions, vote, and show general approval or disapproval of the system.

Participation can be wide or narrow. Wide participation occurs when people who are capable of influencing the political system make an effort to do so. For example, most adults living in the United States have the right to participate in the political process by voting in elections.

Election Commission workers in Libya collect ballot boxes from various polling stations for final counting. Voters went to the polls in July 2012, nine months after the removal of a dictatorship that ruled Libya for more than 40 years. Around 2.8 million Libyans were eligible to vote in this first step toward creating a new constitution and system of government in Libya. The election followed a nasty civil war that exposed Libya's deep regional, tribal, and ethnic differences. How do you think wide political participation can benefit a country and its people?

Source: SABRI ELMHEDWI/EPA/ Newscom

Narrow participation occurs when few people participate. In Kuwait, for example, only citizens who can prove Kuwaiti ancestry can participate in the political process.

Political Ideologies

We can arrange the world's three political ideologies on a horizontal scale, with one on either end and one in the middle:

- At one extreme lies *totalitarianism*—the belief that every aspect of people's lives must be controlled for a nation's political system to be effective. Totalitarianism disregards individual liberties and treats people as slaves of the political system. The state reigns supreme over institutions such as family, religion, business, and labor. Totalitarian political systems include authoritarian regimes such as communism and fascism.
- At the other extreme lies *anarchism*—the belief that only individuals and private groups should control a nation's political activities. An anarchist views public government as unnecessary and unwanted because it tramples personal liberties.
- Between totalitarianism and anarchism lies *pluralism*—the belief that both private and public groups play important roles in a nation's political activities. Each group (consisting of people with different ethnic, racial, class, and lifestyle backgrounds) serves to balance the power that can be gained by the others. Pluralistic political systems include democracies, constitutional monarchies, and some aristocracies.

To better understand how elements of politics influence national business practices, let's examine two prevalent political systems—*totalitarianism* and *democracy*.

TOTALITARIANISM In a **totalitarian system**, individuals govern without the support of the people, tightly control people's lives, and do not tolerate opposing viewpoints. Nazi Germany under Adolf Hitler and the former Soviet Union under Joseph Stalin are historical examples of totalitarian governments. Today, North Korea is the most prominent example of a totalitarian government. Totalitarian leaders attempt to silence those with opposing political views and, therefore, require the near-total centralization of political power. But a "pure" form of totalitarianism is not possible because no totalitarian government is capable of entirely silencing all its critics.

Totalitarian governments tend to share three features:

- **Imposed Authority.** An individual or group forms the political system without the explicit or implicit approval of the people. Leaders often acquire and retain power through

totalitarian system
Political system in which individuals govern without the support of the people, tightly control people's lives, and do not tolerate opposing viewpoints.

military force or fraudulent elections. In some cases, they come to power through legitimate means but then remain in office after their terms expire.

- **Lack of Constitutional Guarantees.**   Totalitarian systems deny citizens the constitutional guarantees woven into the fabric of democratic practice. They limit, abuse, or reject concepts such as freedom of expression, periodically held elections, guaranteed civil and property rights, and minority rights.
- **Restricted Participation.**   Political representation is limited to parties sympathetic to the government or to those who pose no credible threat. In most cases, political opposition is completely banned, and political dissidents are severely punished.

Let's now take a detailed look at the two most common types of totalitarian political systems: *theocratic* and *secular*.

Theocratic Totalitarianism A political system in which a country's religious leaders are also its political leaders is called a **theocracy**. The religious leaders enforce a set of laws and regulations based on religious beliefs. A political system under the control of totalitarian religious leaders is called **theocratic totalitarianism**.

Iran is a prominent example of a theocratic totalitarian state. Iran has been an Islamic state since the 1979 revolution in which the reigning monarch was overthrown. Today, many young Iranians appear disenchanted with the strict code imposed on many aspects of their public and private lives, including stringent laws against products and ideas deemed too "Western." They may not question their religious beliefs but yearn for a more open society.

Secular Totalitarianism A political system in which political leaders rely on military and bureaucratic power is called **secular totalitarianism**. It takes three forms: *communist, tribal,* and *right-wing*.

Under *communist totalitarianism* (referred to here simply as *communism*), the government maintains sweeping political and economic powers. The Communist Party controls all aspects of the political system, and opposition parties are given little or no voice. In general, each party member holding office is required to support all government policies, and dissension is rarely permitted. **Communism** is the belief that social and economic equality can be obtained only by establishing an all-powerful Communist Party and by instituting **socialism**—an economic system in which the government owns and controls all types of economic activity. This includes granting the government ownership of the means of production (such as capital, land, and factories) and the power to decide what the economy produces and the prices at which goods are sold.

However, important distinctions separate communism from socialism. Communists follow the teachings of Marx and Lenin, believe that a violent revolution is needed to seize control over resources, and wish to eliminate political opposition. Socialists believe in none of these. Thus, communists are socialists, but socialists are not necessarily communist.

Under *tribal totalitarianism,* one tribe (or ethnic group) imposes its will on others with whom it shares a national identity. Tribal totalitarianism characterizes the governments of several African nations, including Burundi and Rwanda. When the European colonial powers departed Africa, many national boundaries were created with little regard to ethnic differences among the people. People of different ethnicities found themselves living in the same nation, whereas members of the same ethnicity found themselves living in different nations. In time, certain ethnic groups gained political and military power over other groups. Animosity among them often erupted in bloody conflict.

Nations mired in military conflict pay a hefty price in terms of sustainability. Over the decades, civil war has inflicted enormous human, social, and environmental costs on many African nations, for example. To explore the costs of civil wars (particularly in Africa) and how developed nations can help put an end to them, see the Global Sustainability feature, titled "From Civil War to Civil Society."

Under *right-wing totalitarianism,* the government endorses private ownership of property and a market-based economy but grants few (if any) political freedoms. Leaders generally strive for economic growth while opposing *left-wing totalitarianism* (communism). Argentina, Brazil, Chile, and Paraguay all had right-wing totalitarian governments in the 1980s.

Despite the inherent contradictions between communism and right-wing totalitarianism, China's political system is currently a mix of the two ideologies. China's leaders are engineering high economic growth by implementing certain characteristics of a capitalist economy while

theocracy
Political system in which a country's religious leaders are also its political leaders.

theocratic totalitarianism
Political system under the control of totalitarian religious leaders.

secular totalitarianism
Political system in which leaders rely on military and bureaucratic power.

communism
Belief that social and economic equality can be obtained only by establishing an all-powerful Communist Party and by granting the government ownership and control over all types of economic activity.

socialism
Belief that social and economic equality is obtained through government ownership and regulation of the means of production.

GLOBAL SUSTAINABILITY   From Civil War to Civil Society

Today, most wars occur *within* nations that were once controlled and stabilized by colonial powers. If these nations are to prosper from globalization, they must break the vicious cycle whereby conflict causes poverty and poverty causes conflict.

- ***War's Root Causes.*** Although tribal or ethnic rivalry is typically blamed for starting civil wars, the most common causes are poverty, low economic growth, and dependency on natural resource exports. In fact, the poorest one-sixth of humanity endures four-fifths of the world's civil wars. Still, religious differences increasingly underlie civil conflicts.
- ***What's at Stake.*** It appears that the pitched battles in Bunia, in the eastern part of Democratic Republic of the Congo, are rooted in ethnic conflict. Yet the Hema and the Lendu tribes only began fighting each other when neighboring Uganda (so that it could control mineral-rich Bunia) started arming rival militias in 1999. In the Darfur region of Sudan, Arab Muslims battle black non-Muslims. Depending on whom you ask, the conflict began as a fight over pastures and livestock or over the oil beneath them. Meanwhile, foreign investors remain wary.
- ***What Is Lost.*** On average, a civil conflict lasts eight years. And apart from the terrible human cost in lives and health, there is also a financial cost. Health costs are $5 billion per conflict

because of collapsed health systems and forced migrations (which worsen and spread disease). Gross domestic product (GDP) falls by 2.2 percent, and another 18 percent of income is spent on arms and militias. Full economic recovery takes a decade, which reduces output by about 105 percent of the nation's prewar GDP.

- ***What To Do.*** Because the risk of civil war is cut in half when income per person doubles, conflicts may be *prevented* by funneling more aid to poor nations. Also, war might be *limited* by restricting a nation in conflict from spending the proceeds from its exports on munitions or by lowering the world market price of those exports. Finally, to *halt* nations from slipping back into civil war, health and education aid could be increased after war ends, or a foreign power could intervene to keep the peace.
- ***Want to Know More?*** Visit the Centre for the Study of African Economies (www.csae.ox.ac.uk), Copenhagen Consensus Center (www.copenhagenconsensus.com), and World Bank Conflict Prevention and Reconstruction unit (www.worldbank.org).

Source: "Unloved for Trying to Keep the Peace," *The Economist*, April 17, 2010, pp. 51–52; "Correspondent's Diary: More than Sectarian Strife," *The Economist* (www. economist.com), April 13, 2010; Paul Collier and Anke Hoeffler, *The Challenge of Reducing the Global Incidence of Civil War* (Oxford: Copenhagen Consensus, March 2004); Copenhagen Consensus Center website (www.copenhagenconsensus.com).

retaining a hard line in the political sphere. The Chinese government is selling off money-losing, state-run companies and encouraging the investment needed to modernize its factories. But China's government still has little patience for dissidents who demand greater political freedom, and it does not allow a completely free press.

Doing Business in Totalitarian Countries   What are the costs and benefits of doing business in a totalitarian nation? On the plus side, international companies can be relatively less concerned with local political opposition to their activities. On the negative side, they might need to pay bribes and kickbacks to government officials. Refusal to pay could result in loss of market access or even forfeiture of investments in the country.

In any case, doing business in a totalitarian country can be a risky proposition. In a country such as the United States, laws regarding the resolution of contractual disputes are quite specific. In totalitarian nations, the law can be either vague or nonexistent, and people in powerful government positions can interpret laws largely as they please. In China, for instance, it may not matter so much what the law states but rather how individual bureaucrats interpret the law. The arbitrary nature of totalitarian governments makes it hard for companies to know how laws will be interpreted and applied to their particular business dealings.

Companies that operate in totalitarian nations are sometimes criticized for lacking compassion for people hurt by the oppressive policies of their hosts. Executives must decide whether to refrain from investing in totalitarian countries—and miss potentially profitable opportunities—or invest and bear the brunt of potentially damaging publicity. There are no simple answers to this controversial issue, which amounts to an ethical dilemma.

QUICK STUDY 1

1. What is a *political system*? Explain the relationship between political systems and culture.
2. Identify the three main features of *totalitarianism*.
3. Briefly explain each form of totalitarianism.
4. How might a totalitarian government affect business activities?

democracy
Political system in which government leaders are elected directly by the wide participation of the people or by their representatives.

DEMOCRACY A **democracy** is a political system in which government leaders are elected directly by the wide participation of the people or by their representatives. Democracy differs from totalitarianism in nearly every respect. The foundations of modern democracy go back at least as far as the ancient Greeks.

The Greeks tried to practice a *pure* democracy, one in which all citizens participate freely and actively in the political process. But a pure democracy is more an ideal than a workable system for several reasons. Some people have neither the time nor the desire to get involved in the political process. Also, citizens are less able to participate completely and actively as a population grows and as the barriers of distance and time increase. Finally, leaders in a pure democracy may find it difficult or impossible to form cohesive policies because direct voting can lead to conflicting popular opinion.

representative democracy
Democracy in which citizens elect individuals from their groups to represent their political views.

Representative Democracy For practical reasons, most nations resort to a **representative democracy**, in which citizens elect individuals from their groups to represent their political views. These representatives then help govern the people and pass laws. The people reelect representatives they approve of and replace those they no longer want representing them.

Representative democracies strive to provide some or all of the following:

- **Freedom of Expression.** A constitutional right in most democracies, freedom of expression ideally grants the right to voice opinions freely and without fear of punishment.
- **Periodic Elections.** Each elected representative serves for a period of time, after which the people (or electorate) decide whether to retain that representative. Two examples of periodic elections include the U.S. presidential elections (held every four years) and the French presidential elections (held every five years).
- **Full Civil and Property Rights.** Civil rights include freedom of speech, freedom to organize political parties, and the right to a fair trial. Property rights are the privileges and responsibilities of owners of property (homes, cars, businesses, and so forth).
- **Minority Rights.** In theory, democracies try to preserve peaceful coexistence among groups of people with diverse cultural, ethnic, and racial backgrounds. Ideally, the same rights and privileges extend legally to each group, no matter how few its members.
- **Nonpolitical Bureaucracies.** The bureaucracy is the part of government that implements the rules and laws passed by elected representatives. In *politicized bureaucracies,* bureaucrats tend to implement decisions according to their own political views rather than those of the people's representatives. This clearly contradicts the purpose of the democratic process.

Freedom of expression is a fundamental right that most democracies strive to uphold. On the International Day of Press Freedom, a woman in Tegucigalpa, Honduras, wears tape on her mouth to show support for the right of freedom of expression. To limit and tightly control the news that ordinary people receive, some countries block or scramble the reception of foreign media broadcasts. In what ways do you think freedom of expression can benefit a society?

Source: DANIEL MENDOZA/Newscom

Despite such shared principles, countries vary greatly in the practice of representative democracy. Britain, for example, practices *parliamentary democracy*. The nation divides itself into geographical districts, and people in each district vote for competing *parties* rather than individual candidates. But the party that wins the greatest number of legislative seats in an election does not automatically win the right to run the country. Rather, a party must gain an *absolute majority*—that is, the number of representatives that a party gets elected must exceed the number of representatives elected among all other parties.

If the party with the largest number of representatives lacks an absolute majority, it can join with one or more other parties to form a *coalition government*. In a coalition government, the strongest political parties share power by dividing government responsibilities among themselves. Coalition governments are often formed in Italy, Israel, and the Netherlands, where a large number of political parties make it difficult for any single party to gain an absolute majority.

Nations also differ in the relative power that each political party commands. In some democratic countries, a single political party has effectively controlled the system for decades. In Japan, for example, the Liberal Democratic Party (which is actually conservative) has enjoyed nearly uninterrupted control of the government since the 1950s. In Mexico, the Institutional Revolutionary Party (PRI) ran the country for 71 years until 2001 when Vicente Fox of the conservative National Action Party (PAN) won the presidency. But then in 2012, Enrique Peña Nieto won the presidential election and led the PRI back into power.[3]

Doing Business in Democracies Democracies maintain stable business environments primarily through laws that protect individual property rights. In theory, commerce prospers when the **private sector** includes independently owned firms that seek to earn profits. **Capitalism** is the belief that ownership of the means of production belongs in the hands of individuals and private businesses. Capitalism is also frequently referred to as the *free market*. (We cover the economics of communism and capitalism in Chapter 4.)

Bear in mind that, although participative democracy, property rights, and free markets tend to encourage economic growth, they do not always do so. For instance, although India is the world's largest democracy, it experienced slow economic growth for decades until recently. Meanwhile, some countries achieved rapid economic growth under political systems that were not truly democratic. The four tigers of Asia—Hong Kong, Singapore, South Korea, and Taiwan—built strong market economies in the absence of truly democratic practices.

private sector
Segment of the economic environment comprising independently owned firms that seek to earn profits.

capitalism
Belief that ownership of the means of production belongs in the hands of individuals and private businesses.

Political Systems in Times of Change

People around the world are demanding wider participation in the political process and are forcing a move toward more democratic systems. Capitalism also seems to have won the battle over communist totalitarianism and economic socialism. Shortly after the former Soviet Union implemented its twin policies of *glasnost* (political openness) and *perestroika* (economic reform), its totalitarian government crumbled. Communist governments in Central and Eastern Europe fell soon after, and today countries such as the Czech Republic, Hungary, Poland, Romania, and Ukraine have republican governments. There are far fewer communist nations than there were two decades ago, although Cuba and North Korea remain hard-line communist nations.

One of the most closely watched nations in terms of its political change is China. After 1949, when the communists defeated the nationalists in China's civil war, China imprisoned or exiled most of its capitalists. But private businesspeople are now allowed to join China's Communist Party, and workers can now elect local representatives to the official trade union. These moves represent the leadership's struggle to maintain order in the face of increasingly rapid economic and social change. Part of the reason for this move was explained in a government report that spoke of problems facing the nation. Difficulties reported included the collapse of state-owned industry, a social safety net unable to cope with millions of unemployed, poor relations with the nation's ethnic minorities, an unjust legal system, and an increasingly restless rural population.

QUICK STUDY 2

1. What is *democracy*? Explain the differences between *democracy* and *totalitarianism*.
2. What five freedoms does a representative democracy strive to provide its people?
3. How might a democratic government affect business activities in a nation?

Political Risk

political risk
Likelihood that a society will
undergo political changes that
negatively affect local business
activity.

All companies doing business domestically or internationally confront **political risk**—the likelihood that a society will undergo political changes that negatively affect local business activity. Political risk abroad affects different types of companies in different ways. It can threaten the market of an exporter, the production facilities of a manufacturer, or the ability of a company to extract profits from a country in which they were earned. A solid grasp of local values, customs, and traditions can help reduce a company's exposure to political risk.

Map 3.1 on pages 82–83 shows that political risk levels vary from nation to nation. Some of the factors included in this assessment of political risk levels include government stability, internal and external conflict, military and religion involvement in politics, corruption, law and order, and bureaucracy quality.

Types of Political Risk

The broadest categories of political risk reflect the range of companies affected. *Macro risk* threatens the activities of all domestic and international companies in every industry. Examples include an ongoing threat of violence against corporate assets in a nation and a rising level of government corruption. *Micro risk* threatens companies only within a particular industry (or more narrowly defined group). For example, an international trade war in steel affects the operations of steel producers and companies that require steel as an input to their business activities.

In addition to these two broad categories, we can classify political risk according to the actions or events that cause it to arise, including:

- Conflict and violence
- Terrorism and kidnapping
- Property seizure
- Policy changes
- Local content requirements

CONFLICT AND VIOLENCE Local conflict can discourage international companies from investing in a nation. Violent disturbances impair a company's ability to manufacture and distribute products, obtain materials and equipment, and recruit talented personnel. Open conflict also threatens a company's physical assets (such as offices and factories) and the lives of its employees.

Conflict arises from several sources. First, it may arise from people's resentment toward their own government. When peaceful resolution of disputes between people (or factions) and the government fails, violent attempts to change political leadership can ensue. ExxonMobil (www.exxonmobil.com) suspended production of liquid natural gas at its facility in Indonesia's Aceh province when separatist rebels targeted the complex with violence.

Second, conflict can arise over territorial disputes between countries. For example, a dispute over the Kashmir territory between India and Pakistan resulted in major armed conflict between their two peoples several times. And a border dispute between Ecuador and Peru caused these South American nations to go to war three times.

Third, disputes among ethnic, racial, and religious groups may erupt in violent conflict. Indonesia comprises 13,000 islands, more than 300 ethnic groups, and some 450 languages. Years ago, Indonesia's government relocated people from crowded, central islands to less populated, remote ones without regard to ethnicity and religion. Violence among them later displaced more than one million people.

TERRORISM AND KIDNAPPING Terrorist activities are a means of making political statements. Groups dissatisfied with the current political or social situation sometimes resort to terrorist tactics in order to force change through fear and destruction. On September 11, 2001, the world witnessed terrorism on a scale like never before. Two passenger planes were flown into the twin towers of the World Trade Center in New York City, one plane was crashed into the Pentagon in Washington, DC, and one plane crashed in a Pennsylvania field. The terrorist group Al-Qaida claimed responsibility for those U.S. attacks and for more recent attacks around the world. The terror organization's stated goals are to drive Western influence out of Muslim nations and to implement Islamic law.

Kidnapping and the taking of hostages for ransom may be used to fund a terrorist group's activities. Executives of large international companies are often prime targets for kidnappers because their employers have "deep pockets" to pay large ransoms. Latin American countries have some of the world's highest kidnapping rates, and Mexico City is at or near the top of the list of cities with the highest kidnapping rates. Annual security costs for a company with a sales office in Bogotá, Colombia, can be $125,000 and up to $1 million for a company with operations in rebel-controlled areas. Top executives are forced to spend about a third of their time coordinating their company's security in Colombia. A medium-sized firm that has 5 to 10 employees traveling to Latin America for a week at a time could carry $10 million in kidnap and ransom insurance at a cost of around $5,000 a year.[4]

When high-ranking executives are required to enter countries with high kidnapping rates, they should enter unannounced, meet with only a few key people in secure locations, and leave just as quickly and quietly. Some companies purchase kidnap, ransom, and extortion insurance, but security experts say that training people to avoid trouble in the first place is a far better investment. For additional ways managers can stay safe during overseas assignments, see the Manager's Briefcase, titled "Your Global Security Checklist."

PROPERTY SEIZURE Governments sometimes seize the assets of companies doing business within their borders. Asset seizures fall into one of three categories: *confiscation*, *expropriation*, or *nationalization*.

The forced transfer of assets from a company to the government *without compensation* is called **confiscation**. Usually the former owners have no legal basis for requesting compensation or the return of assets. The 1996 Helms–Burton Law allows U.S. businesses to sue companies from other nations that use their property confiscated by Cuba in its 1959 communist revolution. For example, the Cuban government faces nearly 6,000 company claims valued at $20 billion. But U.S. presidents repeatedly waive the law so as not to harm its relations with other countries.[5]

The forced transfer of assets from a company to the government *with compensation* is called **expropriation**. The expropriating government normally determines the amount of compensation. There is no framework for legal appeal, and compensation is typically far below market value. Today, governments rarely resort to confiscation or expropriation because these acts can jeopardize investment in the country. Still, it does happen. Argentina expropriated 51 percent of that country's largest energy firm, named Yacimientos Petroliferos Fiscales (YPF). The move isolated Argentina internationally and caused even greater uncertainty for international investors. Buenos Aires Waterworks and Aerolineas Argentinas are two other entities in Argentina that saw increasing losses after they were nationalized a second time.[6]

Whereas expropriation involves one or several companies in an industry, **nationalization** means government takeover of an *entire* industry. Nationalization is more common than

confiscation
Forced transfer of assets from a company to the government without compensation.

expropriation
Forced transfer of assets from a company to the government with compensation.

nationalization
Government takeover of an entire industry.

MANAGER'S BRIEFCASE   Your Global Security Checklist

- *Getting There.* Take nonstop flights when possible, as accidents are more likely during takeoffs and landings. Move quickly from an airport's public and check-in areas to more secure areas beyond passport control. Report abandoned packages to airport security.
- *Getting Around.* Kidnappers watch for daily routines. Vary the exits you use to leave your house, office, and hotel, and vary the time that you depart and arrive. Drive with your windows up and doors locked. Swap cars with others occasionally, or take a cab one day and ride the tram/subway the next. Be discreet regarding your itinerary.
- *Keep a Low Profile.* Don't draw attention by pulling out a large wad of currency or paying with large denominations. Avoid public demonstrations. Dress like the locals when possible and leave expensive jewelry at home. Avoid loud conversation and being overheard. If you rent an automobile, avoid the flashy car and choose a local, common model.

- *Guard Personal Data.* Be friendly but cautious when answering questions about you, your family, and your employment. Keep answers short and vague when possible. Give out your work number only—all family members should do the same. Do not list your home or mobile phone numbers in directories. Do not carry items in your purse or wallet that contain your home address.
- *Use Caution.* Be cautious if a local asks directions or the time—it could be a mugging ploy. When possible, travel with others and avoid walking alone after dark. Avoid narrow, dimly lit streets. If you get lost, act as if you know where you are, and ask directions from a place of business, not passersby. Beware of offers by drivers of unmarked or poorly marked cabs.
- *Know Emergency Procedures.* Be familiar with the local emergency procedures before trouble strikes. Keep the phone numbers of police, fire, your hotel, your nation's embassy, and a reputable taxi service in your home and with you at all times.

MAP 3.1
Political Risk around the World

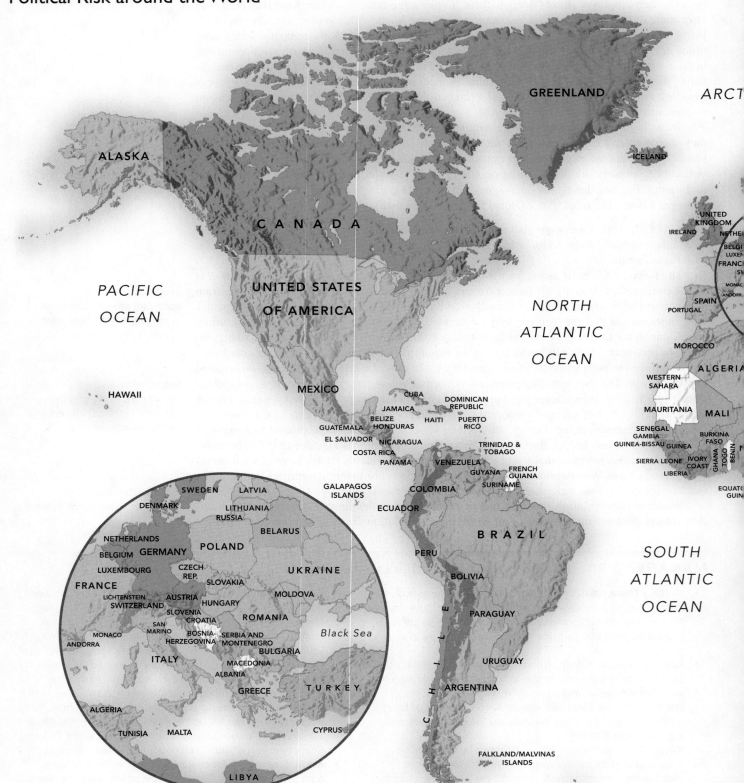

Level of risk

- very high
- high
- moderate
- low
- very low
- no data available

confiscation and expropriation. Likely candidates for nationalization include industries important to a nation's security and those that generate large revenues. In recent years, Venezuela's President Hugo Chavez nationalized that country's telephone, electricity, and oil industries and threatened to nationalize many more. Businesses from other countries reacted to these moves by not investing in Venezuela. In general, a government may nationalize an industry to:

- Use subsidies to protect an industry for ideological reasons.
- Save local jobs in an ailing industry to gain political clout.
- Control industry profits so they cannot be transferred to low tax-rate countries.
- Invest in sectors, such as public utilities, that private companies cannot afford.

The extent of nationalization varies widely from country to country. Whereas the governments of Cuba and North Korea control practically every industry, those of the United States and Canada own very few. Many countries, including France, Mexico, Poland, and India, try to strike a balance between government and private ownership.

POLICY CHANGES Government policy changes are the result of a variety of influences, including the ideals of newly empowered political parties, political pressure from special interests, and civil or social unrest. One common policy tool restricts ownership to domestic companies or limits ownership by nondomestic firms to a minority stake. This type of policy restricted PepsiCo's (www.pepsico.com) ownership of local companies to 49 percent when it first entered India.

Other policies relate to cross-border investments. Facing a slowdown in the technology sector, Taiwan's businesses and politicians called for a scrapping of the nation's "go slow, be patient" policy with China. That policy capped investments in mainland China at $50 million and banned investments in infrastructure and industries sensitive for national security reasons. Taiwan's government created a new policy called "active opening, effective management," which reduced restrictions on cross-border investment.

LOCAL CONTENT REQUIREMENTS Laws stipulating that a specified amount of a good or service be supplied by producers in the domestic market are called **local content requirements**. These requirements can force companies to use locally available raw materials, procure parts from local suppliers, or employ a minimum number of local workers. They ensure that international companies foster local business activity and help ease regional or national unemployment. They also help governments maintain some degree of control over international companies without resorting to extreme measures such as confiscation and expropriation.

But local content requirements can jeopardize an international firm's long-term survival. First, a company required to hire local personnel might be forced to take on an inadequately trained workforce or take on excess workers. Second, a company made to obtain raw materials or parts locally can find its production costs rise or its product quality decline.

local content requirements
Laws stipulating that a specified amount of a good or service be supplied by producers in the domestic market.

Managing Political Risk

International companies benefit from monitoring and attempting to predict political changes that can negatively affect their activities. When an international business opportunity arises in an environment plagued by extremely high risk, simply not investing in the location may be the wisest course of action. Yet when risk levels are moderate and the local market is attractive, international companies find other ways to manage political risks. Let's now examine the three main methods of managing political risk: *adaptation, information gathering,* and *political influence.*

ADAPTATION Adaptation means incorporating risk into business strategies, often with the help of local officials. Companies can incorporate risk by means of four strategies:

- *Partnerships* help companies leverage expansion plans. They can be informal arrangements or include joint ventures, strategic alliances, and cross-holdings of company stock. Partnering helps a company to share the risk of loss, which is especially important in emerging markets. If partners own shares (*equity*) in local operations, they get cuts of the profits; if they loan cash (*debt*), they receive interest. Local partners who can help keep political forces from interrupting operations include firms, trade unions, financial institutions, and government agencies.

- *Localization* entails modifying operations, the product mix, or some other business element—even the company name—to suit local tastes and culture. Consider how MTV (www.mtv.com) demonstrates its sensitivity to local cultural and political issues by localizing its programming to suit regional and national tastes.
- *Development assistance* lets an international business assist the host country or region in improving the quality of life for locals. For example, by developing distribution and communications networks, both a company and a nation benefit. Royal Dutch/Shell (www.shell.com), the oil company, is working in Kenya to increase the incomes of poor villagers and to triple the average period of food security.[7] Canon (www.canon.com), the Japanese copier and printer maker, practices *kyosei* ("spirit of cooperation") to press local governments into making social and political reforms.
- *Insurance* against political risk can be essential to companies entering risky business environments. The *Overseas Private Investment Corporation* (www.opic.gov) insures U.S. companies that invest abroad against loss and can provide project financing. Some policies protect companies when local governments restrict the convertibility of local money into home-country currency, whereas others insure against losses created by violent events, including war and terrorism. The *Foreign Credit Insurance Association* (www.fcia.com) also insures U.S. exporters against loss due to a variety of causes.

INFORMATION GATHERING International firms attempt to gather information that will help them predict and manage political risk. Two sources that companies use to conduct accurate political risk forecasting are:

- **Current Employees with Relevant Information.** Employees who have worked in a country long enough to gain insight into local culture and politics are often good sources of information. Individuals who formerly had decision-making authority while on international assignment probably had contact with local politicians and other officials. Yet it is important that an employee's international experience be recent because political power in a nation can shift rapidly and dramatically.
- **Agencies Specializing in Political-Risk Services.** These include banks, political consultants, news publications, and risk-assessment services. Many of these agencies publish

One way to lessen political risk is to offer development assistance to poor communities. Shown here is Richard Branson, founder of the Virgin Group (www.virgin.com), in Johannesburg, South Africa. Branson is visiting the School of Entrepreneurship his foundation started. The school offers virtually free higher education to students from a financially disadvantaged background. Branson's not-for-profit foundation, Virgin Unite, strives to educate and inspire young leaders in order to unlock the potential of South Africa's youth.

Source: JON HRUSA/EPA/Newscom

reports detailing national levels and sources of political risk. Small companies that cannot afford to pay for these services can consider the many free sources of information available, notably from their federal governments. Government intelligence agencies are excellent and inexpensive sources to consult.

lobbying
Policy of hiring people to represent a company's views on political matters.

POLITICAL INFLUENCE   Managers must work within the established rules and regulations of each national business environment. Business law in most nations undergoes frequent change, with new laws being enacted and existing ones modified. Influencing local politics means dealing with local lawmakers and politicians directly or through lobbyists. **Lobbying** is the policy of hiring people to represent a company's views on political matters. Lobbyists meet with a local public official to influence his or her position on issues relevant to the company. The ultimate goal of the lobbyists is to get favorable legislation enacted and unfavorable legislation rejected. Lobbyists also work to convince local officials that a company benefits the local economy, environment, workforce, and so on.

Foreign Corrupt Practices Act
A 1977 statute that forbids U.S. companies from bribing government officials or political candidates in other nations.

Bribes often represent attempts to gain political influence. Years ago, the president of U.S.-based Lockheed Corp., now Lockheed Martin (www.lockheedmartin.com), bribed Japanese officials in order to obtain large sales contracts. Public disclosure of the incident resulted in passage of the 1977 **Foreign Corrupt Practices Act**, which forbids U.S. companies from bribing government officials or political candidates in other nations (except when a person's life is in danger). A bribe constitutes "anything of value"—money, gifts, and so forth—and cannot be given to any "foreign government official" empowered to make a "discretionary decision" that may be to the payer's benefit. The law also requires firms to keep accounting records that reflect their international activities and assets. (We discuss corruption further in the later section on ethics.)

In our discussion of political systems and how companies deal with political uncertainty, we touched on several important legal issues. Although there is a good deal of overlap between a nation's political and legal systems, they are distinct. Let's now examine several types of legal systems and how they influence the activities of international companies.

QUICK STUDY 3

1. What are the five main types of *political risk*? How might each affect international business activities?
2. Distinguish between *confiscation, expropriation,* and *nationalization.*
3. What three methods can businesses use to manage political risk?

Legal Systems

legal system
Set of laws and regulations, including the processes by which a country's laws are enacted and enforced and the ways in which its courts hold parties accountable for their actions.

A country's **legal system** is its set of laws and regulations, including the processes by which its laws are enacted and enforced and the ways in which its courts hold parties accountable for their actions. Many cultural factors—including ideas on social mobility, religion, and individualism—influence a nation's legal system. Likewise, many laws and regulations are enacted to safeguard cultural values and beliefs. For several examples of how legal systems differ from nation to nation, see this chapter's Culture Matters feature, titled "Playing by the Rules."

A country's political system also influences its legal system. Totalitarian governments tend to favor public ownership of economic resources and enact laws limiting entrepreneurial behavior. By contrast, democracies tend to encourage entrepreneurial activity and protect business with strong property-rights laws. The rights and responsibilities of parties to business transactions also differ from nation to nation. Political systems and legal systems, therefore, are naturally interlocked. A country's political system inspires and endorses its legal system, and its legal system legitimizes and supports its political system.

nationalism
Devotion of a people to their nation's interests and advancement.

Legal systems are frequently influenced by political moods and upsurges of **nationalism**—the devotion of a people to their nation's interests and advancement. Nationalism typically involves intense national loyalty and cultural pride and is often associated with drives toward national independence. In India, for example, most business laws originated when the country was struggling for "self-sufficiency." As a result, the legal system tended to protect local

CULTURE MATTERS Playing by the Rules

Understanding legal systems in other countries begins with an awareness of cultural differences. Here are snapshots of several nations' legal environments:

- **Japan.** Japan's harmony-based, consensus-driven culture considers court battles to be a last resort. But with growing patent disputes and a rise in cross-border mergers, Japan is discovering the value of lawyers. Japan has just 22,000 licensed attorneys compared with more than one million in the United States. So Japan is now minting thousands of new lawyers every year. Japanese businesses now litigate disputes that once might have been settled between parties.
- **Saudi Arabia.** Islam permeates every aspect of Saudi Arabia and affects its laws, politics, economics, and social development. Islamic law is grounded in religious teachings contained in the Koran and governs both criminal and civil cases. The Koran, in fact, is considered Saudi Arabia's constitution. The king and the council of ministers exercise all executive and legislative authority within the framework of Islamic law.
- **China.** Factory workers in China must sometimes endure military-style drills, verbal abuse, and mockery. But labor groups are winning higher wages, better working conditions, and better housing from a flock of lawyers and law students who hold free seminars and argue labor cases in China's courts. Inadequate protection of workers' rights is giving way to better conditions for China's 169 million factory workers.
- **Want to Know More?** Visit the Law Library of Congress (www.loc.gov/law/help/guide/nations/japan.php), the Royal Embassy of Saudi Arabia (www.saudiembassy.net), and China Gate (en.chinagate.cn).

Source: David Barboza, "After Suicides, Scrutiny of China's Grim Factories," *New York Times* (www.nytimes.com), June 6, 2010; "Suicides at Foxconn: Light and Death," *The Economist* (www.economist.com), May 27, 2010; "Saudi Arabia: Our Women Must Be Protected," *The Economist*, April 24, 2008, pp. 64–65; "Japan: Lawyers Wanted. No, Really," *Bloomberg Businessweek* (www.businessweek.com), April 2, 2006.

---

businesses from international competition. Although years ago India had nationalized many industries and closely scrutinized business applications, today its government is embracing globalization by enacting pro-business laws.

With that brief introduction, let's now examine the key characteristics of each type of legal system in use around the world (*common law, civil law,* and *theocratic law*) and discuss the key legal issues facing international companies.

Common Law

The practice of common law originated in eleventh-century England and was adopted in that nation's territories worldwide. The U.S. legal system, therefore, is based largely on the common law tradition (although it integrates some aspects of civil law). A **common law** legal system reflects three elements:

- **Tradition.** A country's legal history
- **Precedent.** Past cases that have come before the courts
- **Usage.** How laws are applied in specific situations

common law
Legal system based on a country's legal history (tradition), past cases that have come before its courts (precedent), and how laws are applied in specific situations (usage).

Under common law, the justice system decides cases by interpreting the law on the basis of tradition, precedent, and usage. Yet each law may be interpreted somewhat differently in each case to which it is applied. In turn, each new interpretation sets a precedent that may be followed in later cases. As new precedents arise, laws are altered to clarify vague wording or to accommodate situations not previously considered.

Business contracts tend to be lengthy in common-law nations (especially the United States) because they must consider many possible contingencies and many possible interpretations of the law in case of a dispute. Companies devote considerable time to devising clear contracts and spend large sums of money on legal advice. On the positive side, common-law systems are flexible. Instead of applying uniformly to all situations, laws take into account particular situations and circumstances. The common-law tradition prevails in Australia, Britain, Canada, Ireland, New Zealand, the United States, and some nations of Asia and Africa.

Civil Law

The origins of the civil law tradition can be traced to Rome in the fifth century B.C. It is the world's oldest and most common legal tradition. A **civil law** system is based on a detailed set of written rules and statutes that constitute a legal *code*. Civil law can be less adversarial than common law because there tends to be less need to interpret what a particular law states. Because

civil law
Legal system based on a detailed set of written rules and statutes that constitute a legal code.

all laws are codified and concise, parties to contracts tend to be more concerned only with the explicit wording of the code. All obligations, responsibilities, and privileges follow directly from the relevant code. Less time and money are typically spent, therefore, on legal matters. But civil law systems can ignore the unique circumstances of particular cases. Civil law is practiced in Cuba, Puerto Rico, Quebec, all of Central and South America, most of Western Europe, and many nations in Asia and Africa.

Theocratic Law

theocratic law
Legal system based on religious teachings.

A legal tradition based on religious teachings is called **theocratic law**. Three prominent theocratic legal systems are Islamic, Hindu, and Jewish law. Although Hindu law was restricted by India's 1950 constitution, in which the state appropriated most legal functions, it does persist as a cultural and spiritual force. Likewise, although Jewish law remains a strong religious force, it has served few legal functions since the eighteenth century, when most Jewish communities lost their judicial autonomy.

Islamic law is the most widely practiced theocratic legal system today. Islamic law was initially a code governing moral and ethical behavior and was later extended to commercial transactions. It restricts the types of investments companies can make and sets guidelines for business transactions. According to Islamic law, for example, banks cannot charge interest on loans or pay interest on deposits. Instead, banks receive a portion of the profits earned by investors who borrow funds and pay depositors from these earnings. Likewise, because the products of alcohol- and tobacco-related businesses violate Islamic beliefs, firms abiding by Islamic law cannot invest in such companies.

QUICK STUDY 4

1. What is meant by the term *legal system*?
2. Explain the role of *nationalism* in politics.
3. Identify the main features of each type of legal system (*common, civil,* and *theocratic law*).

Global Legal Issues

Earlier in this chapter, we saw how international companies work to overcome obstacles that an unfamiliar political system presents. Likewise, companies must adapt to dissimilar legal systems in global markets. Let's examine several important legal issues facing companies that are active in international business.

Standardization

Companies must adapt to dissimilar legal systems because there is no clearly defined body of international law that all nations accept. There is a movement toward *standardizing* the interpretation and application of laws in more than one country, but this does not involve standardizing entire legal systems. Enduring differences in legal systems, therefore, can force companies to continue the costly practice of hiring legal experts in each country where they operate.

Still, international treaties and agreements exist in intellectual property rights, antitrust regulation, taxation, contract arbitration, and general matters of trade. International organizations that promote standardization include the United Nations (UN; www.un.org), the Organization for Economic Cooperation and Development (OECD; www.oecd.org), and the International Institute for the Unification of Private Law (www.unidroit.org). The European Union is standardizing parts of its members' legal systems to facilitate commerce in Western Europe.

Intellectual Property

intellectual property
Property that results from people's intellectual talent and abilities.

property rights
Legal rights to resources and any income they generate.

Property that results from people's intellectual talent and abilities is called **intellectual property**. It includes graphic designs, novels, computer software, machine-tool designs, and secret formulas, such as that for making Coca-Cola. Technically, it results in *industrial property* (in the form of either a *patent* or a *trademark*) or *copyright* and confers a limited monopoly on its holder.

Most national legal systems protect **property rights**—the legal rights to resources and any income they generate. Similar to other types of property, intellectual property can be traded,

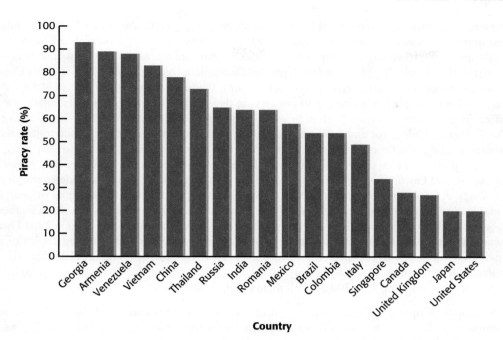

FIGURE 3.1

Business Software Piracy

Source: Based on the *Eighth Annual BSA and IDC Global Software Piracy Study* (Washington, DC; Business Software Alliance, May 2011), pp. 8–9, available at www.bsa.org/globalstudy.

sold, and licensed in return for fees and/or royalty payments. Intellectual property laws are designed to compensate people whose property rights are violated.

Intellectual property laws differ greatly from nation to nation. Business Software Alliance (BSA; www.bsa.org), the trade body for business software makers, conducts an annual study of software piracy rates around the globe. Where illegal copies of business software recently made up 20 percent of the U.S. domestic market (the lowest in the world), pirated software made up 93 percent of the market in Georgia (the highest worldwide). Globally, business software piracy averages around 42 percent and costs business software makers nearly $59 billion annually.[8] Figure 3.1 shows piracy rates for some of the nations included in the BSA study. As these figures suggest, the laws of some countries are softer on piracy than the laws of some other nations. Software companies in the United States and the European Union continually lobby their governments to pressure other nations to adopt stronger laws.

Although peddlers of pirated CDs and DVDs operate openly from sidewalk kiosks in China, China's government did more to tackle piracy recently. The effort was a test case in fighting piracy in the YouTube era of video sharing. Richard Cotton, a general legal counsel at NBC, says, "[Chinese officials] recognize the future of the Chinese economy depends on innovation and creativity, and they have to protect the [intellectual property] that drives it."[9]

INDUSTRIAL PROPERTY **Industrial property** includes patents and trademarks, which are often a firm's most valuable assets. Laws protecting industrial property are designed to reward inventive and creative activity. Industrial property is protected internationally under the Paris Convention for the Protection of Industrial Property (www.wipo.int), to which nearly 100 countries are signatories.

A **patent** is a right granted to the inventor of a product or process that excludes others from making, using, or selling the invention. Current U.S. patent law went into effect on June 8, 1995, and is in line with the systems of most developed nations. Its provisions are those of the World Trade Organization (WTO), the international organization that regulates trade between nations. The WTO (www.wto.org) typically grants patents for a period of 20 years. The 20-year term begins when a patent application is filed with a country's patent office, not when it is finally granted. Patents can be sought for any invention that is new, useful, and not obvious to any individual of ordinary skill in the relevant technical field. Patents motivate companies to pursue inventions and make them available to consumers because they protect investments that companies make in research and development.

Trademarks are words or symbols that distinguish a product and its manufacturer. The Nike (www.nike.com) "swoosh" is a trademark, as is the name "Lexus" (www.lexus.com). Trademark law creates incentives for manufacturers to invest in developing new products. It also benefits

industrial property
Patents and trademarks.

patent
Property right granted to the inventor of a product or process that excludes others from making, using, or selling the invention.

trademark
Property right in the form of words or symbols that distinguish a product and its manufacturer.

consumers because they know what to expect when they buy a particular brand. In other words, you would not expect a canned soft drink labeled "Coca-Cola" to taste like one labeled "Sprite."

Trademark protection typically lasts indefinitely, provided the word or symbol continues to be *distinctive*. Ironically, this stipulation presents a problem for companies such as Coca-Cola (www.coca-cola.com) and Xerox (www.xerox.com), whose trademarks "Coke" and "Xerox" have evolved into *generic* terms for all products in their respective categories. Trademark laws differ from country to country, though some progress toward standardization is occurring. The European Union, for example, opened a trademark-protection office to police trademark infringement against firms that operate in any European Union country.

Designers who own trademarks, such as Chanel (www.chanel.com), Christian Dior (www.dior.com), and Gucci (www.gucci.com), have long been plagued by shoddily made counterfeit handbags, shoes, shirts, and other products. But recently, pirated products of equal or nearly equal quality are turning up, especially in Italy. Most Italian owners of luxury brands of leather goods and jewelry, for example, outsource production to small manufacturers. It is not hard for these same artisans to counterfeit extra copies of a high-quality product. Bootleg copies of a Prada (www.prada.com) backpack that costs $500 in New York can be bought for less than $100 in Rome. Jewelry shops in Milan can buy fake watches labeled Bulgari (www.bulgari.com) and Rolex (www.rolex.com) for $300 and sell them retail for $2,500.

copyright
Property right giving creators of original works the freedom to publish or dispose of them as they choose.

COPYRIGHTS **Copyrights** give creators of original works the freedom to publish or dispose of them as they choose. A copyright is typically denoted by the well-known symbol ©, a date, and the copyright holder's name. A copyright holder has the legal rights to:

• Reproduce the copyrighted work.
• Derive new works from the copyrighted work.
• Sell or distribute copies of the copyrighted work.
• Perform the copyrighted work.
• Display the copyrighted work publicly.

Copyright holders include artists, photographers, painters, literary authors, publishers, musical composers, and software developers. Works created after January 1, 1978, are automatically copyrighted for the creator's lifetime plus 50 years. Publishing houses receive copyrights for either 75 years from the date of publication or 100 years after creation, whichever comes first. Copyrights are protected under the **Berne Convention** (www.wipo.int), which is an international copyright treaty to which the United States is a member, and the 1954 Universal Copyright Convention. More than 50 countries abide by one or both of these treaties.

Berne Convention
International treaty that protects copyrights.

A copyright is granted for the *tangible expression* of an idea, not for the idea itself. For example, no one can copyright the idea for a movie about the sinking of the *Titanic*. But once a film is made that expresses its creator's treatment of the subject, that film can be copyrighted.

Perhaps the most well known song around the world, "Happy Birthday to You," is actually protected by U.S. copyright law. The song was composed in 1859 and copyrighted in 1935. Although the copyright was set to expire in 2010 on the song's 75th copyright birthday, the U.S. Congress extended it until 2030. Time Warner owns the copyright and stands to gain as much as $20 million from the extension.

Product Safety and Liability

Product safety laws in most countries set standards that manufactured products must meet. **Product liability** holds manufacturers, sellers, individuals, and others responsible for damage, injury, or death caused by defective products. Injured parties can sue for monetary compensation through *civil* lawsuits and for fines or imprisonment through *criminal* lawsuits.

product liability
Responsibility of manufacturers, sellers, individuals, and others for damage, injury, or death caused by defective products.

Developed nations have the toughest product liability laws, whereas developing and emerging countries have the weakest laws. Business insurance costs and legal expenses are greater in nations with strong product liability laws, where damage awards can be large. Likewise, enforcement of product liability laws differs from nation to nation. In the most developed nations, for example, tobacco companies are regularly under attack for the negative health effects of tobacco and nicotine. But critics say that the tobacco industry markets aggressively to women and children in developing countries where regulations are weak and many people do not know that smoking is dangerous.[10]

TABLE 3.1 Effect of Value Added Taxes (VAT)

Production Stage	Selling Price	Value Added	10% VAT	Total VAT
Shrimper	$1.00	$1.00	$0.10	$0.10
Processor	1.70	0.70	0.07	0.17
Wholesaler	2.80	1.10	0.11	0.28
Retailer	3.80	1.00	1.10	0.38

Taxation

National governments use income and sales taxes for many purposes. They use tax revenue to pay government salaries, build military capabilities, and shift earnings from people with high incomes to the poor. Nations may also tax imports in order to make them more expensive and give locally made products an advantage among price-sensitive consumers.

Nations pass indirect taxes, called "consumption taxes," which help pay for the consequences of using particular products. Consumption taxes on products such as alcohol and tobacco help pay the health-care costs of treating illnesses that result from using these products. Similarly, gasoline taxes help pay for the road and bridge repairs needed to counteract the effects of traffic and weathering.

Many countries impose a **value added tax (VAT)**—a tax levied on each party that adds value to a product throughout its production and distribution. The United States has not previously implemented a VAT tax, but the nation's considerable debt level is causing speculation that it may soon impose one. Supporters of the VAT system contend that it distributes taxes on retail sales more evenly between producers and consumers. Suppose, for example, that a shrimper sells the day's catch of shrimp for $1 per kilogram and that the country's VAT is 10 percent (see Table 3.1). The shrimper, processor, wholesaler, and retailer pay taxes of $0.10, $0.07, $0.11, and $0.10, respectively, for the value that each adds to the product as it makes its way to consumers. Consumers pay no additional tax at the point of sale because the government has already collected taxes from each party in the value chain. Still, consumers end up paying the tax because producers and distributors must increase prices to compensate for their tax burdens. So that the poor are not overly burdened, many countries exclude the VAT on certain items such as children's clothing.

value added tax (VAT)
Tax levied on each party that adds value to a product throughout its production and distribution.

Antitrust Regulations

Laws designed to prevent companies from fixing prices, sharing markets, and gaining unfair monopoly advantages are called **antitrust (antimonopoly) laws**. These laws try to provide consumers with a wide variety of products at fair prices. The United States and the European Union are the world's strictest antitrust regulators. In Japan, the Fair Trade Commission enforces antitrust laws but is often ineffective because *absolute proof* of wrongdoing is needed to bring charges.

antitrust (antimonopoly) laws
Laws designed to prevent companies from fixing prices, sharing markets, and gaining unfair monopoly advantages.

Companies based in strict antitrust countries often argue that they are at a disadvantage against competitors whose home countries condone *market sharing*, whereby competitors agree to serve only designated segments of a certain market. That is why firms in strict antitrust countries often lobby for exemptions in certain international transactions. Small businesses also argue that they could better compete against large international companies if they could join forces without fear of violating antitrust laws.

In the absence of a global antitrust enforcement agency, international companies must concern themselves with the antitrust laws of each nation where they do business. In fact, a nation (or group of nations) can block a merger or acquisition between two nondomestic companies if those companies do a good deal of business there. This happened to the proposed $43 billion merger between General Electric (GE; www.ge.com) and Honeywell (www.honeywell.com). GE wanted to marry its manufacture of airplane engines to Honeywell's production of advanced electronics for the aviation industry. Although both companies are based in the United States, together they employed 100,000 Europeans. GE alone earned $25 billion in Europe the year before the proposed merger. The European Union blocked the merger because it believed the result would be higher prices for customers, particularly airlines.

1. What are *intellectual property rights*? What is the significance of such rights?
2. Explain the term *industrial property*. What are its two types?
3. What is a *copyright*? Explain its importance to international business.
4. Identify the ramifications of *antitrust (antimonopoly) laws* and *product liability laws*.

Ethics and Social Responsibility

We learned in Chapter 2 that, when a company goes global, its managers encounter many unfamiliar cultural rules that govern human behavior. Although legal systems set boundaries for lawful individual and corporate behavior, they are inadequate for dilemmas of ethics and social responsibility. Frameworks for business law vary in strength from country to country. Unfortunately, the quest for profits may entice a company to exploit differences in legal standards by locating certain business operations in nations where they will be less scrutinized. In this way, national legal differences can become ethical issues for managers.

ethical behavior
Personal behavior in accordance with guidelines for good conduct or morality.

Ethical behavior is personal behavior in accordance with guidelines for good conduct or morality. Ethical dilemmas are not legal questions. When a law exists to guide a manager toward a legally correct action, that path should be followed. In an ethical dilemma, there is no right or wrong decision. There are alternatives, however, that may be equally valid in ethical terms depending on one's perspective.

corporate social responsibility
Practice of companies going beyond legal obligations to actively balance commitments to investors, customers, other companies, and communities.

In addition to the need for individual managers to behave ethically, businesses are expected to exercise **corporate social responsibility**—the practice of going beyond legal obligations to actively balance commitments to investors, customers, other companies, and communities. Corporate social responsibility (or CSR, as it is known) includes a wide variety of activities, including giving to the poor, building schools in developing countries, and protecting the global environment.

We can think of CSR as consisting of three layers of activity. The first layer is *traditional philanthropy,* whereby a corporation donates money and, perhaps, employee time toward a specific social cause. The second layer is related to *risk management,* whereby a company develops a code of conduct that it will follow in its global operations and agrees to operate with greater transparency. The third layer is *strategic CSR,* in which a business builds social responsibility into its core operations to create value and build competitive advantage.[11]

In the next two sections, we present the main theories of ethics and CSR and then examine several important issues.

Philosophies of Ethics and Social Responsibility

There are four commonly cited philosophies of business ethics and social responsibility. The *Friedman view*—named for its main supporter, the late economist Milton Friedman—says that a company's sole responsibility is to maximize profits for its owners (or shareholders) while operating within the law.[12] Imagine a company that moves its pollution-generating operations from a country having strict and expensive environmental-protection laws to a country having no such laws. Managers subscribing to the Friedman philosophy would applaud this decision. They would argue that the company is doing its duty to increase profits for its owners and is operating within the law in the foreign country. Many people disagree with this argument and say the discussion is not *whether* a company has CSR obligations but *how* it will fulfill them.

The *cultural relativist view* says that a company should adopt local ethics wherever it operates because all belief systems are determined within a cultural context. Cultural relativism sees truth, itself, as relative and argues that right and wrong are determined within a specific situation. The expression "When in Rome, do as the Romans do" captures the essence of cultural relativism. Consider a company that opens a factory in a developing market and, following local customs, employs child laborers. The cultural relativist manager would argue that this company is acting appropriately and in accordance with local standards of conduct. Many people strongly oppose this line of ethical reasoning.

The *righteous moralist view* says that a company should maintain its home-country ethics wherever it operates because the home-country's view of ethics and responsibility is superior to others' views. Imagine a company that expands from its developed-country base to an emerging market where local managers commonly bribe officials. Suppose headquarters detests the act of bribery and instructs its subsidiary managers to refrain from bribing any local officials. In this situation, headquarters is imposing its righteous moralist view on local managers.

The *utilitarian view* says that a company should behave in a way that maximizes "good" outcomes and minimizes "bad" outcomes wherever it operates. The utilitarian manager asks the question, "What outcome should I aim for?" and answers, "That which produces the best outcome for all affected parties." In other words, utilitarian thinkers say the right behavior is that which produces the greatest good for the greatest number. Consider, again, the righteous moralist company above that instructs its employees not to bribe local officials in the emerging market. Now suppose a manager learns that, by bribing a local official, the company will finally obtain permission to expand its factory and create 100 well-paying jobs for the local community. If the manager pays the bribe based on his or her calculations that more people will benefit than will be harmed by the outcome, he or she is practicing utilitarian ethics.

Although businesses develop guidelines and policies regarding ethical behavior and social responsibility, issues arise on a daily basis that can cause dilemmas for international managers. Let's examine some of these key issues.

CSR Issues

Companies should not produce public relations campaigns that present a business as socially responsible if it does not truly embrace CSR principles. Conscientious business leaders realize that the futures of their companies rest on healthy workforces and environments worldwide. For example, soft drink makers support all sorts of environmental initiatives because they understand that their futures depend on an ample supply of clean drinking water. Let's now discuss CSR as it pertains to bribery and corruption, labor conditions and human rights, fair trade practices, and the environment.

BRIBERY AND CORRUPTION Similar to other cultural and political elements, the prevalence of corruption varies from nation to nation. In certain countries, bribes are routinely paid to distributors and retailers in order to push a firm's products through distribution channels. Bribes can mean the difference between obtaining an important contract and being completely shut out of a market. But corruption is detrimental to society and business. Among other things, corruption can send resources toward inefficient uses, hurt economic development, distort public policy, and damage national integrity.

Map 3.2 on pages 94–95 shows how countries rate on their perceived levels of corruption. The higher a country's score on the corruption perceptions index (CPI), the less corrupt it is perceived to be by international managers. What stands out immediately on this map is that the poorer and least developed nations tend to be perceived as being most corrupt (such as Russia, much of Africa, and areas in the Middle East). This reflects the hesitancy on the part of international companies about investing in corrupt economies.

Enron Corporation made history when it acknowledged in a federal filing that it had overstated its earnings. Investors fled in droves as Enron stock became worthless and the company went bankrupt. Although executives had earned millions over the years in salaries and bonuses, Enron's rank-and-file employees saw their retirement savings disappear as the firm disintegrated. European banks lost around $2 billion that they had lent to Enron and its subsidiaries. Chairman of the board Kenneth Lay (now deceased) and CEO Jeffrey Skilling were convicted on criminal charges. Then a criminal indictment was filed against accounting firm Arthur Andersen, Enron's auditor, for shredding documents related to its work for Enron. With its reputation irreparably damaged, Andersen also collapsed.

The financial losses and diminished confidence in business that resulted from Enron's collapse prompted the U.S. Congress to pass the *Sarbanes–Oxley Act* (Sarbox) on corporate governance. The law established new, stringent accounting standards and reporting practices for firms. Around the world, governments, accounting standards boards, other regulators, and interest groups won the fight for higher standards and more transparent financial reporting by companies. Businesses worldwide received the message that fudging the accounting numbers, misrepresenting the firm's financial health, and running a company in that gray area between right and wrong is unethical and, now, illegal.

MAP 3.2
Corruption Perceptions Index (CPI)

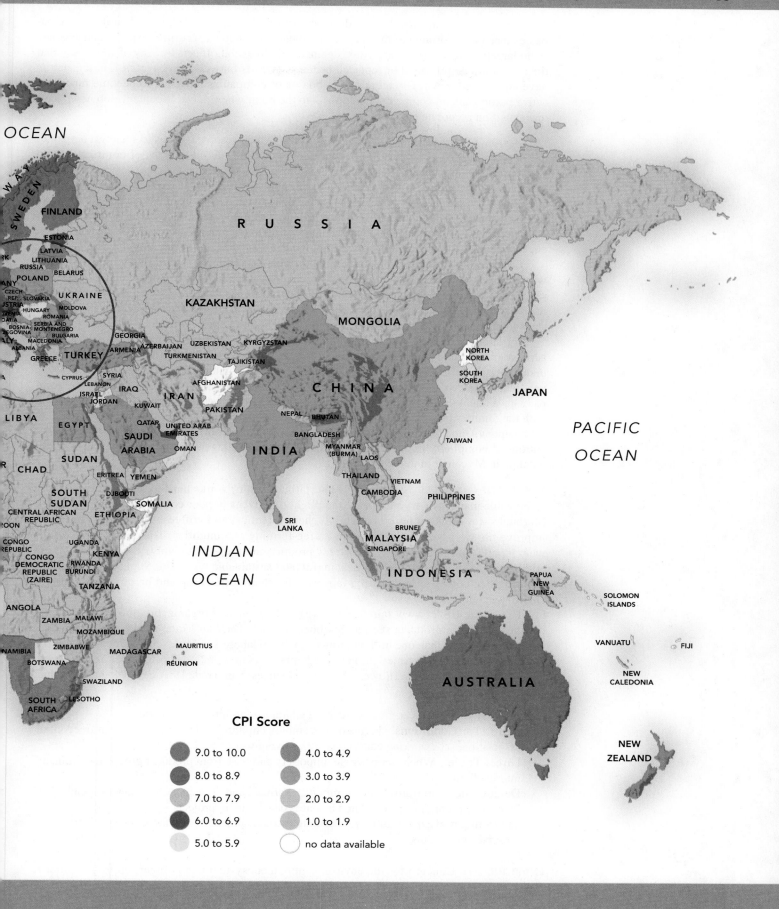

CPI Score

- 9.0 to 10.0
- 8.0 to 8.9
- 7.0 to 7.9
- 6.0 to 6.9
- 5.0 to 5.9
- 4.0 to 4.9
- 3.0 to 3.9
- 2.0 to 2.9
- 1.0 to 1.9
- no data available

Some people believe Sarbox needs to be reformed because of the financial burden that companies face in conforming to the act's requirements. Regulators, securities experts, and scholars (who largely praise Sarbox) are pitted against chief financial officers—many of whom say that the act should be reformed or repealed because its costs outweigh its benefits. But legislators have not backed down. Directors on the boards of companies have had to become far-more-active participants in company operations—to the point where it has become "a job now," says one expert on corporate governance.[13]

LABOR CONDITIONS AND HUMAN RIGHTS To fulfill their responsibilities to society, companies are monitoring the actions of their own employees and the employees of companies with whom they conduct business. Pressure from human rights activists drove conscientious apparel companies to introduce codes of conduct and monitoring mechanisms for their international suppliers. Levi-Strauss (www.levistrauss.com) pioneered the use of practical codes to control working conditions at contractors' facilities. The company does business only with partners who meet its "Terms of Engagement," which sets minimal guidelines regarding ethical behavior, environmental and legal requirements, employment standards, and community involvement.[14]

Consider one case publicized by human rights and labor groups investigating charges of worker abuse at the factory of one of Nike's Vietnamese suppliers. Twelve of 56 female employees reportedly fainted when a supervisor forced them to run around the factory as punishment for not wearing regulation shoes. Nike confirmed the report and, in suspending the supervisor, took steps to implement practices more in keeping with the company's home-country ethics.

International law says that only nations can be held liable for human rights abuses. But activist groups can file a lawsuit against a U.S. business for an alleged human rights violation under the Alien Tort Claims Act by alleging a company's complicity in the abuse. Yahoo! (www.yahoo.com) felt the power of this law when two Chinese dissidents were jailed after the company gave data it had on them to Chinese authorities. Yahoo! reached an out-of-court settlement with the families of the jailed men. And despite denials of any responsibility in the matter, U.S. oil company Unocal, now part of Chevron (www.chevron.com), settled out of court over allegations of complicity in government soldiers' abuse of villagers during construction of an oil pipeline in Myanmar in the 1990s.[15]

FAIR TRADE PRACTICES Starbucks (www.starbucks.com) works hard to operate in a socially responsible manner by trying to ease the plight of citizens in poor coffee-producing countries. Starbucks does this by building schools, health clinics, and coffee-processing facilities to improve the well-being of families in coffee-farming communities. The company also sells what it calls "fair trade coffee." Fair trade products are those that involve companies working with suppliers in more equitable, meaningful, and sustainable ways. For Starbucks, this means ensuring that coffee farmers earn a fair price for their coffee crop and helping them farm in environmentally friendly ways.[16]

Fair Trade USA (www.fairtradeusa.org) is the nonprofit organization that independently certifies fair trade products such as Starbucks coffee. The Fair Trade model of international trade benefits more than one million farmers and farm laborers in 58 developing countries across Africa, Asia, and Latin America. Fair Trade products now include coffee, tea, herbs, cocoa, chocolate, fruit, rice, sugar, flowers, honey, and spices. Fair Trade USA certifies that a product meets the following criteria:[17]

- **Fair Prices.** Producer groups receive a guaranteed minimum floor price.
- **Fair Labor Conditions.** Farms do not employ children, and workers are given freedom of association, safe working conditions, and a living wage.
- **Direct Trade.** Whenever possible, importers purchase from producer groups to eliminate intermediaries.
- **Democratic Community Development.** Farmers and workers decide how to spend their Fair Trade premiums in social and business development projects.
- **Environmental Sustainability.** Farming methods protect the health of farmers and preserve ecosystems.

ENVIRONMENT Concern for the environment and ecosystem is no longer left to government agencies and nongovernmental organizations. Today companies pursue "green" initiatives to

The electric Smart car shown here is docked to a charging station in Stuttgart, Germany. Many people believe that globalization and economic development take a toll on the environment. Companies are working to create all sorts of "green" products to reduce the impact of modern economies on our ecosystem. Besides car manufacturers, can you think of other types of companies that are working to become more environmentally responsible?

Source: Franziska Kraufmann/Newscom

reduce their toll on the environment *and* to reduce operating costs and boost profit margins. **Carbon footprint** is the environmental impact of greenhouse gases (measured in units of carbon dioxide) that results from human activity. It consists of two components:[18]

- **Primary Footprint.** Direct carbon dioxide emissions from the burning of fossil fuels, including domestic energy consumption and transportation (such as electricity and gasoline).
- **Secondary Footprint.** Indirect carbon dioxide emissions from the whole life cycle of products (from their manufacture to eventual breakdown).

carbon footprint
Environmental impact of greenhouse gases (measured in units of carbon dioxide) that results from human activity.

Companies at the leading edge of the green movement are printing a number on their products that represents the grams of carbon dioxide emitted from producing and shipping them to retailers. The number signifies the environmental impact of all the materials, chemicals, and so on, used in producing and distributing a good. For example, the United Kingdom's number-one selling snack food brand, Walker (www.walkers-crisps.co.uk), stamps "75g" on its packets of cheese- and onion-flavored potato chips, or *crisps*—meaning 75 grams of carbon dioxide were emitted in producing and shipping each packet. Footwear and clothing maker Timberland (www.timberland.com) is implementing a different system. It labels its products with a score ranging from 0 to 10. A score of "0" means producing and shipping a product emitted less than 2.5 kilograms of carbon dioxide; a product with a score of "10" emitted 100 kilograms of carbon dioxide—roughly equivalent to driving a car 240 miles.[19]

Another trendsetter in reducing its carbon footprint is Marriott International (www.marriott.com). The hotel company's employee cafeteria replaced paper and plastic containers with real plates and biodegradable potato-based containers called Spudware. Marriott gives employees reusable plastic water bottles and lets them exchange burnt-out regular bulbs, from work or home, for energy-saving compact fluorescent bulbs. And the company has "green ambassadors" who remind employees to print documents double-sided and to turn off lights and electronic devices not in use.[20]

Boisset Family Estates (www.boisset.com), France's third-largest winery, initiated an eco-smart alternative to the glass bottle. Boisset uses aluminum-coated paperboard similar to containers commonly used for juices and milk. Besides protecting the product from oxidation and making it easier to chill, the new packaging helps the environment and improves company profits. It used to take 28 trucks to haul enough empty glass bottles to the winery to package the same volume of wine that today takes just one truck of empty cartons. After the cartons are filled, one truck now hauls away what used to take three trucks. The savings in materials, fuel, and equipment are significant.[21]

On a national level, the German government has gone greener than most others. Germany's energy law guarantees operators of windmills and solar generators prices that are above the market rate for as long as 20 years. That law, combined with German expertise in aerodynamics, is making the country a global leader in renewable energy. Today, 60 companies in Germany specialize in wind systems. The former East Germany is nicknamed Solar Valley because of the large number of companies that manufacture solar cells there. Germany's green-energy sector employs more than 235,000 people and generates $33 billion in sales annually.[22]

Business and International Relations

The political relations between a company's home country and the nations in which it does business affect its international business activities. Favorable political relationships foster stable business environments and increase international cooperation in many areas, including the development of international communications and distribution infrastructures. In turn, a stable environment requires a strong legal system through which disputes can be resolved quickly and fairly. In general, favorable political relations lead to increased business opportunities and lower risk.

To generate stable business environments, some countries have turned to *multilateral agreements*—treaties concluded among several nations, each of whom agrees to abide by treaty terms even if tensions develop. According to the European Union's founding treaty, goods, services, and citizens of member nations are free to move across members' borders. Every nation must continue to abide by such terms even if it has a conflict with another member. For instance, although Britain and France disagree on many issues, neither can treat goods, services, and citizens coming and going between their two nations any differently than it treats any other member nation's goods, services, and citizens. See Chapter 8 for a detailed presentation of the European Union.

The United Nations

United Nations (UN)
International organization formed after World War II to provide leadership in fostering peace and stability around the world.

Although individual nations sometimes have the power to influence the course of events in certain parts of the world, they cannot monitor political activities everywhere at once. The **United Nations** (UN; www.un.org) was formed after the Second World War to provide leadership in fostering peace and stability around the world. The UN and its many agencies provide food and medical supplies, educational supplies and training, and financial resources to poorer member nations. The UN receives its funding from member contributions based primarily on gross national product (GNP). Practically all nations in the world are UN members—except for several small countries and territories that have observer status.

The UN is headed by a secretary general who is elected by all members and who serves for a five-year term. The UN system consists of six main bodies:

- All members have an equal vote in the *General Assembly,* which discusses and recommends action on any matter that falls within the UN Charter. It approves the UN budget and the makeup of the other bodies.
- The *Security Council* consists of 15 members. Five (China, France, the United Kingdom, Russia, and the United States) are permanent. Ten others are elected by the General Assembly for two-year terms. The council is responsible for ensuring international peace and security, and all UN members are supposed to be bound by its decisions.
- The *Economic and Social Council,* which is responsible for economics, human rights, and social matters, administers a host of smaller organizations and specialized agencies.
- The *Trusteeship Council* consists of the five permanent members of the Security Council and administers all trustee territories under UN custody.
- The *International Court of Justice* consists of 15 judges elected by the General Assembly and Security Council. It can hear disputes only between nations, not cases brought against individuals or corporations. It has no compulsory jurisdiction, and its decisions can be, and have been, disregarded by specific nations.
- Headed by the secretary general, the *Secretariat* administers the operations of the UN.

An important body within the UN Economic and Social Council is the United Nations Conference on Trade and Development (UNCTAD; unctad.org). The organization has a broad mandate in the areas of international trade and economic development. It hosts conferences on pressing development issues including entrepreneurship, AIDS, poverty, and national debt. Certain conferences are designed to develop the business management skills of individuals in developing nations.

QUICK STUDY 6

1. Define *ethical behavior* and *corporate social responsibility*.
2. What are four commonly cited philosophies of business ethics and social responsibility?
3. List several issues of ethics and social responsibility relevant to international managers.
4. Why are international relations among countries important to international business?

BOTTOM LINE FOR BUSINESS

Differences in political and legal systems present both opportunities and risks for international companies. Gaining complete control over events in even the most stable national business environment is extremely difficult because of the intricate connections among politics, law, and culture. Still, understanding these connections is the first step in managing the risks of doing business in unfamiliar environments.

Implications for Business in Totalitarian Nations
Political opposition to business from nongovernmental organizations is extremely unlikely if a totalitarian nation sanctions a particular commercial activity. Bribery and kickbacks to government officials will likely prevail, and refusal to pay tends not to be an option. As such, business activities in totalitarian nations are inherently risky. Business law in totalitarian nations is either vague or nonexistent, and interpretation of the law is highly subjective. Finally, certain groups criticize companies for doing business in or with totalitarian nations, saying they are helping sustain oppressive political regimes.

Implications for Business in Democracies
Democracies tend to provide stable business environments through laws that protect individual property rights. Commerce should prosper when the private sector comprises independently owned firms that exist to make profits. Although participative democracy, property rights, and free markets tend to encourage economic growth, they do not always do so. India is the world's largest democracy, yet its economy grew very slowly for decades. Meanwhile, some countries achieved rapid economic growth under political systems that were not genuinely democratic.

Which Type of Government Is Best for Business?
Although democracies pass laws to protect individual civil liberties and property rights, totalitarian governments could also grant such rights. The difference is that, whereas democracies strive to guarantee such rights, totalitarian governments retain the power to repeal them whenever they choose. As for a nation's rate of economic growth, we can say only that a democracy does not guarantee high rates of economic growth and that totalitarianism does not doom a nation to slow economic growth. An economy's growth rate is influenced by many additional factors.

Implications of Legal Issues for Companies
A nation's political system is naturally intertwined with its legal system. Its political system inspires and endorses its legal system, which legitimizes and supports the political system. Flexible business strategies help companies operate within the political and legal frameworks of nations. Managers will benefit if they have a solid grasp of how legal systems affect company operations and strategy.

Implications of Ethical Issues for Companies
Probably every international company of at least moderate size has a policy for corporate social responsibility (CSR). Traditionally, companies practiced CSR through old-fashioned philanthropy. Indeed, donating money and time toward solving social problems helped society and bolstered a company's public image. Companies later developed codes of conduct for their global operations to ensure they were good citizens wherever they operated. Today, companies search for ways to use CSR to create value and build competitive advantage.

Chapter Summary

1. **Describe each main type of political system.**
   - A *political system* consists of the structures, processes, and activities by which a nation governs itself.
   - In a *totalitarian system,* individuals govern without the support of the people, tightly control people's lives, and do not tolerate opposing viewpoints.
   - Totalitarian governments tend to impose authority, lack constitutional guarantees, and restrict participation.

MyManagementLab
Go to **mymanagementlab.com** to complete the problem marked with this icon ⭐.

- Under *theocratic totalitarianism,* a country's religious leaders enforce laws and regulations based on religious and totalitarian beliefs.
- Under *secular totalitarianism,* political leaders rely on military and bureaucratic power.
- Secular totalitarianism takes three forms: *communist totalitarianism, tribal totalitarianism,* and *right-wing totalitarianism.*
- In a *democratic system,* leaders are elected directly by the wide participation of the people or by their representatives.
- Most democracies are *representative democracies,* in which citizens elect individuals from their groups to represent their political views.
- Representative democracies strive to provide freedom of expression, periodic elections, full civil and property rights, minority rights, and nonpolitical bureaucracies.

2. Identify the origins of political risk and how managers can reduce its effects.
- *Political risk* is the likelihood that a society will undergo political changes that negatively affect local business activity.
- *Macro risk* threatens the activities of all domestic and international companies in every industry, whereas *micro risk* threatens companies only within a particular industry or more narrowly defined group.
- Five actions or events that cause political risk are conflict and violence, terrorism and kidnapping, property seizure, policy changes, and local content requirements.
- The seizure of assets by a local government can take one of three forms: *confiscation* (forced transfer of assets without compensation), *expropriation* (forced transfer with compensation), or *nationalization* (forced takeover of an entire industry).
- Managers can reduce the effects of political risk through *adaptation* (incorporating risk into business strategies), *information gathering* (monitoring local political events), and *political influence* (such as by *lobbying* local political leaders).
- The *Foreign Corrupt Practices Act* forbids U.S. companies from bribing government officials or political candidates in other nations.

3. Describe each main type of legal system and some important global legal issues.
- A country's *legal system* is its set of laws and regulations, including the processes by which its laws are enacted and enforced and the ways in which its courts hold parties accountable for their actions.
- *Common law* is a legal system based on a country's legal history (tradition), past cases that have come before its courts (precedent), and how laws are applied in specific situations (usage).
- *Civil law* is a system based on a detailed set of written rules and statutes that constitute a legal code, from which flows all obligations, responsibilities, and privileges.
- *Theocratic law* is a system based on religious teachings.
- Businesses prefer a legal system that protects *property rights* (legal rights to resources and any income they generate) and *intellectual property* (property that results from people's intellectual talent and abilities).
- Intellectual property takes the form of *industrial property* (a patent or trademark) or copyright.
- Many nations have *product liability laws* (responsibility for damage, injury, or death caused by defective products) and *antitrust laws* (designed to prevent companies from fixing prices, sharing markets, and gaining unfair monopoly advantages).

4. Explain ethics and social responsibility and key issues facing international companies.
- *Ethical behavior* is personal behavior in accordance with guidelines for good conduct or morality.
- *Corporate social responsibility* is the practice of companies going beyond legal obligations to actively balance commitments to investors, customers, other companies, and communities.
- The *Friedman view* of CSR says that a company's sole responsibility is to maximize profits for its owners while operating within the law.
- The *cultural relativist view* of CSR says that a company should adopt local ethics wherever it operates.

- The *righteous moralist view* of CSR says that a company should maintain its home-country ethics wherever it operates.
- The *utilitarian view* of CSR says that a company should behave in a way that maximizes "good" outcomes and minimizes "bad" outcomes wherever it operates.

5. Explain how international relations affect international business activities.
   - Political relations between a company's home country and those with which it does business strongly affect its international activities.
   - In general, favorable political relations lead to increased opportunity and stable business environments.
   - The mission of the *United Nations (UN)* is to provide leadership in fostering peace and stability around the world.
   - Although its global peacekeeping efforts have had mixed results, the UN helps poor nations by providing food and medical supplies, educational supplies and training, and financial resources.

Talk It Over

1. The Internet and the greater access to information it can provide are forcing politicians to change their methods of governing. How might the Internet change totalitarian political systems, such as North Korea? What might its future expansion mean for nations with theocratic systems, such as Iran? How might technology change the way that democracies function?
2. Under a totalitarian political system, the Indonesian economy grew strongly for 30 years. Meanwhile, the economy of the world's largest functioning democracy, India, performed poorly for decades until recently. Relying on what you learned in this chapter, do you think the Indonesian economy grew despite or because of a totalitarian regime? What might explain India's relatively poor performance under a democratic political system?

Teaming Up

1. **Debate Project.** Two groups of four students each will debate the ethics of doing business in countries with totalitarian governments. After the first student from each side has spoken, the second student will question the opposing side's arguments, looking for holes and inconsistencies. The third student will attempt to answer these arguments. The fourth student will present a summary of each side's arguments. Finally, the class will vote to determine which team has offered the more compelling argument.
2. **Market Entry Strategy Project.** This exercise corresponds to the *MESP* online simulation. For the nation you are studying, what type of political and legal systems does it have? Do free elections take place? Is the government heavily involved in the economy? Is the legal system effective and impartial? Do political and legal conditions suggest the country could be a potential market? If so, for what kinds of goods or services might the market be appealing? What is the level of corruption in the nation? Is legislation pending that may be relevant to international companies? Integrate your findings into your completed *MESP* report.

Key Terms

antitrust (antimonopoly) laws (p. 91)
Berne Convention (p. 90)
capitalism (p. 79)
carbon footprint (p. 97)
civil law (p. 87)
common law (p. 87)
communism (p. 76)
confiscation (p. 81)
copyright (p. 90)
corporate social responsibility (p. 92)
democracy (p. 78)
ethical behavior (p. 92)
expropriation (p. 81)

Foreign Corrupt Practices Act (p. 86)
industrial property (p. 89)
intellectual property (p. 88)
legal system (p. 86)
lobbying (p. 86)
local content requirements (p. 84)
nationalism (p. 86)
nationalization (p. 81)
patent (p. 89)
political risk (p. 80)
political system (p. 74)
private sector (p. 79)

product liability (p. 90)
property rights (p. 88)
representative democracy (p. 78)
secular totalitarianism (p. 76)
socialism (p. 76)
theocracy (p. 76)
theocratic law (p. 88)
theocratic totalitarianism (p. 76)
totalitarian system (p. 75)
trademark (p. 89)
United Nations (UN) (p. 98)
value added tax (VAT) (p. 91)

Take It to the Web

1. **Video Report.**   Visit this book's channel on YouTube (www.YouTube.com/MyIBvideos). Click on "Videos" near the top of the page and click on the set of videos labeled "Ch 03: Politics, Law, and Business Ethics." Watch one video from the list, and then summarize it in a half-page report. Reflecting on the contents of this chapter, which components of politics, law, and business ethics can you identify in the video? How might a company engaged in international business act on the information contained in the video?

2. **Website Report.**   To attract investment from domestic and foreign companies, nations compete against each other to provide top-notch services.

   Visit the main government portal of Hong Kong, SAR (www.gov.hk). Can you identify several sections of the site that are government-to-business activities and government-to-citizen dealings? Visit the "Environment" section and read about Hong Kong's eco-friendly initiatives. What key milestones has it achieved, and what future initiatives are planned?

   List the types of services that would be available to you as (1) a citizen of Hong Kong, (2) a tourist planning to visit Hong Kong, (3) a person thinking of starting a business in Hong Kong, and (4) a company currently operating in Hong Kong. What additional services should the government offer on its website that it does not currently provide?

Ethical Challenges

1. You are the president of a firm that publishes textbooks for medical students in more than 30 languages. On a recent trip to a university in a developing country (with a GDP per capita of under $1,000 per year), you discover that students are using bound photocopies of your best-selling medical textbook. Speaking with several students, they inform you that if they were required to pay for the actual books, they could not afford medical school. Witnessing the clear copyright violation firsthand, how do you react? What possible courses of action might you take? If additional information would be helpful to you, what would it be?

2. You are the proprietor of a fledging computer graphics company in Shanghai, China. The sophisticated business application software you need for your business normally sells for 2,900 renminbi (around $350) at computer stores in Shanghai. But with an income of just over $5,000 a year, you cannot afford to buy the original graphics software for your business. A friend has told you she can get you all the software you need, and more, at a nearby street market for only $40. Because very few people buy official software, you know the authorities will not punish you if you are caught. Is it unethical for you to purchase the pirated software? Do you believe you are justified in doing so?

3. You are the CEO of a major pharmaceutical firm that holds worldwide patents on several highly successful drugs. Your company invests heavily to develop its drugs because patents allow it to recoup its investment. But your firm has come under pressure from competitors selling cheaper alternatives and from politicians and nongovernmental groups to supply drugs to people in poor nations at reduced prices. Several senior executives in your company feel that the firm is unfairly being asked to discount its drugs that treat diseases afflicting people of poor nations. Some executives suggest that the firm focus on drugs to treat diseases (such as heart disease and cancer) that occur mostly in wealthy nations, but you are uneasy with such a move. Would such a course of action be ethical? Diseases such as AIDS, cancer, and heart disease all kill their victims. Should drugs for only certain diseases be exempt from patent protection?

MyManagementLab

Go to **mymanagementlab.com** for Auto-graded writing questions as well as the following Assisted-graded writing questions:

3-1.   Consider the following statement: "Democratic political systems, as opposed to totalitarian ones, provide international companies with more stable environments in which to do business." Do you agree? Why or why not? Support your argument with specific country examples.

3-2.   What actions can companies and governments take to ensure that products cannot be easily pirated? Be specific.

3-3.   Mymanagementlab Only – comprehensive writing assignment for this chapter.

Practicing International Management Case

Pirates of Globalization

It pays to remember that old Latin phrase, *caveat emptor* ("let the buyer beware"), when tackling the production of counterfeit products on a global scale. Sophisticated pirates routinely violate patents, trademarks, and copyrights to churn out high-quality fakes of the best-known brands. Trademark counterfeiting amounts to between 5 and 7 percent of world trade, or around $500 billion a year. Phony products appear in many industries, including computer software, films, books, music CDs, and pharmaceutical drugs. Fake computer chips, broadband routers, and computers cost the electronics industry alone up to $100 billion annually.

Traditionally peddled by sidewalk vendors and in back-street markets, counterfeiters now employ the latest technology. Just as honest businesses do, they are using the Internet to slash the cost of distributing their fake goods. All merchandise on some Internet sites is counterfeit, and even legitimate website operators, such as eBay (www.ebay.com), have difficulty rooting out pirates.

New York retailer Tiffany & Company (www.tiffany.com) sued eBay when counterfeits of its products appeared on eBay's website. In the complaint, Tiffany said that, of the 186 jewelry pieces bearing the Tiffany name that it randomly purchased on eBay, 73 percent were phony. Tiffany argues that, because eBay profits significantly from the sale of fake merchandise, provides a forum for such sales, and promotes it, the company "should bear responsibility for the sale of counterfeit merchandise on its site." Others disagree, saying it is impractical to require online auctioneers to verify the authenticity of every product sold on its site.

Pirates have not ignored the market for automotive parts, which loses around $12 billion annually to phony goods. Car manufacturers list harmful fakes such as brake linings made of compressed sawdust and transmission fluid that is nothing more than cheap oil with added dye. Boxes bearing legitimate-looking labels make it difficult for consumers to tell the difference between a fake and the real deal. The problem is causing fears of lawsuits because of malfunctioning counterfeits and concerns of lost revenue for producers of the genuine articles. For example, if someone is in an accident because of a counterfeit product, legitimate manufacturers need to prove the product is not their own.

Lax antipiracy regulations and booming economies in emerging markets mean potential intellectual-property traps await companies doing business there. For example, Indian law gives international pharmaceutical firms five- to seven-year patents on *processes used to manufacture drugs*—but *not on the drugs themselves*. This lets Indian companies modify the patented production processes of international pharmaceutical companies to create drugs that are only slightly different.

In China, political protection for pirates of intellectual property remains fairly common. Government officials, people working for the government, and even the People's Liberation Army (China's national army) operate factories that churn out pirated goods. An international company has difficulty fighting piracy in China because filing a lawsuit can severely damage its business relations there.

Yet, opinion is divided on the root causes of intellectual property violations in China. Some argue that Chinese legislation is vaguely worded and difficult to enforce. Others say China's intellectual property laws and regulations are fine, but poor enforcement is to blame for high rates of piracy. Amazingly, China's regulatory body sometimes allows a counterfeiter to remove an infringing trademark and still sell the substandard good. Technology companies said to have been harmed by China's weak intellectual property laws include Microsoft (www.microsoft.com), which claims that its software is widely pirated, and Cisco Systems (www.cisco.com), which sued a Chinese hardware maker for allegedly copying and using Cisco networking software.

Thinking Globally

1. Do you think that the international business community is being too lax about the abuse of intellectual property rights? Are international companies simply afraid to speak out for fear of jeopardizing access to attractive markets?

2. Increased digital communication may pose a threat to intellectual property because technology allows people to create perfect clones of original works. How do you think the Internet is affecting intellectual property laws?

3. Locate information on the Tiffany versus eBay lawsuit mentioned in the case. Identify the arguments of the plaintiff and the defendant and who prevailed. What are the implications of that lawsuit for the sale of counterfeits in online auctions?

Source: "Counterfeit Drugs: Fake Pharma," *The Economist* (www.economist.com), February 15, 2012; Rachael King, "Fighting a Flood of Counterfeit Tech Products," *Bloomberg Businessweek* (www.businessweek.com), March 1, 2010; Andrew Willis, "Europe Awash in Counterfeit Drugs," *Bloomberg Businessweek* (www.businessweek.com), December 8, 2009; Rachel Metz, "eBay Beats Tiffany in Court Case over Trademarks," *USA Today* (www.usatoday.com) July 14, 2008.

Economics and Emerging Markets

LEARNING OBJECTIVES

After studying this chapter, you should be able to

1. Describe what is meant by a centrally planned economy and explain why its use is declining.

2. Identify the main characteristics of a mixed economy and explain the emphasis on privatization.

3. Explain how a market economy functions and identify its distinguishing features.

4. Describe the different ways to measure a nation's level of development.

5. Discuss the process of economic transition and identify the obstacles for business.

A Look Back

Chapter 3 presented the ways in which different political and legal systems affect international business activities. We also explored some of the ways managers can cope with the risks created by political and legal uncertainties.

A Look at This Chapter

This chapter explains the key differences between centrally planned, mixed, and market economies. We also explore economic development and the challenges facing emerging markets and those transforming their economies into free markets.

A Look Ahead

Chapter 5 introduces us to a major form of international business activity—international trade. We examine the patterns of international trade and outline several theories that attempt to explain why nations conduct trade.

INDIA'S TECH KING

BANGALORE, India—Infosys (www.infosys.com) was founded in 1981 with an initial capital outlay of only $250. Today, the company is one of India's top providers of information technology services, with more than 151,000 employees and $7 billion in revenue. Infosys and other Indian firms provide high-quality software and consulting services to global companies. Pictured here, associates walk past the company's Global Education Center in Mysore, India.

Just as China drove down prices worldwide in manufacturing, India is doing the same in services. But China and India are following two distinct paths to development. Whereas China developed its economy by throwing open its doors to investment, India's commitment to free markets was ambiguous and made international companies wary. So India underwent organic growth and spawned homegrown firms in knowledge-based industries, such as Infosys.

Despite its reputation for high taxes and burdensome regulations, India long had some of the most basic foundations of a market economy—including private enterprise, democratic government, and Western accounting practices. Its capital markets

Source: JAGADEESH NV/EPA/Newscom

are also more efficient and transparent than China's, and its legal system is more advanced. The fact that China is following a top-down approach to development while India pursues a bottom-up approach reflects their opposing political systems: India is a democracy, and China is not.

India appears to be the first developing nation to advance economically by relying on the brainpower of its people. China, by contrast, is relying on its natural resources and inexpensive factory labor to develop its economy. The best growth strategy—the organic-led path of India versus the investment-led path of China—depends on a nation's circumstances. As you read this chapter, consider the importance of economic development and how companies can help to improve a nation's standards of living.[1]

S imilar to culture and systems of politics and law, economic systems differ from country to country. In Chapter 2, we saw that one defining element of a culture is its tendency toward *individualism* or *collectivism*. In Chapter 3, we saw how a people's history and culture influence the development of their political and legal systems. In this chapter, we investigate the linkages between culture and economic systems.

National culture can have a strong impact on a nation's economic development. In turn, the development of a country's economy can dramatically influence many aspects of its culture. Economic systems in individualist cultures tend to provide incentives and rewards for individual business initiative. Collectivist cultures tend to offer fewer such incentives and rewards. For example, in individualist cultures, *entrepreneurs*—businesspeople who accept the risks and opportunities involved in creating and operating new business ventures—tend to be rewarded with relatively low tax rates that encourage their activities.

We begin this chapter by introducing the world's different economic systems and exploring the links between culture and economics. We then examine economic development and ways of classifying nations using several indicators of development. We conclude by looking at how countries in transition are implementing market-based economic reforms and the challenges they face. Throughout the chapter, we will encounter anecdotes of how *emerging markets* are faring in their economic development efforts.

Economic Systems

economic system
Structure and processes that a country uses to allocate its resources and conduct its commercial activities.

A country's **economic system** consists of the structure and processes that it uses to allocate its resources and conduct its commercial activities. No nation is either completely individualist or completely collectivist in its cultural orientation. Likewise, the economies of all nations display a blend of individual and group values. In other words, no economy is entirely focused on individual reward at the expense of social well-being. Nor is any economy so completely focused on social well-being that it places no value on individual incentive and enterprise.

Yet every economy displays a *tendency* toward individualist or collectivist economic values. We can arrange national economies on a horizontal scale that is anchored by two extremes. At one end of the scale is a theoretical pure centrally planned economy, at the other end is a theoretical pure market economy, and in between is a mixed economy (see Figure 4.1). Let's now explore the workings of *centrally planned, mixed,* and *market economies.*

Centrally Planned Economy

centrally planned economy
Economic system in which a nation's land, factories, and other economic resources are owned by the government, which plans nearly all economic activity.

A **centrally planned economy** is a system in which a nation's land, factories, and other economic resources are owned by the government. The government makes nearly all economy-related decisions—including who produces what and what the prices of products, labor, and capital will be. Central planning agencies specify production goals for factories and other production units, and they even decide prices. In the former Soviet Union, for example, communist officials set prices for milk, bread, eggs, and other essential goods. The ultimate goal of central planning is to achieve a wide range of political, social, and economic objectives by taking complete control over the production and distribution of a nation's resources.

FIGURE 4.1

Range of Economic Systems

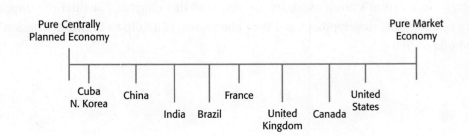

ORIGINS OF THE CENTRALLY PLANNED ECONOMY Central planning is rooted in the ideology that the group's welfare is more important than individual well-being. Just as collectivist cultures emphasize group over individual goals, a centrally planned economy strives to achieve economic and social equality.

German philosopher Karl Marx popularized the idea of central economic planning in the nineteenth century. Marx formulated his ideas while witnessing the hardship endured by working-class people in Europe during and after the Industrial Revolution. Marx argued that the economy could not be reformed, but that it must be overthrown and replaced with a more equitable "communist" system. (See the discussion of communism in Chapter 3.)

Different versions of Marx's ideas were implemented in the twentieth century by means of violent upheaval. Revolutions installed totalitarian economic and political systems in Russia in 1917, in China and North Korea in the late 1940s, and in Cuba in 1959. By the 1970s, central planning was the economic law in lands stretching across Central and Eastern Europe (Albania, Bulgaria, Czechoslovakia, East Germany, Hungary, Poland, Romania, and Yugoslavia), Asia (Cambodia, China, North Korea, and Vietnam), Africa (Angola and Mozambique), and Latin America (Cuba and Nicaragua).

DECLINE OF CENTRAL PLANNING In the late 1980s, nation after nation began to dismantle communist central planning in favor of market-based economies. Economists, historians, and political scientists attribute the decline of centrally planned economies to a combination of several factors.

Failure to Create Economic Value Central planners paid little attention to the task of producing quality goods and services at the lowest possible cost. In other words, they failed to see that commercial activities succeed when they create economic value for customers. Along the way, scarce resources were wasted in the pursuit of commercial activities that were not self-sustaining.

Failure to Provide Incentives Government ownership of economic resources drastically reduced incentives for businesses to maximize the output obtained from those resources. Except for aerospace, nuclear power, and other sciences (in which government scientists excelled), there were few incentives to create new technologies, new products, and new production methods. The result was little or no economic growth and consistently low standards of living.

As the world's most closed economy, North Korea has earned its nickname, "The Hermit Kingdom." For the most part, its policy of *juche* (self-reliance) is causing extreme hardship for North Korea's citizens. The combination of recurring floods and droughts, a shortage of fertilizers,

Although farming is a high-tech endeavor in the world's most advanced nations today, it is labor intensive and inefficient in North Korea. The government's failed communist economic policies hamper development and are at the root of its inability to afford fertilizers and modern machinery that could boost food production. Seemingly endless famines and economic collapse have cut North Korea's life expectancy to 65 years for men and 73 years for women.

Source: KCNA/EPA/Newscom

and a lack of farm machinery restrain the nation from reaching its peak food-production potential. As a result, North Korea often must rely on aid from abroad to feed its people.

Failure to Achieve Rapid Growth Leaders in communist nations took note of the high rates of economic growth in countries such as Hong Kong, Singapore, South Korea, and Taiwan—called Asia's four tigers. That a once-poor region of the world had so rapidly achieved such astounding growth awakened central planners to the possibilities. They realized that an economic system based on private ownership fosters growth much better than one hampered by central planning.

North Korea, once again, provides us with a good example. Each year for a decade until 1999, the North Korean economy contracted. Out of desperation, the country's leaders quietly allowed limited free market reforms, and small bazaars soon dotted the countryside. Street-corner currency exchanges sprang up to help facilitate a tiny but growing trade with bordering Chinese merchants. Impoverished North Koreans could buy mobile phones and found hope for a better life in DVDs of South Korean soap operas. But a disastrous attempt to reform its currency dealt a serious setback to North Korea's experiment with the free market.[2] For now, at least, the last green shoots of capitalism in North Korea seem to be coming from its Kaesong Industrial Complex along its border with South Korea. The one-of-a-kind industrial park buses in around 500 South Korean managers daily to manage around 44,000 North Korean factory workers. But its future is uncertain amid volatile relations between the North and South and because many South Korean businesses involved in the project are losing money.[3]

Failure to Satisfy Consumer Needs People in centrally planned economies were tired of a standard of living that had slipped far below that found in market economies. Ironically, although central planning was conceived as a means to create a more equitable system of distributing wealth, too many central planners failed to provide even basic necessities such as adequate food, housing, and medical care. Underground (shadow) economies for all kinds of goods and services flourished and, in some cases, even outgrew "official" economies. Prices of goods on the black market were much higher than the official (and artificial) prices set by governments.

Emerging Market Focus: China

China began its experiment with central planning in 1949, when communists defeated the nationalists in a long and bloody civil war. Today, the country's leaders describe its economic philosophy as "socialism with Chinese characteristics." There is possibly no country on earth that has done more for its people economically over the past two decades than China. Glistening skyscrapers now dominate the Shanghai and Beijing cityscapes, where most people have good job prospects. The country's immense population, rising incomes, and expanding opportunities are attracting huge sums of investment.

EARLY YEARS From 1949 until reforms were initiated in the late 1970s, China had a unique economic system. Agricultural production was organized into groups of people who formed production "brigades" and production "units." Communes were larger entities responsible for planning agricultural production quotas and industrial production schedules. Rural families owned their homes and parcels of land on which to produce particular crops. Production surpluses could be consumed by the family or sold at a profit on the open market. In 1979, China initiated agricultural reforms that strengthened work incentives in this sector. Family units could then grow whatever crops they chose and could sell the produce at market prices.

At about the same time, township and village enterprises (TVEs) began to appear. Each TVE relied on the open market for materials, labor, and capital and used a nongovernmental distribution system. Each TVE employed managers who were directly responsible for profits and losses. The government initially regarded TVEs as illegal and unrelated to the officially sanctioned communes. But they were legalized in 1984 and helped lay additional groundwork for a market economy.

PATIENCE AND *GUANXI* If there is one trait that is needed by all private companies in China, it is patience. Despite obvious ideological differences between itself and the private sector, China's Communist Party is trying very hard to appear well suited to running the country. Karl Marx once summed up communism as the "abolition of private property," and the name of China's

CULTURE MATTERS   Guidelines for Good *Guanxi*

- ***Importance of Contacts, Not Contracts.*** In China, face-to-face communication and personal relationships take priority over written contracts. Mu Dan Ping of Ernst & Young (www.ey.com) offers this diagram to show the different priorities:

  United States: Reason → Law → Relationship
  China: Relationship → Reason → Law

  Managers from the United States look for rationale or reason first, wondering if there is a market with profit potential. If so, they want a legal contract before spending time on a business relationship. But the Chinese need to establish a trust relationship first and then look for common goals as a reason for doing business. For them, legal contracts are just a formality, serving to ensure mutual understanding.

- ***Pleasure before Business.*** Experts advise managers to leave the sales pitch on the back burner and to follow the lead of their Chinese hosts. If seeking partnerships in China, one cannot overlook the importance of personal relationships. Companies that send their top performers to wow Chinese businesspeople with savvy sales pitches can return empty-handed—friendship comes before business in China.

- ***Business Partners Are Family Members, Too.*** The importance of family means that visiting managers should never turn down invitations to partake in a Chinese executive's family life. Lauren Hsu, market analyst for Kohler Company (www.kohler.com), was responsible for researching and identifying potential joint venture partners in China. She once went bowling with the partner's daughter and then to a piano concert with the entire family. Two years of meetings and visits to get acquainted eventually resulted in a joint venture deal.

- ***Cultural Sensitivity.*** China is not a single market but many different regional markets with different cultures and even different languages. Bob Wilner, of McDonald's Corporation (www.mcdonalds.com), went to China to learn how Chinese people are managed. "Unlike the way we cook our hamburgers exactly the same in all 101 countries," says Wilner, "the way we manage, motivate, reward, and discipline is more sensitive to the culture." Wilner and other McDonald's managers developed that sensitivity only through repeated visits to China.

Source: "The Panda Has Two Faces," *The Economist,* April 3, 2010, p. 70; Paul Maidment, "China's Legal Catch-22," *Forbes* (www.forbes.com), February 17, 2010; Frederik Balfour, "You Say *Guanxi,* I Say Schmoozing," *Bloomberg Businessweek* (www.businessweek.com), November 18, 2007.

Communist Party (in Chinese characters) literally means "common property party." But business was officially embraced when the Communist Party allowed businesspeople to become party members. Private property is now an accepted concept (though property rights violations are commonplace), which encouraged Chinese companies to invest in innovation. For example, Chinese Telecommunications firm Huawei (huawei.com) is now the world's fourth-largest applicant for patents.[4]

A personal touch is another necessary ingredient for success in China. Initially, and in line with communist ideology, non-Chinese companies were restricted from participating in China's economy. But today, outsiders enjoy ever-greater opportunities to create joint ventures with local partners. One of the most important factors in forming a successful venture in China is *guanxi*—the Chinese term for "personal relationships." To learn more about the secrets of *guanxi,* see this chapter's Culture Matters feature, titled "Guidelines for Good *Guanxi.*"

CHALLENGES AHEAD Despite the global recession, China's economy continues to reform itself and grow at between 7 and 9 percent annually. *Political and social problems,* however, pose threats to China's future economic performance. Skirmishes between secular and Muslim Chinese in western provinces still occur, although less frequently today. Meanwhile, for the most part, political leaders restrict advanced democratic reforms. Protests sporadically arise from time to time whenever ordinary Chinese citizens grow impatient with political progress.

Another potential problem is *unemployment.* Intensified competition and the entry of international companies into China are placing greater emphasis on efficiency and the cutting of payrolls in some industries. But the biggest contributor to the unemployed sector seems to be migrant workers. Hundreds of thousands of workers have left their farms and now go from city to city searching for better-paying factory work or construction jobs. Unhappiness with economic progress in the countryside and the misery of migrant workers are serious potential sources of social unrest for the Chinese government. And although factory workers are striking with greater frequency, they are mostly trying to recover ground lost by mandatory pay freezes during a recent economic slowdown.[5]

China has developed its own approach to innovation. First, *flexible networks* fueled by *guanxi* help companies to reduce costs and increase flexibility. Chinese companies spread their production contracts over a large number of parts suppliers and can then increase or decrease orders as demand dictates. Second, some companies exploit China's lax enforcement of property rights to quickly copy new, pricey global products and make cheaper versions available to

Chinese consumers. These companies employ *bandit* or *guerilla innovation* to continually learn innovative ways to produce goods at lower cost, though they are clearly violating the original producer's property rights.[6]

Another key issue is *reunification* of "greater China." China regained control of Hong Kong in 1997 after 99 years under British rule. For the most part, China has kept its promise of "one country, two systems." Although the economic (and, to a lesser extent, political) freedoms of people in Hong Kong would remain largely intact, the rest of China would continue along lines drawn by the communist leadership. In addition, China regained control of its southern coastal territory of Macao in 1999. Only a one-hour ferry ride from Hong Kong, Macao had been under Portuguese administration since it was founded in 1557. Although Macao's main function used to be that of trading post, today it serves mainly as a gambling outpost and is referred to as "Asia's Vegas."[7]

Any chance of Taiwan's eventual reunification with the Chinese mainland depends on how China manages Hong Kong and Macao. For now, reunification seems more likely as economic ties between China and Taiwan steadily grow. Taiwan recently scrapped a 50-year ban that capped the size of investments in China and eased restrictions on direct financial flows between Taiwan businesses and the mainland. Also, the entry of both China and Taiwan into the World Trade Organization (www.wto.org) in recent years has encouraged further integration of their two economies.

QUICK STUDY 1

1. Define *economic system*. What is the relationship between culture and economics?
2. What is a *centrally planned economy*? Describe the link between central planning and communism.
3. Identify several factors that contributed to the decline of centrally planned economies.
4. Describe China's experience with central planning and the challenges it faces.

Mixed Economy

mixed economy
Economic system in which land, factories, and other economic resources are rather equally split between private and government ownership.

A **mixed economy** is a system in which land, factories, and other economic resources are rather equally split between private and government ownership. In a mixed economy, the government owns fewer economic resources than does the government in a centrally planned economy. Yet in a mixed economy, the government tends to control the economic sectors that it considers important to national security and long-term stability. Such sectors usually include iron and steel manufacturing (for building military equipment), oil and gas production (to guarantee continued manufacturing and availability), and automobile manufacturing (to guarantee employment for a large portion of the workforce). Many mixed economies also maintain generous welfare systems to support the unemployed and to provide health care for the general population.

Mixed economies are found all around the world: Denmark, France, Germany, Norway, Spain, and Sweden in Western Europe; India, Indonesia, Malaysia, Pakistan, and South Korea in Asia; Argentina in South America; and South Africa. Although all the governments of these nations do not centrally plan their economies, they all influence economic activity by means of special incentives, including hefty subsidies to key industries, and through significant government involvement in the economy.

ORIGINS OF THE MIXED ECONOMY Advocates of mixed economies contend that a successful economic system not only must be efficient and innovative but also should protect society from the excesses of unchecked individualism and organizational greed. The goal is to achieve low unemployment, low poverty, steady economic growth, and an equitable distribution of wealth by means of the most effective policies.

Proponents point out that European and U.S. rates of productivity and growth were almost identical for decades after the Second World War. Although the United States has created more jobs, it has done so at the cost of widening social inequality, proponents say. They argue that nations with mixed economies should not dismantle their social-welfare institutions but should modernize them so that they contribute to national competitiveness. Austria, the Netherlands, and Sweden are taking this route. In the Netherlands, labor unions and the government agreed to an epic deal involving wage restraint, shorter working hours, budget discipline, new tolerance for part-time and temporary work, and the trimming of social benefits. As a result, unemployment in the Netherlands is hovering around 6 percent. By comparison, the average jobless rate for all nations in the Euro currency area is around 11 percent.[8]

DECLINE OF MIXED ECONOMIES Many mixed economies are remaking themselves to more closely resemble free markets. When assets are owned by the government, there seems to be less incentive to eliminate waste or to practice innovation. Extensive government ownership on a national level tends to result in a lack of accountability, rising costs, defective products, and slow economic growth. Many government-owned businesses in mixed economies need large infusions of taxpayer money to survive as world-class competitors, which raises taxes and prices for goods and services. Underpinning the move toward market-based systems is the sale of government-owned businesses.

Move toward Privatization As discussed earlier, citizens of many European nations prefer a combination of rich benefits and higher unemployment to the low jobless rates and smaller social safety net of the United States. In France, for instance, the French electorate continues to hold fast to a deeply embedded tradition of social welfare and job security in government-owned firms. Many French believe the social security and cohesion benefits of a more collectivist economy outweigh the efficiency advantages of an individualist one. Yet such attitudes are costly in terms of economic efficiency.

The selling of government-owned economic resources to private operators is called **privatization**. Privatization helps eliminate subsidized materials, labor, and capital formerly provided to government-owned companies. It also curtails the practice of appointing managers for political reasons rather than for their professional expertise. To survive, newly privatized companies must produce competitive products at fair prices because they are subject to the forces of the free market. The overall aim of privatization is to increase economic efficiency, boost productivity, and raise living standards.

Market Economy

In a **market economy**, the majority of a nation's land, factories, and other economic resources are privately owned, either by individuals or businesses. This means that who produces what and the prices of products, labor, and capital in a market economy are determined by the interplay of two forces:

- **Supply:** the quantity of a good or service that producers are willing to provide at a specific selling price
- **Demand:** the quantity of a good or service that buyers are willing to purchase at a specific selling price

privatization
Policy of selling government-owned economic resources to private operators.

market economy
Economic system in which the majority of a nation's land, factories, and other economic resources are privately owned, either by individuals or businesses.

supply
Quantity of a good or service that producers are willing to provide at a specific selling price.

demand
Quantity of a good or service that buyers are willing to purchase at a specific selling price.

Citizens and tourists alike go shopping along Myeongdong Street in Seoul, South Korea. The country is open to both foreign investment and foreign tourists. The comparison with North Korea could not be more striking. South Korea is a bustling economy that has benefited greatly from globalization. The life expectancy is 76 years for South Korean men and 83 for women. By contrast, North Korea remains a poor, closed nation where life expectancy is 65 years for men and 73 for women.

Source: imago stock&people/Newscom

As supply and demand change for a good or service, so does its selling price. The lower a product's price, the greater demand will be; the higher its price, the lower demand will be. Likewise, the lower a product's price, the smaller the quantity that producers will supply; the higher the price, the greater the quantity they will supply. In this respect, what is called the "price mechanism" (or "market mechanism") dictates supply and demand.

Market forces and uncontrollable natural forces can affect prices for many products, particularly commodities. Chocolate lovers, for example, should consider how the interplay of several forces affects the price of cocoa, the principal ingredient in chocolate. Suppose cocoa consumption suddenly rises in large cocoa-consuming nations such as Britain, Japan, and the United States. Suppose further that disease and pests plague crops in cocoa-producing countries such as Brazil, Ghana, and the Ivory Coast. As worldwide consumption of cocoa begins to outstrip production, market pressure is felt on both the demand side (consumers) and the supply side (producers). Falling worldwide reserves of cocoa then force the price of cocoa higher.

ORIGINS OF THE MARKET ECONOMY Market economics is rooted in the belief that individual concerns should be placed above group concerns. According to this view, the group benefits when individuals receive incentives and rewards to act in certain ways. It is argued that people take better care of property they own and that individuals have fewer incentives to care for property under a system of public ownership.

Laissez-Faire Economics For many centuries, the world's dominant economic philosophy supported government control of a significant portion of a society's assets and government involvement in its international trade. But in the mid-1700s a new approach to national economics called for less government interference in commerce and greater individual economic freedom. This approach became known as a *laissez-faire* system, loosely translated from French as "allow them to do [without interference]."

Canada and the United States are examples of contemporary market economies. It is no accident that both these countries have individualist cultures (although Canada to a somewhat lesser extent than the United States). As much as an emphasis on individualism fosters a democratic form of government, it also supports a market economy.

FEATURES OF A MARKET ECONOMY To function smoothly and properly, a market economy requires three things: *free choice, free enterprise,* and *price flexibility.*

- *Free choice* gives individuals access to alternative purchase options. In a market economy, few restrictions are placed on consumers' ability to make their own decisions and exercise free choice. For example, a consumer shopping for a new car is guaranteed a variety from which to choose. The consumer can choose among dealers, models, sizes, styles, colors, and mechanical specifications such as engine size and transmission type.
- *Free enterprise* gives companies the ability to decide which goods and services to produce and the markets in which to compete. Companies are free to enter new and different lines of business, select geographic markets and customer segments to pursue, hire workers, and advertise their products. They are, therefore, guaranteed the right to pursue interests profitable to them.
- *Price flexibility* allows most prices to rise and fall to reflect the forces of supply and demand. By contrast, nonmarket economies often set and maintain prices at stipulated levels. Interfering with the price mechanism violates a fundamental principle of the market economy.

GOVERNMENT'S ROLE IN A MARKET ECONOMY In a market economy, the government has relatively little direct involvement in business activities. Even so, it usually plays four important roles: *enforcing antitrust laws, preserving property rights, providing a stable fiscal and monetary environment,* and *preserving political stability.* Let's look briefly at each of these activities.

Enforcing Antitrust Laws When one company is able to control a product's supply—and, therefore, its price—it is considered a monopoly. *Antitrust (antimonopoly) laws* are designed to encourage the development of industries with as many competing businesses as the market will sustain. (These laws are explained fully in Chapter 3.) In competitive industries, prices are kept low by the forces of competition. By enforcing antitrust laws, governments prevent trade-restraining monopolies and business combinations that exploit consumers and constrain the growth of commerce.

The Federal Trade Commission (FTC) of the U.S. government seeks to ensure the competitive and efficient functioning of the nation's markets. But the FTC (www.ftc.gov) can also evaluate proposed deals outside the United States when the U.S. market is likely to be affected. For example, the FTC reviewed the proposed acquisition of Sweden's Svedala Industri by Finland's Metso Corporation (www.metso.com). Metso and Svedala were the world's two largest suppliers of rock-processing equipment at the time. In response to FTC concerns over potential anticompetitive effects in the global market for rock-processing equipment, the two companies agreed to sell parts of the combined business to third parties in return for FTC approval of the acquisition.

Preserving Property Rights A smoothly functioning market economy rests on a legal system that safeguards individual property rights. By preserving and protecting individual property rights, governments encourage individuals and companies to take risks such as investing in technology, inventing new products, and starting new businesses. Strong protection of property rights ensures entrepreneurs that their claims to assets and future earnings are legally safeguarded. This protection also supports a healthy business climate in which a market economy can flourish.

Providing a Stable Fiscal and Monetary Environment Unstable economies are often characterized by high inflation and unemployment. These forces create general uncertainty about a nation's suitability as a place to do business. Governments can help control inflation through effective *fiscal policies* (policies regarding taxation and government spending) and *monetary policies* (policies controlling money supply and interest rates). A stable economic environment helps companies make better forecasts of costs, revenues, and the future of the business in general. Such conditions reduce the risks associated with future investments, such as new product development and business expansion.

Preserving Political Stability A market economy depends on a stable government for its smooth operation and, indeed, for its future existence. Political stability helps businesses engage in activities without worrying about terrorism, kidnappings, and other political threats to their operations. (See Chapter 3 for extensive coverage of political risk and stability.)

ECONOMIC FREEDOM So far we have discussed the essence of market economies as being grounded in freedom: free choice, free enterprise, free prices, and freedom from direct intervention by government. Map 4.1 classifies countries according to their levels of economic freedom. Factors making up each country's rating include trade policy, government intervention in the economy, property rights, black markets, and wage and price controls. Most developed economies are completely or mostly free, but most emerging markets and developing nations are far less free.

Recall from Chapter 3 that the connection between political freedom and economic growth is not at all certain. Likewise, we can say only that countries with the greatest economic freedom *tend to have* the highest standards of living, whereas those with the lowest freedom *tend to have* the lowest standards of living. But greater economic freedom does not *guarantee* a high per capita income. A country can rank very low on economic freedom yet have a higher per capita income than a country with far greater freedom.

QUICK STUDY 2

1. What is a *mixed economy*? Explain the origin of mixed economies.
2. Explain the changes occurring in mixed economies and the role of *privatization*.
3. Define what is meant by *market economy,* and identify its three required features.
4. What is the role of government in a market economy?

Development of Nations

The economic well-being of one nation's people as compared with that of another nation's people is reflected in the country's level of **economic development**. It reflects several economic and human indicators, including a country's economic output (agricultural and industrial), infrastructure (power and transportation facilities), and its people's physical health and level of education.

economic development
Measure for gauging the economic well-being of one nation's people as compared with that of another nation's people.

MAP 4.1
Countries Ranked by Levels of Economic Freedom

C OCEAN

NORWAY
SWEDEN
FINLAND
ESTONIA
LATVIA
DENMARK
LITHUANIA
RUSSIA
BELARUS
LANDS
GERMANY POLAND
URG CZECH
ICHT. REP. SLOVAKIA
AUSTRIA UKRAINE
SLOVENIA HUNGARY
CROATIA MOLDOVA
BOSNIA SERBIA AND ROMANIA
HERZEGOVINA MONTENEGRO BULGARIA
ITALY MACEDONIA
ALBANIA
GREECE TURKEY
UNISIA
CYPRUS
SYRIA
LEBANON
ISRAEL
JORDAN

RUSSIA

KAZAKHSTAN

MONGOLIA

GEORGIA
AZERBAIJAN UZBEKISTAN KYRGYZSTAN
ARMENIA TURKMENISTAN
TAJIKISTAN
IRAN AFGHANISTAN
IRAQ
KUWAIT PAKISTAN
UNITED
QATAR ARAB
EMIRATES
SAUDI
ARABIA OMAN
NEPAL BHUTAN
BANGLADESH

CHINA

NORTH
KOREA
SOUTH
KOREA JAPAN

LIBYA EGYPT

INDIA

TAIWAN

PACIFIC
OCEAN

GER CHAD SUDAN
ERITREA
YEMEN
DJIBOUTI
SOMALIA
SOUTH
SUDAN
CENTRAL
AFRICAN
REPUBLIC ETHIOPIA
UGANDA
CONGO
REPUBLIC KENYA
CONGO RWANDA
DEMOCRATIC BURUNDI
REPUBLIC
(ZAIRE) TANZANIA

ERIA

ROON

ON

MYANMAR HONG
(BURMA) LAOS KONG
THAILAND
VIETNAM
CAMBODIA PHILIPPINES

SRI
LANKA

INDIAN

OCEAN

BRUNEI
MALAYSIA
SINGAPORE

INDONESIA

PAPUA
NEW
GUINEA

SOLOMON
ISLANDS

ANGOLA
ZAMBIA MALAWI
MOZAMBIQUE
NAMIBIA ZIMBABWE MADAGASCAR
BOTSWANA
SWAZILAND
SOUTH LESOTHO
AFRICA

MAURITIUS
RÉUNION

AUSTRALIA

VANUATU FIJI

NEW
CALEDONIA

NEW
ZEALAND

ERDE   MALTA   MAURITIUS

Level of economic freedom

- 80-100% free
- 70-79.9% free
- 60-69.9% free
- 50-59.9% free
- 0-49.9% free
- Not ranked

Cultural, political, legal, and economic differences among nations can cause great differences in economic development.

Economic development is an increasingly important topic as international companies pursue business opportunities in emerging markets. Although much of the population in these countries is poor, there is often a thriving middle class and ambitious development programs.

Productivity is a key factor that drives economic growth and rising living standards. Productivity is simply the ratio of outputs (what is created) to inputs (resources used to create output). We can speak about the productivity of a business, an industry, or an entire economy. For a company to boost its productivity, it must increase the value of its outputs using the same amount of inputs, create the same value of outputs with fewer inputs, or do both at the same time.

Raising living standards in an economy depends in large part on unlocking the gains that productivity offers. Mixed economies in Western Europe continue to privatize state-owned companies in order to boost productivity and competitiveness. Former centrally planned economies in Eastern Europe implemented free market reforms in order to raise living standards. Even North Korea (with one of the lowest standards of living outside Africa) is being compelled to consider economic reform.

Managers can use a variety of measures to estimate a country's level of economic development. But it is wise to consider a combination of measures when analyzing potential markets because each measure has advantages and disadvantages. Let's now look at a few of the main gauges of economic development.

National Production

Recall from Chapter 1 that the broadest measure of economic development is *gross national product (GNP)*, which is the value of all goods and services produced by a country's domestic and international activities over a one-year period. *Gross domestic product (GDP)* is the value of all goods and services produced by a domestic economy over a one-year period. GDP is a narrower figure that excludes a nation's income generated from exports, imports, and the international operations of its companies. A country's *GDP per capita* is simply its GDP divided by its population. GNP per capita is calculated similarly. Both GDP per capita and GNP per capita measure a nation's income per person. Map 4.2 on pages 118–119 shows how the World Bank (www.worldbank.org) classifies countries according to gross national income (GNI) per capita—a measure that is similar to GNP per capita.

Marketers often use GDP or GNP per capita figures to determine whether a country's population is wealthy enough to begin purchasing its products. For example, the Asian nation of Myanmar, with a GDP per capita of about $120 per year, is very poor. You won't find computer companies marketing laptops or designer-apparel firms selling expensive clothing there. Yet several large makers of personal-care products are staking out territory in Myanmar. Companies like Colgate-Palmolive (www.colgate.com) and Unilever (www.unilever.com) are traditional explorers of uncertain but promising markets in which they can offer relatively inexpensive, everyday items such as soap and shampoo. As multinational companies enter such markets, they often try to satisfy the needs of people who live at the *bottom of the pyramid*—the world's poorest populations with the least purchasing power.

Although GDP and GNP are the most popular indicators of economic development, they have several important drawbacks. We detail each of these in the following sections.

UNCOUNTED TRANSACTIONS For a variety of reasons, many of a nation's transactions do not get counted in either GDP or GNP. Some activities not included are:

- Volunteer work
- Unpaid household work
- Illegal activities such as gambling and black market (underground) transactions
- Unreported transactions conducted in cash

In some cases, the unreported (shadow) economy is so large and prosperous that official statistics such as GDP per capita are almost meaningless. Government statistics can mask a thriving shadow economy driven by differences between official and black-market currency exchange rates. In many wealthy nations, the shadow economy is from one-tenth to one-fifth as large as the official economy. But in more than 50 countries, the shadow economy is at least

40 percent the size of the documented GDP. In the Eurasian country of Georgia, for example, unreported transactions are estimated to equal as much as 73 percent of reported transactions. Whereas Georgia's official GDP is around $20.3 billion, its shadow economy is worth another $14.8 billion.[9]

One way in which goods and services flow through shadow economies is through *barter*—the exchange of goods and services for other goods and services instead of money. In one classic incident, Pepsi-Cola (www.pepsi.com) traded soft drinks in the former Soviet Union for 17 submarines, a cruiser, a frigate, and a destroyer. Pepsi then converted its payment into cash by selling the military goods as scrap metal.[10] Russians still use barter extensively because of a lack of currency. In another classic, and bizarre, case, the Russian government paid 8,000 teachers in the Altai republic (1,850 miles east of Moscow) their monthly salaries with 15 bottles of vodka each. Teachers had previously refused an offer to receive part of their salaries in toilet paper and funeral accessories.[11]

QUESTION OF GROWTH Gross product figures do not tell us whether a nation's economy is growing or shrinking—they are simply a snapshot of one year's economic output. Managers will want to supplement this data with information on expected future economic performance. A nation with moderate GDP or GNP figures inspires greater investor confidence and attracts more investment if its expected growth rate is high.

PROBLEM OF AVERAGES Recall that per capita numbers give an average figure for an entire country. These numbers are helpful in estimating national quality of life, but averages do not give us a very detailed picture of development. Urban areas in most countries are more developed and have higher per capita income than rural areas. In less advanced nations, regions near good harbors or other transportation facilities are usually more developed than interior regions. Likewise, an industrial park that boasts companies with advanced technology in production or design can generate a disproportionate share of a country's earnings.

For example, GDP or GNP per capita figures for China are misleading because Shanghai and coastal regions of China are far more developed than the country's interior. Although luxury cars are sold in many of China's coastal cities and regions, bicycles and simple vehicles are still the transportation of choice in China's interior.

PITFALLS OF COMPARISON Country comparisons using gross product figures can be misleading. When comparing gross product per capita, the currency of each nation being compared must be translated into another currency unit (usually the dollar) at official exchange rates. But official exchange rates only tell us how many units of one currency it takes to buy one unit of another. They do not tell us what that currency can buy in its home country. Therefore, to understand the true value of a currency in its home country, we apply the concept of *purchasing power parity*.

Purchasing Power Parity

Using gross product figures to compare production across countries does not account for the different cost of living in each country. **Purchasing power** is the value of goods and services that can be purchased with one unit of a country's currency. **Purchasing power parity (PPP)** is the relative ability of two countries' currencies to buy the same "basket" of goods in those two countries. This basket of goods is representative of ordinary, daily-use items such as apples, rice, soap, toothpaste, and so forth. Estimates of gross product per capita at PPP allow us to see what a currency can actually buy in real terms.

Let's see what happens when we compare the wealth of several countries to that of the United States by adjusting GDP per capita to reflect PPP. If we convert Swiss francs to dollars at official exchange rates, we estimate Switzerland's GDP per capita at $47,900. This is higher than the official GDP per capita of the United States ($39,700). But adjusting Switzerland's GDP per capita for PPP gives us a revised figure of $34,700, which is lower than the U.S. GDP figure of $39,700. Why the difference? GDP per capita at PPP is lower in Switzerland because of that nation's higher cost of living. It simply costs more to buy the same basket of goods in Switzerland than it does in the United States. The opposite phenomenon occurs in the case of the Czech Republic. Because the cost of living there is lower than in the United States, the Czech Republic's GDP per capita rises from $10,600 to $18,600 when PPP is considered.[12] We discuss PPP in greater detail in Chapter 10.

purchasing power
Value of goods and services that can be purchased with one unit of a country's currency.

purchasing power parity (PPP)
Relative ability of two countries' currencies to buy the same "basket" of goods in those two countries.

Map 4.2
Gross National Income

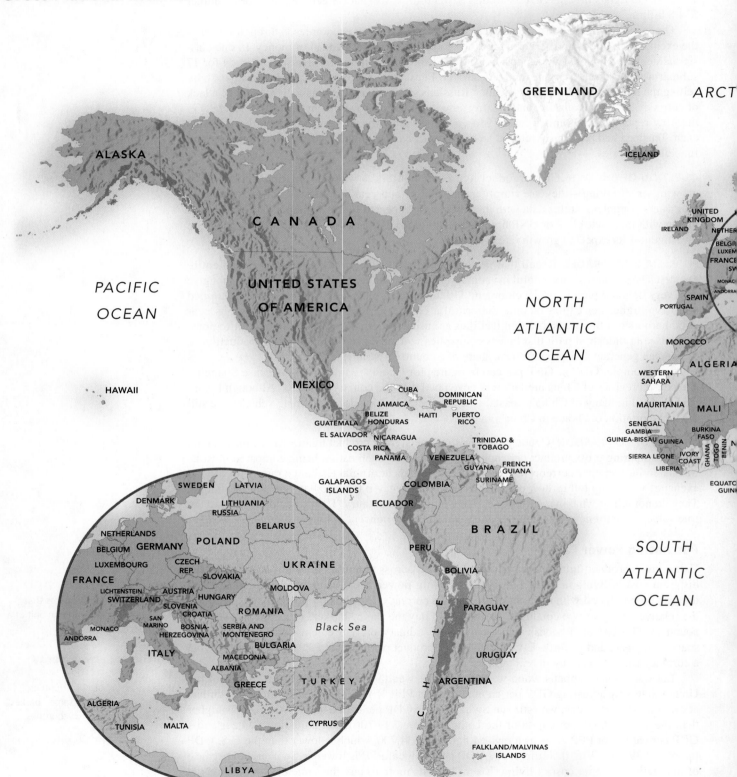

OCEAN

RK WAY

SWEDEN

FINLAND

ESTONIA

LATVIA

LITHUANIA

RUSSIA

BELARUS

ANY

POLAND

CZECH

REP.   SLOVAKIA

USTRIA

HUNGARY

OVENIA

ROATIA

BOSNIA-

RZEGOVINA

'ALY

ALBANIA

GREECE

MOLDOVA

ROMANIA

SERBIA AND

MONTENEGRO

BULGARIA

MACEDONIA

UKRAINE

KAZAKHSTAN

MONGOLIA

RUSSIA

GEORGIA

ARMENIA

AZERBAIJAN

TURKMENISTAN

UZBEKISTAN

KYRGYZSTAN

TAJIKISTAN

TURKEY

CYPRUS

SYRIA

LEBANON

ISRAEL

JORDAN

IRAQ

KUWAIT

IRAN

AFGHANISTAN

PAKISTAN

CHINA

NORTH

KOREA

SOUTH

KOREA

JAPAN

IA

LIBYA

EGYPT

QATAR

UNITED ARAB

EMIRATES

SAUDI

ARABIA

OMAN

NEPAL

BHUTAN

INDIA

BANGLADESH

MYANMAR

(BURMA)

LAOS

TAIWAN

PACIFIC

OCEAN

R

CHAD

SUDAN

ERITREA

YEMEN

THAILAND

VIETNAM

SOUTH

SUDAN

DJIBOUTI

SOMALIA

CAMBODIA

PHILIPPINES

CENTRAL AFRICAN

REPUBLIC

ROON

ETHIOPIA

SRI

LANKA

INDIAN

CONGO

REPUBLIC

UGANDA

KENYA

CONGO

DEMOCRATIC

REPUBLIC

(ZAIRE)

RWANDA

BURUNDI

TANZANIA

BRUNEI

MALAYSIA

SINGAPORE

INDONESIA

OCEAN

PAPUA

NEW

GUINEA

SOLOMON

ISLANDS

ANGOLA

ZAMBIA

MALAWI

MOZAMBIQUE

NAMIBIA

ZIMBABWE

BOTSWANA

MADAGASCAR

MAURITIUS

RÉUNION

VANUATU

FIJI

NEW

CALEDONIA

SWAZILAND

SOUTH

AFRICA

LESOTHO

AUSTRALIA

NEW

ZEALAND

GNI in US dollars

- 7,490 or more
- 2,350 – 7,490
- 1,110 – 2,350
- 430 – 1,110
- less than 430
- no data available

QUICK STUDY 3

1. What is meant by the term *economic development*? Explain the relationship between productivity and living standards.
2. Describe two measures of economic development, and list their advantages and disadvantages.
3. Explain the concept of *purchasing power parity*. What are its implications for a nation's *relative* income per capita?

Human Development

human development index (HDI)
Measure of the extent to which a government equitably provides its people with a long and healthy life, an education, and a decent standard of living.

The PPP concept does a fairly good job of revealing differences between national levels of economic development. Unfortunately, it is *a poor indicator of a people's total well-being*. Table 4.1 shows how selected countries rank according to the United Nations' **human development index (HDI)**—the measure of the extent to which a government equitably provides its people with a long and healthy life, an education, and a decent standard of living.

Table 4.1 also illustrates the disparity that can be present between a nation's wealth and the HDI. For example, we see that the United States ranks 10th in terms of gross national income (GNI) per capita but ranks 4th in providing health care, education, and a decent standard of living. A conspicuous example in the table is the entry for South Africa; the country ranks 79th in terms of GNI per capita but ranks 123rd in terms of HDI. Perhaps most striking is the column showing each nation's life expectancy at birth. We see that the people of first-ranked Norway have a life expectancy that is nearly 33 years longer than the people of last-ranked Democratic Republic of the Congo.

TABLE 4.1 Human Development Index (HDI)

HDI Rank	Country	HDI Value	GNI per Capita Rank	Life Expectancy at Birth (Years)
Very High Human Development				
1	Norway	0.943	7	81.1
4	United States	0.910	10	78.5
6	Canada	0.908	16	81.0
9	Germany	0.905	17	80.4
11	Switzerland	0.903	11	82.3
12	Japan	0.901	23	83.4
20	France	0.884	24	81.5
28	United Kingdom	0.863	21	80.2
45	Argentina	0.797	54	75.9
High Human Development				
57	Mexico	0.770	59	77.0
66	Russia	0.755	53	68.8
84	Brazil	0.718	77	73.5
Medium Human Development				
101	China	0.687	94	73.5
118	Botswana	0.633	62	53.2
123	South Africa	0.619	79	52.8
Low Human Development				
172	Afghanistan	0.398	159	48.7
187	Congo, DPR	0.286	186	48.4

Source: Based on data obtained from *Human Development Report 2011* (New York: United Nations Development Programme, 2011), Table 1, available at www.undp.org.

GLOBAL SUSTAINABILITY   Public Health Goes Global

Beyond the human suffering, three communicable diseases put a drag on economic development and social sustainability.

- **HIV/AIDS.** This disease has killed nearly as many people as the plague that struck fourteenth-century Europe. AIDS has already killed at least 22 million worldwide, and at least 40 million are infected with HIV. In Africa alone, 20 million have died and 30 million are infected. The disease has cut GDP growth by 2.6 percent in some African countries and could *decrease* South Africa's average household income by 8 percent.
- **Tuberculosis.** Each year, tuberculosis (TB) kills 1.7 million people and sickens another 8 million. More than 90 percent of TB cases occur in low- and lower-middle-income countries across Southeast Asia, Eastern Europe, and sub-Saharan Africa. TB is on the rise because of economic hardship, broken health systems, and the emergence of drug-resistant TB. This disease depletes the incomes of the poorest nations by about $12 billion.
- **Malaria.** Each year, malaria kills one million people and indirectly causes the deaths of up to three million. Malaria is prevalent in Vietnam's Mekong Delta, central Africa, and Brazil's Amazon Basin. Central and sub-Saharan Africa account

for 90 percent of all malaria deaths (mostly children and pregnant women) and is where around 20 percent of all children die of malaria before age five. In the worst-affected African nations, malaria costs about 1.3 percent of GDP.
- **The Challenge.** To combat *HIV/AIDS*, rich nations could donate money to train doctors and nurses in poor nations and could invest more in research. To battle *tuberculosis,* more aid money could purchase drugs that cost just $10 per person for the full six-to-eight-month treatment. To fight *malaria,* better distribution of insecticide-treated bed nets could reach the 98 percent of Africa's children who do not sleep under such nets.
- **Want to Know More?** Visit the Global Business Coalition (www.gbchealth.org); the Global Fund to fight AIDS, Tuberculosis, and Malaria (www.theglobalfund.org); the Malaria Foundation International (www.malaria.org); and the World Health Organization TB site (www.who.int/gtb).

Source: "Altogether Now," *The Economist* (www.economist.com), June 3, 2010; Tom Randall, "J&J, Sanofi, Pfizer Speed Testing for New Tuberculosis Drug," *Bloomberg Businessweek* (www.businessweek.com), March 18, 2010; "Twenty-Five Years of AIDS," *The Economist*, June 3, 2006, pp. 24–25; Malaria Foundation International (www.malaria.org), various reports.

Unlike other measures we have discussed, the HDI looks beyond financial wealth. By stressing the human aspects of economic development, it demonstrates that high national income alone does not guarantee human progress—although the importance of national income should not be underestimated. Countries need money to build good schools, provide quality health care, support environmentally friendly industries, and underwrite other programs designed to improve the quality of life.

The spread of communicable diseases in the world's poorest nations is especially worrying. These diseases cause human and economic loss, social disintegration, and political instability. The health care costs required to combat such diseases can significantly impair efforts toward sustainable development. To read about the costs of three particularly lethal diseases, see the Global Sustainability feature, titled "Public Health Goes Global."

Classifying Countries

Nations are commonly classified as being *developed, newly industrialized,* or *developing*. These classifications are based on indicators such as national production, the portion of the economy devoted to agriculture, the amount of exports in the form of industrial goods, and overall economic structure. There is no single, agreed-on list of countries in each category, however, and borderline countries are often classified differently in different listings. Let's take a closer look at each of these classifications.

DEVELOPED COUNTRIES Countries that are highly industrialized and highly efficient, and whose people enjoy a high quality of life, are **developed countries**. People in developed countries usually receive the finest health care and benefit from the best educational systems in the world. Most developed nations also support aid programs for helping poorer nations to improve their economies and standards of living. Countries in this category include Australia, Canada, Japan, New Zealand, the United States, and all western European nations.

NEWLY INDUSTRIALIZED COUNTRIES Countries that have recently increased the portion of their national production and exports derived from industrial operations are **newly industrialized countries (NICs)**. The NICs are located primarily in Asia and Latin America. Most listings of

developed country
Country that is highly industrialized and highly efficient, and whose people enjoy a high quality of life.

newly industrialized country (NIC)
Country that has recently increased the portion of its national production and exports derived from industrial operations.

NICs include Asia's "four tigers" (Hong Kong, South Korea, Singapore, and Taiwan), Brazil, China, India, Malaysia, Mexico, South Africa, and Thailand. Depending on the pivotal criteria used for classification, a number of other countries could be placed in this category, including Argentina, Brunei, Chile, the Czech Republic, Hungary, Indonesia, the Philippines, Poland, Russia, Slovakia, Turkey, and Vietnam.

When we combine newly industrialized countries with countries that have the potential to become newly industrialized, we arrive at a category often called **emerging markets**. Generally, emerging markets have developed some (but not all) of the operations and export capabilities associated with NICs. Debate continues, however, over the defining characteristics of such classifications as *newly industrialized country* and *emerging market*.

emerging markets
Newly industrialized countries plus those with the potential to become newly industrialized.

DEVELOPING COUNTRIES Nations with the poorest infrastructures and lowest personal incomes are called **developing countries** (also called *less-developed countries*). These countries often rely heavily on one or a few sectors of production, such as agriculture, mineral mining, or oil drilling. They might show potential for becoming newly industrialized countries, but they typically lack the necessary resources and skills to do so. Most lists of developing countries include many nations in Africa, the Middle East, and the poorest formerly communist nations in Eastern Europe and Asia.

developing country
Nation that has a poor infrastructure and extremely low personal incomes. Also called less-developed countries.

Developing countries (and NICs as well) are sometimes characterized by a high degree of **technological dualism**—use of the latest technologies in some sectors of the economy coupled with the use of outdated technologies in others. By contrast, developed countries typically incorporate the latest technological advancements in all manufacturing sectors.

technological dualism
Use of the latest technologies in some sectors of the economy coupled with the use of outdated technologies in other sectors.

QUICK STUDY 4

1. Explain the value of the *Human Development Index (HDI)* in measuring a nation's level of development.
2. Identify the main characteristics of (a) *developed countries,* (b) *newly industrialized countries,* (c) *emerging markets,* and (d) *developing countries.*

Economic Transition

Over the past two decades, countries with centrally planned economies have been remaking themselves in the image of stronger market economies. This process, called **economic transition**, involves changing a nation's fundamental economic organization and creating entirely new free-market institutions. Some nations take transition further than others do, but the process typically involves several key reform measures:

economic transition
Process by which a nation changes its fundamental economic organization and creates new free-market institutions.

- Stabilizing the economy, reducing budget deficits, and expanding credit availability
- Allowing prices to reflect supply and demand
- Legalizing private business, selling state-owned companies, and supporting property rights
- Reducing barriers to trade and investment and allowing currency convertibility

Obstacles to Transition

Transition from central planning to free-market economics generates tremendous international business opportunities. Yet, difficulties arising from years of socialist economic principles hampered progress from the start, and some countries still endure high unemployment rates. Let's examine the key remaining obstacles for countries in transition: lack of managerial expertise, shortage of capital, cultural differences, and environmental degradation.

LACK OF MANAGERIAL EXPERTISE In central planning, there was little need for production, distribution, and marketing strategies or for trained individuals to devise them. Central planners decided all aspects of the nation's commercial activities. There was no need to investigate consumer wants and no need for market research. Little thought was given to product pricing or to the need for experts in operations, inventory, distribution, or logistics. Factory managers at government-owned firms had only to meet production requirements set by central planners. In fact, some products rolled off assembly lines merely to be stacked outside the factory because knowing where they were to go after production—and who took them there—was not the factory manager's job.

Recent years, however, are seeing higher-quality management in transition countries. Reasons for this trend include improved education, opportunities to study and work abroad, and changes in work habits caused by companies investing locally. Some managers from former communist nations are even finding managerial opportunities in Western Europe and the United States with large multinational corporations.

SHORTAGE OF CAPITAL Not surprisingly, economic transition is expensive. To facilitate the process and ease the pain, governments usually spend a great deal of money to:

- Develop a telecommunications and infrastructure system, including highways, bridges, rail networks, and sometimes subways.
- Create financial institutions, including stock markets and a banking system.
- Educate people in the ways of market economics.

The governments of many countries in transition cannot afford all the investments required of them. Outside sources of capital are available, however, including national and international companies, other governments, and international financial institutions, such as the World Bank, the International Monetary Fund (IMF), and the Asian Development Bank. Some transition countries owe substantial amounts of money to international lenders, but this is becoming less of a problem today than it was earlier in the era of transition economies.[13]

CULTURAL DIFFERENCES Economic transition and reform make deep cultural impressions on a nation's people. As we saw in Chapter 2, some cultures are more open to change than others. Likewise, certain cultures welcome economic change more easily than others do. Transition replaces dependence on the government with greater emphasis on individual responsibility, incentives, and rights. But sudden deep cuts in welfare payments, unemployment benefits, and guaranteed government jobs can present a major shock to a nation's people.

Importing modern management practices into the culture of a transition country can be difficult. South Korea's Daewoo Motors (www.daewoo.com) faced a culture clash when it entered Central Europe. Korea's management system is based on a rigid hierarchical structure and an intense work ethic. Managers at Daewoo's car plants in South Korea arrived early for work to stand and greet workers at the company gates. But problems arose when Daewoo's managers did not fully comprehend the culture at its factories in Central Europe. Daewoo bridged the cultural and workplace gaps by sending central European workers to staff assembly lines in Korea and sent Korean managers and technicians to work in Central and Eastern Europe.

ENVIRONMENTAL DEGRADATION The economic and social policies of former communist governments in Central and Eastern Europe were disastrous for the natural environment. The direct effects of environmental destruction were evident in high levels of sickness and disease, including asthma, blood deficiencies, and cancer—which lowered productivity in the workplace. Countries in transition often suffer periods during which the negative effects of a market economy seem to outweigh its benefits. In other words, it is hard to enjoy a larger paycheck when smokestacks are polluting the air and the parks and rivers are polluted. But as transition continues, the wider population begins to enjoy the benefits of a market economy.

Emerging Market Focus: Russia

Russia's experience with communism began in 1917. For the next 75 years, factories, distribution, and all other facets of operations, as well as the prices of labor, capital, and products, were controlled by the government. While China was experimenting with private farm ownership and a limited market-price system, Russia and other nations in the Soviet Union remained staunchly communist under a system of complete government ownership. The total absence of market institutions meant that, unlike China, Russia endured massive political change along with economic reform when it embarked on its transition.

ROUGH TRANSITION In the 1980s, the former Soviet Union entered a new era of freedom of thought, freedom of expression, and economic restructuring. For the first time since 1917, people could speak freely about their lives under economic socialism, and speak freely they did.

MANAGER'S BRIEFCASE   Russian Rules of the Game

Although business in Russia can be brutal at times, some go-getting entrepreneurs and brave managers are venturing into this rugged land. If you are one of them, or just an interested observer, here are a few pointers on doing business in Russia:

- **Getting Started.** A visit to your country's local chamber of commerce in Russia should be high on your list. The best organized and managed of these hold regularly scheduled luncheons at which you can make contacts with Russians and others wanting to do business. They might also offer programs on getting acquainted with the business climate in Russia. Many businesses get started in Moscow, St. Petersburg, or Vladivostok, depending in part on their line of business.
- **Be Adventurous.** The kind of person who will succeed in Russia thrives on adventure and enjoys a challenge. He or she also should not demand predictability in day-to-day activities—Russia is anything but predictable. Initially, knowledge of Russian is helpful, though not essential, but eventual proficiency will be

necessary. Prior experience working and living in Eastern Europe would be a big plus.

- **Office Space.** Doing business in Russia demands a personal touch. Locating an office in Russia is crucial if you eventually want to receive income from your operations. Your office does not need to be a suite off Red Square. Almost any local address will do, and a nice flat can double as an office at the start. For business services, upscale hotels commonly have business centers in them. Eventually, renting an average Russian-style office would be more than adequate.
- **Making Deals.** Business in Russia takes time and patience. The Russian negotiating style, like the country itself, is tough and ever changing. During negotiations, emotional outbursts, walkouts, or threats to walk out from your Russian counterparts should not be unexpected. Finally, signed contracts in Russia are not always followed to the letter, as your Russian associate may view new circumstances as a chance to renegotiate terms. All in all, the personalities of individuals involved in business dealings count for much in Russia.

People vented their frustrations over a general lack of consumer goods, poor-quality products, and long lines at banks and grocery stores.

But transition away from government ownership and central planning has been challenging. Except for politicians, bureaucrats, and wealthy businesspeople (called "oligarchs" in Russia), ordinary people are having difficulty maintaining their standard of living and affording many basic items. Some Russians are doing well financially because they were factory managers under the old system and retained their jobs in the new system. Others have turned to the black market to amass personal wealth. Still others are working hard to build legitimate companies but find themselves forced into making "protection" payments to organized crime.

An opaque legal system, rampant corruption, and shifting business laws make Russia a place where non-Russian businesspeople must operate cautiously. Yet some ambitious managers and foreign entrepreneurs are not deterred by such obstacles. For some insights on how to do business in today's Russia, see the Manager's Briefcase feature, titled "Russian Rules of the Game."

CHALLENGES AHEAD FOR RUSSIA As in so many other transitional economies, Russia needs to foster *managerial talent*. Years of central planning delayed the development of managerial skills needed in a market-based economy. Russian managers must improve their skills in every facet of management practice, including financial control, research and development, human resource management, and marketing strategy.

Political instability, especially in the form of intensified nationalist sentiment, is another potential threat to progress. Russia and Georgia had a military confrontation in the summer of 2008 over two of Georgia's restive republics that wanted to align themselves closer to Russia. Strong ethnic and nationalist sentiments in the region can cause misunderstandings to spiral out of control quickly. The lack of security for Russia's nuclear weapons stockpile is also a potential cause of instability. These weapons in the hands of terrorists would threaten global security.

An *unstable investment climate* is another concern within the international business community. Tense uneasiness characterizes relations between Russia's government and its business community. The uneasiness stems from the Russian government's attacks on both business owners who disagree with official policy and on businesses that it wants to control.

The root of many of Russia's problems appears to be *corrupt law enforcement*. Officials of the government, such as the Russian Interior Ministry, are accused of raiding the offices of companies for documents and computers. Records are then falsified and signatures forged to make it appear that another company—one controlled by government officials—has massively overpaid taxes and is due a government refund. Meanwhile, the owners and managers of the raided businesses often find themselves behind Russian prison bars.[14]

The Russian government confiscated oil giant Yukos and threw its chief, Mikhail Khodorkovsky, in jail on charges of fraud, embezzlement, and tax evasion. Observers of events in Russia say that Khodorkovsky's problems were based in his refusal to bow to Russia's bureaucrats and that he ran Yukos as if it were a private company. He also tried to create a new class of people in Russia who would one day push for political reforms there by financing boarding schools for orphans, computer classes for village schools, and civil-society programs for journalists and politicians. His actions clearly made him a threat to the state.[15] If Russia truly wishes to become a location of choice for international companies, it will need to meddle less in business and begin to safeguard property rights.

QUICK STUDY 5

1. What are several reform measures involved in *economic transition*?
2. Describe some of the remaining obstacles to businesses in transitional economies.
3. Explain Russia's experience with economic transition.

BOTTOM LINE FOR BUSINESS

This completes our three-chapter coverage of national business environments. This chapter showed us that economic freedom tends to generate higher standards of living. This relationship is causing mixed economies to remove unnecessary regulation and government interference. Formerly centrally planned economies continue free-market reforms in order to drive domestic entrepreneurial activity and attract international investors. These trends are changing the face of global capitalism. Two topics are likely to dominate conversations on development—the race between China and India and the productivity gap between the United States and Europe.

Economic Development in China versus India

Both China and India have immense potential for growth, and it is only a matter of time before each has a middle class larger than the entire U.S. population. Whether the organic-led path of India or the investment-led path of China is best for a particular nation depends on that nation's circumstances.

Every nation on earth has so far followed a path to development that relied on its natural resources and/or its relatively cheap labor—the model China is following. China's top-down approach to development and India's bottom-up approach reflect their political systems: India is a democracy, whereas China is not. Although China is growing rapidly, it needs homegrown entrepreneurs and Western-style managerial skills to take it to the next level of global competitiveness.

If India can achieve sustained economic growth, it will become the first developing nation to advance economically by relying on the brainpower of its people. India's growth came largely from native competitive firms in cutting-edge, knowledge-based industries. Although India has a long reputation for high taxes and burdensome regulations, it also has had the foundations of a market economy, such as private enterprise, democratic government, and Western accounting practices. India also has a relatively advanced legal system, fairly efficient capital markets, and many talented entrepreneurs.

Productivity in the United States versus Europe

Productivity growth is a key driver of living standards in any nation. Although productivity growth in Europe kept pace with that in the United States for decades, it has fallen behind in recent years. But why is there a productivity gap at all?

Several explanations have been proposed. First, despite its benefits, information technology (IT) spending in Europe lags behind that in the United States. Europeans may be discouraged from spending on IT for reasons related to European business law. Second, stronger labor laws in Europe relative to the United States make it more difficult and costly to shed workers. Thus, even if European companies invest in IT to increase labor productivity, overall productivity gains may be hampered by their inability to rid themselves of excess workers. Third, whereas the U.S. tech sector is a big driver behind higher U.S. productivity growth, the tech sector in Europe is far smaller by comparison. Fourth, Europe spends far less overall on R&D, even though spending on R&D is a big boost to productivity growth.

Strong productivity growth means higher profits, better living standards, and stable prices. Many European officials are calling for a greater shift toward free-market reform to boost productivity. European officials understand that robust productivity growth is the only way for their citizens to close the gap with their U.S. counterparts.

Chapter Summary

MyManagementLab
Go to **mymanagementlab.com** to complete the problem marked with this icon .

1. **Describe what is meant by a centrally planned economy and explain why its use is declining.**
   - In a *centrally planned economy,* the government owns land, factories, and other economic resources and plans nearly all economic-related activities.
   - The philosophy of central planning stresses the group over individual well-being and strives for economic and social equality.
   - One reason for the decline of central planning is that scarce resources were wasted because central planners paid little attention to product quality and buyers' needs.
   - Second, a lack of incentives to innovate resulted in little or no economic growth and consistently low standards of living.
   - Third, central planners realized that other economic systems were achieving far higher growth rates for other countries.
   - Fourth, consumers became fed up with a lack of basic necessities such as adequate food, housing, and health care.

2. **Identify the main characteristics of a mixed economy and explain the emphasis on privatization.**
   - In a *mixed economy,* land, factories, and other economic resources are split between private and government ownership.
   - In mixed economies, governments tend to control economic sectors crucial to national security and long-term stability.
   - Proponents of mixed economies say that a successful economic system not only must be efficient and innovative, but also must protect society from unchecked individualism and organizational greed.
   - Many mixed economies are engaging in *privatization* (the sale of government-owned economic resources) in order to become more efficient in how they use resources.

3. **Explain how a market economy functions and identify its distinguishing features.**
   - In a *market economy,* private individuals or businesses own the majority of land, factories, and other economic resources.
   - Economic decisions in a market economy are influenced by the interplay of *supply* and *demand.*
   - Market economics is rooted in the belief that individual concerns are paramount and that the group benefits when individuals receive proper incentives and rewards.
   - To function smoothly, a market economy requires free choice (in buyers' purchasing options), free enterprise (in producers' competitive decisions), and price flexibility (reflecting supply and demand).
   - Government's role in a market economy involves enforcing antitrust laws, preserving property rights, providing a stable fiscal and monetary environment, and preserving political stability.

4. **Describe the different ways to measure a nation's level of development.**
   - *Economic development* refers to the economic well-being of one nation's people compared with that of another nation's people.
   - One method for gauging economic development is *national production,* which includes measures such as *gross national product* and *gross domestic product.*
   - A second method is *purchasing power parity (PPP),* which refers to the relative ability of two countries' currencies to buy the same "basket" of goods in those two countries.
   - PPP is used to correct international comparisons made at official exchange rates.
   - A third method is the United Nations' *human development index (HDI),* which measures the extent to which a people's needs are satisfied and addressed equally across the population.

5. **Discuss the process of economic transition and identify the obstacles for business.**
   - *Economic transition* is the process whereby a nation changes its fundamental economic organization to create free-market institutions.

- Economic transition typically involves several reform measures: (1) stabilizing the economy; (2) instituting market-based pricing; (3) legalizing business, privatizing state-run businesses, and supporting property rights; and (4) removing barriers to trade, investment, and currency flows.
- One obstacle to transition is a *lack of managerial expertise* because central planners made virtually all business decisions.
- A second obstacle is a *shortage of capital* to pay for new communications and infrastructure, new financial institutions, and education.
- A third obstacle is *cultural differences* between transition economies and the West that can make introducing modern management practices difficult.
- A fourth obstacle is *environmental degradation* that can lower productivity due to poor health conditions.

Talk It Over

1. The Internet has penetrated many aspects of business and culture in developed countries, but it is barely available in many poor countries. Do you think this technology will widen the economic development gap between rich and poor countries? Why or why not? Is there a way for developing countries to use such technologies as tools for economic development?

2. Imagine that you are the director of a major international lending institution supported by funds from member countries. What one area in newly industrialized and developing economies would be your priority for receiving development aid? Do you suspect that any member country will be politically opposed to aid in this area? Why or why not?

Teaming Up

1. **Debate Project.** In this project, two groups of four students each will debate the benefits and drawbacks of both market and mixed economies. After the first student from each side has spoken, the second student will question the opposing side's arguments, looking for holes and inconsistencies. The third student will attempt to answer these arguments. A fourth student will present a summary of each side's arguments. Finally, the class will vote on which team has offered the more compelling argument.

⭐2. **Market Entry Strategy Project.** This exercise corresponds to the *MESP* online simulation. For the country your team is researching, what type of economic system does it have? Has it always had this type of economic system? Is it a developed, newly industrializing, emerging, or developing country? How does it rank on the various measures of economic development? Has it undergone any form of economic transition within the past 20 years? If so, how has that transition affected the culture and the country's political, legal, and economic systems? Integrate your findings into your completed *MESP* report.

Key Terms

centrally planned economy (p. 106)
demand (p. 111)
developed country (p. 121)
developing country (also called *less-developed country*) (p. 122)
economic development (p. 113)
economic system (p. 106)

economic transition (p. 122)
emerging markets (p. 122)
human development index (HDI) (p. 120)
market economy (p. 111)
mixed economy (p. 110)
newly industrialized country (NIC) (p. 121)

privatization (p. 111)
purchasing power (p. 117)
purchasing power parity (PPP) (p. 117)
supply (p. 111)
technological dualism (p. 122)

Take It to the Web

1. **Video Report.** Visit this book's channel on YouTube (www.YouTube.com/MyIBvideos). Click on "Videos" near the top of the page, and click on the set of videos labeled "Ch 04: Economics and Emerging Markets." Watch one video from the list, and then summarize it in a half-page report. Reflecting on the contents of this chapter, which components of economic systems and development can you identify in the video? How might a company engaged in international business act on the information contained in the video?

2. **Website Report.** Governments across Western Europe are privatizing state-owned companies, and nations in Eastern Europe are transitioning toward market-based economies.

   Go to the European Union (EU) website (www.europa.eu), and search for information regarding its progress on issues presented in this chapter. Possible topics include privatization, economic and social development, global competition, and national infrastructure. For the topic(s) of your choice, what are the EU's goals? What specific policies will help the EU achieve those goals? Does the EU directly address the challenges (such as increased competition) that globalization presents to its companies?

   Some countries (such as Estonia, Hungary, and Poland) outperformed others (such as Bulgaria and Romania) during their post-communist transitions. For your topic(s), what specific policies does the EU have in place to help nations in transition develop? Identify as many economic, social, and cultural efforts as you can.

Ethical Challenges

1. You are the CEO of a Canadian–Chinese joint venture that operates in China. Your Chinese partner is the People's Liberation Army (PLA). The PLA has built a sprawling network of businesses that do everything from raise pigs to run airlines and hospitals, mine coal, manage hotels, and operate paging and cellular networks. As a business conglomerate, the PLA does business with international investors. Some argue that a large portion of foreign investment going to China is with companies and cartels controlled by the Chinese military. Others argue that it's easy to read too much into the PLA's foray into business. They point out that there is little centralized coordination among the thousands of businesses with military affiliations. Some companies are run by retired officers, others by civilians. As the CEO of the joint organization, do you have any ethical concerns about partnering with the PLA? If so, what are they? Suppose a clash between pro-democracy demonstrators and the PLA turns bloody. How would this turn of events affect business relations with your PLA partner? Are the ethical issues of partnering with the Chinese military any different from those that arise from exporting to China? Why or why not?

2. You are the managing director of your U.S. firm's subsidiary in southern France. The social-welfare states of Western Europe were founded after the Second World War with specific ethical considerations in mind: reduce social and economic inequality, improve living standards for the poor, and provide nearly free health care for all. Now many of these countries have trimmed social-welfare provisions and increased their reliance on market forces. Do you think that the ethical concerns of half a century ago are a thing of the past? Or do you feel that market reforms will simply re-create the conditions that motivated the development of the welfare state in the first place? What can you do as a manager to alleviate workers' fears that a more open economy will reduce their social safety net?

MyManagementLab

Go to **mymanagementlab.com** for Auto-graded writing questions as well as the following Assisted-graded writing questions:

4-1. Two students are discussing the pros and cons of different measures of economic development. "GDP per capita," declares the first, "is the only true measure of how developed a country's economy is." The second student counters, "I disagree. The only true measure of a country's economic development is its people's quality of life, regardless of its GDP." Why is each of these students incorrect?

4-2. Mymanagementlab Only – comprehensive writing assignment for this chapter.

Practicing International Management Case

Cuba Comes Off Its Sugar High

When the Soviet Union still existed, Cuba would barter sugar with its communist allies in return for oil and other goods. But when the Soviet Union crumbled in 1989, Cuba had to say good-bye to its preferential barter rates and Soviet subsidies. The only option left to Cuba's leader, Fidel Castro, was to sell the nation's sugar on the open market. But whereas sugar exports earned Cuba $5 billion in 1990, they earned a paltry $20 million in 2006. Production fell from a peak of more than eight million tons in 1989 to around one million tons in 2010. With decreasing revenues on world markets, falling production, and inefficient sugar mills that guzzle expensive oil, Castro had no choice but to shut down about half the island-nation's mills. Today, Cuba remains a *net sugar importer,* and power is now in the hands of Fidel's brother, Raul.

With the remaining state-owned industrial dinosaurs wheezing away and the economy under immense strain, the government opened up key state industries to non-Cuban investment. As a result, joint ventures became a key plank in the effort to prop up Cuba through limited economic reforms. The money came chiefly from Canada, Mexico, and Europe—all of whom benefited from the absence of Cuba's neighbor and nemesis, the United States, which has maintained a trade embargo against Cuba since 1960. Much of the investment occurred in another commodity that Cuba has to offer the world—nickel. Cuba holds 30 percent of the world's reserves of nickel, which is used in stainless steel and other alloys, and it exports 75 percent of its nickel to Europe. One of the biggest mining firms active in Cuba today is Canada's Sherritt International Corporation (www.sherritt.com). Sherritt's flag flies outside the island's biggest nickel mine, and Sherritt rigs are reviving output from old oil fields. After turning around the ailing nickel mine at Moa, Sherritt received government approval to develop beach resorts and beef up communications and transport networks.

Although international concerns like Sherritt are free to invest in Cuba, they face some harsh realities and restrictions. Cuba is burdened with complex and contradictory rules and regulations. And once foreigners begin to figure out the rules, the government changes them. "There are times when the Cubans seem to go out of their way to create obstacles," complained one European businessman. "They need us, we can do business here, so I don't understand what the problem is." But it seemed Cuba's government was going to do little to help.

Ricardo Elizondo came to Cuba from Mexico to help manage his company's stake in ETECSA, Cuba's national telecommunications firm. Elizondo reports that anyone who wants to do business in Cuba must accept the reality of partnership with a socialist state. Cuba lacks a legal system to enforce commercial contracts, it lacks a banking system to offer credit, and there are no private-property rights. One thing the government doesn't lack is plenty of labor laws—and those are onerous. Non-Cuban partners cannot hire, fire, or even pay workers directly. They must pay the government to provide laborers who, in turn, are paid only a fraction of these payments. Human rights group Freedom House (www.freedomhouse.org) says one company paid the Cuban government $9,500 per year per worker, but the workers received only $120 to $144 per year. Meanwhile, there are reports that an average of 1.2 buildings collapse in Central Havana every day.

Why do companies investing in Cuba put up with such restrictions? For one thing, they are getting a great return on their investment. "Cuba's assets are incredibly cheap, and the potential return is huge," says Frank Mersch, VP at Toronto's Altamira Management (www.altamira.com), which holds 11 percent of Sherritt. Analysts say that Cuba is offering outsiders deals with rates of return up to 80 percent a year. Moreover, international investors acknowledge that the Castro brothers' regime cannot last forever. In a post-Castro era, the United States may end its embargo, in which case, property prices would soar. Companies such as Sherritt and ETECSA, who stepped in first, will have gained a valuable toehold in what could be a vibrant market economy.

Thinking Globally

1. Why do you think the Cuban government requires non-Cuban businesses to hire and pay workers only through the government? Do you think it is ethical for non-Cuban businesses to enter into partnerships with the Cuban government? Why or why not?

2. Do some research on Cuba, and describe a scenario for economic transition in the event that the current regime collapses. How do you think transition to a market economy in Cuba would differ from the experiences of Russia and China?

3. The United States has enacted a law that permits U.S. companies to sue companies from other nations that traffic in the property of U.S. firms nationalized by Cuba. The law also empowers the U.S. government to deny entry visas to the executives of such firms as well as their families. Why does the United States maintain such a hard line against doing business with Cuba? Do you think this embargo is in the United States' best interests? Why or why not?

Source: Archibald Ritter, "Cuba in the 2010s: Creative Reform or Geriatric Paralysis?" *Focal Point,* April 2010, pp. 12–13; "U.S. Is $500 Million Supermarket to Cuba," CNBC website (www.cnbc.com), May 28, 2010; Steve LeVine and Geri Smith, "New Cuba Policy Is No Business Home Run," *Bloomberg Businessweek* (www.businessweek.com), April 15, 2009; *Cuba* Blog, Foreign Policy Association, (cuba.foreignpolicyblogs.com), various reports and data.

International Trade

LEARNING OBJECTIVES

After studying this chapter, you should be able to

1. Describe the relationship between international trade volume and world output, and identify overall trade patterns.

2. Describe mercantilism and explain its impact on world powers and their colonies.

3. Explain the theories of absolute advantage and comparative advantage.

4. Explain the factor proportions and international product life cycle theories.

5. Explain the new trade and national competitive advantage theories.

A Look Back

Chapters 2, 3, and 4 examined cultural, political, legal, and economic differences among countries. We covered these differences early in the book because of their important influence on international business activities.

A Look at This Chapter

This chapter begins our study of the international trade and investment environment. We explore the oldest form of international business activity—international trade. We discuss the benefits and volume of international trade and explore the major theories that attempt to explain why trade occurs.

A Look Ahead

Chapter 6 explains business–government trade relations. We explore both the motives and methods of government intervention in trade relations and how the global trading system works to promote free trade.

FROM BENTONVILLE TO BEIJING

BENTONVILLE, Arkansas—Walmart (www.walmart.com) first became an international company in 1991 when it built a new store near Mexico City, Mexico. Today, Walmart has around 3,900 stores in the United States and more than 4,200 stores in 15 other countries. With nearly $447 billion in sales globally, Walmart is one of the world's largest companies—yet it is based in a state in which chickens outnumber people. Pictured here is a Walmart store in Beijing, China.

Ambitious global expansion by Walmart (and similar firms) is helping boost international trade. To win over customers as it extends its reach around the world, Walmart relies on the slogan "Save Money. Live Better." To fulfill its promise and deliver the lowest priced goods, Walmart sources inexpensive merchandise from low-cost production locations such as China. The discount retailer has played a big part in increasing Chinese imports to the United States in recent years. In fact, if Walmart were a country, it would be China's sixth-largest trading partner. The actions of Walmart and other global firms have propelled world exports of goods and services to record levels.

Source: TPG Top Photo

Growth in international trade is increasing interdependence between China and the rest of the world. Walmart and others are quickly transforming China into the world's factory. China's international trade is expanding at a rate that is about two to three times faster than trade growth for the rest of the world. Around 18 percent of Japan's imports come from China, and about 12 percent of all goods imported by the United States are Chinese-made. Yet, China's imports are also growing. From the United States, China imports everything from steel that feeds its booming construction industry to x-ray machines and other devices to improve its people's health. China is also becoming a larger market for Walmart and other Western consumer-goods businesses. As you read this chapter, consider why nations trade and how the ambitions of firms such as Walmart are driving growth in world trade.[1]

People around the world are accustomed to purchasing goods and services produced in other countries. In fact, many consumers get their first taste of another country's culture through merchandise purchased from that country. Chanel No. 5 perfume (www.chanel.com) evokes the romanticism of France. The fine artwork on Imari porcelain conveys the Japanese attention to detail and quality. And American Eagle jeans (www.ae.com) portray the casual lifestyle of people in the United States.

In this chapter, we explore international trade in goods and services. We begin by examining the benefits, volume, and patterns of international trade. We then explore a number of important theories that attempt to explain why nations trade with one another.

Overview of International Trade

international trade
Purchase, sale, or exchange of goods and services across national borders.

The purchase, sale, or exchange of goods and services across national borders is called **international trade**. This is in contrast to domestic trade, which occurs between different states, regions, or cities within a country.

In recent years, nations that embrace globalization are seeing trade grow in importance for their economies. One way to measure the importance of trade to a nation is to examine the volume of an economy's trade relative to its total output. Map 5.1 on pages 134–135 shows each nation's trade volume as a share of its gross domestic product (GDP). Trade as a share of GDP is defined as the sum of exports and imports (of goods and services) divided by GDP. Recall that GDP is the value of all goods and services produced by a domestic economy over a one-year period. Map 5.1 demonstrates that the value of trade passing through some nations' borders actually exceeds the amount of goods and services they produce (the "over 100%" category).

Benefits of International Trade

International trade is opening doors to new entrepreneurial opportunities across the globe. It also provides a country's people with a greater choice of goods and services. For example, because Finland has a cool climate, it cannot be expected to grow cotton. But it can sell paper and other products made from lumber (which it has in abundance) to the United States. Finland can then use the proceeds from the sale of products derived from lumber to buy U.S.–grown Pima cotton. Thus, people in Finland get cotton they otherwise would not have. Likewise, although the United States has vast forests, the wood-based products from Finland might be of a certain quality that fills a gap in the U.S. marketplace.

International trade is an important engine for job creation in many countries. The U.S. Department of Commerce (www.commerce.gov) calculates that for every $1 billion increase in exports, 22,800 jobs are created in the United States. It is also estimated that 12 million U.S. jobs depend on exports and that these jobs pay on average from 13 to 18 percent more than those not related to international trade.[2] Expanded trade benefits other countries similarly.

Volume of International Trade

The value and volume of international trade continues to increase. Today, world merchandise exports are valued at more than $14 trillion, and service exports are worth more than $3 trillion.[3] Table 5.1 shows the world's largest exporters of merchandise and services. Perhaps not surprisingly, the United States ranks first in commercial services exports and ranks second in merchandise exports (behind China).

Most of world merchandise trade is composed of trade in manufactured goods. The dominance of manufactured goods in the trade of merchandise has persisted over time and will likely continue to do so. The reason is its growth is much faster than trade in the two other classifications of merchandise—mining and agricultural products. Trade in services accounts for around 20 percent of total world trade. Although the importance of trade in services is growing for many nations, it tends to be relatively more important for the world's richest countries.

TRADE AND WORLD OUTPUT The level of world output in any given year influences the level of international trade in that year. Slower world economic output slows the volume of international trade, and higher output propels greater trade. Trade slows in times of economic recession because when people are less certain about their own financial futures they buy fewer domestic

TABLE 5.1 World's Top Exporters

	World's Top Merchandise Exporters				World's Top Service Exporters		
Rank	Exporter	Value (U.S. $ billions)	Share of World Total (%)	Rank	Exporter	Value (U.S. $ billions)	Share of World Total (%)
1	China	1,578	10.4	1	United States	518	14.0
2	United States	1,278	8.4	2	Germany	232	6.3
3	Germany	1,269	8.3	3	United Kingdom	227	6.1
4	Japan	770	5.1	4	China	170	4.6
5	Netherlands	573	3.8	5	France	143	3.9
6	France	521	3.4	6	Japan	139	3.8
7	South Korea	466	3.1	7	India	123	3.3
8	Italy	448	2.9	8	Spain	123	3.3
9	Belgium	412	2.7	9	Netherlands	113	3.1
10	United Kingdom	406	2.7	10	Singapore	112	3.0

Source: Based on *International Trade Statistics 2011* (Geneva: World Trade Organization, November 2011), Tables I.8 and I.10, available at www.wto.org.

and imported products. Another reason output and trade move together is that a country in recession also often has a currency that is weak relative to other nations. This makes imports more expensive relative to domestic products. (We discuss the relationship between currency values and trade at length in Chapter 10.) In addition to international trade and world output moving in lockstep fashion, trade has consistently grown faster than output.

International Trade Patterns

Exploring the volume of international trade and world output provides useful insights into the international trade environment, but it does not tell us who trades with whom. It does not reveal whether trade occurs primarily between the world's richest nations or whether there is significant trade activity involving poorer nations.

Customs agencies in most countries record the destination of exports, the source of imports, and the physical quantities and values of goods crossing their borders. Although this type of data is sometimes misleading, customs data does reflect overall trade patterns among nations. For example, governments sometimes deliberately distort the reporting of trade in military equipment or other sensitive goods. In other cases, extensive trade in unofficial (underground) economies can distort the real picture of trade between nations.

Large ocean-going cargo vessels are needed to support these patterns in international trade and deliver merchandise from one shore to another. In fact, Greek and Japanese merchant ships own more than 30 percent of the world's total capacity (measured in tons shipped, or tonnage) of merchant ships. Yet, global merchant-shipping companies are feeling the pinch of higher oil prices. And as importers must absorb a portion of higher shipping costs, they may begin producing goods closer to home and reduce the need for additional merchant-ship capacity.[4]

WHO TRADES WITH WHOM? There has been a persistent pattern of merchandise trade among nations. Trade between the world's high-income economies accounts for roughly 60 percent of total world merchandise trade. Two-way trade between high-income countries and low- and middle-income nations accounts for about 34 percent of world merchandise trade. Meanwhile, merchandise trade between low- and middle-income nations accounts for only about 6 percent of total world trade. These figures reveal the low purchasing power of the world's poorest nations and indicate their general lack of economic development.

Table 5.2 shows trade data (in percentages) for the major regions of the world economy. What immediately stands out is the number representing intraregional exports for Europe (the intersection of the row and column titled "Europe"). This number tells us that 71 percent of

MAP 5.1
Importance of Trade

OCEAN

R U S S I A

SWEDEN

FINLAND

ESTONIA

LATVIA

RK

LITHUANIA

RUSSIA

BELARUS

POLAND

ANY

CZECH
REP.   SLOVAKIA   UKRAINE

USTRIA

OVENIA   HUNGARY   MOLDOVA

OATIA   ROMANIA

BOSNIA AND
ZEGOVINA   SERBIA AND
MONTENEGRO   BULGARIA

ALY   MACEDONIA

ALBANIA

GREECE   TURKEY

GEORGIA

ARMENIA   AZERBAIJAN

KAZAKHSTAN

MONGOLIA

UZBEKISTAN   KYRGYZSTAN

TURKMENISTAN

TAJIKISTAN

NORTH
KOREA

SOUTH
KOREA

JAPAN

CYPRUS   SYRIA
LEBANON

ISRAEL
JORDAN   IRAQ   IRAN

AFGHANISTAN

PAKISTAN

C H I N A

KUWAIT

TAIWAN

LIBYA   EGYPT

QATAR
UNITED ARAB
EMIRATES

SAUDI
ARABIA   OMAN

NEPAL   BHUTAN

BANGLADESH

I N D I A

MYANMAR
(BURMA)

HONG KONG

PACIFIC

OCEAN

R

CHAD   SUDAN

SUDAN

LAOS

THAILAND   VIETNAM

CAMBODIA

PHILIPPINES

ERITREA   YEMEN

SOUTH
SUDAN

DJIBOUTI

CENTRAL AFRICAN
REPUBLIC

ROON   ETHIOPIA

SOMALIA

SRI
LANKA

BRUNEI

MALAYSIA

CONGO
REPUBLIC   UGANDA

SINGAPORE

CONGO
DEMOCRATIC
REPUBLIC
(ZAIRE)   KENYA

RWANDA
BURUNDI

TANZANIA

INDIAN

OCEAN

I N D O N E S I A

PAPUA
NEW
GUINEA

SOLOMON
ISLANDS

ANGOLA

ZAMBIA   MALAWI

MOZAMBIQUE

VANUATU   FIJI

NAMIBIA   ZIMBABWE

MADAGASCAR   MAURITIUS

RÉUNION

BOTSWANA

SWAZILAND

NEW
CALEDONIA

SOUTH
AFRICA   LESOTHO

A U S T R A L I A

NEW
ZEALAND

Trade as a percent of GDP

◉ over 100%

◉ 75%–100%

◉ 50%–74%

◉ 25%–49%

◉ less than 25%

◯ no data available

TABLE 5.2 Regional Merchandise Trade (Percentage)

Origin	World	North America	South and Central America	Europe	Commonwealth of Independent States	Africa	Middle East	Asia
				Destination				
North America	16.9	48.7	23.9	7.4	5.6	16.8	8.8	17.1
South and Central America	4.0	8.4	25.6	1.7	1.1	2.7	0.8	3.2
Europe	39.4	16.8	18.7	71.0	52.4	36.2	12.1	17.2
Commonwealth of Independent States	2.7	0.6	1.3	3.2	18.6	0.4	0.5	1.8
Africa	3.0	1.7	2.6	3.1	1.5	12.3	3.2	2.7
Middle East	3.8	2.7	2.6	3.0	3.3	3.7	10.0	4.2
Asia	28.4	21.0	23.2	9.3	14.9	24.1	52.6	52.6

Note: Columns do not equal 100.0 due to mathematical rounding and national differences in data recording methods.

Source: Based on *International Trade Statistics 2009* (Geneva: World Trade Organization, November 2009), Table I.5, available at www.wto.org.

Europe's exports are destined for other European nations. Intraregional exports account for more than 52 percent of all exports in Asia and more than 48 percent of exports in North America. This data underscores the rationale behind the creation of the European Union (which we discuss in Chapter 8).

Data in Table 5.2 also reveals each region's contribution to total world merchandise exports. Europe accounts for more than 39 percent, Asia accounts for around 28 percent and North America accounts for nearly 17 percent. Asia's role in merchandise trade will undoubtedly increase as the region's economies continue to expand. Some economists call this century the "Pacific century," referring to the expected growth of Asian economies and the resulting shift in the majority of trade flows from the Atlantic Ocean to the Pacific. It will be increasingly important for managers to understand the varying and rich cultures in Asia. For some pointers on doing business in Pacific Rim nations, see this chapter's Culture Matters feature, titled "Business Culture in the Pacific Rim."

Trade Dependence and Independence

Countries differ in the extent of their trade interdependencies. Some nations depend almost entirely on trade with one other country, whereas some nations depend on no single trading partner. Complete independence was considered desirable from the sixteenth century through much of the eighteenth century. Some remote island nations were completely independent simply because they lacked methods of transportation to engage in trade. But today, isolationism is generally considered undesirable.

Trade between most nations is characterized by a certain degree of interdependency. Companies in advanced nations trade a great deal with companies in other advanced nations. The level of interdependency between pairs of countries often reflects the amount of trade that occurs between a company's subsidiaries in the two nations.

EFFECT ON DEVELOPING AND TRANSITION NATIONS Developing and transition nations that share borders with developed countries are often dependent on their wealthier neighbors. Trade dependency has been a blessing for many Central and Eastern European nations. A large number of joint ventures now bridge the borders between Germany and its neighbors—Germany recently had more than 6,000 joint ventures in Hungary alone. Germany also is the single most important trading partner of the Central and Eastern European nations that recently joined the European Union (www.europa.eu). To gain an advantage over the competition, German firms are combining German technology with relatively low-cost labor in Central and Eastern Europe. For example, Opel (www.opel.com), the German division of General Motors Corporation (www.gm.com), built a $440 million plant in Szentgotthard, Hungary, to make parts for and assemble its Astra hatchbacks destined for export.

CULTURE MATTERS   Business Culture in the Pacific Rim

Asian customers are as diverse as their cultures and aggressive sales tactics do not work. Before visiting these countries, it is helpful for managers to review some general rules:

- *Make Use of Contacts.* Asians prefer to do business with people they know. Cold calls and other direct-contact methods seldom work. Meeting the right people in an Asian company often depends on having the right introduction. If the person with whom you hope to do business respects your intermediary, chances are that he or she will respect you.
- *Carry Bilingual Business Cards.* To make a good first impression, have bilingual cards printed, even though many Asians speak English. It shows both respect for the language and a commitment to doing business in a country. It also translates your title into the local language. Asians generally are not comfortable until they know what your position is and whom you represent.

- *Respect, Harmony, Consensus.* Asian cultures command respect for their achievements in music, art, science, philosophy, business, and more. Asian businesspeople are tough negotiators, but they dislike argumentative exchanges. Harmony and consensus are the bywords in Asia, so be patient but firm.
- *Drop the Legal Language.* Legal documents are subordinate to personal relationships. Asians tend to dislike detailed contracts. Agreements are often left flexible so that adjustments can be made easily in order to fit changing circumstances. It's important to foster good relations based on mutual trust and benefit. The importance of a contract in many Asian societies is not what it stipulates but rather who signed it.
- *Build Personal Rapport.* Social ease and friendship are prerequisites to doing business across much of Asia. As much business is transacted at informal dinners as it is in corporate settings, so accept invitations, and be sure to reciprocate.

DANGERS OF TRADE DEPENDENCY The dangers of trade dependency become apparent when a nation experiences economic recession or political turmoil, which then also harms dependent nations. Trade dependency was a blessing for Mexico for many years when it was a favorite location for the production and assembly operations of U.S. companies. Mexican factories still assemble all sorts of products headed for the U.S. market, including refrigerators, mobile phones, and many types of garments. But corruption, an outdated infrastructure, and drug-related violence are forcing some companies to abandon Mexico for Asia—leaving unemployed Mexican workers behind. The best way for Mexico to deal with its dependency on the United States is to boost its competitiveness, thereby making it a preferred location among all emerging markets.

QUICK STUDY 1

1. What portion of world trade occurs in (a) merchandise and (b) services?
2. What is the relationship between trade and world output?
3. Describe the broad pattern of *international trade*.
4. Why is a nation's level of trade dependence or independence important?

Theories of International Trade

Trade between different groups of people has occurred for many thousands of years. But it was not until the fifteenth century that people tried to explain why trade occurs and how trade can benefit both parties to an exchange. Figure 5.1 shows a timeline of when the main theories of international trade were proposed. Efforts to refine existing trade theories and to develop new ones continue today. Let's now discuss the first theory developed to explain why nations should engage in international trade—*mercantilism*.

Mercantilism

The trade theory that nations should accumulate financial wealth, usually in the form of gold, by encouraging exports and discouraging imports is called **mercantilism**. It states that other measures of a nation's well-being, such as living standards or human development, are irrelevant. Nation-states in Europe followed this economic philosophy from about 1500 to the late 1700s. The most prominent mercantilist nations included Britain, France, the Netherlands, Portugal, and Spain.

mercantilism
Trade theory that nations should accumulate financial wealth, usually in the form of gold, by encouraging exports and discouraging imports.

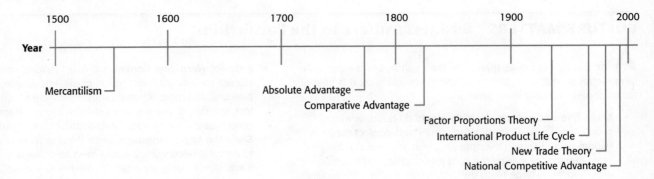

FIGURE 5.1
Trade Theory Timeline

HOW MERCANTILISM WORKED When navigation was a fairly new science, Europeans explored the world by sea and claimed the lands they encountered in the name of the European monarchy that financed their voyage. Early explorers landed in Africa, Asia, and the Americas, where they established colonies. Colonial trade was conducted for the benefit of mother countries, and the appeal of the colonies was their abundant resources.

In recent times, former colonies have struggled to diminish their reliance on the former colonial powers. For example, in an effort to decrease their dependence on their former colonial powers, African nations are welcoming trade relationships with partners from Asia and North America. But because of geographic proximity, the European Union is still often preferred as a trading partner.

Just how did countries implement mercantilism? The practice of mercantilism rested on three essential pillars: trade surpluses, government intervention, and colonialism.

trade surplus
Condition that results when the value of a nation's exports is greater than the value of its imports.

trade deficit
Condition that results when the value of a country's imports is greater than the value of its exports.

Trade Surpluses Nations believed they could increase their wealth by maintaining a **trade surplus**—the condition that results when the value of a nation's exports is greater than the value of its imports. In mercantilism, a trade surplus means that a country takes in more gold on the sale of its exports than it pays out for its imports. A **trade deficit** is the opposite condition—one that results when the value of a country's imports is greater than the value of its exports. In mercantilism, trade deficits are to be avoided at all costs. (We discuss the importance of national trade balance at length in Chapter 7.)

Government Intervention Governments actively intervened in international trade in order to maintain a trade surplus. According to mercantilism, the accumulation of wealth depends on increasing a nation's trade surplus, not necessarily expanding its total value or volume of trade. The governments of mercantilist nations did this by either banning certain imports or imposing various restrictions on them, such as tariffs or quotas. At the same time, the nations subsidized industries based in the home country in order to expand exports. Governments also typically outlawed the removal of their gold and silver to other nations.

Colonialism Mercantilist nations acquired territories (colonies) around the world to serve as sources of inexpensive raw materials and as markets for higher-priced finished goods. These colonies were the source of essential raw materials, including tea, sugar, tobacco, rubber, and cotton. These resources would be shipped to the mercantilist nation, where they were incorporated into finished goods such as clothing, cigars, and other products. These finished goods would then be sold to the colonies. Trade between mercantilist countries and their colonies were a huge source of profits for the mercantilist powers. The colonies received low prices for basic raw materials but paid high prices for finished goods.

The mercantilist and colonial policies greatly expanded the wealth of nations that implemented them. This wealth allowed nations to build armies and navies to control their far-flung colonial empires and to protect their shipping lanes from attack by other nations. It was a source of a nation's economic power that in turn increased its political power relative to other countries. Today, countries seen by others as trying to maintain a trade surplus and expand their national treasuries at the expense of other nations are accused of practicing *neomercantilism* or *economic nationalism*.

Employees in Mexico churn out all sorts of products destined for the United States. For decades, trade with the United States brought well-paying jobs to ordinary Mexicans, like this man helping to build a Volkswagen Jetta at an assembly plant in Puebla, Mexico. But some businesses in Mexico are moving production to cheaper locations, such as China and Vietnam. When this happens, Mexico experiences the negative effects of its dependence on U.S. trade.

Source: Susana Gonzalez/Newscom

FLAWS OF MERCANTILISM Despite its seemingly positive benefits for any nation implementing it, mercantilism is inherently flawed. Mercantilist nations believed that the world's wealth was limited and that a nation could increase its share of the pie only at the expense of its neighbors—a situation called a *zero-sum game*. The main problem with mercantilism is that, if all nations were to barricade their markets from imports and push their exports onto others, international trade would be severely restricted. In fact, trade in all nonessential goods would likely cease altogether.

In addition, paying colonies little for their exports but charging them high prices for their imports impaired their economic development. Thus, their appeal as markets for goods was less than it would have been if they had been allowed to accumulate greater wealth. These negative aspects of mercantilism were made apparent by a trade theory developed in the late 1700s—*absolute advantage*.

QUICK STUDY 2

1. How did *mercantilism* work? Identify its three essential pillars.
2. What types of policies might a country have in place to be called neomercantilist?
3. Describe the main flaws of mercantilism. What is meant by the term *zero-sum game*?

Absolute Advantage

Scottish economist Adam Smith first put forth the trade theory of absolute advantage in 1776.[5] The ability of a nation to produce a good more efficiently than any other nation is called an **absolute advantage**. In other words, a nation with an absolute advantage can produce a greater output of a good or service than other nations using the same amount of, or fewer, resources.

Among other things, Smith reasoned that international trade should not be banned or restricted by tariffs and quotas but allowed to flow as dictated by market forces. If people in

absolute advantage
Ability of a nation to produce a good more efficiently than any other nation.

different countries were able to trade as they saw fit, no country would need to produce all the goods it consumed. Instead, a country could concentrate on producing the goods in which it holds an absolute advantage. It could then trade with other nations to obtain the goods it needs but does not produce.

Suppose a talented CEO wants to install a hot tub in her home. Should she do the job herself or hire a professional installer to do it for her? Suppose the CEO (who has never installed a hot tub before) would have to take one month off from work and forgo $800,000 in salary in order to complete the job. On the other hand, the professional installer (who is not a talented CEO) can complete the job for $10,000 and do it in two weeks. Whereas the CEO has an absolute advantage in running a company, the installer has an absolute advantage in installing hot tubs. It takes the CEO one month to do the job the installer can do in two weeks. Thus, the CEO should hire the professional to install the hot tub to save both time and money resources.

Let's now apply the absolute advantage concept to an example of two trading countries to see how trade can increase production and consumption in both nations.

CASE: RICELAND AND TEALAND   Suppose that we live in a world of just two countries (Riceland and Tealand), with two products (rice and tea), and that transporting goods between these two countries costs nothing. Riceland and Tealand currently produce and consume their own rice and tea. The following table shows the number of units of resources (labor) each country expends in creating rice and tea. In Riceland, just one resource unit is needed to produce a ton of rice, but five units of resources are needed to produce a ton of tea. In Tealand, six units of resources are needed to produce a ton of rice, whereas three units are needed to produce a ton of tea.

| | Units Required for Production | |
	Rice	Tea
Riceland	1	5
Tealand	6	3

Another way of stating each nation's efficiency in the production of rice and tea is:

- In Riceland, 1 unit of resources = 1 ton of rice or 1/5 ton of tea
- In Tealand, 1 unit of resources = 1/6 ton of rice or 1/3 ton of tea

These numbers also tell us one other thing about rice and tea production in these two countries. Because one unit of resources produces one ton of rice in Riceland compared with Tealand's output of only 1/6 ton of rice, Riceland has an absolute advantage in rice production— it is the more efficient rice producer. However, because one resource unit produces 1/3 ton of tea in Tealand compared with Riceland's output of just 1/5 ton, Tealand has an absolute advantage in tea production.

Gains from Specialization and Trade   Suppose now that Riceland specializes in rice production to maximize the output of rice in our two-country world. Likewise, Tealand specializes in tea production to maximize the world output of tea. Although each country now specializes and world output increases, both countries face a problem. Riceland can consume only its rice production, and Tealand can consume only its tea production. The problem can be solved if the two countries trade with each other to obtain the good that it needs but does not produce.

Suppose that Riceland and Tealand agree to trade rice and tea on a one-to-one basis—a ton of rice costs a ton of tea, and vice versa. Thus, Riceland can produce one extra ton of rice with an additional resource unit and can trade with Tealand to get one ton of tea. This is much better than the 1/5 ton of tea that Riceland would have gotten by investing that additional resource unit in making tea for itself. Thus, Riceland definitely benefits from the trade. Likewise, Tealand can produce 1/3 extra ton of tea with an additional resource unit and trade with Riceland to get 1/3 ton of rice. This is twice as much as the 1/6 ton of rice it could have produced using that additional resource unit to make its own rice. Thus, Tealand also benefits from the trade. The gains resulting from this simple trade are shown in Figure 5.2.

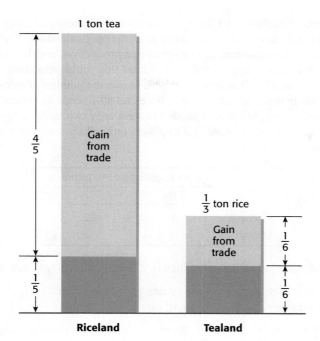

FIGURE 5.2

Gains from Specialization and Trade: Absolute Advantage

Although Tealand does not gain as much as Riceland does from the trade, it does get more rice than it would without trade. The gains from trade for actual countries would depend on the total number of resources each country has at its disposal and the demand for each good in each country.

As this example shows, the theory of absolute advantage destroys the mercantilist idea that international trade is a *zero-sum game*. Instead, because there are gains to be had by both countries party to an exchange, international trade is a *positive-sum game*. The theory also calls into question the objective of national governments to acquire wealth through restrictive trade policies. It argues that nations should instead open their doors to trade so that their people can obtain a greater quantity of goods more cheaply. The theory does not measure a nation's wealth by how much gold and silver it has on reserve but by the living standards of its people.

Despite the power of the theory of absolute advantage in showing the gains from trade, there is one potential problem. What happens if a country does not hold an absolute advantage in the production of any product? Are there still benefits to trade, and will trade even occur? To answer these questions, let's take a look at an extension of absolute advantage: the theory of *comparative advantage*.

Comparative Advantage

An English economist named David Ricardo developed the theory of comparative advantage in 1817.[6] He proposed that if one country (in our example of a two-country world) held absolute advantages in the production of both products, specialization and trade could still benefit both countries. A country has a **comparative advantage** when it is unable to produce a good more efficiently than other nations but produces the good more efficiently than it does any other good. In other words, *trade is still beneficial even if one country is less efficient in the production of two goods, as long as it is less inefficient in the production of one of the goods.*

Let's return to our hot tub example. Now suppose that the talented CEO has previously installed many hot tubs and can do the job in one week—twice as fast as the hot tub installer. Thus, the CEO now holds absolute advantages in both running a company and hot tub installation. Although the professional installer is at an absolute disadvantage in both hot tub installation and running a company, he is less inefficient in hot tub installation. Despite her absolute advantage in both areas, however, the CEO would still have to give up $200,000 (one week's pay) to take time off from running the company to complete the work. Is this a wise decision? No. The CEO should hire the professional installer to do the work for $10,000. The installer earns money he would not earn if the CEO did the job herself. And the CEO earns more money by focusing on running the company than she would save by installing the hot tub herself.

comparative advantage
Inability of a nation to produce a good more efficiently than other nations but an ability to produce that good more efficiently than it does any other good.

Gains from Specialization and Trade   To see how the theory of comparative advantage works with international trade, let's return to our example of Riceland and Tealand. In our earlier discussion, Riceland had an absolute advantage in rice production, and Tealand had an absolute advantage in tea production. Suppose that Riceland now holds absolute advantages in the production of both rice *and* tea. The following table shows the number of units of resources each country now expends in creating rice and tea. Riceland still needs to expend just one resource unit to produce a ton of rice, but now it needs to invest only two units of resources (instead of five) to produce one ton of tea. Tealand still needs six units of resources to produce a ton of rice and three units to produce a ton of tea.

	Units Required for Production	
	Rice	Tea
Riceland	1	2
Tealand	6	3

Another way of stating each nation's efficiency in the production of rice and tea is:

- In Riceland, 1 unit of resources = 1 ton of rice or 1/2 ton of tea
- In Tealand, 1 unit of resources = 1/6 ton of rice or 1/3 ton of tea

Thus, for every unit of resource used, Riceland can produce more rice and tea than Tealand can. Riceland has *absolute* advantages in the production of both goods. But Riceland can still gain from trading with a less-efficient producer. Although Tealand has absolute disadvantages in both rice and tea production, it has a *comparative* advantage in tea. In other words, although Tealand is unable to produce either rice or tea more efficiently than Riceland, it produces tea more efficiently than it produces rice.

Assume once again that Riceland and Tealand decide to trade rice and tea on a one-to-one basis. Tealand could use one unit of resources to produce 1/6 ton of rice. But it would do better to produce 1/3 ton of tea with this unit of resources and trade with Riceland to get 1/3 ton of rice. By specializing and trading, Tealand gets twice as much rice as it could get if it were to produce the rice itself. There are also gains from trade for Riceland despite its dual absolute advantages. Riceland could invest one unit of resources in the production of 1/2 ton of tea. It would do better, however, to produce one ton of rice with the one unit of resources and trade that rice to Tealand in exchange for one ton of tea. Thus, Riceland gets twice as much tea through trade than if it were to produce the tea itself. This is in spite of the fact that it is a more efficient producer of tea than Tealand.

The benefits for each country from this simple trade are shown in Figure 5.3. Again, the benefits actual countries obtain from trade depend on the amount of resources at their disposal and each market's desired level of consumption of each product.

ASSUMPTIONS AND LIMITATIONS   Throughout the discussion of absolute and comparative advantage, we made several important assumptions that limit real-world application of the theories. First, we assumed that countries are driven only by the maximization of production and consumption. This is often not the case. Governments often get involved in international trade out of a concern for workers or consumers. (We discuss the role of government in international trade in Chapter 6.)

Second, the theories assume that there are only two countries engaged in the production and consumption of just two goods. This is obviously not the situation that exists in the real world. There currently are more than 180 countries and a countless number of products being produced, traded, and consumed worldwide.

Third, it is assumed that there are no costs for transporting traded goods from one country to another. In reality, transportation costs are a major expense of international trade for some products. If transportation costs for a good are higher than the savings generated through specialization, trade will not occur.

Fourth, the theories consider labor to be the only resource used in the production process because labor accounted for a large portion of the total production cost of goods at the time the theories were developed. Moreover, it is assumed that resources are mobile within each nation

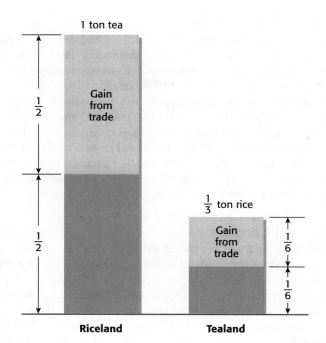

FIGURE 5.3

Gains from Specialization and Trade: Comparative Advantage

but cannot be transferred between nations. But labor and natural resources can be transferred between nations, although doing so can be difficult and costly.

Finally, it is assumed that specialization in the production of one particular good does not result in gains in efficiency. But we know that specialization results in increased knowledge of a task and perhaps even future improvements in how that task is performed. Thus, the amount of resources needed to produce a specific amount of a good should decrease over time.

Despite the assumptions made in the theory of comparative advantage, research reveals that it appears to be supported by a substantial body of evidence. Nevertheless, economic researchers continue to develop and test new theories to explain international trade.

QUICK STUDY 3

1. What is meant by the term *absolute advantage*? Describe how it works using a numerical example.
2. What is meant by the term *comparative advantage*? How does it differ from an absolute advantage?
3. Explain why countries can gain from trade even without having an absolute advantage.

Factor Proportions Theory

In the early 1900s, an international trade theory emerged that focused attention on the proportion (supply) of resources in a nation. The cost of any resource is simply the result of supply and demand: Factors in great supply relative to demand will be less costly than factors in short supply relative to demand. **Factor proportions theory** states that countries produce and export goods that require resources (factors) that are abundant and import goods that require resources in short supply.[7] The theory resulted from the research of two economists, Eli Heckscher and Bertil Ohlin, and is therefore sometimes called the Heckscher–Ohlin theory.

Factor proportions theory differs considerably from the theory of comparative advantage. Recall that the theory of comparative advantage states that a country specializes in producing the good that it can produce more efficiently than any other good. Thus, the focus of the theory (and absolute advantage, as well) is on the *productivity* of the production process for a particular good. By contrast, factor proportions theory says that a country specializes in producing and exporting goods using the factors of production that are most *abundant* and thus *cheapest*—not the goods in which it is most productive.

factor proportions theory
Trade theory stating that countries produce and export goods that require resources (factors) that are abundant and import goods that require resources in short supply.

LABOR VERSUS LAND AND CAPITAL EQUIPMENT Factor proportions theory breaks a nation's resources into two categories: labor on the one hand, land and capital equipment on the other. It predicts that a country will specialize in products that require labor if the cost of labor is low relative to the cost of land and capital. Alternatively, a country will specialize in products that require land and capital equipment if their cost is low relative to the cost of labor.

Factor proportions theory is conceptually appealing. For example, Australia has a great deal of land (nearly 60 percent of which is meadows and pastures) and a small population relative to its size. Australia's exports consist largely of mined minerals, grain, beef, lamb, and dairy products—products that require a great deal of land and natural resources. Australia's imports, on the other hand, consist mostly of manufactured raw materials, capital equipment, and consumer goods—things needed in capital-intensive mining and modern agriculture. But instead of looking only at anecdotal evidence, let's see how well factor proportions theory stands up to scientific testing.

EVIDENCE ON FACTOR PROPORTIONS THEORY: THE LEONTIEF PARADOX Despite its conceptual appeal, factor proportions theory is not supported by studies that examine the trade flows of nations. The first large-scale study to document such evidence was performed by a researcher named Wassily Leontief in the early 1950s.[8] Leontief tested whether the United States, which uses an abundance of capital equipment, exports goods requiring capital-intensive production and imports goods requiring labor-intensive production. Contrary to the predictions of the factor proportions theory, his research found that U.S. exports require more labor-intensive production than its imports. This apparent paradox between the predictions using the theory and the actual trade flows is called the *Leontief paradox*. Leontief's findings are supported by more-recent research on the trade data of a large number of countries.

What might account for the paradox? One possible explanation is that factor proportions theory considers a country's production factors to be homogeneous—particularly labor. But we know that labor skills vary greatly within a country—more highly skilled workers emerge from training and development programs. When expenditures on improving the skills of labor are taken into account, the theory seems to be supported by actual trade data. Further studies examining international trade data will help us better understand what reasons actually account for the Leontief paradox.

Because of the drawbacks of each of the international trade theories mentioned so far, researchers continue to propose new ones. Let's now examine a theory that attempts to explain international trade based on the life cycle of products.

International Product Life Cycle

Raymond Vernon put forth an international trade theory for manufactured goods in the mid-1960s. His **international product life cycle** theory says that a company will begin by exporting its product and later undertake foreign direct investment as the product moves through its life cycle. The theory also says that, for a number of reasons, a country's export eventually becomes its import.[9]

Although Vernon developed his model around the United States, we can generalize it to apply to any developed and innovative market such as Australia, the European Union, and Japan. Let's examine how this theory attempts to explain international trade flows.

STAGES OF THE PRODUCT LIFE CYCLE The international product life cycle theory follows the path of a good through its life cycle (from new to maturing to standardized product) in order to determine where it will be produced (see Figure 5.4). In Stage 1, the *new product stage,* the high purchasing power and demand of buyers in an industrialized country drive a company to design and introduce a new product concept. Because the exact level of demand in the domestic market is highly uncertain at this point, the company keeps its production volume low and based in the home country. Keeping production where initial research and development occurred and staying in contact with customers allow the company to monitor buyer preferences and to modify the product as needed. Although initially there is virtually no export market, exports do begin to pick up late in the new product stage.

In Stage 2, the *maturing product stage,* the domestic market and markets abroad become fully aware of the existence of the product and its benefits. Demand rises and is sustained over a fairly lengthy period of time. As exports begin to account for an increasingly greater share of

international product life cycle
Theory stating that a company will begin by exporting its product and later undertake foreign direct investment as the product moves through its life cycle.

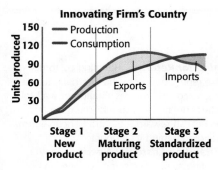
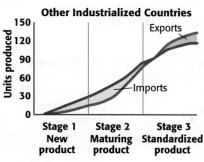
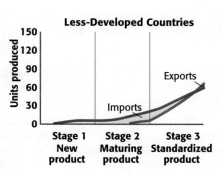

FIGURE 5.4

International Product Life Cycle

Source: Raymond Vernon and Louis T. Wells Jr., *The Economic Environment of International Business,* 5th ed. (Upper Saddle River, NJ: Prentice Hall, 1991), p. 85.

total product sales, the innovating company introduces production facilities in the countries with the highest demand. Near the end of the maturity stage, the product begins generating sales in developing nations, and perhaps some manufacturing presence is established there.

In Stage 3, the *standardized product stage,* competition from other companies selling similar products pressures companies to lower prices in order to maintain sales levels. As the market becomes more price sensitive, the company begins searching aggressively for low-cost production bases in developing nations to supply a growing worldwide market. Furthermore, as most production now takes place outside the innovating country, demand in the innovating country is supplied with imports from developing countries and other industrialized nations. Late in this stage, domestic production might even cease altogether.

LIMITATIONS OF THE THEORY Vernon developed his theory at a time when most new products were being developed and sold first in the United States. One reason U.S. companies were strong globally in the 1960s was that their domestic production bases were not destroyed during the Second World War, as was the case in Europe (and to some extent Japan). In addition, during the war, the production of many durable goods in the United States, including automobiles, was shifted to the production of military transportation and weaponry. This laid the foundation for enormous postwar demand for new capital-intensive consumer goods, such as automobiles and home appliances. Furthermore, advances in technology that were originally developed with military purposes in mind were integrated into consumer goods. A wide range of new and innovative products like TVs, photocopiers, and computers met the seemingly insatiable appetite of consumers in the United States.

The theory seemed to explain world trade patterns quite well when the United States dominated world trade. But today, the theory's ability to accurately depict the trade flows of nations is weak. The United States is no longer the sole innovator of products in the world. New products spring up everywhere as companies continue to globalize their research-and-development activities.

Furthermore, companies today design new products and make product modifications at a very quick pace. The result is quicker product obsolescence and a situation in which companies replace their existing products with new product introductions. This is forcing companies to introduce products in many markets simultaneously in order to recoup a product's research-and-development costs before sales decline and the product is dropped. The theory has a difficult time explaining the resulting trade patterns.

In fact, older theories might better explain today's global trade patterns. Much production in the world today more closely resembles what is predicted by the theory of comparative advantage. Boeing's (www.boeing.com) assembly plant in Everett, Washington, assembles its 787 Dreamliner wide-body aircraft. But companies around the world build the parts used in the 787. Cargo doors arrive stamped "Made in Sweden" and are supplied by Saab Aerostructures. The plane's lavatories are made by Jamco in Japan, its flight deck seats are supplied by Ipeco of the United Kingdom, its landing gear is made by Messier-Bugatti-Dowty of France, and so forth.[10] Components are later assembled in a chosen location. This pattern resembles the theory of comparative advantage in that a product's components are made in the country that can produce them at a high level of productivity.

Finally, the theory is challenged by the fact that more companies are operating in international markets from their inception. Many small companies are teaming up with companies in

MANAGER'S BRIEFCASE   Five Fulfillment Mistakes

Although there's no way to completely foolproof logistics when selling online, a company should enjoy greater customer satisfaction if it can avoid these five key mistakes:

- **Mistake 1: Misunderstanding the Supply Chain.** How many orders can fulfillment centers fill in an hour, a day, and a week? How long does it take a package to reach a customer from the fulfillment center using standard, nonexpedited delivery? And how much inventory can the centers receive on any given day? If a company doesn't know the answers, it could be in serious danger of making delivery promises it can't keep.
- **Mistake 2: Overpromising on Delivery.** The entrepreneur owner/manager should not advertise aggressive delivery times without a qualifier for uncontrollable factors, such as the weather. Care must also be taken to ensure that a customer is not promised an unrealistically quick order-turnaround time. Flexibility must be built into fulfillment operations.

- **Mistake 3: Not Planning for Returns.** Handling customer returns well can increase repeat business. The internal returns process needs to be organized, and returns should not wait to go out until products start coming back to fulfillment centers. Prompt credit to customers can reward the entrepreneurial firm with a reputation as standing behind its products.
- **Mistake 4: Misunderstanding Customer Needs.** Many Internet shoppers are willing to sacrifice shipping speed in exchange for lower shipping costs. Balancing this cost–service differential is an opportunity for online marketers to cut order-fulfillment costs.
- **Mistake 5: Poor Internal Communication.** Marketing departments must communicate with logistics people. A public relations nightmare can result if logistics professionals are not told and the big planned marketing push crashes the company website.

other markets to develop new products or production technologies. This strategy is particularly effective for small companies that would otherwise be unable to participate in international production or sales. French company Ingenico (www.ingenico.com) is a leading global supplier of secure transaction systems, including terminals and their associated software. The company began small and worked with a global network of entrepreneurs who acted as Ingenico's local agents and helped it to conquer local markets. The cultural knowledge embedded in Ingenico's global network helped it to design and sell products appropriate for each market.[11]

The Internet also makes it easier for companies of all sizes to reach a global audience. For a discussion of several pitfalls companies can avoid in fulfilling their international orders taken on the Internet, see the Manager's Briefcase, titled "Five Fulfillment Mistakes."

QUICK STUDY 4

1. What does the *factor proportions theory* have to say about a nation's imports and exports?
2. Identify the two categories of national resources in the factor proportions theory. What is the *Leontief paradox*?
3. What are the three stages of the *international product life cycle theory*? Identify its limitations.

New Trade Theory

new trade theory
Trade theory stating that (1) there are gains to be made from specialization and increasing economies of scale, (2) the companies first to market can create barriers to entry, and (3) government may play a role in assisting its home companies.

During the 1970s and 1980s, another theory emerged to explain trade patterns.[12] The **new trade theory** states that (1) there are gains to be made from specialization and increasing economies of scale, (2) the companies first to market can create barriers to entry, and (3) government may play a role in assisting its home companies. Because the theory emphasizes productivity rather than a nation's resources, it is in line with the theory of comparative advantage but at odds with factor proportions theory.

FIRST-MOVER ADVANTAGE According to the new trade theory, as a company increases the extent to which it specializes in the production of a particular good, output rises because of gains in efficiency. Regardless of the amount of a company's output, it has fixed production costs such as the cost of research and development and the plant and equipment needed to produce the product. The theory states that, as specialization and output increase, companies can realize economies of scale, thereby pushing the unit costs of production lower. That is why as many companies expand, they lower prices to buyers and force potential new competitors to produce at a similar level of output if they want to be competitive in their pricing. Thus, the presence of large economies of scale can create an industry that supports only a few large firms.

A **first-mover advantage** is the economic and strategic advantage gained by being the first company to enter an industry. This first-mover advantage can create a formidable barrier to entry for potential rivals. The new trade theory also states that a country may dominate in the export of a certain product because it has a home-based firm that has acquired a first-mover advantage.[13]

Because of the potential benefits of being the first company to enter an industry, some businesspeople and researchers make a case for government assistance to companies. They say that by working together to target potential new industries, a government and its home companies can take advantage of the benefits of being the first mover in an industry. Government involvement has always been widely accepted in undertakings such as space exploration for national security reasons, but has been less so in purely commercial ventures. But the fear that governments of other countries might participate with industry to gain first-mover advantages drives many governments into action.

first-mover advantage
Economic and strategic advantage gained by being the first company to enter an industry.

National Competitive Advantage

What aspects of a nation's economic development can supply it with a national competitive advantage? The poorest nations tend to invest in the fundamental drivers of productivity growth (such as basic infrastructure). The richest nations typically exploit the latest technological advancements in order to boost productivity. Research into how nations achieve sustainable economic development has examined the potential roles of (1) culture, (2) geography, and (3) innovation. To read more about whether these factors drive economic growth, see this chapter's Global Sustainability feature, titled "Foundations of Development."

A related question researchers have tried to answer is, How do firms in certain nations develop competitive advantage in specific industries? Michael Porter put forth a theory in 1990 to explain why certain countries are leaders in the production of certain products.[14] His **national competitive advantage theory** states that a nation's competitiveness in an industry depends on the capacity of the industry to innovate and upgrade. Porter's work incorporates certain elements of previous international trade theories but also makes some important new discoveries.

Porter is not preoccupied with explaining the export and import patterns of nations but rather with explaining why some nations are more competitive in certain industries. He identifies four elements that are present to varying degrees in every nation and that form the basis of national competitiveness. The *Porter diamond* consists of (1) factor conditions, (2) demand

national competitive advantage theory
Trade theory stating that a nation's competitiveness in an industry depends on the capacity of the industry to innovate and upgrade.

GLOBAL SUSTAINABILITY   Foundations of Development

Researchers debate which aspects of a nation might influence sustainable economic development, including the following:

- **Culture.** Some researchers believe cultural differences among nations can explain differences in development, material well-being, and socioeconomic equity. They argue that any culture can attain high productivity and economic growth if it values the benefits that development brings. Critics say that this perspective unfairly judges other cultures. They argue that each culture defines its own values, practices, goals, and ethics, and that Western nations should not impose their concept of "progress" on other cultures.

- **Geography.** Other researchers claim geography is central to productivity and economic development. Factors thought to hinder development include being a landlocked nation far from the coast, having poor access to markets, possessing few natural resources, and having a tropical climate. But Hong Kong, Singapore, South Korea, and Taiwan built competitive market economies despite their small size and lack of vast natural

resources. Each of these nations also threw off dependence on a colonial power.

- **Innovation.** Nations that want to join the European Union must satisfy strict and innovative requirements. This is pulling Eastern Europe's culture closer to Western Europe's, along with shifting habits, attitudes, and values. In emerging markets today, innovation is being driven by ambition to improve one's lot in life and the fear of being replaced by an even cheaper production location. Homegrown businesses in emerging markets have developed very inexpensive yet highly functional automobiles, computers, and mobile phones that appeal to consumers at home and abroad.

- **Want to Know More?** Visit the Culturelink Network (www .culturelink.org), the Observatory of Cultural Policies in Africa (ocpa.irmo.hr), and the North-South Institute (www.nsi-ins.ca).

Source: Mark Johnson, "Innovation in Emerging Markets," *Bloomberg Businessweek* (www.businessweek.com), May 28, 2010; "The World Turned Upside Down," *The Economist*, April 17, 2010, pp. 3–6; William Fischer, "Dealing with Innovation from Emerging Markets," IMD website (www.imd.org), November 2008.

conditions, (3) related and supporting industries, and (4) firm strategy, structure, and rivalry. Let's look at these elements and see how they interact to support national competitiveness.

FACTOR CONDITIONS Factor proportions theory considers a nation's resources, such as a large labor force, natural resources, climate, or surface features, as paramount factors in what products a country will produce and export. Porter acknowledges the value of such resources, which he terms *basic* factors, but he also discusses the significance of what he calls *advanced* factors.

Advanced Factors Advanced factors include the skill levels of different segments of the workforce and the quality of the technological infrastructure in a nation. Advanced factors are the result of investments in education and innovation, including worker training and technological research and development. Whereas basic factors can be the initial spark for why an economy begins producing a certain product, advanced factors account for the sustained competitive advantage a country enjoys in that product.

Today, for example, Japan has an advantage in automobile production and the United States in the manufacture of airplanes. In the manufacture of computer components, Taiwan reigns supreme, although China is an increasingly important competitor. These countries did not attain their status in their respective areas because of basic factors. For example, Japan did not acquire its advantage in automobiles because of its natural resources of iron ore—it has virtually none and must import most of the iron it needs. These countries developed their productivity and advantages in producing these products through deliberate efforts.

DEMAND CONDITIONS Sophisticated buyers in the home market are also important to national competitive advantage in a product area. A sophisticated domestic market drives companies to add new design features to products and to develop entirely new products and technologies. Companies in markets with sophisticated buyers should see the competitiveness of the entire group improve. For example, the sophisticated U.S. market for computer software has helped give companies based in the United States an edge in developing new software products.

RELATED AND SUPPORTING INDUSTRIES Companies that belong to a nation's internationally competitive industries do not exist in isolation. Rather, supporting industries spring up to provide the inputs required by the industry. This happens because companies that can benefit from the product or process technologies of an internationally competitive industry begin to form clusters of related economic activities in the same geographic area. Each industry in the cluster serves to reinforce the productivity and, therefore, competitiveness of every other industry within the cluster. For example, Italy is home to a successful cluster in the footwear industry that greatly benefits from the country's closely related leather-tanning and fashion-design industries. And within the United States, Phoenix, Arizona, is home to companies that specialize in semiconductors, optics, and electronic testing—all heavily incorporated into the activities of Boeing (www.boeing.com) and Motorola (www.motorola.com), which have a significant presence there.

A relatively small number of clusters usually account for a major share of regional economic activity. They also often account for an overwhelming share of the economic activity that is "exported" to other locations. *Exporting clusters*—those that export products or make investments to compete outside the local area—are the primary source of an area's long-term prosperity. Although demand for a local industry is inherently limited by the size of the local market, an exporting cluster can grow far beyond that limit.[15]

FIRM STRATEGY, STRUCTURE, AND RIVALRY The strategies of firms and the actions of their managers have lasting effects on future competitiveness. Essential to successful companies are managers who are committed to producing quality products valued by buyers while maximizing the firm's market share and/or financial returns. Equally as important is the industry structure and rivalry between a nation's companies. The more intense the struggle to survive between a nation's domestic companies, the greater will be their competitiveness. This heightened competitiveness helps them to compete against imports and against companies that might develop a production presence in the home market.

GOVERNMENT AND CHANCE Apart from the four factors identified as part of the diamond, Porter identifies the roles of government and chance in fostering the national competitiveness of industries.

First, governments, by their actions, can often increase the competitiveness of firms and perhaps even entire industries. Governments of emerging markets could increase economic growth by increasing the pace of privatization of state-owned companies, for example. Privatization forces those companies to grow more competitive in world markets if they are to survive.

Second, although chance events can help the competitiveness of a firm or an industry, it can also threaten it. McDonald's (www.mcdonalds.com) holds a clear competitive advantage worldwide in the fast-food industry. But its overwhelming dominance was threatened by the discovery of mad cow disease several years ago. To keep customers from flocking to the nonbeef substitute products of competitors, McDonald's introduced the McPork sandwich and other nonbeef products.

There are important implications for companies and governments if Porter's theory accurately identifies the important drivers of national competitiveness. For instance, government policies should not be designed to protect national industries that are not internationally competitive but should develop the components of the diamond that contribute to increased competitiveness.

QUICK STUDY 5

1. What is the *new trade theory*? Explain what is meant by the term *first-mover advantage*.
2. Describe the *national competitive advantage theory*. What is an "advanced" factor?
3. What are the four elements and two influential factors of the Porter diamond?

BOTTOM LINE FOR BUSINESS

Trade can liberate the entrepreneurial spirit and bring economic development to a nation and its people. As the value and volume of trade continue to expand worldwide, new theories will likely emerge to explain why countries trade and why nations have advantages in producing certain products.

Globalization and Trade

An underlying theme of this book is how companies are adapting to globalization. Globalization and the increased competition it causes are forcing companies to locate particular operations to where they can be performed most efficiently. Firms are doing this either by relocating their own production facilities to other nations or by outsourcing certain activities to companies abroad. Companies undertake such action in order to boost competitiveness.

The relocation and outsourcing of business activities are altering international trade in both goods and services. In this chapter's opening company profile, we saw that Walmart relies on the sourcing of products from low-cost production locations such as China to deliver low-priced goods. Hewlett-Packard also makes use of globalization and international trade to minimize costs while maximizing output. The company dispersed the design and production of a new computer server throughout an increasingly specialized electronics-manufacturing system. HP conceptualized and designed the computer in Singapore, engineered and manufactured many parts for it in Taiwan, and assembled it in Australia, China, India, and Singapore. Companies are using such production and distribution techniques to maximize efficiency.

Not only is the production of goods being sent to distant locations, but so too is the delivery of business services, including financial accounting, data processing, and the handling of credit card and insurance inquiries. Even jobs requiring higher-level skills such as engineering, computer programming, and scientific research are migrating to distant locations. The motivation for companies is the same as when they send manufacturing jobs to more cost-effective locations—remaining viable in the face of increasing competitive pressure.

Supporting Free Trade

International trade theory is fundamentally no different when it comes to the relocation of services production as compared with the production of goods. As we've seen in this chapter, trade theory tells us that if a refrigerator bound for a Western market can be made more cheaply in China, it should be. The same reasoned logic tells us that if a credit card inquiry from a Western market can be more cheaply (but adequately) processed in India, it should be. In both cases, the importing country benefits from a less-expensive product, and the exporting country benefits from inward-flowing investment and more numerous and better-paying jobs.

Finally, there are policy implications for governments. Although employment in developed countries should not be negatively affected in the aggregate, job dislocation is a concern. Many governments are encouraging lifelong education among workers to guard against the possibility that an individual may become "obsolete" in terms of lacking marketable skills relative to workers in other nations. And no matter how loud the calls for protectionism grow in the service sector, governments will do well to resist such temptations. Experience tells us that erecting barriers to competition results in less competitive firms and industries, greater job losses, and lower standards of living than would be the case under free trade.

Chapter Summary

MyManagementLab

Go to **mymanagementlab.com** to complete the problems marked with this icon .

1. **Describe the relationship between international trade volume and world output, and identify overall trade patterns.**
   - *International trade* is the purchase, sale, or exchange of goods and services across national borders.
   - Trade provides a country's people with a greater choice of goods and services and is an important engine for job creation in many countries.
   - Merchandise comprises most world trade, although services account for around 20 percent.
   - Slower world economic output slows international trade, and higher output drives greater trade.
   - The pattern of international trade in merchandise is dominated by flows among wealthy nations.

2. **Describe mercantilism and explain its impact on world powers and their colonies.**
   - *Mercantilism* states that nations should accumulate financial wealth, usually in the form of gold, by encouraging exports and discouraging imports.
   - Mercantilism assumes that a nation increases its wealth only at the expense of other nations—a *zero-sum game*.
   - One key element of mercantilism is to increase wealth by maintaining a *trade surplus*, the condition that results when the value of a nation's exports is greater than the value of its imports.
   - A second key element is to intervene actively in international trade in order to maintain a surplus.
   - A third key element is the acquisition of colonies to serve as sources of inexpensive raw materials and as markets for higher-priced finished goods.

3. **Explain the theories of absolute advantage and comparative advantage.**
   - The ability of a nation to produce a good more efficiently than any other nation is called an *absolute advantage,* which advocates letting market forces dictate trade flows.
   - Absolute advantage allows a country to produce goods in which it holds an absolute advantage and trade with other nations to obtain goods it needs but does not produce—a *positive-sum game.*
   - A nation holds a *comparative advantage* in production of a good when it is unable to produce the good more efficiently than other nations but can produce it more efficiently than it can any other good.
   - Trade is still beneficial if one country is less efficient in the production of two goods, so long as it is less inefficient in the production of one of the goods.

4. **Explain the factor proportions and international product life cycle theories.**
   - The *factor proportions theory* states that countries produce and export goods that require resources (factors) that are abundant and import goods that require resources that are in short supply.
   - Factor proportions theory predicts that a country will specialize in products that require labor if its cost is low relative to the cost of land and capital, and vice versa.
   - The apparent paradox between predictions of the theory and actual trade flows is called the *Leontief paradox.*
   - The *international product life cycle theory* says that a company will begin exporting its product and later undertake foreign direct investment as the product moves through its life cycle.
   - In the *new product stage,* production remains based in the home country; in the *maturing product stage,* production begins in countries with the highest demand; and in the *standardized product stage,* production moves to low-cost locations to supply a global market.

5. Explain the new trade and national competitive advantage theories.
   - The *new trade theory* argues that, as specialization and output increase, companies realize economies of scale that push the unit costs of production lower.
   - These economies of scale allow a firm to gain a *first-mover advantage*—the economic and strategic advantage gained by being the first company to enter an industry.
   - *National competitive advantage theory* states that a nation's competitiveness in an industry (and, therefore, trade flows) depends on the capacity of the industry to innovate and upgrade.
   - The *Porter diamond* identifies four elements that form the basis of national competitiveness: (1) *factor conditions,* (2) *demand conditions,* (3) *related and supporting industries,* and (4) *firm strategy, structure, and rivalry.*
   - The actions of *governments* and the occurrence of *chance events* can also affect the competitiveness of a nation's companies.

Talk It Over

1. If the nations of the world were to suddenly cut off all trade with one another, what products might you no longer be able to obtain in your country? Choose one country other than your own, and identify the products it would need to do without.

Teaming Up

1. **Debate Project.** In this project, two groups of four students will debate the advantages and disadvantages of completely free international trade. After the first student from each side has spoken, the second student will question the opponent's arguments, looking for holes and inconsistencies. The third student will attempt to answer these arguments. The fourth student will present a summary of each side's arguments. Finally, the class will vote on which team has offered the more compelling argument.

⭐2. **Market Entry Strategy Project.** This exercise corresponds to the *MESP* online simulation. For the country your team is researching, how important is trade (trade as a share of GDP)? What products and services does it export and import? Is there a concerted effort to promote exports to stimulate the economy? With whom does the nation trade? Is it dependent on any particular nation for trade, or does another nation depend on it? Is outsourcing affecting its trade patterns? Does the nation trade only with high-income countries or with low- and middle-income countries, as well? Integrate your findings into your completed *MESP* report.

Key Terms

absolute advantage (p. 139)	international product life cycle theory (p. 144)	national competitive advantage theory (p. 147)
comparative advantage (p. 141)	international trade (p. 132)	new trade theory (p. 146)
factor proportions theory (p. 143)	mercantilism (p. 137)	trade deficit (p. 138)
first-mover advantage (p. 147)		trade surplus (p. 138)

Take It to the Web

1. **Video Report.** Visit this book's channel on YouTube (www.YouTube.com/MyIBvideos). Click on "Videos" near the top of the page, and click on the set of videos labeled "Ch 05: International Trade." Watch one video from the list, and then summarize it in a half-page report. Reflecting on the contents of this chapter, which components of international trade can you identify in the video? How might a company engaged in international business act on the information contained in the video?
2. **Website Report.** Trade theories say that a country gains a competitive advantage in an industry when its companies form a cluster of activities and that governments can help their firms become strong internationally.

The government of France invested heavily in a rather unique public–private venture in Europe called Genopole. Located in a specially designated area within France, the genetic research and development project is designed to thrust France to the forefront of life sciences research. Visit the website of Genopole (www.genopole.com). Report on (1) the various participants (public and private) involved in the venture, (2) specific types of research (genetics, biotechnology, etc.) the organization carries out, and (3) several specific scientific achievements of the project.

Regarding the aims of Genopole, what does each group offer the cluster to encourage the cross-fertilization of ideas and innovations? Why do you think governments today try to create clusters around groundbreaking research in high-technology products and processes? Do you think governments should undertake such efforts or let markets, on their own, decide who should succeed or fail? Can you identify a cluster in your city? If so, identify its members and the contribution of each to the cluster.

Ethical Challenges

1. You are a research fellow for a Washington, DC–based research institute investigating the ethics of restrictions on the international movement of labor. In the practice of international trade, both physical resources and capital cross international borders rather freely, whereas labor is heavily restricted. In fact, it can be extremely difficult for individuals to obtain a permit that allows them to be gainfully employed within many countries. Thus, whereas companies are free to set up production in markets where labor is cheap, labor cannot move to markets where wages are higher. Some argue this locks poor people to their poor geographies and gives them little hope for advancement. Why do you think this situation prevails? Is it ethical that, of all the components of production, labor is the one most subject to restrictions on its international mobility? Explain.

2. You are the production manager for a European-based firm that is considering outsourcing its manufacturing to a producer in China. You are asked by your firm's CEO to prepare a report that outlines the benefits and drawbacks of this potential change. During your research, you find international trade theories that say protectionist actions restrict imports and harm a nation's standard of living—an argument for free trade. Yet you know that free trade and global competition is driving firms like your own to move production to cheaper locations abroad, thereby eliminating jobs in their home countries. Clearly, the gains and losses of free trade are not always distributed evenly across the population. As part of your report to the CEO, argue either for or against the need for measures that protect domestic production and, therefore, jobs at home.

3. You are a member of a World Trade Organization task force that is reviewing the recent banana conflict between the United States and the European Union (EU). The EU and the United States recently ended a nine-year battle over trade in bananas. The EU was giving preferential treatment to banana exporters from Africa, the Caribbean, and the Pacific island nations. But the United States challenged what it saw as unfair trading practices, and the World Trade Organization agreed. Large global fruit companies such as Dole, Chiquita, and Del Monte—which alone account for nearly two-thirds of the fruit traded worldwide—supported the U.S. action. The EU argued it was trying to support struggling economies, for which bananas make up a large portion of their income. Discuss the ethics of managing trade in the interests of countries vulnerable in the global economy. Would you have argued on behalf of the United States or the EU? Why? What are the pros and cons of each side's arguments?

MyManagementLab

Go to **mymanagementlab.com** for Auto-graded writing questions as well as the following Assisted-graded writing questions:

5-1. Many economists believe that China will soon achieve "superpower" status because of its economic reforms, along with the work ethic and high education of its population. How is the rise of China affecting trade among Asia, Europe, and North America?

5-2. Despite its abundance of natural resources, Brazil was once considered an economic "basket case." Yet in recent years, Brazil's economy has performed very well. What forces do you think are propelling Brazil's economic progress?

5-3. Mymanagementlab Only – comprehensive writing assignment for this chapter.

Practicing International Management Case

First in Asia and the World

What company is the leading international express carrier? If you answered Federal Express (www.fedex.com) or UPS (www.ups.com), you're wrong. Try DHL International (www.dhl.com). This company, founded in San Francisco by three entrepreneurs, carved out the niche for combined land-sea express services in 1969 when it began shipping bills of lading and other documents from San Francisco to Honolulu. Soon the company got requests to deliver and pick up in Japan and other Asian countries, and the business of international express delivery was born.

Today, the company services 120,000 destinations in more than 220 countries and territories from its base in Leipzig, Germany. DHL employs more than 300,000 people worldwide, many of them based in Asia, the company's first and most important international market. DHL prides itself on its customer service and reliability. The company hires personnel in the countries where it operates and sees this practice as key to forging relationships with customers in its overseas markets. "Unlike many of our competitors," says one DHL executive, "we don't take a package and hand it off to an agent. We ensure that our deliveries and pick-ups are made by DHL personnel and that we can manage business locally by using local people who know local customs." Relationships are the name of the game in service businesses. DHL cultivates relationships with customs agents because the archaic clearance procedures in many countries are the biggest obstacle to speedy international deliveries.

Express air delivery is now a huge business in Asia, and DHL has several formidable competitors snapping at its heels. These include Federal Express, which offers competitive rates, and local players like Hong Kong Delivery, whose small size makes it highly flexible. DHL cannot simply rest on its number-one position or boast of its long years of experience to stay ahead. The dangers of complacency were brought home to the company when its DHL Japan office faced customer resistance to a price hike. DHL employees had simply assumed that the firm would always be number one and had grown lax on service. In fact, an objective "shipment test" revealed that DHL Japan provided the worst service at what were already the highest prices. Japanese customers had simply continued to use DHL because it was the first in the business and because loyalty was important. Yet the proposed price hike might have been the decisive factor in convincing formerly compliant customers to defect. Fortunately, DHL Japan was able to get back on track through aggressive initiatives.

Today, DHL's customer service record is winning repeated kudos in Asia and around the world. For example, a division called DHL Logistics earned a second consecutive gold medal for excellence in the eighteenth annual Quest for Quality survey conducted by the industry's Logistics Management and Distribution Report. It is also often voted the "Best Express Service" at the annual Asian Freight Industry Awards. These days, competition in the express delivery industry is increasingly intense. Slow global economic growth in recent years has served to strengthen this intensity as DHL and other industry players compete for business. DHL will need to continue listening to its customers, working hard to deliver higher-level services, and fulfilling their advanced logistics needs.

DHL purchased Airborne Express in 2003 for around $1 billion. The merger, designed to restructure the business and slash overhead expenses, integrated the two companies' ground and courier networks and offered customers a seamless global network. The idea was that DHL could then offer its U.S. customers the best of both worlds: the world-class international services of DHL combined with the strong domestic service offerings of Airborne. DHL has been losing money in the United States, but it will not pull out of the U.S. market altogether. Instead, its U.S. arm closed about a third of its stations, cut its ground-hauling network by 18 percent, and reduced its pickup and delivery routes by 17 percent. DHL is also working out a deal whereby UPS will provide air freight for DHL Express shipments within North America.

Thinking Globally

1. As the first to set up an international air express business in 1969, DHL had the first-mover advantage over other companies. Is being a first mover as advantageous for a service company such as DHL as it is for a manufacturing company such as Boeing? Explain.
2. When it comes to global expansion and setting up affiliates abroad, how is a service company's focus different from that of a manufacturing company? What elements are necessary for a service company to achieve global success? What are the obstacles to global expansion?
3. DHL prides itself on having its own staff of more than 300,000 people spread across the globe, instead of relying on local agents. Discuss the merits and drawbacks of this international staffing approach.
4. Why do you think DHL faltered in the United States? What do you think are the dangers, if any, of being a first mover?

Source: Ellie Duncan, "DHL Receives Five Awards at AFSCA 2010," *Supply Chain Digital* (www.supplychaindigital.com), June 14, 2010; Eric Joiner Jr., "DHL Brussels Farewell Party—June 11, 2010," *Freight Dawg* Blog (www.freightdawg.com), April 20, 2010; Jane Roberts, "FedEx, UPS Look to Gain if DHL Scales Back," *Memphis Commercial Appeal* (www.commercialappeal.com), March 6, 2008; DHL website (www.dhl.com), select reports and press releases.

Business–Government Trade Relations

LEARNING OBJECTIVES

After studying this chapter, you should be able to

1. Describe the political, economic, and cultural motives behind governmental intervention in trade.

2. List and explain the methods governments use to promote international trade.

3. List and explain the methods governments use to restrict international trade.

4. Discuss the importance of the World Trade Organization in promoting free trade.

A Look Back

Chapter 5 explored theories that have been developed to explain the pattern international trade should take. We examined the important concept of comparative advantage and the conceptual basis for how international trade benefits nations.

A Look at This Chapter

This chapter discusses the active role of national governments in international trade. We examine the motives for government intervention and the tools that nations use to accomplish their goals. We then explore the global trading system and show how it promotes free trade.

A Look Ahead

Chapter 7 continues our discussion of the international business environment. We explore recent patterns of foreign direct investment, theories that try to explain why it occurs, and governments' role in influencing investment flows.

TIME WARNER RISES

HOLLYWOOD, California—Time Warner (www.timewarner.com) is a global leader in the media and entertainment industry. Its businesses include television networks (HBO, Turner Broadcasting), publishing (*Time, Sports Illustrated*), and film entertainment (New Line Cinema, Warner Bros.). As Time Warner marches across the globe, people in almost every nation on the planet view its media creations.

New Line Cinema's *The Lord of the Rings* trilogy, based on the books by J.R.R. Tolkien and directed by filmmaker Peter Jackson, is the most successful film franchise in history. The final installment in the trilogy, *The Lord of the Rings: The Return of the King,* earned more than $1 billion at the worldwide box office. The entire trilogy earned nearly $3 billion worldwide and won 17 Academy Awards. New Line is also producing the *The Hobbit* trilogy, again under the direction of Peter Jackson.

Warner Bros.'s ongoing *Harry Potter* films, based on the novels of former British schoolteacher J.K. Rowling, have been magically successful. Kids worldwide snatched up *Harry Potter* books in every major language and poured into cinemas to watch young Harry on the silver screen. Warner Bros. also hit it big with the *Batman* film *The Dark Knight*—one of the highest-grossing films ever. Shown here, Catwoman rides the "Batpod" motorcycle in the film *The Dark Knight Rises*. Warner Bros. also produces mini-movies and games exclusively for its website.

Source: WARNER BROS PICTURES/Newscom

Yet Time Warner must tread carefully as it expands its reach. Some governments fear that their own nations' writers, actors, directors, and producers will be drowned out by big-budget Hollywood productions such as *The Lord of the Rings, Harry Potter,* and *Batman.* Others fear the replacement of their traditional values with those depicted in imported entertainment. As you read this chapter, consider all the cultural, political, and economic reasons why governments regulate international trade.[1]

Chapter 5 presented theories that describe what the patterns of international trade *should* look like. The theory of comparative advantage says that the country that has a comparative advantage in the production of a certain good will produce that good when barriers to trade do not exist. But this ideal does not accurately characterize trade in today's global marketplace. Despite efforts by organizations such as the World Trade Organization (www.wto.org) and smaller groups of countries, nations still retain many barriers to trade.

In this chapter, we investigate business–government trade relations. We first explain why nations erect barriers to trade, exploring the cultural, political, and economic motives for such barriers. We then examine the instruments countries use to restrict imports and exports. Efforts to promote trade by reducing barriers within the context of the global trading system are then presented. In Chapter 8 we discuss how smaller groups of countries are eliminating barriers to both trade and investment.

Why Do Governments Intervene in Trade?

The pattern of imports and exports that occurs in the absence of trade barriers is called **free trade**. Despite the advantages of open and free trade among nations, governments have long intervened in the trade of goods and services. Why do governments impose restrictions on free trade? In general, they do so for reasons that are political, economic, or cultural—or some combination of the three. Countries often intervene in trade by strongly supporting their domestic companies' exporting activities. But the more emotionally charged intervention occurs when a nation's economy is underperforming. In tough economic times, businesses and workers often lobby their governments for protection from imports that are eliminating jobs in the domestic market. Let's take a closer look at the political, economic, and cultural motives for intervention.

Political Motives

Government officials often make trade-related decisions based on political motives because a politician's career can depend on pleasing voters and getting reelected. Yet, a trade policy based purely on political motives is seldom wise in the long run. The main political motives behind government intervention in trade include protecting jobs, preserving national security, responding to other nations' unfair trade practices, and gaining influence over other nations.[2]

PROTECT JOBS Short of an unpopular war, nothing will oust a government faster than high rates of unemployment. Thus, practically all governments become involved when free trade creates job losses at home. For example, Ohio lost around 215,000 manufacturing jobs over a recent 14-year period. Most of those jobs went to China and the nations of Central and Eastern Europe. The despair of unemployed workers and the pivotal role of Ohio in presidential elections lured politicians to the state, who promised Ohio lower income taxes, expanded worker retraining, and greater investment in the state's infrastructure.

But politicians' efforts to protect jobs can draw attention away from free trade's real benefits. General Electric (GE) sent many jobs from the United States to Mexico over the years. GE now employs 30,000 Mexicans at 35 factories that manufacture all sorts of its appliances and other goods. But GE also sold Mexican companies $350 million worth of its turbines made in Texas, 100 of its locomotives made in Pennsylvania, and dozens of its U.S.-made aircraft engines. Mexico specializes in making products that require less-expensive labor, and the United States specializes in producing goods that require advanced technology and a large investment of capital.[3]

PRESERVE NATIONAL SECURITY Human, economic, and environmental security are closely related to national security. The globalization of markets and production creates new security risks for companies. To read about these risks, see this chapter's Global Sustainability feature, titled "Managing Security in the Age of Globalization."

National Security and Imports Certain imports are often restricted in the name of preserving national security. In the event of war, governments must have access to a domestic supply of certain items such as weapons, fuel, and air, land, and sea transportation in case their availability is restricted. Many nations continue to search for oil within their borders in case war disrupts its

GLOBAL SUSTAINABILITY   Managing Security in the Age of Globalization

As well as the need to secure lengthy supply chains and distribution channels, companies must secure their facilities, information systems, and reputations.

- **Facilities Risk.** Large companies with top-notch property risk–management programs produce more stable earnings. Companies practicing weak risk management experience 55 times greater risk of property loss due to fire and 29 times greater risk of property loss caused by natural hazards. Planning and facilities assessment (around $12,000 for a midsized company, $1 million for a large firm) can be well worth the cost.
- **Information Risk.** Computer viruses, software worms, malicious code, and cyber criminals cost companies around the world many billions of dollars each year. Disgruntled employees, dishonest competitors, and hackers who steal customers' personal and financial data can then sell it to the highest bidder. Upon termination, employees sometimes leave with digital devices containing confidential memos, competitive data, and private e-mails.
- **Reputational Risk.** News today travels worldwide quickly. Reputational risk is anything that can harm a firm's image, including

product recalls, workers' rights violations, and lawsuits. The damaged reputation of Goldman Sachs following a $550 million settlement with the Securities and Exchange Commission for its actions before and during recent financial crises cost the firm 40 percent ($6 billion) of its brand value in one year.
- **What to Do.** Like the risks themselves, the challenges are varied. Companies should identify all potential risks to their facilities and then develop a best-practice property risk program. It sounds simple, but employees must change passwords frequently, safeguard their computers and mobile devices from attack, and return company-owned digital devices when leaving the firm. Finally, ever-increasing scrutiny means that companies should act ethically and within the law to protect their reputations.
- **Want to Know More?** Visit Sustainable Security (sustainablesecurity.org), the Foundation for Environmental Security and Sustainability (www.fess-global.org), Kroll (www.krollworldwide.com), and Check Point Software Technologies (www.checkpoint.com).

flow from outside sources. Legitimate national security reasons for intervention can be difficult to argue against, particularly when they have the support of most of a country's people.

Some countries claim that national security is the reason for fierce protection of their agricultural sector, since food security is essential at a time of war. France has been criticized by many nations for ardently protecting its agricultural sector. French agricultural subsidies are intended to provide a fair financial return for French farmers, who traditionally operate on a small scale and therefore have high production costs and low profit margins. But many developed nations are exposing agribusiness to market forces and prompting their farmers to discover new ways to manage risk and increase efficiency. Innovative farmers are experimenting with more intensive land management, high-tech precision farming, and greater use of biotechnology.

Yet, protection from import competition does have its drawbacks. Perhaps the main one is the added cost of continuing to produce a good or provide a service domestically that could be supplied more efficiently from abroad. Also, a policy of protection may remain in place much longer than necessary once it is adopted. Thus, policy makers should consider whether an issue truly is a matter of national security before intervening in trade.

National Security and Exports Governments also have national security motives for banning certain defense-related goods from export to other nations. Most industrialized nations have agencies that review requests to export technologies or products that are said to have *dual uses*—meaning they have both industrial and military applications. Products designated as dual use are classified as such and require special governmental approval before export can take place.

Products on the dual-use lists of most nations include nuclear materials, technological equipment, certain chemicals and toxins, some sensors and lasers, and specific devices related to weapons, navigation, aerospace, and propulsion. Bans on the export of dual-use products were strictly enforced during the Cold War years between the West and the former Soviet Union. Whereas many countries relaxed enforcement of these controls in recent years, the continued threat of terrorism and fears of weapons of mass destruction are renewing support for such bans.

Nations also place certain companies and organizations in other countries on a list of entities that are restricted from receiving their exports. For example, the owner of an electronics firm pleaded guilty to charges of conspiracy to illegally export dual-use items from the United States to India for possible use in ballistic missiles, space launch vehicles, and fighter jets. Parthasarathy Sudarshan admitted that he provided the components to government entities in India, including two companies on the U.S. Department of Commerce's "Entity List." Sudarshan was sentenced to 35 months in a U.S. federal prison and was fined $60,000.[4]

RESPOND TO "UNFAIR" TRADE Many observers argue that it makes no sense for one nation to allow free trade if other nations actively protect their own industries. Governments often threaten to close their ports to another nation's ships or to impose extremely high tariffs on its goods if the other nation does not concede on some trade issue that is seen as being unfair. In other words, if one government thinks another nation is not "playing fair," it will often threaten to retaliate unless certain concessions are made.

GAIN INFLUENCE Governments of the world's largest nations may become involved in trade to gain influence over smaller nations. The United States goes to great lengths to gain and maintain control over events in all of Central, North, and South America, and the Caribbean basin.

The United States has banned all trade and investment with Cuba since 1962 in the hope of exerting political influence against its communist leaders. Designed to pressure Cuba's government to change, the policy has caused suffering among Cuba's citizens. Many Cubans have perished trying to reach the United States on homemade rafts. But change is occurring in Cuba, and since 2008, its people can buy DVD players, stay in tourist hotels, and use mobile phones. Even the concept of performance-related pay was introduced. These seemingly trivial freedoms represent monumental change to ordinary Cubans, who now hope for the right to buy cars, travel, and buy and sell property.[5]

Economic Motives

Although governments intervene in trade for highly charged cultural and political reasons, they also have economic motives for their intervention. The most common economic reasons for nations' attempts to influence international trade are the protection of young industries from competition and the promotion of a strategic trade policy.

PROTECT INFANT INDUSTRIES According to the *infant industry argument,* a country's emerging industries need protection from international competition during their development phase until they become sufficiently competitive internationally. This argument is based on the idea that infant industries need protection because of a steep learning curve. In other words, only as an industry grows and matures does it gain the knowledge it needs to become more innovative, efficient, and competitive.

Although this argument is conceptually appealing, it does have several problems. First, the argument requires governments to distinguish between industries that are worth protecting and those that are not. This is difficult, if not impossible, to do. For years, Japan has targeted infant industries for protection, low interest loans, and other benefits. Its performance on assisting these industries was very good through the early 1980s but has been less successful since then.

Environmental activists protest against genetically modified (GM) food in front of the European Council in Brussels, Belgium. All types of crops today, including corn, soybeans, and wheat, are grown with genetically enhanced seed technology to resist insects and disease. Many people in Europe fiercely resist U.S. efforts to export GM crops to their markets. Do you believe Europeans are right to be wary of the importation of GM crops?

Source: Wiktor Dabkowski/Newscom

Until the government achieves future success in identifying and targeting industries, supporting this type of policy remains questionable.

Second, protection from international competition can cause domestic companies to become complacent toward innovation. This can limit a company's incentives to obtain the knowledge it needs to become more competitive. The most extreme examples of complacency are industries within formerly communist nations. When their communist protections collapsed, nearly all companies that were run by the state were decades behind their competitors from capitalist nations. To survive, many government-owned businesses required financial assistance in the form of infusions of capital or outright purchase.

Third, protection can do more economic harm than good. Consumers often end up paying more for products because a lack of competition typically creates fewer incentives to cut production costs or improve quality. Meanwhile, companies become less competitive and more reliant on protection. Protection in Japan created a two-tier economy where, in one tier, highly competitive multinational corporations faced rivals in overseas markets and learned to become strong competitors. In the other tier, domestic industries were made noncompetitive through protected markets, high wages, and barriers to imports.

Fourth, the infant industry argument also says that it is not always possible for small, promising companies to obtain funding in capital markets, and thus they need financial support from their government. However, international capital markets today are far more sophisticated than in the past, and promising business ventures can normally obtain funding from private sources.

PURSUE STRATEGIC TRADE POLICY   Recall from our discussion in Chapter 5 that new trade theorists believe government intervention can help companies take advantage of economies of scale and become the first movers in their industries. First-mover advantages arise because economies of scale in production limit the number of companies that an industry can sustain.

Benefits of Strategic Trade Policy   Supporters of strategic trade policy argue that it results in increased national income. Companies should earn a good profit if they obtain first-mover advantages and solidify positions in their markets around the world. Advocates claim that strategic trade policies helped South Korea build global conglomerates (called *chaebol*) that dwarf competitors. For years, South Korean shipbuilders received a variety of government subsidies, including low-cost financing. The *chaebol* helped South Korea to emerge strongly from the global economic crisis because of their market power and the wide range of industries in which they compete. Such policies had spin-off effects on related industries, and local suppliers to the *chaebol* are now thriving.[6]

Drawbacks of Strategic Trade Policy   Although it sounds as if strategic trade policy only has benefits, there can be drawbacks as well. Lavish government assistance to domestic companies in the past caused inefficiency and high costs for both South Korean and Japanese companies. Large government concessions to local labor unions hiked wages and forced Korea's *chaebol* to accept low profit margins.[7]

In addition, when governments decide to support specific industries, their choice is often subject to political lobbying by the groups seeking government assistance. It is possible that special interest groups could capture all the gains from assistance with no benefit for consumers. If this were to occur, consumers could end up paying more for lower-quality goods than they could otherwise obtain.

Cultural Motives

Nations often restrict trade in goods and services to achieve cultural objectives, the most common being protection of national identity. Culture and trade are intertwined and greatly affect one another. The cultures of countries are slowly altered by exposure to the people and products of other cultures. Unwanted cultural influence in a nation can cause great distress and cause governments to block imports that it believes are harmful (recall our discussion of *cultural imperialism* in Chapter 2).

French law bans foreign-language words from virtually all business and government communications, radio and TV broadcasts, public announcements, and advertising messages—at least whenever a suitable French alternative is available. You can't advertise a *best seller*; it has to be a *succès de librairie*. You can't sell *popcorn* at *le cinéma*; French moviegoers must snack

CULTURE MATTERS   Myths of Small Business Exporting

- **Myth 1:** Only large companies can export successfully. **Fact:** Most exporters are small and medium-sized enterprises with fewer than 50 employees. Exporting can reduce the dependency of small firms on domestic markets and can help them avoid seasonal sales fluctuations. A product popular domestically, or perhaps even unsuccessful at home, may be wanted elsewhere in the global market.

- **Myth 2:** Small businesses can find little export advice. **Fact:** Novice and experienced exporters alike can receive comprehensive export assistance from federal agencies (www .export.gov). International trade specialists can help small businesses locate and use federal, state, local, and private-sector programs. They are also an excellent source of market research, trade leads, financing, and trade events.

- **Myth 3:** Licensing requirements needed to export are too complicated. **Fact:** Most products do not need export licenses. Exporters need only to write "NLR" for "no license required" on their Shipper's Export Declaration. A license is generally needed only for high-tech or defense-related goods or when the receiving country is under a U.S. embargo or other restriction.

- **Myth 4:** Small businesses cannot obtain export financing. **Fact:** The Small Business Administration (www.sba.gov) and the Export-Import Bank (www.exim.gov) work together in lending money to small businesses. Whereas the SBA is responsible for loan requests below $750,000, the Export-Import Bank handles transactions over $750,000. The Trade and Development Agency (www.ustda.gov) also helps small and medium-sized firms obtain financing for international projects.

on *mais soufflé*. The Higher Council on French Language works against the inclusion of so-called Franglais phrases such as *le marketing, le cash flow,* and *le brainstorming* into commerce and other areas of French culture. Not to be outdone by neighboring France, German bureaucrats plan to exchange governmental use of English words with German ones, for example, replacing *brainstorming* with *ideensammlung* and *meeting points* with *treffpukte*.[8]

Canada also tries to mitigate the cultural influence of entertainment products imported from the United States. Canada requires at least 35 percent of music played over Canadian radio to be by Canadian artists. In fact, many countries are considering laws to protect their media programming for cultural reasons. The downside of such restrictions is they reduce the selection of products available to consumers.

CULTURAL INFLUENCE OF THE UNITED STATES International trade is the vehicle by which the English language swiftly infiltrates the cultures of other nations. International trade in all sorts of goods and services is exposing people around the world to new words, ideas, products, and ways of life. Still, as international trade continues to expand, many governments try to limit potential adverse effects on their cultures and economies.

The United States, more than any other nation, is seen by many around the world as a threat to local culture. The reason is the global strength of the United States in entertainment and media (such as movies, magazines, and music) and consumer goods. These products are highly visible to all consumers and cause groups of various kinds to lobby government officials for protection from their cultural influence. Domestic producers find it easy to join in the calls for protection because the rhetoric of protectionism often receives widespread public support.

Oddly, many small businesses capable of exporting have not yet begun to do so. By some estimates, only 10 percent of U.S. companies with fewer than 100 employees export. Encouraging greater export activity may require U.S. companies to undergo a *cultural shift in mindset*. Although a lack of investment capital can be a real obstacle to exporting for small businesses, some common myths in the business culture create artificial obstacles. To explore some of these myths and the facts that dispute them, see this chapter's Culture Matters feature, titled "Myths of Small Business Exporting."

QUICK STUDY 1

1. What are some political reasons why governments intervene in trade? Explain the role of national security concerns.
2. Identify the main economic motives for government trade intervention. What are the drawbacks of each method of intervention?
3. What cultural motives do nations have for intervening in free trade?

TABLE 6.1 Methods of Promoting and Restricting Trade

Trade Promotion	Trade Restriction
Subsidies	Tariffs
Export financing	Quotas
Foreign trade zones	Embargoes
Special government agencies	Local content requirements
	Administrative delays
	Currency controls

Methods of Promoting Trade

In the previous discussion, we alluded to the types of instruments governments use to promote or restrict trade with other nations. The most common instruments that governments use are shown in Table 6.1. In this section, we examine methods of trade promotion. We cover methods of trade restriction in the next section.

Subsidies

Financial assistance to domestic producers in the form of cash payments, low-interest loans, tax breaks, product price supports, or other forms is called a **subsidy**. Regardless of the form a subsidy takes, it is intended to assist domestic companies in fending off international competitors. This can mean becoming more competitive in the home market or increasing competitiveness in international markets through exports. It is nearly impossible to calculate the amount of subsidies a country offers its producers because of the many forms subsidies take. This makes the work of the World Trade Organization difficult when it is called on to settle arguments over subsidies (the World Trade Organization is discussed later in this chapter).

subsidy
Financial assistance to domestic producers in the form of cash payments, low-interest loans, tax breaks, product price supports, or other forms.

DRAWBACKS OF SUBSIDIES Critics say that subsidies encourage inefficiency and complacency by covering costs that truly competitive industries should be able to absorb on their own. Many believe subsidies benefit companies and industries that receive them but harm consumers because they tend to be paid for with income and sales taxes. Thus, although subsidies provide short-term relief to companies and industries, whether they help a nation's citizens in the long term is questionable.

Some observers say that far more devastating is the effect of subsidies on farmers in developing and emerging markets. We've already seen that many wealthy nations award subsidies to their farmers to ensure an adequate food supply for their people. It is said that these subsidies, worth billions of dollars, make it difficult if not impossible for farmers from poor countries to sell their unsubsidized (i.e., more expensive) food on world markets. Compounding the plight of these farmers is the fact that their nations are being forced to eliminate trade barriers by international organizations. The economic consequences for poor farmers in Africa, Asia, and Latin America are higher unemployment and poverty.[9]

Subsidies can lead to an overuse of resources, negative environmental effects, and higher costs for commodities. As fuel prices soared in China, governments fearing inflation and street protests increased their heavy subsidies of energy. China's fuel subsidies for a single year were estimated at a whopping $40 billion. These subsidies eliminate incentives to conserve fuel and drive fuel prices higher. Whereas countries without fuel subsidies saw steady or falling demand, subsidizing countries saw rising demand that threatened to outstrip growth in global fuel supplies.[10]

Export Financing

Governments often promote exports by helping companies finance their export activities. They can offer loans that a company could otherwise not obtain or can charge them an interest rate that is lower than the market rate. Another option is for a government to guarantee that it will repay the loan of a company if the company should default on repayment; this is called a *loan guarantee*.

MANAGER'S BRIEFCASE   Experts in Export Financing

Several Ex-Im Bank (www.exim.gov) programs can help U.S. businesses expand abroad:

- *City/State Program.* This program brings financing services to small and medium-sized U.S. companies that are ready to export. This program currently exists with 38 state and local government offices and private sector organizations.
- *Working Capital Guarantee Program.* This program encourages commercial banks to loan money to companies with export potential. The guarantee covers 90 percent of the loan's principal and accrued interest. The guaranteed financing can help purchase finished products for export or pay for raw materials, for example.
- *Credit Information Services.* The Ex-Im Bank supplies credit information to U.S. exporters and commercial lenders. It provides information on a country or specific company abroad. But the bank does not divulge either confidential financial data on non–U.S. buyers to whom it has extended credit or confidential information on specific conditions in other countries.

- *Credit Insurance.* This program helps U.S. exporters by protecting them against loss should a non–U.S. buyer or other non–U.S. debtor default for political or commercial reasons. The proceeds of the policy can be used as collateral and therefore can make obtaining export financing easier.
- *Guarantee Program.* This program provides repayment protection for private sector loans made to creditworthy buyers of U.S. capital equipment, projects, and services. The bank guarantees the principal and interest on the loan if the borrower defaults. Most guarantees provide comprehensive coverage against political and commercial risks.
- *Loan Program.* The bank makes loans directly to non–U.S. buyers of U.S. exports and intermediary loans to creditworthy parties that provide loans to non–U.S. buyers. The program provides fixed-interest-rate financing for export sales of U.S. capital equipment and related services.

Source: Export-Import Bank of the United States website (www.exim.gov).

Many nations have special agencies dedicated to helping their domestic companies obtain export financing. For example, a very well-known institution is called the *Export-Import Bank of the United States*—or *Ex-Im Bank* for short. The Ex-Im Bank (www.exim.gov) finances the export activities of companies in the United States and offers insurance on foreign accounts receivable. Another U.S. government agency, the *Overseas Private Investment Corporation (OPIC),* also provides insurance services but for investors. Through OPIC (www.opic.gov), companies that invest abroad can insure against losses due to (1) expropriation, (2) currency inconvertibility, and (3) war, revolution, and insurrection.

Receiving financing from government agencies is often crucial to the success of small businesses that are just beginning to export. Taken together, small businesses account for more than 80 percent of all transactions handled by the Ex-Im Bank. For instance, the Ex-Im Bank guaranteed to cover a loan of nearly $4 million to help fund development of an amusement park in Accra, Ghana. The investment in Africa is in response to rising demand for world-class amusement parks across West Africa. The park will employ at least 175 local Ghanaians under the supervision of U.S. expatriate managers. For more on how the Ex-Im Bank helps businesses gain export financing, see the Manager's Briefcase, titled "Experts in Export Financing."

Foreign Trade Zones

foreign trade zone (FTZ)
Designated geographic region through which merchandise is allowed to pass with lower customs duties (taxes) and/or fewer customs procedures.

Most countries promote trade with other nations by creating what is called a **foreign trade zone (FTZ)**—a designated geographic region through which merchandise is allowed to pass with lower customs duties (taxes) and/or fewer customs procedures. Increased employment is often the intended purpose of FTZs, with a by-product being increased trade. A good example of a foreign trade zone is Turkey's Aegean Free Zone, in which the Turkish government allows companies to conduct manufacturing operations free from taxes.

Customs duties increase the total amount of a good's production cost and increase the time needed to get it to market. Companies can reduce such costs and time by establishing a facility inside an FTZ. A common purpose of many companies' facilities in such zones is final product assembly. The U.S. Department of Commerce (www.commerce.gov) administers dozens of FTZs within the United States. Many of these zones allow components to be imported at a discount from the normal duty. Once assembled, the finished product can be sold within the U.S. market with no further duties charged. State governments welcome such zones in order to obtain the jobs that the assembly operations create.

China has established a number of large FTZs in order to reap the employment advantages they offer. Goods imported into these zones do not require import licenses or other documents, nor are they subject to import duties. International companies can also store goods in these zones before shipping them to other countries without incurring taxes in China. Moreover, five of these zones are located within specially designated economic zones in which local governments can offer additional opportunities and tax breaks to international investors.

Another country that has enjoyed the beneficial effects of FTZs is Mexico. Decades ago, Mexico established such a zone along its northern border with the United States. Creation of the zone caused development of companies called *maquiladoras* along the border inside Mexico. The *maquiladoras* import materials or parts from the United States duty free, process them to some extent, and export them back to the United States, which charges duties only on the value added to the product in Mexico. The program has expanded rapidly over the five decades since its inception, employing hundreds of thousands of people from all across Mexico who move north looking for work.

Special Government Agencies

Learning the government regulations of other countries can be a daunting task. A company must know whether its product is subject to a tariff or quota, for example. Governments of most nations, therefore, have special agencies responsible for promoting exports. Such agencies can be particularly helpful to small and medium-sized businesses that have limited financial resources.

Government trade-promotion agencies often organize trips for trade officials and business-people to visit other countries in order to meet potential business partners and generate contacts for new business. They also typically open trade offices in other countries. These offices are designed to promote the home country's exports and introduce businesses to potential partners in the host nation. Government trade-promotion agencies typically do a great deal of advertising in other countries promoting the nation's exports. For example, Chile's Trade Commission, ProChile, has commercial offices in 40 countries and a website (www.chileinfo.com).

Governments not only promote trade by encouraging exports but also encourage imports that the nation does not or cannot produce. For example, the Japan External Trade Organization (JETRO; www.jetro.go.jp) is a trade-promotion agency of the Japanese government. The agency coaches small and medium-sized overseas businesses on the protocols of Japanese deal making, arranges meetings with suitable Japanese distributors and partners, and even assists in finding temporary office spaces.

QUICK STUDY 2

1. How do governments use *subsidies* to promote trade? Identify the drawbacks of subsidies.
2. How does export financing promote trade? Explain its importance to small and medium-sized firms.
3. Define the term *foreign trade zone*. How can it be used to promote trade?
4. How can special government agencies help promote trade?

Methods of Restricting Trade

Earlier in this chapter, we read about the political, economic, and cultural reasons for governmental intervention in trade. In this section, we discuss the methods governments can use to restrict unwanted trade. There are two general categories of trade barriers available to governments. A **tariff** is a government tax levied on a product as it enters or leaves a country. A tariff increases the price of an imported product *directly* and, therefore, reduces its appeal to buyers. A nontariff barrier limits the availability of an imported product, which increases its price *indirectly* and, therefore, reduces its appeal to buyers. Let's take a closer look at tariffs and the various types of nontariff barriers.

tariff
Government tax levied on a product as it enters or leaves a country.

Tariffs

We can classify a tariff into one of three categories. An *export tariff* is levied by the government of a country that is exporting a product. Countries can use export tariffs when they believe an export's price is lower than it should be. Developing nations whose exports consist mostly of low-priced natural resources often levy export tariffs. A *transit tariff* is levied by the government of a country that a product is passing through on its way to its final destination. Transit tariffs have been almost entirely eliminated worldwide through international trade agreements. An *import tariff* is levied by the government of a country that is importing a product. The import tariff is by far the most common tariff used by governments today.

We can further break down the import tariff into three subcategories based on the manner in which it is calculated. An **ad valorem tariff** is levied as a percentage of the stated price of an imported product. A **specific tariff** is levied as a specific fee for each unit (measured by number, weight, etc.) of an imported product. A **compound tariff** is levied on an imported product and calculated partly as a percentage of its stated price and partly as a specific fee for each unit. Let's now discuss the two main reasons why countries levy tariffs.

PROTECT DOMESTIC PRODUCERS Nations can use tariffs to protect domestic producers. For example, an import tariff raises the cost of an imported good and increases the appeal of domestically produced goods. In this way, domestic producers gain a protective barrier against imports. Although producers that receive tariff protection can gain a price advantage, in the long run protection can keep them from increasing efficiency. A protected industry can be devastated if protection encourages complacency and inefficiency and it is later thrown into the lion's den of international competition. Mexico began reducing tariff protection in the mid-1980s as a prelude to NAFTA negotiations, and many Mexican producers went bankrupt despite attempts to grow more efficient.

GENERATE REVENUE Tariffs are also a source of government revenue, but mostly among developing nations. The main reason is that less-developed nations tend to have less-formal domestic economies that lack the capability to record domestic transactions accurately. The lack of accurate record keeping makes collection of sales taxes within the country extremely difficult. Nations solve the problem by simply raising their needed revenue through import and export tariffs. As countries develop, however, they tend to generate a greater portion of their revenues from taxes on income, capital gains, and other economic activity.

The discussion so far leads us to question who benefits from tariffs. We've already learned the two principal reasons for tariff barriers—protecting domestic producers and raising government revenue. On the surface, it appears that governments and domestic producers benefit. We also saw that tariffs raise the price of a product because importers typically charge a higher price to recover the cost of this additional tax. Thus, it appears on the surface that consumers do not benefit. As we also mentioned earlier, there is the danger that tariffs will create inefficient domestic producers that may go out of business once protective import tariffs are removed. Analysis of the total cost to a country is far more complicated and goes beyond the scope of our discussion. Suffice it to say that tariffs tend to exact a cost on countries as a whole because they lessen the gains that a nation's people obtain from trade.

Quotas

A restriction on the amount (measured in units or weight) of a good that can enter or leave a country during a certain period of time is called a **quota**. After tariffs, quotas are the second most common type of trade barrier. Governments typically administer their quota systems by granting quota licenses to the companies or governments of other nations (in the case of import quotas) and domestic producers (in the case of export quotas). Governments normally grant such licenses on a year-by-year basis.

REASON FOR IMPORT QUOTAS A government may impose an *import quota* to protect its domestic producers by placing a limit on the amount of goods allowed to enter the country. This helps domestic producers maintain their market shares and prices because competitive forces are restrained. In this case, domestic producers win because their market is protected. Consumers lose because of higher prices and limited selection attributable to lower competition. Other losers include domestic producers whose own production requires the import subjected to a quota. Companies relying on the importation of so-called intermediate goods will find the final cost of their own products increase.

Historically, countries placed import quotas on the textile and apparel products of other countries under the Multi-Fibre Arrangement. This arrangement at one time affected countries accounting for more than 80 percent of world trade in textiles and clothing. When that

ad valorem tariff
Tariff levied as a percentage of the stated price of an imported product.

specific tariff
Tariff levied as a specific fee for each unit (measured by number, weight, etc.) of an imported product.

compound tariff
Tariff levied on an imported product and calculated partly as a percentage of its stated price and partly as a specific fee for each unit.

quota
Restriction on the amount (measured in units or weight) of a good that can enter or leave a country during a certain period of time.

Vietnamese women manufacture woven rugs at a craft center in Hoi An, Vietnam. Across Vietnam, hundreds of small clothing factories have thrived following removal of worldwide import quotas allowed under the Multi-Fibre Agreement. Under the Multi-Fibre Agreement, wealthy nations guaranteed imports of textiles and garments from poor countries under a quota system. Under what conditions do you think nations should be allowed to impose import quotas?

Source: David R. Frazier/Newscom

arrangement expired in 2005, many textile producers in poor nations feared the loss of jobs to China. But some countries with a large textile industry, such as Bangladesh, are benefiting from cheap labor and the reluctance among purchasers to rely exclusively on China for all supplies.

REASONS FOR EXPORT QUOTAS There are at least two reasons why a country imposes *export quotas* on its domestic producers. First, it may wish to maintain adequate supplies of a product in the home market. This motive is most common among countries that export natural resources that are essential to domestic business or the long-term survival of a nation.

Second, a country may limit the export of a good in order to restrict its supply on world markets, thereby increasing the international price of the good. This is the motive behind the formation and activities of the Organization of Petroleum Exporting Countries (OPEC; www.opec.org). This group of nations from the Middle East and Latin America attempts to restrict the world's supply of crude oil in order to earn greater profits.

Voluntary Export Restraints A unique version of the export quota is called a **voluntary export restraint (VER)**—a quota that a nation imposes on its own exports, usually at the request of another nation. Countries normally self-impose a voluntary export restraint in response to the threat of an import quota or a total ban on the product by an importing nation. The classic example of the use of a voluntary export restraint is from the 1980s when Japanese carmakers were making significant market-share gains in the United States. The closing of U.S. carmakers' production facilities in the United States was creating a volatile anti-Japan sentiment among the population and the U.S. Congress. Fearing punitive legislation if Japan did not limit its automobile exports to the United States, the Japanese government and its carmakers self-imposed a voluntary export restraint on cars headed for the United States.

Consumers in the country that imposes an export quota benefit from lower-priced products (due to their greater supply) as long as domestic producers do not curtail production. Producers in an importing country benefit because the goods of producers from the exporting country are restrained, which may allow them to increase prices. Export quotas hurt consumers in the importing nation because of reduced selection and perhaps higher prices. Yet export quotas might allow these same consumers to retain their jobs if imports were threatening to put domestic producers out of business. Again, detailed economic studies are needed to determine the winners and losers in any particular export quota case.

TARIFF-QUOTAS A hybrid form of trade restriction is called a **tariff-quota**—a lower tariff rate for a certain quantity of imports and a higher rate for quantities that exceed the quota. Imports entering a nation under a quota limit of, say, 1,000 tons are charged a 10-percent tariff. But

voluntary export restraint (VER)
Unique version of export quota that a nation imposes on its exports, usually at the request of an importing nation.

tariff-quota
Lower tariff rate for a certain quantity of imports and a higher rate for quantities that exceed the quota.

FIGURE 6.1

How a Tariff-Quota Works

Source: World Trade Organization
Web site (www.wto.org)

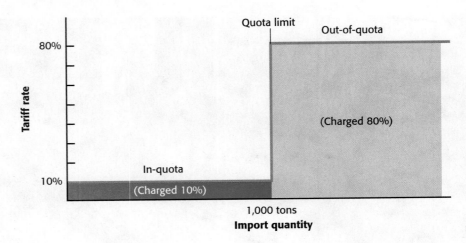

subsequent imports that do not make it under the quota limit of 1,000 tons are charged a tariff of 80 percent. Figure 6.1 shows how a tariff-quota actually works. Tariff-quotas are used extensively in the trade of agricultural products. Many countries implemented tariff-quotas in 1995 after their use was permitted by the World Trade Organization, the agency that regulates trade among nations.

Embargoes

A complete ban on trade (imports and exports) in one or more products with a particular country is called an **embargo**. An embargo may be placed on one or a few goods, or it may completely ban trade in all goods. It is the most restrictive nontariff trade barrier available, and it is typically applied to accomplish political goals. Embargoes can be decreed by individual nations or by supranational organizations such as the United Nations. Because they can be very difficult to enforce, embargoes are used less today than they have been in the past. One example of a total ban on trade with another country is the U.S. embargo on trade with Cuba, although some medicines and foods from the United States are now allowed to enter Cuba.

After a military coup ousted elected President Aristide of Haiti in the early 1990s, restraints were applied to force the military junta either to reinstate Aristide or to hold new elections. One restraint was an embargo by the Organization of American States. Because of difficulties in actually enforcing the embargo and after two years of fruitless United Nations diplomacy, the embargo failed. The United Nations then stepped in with a ban on trade in oil and weapons. Despite some smuggling through the Dominican Republic, which shares the island of Hispaniola with Haiti, the embargo was generally effective and Aristide was eventually reinstated.

Local Content Requirements

Recall from Chapter 3 that *local content requirements* are laws stipulating that producers in the domestic market must supply a specified amount of a good or service. These requirements can state that a certain portion of the end product must consist of domestically produced goods or that a certain portion of the final cost of a product must come from domestic sources.

The purpose of local content requirements is to force companies from other nations to use local resources in their production processes—particularly labor. Similar to other restraints on imports, such requirements help protect domestic producers from the price advantage of companies based in other, low-wage countries. Today, many developing countries use local content requirements as a strategy to boost industrialization. Companies often respond to local content requirements by locating production facilities inside the nation that stipulates such restrictions.

For example, although many people consider music to be the universal language, not all cultures are equally open to the world's diverse musical influences. To prevent Anglo-Saxon music from invading French culture, French law requires radio programs to include at least 40-percent French content. Such local content requirements are intended to protect both the French cultural identity and the jobs of French artists against other nations' pop culture that may wash up on French shores.

embargo
Complete ban on trade (imports and exports) in one or more products with a particular country.

Administrative Delays

Regulatory controls or bureaucratic rules designed to impair the flow of imports into a country are called **administrative delays**. This nontariff barrier includes a wide range of government actions, such as requiring international air carriers to land at inconvenient airports, requiring product inspections that damage the product itself, purposely understaffing customs offices to cause unusual time delays, and requiring special licenses that take a long time to obtain. The objective of all such administrative delays for a country is to discriminate against imported products—it is, in a word, protectionism.

administrative delays
Regulatory controls or bureaucratic rules designed to impair the flow of imports into a country.

Currency Controls

Restrictions on the convertibility of a currency into other currencies are called **currency controls**. A company that wishes to import goods generally must pay for those goods in a common, internationally acceptable currency such as the U.S. dollar, European Union euro, or Japanese yen. Generally, it must also obtain the currency from its nation's domestic banking system. Governments can require companies that desire such a currency to apply for a license to obtain it. Thus, a country's government can discourage imports by restricting who is allowed to convert the nation's currency into the internationally acceptable currency.

currency controls
Restrictions on the convertibility of a currency into other currencies.

Another way governments apply currency controls to reduce imports is by stipulating an exchange rate that is unfavorable to potential importers. Because the unfavorable exchange rate can force the cost of imported goods to an impractical level, many potential importers simply give up on the idea. Meanwhile, the country will often allow exporters to exchange the home currency for an international currency at favorable rates to encourage exports.

QUICK STUDY 3

1. How do *tariffs* and *quotas* differ from one another? Identify the different forms each can take.
2. Describe how a *voluntary export restraint* works and how it differs from a quota.
3. What is an *embargo*? Explain why it is seldom used today.
4. Explain how *local content requirements, administrative delays,* and *currency controls* restrict trade.

Global Trading System

The global trading system certainly has seen its ups and downs. World trade volume reached a peak in the late 1800s, only to be devastated when the United States passed the Smoot–Hawley Act in 1930. The act represented a major shift in U.S. trade policy from one of free trade to one of protectionism. The act set off round after round of competitive tariff increases among the major trading nations. Other nations felt that, if the United States was going to restrict its imports, they were not going to give exports from the United States free access to their domestic markets. The Smoot–Hawley Act, and the global trade wars that it helped to usher in, crippled the economies of the industrialized nations and helped spark the Great Depression. Living standards around the world were devastated throughout most of the 1930s.

We begin this section by looking at early attempts to develop a global trading system—the *General Agreement on Tariffs and Trade*—and then examine its successor, the *World Trade Organization*.

General Agreement on Tariffs and Trade (GATT)

Attitudes toward free trade changed markedly in the late 1940s. For the previous 50 years, extreme economic competition among nations and national quests to increase their resources for production helped create two world wars and the worst global economic recession ever. As a result, economists and policy makers proposed that the world band together and agree on a trading system that would help to avoid similar calamities in the future. A system of multilateral agreements was developed that became known as the *General Agreement on Tariffs and Trade (GATT)*—a treaty designed to promote free trade by reducing both tariff and nontariff barriers to international trade. The GATT was formed in 1947 by 23 nations—12 developed and 11 developing economies—and came into force in January 1948.[11]

TABLE 6.2 Completed Rounds of GATT

Year	Site	Number of Countries Involved	Topics Covered
1947	Geneva, Switzerland	23	Tariffs
1949	Annecy, France	13	Tariffs
1951	Torquay, England	38	Tariffs
1956	Geneva	26	Tariffs
1960–1961	Geneva (Dillon Round)	26	Tariffs
1964–1967	Geneva (Kennedy Round)	62	Tariffs, antidumping measures
1973–1979	Geneva (Tokyo Round)	102	Tariffs, nontariff measures, "framework agreements"
1986–1994	Geneva (Uruguay Round)	123	Tariffs, nontariff measures, rules, services, intellectual property, dispute settlement, investment measures, agriculture, textiles and clothing, natural resources, creation of the World Trade Organization

Source: Based on *About the WTO*, World Trade Organization website (www.wto.org).

The GATT was highly successful throughout its early years. Between 1947 and 1988, it helped to reduce average tariffs from 40 percent to 5 percent and to multiply the volume of international trade by a factor of 20. But by the middle to late 1980s, rising nationalism worldwide and trade conflicts led to a nearly 50 percent increase in nontariff barriers to trade. Also, services (not covered by the original GATT) had become increasingly important and had grown to account for a much greater share of total world trade. It was clear that a revision of the treaty was necessary, and in 1986 a new round of trade talks began.

URUGUAY ROUND OF NEGOTIATIONS The ground rules of the GATT resulted from periodic "rounds" of negotiations among its members. Though relatively short and straightforward in the early years, negotiations later became protracted as issues grew more complex. Table 6.2 shows the eight completed negotiating rounds that occurred under the auspices of the GATT. Note that whereas tariffs were the only topic of the first five rounds of negotiations, other topics were added in subsequent rounds.

The Uruguay Round of GATT negotiations, begun in 1986 in Punta del Este, Uruguay (hence its name), was the largest trade negotiation in history. It was the eighth round of GATT talks within a span of 40 years and took more than 7 years to complete. The Uruguay Round made significant progress in reducing trade barriers by revising and updating the 1947 GATT. In addition to developing plans to further reduce barriers to merchandise trade, the negotiations modified the original GATT treaty in several important ways.

Agreement on Services Because of the ever-increasing importance of services to the total volume of world trade, nations wanted to include GATT provisions for trade in services. The General Agreement on Trade in Services (GATS) extended the principle of nondiscrimination to cover international trade in all services, although talks regarding some sectors were more successful than were others. The problem is that, although trade in goods is a straightforward concept—goods are exported from one country and imported to another—defining exactly what a service is can be difficult. Nevertheless, the GATS created during the Uruguay Round identifies four different forms that international trade in services can take:

1. *Cross-border supply.* Services supplied from one country to another (for example, international telephone calls).
2. *Consumption abroad.* Consumers or companies using a service while in another country (for example, tourism).

3. *Commercial presence.* A company establishing a subsidiary in another country in order to provide a service (for example, banking operations).

4. *Presence of natural persons.* Individuals traveling to another country in order to supply a service (for example, business consultants).

Agreement on Intellectual Property Like services, products consisting entirely or largely of intellectual property account for an increasing portion of international trade. Recall from Chapter 3 that *intellectual property* refers to property resulting from people's intellectual talent and abilities. Products classified as intellectual property are supposed to be legally protected by copyrights, patents, and trademarks.

Although international piracy continues, the Uruguay Round took an important step toward getting it under control. It created the Agreement on Trade-Related Aspects of Intellectual Property (TRIPS) to help standardize intellectual property rules around the world. The TRIPS Agreement acknowledges that protection of intellectual property rights benefits society because it encourages the development of new technologies and other creations. It supports the articles of both the Paris Convention and the Berne Convention (see Chapter 3) and in certain instances takes a stronger stand on intellectual property protection.

Agreement on Agricultural Subsidies Trade in agricultural products has been a bone of contention for most of the world's trading partners at one time or another. Some of the more popular barriers that countries use to protect their agricultural sectors include import quotas and subsidies paid directly to farmers. The Uruguay Round addressed the main issues of agricultural tariffs and nontariff barriers in its Agreement on Agriculture. The result is increased exposure of national agricultural sectors to market forces and increased predictability in international agricultural trade. The agreement forces countries to convert all nontariff barriers to tariffs—a process called "tariffication." It then calls on developed and developing nations to cut agricultural tariffs significantly, but it places no requirements on the least-developed economies.

World Trade Organization (WTO)

Perhaps the greatest achievement of the Uruguay Round was the creation of the *World Trade Organization (WTO)*—the international organization that regulates trade among nations. The three main goals of the WTO (www.wto.org) are to help the free flow of trade, to help negotiate further opening of markets, and to settle trade disputes among its members. One key component of the WTO that was carried over from the GATT is the principle of nondiscrimination called **normal trade relations** (formerly called "most favored nation status")—a requirement that WTO members extend the same favorable terms of trade to all members that they extend to any single member. For example, if Japan were to reduce its import tariff on German automobiles to 5 percent, it must reduce the tariff it levies against automobile imports from all other WTO nations to 5 percent.

normal trade relations (formerly "most favored nation status") Requirement that WTO members extend the same favorable terms of trade to all members that they extend to any single member.

The WTO replaced the *institution* of the GATT but absorbed the GATT *agreements* (such as on services, intellectual property, and agriculture) into its own agreements. Thus, the GATT institution no longer officially exists. The WTO recognizes 157 members and 27 observers.

DISPUTE SETTLEMENT IN THE WTO The power of the WTO to settle trade disputes is what really sets it apart from the GATT. Under the GATT, nations could file a complaint against another member and a committee would investigate the matter. If appropriate, the GATT would identify the unfair trade practices, and member countries would pressure the offender to change its ways. But in reality most nations simply ignored GATT rulings, which were usually made only after very long investigative phases that sometimes lasted years.

By contrast, the various WTO agreements are essentially contracts between member nations that commit them to maintaining fair and open trade policies. When one WTO member files a complaint against another, the Dispute Settlement Body of the WTO moves into action swiftly. Decisions are to be rendered in less than one year—although within nine months if the case is urgent and 15 months if the case is appealed. The WTO dispute settlement system is not only faster and automatic, but its rulings cannot be ignored or blocked by members. Offenders must realign their trade policies according to WTO guidelines or suffer financial penalties and perhaps trade sanctions. Because of its ability to penalize offending member nations, the WTO's dispute settlement system is the spine of the global trading system.

dumping
Exporting a product at a price either lower than the price that the product normally commands in its domestic market or lower than the cost of production.

DUMPING AND THE WTO The WTO also gets involved in settling disputes that involve "dumping" and the granting of subsidies. When a company exports a product at a price that is either lower than the price normally charged in its domestic market or lower than the cost of production, it is said to be **dumping**. Charges of dumping are made (fairly or otherwise) against companies from almost every nation at one time or another and can occur in any type of industry. For example, Western European plastic producers considered retaliating against Asian competitors whose prices were substantially lower in European markets than at home. More recently, U.S. steel producers and their powerful union charged that steelmakers in Brazil, Japan, and Russia were dumping steel on the U.S. market at low prices. The problem arose as those nations tried to improve their economies through increased exporting of all products, including steel.

The WTO cannot punish the country in which the company accused of dumping is based because dumping is an act by a company, not a country. The WTO can respond only to the actions of a country that retaliates against a company that is dumping. The WTO allows a nation to retaliate against dumping if it can show that dumping is actually occurring, can calculate the damage to its own companies, and can show that the damage is significant. The normal way a country retaliates is to charge an **antidumping duty**—an additional tariff placed on an imported product that a nation believes is being dumped on its market. But such measures must expire within five years of the time they are initiated unless a country can show that circumstances warrant their continuation. A large number of antidumping cases have been brought before the WTO in recent years.

antidumping duty
Additional tariff placed on an imported product that a nation believes is being dumped on its market.

countervailing duty
Additional tariff placed on an imported product that a nation believes is receiving an unfair subsidy.

SUBSIDIES AND THE WTO Governments often retaliate when the competitiveness of their companies is threatened by a subsidy that another country pays its own domestic producers. Like antidumping measures, nations can retaliate against product(s) that receive an unfair subsidy by charging a **countervailing duty**—an additional tariff placed on an imported product that a nation believes is receiving an unfair subsidy. Unlike dumping, because payment of a subsidy is an action by a country, the WTO regulates the actions of the government that reacts to the subsidy as well as those of the government that originally paid the subsidy.

DOHA ROUND OF NEGOTIATIONS The WTO launched a new round of negotiations in Doha, Qatar, in late 2001. The renewed negotiations were designed to lower trade barriers further and to help poor nations in particular. Agricultural subsidies that rich countries pay to their own farmers are worth $1 billion per day—more than six times the value of their combined aid budgets to poor nations. Because 70 percent of the exports of poor nations are agricultural products and textiles, wealthy nations had intended to open these and other labor-intensive industries further. Poor nations were encouraged to reduce tariffs among themselves and were to receive help from rich nations in integrating themselves into the global trading system. Although the Doha round was to conclude by the end of 2004, negotiations continue to limp along.[12]

WTO AND THE ENVIRONMENT Steady gains in global trade and rapid industrialization in many developing and emerging economies have generated environmental concerns among both governments and special interest groups. Of concern to many people are levels of carbon dioxide emissions—the principal greenhouse gas believed to contribute to global warming. Most carbon dioxide emissions are created from the burning of fossil fuels and the manufacture of cement.

The WTO has no separate agreement that deals with environmental issues. The WTO explicitly states that it is not to become a global environmental agency responsible for setting environmental standards. It leaves such tasks to national governments and the many intergovernmental organizations that already exist for such purposes. The WTO works alongside existing international agreements on the environment, including the Montreal Protocol for protection of the ozone layer, the Basel Convention on international trade or transport of hazardous waste, and the Convention on International Trade in Endangered Species.

Nevertheless, the preamble to the agreement that established the WTO does mention the objectives of environmental protection and sustainable development. The WTO also has an internal committee called the Committee on Trade and Environment. The committee's responsibility is to study the relationship between trade and the environment and to recommend possible changes in the WTO trade agreements.

In addition, the WTO does take explicit positions on some environmental issues related to trade. Although the WTO supports national efforts at labeling "environmentally friendly" products as such, it states that labeling requirements or policies cannot discriminate against the products of other WTO members. Also, the WTO supports policies of the least developed countries that require full disclosure of potentially hazardous products entering their markets for reasons of public health and environmental damage.

QUICK STUDY 4

1. What was the *General Agreement on Tariffs and Trade (GATT)*? List its main accomplishments.
2. What is the *World Trade Organization (WTO)*? Describe how the WTO settles trade disputes.
3. Explain the difference between an *antidumping duty* and a *countervailing duty*.

BOTTOM LINE FOR BUSINESS

Despite the theoretical benefits of free trade, nations do not simply throw open their doors to trade and force their domestic businesses to sink or swim. This chapter explained why governments protect their industries and how they go about it. The WTO tries to strike a balance between national desires for protection and international desires for free trade.

Implications of Trade Protection
Free trade allows firms to move production to locations that maximize efficiency. Yet, government interference in the free flow of trade has implications for production efficiency and firm strategy. *Subsidies* often encourage complacency on the part of companies receiving them because they discourage competition. Subsidies can be thought of as a redistribution of wealth in society whereby international firms not receiving subsidies are at a disadvantage. Unsubsidized firms either must cut production and distribution costs or must differentiate in some way to justify a higher selling price.

Import tariffs raise the cost of an imported good and make domestically produced goods more attractive to consumers. But because a tariff can create inefficient domestic producers, deteriorating competitiveness may offset the benefits of import tariffs. Companies trying to enter markets having high import tariffs often produce within that market. *Import quotas* help domestic producers maintain market share and prices by restraining competitive forces. Domestic producers protected by the quota win because the market is protected. Yet other producers that require the import subjected to a quota lose. These companies will need to pay more for their intermediate products or locate production outside the market imposing the quota.

Local content requirements protect domestic producers from producers based in low-cost countries. A firm trying to sell to a market imposing local content requirements may have no alternative but to produce locally. The objective of *administrative delays* is to discriminate against imported products, but it can discourage efficiency. *Currency controls* can require firms to apply for a license to obtain an internationally accepted currency. The nation thus discourages imports by restricting who is allowed to obtain such a currency to pay for imports. A government may also block imports by stipulating an exchange rate that is unfavorable to potential importers. The unfavorable exchange rate forces the cost of imported goods to an impractical level. The same country then often stipulates an exchange rate that is favorable for exporters.

Government subsidies are typically paid for by levying taxes across the economy. Whether subsidies help a nation's people long term is questionable, and they may actually harm a nation. Import tariffs also hurt consumers because they raise the price of imports and protect domestic firms that may raise prices. Import quotas hurt consumers because they lessen competition, boost prices, and decrease selection. Protection tends to lessen the long-term gains a people can obtain from free trade.

Implications of the Global Trading System
Development of the global trading system benefits international companies by promoting free trade through the reduction of both tariffs and nontariff barriers to international trade. The GATT treaty was successful in its early years, and its revision significantly improved the climate for trade. Average tariffs on merchandise trade were reduced and subsidies for agricultural products were lowered. Firms also benefited from an agreement that extended the principle of nondiscrimination to cover trade in services. The revision of the GATT also clearly defined intellectual property rights—giving protection to copyrights, trademarks and service marks, and patents. This encourages firms to develop new products and processes because they know their rights to the property will be protected.

Creation of the WTO is also good for international firms because the various WTO agreements commit member nations to maintaining fair and open trade policies. Both domestic and international firms based in relatively poor nations should benefit most from future rounds of trade negotiations. Because poor nations tend to export agricultural products and textiles, their firms in these industries will benefit from wealthy nations reducing barriers to imports in these sectors. Companies based in poor countries should also benefit from better cooperation among poor countries and their further integration into the global trading system.

Chapter Summary

MyManagementLab

Go to **mymanagementlab.com** to complete the problems marked with this icon .

1. **Describe the political, economic, and cultural motives behind governmental intervention in trade.**
   - *Political* motives behind government intervention in trade include (a) protecting jobs, (b) preserving national security, (c) responding to other nations' unfair trade practices, and (d) gaining influence over other nations.
   - *Economic* reasons for government intervention in trade are (a) protection of infant industries and (b) promotion of a strategic trade policy.
   - The *infant industry argument* says that a country's emerging industries need protection from international competition during their development until they become sufficiently competitive, but this may reduce competitiveness and inflate prices.
   - *Strategic trade policy* argues for government intervention to help companies take advantage of economies of scale and be first movers in their industries, but this may cause inefficiency, higher costs, and trade wars.
   - The most common *cultural* motive for trade intervention is protection of national identity.

2. **List and explain the methods governments use to promote international trade.**
   - A *subsidy* is financial assistance to domestic producers in the form of cash payments, low-interest loans, tax breaks, product price supports, or other forms.
   - Although subsidies are intended to help domestic companies fend off international competitors, critics say that they amount to corporate welfare and are detrimental in the long term.
   - *Export financing* includes loans at below-market interest rates, loans that would otherwise be unavailable, and *loan guarantees* that a government will repay a loan if the company defaults.
   - A *foreign trade zone (FTZ)* is a designated geographic region through which merchandise is allowed to pass with lower customs duties (taxes) and/or fewer customs procedures.
   - *Special government agencies* organize trips abroad for trade officials and businesspeople and open offices abroad to promote home country exports.

3. **List and explain the methods governments use to restrict international trade.**
   - A *tariff* is a government tax levied on a product as it enters or leaves a country; its three types are the *export tariff, transit tariff,* and *import tariff.*
   - An import tariff can be an *ad valorem tariff,* a *specific tariff,* or a *compound tariff.*
   - A restriction on the amount of a good that can enter or leave a country during a certain period of time is called a *quota.*
   - *Import quotas* protect domestic producers, whereas *export quotas* maintain adequate supplies domestically or increase the world price of a product.
   - A complete ban on trade with a particular country is an *embargo.*
   - *Local content requirements* are laws stipulating that a specified amount of a good or service be supplied by producers in the domestic market.
   - Imports can also be discouraged using *administrative delays* (regulatory controls or bureaucratic rules) or *currency controls* (restrictions on currency convertibility).

4. **Discuss the importance of the World Trade Organization in promoting free trade.**
   - The *General Agreement on Tariffs and Trade (GATT)* was a treaty designed to promote free trade by reducing tariff and nontariff barriers to trade.
   - The *Uruguay Round* of GATT negotiations (a) for the first time included trade in services, (b) defined intellectual property rights, (c) reduced trade barriers in agriculture, and (d) created the *World Trade Organization (WTO).*
   - The three goals of the WTO are to help the free flow of trade, to help negotiate further opening of markets, and to settle trade disputes among its members.
   - A key component of the WTO is the principle of nondiscrimination called *normal trade relations,* which requires WTO members to treat all members equally.
   - *Dumping* is said to occur when a company exports a product at a price either lower than the price it normally charges in its domestic market or lower than the cost of production.

Talk It Over

⭐1. Most countries create a list of "hostile" countries that require special permission before an exporter will be allowed to proceed. Which countries and products would you place on such a list for your nation, and why?

2. Two students are discussing efforts within the global trading system to reduce trade's negative effects on the environment. One student says, "Sure, there may be pollution effects, but they're a small price to pay for a higher standard of living." The other student agrees, saying, "Yeah, those 'tree-huggers' are always exaggerating those effects anyway. Who cares if some little toad in the Amazon goes extinct? I sure don't." What counterarguments can you offer to these students?

Teaming Up

1. **Research Project.** As a group, select a company in your city or town that is involved in importing and/or exporting, and interview the owner or a top manager. Your goal is to understand how government involvement in international trade has helped or harmed the company's business activities. Prepare for your appointment by researching the topic of government trade intervention in a business periodical (in print or online), and follow up the interview with additional research. Ask for past examples and specific potential impacts of government intervention on the business.

⭐2. **Market Entry Strategy Project.** This exercise corresponds to the *MESP* online simulation. For the country your team is researching, to what extent does its government intervene in trade? What are its political, economic, or cultural motives for intervention? What methods, if any, does the government use to (a) promote exports and (b) restrict imports? Does the nation maintain a free trade zone within its borders? Has the country filed a complaint with the WTO against another member nation? Has it been reported by another nation for unfair trade practices? Integrate your findings into your completed *MESP* report.

Key Terms

administrative delays (p. 167)
ad valorem tariff (p. 164)
antidumping duty (p. 170)
compound tariff (p. 164)
countervailing duty (p. 170)
currency controls (p. 167)

dumping (p. 170)
embargo (p. 166)
foreign trade zone (FTZ) (p. 162)
free trade (p. 156)
normal trade relations (p. 169)
quota (p. 164)

specific tariff (p. 164)
subsidy (p. 161)
tariff (p. 163)
tariff-quota (p. 165)
voluntary export restraint (VER) (p. 165)

Take It to the Web

1. **Video Report.** Visit this book's channel on YouTube (www.YouTube.com/MyIBvideos). Click on "Videos" near the top of the page, and click on the set of videos labeled "Ch 06: Business–Government Trade Relations." Watch one video from the list, and then summarize it in a half-page report. Reflecting on the contents of this chapter, which aspects of governmental trade intervention can you identify in the video? How might a company engaged in international business act on the information contained in the video?

2. **Website Report.** The WTO recently ordered the United States to repeal $4 billion of tax breaks for U.S. exporters who operate through offshore subsidiaries or face possible sanctions. Although the case was brought by the European Union, many European companies were ambivalent about the tax breaks because they have U.S. subsidiaries that benefit from them.

Visit the website of the WTO (www.wto.org) and the websites of business periodicals on the Internet. Identify a case on which the WTO has recently ruled. What countries are involved? List as many cultural, political, or economic reasons you can think of that motivated the country to bring the case. Do you think it was a fair charge, and do you think the ruling was correct? Explain your answer.

Do you think the WTO should have the power to dictate the trade policies of individual nations and to punish them if they do not comply? Why or why not? Do you think countries experiencing economic difficulties should be allowed to erect temporary tariff and nontariff barriers? Why or why not? What effect do you think such an allowance would have on the future of the global trading system?

Ethical Challenges

1. You are a consultant advising the WTO on the U.S. Supreme Court decision regarding the state of Massachusetts and the country of Myanmar. A nonprofit trade and industry group, the National Foreign Trade Council (NFTC), based in Washington, DC, won a court battle against the state of Massachusetts. In a unanimous decision, the U.S. Supreme Court sided with the NFTC and struck down a Massachusetts law that was designed to deny state contracts to any company doing business in Myanmar. The Court ruled that the Massachusetts law intruded on the federal government's authority and was preempted by federal law regarding Myanmar. In fact, the U.S. Constitution states that "foreign policy is exclusively reserved for the federal government." The NFTC says that it shares concern over human rights abuses occurring in Myanmar but believes that a coordinated, multinational effort would be most effective at instilling change in the nation.

   Do you think companies should be penalized in their domestic business dealings because of where they do business abroad? Should the WTO get involved in these types of political matters? Why or why not? How might domestic firms be affected if each state were allowed to punish firms based on its individual foreign policy ideals?

MyManagementLab

Go to **mymanagementlab.com** for Auto-graded writing questions as well as the following Assisted-graded writing questions:

6-1. You are the president of a sugar company based in southern Florida. Your firm is struggling lately to meet demand because of poor harvests in the Caribbean Islands, where your firm sources much of its raw product. Because of the Helms–Burton Act and the U.S. embargo on Cuba, your firm is not allowed to trade with Cuba. If the embargo were dropped, your firm would have an excellent source of cheap sugar, and profits would improve significantly. A U.S. senator from your state of Florida serves on an influential committee in Washington, DC, that is reviewing the status of the embargo on Cuba. What arguments would you provide your senator that could help eliminate this trade barrier?

6-2. Imagine that people in your country believe international trade is harmful to their wages and jobs, and your task is to change their minds. What kinds of programs would you implement to educate your people about the benefits of trade? Describe how each program would help change people's attitudes.

6-3. Mymanagementlab Only – comprehensive writing assignment for this chapter.

Practicing International Management Case

Down with Dumping

"**W**TO Agrees to Probe EU Duties on Chinese Footwear" . . . "Canada Launches WTO Challenge to U.S." . . . "Mexico Widens Anti-dumping Measure" . . . "Rough Road Ahead for U.S.–China Trade" . . . "It Must Be Stopped" are just a sampling of headlines from around the world.

International trade theories argue that nations should open their doors to trade. Conventional free-trade wisdom says that, by trading with others, a country can offer its citizens a greater quantity and selection of goods at cheaper prices than it could in the absence of trade. Nevertheless, truly free trade still does not exist because national governments intervene. On average, 234 anti-dumping cases are initiated each year with the WTO. And whereas the United States and the European Union initiated half of all WTO cases in prior years, they now initiate only about a quarter of all cases—more than half are now brought by emerging markets.

China launched an inquiry to determine whether synthetic rubber imports (used in tires and footwear) from Japan, South Korea, and Russia are being dumped in the country. Mexico expanded the use of its system that requires exporters (from a select list of countries) to notify Mexican officials of the amount and price of a shipment 10 days prior to its expected arrival in Mexico. The 10-day notice gives domestic producers advanced warning of low-priced products so they can report dumping before the products clear customs and enter the marketplace. Argentina, India, Indonesia, South Africa, South Korea, and Thailand are also using this increasingly popular tool of protectionism.

Why is dumping so popular? Oddly enough, the WTO allows it. The WTO has made major inroads on the use of tariffs, slashing them across almost every product category in recent years. But it does not have authority to punish companies, only governments. Thus, the WTO cannot make judgments against individual companies that are dumping products in other markets. It can only pass rulings against the government of the country that imposes an anti-dumping duty. But the WTO allows countries to retaliate against nations whose producers are suspected of dumping when it can be shown that (1) alleged offenders are significantly hurting domestic producers, and (2) the export price is lower than the cost of production or lower than the home market price.

Alternatives to bringing antidumping cases before the WTO do exist. U.S. President George W. Bush relied on a Section 201, or "global safeguard," investigation under U.S. trade law to slap tariffs of up to 30 percent on steel imports. The U.S. steel industry had been suffering under an onslaught of steel imports from Brazil, the European Union, Japan, and South Korea. Yet nations still brought complaints about the action before the WTO.

Similarly, in 2004 the U.S. government slapped around 100 percent tariffs on shrimp imported from China and Vietnam, charging those nations with dumping their crustaceans on U.S. shores.

Supporters of antidumping tariffs claim that they prevent dumpers from undercutting the prices charged by producers in a target market, driving them out of business. Another claim in support of antidumping is that it is an excellent way of retaining some protection against the potential dangers of totally free trade. Detractors of antidumping tariffs charge that once such tariffs are imposed they are rarely removed. They also claim that it costs companies and governments a great deal of time and money to file and argue their cases. It is also argued that the fear of being charged with dumping causes international competitors to keep their prices higher in a target market than would otherwise be the case. This would allow domestic companies to charge higher prices and not lose market share—forcing consumers to pay more for their goods.

Thinking Globally

1. "You can't tell consumers that the low price they are paying for that video game console or automobile is somehow unfair. They're not concerned with the profits of some company. To them, it's just a great bargain, and they want it to continue." Do you agree with this statement? Do you think that people from different cultures would respond differently to this statement? Explain your answers.

2. As we have seen, currently the WTO cannot get involved in punishing individual companies—its actions can only be directed toward governments of countries. Do you think this is a wise policy? Why or why not? Why do you think the WTO was not given authority to charge individual companies with dumping? Explain.

3. Identify a recent antidumping case that was brought before the WTO. Locate as many articles in the press as you can that discuss the case. Identify the nations, product(s), and potential punitive measures involved. If you were part of the WTO dispute settlement body, would you vote in favor of the measures taken by the retaliating nation? Why or why not?

Source: Jennifer M. Freedman, "WTO Agrees to Probe EU Duties on Chinese Footwear," *Bloomberg Businessweek* (www.businessweek.com), May 18, 2010; "Settling Trade Disputes: When Partners Attack," *The Economist* (www.economist.com), February 11, 2010; "Global Trade Disputes: Trading Blows," *The Economist* (www.economist.com), December 1, 2009; Frederik Balfour, "Rough Road Ahead for U.S.-China Trade," *Bloomberg Businessweek* (www.businessweek.com), April 4, 2007.

Foreign Direct Investment

LEARNING OBJECTIVES

After studying this chapter, you should be able to

1. Describe worldwide patterns of foreign direct investment (FDI) and reasons for those patterns.

2. Describe each of the theories that attempt to explain why FDI occurs.

3. Discuss the important management issues in the FDI decision.

4. Explain why governments intervene in the free flow of FDI.

5. Discuss the policy instruments that governments use to promote and restrict FDI.

A Look Back

Chapter 6 explained business–government relations in the context of world trade in goods and services. We explored the motives and methods of government intervention. We also examined the global trading system and how it promotes free trade.

A Look at This Chapter

This chapter examines another significant form of international business: foreign direct investment (FDI). Again, we are concerned with the patterns of FDI and the theories on which it is based. We also explore why and how governments intervene in FDI activity.

A Look Ahead

Chapter 8 explores the trend toward greater regional integration of national economies. We explore the benefits of closer economic cooperation and examine prominent regional trading blocs that exist around the world.

DAS AUTO

FRANKFURT, Germany—The Volkswagen Group (www.vw.com) owns 10 of the most prestigious and best-known automotive brands in the world, including Audi, Bentley, Bugatti, Lamborghini, Porsche, and Volkswagen. From its 48 production facilities worldwide, the company produces and sells around eight million cars annually to more than 150 countries. Volkswagen is the top-selling manufacturer in China and South America. It has been active in China since 1985 and plans to double production capacity there to three million cars a year by 2014.

Volkswagen is building four new assembly plants in China, one being the first in western China. Shown here is a worker on the assembly line at a Volkswagen plant in Brazil.

Volkswagen also has ambitious goals for its U.S. expansion. It is adapting designs to domestic tastes, cutting prices, and adding inexpensive production capacity. The company employs more than 2,000 people at its state-of-the-art assembly plant in Chattanooga, Tennessee. Volkswagen pays wages and benefits at the plant equal to $27 an hour, whereas Japanese auto-makers in the United States pay $50 an hour and General Motors pays around $60 an hour. The company uses a *modular strategy* in production that lets it use the same key components in 16 different vehicles and seven

Source: Julian Stratenschulte/Newscom

million units across its brands. The strategy should shave $500 off the cost of each car by cutting product development and parts costs by 20 percent and reducing production time by 30 percent.

Volkswagen, like companies everywhere, received plenty of help in getting where it is today. Until recently, Volkswagen received special protection from its own legislation known as the VW Law. The law gave the German state of Lower Saxony, which owns 20.1 percent of Volkswagen, the power to block any takeover attempt that threatened local jobs and the economy. Volkswagen's special treatment lies in the close ties between government and management in Germany and its importance to the nation's economy, where it employs tens of thousands of people. As you read this chapter, consider all the issues that affect the foreign investment decisions of companies.[1]

Many early trade theories were created at a time when most production factors (such as labor, financial capital, capital equipment, and land or natural resources) either could not be moved or could not be moved easily across national borders. But today, all those production factors except land are internationally mobile and flow across borders to wherever they are needed. Financial capital is readily available from international financial institutions to finance corporate expansion, and whole factories can be picked up and moved to another country. Even labor is more mobile than in years past, although many barriers restrict the complete mobility of labor.

International flows of capital are at the core of **foreign direct investment (FDI)**—the purchase of physical assets or a significant amount of the ownership (stock) of a company in another country in order to gain a measure of management control. But there is wide disagreement on what exactly constitutes FDI. Nations set different thresholds at which they classify an international capital flow as FDI. The U.S. Commerce Department sets the threshold at 10 percent of stock ownership in a company abroad, but most other governments set it at anywhere from 10 to 25 percent. By contrast, an investment that does not involve obtaining a degree of control in a company is called a **portfolio investment**.

In this chapter, we examine the importance of FDI to the operations of international companies. We begin by exploring the growth of FDI in recent years and investigating its sources and destinations. We then look at several theories that attempt to explain FDI flows. Next, we turn our attention to several important management issues that arise in most decisions about whether a company should undertake FDI. This chapter closes by discussing the reasons why governments encourage or restrict FDI and the methods they use to accomplish these goals.

Patterns of Foreign Direct Investment

Just as international trade displays distinct patterns (see Chapter 5), so too does FDI. In this section, we first look at the factors that have propelled growth in FDI over the past decade. We then turn our attention to the destinations and sources of FDI.

Ups and Downs of FDI

FDI inflows grew around 20 percent per year in the first half of the 1990s and expanded about 40 percent per year in the second half of the decade. As shown in Figure 7.1, global FDI inflows averaged $548 billion annually between 1994 and 1999. FDI inflows peaked at around $1.4 trillion in 2000 and then slowed. Strong economic performance and high corporate profits in many countries lifted FDI inflows in 2004, 2005, 2006, and reached an all-time record of more than $1.9 trillion in 2007.

Global financial crises and slower global economic growth meant declining FDI inflows in 2008 and 2009. FDI inflows climbed again in 2010 and 2011 and are expected to rise slowly but

foreign direct investment
Purchase of physical assets or a significant amount of the ownership (stock) of a company in another country to gain a measure of management control.

portfolio investment
Investment that does not involve obtaining a degree of control in a company.

FIGURE 7.1

Yearly Foreign Direct Investment Inflows

Source: Based on *World Investment Report* (Geneva, Switzerland: UNCTAD), various years.

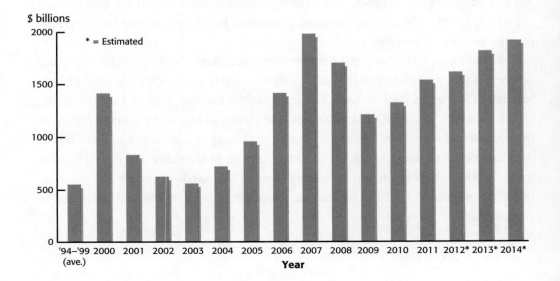

steadily as the world emerges from recession. The long-term trend points toward greater FDI inflows worldwide. The two main drivers of FDI flows are *globalization* and international *mergers and acquisitions*.

GLOBALIZATION   Recall from Chapter 6 that, years ago, barriers to trade were not being reduced, and new, creative barriers seemed to be popping up in many nations. This presented a problem for companies that were trying to export their products to markets around the world. A wave of FDI began as many companies entered promising markets to get around growing trade barriers. But then the Uruguay Round of GATT negotiations created renewed determination to further reduce barriers to trade. As countries lowered their trade barriers, companies realized that they could now produce in the most efficient and productive locations and simply export to their markets worldwide. This set off another wave of FDI flows into low-cost emerging markets. Forces causing globalization to occur are, therefore, part of the reason for long-term growth in FDI.

Increasing globalization is also causing a growing number of international companies from emerging markets to undertake FDI. For example, companies from Taiwan began investing heavily in other nations two decades ago. Acer (www.acer.com), headquartered in Singapore but founded in Taiwan, manufactures personal computers and computer components. Just 20 years after it opened for business, Acer had spawned 10 subsidiaries worldwide and had become the dominant industry player in many emerging markets.

MERGERS AND ACQUISITIONS   The number of *mergers and acquisitions (M&As)* and their rising values over time also underlie long-term growth in FDI. In fact, cross-border M&As are the main vehicle through which companies undertake FDI. Companies based in developed nations have historically been the main participants behind cross-border M&As, but firms from emerging markets are accounting for an ever greater share of global M&A activity. The value of cross-border M&As peaked in 2000 at around $1.2 trillion. This figure accounted for about 3.7 percent of the market capitalization of all stock exchanges worldwide. Reasons previously mentioned for the ups and downs of FDI inflows also cause the pattern we see in cross-border M&A deals (see Figure 7.2). By 2007, the value of cross-border M&As rose to around $1 trillion. But M&A activity was significantly lower in 2008, 2009, and 2010 due to effects of the global financial crisis and global economic slowdown. By 2011, the value of cross-border M&A activity had climbed back to $526 billion.

Many cross-border M&A deals are driven by the desire of companies to:

* Get a foothold in a new geographic market.
* Increase a firm's global competitiveness.
* Fill gaps in companies' product lines in a global industry.
* Reduce costs of research and development, production, distribution, and so forth.

Entrepreneurs and small businesses also play a role in the expansion of FDI inflows. There is no data on the portion of FDI contributed by small businesses, but we know from anecdotal evidence that these companies are engaged in FDI. Unhindered by many of the constraints of a large company, entrepreneurs investing in other markets often demonstrate an inspiring can-do spirit mixed with ingenuity and bravado. Another advantage individuals can possess is an

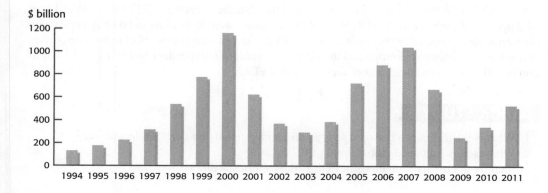

FIGURE 7.2

Value of Cross-Border Mergers and Acquisitions

Source: Based on *World Investment Report* (Geneva, Switzerland: UNCTAD), various years.

CULTURE MATTERS   The Cowboy of Manchuria

Tom Kirkwood turned his dream of introducing his grandfather's taffy to China into a fast-growing business. Kirkwood's story—his hassles and hustling—provides some lessons on the purest form of global investing. The basics that small investors in China can follow are as rudimentary as they get. Find a product that's easy to make, widely popular, and cheap to sell, and then choose the least expensive, investor-friendliest place to make it.

Kirkwood, whose family runs the Shawnee Inn, a ski and golf resort in Shawnee-on-Delaware, Pennsylvania, decided to make candy in Manchuria—China's gritty, heavily populated, industrial northeast. Chinese people often give individually wrapped candies as a gift, and Kirkwood reckoned that China's rising, increasingly prosperous urbanites would have a lucrative sweet tooth. "You can't be M&Ms, but you don't have to be penny candy, either," Kirkwood says. "You find your niche because a niche in China is an awful lot of people."

Kirkwood concluded early on that he wanted to do business in China. In the mid-1980s after prep school, he spent a year in Taiwan and China learning Chinese and working in a Shanghai engineering company. The experience gave him a taste for adventure capitalism on the frontier of China's economic development. Using $400,000 of Kirkwood's family money, Kirkwood and his friend Peter Moustakerski bought equipment and rented a factory in Shenyang, a city of six million people in the heart of Manchuria. Roads and rail transport were convenient, and wages were low. The local government seemed amenable to a 100 percent foreign-owned factory, and the Shenyang Shawnee Cowboy Food Company was born.

Although it's a small operation, it now has 89 employees and is growing. Kirkwood is determined to succeed selling his candies with names such as Longhorn Bars. As he boarded a flight to Beijing for a meeting with a distributor recently, Kirkwood realized he had a bag full of candy. He offered one to a flight attendant. When lunch is over, he vowed, "Everybody on this plane will know Cowboy Candy."

---

understanding of the local language and culture of the market being entered. For a day-in-the-life look at a young entrepreneur who is realizing his dreams in China, see the Culture Matters feature, titled "The Cowboy of Manchuria."

Worldwide Flows of FDI

Driving FDI growth are more than 82,000 multinational companies with more than 810,000 affiliates abroad, roughly half of which are in developing countries.[2] Developed countries account for 49 percent ($748 billion) of total global FDI inflows (more than $1.5 trillion in 2011). By comparison, FDI inflows to developing countries were valued at $684 billion—about 45 percent of world FDI inflows. The remaining 6 percent of global FDI inflows went to countries across Southeast Europe in various stages of transition from communism to capitalism.

Among developed countries, European Union (EU) nations, the United States, and Japan account for the majority of world FDI inflows. The EU remains the world's largest FDI recipient, garnering nearly $421 billion in 2011 (nearly 28 percent of the world's total). Behind the large FDI figure for the EU is consolidation among large national competitors and further efforts at EU regional integration.

Developing nations had varying experiences in 2011. FDI inflows to developing nations in Asia were $423 billion in 2011, with China attracting a historic high of more than $124 billion of that total. India, the largest recipient on the Asian subcontinent, had inflows of nearly $31 billion. FDI flowing from developing nations in Asia is also on the rise, coinciding with the rise of these nations' own global competitors.

Elsewhere, all of Africa drew in $43 billion of FDI in 2011, or about 2.8 percent of the world's total. FDI flows into Latin America and the Caribbean grew to $217 billion in 2011, or 14.2 percent of the total world FDI. Most of these inflows went to markets in South America with their growing economies, expanding consumer bases, and rich endowments of natural resources. FDI inflows to Southeast Europe and the Commonwealth of Independent States reached $92 billion in 2011, or around 6 percent of the total world FDI.

QUICK STUDY 1

1. What is the difference between *foreign direct investment* and *portfolio investment*?
2. What factors influence global flows of FDI?
3. Identify the main destinations of FDI. Is the pattern shifting?

Explanations for Foreign Direct Investment

So far, we have examined the flows of FDI, but we have not investigated explanations for why FDI occurs. Let's now investigate the four main theories that attempt to explain why companies engage in FDI.

International Product Life Cycle

Although we introduced it in Chapter 5 in the context of international trade, the international product life cycle is also used to explain FDI.[3] The **international product life cycle** theory states that a company begins by exporting its product and then later undertakes FDI as a product moves through its life cycle. In the *new product stage,* a good is produced in the home country because of uncertain domestic demand and to keep production close to the research department that developed the product. In the *maturing product stage,* the company directly invests in production facilities in countries where demand is great enough to warrant its own production facilities. In the final *standardized product stage,* increased competition creates pressures to reduce production costs. In response, a company builds production capacity in low-cost developing nations to serve its markets around the world.

Despite its conceptual appeal, the international product life cycle theory is limited in its power to explain why companies choose FDI over other forms of market entry. A local firm in the target market could pay for (license) the right to use the special assets needed to manufacture a particular product. In this way, a company could avoid the additional risks associated with direct investments in the market. The theory also fails to explain why firms choose FDI over exporting activities. It might be less expensive to serve a market abroad by increasing output at the home country factory rather than by building additional capacity within the target market.

The theory explains why the FDI of some firms follows the international product life cycle of their products. But it does not explain why other market entry modes are inferior or less advantageous options.

Market Imperfections (Internalization)

A market that is said to operate at peak efficiency (prices are as low as they can possibly be) and where goods are readily and easily available is said to be a *perfect market.* But perfect markets are rarely, if ever, seen in business because of factors that cause a breakdown in the efficient operation of an industry—called *market imperfections.* **Market imperfections** theory states that when an imperfection in the market makes a transaction less efficient than it could be, a company will undertake FDI to internalize the transaction and thereby remove the imperfection. There are two market imperfections that are relevant to this discussion—trade barriers and specialized knowledge.

TRADE BARRIERS One common market imperfection in international business is trade barriers, such as tariffs. For example, the North American Free Trade Agreement stipulates that a sufficient portion of a product's content must originate within Canada, Mexico, or the United States for the product to avoid tariff charges when it is imported to any of these three markets. That is why a large number of Korean manufacturers invested in production facilities in Tijuana, Mexico, just south of Mexico's border with California. By investing in production facilities in Mexico, the Korean companies were able to skirt the North American tariffs that would have been levied if they were to export goods from Korean factories. The presence of a market imperfection (tariffs) caused those companies to undertake FDI.

SPECIALIZED KNOWLEDGE The unique competitive advantage of a company sometimes consists of specialized knowledge. This knowledge could be the technical expertise of engineers or the special marketing abilities of managers. When the knowledge is technical expertise, companies can charge a fee to companies in other countries for use of the knowledge in producing the same or a similar product. But when a company's specialized knowledge is embodied in its employees, the only way to exploit a market opportunity in another nation may be to undertake FDI.

The possibility that a company will create a future competitor by charging another company for access to its knowledge is another market imperfection that can encourage FDI. Rather than trade a short-term gain (the fee charged another company) for a long-term loss (lost competitiveness), a company will prefer to undertake investment. For example, as Japan rebuilt its industries

At one time, Boeing aircraft were made entirely in the United States. But today, Boeing can source its landing gear doors from Northern Ireland, outboard wing flaps from Italy, wing tip assemblies from Korea, and rudders from Australia. Shown here, the core wing components of a Boeing 787 Dreamliner are loaded into a cargo jet at Japan International Airport to be shipped to Washington for assembly. The wings were manufactured in Japan by Mitsubishi Heavy Industry.

Source: STR/AFP/Newscom

following the Second World War, many Japanese companies paid Western firms for access to the special technical knowledge embodied in their products. Those Japanese companies became adept at revising and improving many of these technologies and became leaders in their industries, including electronics and automobiles.

Eclectic Theory

eclectic theory
Theory stating that firms undertake foreign direct investment when the features of a particular location combine with ownership and internalization advantages to make a location appealing for investment.

The **eclectic theory** states that firms undertake FDI when the features of a particular location combine with ownership and internalization advantages to make a location appealing for investment.[4] A *location advantage* is the advantage of locating a particular economic activity in a specific location because of the characteristics (natural or acquired) of that location.[5] These advantages have historically been natural resources such as oil in the Middle East, timber in Canada, or copper in Chile. But the advantage can also be an acquired one, such as a productive workforce. An *ownership advantage* refers to company ownership of some special asset, such as brand recognition, technical knowledge, or management ability. An *internalization advantage* is one that arises from internalizing a business activity rather than leaving it to a relatively inefficient market. The eclectic theory states that when all of these advantages are present, a company will undertake FDI.

Market Power

market power
Theory stating that a firm tries to establish a dominant market presence in an industry by undertaking foreign direct investment.

vertical integration
Extension of company activities into stages of production that provide a firm's inputs (backward integration) or that absorb its output (forward integration).

Firms often seek the greatest amount of power possible relative to rivals in their industries. The **market power** theory states that a firm tries to establish a dominant market presence in an industry by undertaking FDI. The benefit of market power is greater profit because the firm is far better able to dictate the cost of its inputs and/or the price of its output.

One way a company can achieve market power (or dominance) is through **vertical integration**—the extension of company activities into stages of production that provide a firm's inputs (*backward integration*) or that absorb its output (*forward integration*). Sometimes a company can effectively control the world supply of an input needed by its industry if it has the resources or ability to integrate backward into supplying that input. Companies may also be able to achieve a great deal of market power if they can integrate forward to increase control over output. For example, they could perhaps make investments in distribution to leapfrog channels of distribution that are tightly controlled by competitors.

QUICK STUDY 2

1. Explain the international *product life cycle theory* of FDI.
2. How does the theory of *market imperfections* (internalization) explain FDI?
3. Explain the *eclectic theory,* and identify the three advantages necessary for FDI to occur.
4. How does the theory of *market power* explain the occurrence of FDI?

Management Issues and Foreign Direct Investment

Decisions about whether to engage in FDI involve several important issues regarding management of the company and its market. Some of these issues are grounded in the inner workings of firms that undertake FDI, such as the control desired over operations abroad or the firm's cost of production. Others are related to the market and the industry in which a firm competes, such as the preferences of customers or the actions of rivals. Let's now examine each of these important issues.

Control

Many companies investing abroad are greatly concerned with controlling the activities that occur in the local market. Perhaps the company wants to be certain that its product is being marketed in the same way in the local market as it is at home. Or maybe it wants to ensure that the selling price remains the same in both markets. Some companies try to maintain ownership of a large portion of the local operation, say, even up to 100 percent, in the belief that greater ownership gives them greater control.

Yet for a variety of reasons, even complete ownership does not *guarantee* control. For example, the local government might intervene and require a company to hire some local managers rather than bringing them all in from the home office. Companies may need to prove a scarcity of skilled local managerial talent before the government will let them bring managers in from the home country. Governments might also require that all goods produced in the local facility be exported so that they do not compete with products of the country's domestic firms.

PARTNERSHIP REQUIREMENTS Many companies have strict policies regarding how much ownership they take in firms abroad because of the importance of maintaining control. In the past, IBM (www.ibm.com) strictly required that the home office own 100 percent of all international subsidiaries. But companies must sometimes abandon such policies if a country demands shared ownership in return for market access.

Some governments saw shared ownership requirements as a way to shield their workers from exploitation and their industries from domination by large international firms. Companies would sometimes sacrifice control in order to pursue a market opportunity, but frequently they did not. Most countries today do not take such a hard-line stance and have opened their doors to investment by multinational companies. Mexico used to make decisions on investment by multinational corporations on a case-by-case basis. IBM was negotiating with the Mexican government for 100 percent ownership of a facility in Guadalajara and got the go-ahead only after the company made numerous concessions in other areas.

BENEFITS OF COOPERATION Many nations have grown more cooperative toward international companies in recent years. Governments of developing and emerging markets realize the benefits of investment by multinational corporations, including decreased unemployment, increased tax revenues, training to create a more highly skilled workforce, and the transfer of technology. A country known for overly restricting the operations of multinational enterprises can see its inward investment flow dry up. Indeed, the restrictive policies of India's government hampered FDI inflows for many years.

Cooperation also frequently opens important communication channels that help firms to maintain positive relationships in the host country. Both parties tend to walk a fine line—cooperating most of the time, but holding fast on occasions when the stakes are especially high.

Cooperation with a local partner and respect for national pride in Central Europe contributed to the successful acquisition of Hungary's Borsodi brewery (formerly a state-owned enterprise) by Belgium's Interbrew, now part of Anheuser-Busch InBev (www.ab-inbev.com). From the start, Interbrew wisely insisted that it would move ahead with its purchase only if local management would be in charge. Interbrew then assisted local management with technical, marketing, sales, distribution, and general management training.

Purchase-or-Build Decision

Another important matter for managers is whether to purchase an existing business or to build a subsidiary abroad from the ground up—called a *greenfield investment*. An acquisition generally provides the investor with an existing plant, equipment, and personnel. The acquiring firm may also benefit from the goodwill the existing company has built up over the years and, perhaps,

MANAGER'S BRIEFCASE   Surprises of Investing Abroad

The decision of whether to build facilities in a market abroad or to purchase existing operations in the local market can be a difficult one. Managers can minimize risk by preparing their companies for a number of surprises they might face:

- **Human Resource Policies.** Companies cannot always import home country policies without violating local laws or offending local customs. Countries have differing requirements for plant operations and have their own regulations regarding business operations.
- **Mandated Benefits.** These include company-supplied clothing and meals, required profit sharing, guaranteed employment contracts, and generous dismissal policies. These costs can exceed an employee's wages and are typically not negotiable.
- **Labor Costs.** France has a minimum wage of about $12 an hour, whereas Mexico has a minimum wage of nearly $5 a day. But Mexico's real minimum wage is nearly double that due to

government-mandated benefits and employment practices. Such differences are not always obvious.

- **Labor Unions.** In some countries, organized labor is found in nearly every industry and at almost every company. Rather than dealing with a single union, managers may need to negotiate with five or six different unions, each of which represents a distinct skill or profession.
- **Information.** Sometimes there simply is no reliable data on factors such as labor availability, cost of energy, and national inflation rates. These data are generally high quality in developed countries but suspect in emerging and developing ones.
- **Personal and Political Contacts.** These contacts can be extremely important in developing and emerging markets and can be the only way to establish operations. But complying with locally accepted practices can cause ethical dilemmas for managers.

---

brand recognition of the existing firm. The purchase of an existing business may also allow for alternative methods of financing the purchase, such as an exchange of stock ownership between the companies. Factors that can reduce the appeal of purchasing existing facilities include obsolete equipment, poor relations with workers, and an unsuitable location. For insight into several issues managers consider when deciding to build or purchase operations, see the Manager's Briefcase, titled "Surprises of Investing Abroad."

Mexico's Cemex, S.A. (www.cemex.com), is a multinational company that made a fortune by buying struggling, inefficient plants around the world and reengineering them. Chairman Lorenzo Zambrano has long figured that the overriding principle is "Buy big globally, or be bought." The success of Cemex in using FDI has confounded, even rankled, its competitors in developed nations. For example, Cemex shocked global markets when it carried out a $1.8 billion purchase of Spain's two largest cement companies, Valenciana and Sanson.

But adequate facilities in the local market are sometimes unavailable, and a company must go ahead with a greenfield investment. For example, because Poland is a source of skilled and inexpensive labor, it is an appealing location for automobile manufacturers. But the country had little in the way of advanced automobile-production facilities when General Motors (GM; www .gm.com) considered investing there. So GM built a $320 million facility in Poland's Silesian region. The factory has the potential to produce 200,000 units annually—some of which are destined for export to profitable markets in Western Europe. However, greenfield investments can have their share of headaches. Obtaining the necessary permits, financing, and hiring local personnel can be a real problem in some markets.

Production Costs

Many factors contribute to production costs in every national market. Labor regulations can add significantly to the overall cost of production. Companies may be required to provide benefits packages for their employees that are over and above hourly wages. More time than was planned for might be required to train workers adequately in order to bring productivity up to an acceptable standard. Although the cost of land and the tax rate on profits can be lower in the local market (or purposely lowered to attract multinational corporations), the fact that they will remain constant cannot be assumed. Companies from around the world using China as a production base have witnessed rising wages erode their profits as the economy continues to industrialize. Some companies are therefore finding that Vietnam is now their low-cost location of choice.

rationalized production
System of production in which each of a product's components is produced where the cost of producing that component is lowest.

RATIONALIZED PRODUCTION One approach companies use to contain production costs is called **rationalized production**—a system of production in which each of a product's components is produced where the cost of producing that component is lowest. All the components are then brought together at one central location for assembly into the final product. Consider the typical stuffed animal made in China whose components are all imported to China (with the exception of the polycore thread with which it's sewn). The stuffed animal's eyes are molded in Japan. Its outfit is imported from France. The polyester-fiber stuffing comes from either Germany or the United States, and the pile-fabric fur is produced in Korea. Only final assembly of these components occurs in China.

Although this production model is highly efficient, a potential problem is that a work stoppage in one country can bring the entire production process to a standstill. For example, the production of automobiles is highly rationalized, with parts coming in from a multitude of countries for assembly. When the United Auto Workers (www.uaw.org) union held a strike for weeks against GM (www.gm.com), many of GM's international assembly plants were threatened. The UAW strategically launched their strike at GM's plant that supplied brake pads to virtually all of its assembly plants throughout North America.

MEXICO'S *MAQUILADORA* Stretching 2,000 miles from the Pacific Ocean to the Gulf of Mexico lies a 130-mile-wide strip along the U.S.–Mexican border that comprises a special economic region. The region's economy encompasses 11 million people and $150 billion in output. The combination of a low-wage economy nestled next to a prosperous giant is now becoming a model for other regions that are split by wage or technology gaps. Some analysts compare the U.S.–Mexican border region with that between Hong Kong and its manufacturing realm, China's Guangdong province. Officials from cities along the border between Germany and Poland studied the U.S.–Mexican experience to see what lessons could be applied to their unique situation.

COST OF RESEARCH AND DEVELOPMENT As technology becomes an increasingly powerful competitive factor, the soaring cost of developing subsequent stages of technology has led multinational corporations to engage in cross-border alliances and acquisitions. For instance, huge multinational pharmaceutical companies are intensely interested in the pioneering biotechnology work done by smaller, entrepreneurial start-ups. Cadus Pharmaceutical Corporation of New York discovered the function of 400 genes related to so-called receptor molecules. Many disorders are associated with the improper functioning of these receptors—making them good targets for drug development. Britain's SmithKline Beecham (www.gsk.com) then invested around $68 million in Cadus in return for access to its research knowledge.

One indicator of technology's significance in FDI is the amount of research and development (R&D) conducted by company affiliates in other countries. The globalization of innovation and the phenomenon of foreign investment in R&D are not necessarily motivated by demand factors such as the size of local markets. They instead appear to be encouraged by supply factors, including gaining access to high-quality scientific and technical human capital.

Customer Knowledge

The behavior of buyers is frequently an important issue in the decision of whether to undertake FDI. A local presence can help companies gain valuable knowledge about customers that could not be obtained from the home market. For example, when customer preferences for a product differ a great deal from country to country, a local presence might help companies better understand such preferences and tailor their products accordingly.

Some countries have quality reputations in certain product categories. German automotive engineering, Italian shoes, French perfume, and Swiss watches impress customers as being of superior quality. Because of these perceptions, it can be profitable for a firm to produce its product in the country with the quality reputation, even if the company is based in another country. For example, a cologne or perfume producer might want to bottle its fragrance in France and give it a French name. This type of image appeal can be strong enough to encourage FDI.

Following Clients

Firms commonly engage in FDI when the firms they supply have already invested abroad. This practice of "following clients" is common in industries in which producers source component parts from suppliers with whom they have close working relationships. The practice tends to result in companies clustering within close geographic proximity to each other because they

GLOBAL SUSTAINABILITY   Greening the Supply Chain

- The Rainforest Action Network (RAN) wanted to get paper and wood products manufacturer Boise Cascade (www.bc.com) to protect endangered forests. Instead of approaching Boise Cascade directly, RAN contacted 400 of its customers, including Home Depot. RAN convinced Home Depot (www.homedepot .com) to phase out wood products not certified as originating from well-managed forests. It also convinced Kinkos (www.fedex .com/us/office) to drop Boise Cascade as a supplier. The strategy encouraged Boise Cascade to adopt an environmental policy, part of which involved no longer harvesting U.S. virgin forests.
- When furniture manufacturer Herman Miller (www.hermanmiller .com) started creating its environmentally friendly chair the Mirra, it asked potential suppliers to provide a list of ingredients that went into the part it would supply. Every material and chemical inside each component was assigned a color code of green (environmentally friendly), yellow (neutral), or red (like PVC plastic). The goal was to avoid red-coded materials, minimize yellows, and maximize the greens. Herman Miller bought

components only from companies that (1) supplied its list of ingredients, and (2) had "greener" components than competitors had.
- When Apple (www.apple.com) decided to pull its products from the Electronic Product Environmental Assessment Tool (EPEAT) environmental registry, it expected no one would notice. But some major Apple customers, like educational institutions and governments, must make most or all of their technology purchases from products on the EPEAT–certified list, comprising $65 billion worth of goods annually. The backlash from consumers, corporations, and government agencies forced Apple to backtrack. Apple said its products would again be submitted for certification and that its relationship with EPEAT "has become stronger as a result of this experience."

Source: Jon Fortt, "EPEAT CEO: Apple's Exit Spurred a Customer Backlash," CNBC website (www.cnbc.com), July 13, 2012; Peter Senge, *The Necessary Revolution* (New York: Broadway Books, 2010), pp. 107–108; Daniel C. Esty and Andrew S. Winston, *Green to Gold* (New Haven, CT: Yale University Press, 2006), pp. 84–85, 176–177.

supply each other's inputs (see Chapter 5). When Mercedes (www.mercedes.com) opened its first international car plant in Tuscaloosa County, Alabama, automobile-parts suppliers also moved to the area from Germany—bringing with them additional investment in the millions of dollars.

With firms working closely together to deliver a product on a global basis, they get to know one another rather well. And the movement toward making business activities more environmentally, economically, and socially sustainable means that companies sometimes pressure their suppliers and their clients to "green" their activities. For several examples of how businesses have done this, read this chapter's Global Sustainability feature, titled "Greening the Supply Chain."

Following Rivals

FDI decisions frequently resemble a "follow the leader" scenario in industries that have a limited number of large firms. In other words, many of these firms believe that choosing not to make a move parallel to that of the "first mover" might result in being shut out of a potentially lucrative market. When firms based in industrial countries moved back into South Africa after the end of apartheid, their competitors followed. Of course, each market can sustain only a certain number of rivals and firms that cannot compete often choose to exit the market. This seems to have been the case for Pepsi (www.pepsi.com), which went back into South Africa in 1994 but withdrew in 1997 after being crushed there by Coke (www.cocacola.com).

In this section, we have presented several key issues managers consider when investing abroad. We will have more to say on this topic in Chapter 15, when we learn how companies take on such an ambitious goal.

QUICK STUDY 3

1. Why is control important to companies considering the FDI decision?
2. What is the role of production costs in the FDI decision? Define *rationalized production.*
3. Explain the need for customer knowledge, following clients, and following rivals in the FDI decision.

Government Intervention in Foreign Direct Investment

Nations often intervene in the flow of FDI in order to protect their cultural heritages, domestic companies, and jobs. They can enact laws, create regulations, or construct administrative hurdles that companies from other nations must overcome if they want to invest in the nation. Yet, rising competitive pressure is forcing nations to compete against each other to attract multinational companies. The increased national competition for investment is causing governments to enact regulatory changes that encourage investment. The majority of regulatory changes that governments introduced in recent years are *more favorable to FDI.*[6]

In a general sense, a bias toward protectionism or openness is rooted in a nation's culture, history, and politics. Values, attitudes, and beliefs form the basis for much of a government's position regarding FDI. For example, South American nations with strong cultural ties to a European heritage (such as Argentina) are generally enthusiastic about investment received from European nations. South American nations with stronger indigenous influences (such as Ecuador) are generally less enthusiastic.

Opinions vary widely on the appropriate amount of FDI a country should encourage. At one extreme are those who favor complete economic self-sufficiency and who oppose any form of FDI. At the other extreme are those who favor no governmental intervention and who favor booming FDI inflows. Between these two extremes lie most countries, which believe a certain amount of FDI is desirable to raise national output and enhance the standard of living for their people.

Besides philosophical ideals, countries intervene in FDI for a host of very practical reasons. But to fully appreciate those reasons, we must first understand what is meant by a country's *balance of payments.*

Balance of Payments

A country's **balance of payments** is a national accounting system that records all receipts coming into the nation and all payments to entities in other countries. International transactions that result in inflows from other nations add to the balance of payments accounts. International transactions that result in outflows to other nations reduce the balance of payments accounts. Table 7.1 shows the balance of payments accounts for the United States, which has two major components—the *current account* and the *capital account*. The balances of the current and capital accounts should be equal.

balance of payments
National accounting system that records all receipts coming into the nation and all payments to entities in other countries.

TABLE 7.1 U.S. Balance of Payments Accounts

CURRENT ACCOUNT	
Exports of goods and services and income receipts	+
Merchandise	+
Services	+
Income receipts on U.S. assets abroad	+
Imports of goods and services and income payments	−
Merchandise	−
Services	−
Income payments on foreign assets in United States	−
Unilateral transfers	−
Current account balance	+ / −
CAPITAL ACCOUNT	
Increase in U.S. assets abroad (capital outflow)	−
U.S. official reserve assets	−
Other U.S. government assets	−
U.S. private assets	−
Foreign assets in the United States (capital inflow)	+
Foreign official assets	+
Other foreign assets	+
Capital account balance	+ / −

current account
National account that records transactions involving the export and import of goods and services, income receipts on assets abroad, and income payments on foreign assets inside the country.

CURRENT ACCOUNT The **current account** is a national account that records transactions involving the export and import of goods and services, income receipts on assets abroad, and income payments on foreign assets inside the country. The *merchandise* account in Table 7.1 covers tangible goods such as computer software, electronic components, and apparel. An "Export" of merchandise is assigned a positive value in the balance of payments because income is received. An "Import" is assigned a negative value because money is paid to a firm abroad.

The *services* account involves tourism, business consulting, banking, and other services. Suppose a business in the United States receives payment for consulting services provided to a company in another country. The receipt is recorded as an "Export" of services and is assigned a positive value. An "Import" of services requires money to be sent out of a nation and therefore receives a negative value.

The *income receipts* account is income earned on U.S. assets held abroad. When a U.S. company's subsidiary abroad remits profits back to the parent in the United States, it is recorded as an "Income receipt" and is assigned a positive value.

Finally, the *income payments* account is money paid to entities in other nations that was earned on assets held in the United States. For example, when a French company's U.S. subsidiary sends its profits back to the parent company in France, the transaction is recorded as an "Income payment" and is assigned a negative value.

current account surplus
When a country exports more goods and services and receives more income from abroad than it imports and pays abroad.

current account deficit
When a country imports more goods and services and pays more abroad than it exports and receives from abroad.

A **current account surplus** occurs when a country exports more goods and services and receives more income from abroad than it imports and pays abroad. Conversely, a **current account deficit** occurs when a country imports more goods and services and pays more abroad than it exports and receives from abroad.

capital account
National account that records transactions involving the purchase and sale of assets.

CAPITAL ACCOUNT The **capital account** is a national account that records transactions involving the purchase and sale of assets. Suppose a U.S. citizen buys shares of stock in a Mexican company on Mexico's stock market. The transaction is recorded as an "Increase in U.S. assets abroad (capital outflow)" and is assigned a negative value. If a Mexican investor buys real estate in the United States, the transaction increases "Foreign assets in the United States (capital inflow)" and is assigned a positive value.

Reasons for Intervention by the Host Country

A number of reasons underlie a government's decisions regarding FDI by international companies. Let's look at the two main reasons—to control the *balance of payments* and *to obtain resources and benefits*.

CONTROL BALANCE OF PAYMENTS Many governments see intervention as the only way to keep their balance of payments under control. First, because FDI inflows are recorded as additions to the balance of payments, a nation gets a balance-of-payments boost from an initial FDI inflow. Second, countries can impose local content requirements on investors from other nations for the purpose of local production. This gives local companies the chance to become suppliers to the production operation, which can help reduce the nation's imports and thereby improve its balance of payments. Third, exports (if any) generated by the new production operation can have a favorable impact on the host country's balance of payments.

But when companies repatriate profits back to their home countries, they deplete the foreign exchange reserves of their host countries. These capital outflows decrease the balance of payments of the host country. To shore up its balance of payments, the host nation may prohibit or restrict the nondomestic company from removing profits to its home country.

Alternatively, host countries conserve their foreign exchange reserves when international companies reinvest their earnings. Reinvesting in local manufacturing facilities can also improve the competitiveness of local producers and boost a host nation's exports—thus improving its balance-of-payments position.

OBTAIN RESOURCES AND BENEFITS Beyond balance-of-payments reasons, governments might intervene in FDI flows to acquire resources and benefits such as technology, management skills, and employment.

Access to Technology Investment in technology, whether in products or processes, tends to increase the productivity and the competitiveness of a nation. That is why host nations have a strong incentive to encourage the importation of technology. For years, developing countries

Two boys walk past an advertisement for Pizza Hut in Shanghai, China. China's liberal economic policies have caused its inward FDI to surge. The investments of multinational corporations brings badly needed jobs to China's 130 million migrant workers, who travel from one city and job site to another doing day labor on construction sites. How might such investments impact China's balance of payments?

Source: LIU JIN/Newscom

in Asia were introduced to expertise in industrial processes as multinational corporations set up factories within their borders. But today, some of them are trying to acquire and develop their own technological expertise. When German industrial giant Siemens (www.siemens.com) chose Singapore as the site for an Asia-Pacific microelectronics design center, Singapore gained access to valuable technology. Singapore also accessed valuable semiconductor technology by joining with U.S.-based Texas Instruments (www.ti.com) and others to set up the country's first semiconductor-production facility.

Management Skills and Employment   As we saw in Chapter 4, formerly communist nations lack some of the management skills needed to succeed in the global economy. By encouraging FDI, these nations can attract talented managers to come in and train locals and thereby improve the international competitiveness of their domestic companies. Furthermore, locals who are trained in modern management techniques may eventually start their own local businesses— further expanding employment opportunities. Yet detractors argue that although FDI can create jobs, it can also destroy jobs if less-competitive local firms are forced out of business.

Reasons for Intervention by the Home Country

Home nations (those from which international companies launch their investments) may also seek to encourage or discourage *outflows* of FDI for a variety of reasons. But home nations tend to have fewer concerns because they are often prosperous, industrialized nations. For these countries, an outward investment seldom has a national impact—unlike the impact on developing or emerging nations that receive the FDI. Nevertheless, the following are among the most common reasons for discouraging outward FDI:

- *Investing in other nations sends resources out of the home country.* As a result, fewer resources are used for development and economic growth at home. On the other hand, profits on assets abroad that are returned home increase both a home country's balance of payments and its available resources.
- *Outgoing FDI may ultimately damage a nation's balance of payments by taking the place of its exports.* This can occur when a company creates a production facility in a market abroad, the output of which replaces exports that used to be sent there from the home country. For example, if a Volkswagen (www.vw.com) plant in the United States fills a demand that U.S. buyers would otherwise satisfy with purchases of German-made automobiles, Germany's balance of payments is correspondingly decreased. Still, Germany's balance of payments would be positively affected when Volkswagen repatriates U.S. profits, which

helps negate the investment's initial negative balance-of-payments effect. Thus, an international investment might make a positive contribution to the balance-of-payments position of the country in the long term and offset an initial negative impact.

- *Jobs resulting from outgoing investments may replace jobs at home.* This is often the most contentious issue for home countries. The relocation of production to a low-wage nation can have a strong impact on a locale or region. However, the impact is rarely national, and its effects are often muted by other job opportunities in the economy. In addition, there may be an offsetting improvement in home country employment if additional exports are needed to support the activity represented by the outgoing FDI. For example, if Hyundai (www .hyundai-motor.com) of South Korea builds an automobile manufacturing plant in Brazil, Korean employment may increase in order to supply the Brazilian plant with parts.

FDI is not always a negative influence on home nations. In fact, countries promote outgoing FDI for the following reasons:

- *Outward FDI can increase long-term competitiveness.* Businesses today frequently compete on a global scale. The most competitive firms tend to be those that conduct business in the most favorable locations anywhere in the world, continuously improve their performance relative to competitors, and derive technological advantages from alliances formed with other companies. Japanese companies have become masterful at benefiting from FDI and cooperative arrangements with companies from other nations. The key to their success is that Japanese companies see every cooperative venture as a learning opportunity.
- *Nations may encourage FDI in industries identified as "sunset" industries.* Sunset industries are those that use outdated and obsolete technologies or that employ low-wage workers with few skills. These jobs are not greatly appealing to countries having industries that pay skilled workers high wages. By allowing some of these jobs to go abroad and by retraining workers in higher-paying skilled work, they can upgrade their economies toward "sunrise" industries. This represents a trade-off for governments between a short-term loss of jobs and the long-term benefit of developing workers' skills.

QUICK STUDY 4

1. What is a country's *balance of payments*? Briefly explain its usefulness.
2. Explain the difference between the *current account* and the *capital account*.
3. For what reasons do *host* countries intervene in FDI?
4. For what reasons do *home* countries intervene in FDI?

Government Policy Instruments and Foreign Direct Investment

Over time, both host and home nations have developed a range of methods either to promote or to restrict FDI (see Table 7.2). Governments use these tools for many reasons, including improving balance-of-payments positions, acquiring resources, and, in the case of outward investment, keeping jobs at home. Let's take a look at these methods.

TABLE 7.2 Methods of Promoting and Restricting Foreign Direct Investment (FDI)

	FDI Promotion	FDI Restriction
Host Countries	Tax incentives	Ownership restrictions
	Low-interest loans	Performance demands
	Infrastructure improvements	
Home Countries	Insurance	Differential tax rates
	Loans	Sanctions
	Tax breaks	
	Political pressure	

Host Countries: Promotion

Host countries offer a variety of incentives to encourage FDI inflows. These take two general forms—financial incentives and infrastructure improvements.

FINANCIAL INCENTIVES Host governments of all nations grant companies financial incentives to invest within their borders. One method includes tax incentives, such as lower tax rates or offers to waive taxes on local profits for a period of time—extending as far out as five years or more. A country may also offer *low-interest loans* to investors.

The downside of these types of incentives is that they can allow multinational corporations to create bidding wars between locations that are vying for the investment. In such cases, the company typically invests in the most appealing region after the locations endure rounds of escalating incentives. Companies have even been accused of engaging other governments in negotiations to force concessions from locations already selected for investment. The cost to taxpayers of attracting FDI can be several times what the actual jobs themselves pay—especially when nations try to one-up each other to win investment.

INFRASTRUCTURE IMPROVEMENTS Because of the problems associated with financial incentives, some governments are taking an alternative route to luring investment. Lasting benefits for communities surrounding the investment location can result from making local *infrastructure improvements*—better seaports suitable for containerized shipping, improved roads, and increased telecommunications systems. For instance, Malaysia is carving an enormous Multimedia Super Corridor (MSC) into a region's forested surroundings. The MSC promises a paperless government, an intelligent city called Cyberjaya, two telesuburbs, a technology park, a multimedia university, and an intellectual property–protection park. The MSC is dedicated to creating the most advanced technologies in telecommunications, medicine, distance learning, and remote manufacturing.

Host Countries: Restriction

Host countries also have a variety of methods to restrict incoming FDI. Again, these take two general forms—ownership restrictions and performance demands.

OWNERSHIP RESTRICTIONS Governments can impose *ownership restrictions* that prohibit nondomestic companies from investing in certain industries or from owning certain types of businesses. Such prohibitions typically apply to businesses in cultural industries and companies vital to national security. For example, as some cultures try to protect traditional values, accepting investment by multinational companies can create controversy among conservatives, moderates, and liberals. Also, most nations do not allow FDI in their domestic weapons or national defense firms. Another ownership restriction is a requirement that nondomestic investors hold less than a 50 percent stake in local firms when they undertake FDI.

But nations are eliminating such restrictions because companies today often can choose another location that has no such restriction in place. When GM was deciding whether to invest in an aging automobile plant in Jakarta, Indonesia, the Indonesian government scrapped its ownership restriction of an eventual forced sale to Indonesians because China and Vietnam were also courting GM for the same financial investment.

PERFORMANCE DEMANDS More common than ownership requirements are *performance demands* that influence how international companies operate in the host nation. Although typically viewed as intrusive, most international companies allow for them in the same way they allow for home-country regulations. Performance demands include ensuring that a portion of the product's content originates locally, stipulating that a portion of the output must be exported, or requiring that certain technologies be transferred to local businesses.

Home Countries: Promotion

To encourage outbound FDI, home-country governments can do any of the following:

- Offer *insurance* to cover the risks of investments abroad, including, among others, insurance against expropriation of assets and losses from armed conflict, kidnappings, and terrorist attacks.
- Grant *loans* to firms wishing to increase their investments abroad. A home-country government may also guarantee the loans that a company takes from financial institutions.

- Offer *tax breaks* on profits earned abroad or negotiate special tax treaties. For example, several multinational agreements reduce or eliminate the practice of double taxation—profits earned abroad being taxed both in the home and host countries.
- Apply *political pressure* on other nations to get them to relax their restrictions on inbound investments. Non-Japanese companies often find it very difficult to invest inside Japan. The United States, for one, repeatedly pressures the Japanese government to open its market further to FDI. But because such pressure has achieved little success, many U.S. companies cooperate with local Japanese businesses.

Home Countries: Restriction

On the other hand, to limit the effects of outbound FDI on the national economy, home governments may exercise either of the following two options:

- Impose *differential tax rates* that charge income from earnings abroad at a higher rate than domestic earnings
- Impose outright *sanctions* that prohibit domestic firms from making investments in certain nations

QUICK STUDY 5

1. Identify the main methods host countries use to promote and restrict FDI.
2. What methods do home countries use to promote and restrict FDI?

BOTTOM LINE FOR BUSINESS

Companies ranging from massive global corporations to adventurous entrepreneurs all contribute to FDI flows, and the long-term trend in FDI is upward. Here we briefly discuss the influence of national governments on FDI flows and flows of FDI in Asia and Europe.

National Governments and Foreign Direct Investment
The actions of national governments have important implications for business. Companies can either be thwarted in their efforts or be encouraged to invest in a nation, depending on the philosophies of home and host governments. The balance-of-payments positions of both home and host countries are also important because FDI flows affect the economic health of nations. To attract investment, a nation must provide a climate conducive to business operations, including pro-growth economic policies, a stable regulatory environment, and a sound infrastructure, to name just a few.

Increased competition for investment by multinational corporations has caused nations to make regulatory changes more favorable to FDI. Moreover, just as nations around the world are creating free trade agreements (covered in Chapter 8), they are also embracing bilateral investment treaties. These bilateral investment treaties are becoming prominent tools used to attract investment. Investment provisions within free trade agreements are also receiving greater attention than in the past. These efforts to attract investment have direct implications for the strategies of multinational companies, particularly when it comes to deciding where to locate production, logistics, and back-office service activities.

Foreign Direct Investment in Europe
FDI inflows into the developing (transition) nations of Southeast Europe and the Commonwealth of Independent States hit an all-time high in 2008. Countries that recently entered the European Union did particularly well. They saw less investment in areas supporting low-wage, unskilled occupations and greater investment in higher value-added activities that take advantage of a well-educated workforce.

The main reason for the fast pace at which FDI is occurring in Western Europe is regional economic integration. Some of the foreign investment reported by the European Union certainly went to the relatively less-developed markets of the new Central and Eastern European members. But much of the activity occurring among Western European companies is industry consolidation brought on by the opening of markets and the tearing down of barriers to free trade and investment. Change in the economic landscape across Europe is creating a more competitive business climate there.

Foreign Direct Investment in Asia
China attracts the majority of Asia's FDI, luring companies with a low-wage workforce and access to an enormous domestic market. Many companies already active in China are upping their investment further, and companies not yet there are developing strategies for how to include China in their future plans. The "off-shoring" of services will likely propel continued FDI in the coming years, for which India is the primary destination. India's attraction is its well-educated, low-cost, and English-speaking workforce.

An aspect of national business environments that has implications for future business activity is the natural environment. By their actions, businesses lay the foundation for people's attitudes in developing nations toward FDI by multinational corporations. For example, greater decentralization in China's politics has placed local Communist Party bosses and bureaucrats at the center of many FDI deals there. These individuals are often more motivated by their personal financial gain than they are worried about pollution. But China's government is increasing its spending on the environment, and multinational corporations are helping in cleaning up the environment.

Chapter Summary

MyManagementLab

Go to **mymanagementlab.com** to complete the problems marked with this icon .

1. **Describe worldwide patterns of foreign direct investment (FDI) and reasons for those patterns.**
   - FDI inflows reached $1.4 trillion in 2000, slowed through 2003, and then rebounded to more than $1.9 trillion in 2007. FDI slowed in 2008 and 2009 but reached $1.5 trillion in 2011.
   - Developed countries account for around 49 percent of global FDI inflows, and developing countries account for about 45 percent.
   - Among developed countries, the EU, the United States, and Japan account for the majority of FDI inflows. The EU garnered $421 billion of FDI in 2011 (28 percent of the world total).
   - FDI inflows to developing Asian nations were nearly $423 billion in 2011, with China attracting more than $124 billion and India attracting nearly $31 billion.
   - FDI inflows to all of Africa accounted for about 2.8 percent of total world FDI inflows in 2011.
   - *Globalization* and a growing number of *mergers and acquisitions* account for the rising tide of FDI flows.

2. **Describe each of the theories that attempt to explain why FDI occurs.**
   - The *international product life cycle theory* says that a company begins by exporting its product and then later undertakes FDI as the product moves through its life cycle of three stages: new product, maturing product, and standardized product.
   - *Market imperfections theory* says that when an imperfection in the market makes a transaction less efficient than it could be, a company will undertake FDI to internalize the transaction and thereby remove the imperfection.
   - The *eclectic theory* says that firms undertake FDI when the features of a particular location combine with ownership and internalization advantages to make a location appealing for investment.
   - The *market power theory* states that a firm tries to establish a dominant market presence in an industry by undertaking FDI.

3. **Discuss the important management issues in the FDI decision.**
   - Although companies investing abroad often wish to *control* activities in the local market, they may be forced to hire local managers or to export all goods produced locally.
   - Acquisition of an existing business is preferred when the existing business entails updated equipment, good relations with workers, and a suitable location.
   - When adequate facilities are unavailable, a company might need to pursue a *greenfield investment*.
   - A local market presence can give a company valuable knowledge of local *buyer behavior*.
   - Firms commonly engage in FDI when the investment locates them close to *client* firms and *rival* firms.

4. **Explain why governments intervene in the free flow of FDI.**
   - *Host nations* receive a *balance-of-payments* boost from initial FDI and from any exports the FDI generates, but they see a decrease in balance of payments when a company sends profits to the home country.
   - FDI in *technology* brings in people with *management skills* who can train locals and increase a nation's productivity and competitiveness.
   - *Home countries* intervene in FDI outflows because they can lower the balance of payments, but profits sent home that are earned on assets abroad increase the balance of payments.
   - FDI outflows may replace jobs at home that were based on exports to the host country and may damage the home nation's balance of payments if they reduce prior exports.

5. Discuss the policy instruments that governments use to promote and restrict FDI.
   - Host countries can promote FDI inflows by offering companies *tax incentives* (such as lower tax rates or waived taxes), extending *low interest loans,* and making local *infrastructure improvements*.
   - Host countries can restrict FDI inflows by imposing *ownership restrictions* (prohibitions from certain industries) and by creating *performance demands* that influence how a company can operate.
   - Home countries can promote FDI outflows by offering *insurance* to cover investment risks abroad, granting loans to firms investing abroad, guaranteeing company loans from financial institutions, offering *tax breaks* on profits earned abroad, negotiating special tax treaties, and applying *political pressure* to get other nations to accept FDI.
   - Home countries can restrict FDI outflows by imposing *differential tax rates* that charge income from earnings abroad at a higher rate than domestic earnings and by imposing *sanctions* that prohibit domestic firms from making investments in certain nations.

Talk It Over

1. You overhear your superior tell another manager in the company, "I'm fed up with our nation's companies sending manufacturing jobs abroad and offshoring service work to lower-wage nations. Don't any of them have any national pride?" The other manager responds, "I disagree. It is every company's duty to make as much profit as possible for its owners. If that means going abroad to reduce costs, so be it." Do you agree with either of these managers? Why or why not? Now step into the conversation and explain where you stand on this issue.
2. The global automaker you work for is investing in an automobile assembly facility in Costa Rica with a local partner. Explain the potential reasons for this investment. Will your company want to exercise a great deal of control over this operation? Why or why not? In what areas might your company want to exercise control, and in what areas might it cede control to the partner?
3. This chapter presented several theories that attempt to explain why firms undertake FDI. Which of these theories seems most appealing to you? Why is it appealing? Can you think of one or more companies that seem to fit the pattern described by the theory? In your opinion, what faults do the alternative theories have?

Teaming Up

1. **Research Project.** In a small group, locate an article in the business press that discusses a cross-border merger or acquisition within the past year. Gather additional information on the deal from any sources available. What reasons did each company give for the merger or acquisition? Was it a marriage of equals, or did a larger partner absorb a far smaller one? Do the articles identify any internal issues managers had to deal with following the merger or acquisition? What is the current performance of the new company? Write a two- to three-page report of your group's findings.
2. **Market Entry Strategy Project.** This exercise corresponds to the *MESP* online simulation. For the country your team is researching, does it attract large amounts of FDI? Is it a major source of FDI for other nations? What is the nation's balance-of-payments position? What is its current account balance? List some possible causes for its surplus or deficit. How is this surplus or deficit affecting the nation's economic performance? What is its capital account balance? How does the government encourage or restrict trade with other nations? Integrate your findings into your completed *MESP* report.

Key Terms

balance of payments (p. 187)	eclectic theory (p. 182)	market power (p. 182)
capital account (p. 188)	foreign direct investment (FDI) (p. 178)	portfolio investment (p. 178)
current account (p. 188)	international product life cycle (p. 181)	rationalized production (p. 184)
current account deficit (p. 188)	market imperfections (p. 181)	vertical integration (p. 182)
current account surplus (p. 188)		

Take It to the Web

1. **Video Report.** Visit this book's channel on YouTube (www.YouTube.com/MyIBvideos). Click on "Videos" near the top of the page, and click on the set of videos labeled "Ch 07: Foreign Direct Investment." Watch one video from the list, and then summarize it in a half-page report. Reflecting on the contents of this chapter, which aspects of FDI can you identify in the video? How might a company engaged in international business act on the information contained in the video?

2. **Website Report.** This chapter presented many reasons why companies directly invest in other nations and many factors in the decision of whether and where to invest abroad.

   Research the economy of the Philippines and its neighbors. In what economic sectors is each country strong? Do the strengths of each country really complement one another, or do they compete directly with one another? If you were considering investing in the Philippines, what management issues would concern you? Be specific in your answer. (*Hint:* A good place to begin your research is the CIA's World Factbook at https://www.cia.gov/library/publications/the-world-factbook).

   In this era of intense national competition to attract jobs, Southeast Asian governments fear losing ground to China in the race for investment. What do you think those governments could do to increase the attractiveness of their homelands for multinational corporations?

   Find an article on the Internet that describes a company's decision to relocate some or all of its business operations (goods or services). What reasons are stated for the relocation? Was any consideration given to the plight of employees being put out of work?

Ethical Challenges

1. You are a sales manager working in international sales for a major U.S. beef distributor. Your firm is attempting to sell a large quantity of beef to a developing market in northern Africa where U.S. beef is a rarity. The vice president for new business development has instructed you to quickly sell the beef well below market price. Standing at the coffee machine, you overhear two quality assurance managers discussing "the potentially tainted beef heading for Africa." You are aware that in the past your firm has come across small traces of typhoid in some of its products. What do you do? Do you go through with the northern Africa deal? Do you first contact someone inside or outside the company? If additional information would be helpful to you, what would it be?

2. You are the U.S. senator deciding whether to vote yes or no on a new piece of legislation. The potential new law places restrictions on the practice of outsourcing work to low-wage countries and is designed to protect U.S. workers' jobs. These days it is increasingly common for companies to promise manufacturing contracts to overseas suppliers in exchange for entry into that country's market. Labor union representatives argue that these kinds of deals are made at the expense of jobs at home. After all, if a company can have parts made in China at lower wages, why keep factories operating at home? They also are concerned that the transfer of technology will breed strong competitors in other nations and thereby threaten even more domestic jobs in the future. But others argue that increased sales abroad actually helps create more jobs at home. Discuss the ethics of companies contracting out production to factories abroad in exchange for sales contracts. How would you vote on the pending legislation? What other issues must you consider?

3. You are the U.S. ambassador to Malaysia. In order to become a major export platform for the semiconductor industry, Malaysia's government not only offered tax breaks but also guaranteed that electronics workers would be prohibited from organizing independent labor unions. The government decreed that the goal of national development required a "union-free" environment for the "pioneers" of semiconductors. Under pressure from U.S. labor unions, the Malaysian government offered a weak alternative to industry unions—company-by-company "in-house" unions. Yet as soon as workers organized one at a Harris Electronics plant, the 21 union leaders were fired, and the new union was disbanded. In another instance, when French-owned Thomson Electronics inherited a Malaysian factory with a union of 3,000, it closed the plant and moved the work to Vietnam. Newly industrialized nations such as Malaysia feel that their futures depend on investment by multinational corporations. Yet their governments are acutely aware that in the absence of incentives such as a "union-free" workforce, international companies can easily take their investment money elsewhere. Discuss the problems that these governments face in balancing the needs of their citizens with the long-term quest for economic development. As the ambassador, what advice do you give Malaysian business and government leaders? Can you think of examples from other nations that can help you make the case for local unions?

MyManagementLab

Go to **mymanagementlab.com** for Auto-graded writing questions as well as the following Assisted-graded writing questions:

7-1. What do you see as the pros and cons of Mercedes' approach to managing FDI—abandoning the culture and some of its home-country practices?

7-2. Mymanagementlab Only – comprehensive writing assignment for this chapter.

Practicing International Management Case

World Class in Dixieland

"**A**loof." "Serious." "Not youthful." Definitely "not fun." These were the unfortunate epithets applied to Mercedes-Benz by a market research firm that assesses product personalities. Research among dealers in the United States also revealed that consumers felt so intimidated by Mercedes that they wouldn't sit in the cars at the showroom.

To boost sales and broaden the market to a more youthful and value-conscious consumer, Mercedes-Benz U.S. International (www.mbusi.com) came up with a series of inventive, free-spirited ads featuring stampeding rhinos and bobbing aliens. Although the new ads boosted sales, the company needed more than a new marketing message to ensure its future growth. What it needed was an all-new Mercedes. Enter the Mercedes M-Class, a sports utility vehicle (SUV). Mercedes placed its M-Class to compete squarely against the Ford Explorer and Jeep Grand Cherokee.

Not only was the M-Class Mercedes' first SUV, it was also the first car that Mercedes had manufactured outside Germany—in the heart of Dixie, no less. The rough-hewn town of Vance, Alabama (population 400), in Tuscaloosa County is where people hang out at the local barbecue joint. And it is the last place you'd expect to find button-down engineers from Stuttgart, Germany. But this small town appealed to Mercedes for several reasons. Labor costs in the U.S. Deep South are 50 percent lower than in Germany. Also, Alabama offered an attractive $250 million in tax refunds and other incentives to win the much-needed Mercedes jobs. Mercedes also wanted to be closer to the crucial U.S. market and to create a plant from the ground up, one that would be a model for its future international operations.

When Japanese automakers entered the U.S. market, they reproduced their automobile-building philosophies, cultures, production practices, and management styles. By contrast, Mercedes started with the proverbial blank sheet of paper at Tuscaloosa. To appeal to U.S. workers, Mercedes knew it had to abandon the rigid hierarchy of its typical production line and create a more egalitarian shop floor. Administrative offices in the gleaming, *E*-shaped Mercedes plant run through the middle of the manufacturing area, and administrators are accessible to team members on the shop floor. Also, the plant's design lets workers unilaterally stop the assembly line to correct manufacturing problems.

So far, the system has been a catalyst to communication among the Tuscaloosa plant's U.S. workers, German trainers, and a diverse management team that includes executives from Detroit and Japan. Even so, an enormous amount of time and effort was invested in training the U.S. workforce. Explains Sven Schoolman, a 31-year-old trainer from Sindelfingen, "In Germany, we don't say we build a car. We say we build a Mercedes. We had to teach that." The innovative production system is a combination of German, Japanese, and U.S. automotive best practices within a young corporate culture.

The Tuscaloosa plant uses a "just-in-time" manufacturing method that requires only about two hours of inventory on line and about three hours of inventory in the body shop. French company Faurecia opened a brand new facility in 2011 to make fully assembled automotive seats for Mercedes-Benz's 2012 model vehicles made in Tuscaloosa. Mercedes' experience is so successful that Honda, Toyota, and Hyundai followed it to Alabama, and Volkswagen may soon, as well.

Mercedes has expanded its Tuscaloosa operations to nearly triple the size of its original factory. The plant now uses flexible manufacturing technology to accommodate the M-Class, R-Class, and GL-Class. Around 65 percent of each vehicle's content comes from Canada, Mexico, and the United States, and engines and transmissions are imported from Germany. Every vehicle built at the Tuscaloosa plant is for an order from one of Mercedes' 135 markets worldwide.

The company is gaining valuable experience in how to set up and operate a plant in another country. "It was once sacrosanct to talk about our cars being 'Made in Germany,'" said Jürgen E. Schrempp, then CEO of Mercedes' parent company. "We have to change that to 'Made by Mercedes,' and never mind where they are assembled."

Thinking Globally

1. What do you think were the chief factors involved in Mercedes' decision to undertake FDI in the United States rather than build the M-Class in Germany?
2. Why do you think Mercedes decided to build the plant from the ground up in Alabama rather than buy an existing plant in, say, Detroit? List as many reasons as you can, and explain your answer.
3. Do you think Mercedes risks diluting its "Made in Germany" reputation for engineering quality by building its M-class outside Germany? Why or why not?

Source: Patrick Rupinski, "Riley Joins Officials to Welcome Auto Plant," *Tuscaloosa News* (www.tuscaloosanews.com), April 8, 2010; "Love Me, Love Me Not," *The Economist* (www.economist.com), July 10, 2008; Mercedes-Benz U.S. International website (www.mbusi.com), select reports.

Regional Economic Integration

LEARNING OBJECTIVES

After studying this chapter, you should be able to

1. Define regional economic integration and identify its five levels.

2. Discuss the benefits and drawbacks of regional economic integration.

3. Describe regional integration in Europe and its pattern of enlargement.

4. Discuss regional integration in the Americas and analyze its future prospects.

5. Characterize regional integration in Asia and how it differs from integration elsewhere.

6. Describe integration in the Middle East and Africa, and explain the slow progress.

A Look Back

Chapter 7 examined recent patterns of foreign direct investment. We explored the theories that try to explain why foreign direct investment occurs and discussed how governments influence investment flows.

A Look at This Chapter

This chapter explores the trend toward greater integration of national economies. We first examine the reasons why nations are making significant efforts at regional integration. We then study the most prominent regional trading blocs in place around the world today.

A Look Ahead

Chapter 9 begins our inquiry into the international financial system. We describe the structure of the international capital market and explain how the foreign exchange market operates.

NESTLÉ'S GLOBAL RECIPE

VEVEY, Switzerland—Nestlé (www.nestle.com), the largest food company in the world, is active in nearly every country on the planet. It earns just 2 percent of its sales at home in Switzerland, and it operates across cultural borders 24 hours a day.

Nestlé has a knack for turning humdrum products like bottled water and pet food into well-known global brands. It also takes regional products to the global market when the opportunity arises. For example, Nestlé launched a cereal bar for diabetics first in Asia under the brand name Nutren Balance and then introduced it to other markets worldwide.

Food is integral to every culture's social fabric. Nestlé must carefully navigate the cultural landscape in other countries in order to remain sensitive to local dietary traditions. Nestlé learned from past mistakes and now tries to ensure that mothers in developing nations use purified water to mix its baby milk formulas, for example. As Nestlé expands into emerging markets, it watches for changes in consumer attitudes resulting from greater cross-cultural contact due to regional integration. Pictured here, a woman in Ryazan, Russia, reads the labeling on a package of Nestlé brand baby food.

Source: Ryumin Alexander/Newscom

Nestlé also needs to tread carefully when it comes to global sustainability. Greenpeace charged that Nestlé (and others) source palm oil for their products from delicate Indonesian rainforests and peatlands. Nestlé said it would stop purchasing such palm oil and pledged that by 2015, its palm oil will be certified sustainable. It also committed itself to a "no deforestation" target by 2020.

When Nestlé and Coca-Cola announced a joint venture to develop coffee and tea drinks, they first had to show the European Union (EU) Commission that they would not stifle competition across the region. Firms operating within the EU must also abide by EU environmental protection laws. Nestlé works with governments to minimize packaging waste that results from the use of its products by developing and managing waste-recovery programs. As you read this chapter, consider all the business implications of nations banding together in regional trading blocs.[1]

Regional trade agreements are changing the landscape of the global marketplace. Companies like Nestlé of Switzerland are finding that these agreements lower trade barriers and open new markets for goods and services. Markets otherwise off-limits because tariffs made imported products too expensive can become quite attractive once tariffs are lifted. But trade agreements can be double-edged swords for many companies. Not only do regional trade agreements allow domestic companies to seek new markets abroad, but they also let competitors from other nations enter the domestic market. Such mobility increases competition in every market that takes part in an agreement.

Trade agreements can allow companies to alter their strategies, sometimes radically. As we will see in this chapter, for example, nations in the Americas want to create a free trade area that runs from the northern tip of Alaska to the southern tip of South America. Companies that do business throughout this region could save millions of dollars annually from the removal of import tariffs under an eventual agreement. Multinational corporations could also save money by supplying entire regions from just a few regional factories, rather than having a factory in each nation.

We began Part 3 of this book by discussing the gains resulting from specialization and trade. We now close this part of the book by showing how groups of countries are cooperating to dismantle barriers that threaten these potential gains. In this chapter, we focus on regional efforts to encourage freer trade and investment. We begin by defining *regional economic integration* and describing its five different levels. We then examine the benefits and drawbacks of regional trade agreements. Finally, we explore several long-established trade agreements and several agreements in the early stages of development.

What Is Regional Economic Integration?

The process whereby countries in a geographic region cooperate to reduce or eliminate barriers to the international flow of products, people, or capital is called **regional economic integration (regionalism)**. A group of nations in a geographic region undergoing economic integration is called a *regional trading bloc*.

The goal of nations pursuing economic integration is not only to increase cross-border trade and investment but also to raise living standards for their people. We saw in Chapter 5, for example, how specialization and trade create real gains in terms of greater choice, lower prices, and increased productivity. Regional trade agreements are designed to help nations accomplish these objectives. Regional economic integration sometimes has additional goals, such as protection of intellectual property rights or the environment, or even eventual political union.

Levels of Regional Integration

Nations have tried to reap the potential gains of international trade in a variety of ways. Figure 8.1 shows five potential levels (or degrees) of economic and political integration for regional trading blocs. A *free trade area* is the lowest extent of national integration; *political union* is the greatest. Each level of integration incorporates the properties of those levels that precede it.

FREE TRADE AREA Economic integration whereby countries seek to remove all barriers to trade among themselves but where each country determines its own barriers against nonmembers is called a **free trade area**. A free trade area is the lowest level of economic integration that is possible between two or more countries. Countries belonging to the free trade area strive to remove all tariffs and nontariff barriers, such as quotas and subsidies, on international trade in goods and services. However, each country is able to maintain whatever policy it sees fit against nonmember countries. These policies can differ widely from country to country. Countries belonging to a free trade area also typically establish a process by which trade disputes can be resolved.

CUSTOMS UNION Economic integration whereby countries remove all barriers to trade among themselves and set a common trade policy against nonmembers is called a **customs union**. Thus, the main difference between a free trade area and a customs union is that the members of a customs union agree to treat trade with all nonmember nations in a similar manner. Countries

regional economic integration (regionalism)
Process whereby countries in a geographic region cooperate to reduce or eliminate barriers to the international flow of products, people, or capital.

free trade area
Economic integration whereby countries seek to remove all barriers to trade among themselves but where each country determines its own barriers against nonmembers.

customs union
Economic integration whereby countries remove all barriers to trade among themselves and set a common trade policy against nonmembers.

FIGURE 8.1

Levels of Regional Integration

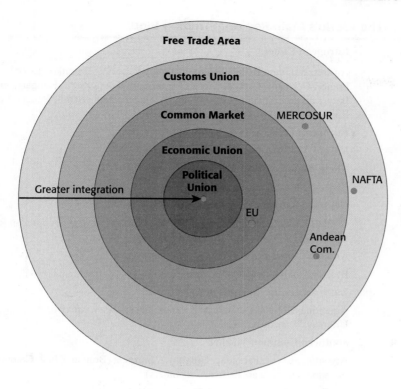

belonging to a customs union might also negotiate as a single entity with other supranational organizations, such as the World Trade Organization.

COMMON MARKET Economic integration whereby countries remove all barriers to trade and to the movement of labor and capital among themselves and set a common trade policy against nonmembers is called a **common market**. Thus, a common market integrates the elements of free trade areas and customs unions and adds the free movement of important factors of production—people and cross-border investment. This level of integration is very difficult to attain because it requires members to cooperate to at least some extent on economic and labor policies. Furthermore, the benefits to individual countries can be uneven because skilled labor may move to countries where wages are higher, and investment capital may flow to areas where returns are greater.

ECONOMIC UNION Economic integration whereby countries remove barriers to trade and the movement of labor and capital among members, set a common trade policy against nonmembers, and coordinate their economic policies is called an **economic union**. An economic union goes beyond the demands of a common market by requiring member nations to harmonize their tax, monetary, and fiscal policies and to create a common currency. Economic unions require that member countries concede a certain amount of their national autonomy (or sovereignty) to the supranational union of which they are a part.

POLITICAL UNION Economic and political integration whereby countries coordinate aspects of their economic *and* political systems is called a **political union**. A political union requires member nations to accept a common stance on economic and political matters regarding nonmember nations. However, nations are allowed a degree of freedom in setting certain political and economic policies within their territories. Individually, Canada and the United States provide examples of political unions early in their histories. In both these nations, smaller states and provinces combined to form larger entities. A group of nations currently taking steps in this direction is the European Union—discussed later in this chapter.

Table 8.1 identifies the members of every regional trading bloc presented in this chapter. As you work through this chapter, refer back to this table for a quick summary of each bloc's members.

common market
Economic integration whereby countries remove all barriers to trade and to the movement of labor and capital among themselves and set a common trade policy against nonmembers.

economic union
Economic integration whereby countries remove barriers to trade and the movement of labor and capital among members, set a common trade policy against nonmembers, and coordinate their economic policies.

political union
Economic and political integration whereby countries coordinate aspects of their economic and political systems.

TABLE 8.1 The World's Main Regional Trading Blocs

EU	**European Union**
	Austria, Belgium, Britain, Bulgaria, Czech Republic, Denmark, Estonia, Finland, France, Germany, Greece, Greek Cyprus (southern portion), Hungary, Ireland, Italy, Latvia, Lithuania, Luxembourg, Malta, the Netherlands, Poland, Portugal, Romania, Slovakia, Slovenia, Spain, Sweden
EFTA	**European Free Trade Association**
	Iceland, Liechtenstein, Norway, Switzerland
NAFTA	**North American Free Trade Agreement**
	Canada, Mexico, United States
CAFTA-DR	**Central American Free Trade Agreement**
	Costa Rica, El Salvador, Guatemala, Honduras, Nicaragua, Dominican Republic, United States
CAN	**Andean Community**
	Bolivia, Colombia, Ecuador, Peru
ALADI	**Latin American Integration Association**
	Argentina, Bolivia, Brazil, Chile, Colombia, Ecuador, Mexico, Paraguay, Peru, Uruguay, Venezuela
MERCOSUR	**Southern Common Market**
	Argentina, Brazil, Paraguay, Uruguay, Venezuela (Bolivia, Chile, Colombia, Ecuador, and Peru are associate members)
CARICOM	**Caribbean Community and Common Market**
	Antigua and Barbuda, Bahamas, Barbados, Belize, Dominica, Grenada, Guyana, Haiti, Jamaica, Montserrat, St. Kitts and Nevis, St. Lucia, St. Vincent and the Grenadines, Suriname, Trinidad and Tobago
CACM	**Central American Common Market**
	Costa Rica, El Salvador, Guatemala, Honduras, Nicaragua
FTAA	**Free Trade Area of the Americas**
	34 nations from Central, North, and South America and the Caribbean
ASEAN	**Association of Southeast Asian Nations**
	Brunei, Cambodia, Indonesia, Laos, Malaysia, Myanmar, the Philippines, Singapore, Thailand, Vietnam
APEC	**Asia Pacific Economic Cooperation**
	Australia, Brunei, Canada, Chile, China, Hong Kong, Indonesia, Japan, South Korea, Malaysia, Mexico, New Zealand, Papua New Guinea, Peru, the Philippines, Russia, Singapore, Taiwan, Thailand, United States, Vietnam
CER	**Closer Economic Relations Agreement**
	Australia, New Zealand
GCC	**Gulf Cooperation Council**
	Bahrain, Kuwait, Oman, Qatar, Saudi Arabia, United Arab Emirates
ECOWAS	**Economic Community of West African States**
	Benin, Burkina Faso, Cape Verde, Gambia, Ghana, Guinea, Guinea-Bissau, Ivory Coast, Liberia, Mali, Niger, Nigeria, Senegal, Sierra Leone, Togo
AU	**African Union**
	Total of 53 nations on the continent of Africa

Effects of Regional Economic Integration

Few topics in international business are as hotly contested and involve as many groups as the effects of regional trade agreements on people, jobs, companies, cultures, and living standards. The topic often spurs debate over the merits and demerits of such agreements. On one side of the debate are people who see the negative effects that regional trade agreements cause; on the other, those who see the positive. Each party to the debate cites data on trade and jobs that bolsters their position. They point to companies that have picked up and moved to another country where wages are lower after a new agreement was signed or to companies that have stayed at home and kept jobs there. The only thing made clear as a result of such debates is that both sides are right some of the time.

There is also the cultural aspect of such agreements. Some people argue that they will lose their unique cultural identity if their nation cooperates too much with other nations. As we saw in this chapter's opening company profile, Nestlé tries to be sensitive to cultural differences across markets. But such large global companies are often lightning rods for those warning of cultural homogenization. Let's take a closer look at the main benefits and drawbacks of regional integration.

Benefits of Regional Integration

Recall from Chapter 5 that nations engage in specialization and trade because of the potential for gains in output and consumption. Higher levels of trade between nations should result in greater specialization, increased efficiency, greater consumption, and higher standards of living.

TRADE CREATION Economic integration removes barriers to trade and/or investment for nations belonging to a trading bloc. The increase in the level of trade between nations that results from regional economic integration is called **trade creation**. One result of trade creation is that consumers and industrial buyers in member nations are faced with a wider selection of goods and services not previously available. For example, the United States has many popular brands of bottled water, including Coke's Dasani (www.dasani.com) and Pepsi's Aquafina (www.pepsi.com). But grocery and convenience stores inside the United States stock a wide variety of lesser-known imported brands of bottled water, such as Stonepoint from Canada. Certainly, the free trade agreement between Canada, Mexico, and the United States (discussed later in this chapter) created export opportunities for this and other Canadian brands.

trade creation
Increase in the level of trade between nations that results from regional economic integration.

Trade creation can also increase aggregate demand in an economy. The wider selection of products that results from trade creation can lower prices. Lower product prices then increase purchasing power, which in turn tend to increase demand for goods and services.

GREATER CONSENSUS In Chapter 6, we saw how the World Trade Organization (WTO) works to lower barriers on a global scale. Efforts at regional economic integration differ in that they comprise smaller groups of nations—ranging from several countries to as many as 30 or more. The benefit of trying to eliminate trade barriers in smaller groups of countries is that it can be easier to gain consensus from fewer members as opposed to, say, the 157 countries that comprise the WTO.

POLITICAL COOPERATION There can also be *political* benefits from efforts toward regional economic integration. A group of nations can have significantly greater political weight than each nation has individually. Thus, the group, as a whole, can have more say when negotiating with other countries in forums such as the WTO. Integration involving political cooperation can also reduce the potential for military conflict between member nations. In fact, peace was at the center of early efforts at integration in Europe in the 1950s. The devastation of two world wars in the first half of the twentieth century caused Europe to see integration as one way of preventing further armed conflicts.

EMPLOYMENT OPPORTUNITIES Regional integration can expand employment opportunities by enabling people to move from one country to another to find work or, simply, to earn a higher wage. Regional integration has opened doors for young people in Europe. Forward-looking young people have abandoned extreme nationalism and have taken on what can only be described as a "European" attitude that embraces a shared history. Those with language skills and a willingness to pick up and move to another EU country get to explore a new culture's way of life while earning a living. As companies seek their future leaders in Europe, they will hire people who can think across borders and across cultures.

Drawbacks of Regional Integration

Although regional integration tends to benefit countries, it can also have substantial negative effects. Let's examine each of these potential consequences.

TRADE DIVERSION The flip side of trade creation is **trade diversion**—the diversion of trade away from nations not belonging to a trading bloc and toward member nations. Trade diversion can occur after the formation of a trading bloc because of the lower tariffs charged among member nations. It can actually result in increased trade with a less-efficient producer within the trading bloc and in reduced trade with a more efficient, nonmember producer. So, economic integration can unintentionally reward a less efficient producer within the trading bloc. Unless there is other internal competition for the producer's good or service, buyers will likely pay more after trade diversion because of the inefficient production methods of the producer.

A World Bank report caused a stir over the results of the free trade bloc among Latin America's largest countries, MERCOSUR (discussed later in this chapter). The report suggested that the bloc's formation only encouraged free trade in the lowest-value products of local origin, while deterring competition for more sophisticated goods manufactured outside the market. Closer analysis showed that, while imports from one member state to another tripled during the period studied, imports from the rest of the world also tripled. Thus, the net effect of the agreement was trade creation, not trade diversion, as critics had charged. Also, the Australian Department of Foreign Affairs and Trade released the results of a study that examined the impact of the North American Free Trade Agreement (NAFTA) on Australia's trade with and investment in North America. The study found no evidence of trade diversion following the agreement's formation.[2]

SHIFTS IN EMPLOYMENT Perhaps the most controversial aspect of regional economic integration is its effect on people's jobs. The formation of a trading bloc promotes efficiency by significantly reducing or eliminating barriers to trade among its members. The surviving producer of a particular good or service, then, is likely to be the bloc's most efficient producer. Industries requiring mostly unskilled labor, for example, tend to respond to the formation of a trading bloc by shifting production to a low-wage nation within the bloc.

Yet figures on jobs lost or gained as a result of trading bloc formation vary depending on the source. The U.S. government contends that rising U.S. exports to Mexico and Canada have created a minimum of 900,000 jobs.[3] But the AFL-CIO (www.aflcio.org), the federation of U.S. unions, disputes these figures and claims a loss of jobs due to NAFTA. Trade agreements do cause dislocations in labor markets; some jobs are lost while others are gained.

It is likely that once trade and investment barriers are removed, countries protecting low-wage domestic industries from competition will see these jobs move to the country where wages are lower. This can be an opportunity for workers who lose their jobs to upgrade their skills and gain more advanced job training. This can help nations increase their competitiveness because a more educated and skilled workforce attracts higher-paying jobs than does a less skilled workforce.[4]

LOSS OF NATIONAL SOVEREIGNTY Successive levels of integration require that nations surrender more of their national sovereignty. The least amount of sovereignty that must be surrendered to the trading bloc occurs in a free trade area. By contrast, a political union requires nations to give up a high degree of sovereignty in foreign policy. This is why a political union is so hard to achieve. Long histories of cooperation or animosity between nations do not become irrelevant when a group of countries forms a union. Because one member nation may have very delicate ties with a nonmember nation with which another member may have very strong ties, the setting of a common foreign policy can be extremely tricky.

Economic integration is taking place throughout the world because of the benefits and despite the drawbacks of regional trade agreements. Europe, the Americas, Asia, the Middle East, and Africa are all undergoing integration to varying degrees (see Map 8.1 on pages 206–207). Let's now begin our coverage of specific efforts toward economic integration by exploring Europe, which has the longest history and highest level of integration to date.

1. What is the ultimate goal of *regional economic integration*?
2. Define each of the five levels, or degrees, of regional integration.
3. Identify several potential benefits and several potential drawbacks of regional integration.
4. What is meant by the terms *trade creation* and *trade diversion*? Why are these concepts important?

Integration in Europe

The most sophisticated and advanced example of regional integration that we can point to today is occurring in Europe. European efforts at integration began shortly after the Second World War as a cooperative endeavor among a small group of countries and involved a few select industries. Regional integration now encompasses practically all of Western Europe and all industries.

European Union

In the middle of the twentieth century, many would have scoffed at the idea that European nations, which had spent so many years at war with one another, could present a relatively unified whole more than 50 years later. Let's investigate how Europe came so far in such a relatively short time.

EARLY YEARS A war-torn Europe emerged from the Second World War in 1945 facing two challenges: (1) It needed to rebuild itself and avoid further armed conflict, and (2) it needed to increase its industrial strength to stay competitive with an increasingly powerful United States. Cooperation seemed to be the only way of facing these challenges. Belgium, France, West Germany, Italy, Luxembourg, and the Netherlands signed the Treaty of Paris in 1951, creating the *European Coal and Steel Community*. These nations were determined to remove barriers to trade in coal, iron, steel, and scrap metal in order to coordinate coal and steel production among themselves, thereby controlling the postwar arms industry.

The members of the European Coal and Steel Community signed the Treaty of Rome in 1957, creating the *European Economic Community*. The Treaty of Rome outlined a future common market for these nations. It also aimed to establish common transportation and agricultural policies among members. In 1967, the community's scope was broadened to include additional industries, notably atomic energy, and it changed its name to the *European Community*. As the goals of integration continued to expand, so too did the bloc's membership. Waves of enlargement occurred in 1973, 1981, 1986, 1995, 2004, and 2007. In 1994, the bloc once again changed its name to the *European Union (EU)*. Today, the 27-member EU (www.europa.eu) has a population of about 500 million people and a gross domestic product (GDP) of around $15 trillion (see Map 8.2 on page 208).

In recent years, two important milestones contributed to the continued progress of the EU: the *Single European Act* and the *Maastricht Treaty*.

Single European Act By the mid-1980s, EU member nations were frustrated by remaining trade barriers and a lack of progress on several important matters, including taxation, law, and regulations. The important objective of harmonizing laws and policies was beginning to appear unachievable. A commission that was formed to analyze the potential for a common market by the end of 1992 put forth several proposals. The goal was to remove remaining barriers, increase harmonization, and thereby enhance the competitiveness of European companies. The proposals became the *Single European Act (SEA),* which went into effect in 1987.

A wave of mergers and acquisitions swept across Europe as companies took advantage of the opportunities that the SEA offered. Large firms combined their special understanding of European needs, capabilities, and cultures with their advantage of economies of scale. Small and medium-sized companies networked with one another to increase their competitiveness.

Maastricht Treaty Some members of the EU wanted to take European integration further still. A 1991 summit meeting of EU member nations took place in Maastricht, the Netherlands. The meeting resulted in the *Maastricht Treaty,* which went into effect in 1993.

The Maastricht Treaty had three aims. First, it called for banking in a single, common currency after January 1, 1999, and circulation of coins and paper currency on January 1, 2002.

MAP 8.1
Most Active
Economic Blocs

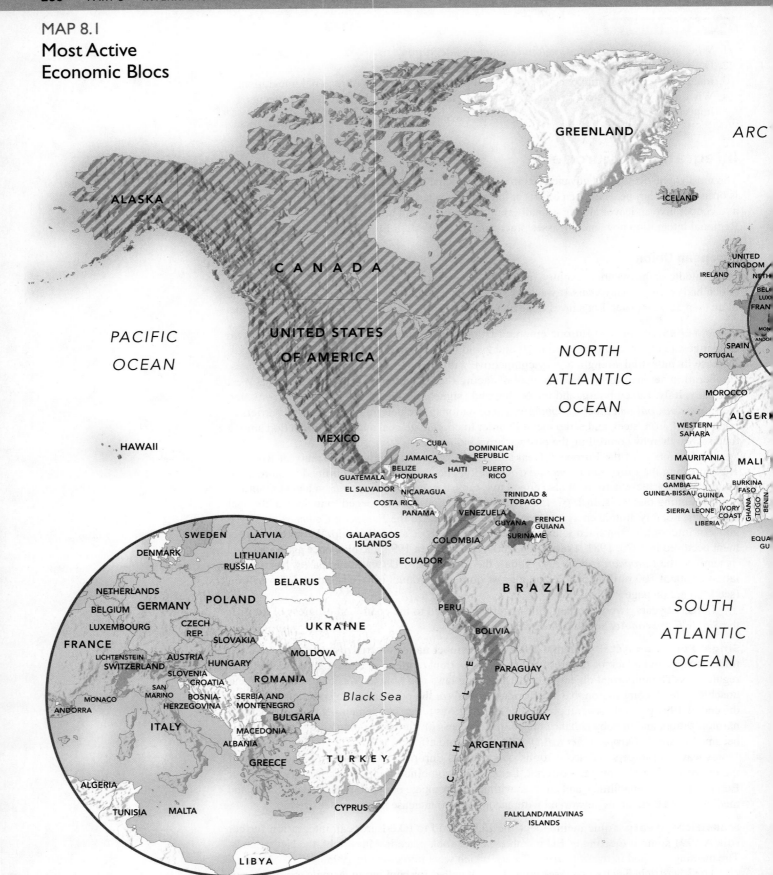

OCEAN

NORWAY
SWEDEN
FINLAND
ESTONIA
LATVIA
DENMARK
LITHUANIA
RUSSIA
BELARUS
GERMANY
POLAND
CZECH
REP. SLOVAKIA
AUSTRIA HUNGARY
SLOVENIA
CROATIA ROMANIA
BOSNIA AND
HERZEGOVINA MONTENEGRO
ITALY SERBIA AND
MONTENEGRO
ALBANIA BULGARIA
MACEDONIA
GREECE TURKEY

RUSSIA

KAZAKHSTAN

MONGOLIA

UKRAINE
MOLDOVA

GEORGIA
ARMENIA AZERBAIJAN UZBEKISTAN KYRGYZSTAN
TURKMENISTAN TAJIKISTAN

CYPRUS
SYRIA
LEBANON
ISRAEL IRAQ
JORDAN
KUWAIT
IRAN
AFGHANISTAN
PAKISTAN

CHINA

NORTH
KOREA
SOUTH
KOREA
JAPAN

LIBYA
EGYPT
QATAR
UNITED ARAB
EMIRATES
SAUDI
ARABIA
OMAN
NEPAL BHUTAN
BANGLADESH
INDIA
MYANMAR
(BURMA)
LAOS
THAILAND
VIETNAM
CAMBODIA
PHILIPPINES

TAIWAN

PACIFIC
OCEAN

NIGER CHAD
SUDAN
ERITREA YEMEN
DJIBOUTI
SOUTH
SUDAN
SOMALIA
ETHIOPIA
CENTRAL AFRICAN
REPUBLIC
CAMEROON
SRI
LANKA
INDIAN
OCEAN

CONGO
REPUBLIC
CONGO
DEMOCRATIC
REPUBLIC
(ZAIRE)
UGANDA
KENYA
RWANDA
BURUNDI
TANZANIA

BRUNEI
MALAYSIA
SINGAPORE

INDONESIA

PAPUA
NEW
GUINEA

SOLOMON
ISLANDS

ANGOLA
ZAMBIA MALAWI
MOZAMBIQUE
NAMIBIA ZIMBABWE
BOTSWANA MADAGASCAR
MAURITIUS
RÉUNION

SWAZILAND
SOUTH LESOTHO
AFRICA

VANUATU FIJI

NEW
CALEDONIA

AUSTRALIA

NEW
ZEALAND

The most active economic blocs

- EU
- EFTA
- NAFTA
- MERCOSUR
- CARICOM
- CAN
- ASEAN
- APEC
- CER

MAP 8.2

Economic Integration in Europe

Second, the treaty set up monetary and fiscal targets for countries that wished to take part in monetary union. Third, the treaty called for political union of the member nations—including development of a common foreign and defense policy and common citizenship. Member countries will hold off further political integration until they gauge the success of the final stages of economic and monetary union. Let's take a closer look at monetary union in Europe.

EUROPEAN MONETARY UNION As stated previously, EU leaders were determined to create a single, common currency. **European monetary union** is the EU plan that established its own central bank and currency in January 1999. The Maastricht Treaty stated the economic criteria with which member nations must comply in order to partake in the single currency, the *euro*. First, consumer price inflation must be below 3.2 percent and must not exceed that of the three best-performing countries by more than 1.5 percent. Second, the debt of government must be no higher than 60 percent of GDP. An exception is made if the ratio is diminishing and approaching the 60 percent mark.

European monetary union
European Union plan that established its own central bank and currency.

Third, the general government deficit must be no higher than 3.0 percent of GDP. An exception is made if the deficit is close to 3.0 percent or if the deviation is temporary and unusual. Fourth, interest rates on long-term government securities must not exceed, by more than 2.0 percent, those of the three countries with the lowest inflation rates. Meeting these criteria better aligned countries' economies and paved the way for smoother policy making under a single European Central Bank. The 17 EU member nations that adopted the single currency are Austria, Belgium, Cyprus, Estonia, Finland, France, Germany, Greece, Ireland, Italy, Luxembourg, Malta, the Netherlands, Portugal, Slovakia, Slovenia, and Spain.

Members of the EU were not immune to the recent global financial crisis and recession. The countries that had amassed the largest debts relative to their GDPs included Greece, Ireland, Italy, Portugal, and Spain. In 2012, the EU supported the economies of Greece and Spain with emergency funding when they began to buckle due to a lack of confidence in their banking and finance sectors. The EU later announced that it would act as a lender of last resort for troubled countries and pledged to create a banking union in order to support the financial institutions of the weakest economies. At this point, we do not know if these moves will solve Europe's lengthy financial crisis. But the newly pledged banking union may, in fact, serve as a stepping stone to a future fiscal union in the EU.[5]

Management Implications of the Euro The move to a single currency influences the activities of companies within the EU. First, the euro removes financial obstacles created by the use of multiple currencies. It completely eliminates exchange-rate risk for business deals between member nations using the euro. The euro also reduces transaction costs by eliminating the cost of converting from one currency to another. In fact, the EU leadership estimates the financial gains to Europe could eventually be 0.5 percent of GDP. The efficiency of trade between participating members resembles that of interstate trade in the United States because only a single currency is involved.

Second, the euro makes prices between markets more transparent, making it difficult to charge different prices in adjoining markets. As a result, shoppers feel less of a need to travel to other countries to save money on high-ticket items. For example, shortly before monetary union, a Mercedes-Benz S320 (www.mercedes.com) cost $72,614 in Germany but only $66,920 in Italy. A Renault Twingo (www.renault.com) that sold for $13,265 in France cost $11,120 in Spain. Automobile brokers and shopping agencies even sprang up specifically to help European consumers reap such savings. The euro has greatly reduced or eliminated this type of situation.

ENLARGEMENT OF THE EUROPEAN UNION One of the most historic events across Europe in recent memory was the EU enlargement from 15 to 27 members. Croatia, Turkey, and the former Yugoslav Republic of Macedonia remain candidates for EU membership and are to become members after they meet certain demands laid down by the EU. These so-called *Copenhagen Criteria* require each country to demonstrate that it:

- Has stable institutions, which guarantee democracy, the rule of law, human rights, and respect for and protection of minorities.
- Has a functioning market economy, capable of coping with competitive pressures and market forces within the EU.

CULTURE MATTERS   Czech List

The countries of Central and Eastern Europe that belong to the EU represent a land of opportunity. But like doing business anywhere, understanding of local culture can be a big advantage. Successful businesspeople in the Czech Republic offer the following advice:

- **Formalities.** Czech society is rather formal, and it is best to tend toward the more formal unless you know your colleague well. This includes using titles like "Doctor" and "Mister." It's rarely appropriate to use first names unless you're close friends.
- **Business Relationships.** Making money is obviously important and is the ultimate goal for any business. Still, building personal relationships, establishing good references, and doing favors for others can smooth the way for newcomers.

- **Czech Partners.** Being communist for 40 years before it became a capitalist democracy has left its mark on the Czech people and their culture. Finding a local partner who can handle the inevitable cultural difficulties that arise is crucial.
- **Local Professionals.** It is a good idea to hire a Czech accountant or someone familiar with Czech laws, taxes, and red tape. An attorney who is bilingual can also interpret differences between Czech and U.S. laws.
- **The Jednatel.** Companies need a "responsible person" (or *jednatel* in Czech) who is in charge of all aspects of the business. Some Czechs still feel more comfortable working with this *jednatel* rather than foreign and unfamiliar company reps.

- Is able to assume the obligations of membership, including adherence to the aims of economic, monetary, and political union.
- Has the ability to adopt the rules and regulations of the community, the rulings of the European Court of Justice, and the treaties.

Although it has applied for membership, negotiations for Turkey are expected to be difficult. One reason for Turkey's lack of support in the EU is charges (fair or not) of human rights abuses with regard to its Kurdish minority. Another reason is intense opposition by Greece, Turkey's longtime foe. Turkey does have a customs union with the EU, however, and trade between them is growing. Despite disappointment among some EU hopefuls and despite intermittent setbacks in the enlargement process, integration is progressing. To read about how culture affects business activities in one EU country, see the Culture Matters feature, titled "Czech List."

STRUCTURE OF THE EU   Five EU institutions play particularly important roles in monitoring and enforcing economic and political integration (see Figure 8.2). Two other EU institutions (Ombudsman and Data Protection Supervisor) fulfill secondary and support roles and are not discussed here.

European Parliament   The European Parliament consists of 736 members elected by popular vote within each member nation every five years. As such, they are expected to voice their particular political views on EU matters. The European Parliament fulfills its role of adopting EU law by debating and amending legislation proposed by the European Commission. It exercises political supervision over all EU institutions—giving it the power to supervise commissioner appointments and to censure the commission. It also has veto power over some laws (including the annual budget of the EU). There is a call for increased democratization within the EU, and some believe this could be achieved by strengthening the powers of the Parliament. The Parliament conducts its activities in Belgium (in the city of Brussels), France (in the city of Strasbourg), and Luxembourg.

Council of the EU   The council is the legislative body of the EU. When it meets, it brings together representatives of member states at the ministerial level. The makeup of the council changes depending on the topic under discussion. For example, when the topic is agriculture, the council is composed of the ministers of agriculture from each member nation. No proposed legislation becomes EU law unless the council votes it into law. Although passage into law for sensitive issues such as immigration and taxation still requires a unanimous vote, some legislation today requires only a simple majority to win approval. The council also concludes, on behalf of the EU, international agreements with other nations or international organizations. The council is headquartered in Brussels, Belgium.

European Commission   The commission is the executive body of the EU. It is comprised of commissioners appointed by each member country—larger nations get two commissioners, smaller countries get one. Member nations appoint the president and commissioners after being approved by the European Parliament. The commission has the right to draft legislation,

FIGURE 8.2

Institutions of the European Union

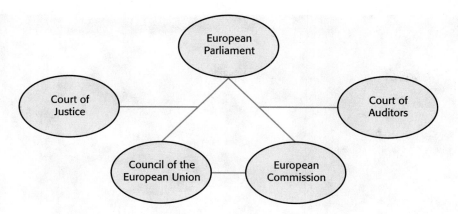

is responsible for managing and implementing policy, and monitors member nations' implementation of, and compliance with, EU law. Each commissioner is assigned a specific policy area, such as competitive policy or agricultural policy. Although commissioners are appointed by their national governments, they are expected to behave in the best interest of the EU as a whole, not in the interest of their own country. The European Commission is headquartered in Brussels, Belgium.

Court of Justice The Court of Justice is the court of appeals of the EU and is composed of 27 judges (one from each member nation) and 8 advocates general who hold renewable six-year terms. One type of case that the Court of Justice hears is one in which a member nation is accused of not meeting its treaty obligations. Another type is one in which the commission or council is charged with failing to live up to its responsibilities under the terms of a treaty. Like the commissioners, justices are required to act in the interest of the EU as a whole, not in the interest of their own countries. The Court of Justice is located in Luxembourg.

Court of Auditors The Court of Auditors is made up of 27 members (one from each member nation) appointed for renewable six-year terms. The court is assigned the duty of auditing the EU accounts and implementing its budget. It also aims to improve financial management in the EU and to report to member nations' citizens on the use of public funds. As such, it issues annual reports and statements on the implementation of the EU budget. The court employs roughly 800 auditors and staff to assist it in carrying out its functions. The Court of Auditors is based in Luxembourg.

European Free Trade Association (EFTA)

Certain nations in Europe were reluctant to join in the ambitious goals of the EU, fearing destructive rivalries and a loss of national sovereignty. Some of these nations did not want to be part of a common market but instead wanted the benefits of a free trade area. So in 1960, several countries banded together and formed the *European Free Trade Association (EFTA)* to focus on trade in industrial, not consumer, goods. Because some of the original members joined the EU and some new members joined EFTA (www.efta.int), today the group consists of only Iceland, Liechtenstein, Norway, and Switzerland (see Map 8.2).

The population of EFTA is around 12.5 million, and it has a combined GDP of around $707 billion. Despite its relatively small size, members remain committed to free trade principles and raising standards of living for their people. The EFTA and the EU created the *European Economic Area (EEA)* to cooperate on matters such as the free movement of goods, persons, services, and capital among member nations. The two groups also cooperate in other areas, including the environment, social policy, and education.

QUICK STUDY 2

1. Why did Europe initially desire to form a regional trading bloc?
2. Describe the evolution of the European Union. What are its five primary institutions?
3. What is *European monetary union*? Explain its importance to business in Europe.
4. Briefly describe the European Free Trade Association.

Shoppers step into a local bakery to buy fresh bread in Varna, Bulgaria. The country has benefited from membership in the European Union (EU), but it still has much work to do. Bulgaria and Romania were the most recent countries to join the EU, whose membership now totals 27. The need to balance the divergent national interests of its members meant that the EU needed a unique system of government. So, the EU designed the role of each of its institutions to reflect this delicate balancing act.

Source: FRANCIS DEAN/DEAN PICTURES/Newscom

Integration in the Americas

Europe's success at economic integration caused other nations to consider the benefits of forming their own regional trading blocs. Latin American countries began forming regional trading arrangements in the early 1960s, but they made substantial progress only in the 1980s and 1990s. North America was about three decades behind Europe in taking major steps toward economic integration. Let's now explore the major efforts toward economic integration in North, South, and Central America, beginning with North America.

North American Free Trade Agreement (NAFTA)

There has always been a good deal of trade between Canada and the United States. Canada and the United States had in the past established trade agreements in several industrial sectors of their economies, including automotive products. In January 1989, the *U.S.–Canada Free Trade Agreement* went into effect. The goal was to eliminate all tariffs on bilateral trade between Canada and the United States by 1998.

Accelerating integration in Europe caused new urgency in the task of creating a North American trading bloc that included Mexico. Mexico joined what is now the World Trade Organization in 1987 and began privatizing state-owned enterprises in 1988. Talks among Canada, Mexico, and the United States in 1991 eventually resulted in the formation of the *North American Free Trade Agreement (NAFTA)*. NAFTA (www.nafta-sec-alena.org) became effective in January 1994 and superseded the U.S.–Canada Free Trade Agreement. Today NAFTA comprises a market with 445 million consumers and a GDP of around $16 trillion (see Map 8.1).

As a free trade agreement, NAFTA seeks to eliminate all tariffs and nontariff trade barriers on goods originating from within North America. The agreement also calls for liberalized rules regarding government procurement practices, the granting of subsidies, and the imposition of countervailing duties (see Chapter 6). Other provisions deal with issues such as trade in services, intellectual property rights, and standards of health, safety, and the environment.

LOCAL CONTENT REQUIREMENTS AND RULES OF ORIGIN While NAFTA encourages free trade among Canada, Mexico, and the United States, manufacturers and distributors must abide by local content requirements and rules of origin. Although producers and distributors rarely know the precise origin of every part or component in a piece of industrial equipment, they are responsible for determining whether a product has sufficient North American content to qualify for tariff-free status. The producer or distributor must also provide a NAFTA "certificate of origin" to an importer to claim an exemption from tariffs. Four criteria determine whether a good meets NAFTA rules of origin:

- Goods wholly produced or obtained in the NAFTA region
- Goods containing nonoriginating inputs but meeting Annex 401 origin rules (which covers regional input)
- Goods produced in the NAFTA region wholly from originating materials
- Unassembled goods and goods classified in the same harmonized system category as their parts that do not meet Annex 401 rules but that have sufficient North American regional value content

EFFECTS OF NAFTA Since NAFTA came into effect, trade among the three participating nations has increased markedly, with the greatest gains occurring between Mexico and the United States. Today, the United States exports more to Mexico than it does to Britain, France, Germany, and Italy combined. In fact, Mexico is the third largest source of U.S. imports (behind China and Canada) and is the second largest market for U.S exports (behind Canada).

Overall, NAFTA has helped trade among the three countries to grow from $297 billion in 1993 to around $1.6 trillion. Since the start of NAFTA, Mexico's exports to the United States have jumped to around $230 billion, and U.S. exports to Mexico have grown to more than $163 billion.[6] As these numbers suggest, the United States has developed a trade deficit with Mexico. Over the same period, Canada's exports to the United States more than doubled to nearly $277 billion, and U.S. exports to Canada grew to $248 billion. Canada exported very little to Mexico before NAFTA, but afterward, exports grew more than threefold, to nearly $2.7 billion.[7]

The agreement's effect on employment and wages is not as easy to determine. The U.S. Trade Representative Office claims that exports to Mexico and Canada support 2.9 million U.S. jobs (900,000 more than in 1993), which pay 13 to 18 percent more than national averages for production workers.[8] But the AFL-CIO group of unions disputes this claim; it argues that, since its formation, NAFTA has cost the United States more than one million jobs and job opportunities.[9]

In addition to claims of job losses, opponents claim that NAFTA has damaged the environment, particularly along the United States–Mexico border. Although the agreement included provisions for environmental protection, Mexico is finding it difficult to deal with the environmental impact of greater economic activity. But Mexico's *Instituto Nacional de Ecologia* (www. ine.gob.mx) has developed an industrial waste–management program, including an incentive system to encourage waste reduction and recycling. The U.S. and Mexican federal governments have invested several billion dollars in environmental protection efforts since the creation of NAFTA.[10]

EXPANSION OF NAFTA Continued ambivalence among union leaders and environmental watchdogs regarding the long-term effects of NAFTA is delaying its expansion. The pace at which NAFTA expands will depend to a large extent on whether the U.S. Congress grants successive U.S. presidents trade-promotion ("fast track") authority. Trade-promotion authority allows a U.S. administration to engage in all necessary talks surrounding a trade deal without the official involvement of Congress. After details of the deal are decided, Congress then simply votes yes or no on the deal and cannot revise the treaty's provisions.

But there is little doubt that integration will expand some day in the Americas. In fact, it is even possible that the North American economies will one day adopt a single currency. As trade among Canada, Mexico, and the United States strengthens, a single currency (most likely the U.S. dollar) would benefit companies in these countries with reduced exposure to changes in exchange rates. Although this would be difficult for Canada and Mexico to accept politically, in the long run we could see one currency for all of North America.

Central American Free Trade Agreement (CAFTA-DR)

The potential benefits from freer trade induced another trading bloc between the United States and six far smaller economies. The *Central American Free Trade Agreement (CAFTA-DR)* was established in 2006 between the United States and Costa Rica, El Salvador, Guatemala, Honduras, Nicaragua, and, later, the Dominican Republic.

Shown here is a handful of freshly picked coffee cherries at a cooperative named Las Brumas in Nicaragua. Like any free trade agreement, CAFTA-DR has supporters and detractors. Supporters say the agreement will encourage trade efficiency and promote investment that will bring good-paying jobs to the region. Others fear the agreement will benefit large U.S. companies and badly damage small businesses and farmers across Central America.

Source: © dinozzaver/Fotolia

Prior to its creation, CAFTA-DR nations had already traded a great deal. The Central American nations and the Dominican Republic are already the second-largest U.S. export market in Latin America behind Mexico. The CAFTA-DR nations represent a U.S. export market larger than India, Indonesia, and Russia combined. Likewise, nearly 80 percent of exports from the Central American nations and the Dominican Republic already enter the United States tariff free. And Central American nations have already cut average tariffs from 45 percent in 1985 to around 7 percent today. The combined value of goods traded between the United States and the six other CAFTA-DR countries is around $32 billion.[11]

The agreement benefits the United States in several ways. CAFTA-DR aims to reduce tariff and nontariff barriers against U.S. exports to the region. It also ensures that U.S. companies are not disadvantaged by Central American nations' trade agreements with Mexico, Canada, and other countries. The agreement also requires the Central American nations and the Dominican Republic to reform their legal and business environments to encourage competition and investment, protect intellectual property rights, and promote transparency and the rule of law. CAFTA-DR is also designed to support U.S. national security interests by advancing regional integration, peace, and stability.

QUICK STUDY 3

1. What was the impetus for the formation of the North American Free Trade Agreement (NAFTA)?
2. What effect has NAFTA had on trade among its member nations?
3. List the main benefits the United States obtains from the Central American Free Trade Agreement.

Andean Community (CAN)

Attempts at integration among Latin American countries had a rocky beginning. The first try, the *Latin American Free Trade Association (LAFTA)*, was formed in 1961. The agreement first called for the creation of a free trade area by 1971 but then extended that date to 1980. Yet because of a crippling debt crisis in South America and a reluctance of member nations to do away with protectionism, the agreement was doomed to an early demise. Disappointment with LAFTA led to the creation of two other regional trading blocs—the Andean Community and the Latin American Integration Association.

Formed in 1969, the *Andean Community* (in Spanish *Comunidad Andina de Naciones, or CAN*) includes four South American countries located in the Andes mountain range—Bolivia, Colombia, Ecuador, and Peru (see Map 8.1). Today, the Andean Community (www.comunidadandina.org) comprises a market of around 97 million consumers and a combined GDP of about $220 billion. The main objectives of the group include tariff reduction for trade among member nations, a common external tariff, and common policies in both transportation and certain industries. The Andean Community had the ambitious goal of establishing a common market by 1995, but delays mean that it remains a somewhat incomplete customs union.

Several factors hamper progress. Political ideology among member nations is somewhat hostile to the concept of free markets and favors a good deal of government involvement in business affairs. Also, inherent distrust among members makes lower tariffs and more open trade hard to achieve. The common market will be difficult to implement within the framework of the Andean Community. One reason is that each country has been given significant exceptions in the tariff structure that they have in place for trade with nonmember nations. Another reason is that countries continue to sign agreements with just one or two countries outside the Andean Community framework. Independent actions impair progress internally and hurt the credibility of the Andean Community with the rest of the world.

Latin American Integration Association (ALADI)

The *Latin American Integration Association (ALADI)* was formed in 1980 and consists of 11 countries today. Because of the failure of the first attempt at integration (LAFTA), the objectives of ALADI were scaled back significantly. The ALADI agreement calls for preferential tariff agreements (*bilateral* agreements) to be made between pairs of member nations that reflect the economic development of each nation. Although the agreement resulted in roughly 24 bilateral agreements and 5 subregional pacts, it did not accomplish a great deal of cross-border trade. Dissatisfaction with progress once again caused certain nations to form a trading bloc of their own—the Southern Common Market.

Southern Common Market (MERCOSUR)

The *Southern Common Market* (in Spanish *El Mercado Comun del Sur,* or *MERCOSUR*) was established in 1988 between Argentina and Brazil but expanded to include Paraguay and Uruguay in 1991 and Venezuela in 2006. Associate members of MERCOSUR (www.mercosur.int) include Bolivia, Chile, Colombia, Ecuador, and Peru (see Map 8.1). Mexico has been granted observer status in the bloc.

Today, MERCOSUR acts as a customs union and boasts a market of more than 266 million consumers (nearly half of Latin America's total population) and a GDP of around $2.8 trillion. Its first years of existence were very successful, with trade among members growing nearly fourfold. MERCOSUR is progressing on trade and investment liberalization and is emerging as the most powerful trading bloc in all of Latin America. Latin America's large consumer base and its potential as a low-cost production platform for worldwide export appeal to both the European Union and the United States.

Central America and the Caribbean

Attempts at economic integration in Central American countries and throughout the Caribbean basin have been much more modest than efforts elsewhere in the Americas. Nevertheless, let's look at two efforts at integration in these two regions—CARICOM and CACM.

CARIBBEAN COMMUNITY AND COMMON MARKET (CARICOM) The *Caribbean Community and Common Market (CARICOM)* trading bloc was formed in 1973. There are 15 full members, 5 associate members, and 8 observers active in CARICOM (www.caricom.org). Although the Bahamas is a member of the community, it does not belong to the common market. As a whole, CARICOM has a combined GDP of nearly $30 billion and a market of almost 6 million people.

A key CARICOM agreement calls for the establishment of a CARICOM Single Market, which would permit the free movement of factors of production including goods, services, capital, and labor. The main difficulty CARICOM will continue to face is that most members trade more with nonmembers than they do with one another simply because members do not have the imports each other needs.

CENTRAL AMERICAN COMMON MARKET (CACM) The *Central American Common Market (CACM)* was formed in 1961 to create a common market among Costa Rica, El Salvador, Guatemala, Honduras, and Nicaragua. Together, the members of CACM (www.sieca.org.gt) comprise a market of 33 million consumers and have a combined GDP of about $120 billion. The common market was never realized, however, because of a long war between El Salvador and Honduras and guerrilla conflicts in several countries. Yet, renewed peace is creating more business confidence and optimism, which is driving double-digit growth in trade between members.

Furthermore, the group has not yet created a customs union. External tariffs among members range between 4 and 12 percent. The tentative nature of cooperation was obvious when Honduras and Nicaragua slapped punitive tariffs on each other's goods during a recent dispute. But officials remain positive, saying that their ultimate goal is European-style integration, closer political ties, and adoption of a single currency—probably the dollar. In fact, El Salvador has adopted the U.S. dollar as its official currency, and Guatemala already uses the dollar alongside its own currency, the quetzal.

Free Trade Area of the Americas (FTAA)

A truly daunting trading bloc would be the creation of a *Free Trade Area of the Americas (FTAA)*. The objective of the FTAA (www.alca-ftaa.org) is to create the largest free trade area on the planet, stretching from the northern tip of Alaska to the southern tip of Tierra del Fuego, in South America. The FTAA would comprise 34 nations and 830 million consumers, with Cuba being the only Western Hemisphere nation excluded from participating. The FTAA would work alongside existing trading blocs throughout the region.

The first official meeting, the 1994 Summit of the Americas, created the broad blueprint for the agreement. Nations reaffirmed their commitment to the FTAA at the Second Summit of the Americas four years later when negotiations began. The Third Summit of the Americas in 2001 met with fierce protests. The ambitious plan of the FTAA means that it will likely be many years before such an agreement would be realized.

QUICK STUDY 4

1. What is the Andean Community? Identify why its progress is behind schedule.
2. Identify the members of the Southern Common Market (MERCOSUR). How has it performed?
3. Characterize economic integration efforts throughout Central America and the Caribbean.
4. What is the objective of the Free Trade Area of the Americas? What are its current prospects for success?

Integration in Asia

Efforts toward economic and political integration outside Europe and the Americas tend to be looser arrangements. Let's take a look at important coalitions in Asia and among Pacific Rim nations—the Association of Southeast Asian Nations, the organization for Asia Pacific Economic Cooperation, and the Australian and New Zealand Closer Economic Relations Agreement.

Association of Southeast Asian Nations (ASEAN)

Indonesia, Malaysia, the Philippines, Singapore, and Thailand formed the *Association of Southeast Asian Nations (ASEAN)* in 1967. Brunei joined in 1984, Vietnam in 1995, Laos and Myanmar in 1997, and Cambodia in 1998 (see Map 8.1). Together, the 10 ASEAN (www.aseansec.org) countries comprise a market of about 560 million consumers and a GDP of nearly $1.1 trillion. The three main objectives of the alliance are to (1) promote economic, cultural, and social development in the region; (2) safeguard the region's economic and political stability; and (3) serve as a forum in which differences can be resolved fairly and peacefully.

The decision to admit Cambodia, Laos, and Myanmar was criticized by some Western nations. The concern regarding Laos and Cambodia being admitted stems from their roles in supporting the communists during the Vietnam War. The quarrel with Myanmar centered on evidence cited by the West of its human rights violations. Yet, ASEAN felt that adding these countries to the coalition could help it to counter China's rising strength, resources of cheap labor, and abundant raw materials.

MANAGER'S BRIEFCASE The Ins and Outs of ASEAN

Businesses unfamiliar with operating in ASEAN countries should exercise caution in their dealings. Some inescapable facts about ASEAN that warrant consideration are the following:

- *Diverse Cultures and Politics.* The Philippines is a representative democracy, Brunei is an oil-rich sultanate, and Vietnam is a state-controlled country. Business policies and protocols must be adapted to suit each country.
- *Economic Competition.* Many ASEAN nations are feeling the effects of China's power to attract investment from multinational corporations worldwide. Whereas ASEAN members used to attract around 30 percent of foreign direct investment into Asia's developing economies, they now attract about half that amount.
- *Corruption and Shadow Markets.* Bribery and shadow (unofficial) markets are common in many ASEAN countries,

including Indonesia, Myanmar, the Philippines, and Vietnam. Studies typically place these countries very high on the list of nations surveyed for corruption.

- *Political Change and Turmoil.* Several nations in the region recently elected new leaders and some go through presidents at a fast clip. Companies must remain alert to shifting political winds and laws regarding trade and investment.
- *Border Disputes.* Parts of Thailand's borders with Cambodia and Laos are tested frequently. Hostilities break out sporadically between Thailand and Myanmar over border alignment and ethnic Shan rebels operating along the border.
- *Lack of Common Tariffs and Standards.* Doing business in ASEAN nations can be costly. Harmonized tariffs, quality and safety standards, customs regulations, and investment rules could cut transaction costs significantly.

Companies involved in Asia's developing economies are likely to be doing business with an ASEAN member. This is even a more likely prospect as China, Japan, and South Korea accelerate their efforts to join ASEAN. China's admission would allow the club to bridge the gap between less advanced and more advanced economies. Some key facts about ASEAN that companies should consider are contained in the Manager's Briefcase, titled "The Ins and Outs of ASEAN."

Asia Pacific Economic Cooperation (APEC)

The organization for *Asia Pacific Economic Cooperation (APEC)* was formed in 1989. Begun as an informal forum among 12 trading partners, APEC (www.apec.org) now has 21 members (see Map 8.1). Together, the APEC nations account for more than 40 percent of world trade and have a combined GDP of more than $19 trillion.

The stated aim of APEC is not to build another trading bloc. Instead, it desires to strengthen the multilateral trading system and expand the global economy by simplifying and liberalizing trade and investment procedures among member nations. In the long term, APEC hopes to have completely free trade and investment throughout the region by 2020.

THE RECORD OF APEC APEC has succeeded in halving its members' tariff rates from an average of 15 to 7.5 percent. The early years saw the greatest progress, but liberalization received a setback when the Asian financial crisis struck in the late 1990s. APEC is at least as much a political body as it is a movement toward freer trade. After all, APEC certainly does not have the focus or the record of accomplishments of NAFTA or the EU. Nonetheless, open dialogue and attempts at cooperation should continue to encourage progress, however slow.

Further progress may create some positive benefits for people doing business in APEC nations. APEC is changing the granting of business visas so that businesspeople can travel throughout the region without obtaining multiple visas. It is recommending mutual recognition agreements on professional qualifications so that engineers, for example, can practice in any APEC country, regardless of nationality. And APEC is ready to simplify and harmonize customs procedures. Eventually, businesses could use the same customs forms and manifests for all APEC economies.

Closer Economic Relations (CER) Agreement

Australia and New Zealand created a free trade agreement in 1966 that slashed tariffs and quotas 80 percent by 1980. The agreement's success encouraged the pair to form the *Closer Economic Relations (CER) Agreement* in 1983 to advance free trade and further integrate their two economies (see Map 8.1).

The CER was an enormous success in that it totally eliminated tariffs and quotas between Australia and New Zealand in 1990, five years ahead of schedule. Each nation allows goods (and most services) to be sold within its borders that can be legally sold in the other country. Each nation also recognizes most professionals who are registered to practice their occupation in the other country.

Integration in the Middle East and Africa

Economic integration has not left out the Middle East and Africa, although progress there is more limited than in any other geographic region. Its limited success is due mostly to the small size of the countries involved and their relatively low level of development. The largest of these coalitions are the Gulf Cooperation Council and the Economic Community of West African States.

Gulf Cooperation Council (GCC)

Several Middle Eastern nations formed the *Gulf Cooperation Council (GCC)* in 1980. Members of the GCC are Bahrain, Kuwait, Oman, Qatar, Saudi Arabia, and the United Arab Emirates. The primary purpose of the GCC at its formation was to cooperate with the increasingly powerful trading blocs in Europe at the time—the EU and EFTA. The GCC has evolved, however, to become as much a political entity as an economic one. Its cooperative thrust allows citizens of member countries to travel freely in the GCC without visas. It also permits citizens of one member nation to own land, property, and businesses in any other member nation without the need for local sponsors or partners.

Economic Community of West African States (ECOWAS)

The *Economic Community of West African States (ECOWAS)* was formed in 1975 but its efforts at economic integration were restarted in 1992 because of a lack of early progress. The most important goals of ECOWAS (www.ecowas.int) include the formation of a customs union, an eventual common market, and a monetary union. Together, the ECOWAS nations comprise a large portion of the economic activity in sub-Saharan Africa.

   Progress on market integration is almost nonexistent. In fact, the value of trade occurring among ECOWAS nations is just 11 percent of the value that the trade members undertake with third parties. But ECOWAS has made progress in the free movement of people, construction of international roads, and development of international telecommunication links. Some of its main problems are due to political instability, poor governance, weak national economies, poor infrastructure, and poor economic policies.

African Union (AU)

A group of 53 nations on the African continent joined forces in 2002 to create the *African Union (AU)*. Heads of state of the nations belonging to the Organization of African Unity paved the way for the AU (www.africa-union.org) when they signed the Sirte Declaration in 1999.

Community members stand by fishing boats at the Agodo fishing settlement near Lagos in southwest Nigeria. Nigeria participates in the regional trading bloc known as ECOWAS in order to improve the lives of its people. The latest food crisis to hit Africa brought participants to Lagos from 25 African countries to exchange ideas with international organizations. Africa is the only region in the world where fish consumption is falling, which has led to calls for massive investment in fish farms in order to encourage better nutrition.

Source: ONOME OGHENE/Newscom

The AU is based on the vision of a united and strong Africa and on the need to build a partnership among governments and all segments of civil society in order to strengthen cohesion among the peoples of Africa. Its ambitious goals are to promote peace, security, and stability across Africa and to accelerate economic and political integration while addressing problems compounded by globalization. Specifically, the stated aims of the AU are to (1) rid the continent of the remaining vestiges of colonialism and apartheid, (2) promote unity and solidarity among African states, (3) coordinate and intensify cooperation for development, (4) safeguard the sovereignty and territorial integrity of members, and (5) promote international cooperation within the framework of the United Nations.

It is too early to judge the success of the AU, but there is no shortage of opportunities on the continent for it to demonstrate its capabilities. The people of Africa have much to gain from an effective and successful AU.

QUICK STUDY 5

1. Identify the three main objectives of the Association of Southeast Asian Nations.
2. How do the goals of the Asia Pacific Economic Cooperation forum differ from those of other regional blocs?
3. What is the Gulf Cooperation Council? Identify its members.
4. List the aims of both the Economic Community of West African States and the African Union.

BOTTOM LINE FOR BUSINESS

Regional economic integration can expand buyer selection, lower prices, increase productivity, and boost national competitiveness. Yet integration has its drawbacks, and governments and independent organizations work to counter those negative effects. Here, we review regional integration as it relates to business operations and employment.

Integration and Business Operations

Regional trade agreements are changing the landscape of the global marketplace. They are lowering trade barriers and opening up new markets for goods and services. Markets otherwise off-limits because tariffs made imported products too expensive can become attractive after tariffs are lifted. But trade agreements can also be double-edged swords for companies. Not only do they allow domestic companies to seek new markets abroad, they also let competitors from other nations enter the domestic market. Such mobility increases competition in every market that participates in such an agreement.

Despite increased competition that often accompanies regional integration, there can be economic benefits, such as those provided by a single currency. Companies in the European Union clearly benefit from its common currency, the euro. First, charges for converting from one member nation's currency to that of another can be avoided. Second, business owners need not worry about potential losses due to shifting exchange rates on cross-border deals. Not having to cover such costs and risks frees up capital for greater investment. Third, the euro makes prices between markets more transparent, making it more difficult to charge different prices in different markets. This helps companies compare prices among suppliers of a raw material, intermediate product, or service.

Another benefit is lower tariffs or none at all. This allows a multinational company to reduce its number of factories that supply a region and thereby reap economies of scale benefits. This is possible because a company can produce in one location and then ship products throughout the low-tariff region at little additional cost. This lowers costs and increases productivity.

One potential drawback of regional integration is that lower tariffs between members of a trading bloc can result in trade diversion. This can increase trade with less-efficient producers within the trading bloc and reduce trade with more-efficient nonmember producers. Unless there is other internal competition for the producer's good or service, buyers will likely pay more after trade diversion.

Integration and Employment

Perhaps most controversial is the impact of regional integration on jobs. Companies can affect the job environment by contributing to dislocations in labor markets. The nation that supplies a particular good or service within a trading bloc is likely to be the most-efficient producer. When that product is labor intensive, the cost of labor in that market is likely to be quite low. Competitors in other nations may shift production to that relatively lower-wage nation within the trading bloc to remain competitive. This can mean lost jobs in the relatively higher-wage nation.

Yet job dislocation can be an opportunity for workers to upgrade their skills and gain more advanced training. This can help nations increase their competitiveness because a more educated and skilled workforce attracts higher-paying jobs. An opportunity for a nation to improve its competitiveness, however, is little consolation to people finding themselves suddenly out of work.

Although there are drawbacks to integration, there are potential gains from increased trade such as raising living standards. Regional economic integration efforts are likely to continue rolling back barriers to international trade and investment because of their potential benefits.

Chapter Summary

1. **Define regional economic integration and identify its five levels.**
   - The process whereby countries in a geographic region cooperate with one another to reduce or eliminate barriers to the international flow of products, people, or capital is called *regional economic integration*.
   - *Free trade area*: countries seek to remove all barriers to trade among themselves but where each country determines its own barriers against nonmembers.
   - *Customs union*: countries remove all barriers to trade among themselves and set a common trade policy against nonmembers.
   - *Common market*: countries remove all barriers to trade and to the movement of labor and capital among themselves and set a common trade policy against nonmembers.
   - *Economic union*: countries remove barriers to trade and the movement of labor and capital among themselves, set a common trade policy against nonmembers, and coordinate their economic policies.
   - *Political union*: countries coordinate aspects of their economic *and* political systems.

2. **Discuss the benefits and drawbacks of regional economic integration.**
   - *Trade creation* is the increase in trade that results from regional economic integration, which can expand buyer selection, lower prices, increase productivity, and boost national competitiveness.
   - Smaller, regional groups of nations can find it easier to reduce trade barriers than can larger groups.
   - Nations can have more say when negotiating with other countries or organizations, reduce the potential for military conflict, and expand employment opportunities.
   - *Trade diversion* is the diversion of trade away from nations not belonging to a trading bloc and toward member nations; it can result in increased trade with a less-efficient producer within the trading bloc.

3. **Describe regional integration in Europe and its pattern of enlargement.**
   - The *European Coal and Steel Community* was formed in 1951 to remove trade barriers for coal, iron, steel, and scrap metal among the member nations.
   - Following several waves of expansion, broadenings of its scope, and name changes, the community is now known as the European Union (EU) and has 27 members.
   - Five main institutions of the EU are the European Parliament, European Commission, Council of the European Union, Court of Justice, and Court of Auditors.
   - The EU single currency has been adopted by 17 member nations, which benefit from the elimination of exchange-rate risk and currency conversion costs within the euro zone.
   - The *European Free Trade Association (EFTA)* has four members and was created to focus on trade in industrial goods.

4. **Discuss regional integration in the Americas and analyze its future prospects.**
   - The *North American Free Trade Agreement (NAFTA)* began in 1994 among Canada, Mexico, and the United States; it seeks to eliminate all tariffs and nontariff trade barriers on goods originating from within North America.
   - The *Central American Free Trade Agreement (CAFTA-DR)* was established in 2006 between the United States and six Central American nations to boost the efficiency of trade.
   - The *Andean Community* was formed in 1969 and calls for tariff reduction for trade among member nations, a common external tariff, and common policies in transportation and certain industries.
   - The *Latin American Integration Association (ALADI),* formed in 1980 between Mexico and 10 South American nations, has had little impact on cross-border trade.
   - The *Southern Common Market (MERCOSUR),* established in 1988, acts as a customs union.
   - The *Caribbean Community and Common Market (CARICOM)* trading bloc was formed in 1973, and the *Central American Common Market (CACM)* was formed in 1961.

5. Characterize regional integration in Asia and how it differs from integration elsewhere.
   * The *Association of Southeast Asian Nations (ASEAN)* formed in 1967 and seeks to (1) promote economic, cultural, and social development; (2) safeguard economic and political stability; and (3) serve as a forum to resolve differences peacefully.
   * The organization for *Asia Pacific Economic Cooperation (APEC)* was formed in 1989 and strives to strengthen the multilateral trading system and expand the global economy by simplifying and liberalizing trade and investment procedures.
   * The *Closer Economic Relations (CER)* agreement in 1983 between Australia and New Zealand totally eliminated tariffs and quotas between the two economies.
6. Describe regional integration in the Middle East and Africa, and explain its slow progress.
   * Several Middle Eastern nations in 1980 formed the *Gulf Cooperation Council (GCC),* which allows citizens of member countries to travel freely without visas and to own properties in other member nations without the need for local sponsors or partners.
   * The *Economic Community of West African States (ECOWAS)* formed in 1975, with a major goal being the formation of a customs union and an eventual common market.
   * The *African Union (AU)* was started in 2002 among 53 nations to promote peace, security, and stability and to accelerate economic and political integration across Africa.

Talk It Over

1. Some people believe that the rise of regional trading blocs threatens free trade progress made by the World Trade Organization (WTO). Do you agree? Why or why not?

Teaming Up

1. **Debate Project.** In this project, two groups of four students each will debate the merits of extending NAFTA to more advanced levels of economic (and even political) integration. After the first student from each side has spoken, the second student will question the opposing side's arguments, looking for holes and inconsistencies. The third student will attempt to answer these arguments. The fourth student will present a summary of each side's arguments. Finally, the class will vote to determine which team has offered the more compelling argument.

⭐2. **Market Entry Strategy Project.** This exercise corresponds to the *MESP* online simulation. For the country your team is researching, identify any regional integration efforts in which the nation may be participating. What other nations are members? What economic, political, and social objectives drive integration? So far, what have been the positive and negative results of integration? How are international companies (domestic and nondomestic) coping? Explain why companies' coping strategies are, or are not, succeeding. Integrate your findings into your completed *MESP* report.

Key Terms

common market (p. 201)	free trade area (p. 200)	trade creation (p. 203)
customs union (p. 200)	political union (p. 201)	trade diversion (p. 204)
economic union (p. 201)	regional economic integration	
European monetary union (p. 209)	(regionalism) (p. 200)	

Take It to the Web

1. **Video Report.** Visit this book's channel on YouTube (www.YouTube.com/MyIBvideos). Click on "Videos" near the top of the page, and click on the set of videos labeled "Ch 08: Regional Economic Integration." Watch one video from the list, and then summarize it in a half-page report. Reflecting on the contents of this chapter, which aspects of regional integration can you identify in the video? How might a company engaged in international business act on the information contained in the video?

2. **Website Report.** Visit the official website of the FTAA (www.alca-ftaa.org). What are the stated reasons why governments across the Americas are pushing for the free trade area? Why do some groups protest implementation of the FTAA? Do you think the FTAA would help lift living standards in small countries (such as Ecuador and Nicaragua) or be a boon only for the largest nations such as Canada and the United States?

Small companies typically have difficulty competing against large multinational corporations when their governments take part in regional trading blocs. What could governments do to help their small companies compete in such blocs? Do you think subregional trading blocs can help *small nations* strengthen their negotiating positions against large nations? Do you think that very small nations should even participate in regional trade agreements with very large nations? Why or why not?

Do you think subregional or regional trade agreements cause instability on a subregional, regional, or global scale, or do you believe they foster cooperation? After all you have read in this chapter about regional trade agreements, what is your assessment of their value? Should their progress continue or be rolled back?

Ethical Challenges

1. You are a member of the U.S. Congress from the state of Florida. Many constituents in your district have complained that NAFTA and CAFTA-DR are unfair to their extended families living on the Caribbean islands. Some experts argue that the term *free trade agreement* is misleading. They say these agreements are really "preferential trade agreements" that offer free trade only to members and relative protection against nonmembers. You worry that this is the case for Caribbean nations excluded from NAFTA and CAFTA-DR. Some argue that, from apparel factories in Jamaica to sugar cane fields in Trinidad, these trade agreements have cost jobs, market share, and income for the vulnerable island nations as jobs moved to Mexico. Given the impact on nonmember nations, do you think such trade agreements are ethical? Why do you think islands in the Caribbean basin were not invited to be part of NAFTA or CAFTA-DR? As a member of the U.S. Congress, what arguments do you make for including the Caribbean in the expansion of NAFTA or CAFTA-DR?

★2. You are a world-renowned economist hired by Ecuador's government to advise it on its current involvement with the Andean Community. The Andean Community is a customs union that consists of four nations in South America: Bolivia, Colombia, Ecuador, and Peru. Member nations are permitted free access to one another's markets, with nonmember nations required to negotiate tariffs with community members. Because Ecuador recently adopted the U.S. dollar as its currency, some believe that the other Andean members are perhaps holding Ecuador back from more rapid development. As the consultant, what pros and cons do you present to the Ecuadorean government for breaking free from the Andean Community?

3. You are the economic adviser to the president of Mexico. Labor unions and environmentalists in the United States are not the only ones speaking out against NAFTA. There continues to be opposition in Mexico by those complaining of a loss of national sovereignty and those who feel that the income gap between the two countries will never be narrowed. Average hourly wages on the U.S. side of the border can be six times that on the Mexican side. Mexican critics fear that their entire country will be subsumed by companies from the United States, which do not contribute to Mexico's higher standard of living but which instead use Mexico as a low-cost assembly site while keeping high-paying, high-skilled jobs at home. Do you think that there is a way for trade agreements to help close the economic gap between poor and wealthy partners? Or will the interests of poorer nations always be subordinate to wealthier countries within regional trading blocs? As the economic adviser, how do you suggest that the president protect Mexico's workforce?

MyManagementLab

Go to **mymanagementlab.com** for Auto-graded writing questions as well as the following Assisted-graded writing questions:

8-1. Proliferation and growth of regional trading blocs will likely continue into the foreseeable future. At what point do you think the integration process will stop (if ever)? Explain your answer.

8-2. Certain groups of countries, particularly in Africa, are far less economically developed than other regions, such as Europe and North America. What sort of integration arrangement do you think developed countries could create with less developed nations to improve living standards? Be as specific as you can.

8-3. Mymanagementlab Only – comprehensive writing assignment for this chapter.

Practicing International Management Case

Global Trade Deficit in Food Safety

Today, U.S. citizens trudging through a freezing Minnesota winter can indulge their cravings for summer-fresh raspberries. Europeans who are thousands of miles away from North America can put Mexican mangoes in their breakfast cereal. Japanese shoppers can buy radishes that were grown from seeds cultivated in Oregon. Globalization of the food industry, falling trade barriers, and the formation of regional trading blocs make it possible for people to choose from produce grown all over the world. Unfortunately, these forces have also made it more likely that consumers will contract illnesses from food-borne pathogens.

In recent years, several outbreaks linked to the burgeoning global trade in produce have made headlines. One serious case occurred when 2,300 people were victims of a parasite called *Cyclospora* that had hitched a ride on raspberries grown in Guatemala. Outbreaks of hepatitis A and *Salmonella* from tainted strawberries and alfalfa sprouts, respectively, have also sickened consumers. The outbreak of severe acute respiratory syndrome (SARS) killed hundreds and sickened hundreds more, mainly in China, Singapore, and Canada. Some scientists believe a fair amount of those cases might actually have been cases of H5N1, also called Avian (bird) flu. Avian flu is particularly virulent and can cross barriers between species. It is most likely transmitted through the handling of poultry and poor sanitation.

Although health officials say that there is no evidence that imports are inherently more dangerous, they do cite several reasons for concern. For one thing, produce is often imported from less-advanced countries where food hygiene and sanitation are lacking in important ways. Also, some microbes that cause no damage in their home country can be deadly when introduced to other countries. Finally, the longer the journey from farm to table, the greater is the chance of contamination. Just consider the journey taken by the *Salmonella*-ridden alfalfa sprouts: The seeds for the sprouts were bought from Uganda and Pakistan, among other nations, shipped through the Netherlands, flown into New York, trucked to retailers all across the United States, and then purchased by consumers.

Incidences of food contamination show no sign of abating. Since the passage of NAFTA, cross-border trade in food among Canada, Mexico, and the United States has skyrocketed. Meanwhile, federal inspections of U.S. imports by the Food and Drug Administration (FDA) have declined. Increasing imports have strained the U.S. food-safety system, which was built 100 years ago for a country contained within its own borders. Yet the U.S. Congress continues to try to advance the cause of greater food safety when it comes to trade. Changes that have been considered include giving the FDA mandatory recall authority, increasing the frequency of food inspections, and requiring food safety plans for food makers.

Although it isn't feasible for the United States to plant FDA inspectors in every country, options are available. The U.S. Congress could further tighten the ban on importing fruit and vegetables from countries that fail to meet expanded U.S. food-safety standards. Better inspections could be performed of farming methods and government safety systems in other countries. Countries that blocked the new inspections could be forbidden to sell fruit and vegetables in the United States. The World Health Organization (WHO) also proposes new policies for food safety, such as introducing food irradiation and other technologies. The WHO believes the most critical intervention in preventing food-borne diseases is promoting good manufacturing practices and educating retailers and consumers on appropriate food handling.

Thinking Globally

1. How do you think countries with a high volume of exports to the United States, such as Mexico, would respond to stricter food-safety rules? Do you think such measures are a good way to stem the tide of food-related illnesses? Why or why not?

2. Sue Doneth of Marshall, Michigan, is a mother of one of the schoolchildren who was exposed to the hepatitis A virus after eating tainted frozen strawberry desserts. Speaking before Congress, she said, "We are forcing consumers to trade the health and safety of their families for free trade. That is not fair trade. NAFTA is not a trade issue; it is a safety issue." Do you think food-safety regulations should be built into an extension of NAFTA? Why or why not? What are the benefits and drawbacks of putting food-safety regulations into international trade pacts?

⭐3. The lack of harmonized food-safety practices and standards is just one of the challenges faced by the food industry as it becomes more global. What other challenges face the food industry in an era of economic integration and opening markets?

Source: Christopher Doering and Roberta Rampton, "Delauro Sees U.S. Food Safety Law in 2010," *Reuters* (www.reuters.com), March 17, 2010; "A Game of Chicken," *The Economist* (www.economist.com), June 26, 2008; "Food Safety and Foodborne Illness," World Health Organization Fact Sheet No. 237, March 2007; "Preparing for a Pandemic," *Harvard Business Review,* Special Report, May 2006, pp. 20–40.

International Financial Markets

LEARNING OBJECTIVES

After studying this chapter, you should be able to

1. Discuss the purposes, development, and financial centers of the international capital market.

2. Describe the international bond, international equity, and Eurocurrency markets.

3. Discuss the four primary functions of the foreign exchange market.

4. Explain how currencies are quoted and the different rates that are given.

5. Identify the main instruments and institutions of the foreign exchange market.

6. Explain why and how governments restrict currency convertibility.

A Look Back

Chapter 8 introduced the most prominent efforts at regional economic integration occurring around the world. We saw how international companies are responding to the challenges and opportunities that regional integration is creating.

A Look at This Chapter

This chapter introduces us to the international financial system by describing the structure of international financial markets. We learn first about the international capital market and its main components. We then turn to the foreign exchange market, explaining how it works and outlining its structure.

A Look Ahead

Chapter 10 concludes our study of the international financial system. We discuss the factors that influence exchange rates and explain why and how governments and other institutions try to manage exchange rates. We also present recent monetary problems in emerging markets worldwide.

Wii IS THE CHAMPION

KYOTO, Japan—Nintendo (www.nintendo.com) has been feeding the addiction of video-gaming fans worldwide since 1989. One hundred years earlier, in 1889, Fusajiro Yamauchi started Nintendo when he began manufacturing *Hanafuda* playing cards in Kyoto, Japan. Today, Nintendo produces and sells mobile gaming devices and home gaming systems, including Wii U, Wii, Nintendo DS, GameCube, and Game Boy Advance, which feature such global icons as Mario, Donkey Kong, Pokémon, and others.

Nintendo took the global gaming industry by storm when it introduced the Wii game console. With wireless motion-sensitive remote controllers, built-in Wi-Fi capability, and other features, the Wii outdid Sony's PlayStation and Microsoft's Xbox game consoles. Nintendo's Wii Fit game forces players through 40 exercises consisting of yoga, strength training, cardio, and even the hula-hoop. Pictured here, the new Nintendo Wii U is presented at the electronic entertainment expo (E3) in Los Angeles, California.

Yet, Nintendo's marketing and game-design talents are not all that affect its performance—so, too, do exchange rates between the Japanese *yen* (¥) and other currencies. The earnings of Nintendo's subsidiaries and affiliates outside Japan must be integrated into consolidated financial statements at the end of each year. Translating subsidiaries' earnings from other currencies into a strong *yen* decreases Nintendo's stated earnings in *yen*.

Nintendo recently reported an annual net income of ¥ 257.3 billion ($2.6 billion), but it also reported that its income included a foreign exchange loss of ¥ 92.3 billion ($923.5 million). A rise of the *yen* against foreign currencies prior to the translation of subsidiaries' earnings into *yen* caused the loss. As you read this chapter, consider how shifting currency values affect financial performance and how managers can reduce their impact.[1]

Source: JOE KLAMAR/Getty Images/Newscom

Well-functioning financial markets are an essential element of the international business environment. They funnel money from organizations and economies with excess funds to those with shortages. International financial markets also allow companies to exchange one currency for another. The trading of currencies and the rates at which they are exchanged are crucial to international business.

Suppose you purchase an MP3 player imported from a company based in the Philippines. Whether you realize it or not, the price you paid for that MP3 player was affected by the exchange rate between your country's currency and the Philippine *peso*. Ultimately, the Filipino company that sold you the MP3 player must convert the purchase made in your currency into Philippine *pesos*. Thus, the profit earned by the Filipino company is also influenced by the exchange rate between your currency and the *peso*. Managers must understand how changes in currency values—and thus in exchange rates—affect the profitability of their international business activities. Among other things, our hypothetical company in the Philippines must know how much to charge you for its MP3 player.

In this chapter, we launch our study of the international financial system by exploring the structure of the international financial markets. The two interrelated systems that comprise the international financial markets are the international capital market and foreign exchange market. We start by examining the purposes of the international capital market and tracing its recent development. We then take a detailed look at the international bond, equity, and Eurocurrency markets, each of which helps companies to borrow and lend money internationally. Later, we take a look at the functioning of the foreign exchange market—an international market for currencies that facilitates international business transactions. We close this chapter by exploring how currency convertibility affects international transactions.

International Capital Market

A **capital market** is a system that allocates financial resources in the form of debt and equity according to their most efficient uses. Its main purpose is to provide a mechanism through which those who wish to borrow or invest money can do so efficiently. Individuals, companies, governments, mutual funds, pension funds, and all types of nonprofit organizations participate in capital markets. For example, an individual might want to buy her first home, a midsized company might want to add production capacity, and a government might want to support the development

capital market
System that allocates financial resources in the form of debt and equity according to their most efficient uses.

Here, a customer counts her Philippine *pesos* after exchanging U.S. dollars at a moneychanger in Manila, the Philippines. The foreign exchange market gives Filipinos working overseas a safe way to wire money to relatives back home. The prices of currencies on the foreign exchange market also help determine the prices of imports and exports. And exchange rates affect the amount of profit a company receives when it translates revenue earned abroad into the home currency.

Source: ROMEO GACAD/Getty Images/ Newscom

of a new wireless communications system. Sometimes, these individuals and organizations have excess cash to lend, and, at other times, they need funds.

Purposes of National Capital Markets

There are two primary means by which companies obtain external financing: *debt* and *equity*. National capital markets help individuals and institutions borrow the money that other individuals and institutions want to lend. Although in theory borrowers could search individually for various parties who are willing to lend or invest, this would be an extremely inefficient process.

ROLE OF DEBT **Debt** consists of loans, for which the borrower promises to repay the borrowed amount (the *principal*) plus a predetermined rate of *interest*. Company debt normally takes the form of **bonds**—instruments that specify the timing of principal and interest payments. The holder of a bond (the *lender*) can force the borrower into bankruptcy if the borrower fails to pay on a timely basis. Bonds issued for the purpose of funding investments are commonly issued by private-sector companies and by municipal, regional, and national governments.

ROLE OF EQUITY **Equity** is part ownership of a company in which the equity holder participates with other part owners in the company's financial gains and losses. Equity normally takes the form of **stock**—shares of ownership in a company's assets that give *shareholders (stockholders)* a claim on the company's future cash flows. Shareholders may be rewarded with *dividends*—payments made out of surplus funds—or by increases in the value of their shares. Of course, they may also suffer losses due to poor company performance—and thus decreases in the value of their shares. Dividend payments are not guaranteed but are determined by the company's board of directors and are based on financial performance. In capital markets, shareholders can sell one company's stock for that of another or can *liquidate* them—exchange them for cash. **Liquidity**, which is a feature of both debt and equity markets, refers to the ease with which bondholders and shareholders can convert their investments into cash.

Purposes of the International Capital Market

The **international capital market** is a network of individuals, companies, financial institutions, and governments that invest and borrow across national boundaries. It consists of both formal exchanges (in which buyers and sellers meet to trade financial instruments) and electronic networks (in which trading occurs anonymously). This market makes use of unique and innovative financial instruments specially designed to fit the needs of investors and borrowers located in different countries. Large international banks play a central role in the international capital market. They gather the excess cash of investors and savers around the world and then channel this cash to borrowers across the globe.

EXPANDS THE MONEY SUPPLY FOR BORROWERS The international capital market is a conduit for joining borrowers and lenders in different national capital markets. A company that is unable to obtain funds from investors in its own nation can seek financing from investors elsewhere. The option of going outside the home nation is particularly important to firms in countries with small or developing capital markets of their own.

REDUCES THE COST OF MONEY FOR BORROWERS An expanded money supply reduces the cost of borrowing. Similar to the prices of potatoes, wheat, and other commodities, the "price" of money is determined by supply and demand. If its supply increases, its price—in the form of interest rates—falls. That is why excess supply creates a borrower's market, forcing down interest rates and the cost of borrowing. Projects regarded as infeasible because of low expected returns might be viable at a lower cost of financing.

REDUCES RISK FOR LENDERS The international capital market expands the available set of lending opportunities. In turn, an expanded set of opportunities helps reduce risk for lenders (investors) in two ways:

1. *Investors enjoy a greater set of opportunities from which to choose.* They can thus reduce overall portfolio risk by spreading their money over a greater number of debt and equity instruments. In other words, if one investment loses money, the loss can be offset by gains elsewhere.

debt
Loan in which the borrower promises to repay the borrowed amount (the principal) plus a predetermined rate of interest.

bond
Debt instrument that specifies the timing of principal and interest payments.

equity
Part ownership of a company in which the equity holder participates with other part owners in the company's financial gains and losses

stock
Shares of ownership in a company's assets that give shareholders a claim on the company's future cash flows.

liquidity
Ease with which bondholders and shareholders may convert their investments into cash.

international capital market
Network of individuals, companies, financial institutions, and governments that invest and borrow across national boundaries.

2. *Investing in international securities benefits investors because some economies are growing while others are in decline.* For example, the prices of bonds in Thailand may follow a pattern that is different from bond-price fluctuations in the United States. Thus, investors reduce risk by holding international securities whose prices move independently.

Would-be borrowers in developing nations often face difficulties trying to secure loans. Interest rates are often high, and borrowers typically have little or nothing to put up as collateral. For some unique methods of getting capital to small business owners in developing nations, see this chapter's Global Sustainability feature, titled "Big Results from Microfinance."

Forces Expanding the International Capital Market

Around 40 years ago, national capital markets functioned largely as independent markets. But since that time, the amount of debt, equity, and currencies traded internationally has increased dramatically. This rapid growth can be traced to three main factors:

- **Information Technology.** Information is the lifeblood of every nation's capital market because investors need information about investment opportunities and their corresponding risk levels. Large investments in information technology over the past two decades have drastically reduced the costs, in both time and money, of communicating around the globe. Investors and borrowers can now respond in record time to events in the international capital market. The introduction of electronic trading that can occur after the daily close of formal exchanges also facilitates faster response times.
- **Deregulation.** Deregulation of national capital markets has been instrumental in the expansion of the international capital market. The need for deregulation became apparent in the early 1970s, when heavily regulated markets in the largest countries were facing fierce competition from less regulated markets in smaller nations. Deregulation increased competition, lowered the cost of financial transactions, and opened many national markets to global investing and borrowing. But the pendulum is now swinging the other direction as legislators demand tighter regulation to help avoid another global financial crisis like that of 2008–2009.[2]
- **Financial Instruments.** Greater competition in the financial industry is creating the need to develop innovative financial instruments. One result of the need for new types of financial instruments is **securitization**—the unbundling and repackaging of hard-to-trade financial assets into more liquid, negotiable, and marketable financial instruments (or *securities*). For example, a mortgage loan from a bank is not liquid or negotiable because it is a customized

securitization
Unbundling and repackaging of hard-to-trade financial assets into more liquid, negotiable, and marketable financial instruments (or *securities*).

GLOBAL SUSTAINABILITY   Big Results from Microfinance

Developing nations are teeming with budding entrepreneurs who need a bit of start-up capital to get going. A practice called microfinance has several key characteristics.

- *Overcoming Obstacles.* If a person in a developing country is lucky enough to obtain a loan, it is typically from a loan shark, whose sky-high interest rates devour most of the entrepreneur's profits. Thus, microfinance is an increasingly popular alternative to lend money to low-income entrepreneurs at competitive interest rates (around 10 to 20 percent) without requiring collateral. Now institutions are warming to the idea of "microsavings" so that people can manage their small but highly uneven flows of income over time.
- *One for All, and All for One.* Sometimes a loan is made to a group of entrepreneurs who sink or swim together. If one member fails to pay off a loan, all members of the group may lose future credit. Peer pressure and support often defend against defaults, however. Support networks in developing countries often incorporate extended family ties. One bank in Bangladesh boasts 98 percent on-time repayment.

- *No Glass Ceiling Here.* Although outreach to male borrowers is increasing, most microfinance borrowers are female. Women tend to be better at funneling profits into family nutrition, clothing, and education, as well as into business expansion. The successful use of microfinance in Bangladesh has increased wages, community income, and the status of women. The microfinance industry is estimated at around $8 billion worldwide.
- *Developed Country Agenda.* The microfinance concept was pioneered in Bangladesh as a way for developing countries to create the foundation for a market economy. It now might be a way to spur economic growth in depressed areas of developed nations, such as in decaying city centers. But whereas microfinance loans in developing countries typically average about $350, those in developed nations would need to be significantly larger.

Source: "A Better Mattress," *The Economist*, March 13, 2010, pp. 75–76; Steve Hamm, "Setting Standards for Microfinance," *Bloomberg Businessweek* (www.businessweek.com), July 28, 2008; Jennifer L. Schenker, "Taking Microfinance to the Next Level," *Bloomberg Businessweek* (www.businessweek.com), February 26, 2008; Grameen Bank website (www.grameen-info.org), select reports.

contract between the bank and the borrower. But agencies of the U.S. government, such as the Federal National Mortgage Association (www.fanniemae.com), guarantee mortgages against default and accumulate them as pools of assets. Securities that are backed by these mortgage pools are then sold in capital markets to raise capital for investment.

Securitization is criticized for the excessive debt that financial institutions took on in the boom years prior to 2007. When investors lost faith in securities backed by sub-prime mortgages, they sold their investments and helped spark the global credit crisis of 2008–2009. Although the trigger for the crisis was lost value in mortgage-backed securities, legislators soon began exploring the option of placing reasonable limits on securitization in order to discourage an appetite for excessive levels of debt.[3]

World Financial Centers

The world's three most important financial centers are London, New York, and Tokyo. But traditional exchanges may become obsolete unless they continue to modernize, cut costs, and provide new customer services. In fact, trading over the Internet and other systems might increase the popularity of *offshore financial centers.*

OFFSHORE FINANCIAL CENTERS An **offshore financial center** is a country or territory whose financial sector features very few regulations and few, if any, taxes. These centers tend to be economically and politically stable and tend to provide access to the international capital market through an excellent telecommunications infrastructure. Most governments protect their own currencies by restricting the amount of activity that domestic companies can conduct in foreign currencies. So, companies that find it hard to borrow funds in foreign currencies can turn to offshore centers. Offshore centers are sources of (usually cheaper) funding for companies with multinational operations.

offshore financial center
Country or territory whose financial sector features very few regulations and few, if any, taxes.

Offshore financial centers fall into two categories:

- *Operational centers* see a great deal of financial activity. Prominent operational centers include London (which does a good deal of currency trading) and Switzerland (which supplies a great deal of investment capital to other nations).
- *Booking centers* are usually located on small island nations or territories with favorable tax and/or secrecy laws. Little financial activity takes place here. Rather, funds simply pass through on their way to large operational centers. Booking centers are typically home to offshore branches of domestic banks that use them merely as bookkeeping facilities to record tax and currency-exchange information. Some important booking centers are the Cayman Islands and the Bahamas in the Caribbean; Gibraltar, Monaco, and the Channel Islands in Europe; Bahrain and Dubai in the Middle East; and Singapore in Southeast Asia.

QUICK STUDY 1

1. What are the three main purposes of the *international capital market*? Explain each briefly.
2. Identify the factors expanding the international capital market.
3. What is an *offshore financial center*? Explain its appeal to businesses.

Main Components of the International Capital Market

Now that we have covered the basic features of the international capital market, let's take a closer look at its main components: the international bond, international equity, and Eurocurrency markets.

International Bond Market

The **international bond market** consists of all bonds sold by issuing companies, governments, or other organizations *outside their own countries*. Issuing bonds internationally is an increasingly popular way to obtain needed funding. Typical buyers include medium-sized to large banks, pension funds, mutual funds, and governments with excess financial reserves. Large international banks typically manage the sales of new international bond issues for corporate and government clients.

international bond market
Market consisting of all bonds sold by issuing companies, governments, or other organizations outside their own countries.

Eurobond
Bond issued outside the country in whose currency it is denominated.

TYPES OF INTERNATIONAL BONDS One instrument used by companies to access the international bond market is called a **Eurobond**—a bond issued outside the country in whose currency it is denominated. In other words, a bond issued by a Venezuelan company, denominated in U.S. dollars, and sold in Britain, France, Germany, and the Netherlands (but not available in the United States or to its residents) is a Eurobond. Because this Eurobond is denominated in U.S. dollars, the Venezuelan borrower both receives dollars and makes its interest payments in dollars.

Eurobonds are popular (accounting for 75 to 80 percent of all international bonds) because the governments of countries in which they are sold do not regulate them. The absence of regulation substantially reduces the cost of issuing a bond. Unfortunately, it increases its risk level—a fact that may discourage some potential investors. The traditional markets for Eurobonds are Europe and North America.

Companies also obtain financial resources by issuing so-called **foreign bonds**—bonds sold outside the borrower's country and denominated in the currency of the country in which they are sold. For example, a *yen*-denominated bond issued by the German carmaker BMW in Japan's domestic bond market is a foreign bond. Foreign bonds account for about 20 to 25 percent of all international bonds.

foreign bond
Bond sold outside the borrower's country and denominated in the currency of the country in which it is sold.

Foreign bonds are subject to the same rules and regulations as the domestic bonds of the country in which they are issued. Countries typically require issuers to meet certain regulatory requirements and to disclose details about company activities, owners, and upper management. Thus BMW's *samurai bonds* (the name for foreign bonds issued in Japan) would need to meet the same disclosure and other regulatory requirements that Toyota's bonds in Japan must meet. Foreign bonds in the United States are called *yankee bonds,* and those in the United Kingdom are called *bulldog bonds*. Foreign bonds issued and traded in Asia outside Japan (and normally denominated in dollars) are called *dragon bonds*.

INTEREST RATES: A DRIVING FORCE Today, low interest rates (the cost of borrowing) are fueling growth in the international bond market. But low interest rates in developed nations mean that investors earn relatively little interest on bonds in those markets. So, banks, pension funds, and mutual funds are seeking higher returns in emerging markets, where higher interest payments reflect the greater risk of the bonds. At the same time, corporate and government borrowers in emerging markets badly need capital to invest in corporate expansion plans and public works projects.

This situation raises an interesting question: How can investors who are seeking higher returns and borrowers who are seeking to pay lower interest rates both come out ahead? The answer, at least in part, lies in the international bond market:

- By issuing bonds in the international bond market, borrowers from emerging markets can borrow money from other nations where interest rates are lower.
- By the same token, investors in developed countries buy bonds in emerging markets in order to obtain higher returns on their investments (although they also accept greater risk).

Despite the attraction of the international bond market, many emerging markets see the need to develop their own national markets because of volatility in the global currency market. A currency whose value is rapidly declining can wreak havoc on companies that earn profits in, say, Indonesian rupiahs but must pay off debts in dollars. Why? A drop in a country's currency forces borrowers to shell out more local currency in order to pay off the interest owed on bonds denominated in a stable currency.

International Equity Market

international equity market
Market consisting of all stocks bought and sold outside the issuer's home country.

The **international equity market** consists of all stocks bought and sold outside the issuer's home country. Companies and governments frequently sell shares in the international equity market. Buyers include other companies, banks, mutual funds, pension funds, and individual investors. The stock exchanges that list the greatest number of companies from outside their own borders are Frankfurt, London, and New York. Large international companies frequently list their stocks on several national exchanges simultaneously and sometimes offer new stock issues only outside their country's borders. Four factors are responsible for much of the past growth in the international equity market, discussed in the following sections.

SPREAD OF PRIVATIZATION As many countries abandoned central planning and socialist-style economics, the pace of privatization accelerated worldwide. A single privatization often places billions of dollars of new equity on stock markets. When the government of Peru sold its 26-percent share of the national telephone company, Telefonica del Peru (www.telefonica.com.pe), it raised $1.2 billion. Of the total value of the sale, 48 percent was sold in the United States, 26 percent to other international investors, and another 26 percent to domestic retail and institutional investors in Peru.

ECONOMIC GROWTH IN EMERGING MARKETS Continued economic growth in emerging markets is contributing to growth in the international equity market. Companies based in these economies require greater investment as they succeed and grow. The international equity market becomes a major source of funding because only a limited supply of funds is available in these nations.

ACTIVITY OF INVESTMENT BANKS Global banks facilitate the sale of a company's stock worldwide by bringing together sellers and large potential buyers. Increasingly, investment banks are searching for investors outside the national market in which a company is headquartered. In fact, this method of raising funds is becoming more common than listing a company's shares on another country's stock exchange.

ADVENT OF CYBERMARKETS The automation of stock exchanges is encouraging growth in the international equity market. The term *cybermarkets* denotes stock markets that have no central geographic locations. Rather, they consist of global trading activities conducted on the Internet. Cybermarkets (consisting of supercomputers, high-speed data lines, satellite uplinks, and individual personal computers) match buyers and sellers in nanoseconds. They allow companies to list their stocks worldwide through an electronic medium in which trading takes place 24 hours a day.

Eurocurrency Market

All the world's currencies that are banked outside their countries of origin are referred to as *Eurocurrency* and trade on the **Eurocurrency market**. Thus, U.S. dollars deposited in a bank in Tokyo are called *Eurodollars,* and British pounds deposited in New York are called *Europounds.* Japanese yen deposited in Frankfurt are called *Euroyen,* and so forth.

Eurocurrency market
Market consisting of all the world's currencies (referred to as "Eurocurrency") that are banked outside their countries of origin.

Because the Eurocurrency market is characterized by very large transactions, only the very largest companies, banks, and governments are typically involved. Deposits originate primarily from four sources:

- Governments with excess funds generated by a prolonged trade surplus
- Commercial banks with large deposits of excess currency
- International companies with large amounts of excess cash
- Extremely wealthy individuals

Eurocurrency originated in Europe during the 1950s—hence the "Euro" prefix. Governments across Eastern Europe feared they might forfeit dollar deposits made in U.S. banks if U.S. citizens were to file claims against them. To protect their dollar reserves, they deposited them in banks across Europe. Banks in the United Kingdom began lending these dollars to finance international trade deals, and banks in other countries (including Canada and Japan) followed suit. The Eurocurrency market is valued at around $6 trillion, with London accounting for about 20 percent of all deposits. Other important markets include Canada, the Caribbean, Hong Kong, and Singapore.

APPEAL OF THE EUROCURRENCY MARKET Governments tend to strictly regulate commercial banking activities in their own currencies within their borders. For example, they often force banks to pay deposit insurance to a central bank, where they must keep a certain portion of all deposits "on reserve" in noninterest-bearing accounts. Although such restrictions protect investors, they add costs to banking operations. By contrast, the main appeal of the Eurocurrency market is the complete absence of regulation, which lowers the cost of banking. The large size of transactions in this market further reduces transaction costs. Thus, banks can charge borrowers less, pay investors more, and still earn healthy profits.

Interbank interest rates—rates that the world's largest banks charge one another for loans—are determined in the free market. The most commonly quoted rate of this type in the Eurocurrency market is the *London Interbank Offer Rate (LIBOR)*—the interest rate that London

interbank interest rates
Interest rates that the world's largest banks charge one another for loans.

banks charge other large banks that borrow Eurocurrency. The *London Interbank Bid Rate (LI-BID)* is the interest rate offered by London banks to large investors for Eurocurrency deposits.

An unappealing feature of the Eurocurrency market is greater risk; government regulations that protect depositors in national markets are nonexistent here. Despite the greater risk of default, however, Eurocurrency transactions are fairly safe because the banks involved are large, with well-established reputations.

Foreign Exchange Market

foreign exchange market
Market in which currencies are bought and sold and their prices determined.

exchange rate
Rate at which one currency is exchanged for another.

Unlike domestic transactions, international transactions involve the currencies of two or more nations. To exchange one currency for another in international transactions, companies rely on a mechanism called the **foreign exchange market**—a market in which currencies are bought and sold and their prices determined. Financial institutions can convert currencies using an **exchange rate**—the rate at which one currency is exchanged for another. Rates depend on the size of the transaction, the trader conducting it, general economic conditions, and, sometimes, government mandate.

The forces of supply and demand determine currency prices, and transactions are conducted through a process of *bid* and *ask quotes*. If someone asks for the current exchange rate of a certain currency, the bank does not know whether it is dealing with a prospective buyer or seller. Thus, it quotes two rates: The *bid quote* is the price at which it will buy, and the *ask quote* is the price at which it will sell. For example, say that the British pound is quoted in U.S. dollars at $1.5054. The bank may then bid $1.5052 to *buy* British pounds and offer to *sell* them at $1.5056. The difference between the two rates is the *bid–ask spread*. Naturally, banks will buy currencies at a lower price than they sell them and earn their profits from the bid–ask spread.

Functions of the Foreign Exchange Market

The foreign exchange market is not really a source of corporate finance. Rather, it facilitates corporate financial activities and international transactions. Investors use the foreign exchange market for four main reasons, as discussed in the following sections.

Displayed on the monitor is the exchange rate between the Chinese *yuan* and the Japanese *yen*. The two countries began direct trading between their currencies in Tokyo, Japan, and Shanghai, China, in 2012. Average daily turnover on Tokyo's foreign exchange market is about $240 billion. Yet this is still significantly lower than trading volume in the U.K. market ($1.33 trillion) and the U.S. market ($618 billion). Around $3.2 trillion worth of currency is traded on global foreign exchange markets every day.

*Source: */Kyodo/Newscom*

CURRENCY CONVERSION Companies use the foreign exchange market to convert one currency into another. Suppose a Malaysian company sells a large number of computers to a customer in France. The French customer wants to pay for the computers in euros, the European Union currency, whereas the Malaysian company wants to be paid in its own *ringgit*. How do the two parties resolve this dilemma? They turn to banks that will exchange the currencies for them.

Companies also must convert to local currencies when they undertake foreign direct investment. Later, when a firm's international subsidiary earns a profit and the company wants to return some of it to the home country, it must convert the local money into the home currency.

CURRENCY HEDGING The practice of insuring against potential losses that result from adverse changes in exchange rates is called **currency hedging**. International companies commonly use hedging for one of two purposes:

1. To lessen the risk associated with international transfers of funds
2. To protect themselves in credit transactions in which there is a time lag between billing and receipt of payment

Suppose a South Korean automaker has a subsidiary in Britain. The parent company in Korea knows that in 30 days—say, on February 1—its British subsidiary will be sending it a payment in British pounds. Because the parent company is concerned about the value of that payment in South Korean *won* a month in the future, it wants to insure against the possibility that the pound's value will fall over that period—meaning, of course, that it will receive less money. Therefore, on January 2, the parent company contracts with a financial institution, such as a bank, to exchange the payment in one month at an agreed-upon exchange rate specified on January 2. In this way, as of January 2, the Korean company knows exactly how many *won* the payment will be worth on February 1.

CURRENCY ARBITRAGE **Currency arbitrage** is the instantaneous purchase and sale of a currency in different markets for profit. Suppose a currency trader in New York notices that the value of the European Union euro is lower in Tokyo than it is in New York. The trader can buy euros in Tokyo, sell them in New York, and earn a profit on the difference. High-tech communication and trading systems allow the entire transaction to occur within seconds. But note that the trade is not worth making if the difference between the value of the euro in Tokyo and the value of the euro in New York is not greater than the cost of conducting the transaction.

Currency arbitrage is a common activity among experienced traders of foreign exchange, very large investors, and companies in the arbitrage business. Firms whose profits are generated primarily by another economic activity, such as retailing or manufacturing, take part in currency arbitrage only if they have very large sums of cash on hand.

Interest Arbitrage **Interest arbitrage** is the profit-motivated purchase and sale of interest-paying securities denominated in different currencies. Companies use interest arbitrage to find better interest rates abroad than those that are available in their home countries. The securities involved in such transactions include government treasury bills, corporate and government bonds, and even bank deposits. Suppose a trader notices that the interest rates paid on bank deposits in Mexico are higher than those paid in Sydney, Australia (after adjusting for exchange rates). He can convert Australian dollars to Mexican *pesos* and deposit the money in a Mexican bank account for, say, one year. At the end of the year, he converts the *pesos* back into Australian dollars and earns more in interest than the same money would have earned had it remained on deposit in an Australian bank.

CURRENCY SPECULATION **Currency speculation** is the purchase or sale of a currency with the expectation that its value will change and generate a profit. The shift in value might be expected to occur suddenly or over a longer period. The foreign exchange trader may bet that a currency's price will go either up or down in the future. Suppose a trader in London believes that the value of the Japanese *yen* will increase over the next three months. She buys *yen* with pounds at today's current price, intending to sell them in 90 days. If the price of *yen* rises in that time, she earns a profit; if it falls, she takes a loss. Speculation is much riskier than arbitrage because the value, or price, of currencies is quite volatile and is affected by many factors. Similar to arbitrage, currency speculation is commonly the realm of foreign exchange specialists rather than the managers of firms engaged in other endeavors.

currency hedging
Practice of insuring against potential losses that result from adverse changes in exchange rates.

currency arbitrage
Instantaneous purchase and sale of a currency in different markets for profit.

interest arbitrage
Profit-motivated purchase and sale of interest-paying securities denominated in different currencies.

currency speculation
Purchase or sale of a currency with the expectation that its value will change and generate a profit.

A classic example of currency speculation unfolded in Southeast Asia in 1997. After news emerged in May about Thailand's slowing economy and political instability, currency traders sprang into action. They responded to poor economic growth prospects and an overvalued currency, the Thai *baht,* by dumping the *baht* on the foreign exchange market. When the supply glutted the market, the value of the *baht* plunged. Meanwhile, traders began speculating that other Asian economies were also vulnerable. From the time the crisis first hit until the end of 1997, the value of the Indonesian *rupiah* fell by 87 percent, the South Korean *won* by 85 percent, the Thai *baht* by 63 percent, the Philippine *peso* by 34 percent, and the Malaysian *ringgit* by 32 percent.[4] Although many currency speculators made a great deal of money, the resulting hardship experienced by these nations' citizens caused some to question the ethics of currency speculation on such a scale.

QUICK STUDY 2

1. Describe the *international bond market.* What single factor is most responsible for fueling its growth?
2. What is the *international equity market*? Identify the factors responsible for its expansion.
3. Describe the *Eurocurrency market.* What is its main appeal?
4. For what four reasons do investors use the foreign exchange market?

How the Foreign Exchange Market Works

Because of the importance of foreign exchange to trade and investment, businesspeople must understand how currencies are quoted in the foreign exchange market. Managers must know what financial instruments are available to help them protect the profits earned by their international business activities. And they must be aware of government restrictions that may be imposed on the convertibility of currencies and know how to work around these and other obstacles.

Quoting Currencies

quoted currency
The numerator in a quoted exchange rate, or the currency with which another currency is to be purchased.

base currency
The denominator in a quoted exchange rate, or the currency that is to be purchased with another currency.

There are two components to every quoted exchange rate: the quoted currency and the base currency. If an exchange rate quotes the number of Japanese yen needed to buy one U.S. dollar (¥/$), the yen is the **quoted currency** and the dollar is the **base currency**. When you designate any exchange rate, the quoted currency is always the *numerator* and the base currency is the *denominator*. For example, if you were given a yen/dollar exchange rate quote of 90/1 (meaning that 90 yen are needed to buy one dollar), the numerator is 90 and the denominator is 1. We can also designate this rate as ¥ 90/$.

DIRECT AND INDIRECT RATE QUOTES Table 9.1 lists exchange rates between the U.S. dollar and a number of other currencies. The columns under the heading "Currency per U.S. $" tells us *how many units of each listed currency can be purchased with one U.S. dollar.* For example, in the row labeled "Japan (*yen*)," we see that 84.3770 Japanese *yen* can be bought with one U.S. dollar. We state this exchange rate as ¥ 84.3770/$. Because the *yen* is the quoted currency, we say that this is a *direct quote* on the *yen* and an *indirect quote* on the dollar. Note that the exchange rate for a nation participating in the single currency (euro) of the European Union is found on the line in the table that reads "Euro area (euro)."

When we have a direct quote on a currency and wish to calculate the indirect quote, we simply divide the currency quote into the numeral 1. The following formula is used to derive a direct quote from an indirect quote:

$$\text{Direct quote} = \frac{1}{\text{Indirect quote}}$$

And for deriving an indirect quote from a direct quote:

$$\text{Indirect quote} = \frac{1}{\text{Direct quote}}$$

TABLE 9.1 Exchange Rates of Major Currencies

Country (Currency)	Currency per U.S. $	Country (Currency)	Currency per U.S. $
Argentina (*peso*)	3.9512	Malaysia (*ringgit*)	3.1405
Australia (dollar)	1.1189	Mexico (*peso*)	13.2040
Bahrain (*dinar*)	0.3770	New Zealand (dollar)	1.4286
Brazil (*real*)	1.7559	Norway (*krone*)	6.3030
Britain (pound)	0.6515	Pakistan (*rupee*)	85.470
Canada (dollar)	1.0645	Peru (*new sol*)	2.7970
Chile (*peso*)	502.75	Philippines (*peso*)	45.2250
China (*yuan*)	6.8090	Poland (*zloty*)	3.1551
Colombia (*peso*)	1,826.45	Romania (*leu*)	3.3659
Czech Rep. (*koruna*)	19.5210	Russia (*ruble*)	30.8040
Denmark (*krone*)	5.8684	Saudi Arabia (*riyal*)	3.7509
Ecuador (U.S. dollar)	1	Singapore (dollar)	1.3546
Egypt (pound)	5.7055	Slovak Rep (*koruna*)	23.7470
Euro area (euro)	0.7883	South Africa (rand)	7.3872
Hong Kong (dollar)	7.7788	South Korea (*won*)	1,191.55
Hungary (*forint*)	226.3250	Sweden (*krona*)	7.3773
India (*rupee*)	47.0750	Switzerland (*franc*)	1.0163
Indonesia (*rupiah*)	9040.0	Taiwan (dollar)	32.0250
Israel (*shekel*)	3.8147	Thailand (*baht*)	31.2170
Japan (*yen*)	84.3770	Turkey (*lira*)	1.5266
Jordan (*dinar*)	0.7057	U.A.E. (*dirham*)	3.6724
Kenya (shilling)	81.0200	Uruguay (*peso*)	20.83
Kuwait (*dinar*)	0.2885	Venezuela (*b. fuerte*)	4.2946
Lebanon (pound)	1,507.39	Vietnam (*dong*)	19,495

In the previous example, we were given an *indirect quote* on the U.S. dollar of ¥ 84.3770/$. To find the *direct quote* on the dollar we simply divide ¥ 84.3770 into $1:

$$\$1 \div ¥ 84.3770 = \$0.011852/¥$$

This means that it costs $0.011852 to purchase one *yen* (¥)—slightly more than one U.S. cent. We state this exchange rate as $0.011852/¥. In this case, because the dollar is the quoted currency, we have a *direct quote* on the dollar and an *indirect quote* on the *yen*.

Businesspeople and foreign exchange traders track currency values over time because changes in currency values can benefit or harm international transactions. **Exchange-rate risk (foreign exchange risk)** is the risk of adverse changes in exchange rates. Managers develop strategies to minimize this risk by tracking percentage changes in exchange rates. To see how to calculate percentage change in the value of currencies, read this chapter's appendix on page 248.

exchange-rate risk (foreign exchange risk)
Risk of adverse changes in exchange rates.

CROSS RATES International transactions between two currencies other than the U.S. dollar often use the dollar as a vehicle currency. For example, a retail buyer of merchandise in the Netherlands might convert its euros (recall that the Netherlands uses the European Union currency) to U.S. dollars and then pay its Japanese supplier in U.S. dollars. The Japanese supplier may then take those U.S. dollars and convert them to Japanese *yen*. This process was more common years ago, when fewer currencies were freely convertible and when the United States greatly dominated world trade. Today, a Japanese supplier may want payment in euros. In this case, both the Japanese and the Dutch companies need to know the exchange rate between their respective currencies. To find this rate using their respective exchange rates with the U.S.

TABLE 9.2 Key Currency Cross Rates

	Dollar	Euro	*Yen*	Pound	Swiss *Franc*	Canadian Dollar
Canada	1.0646	1.3505	0.0126	1.6345	1.0476	...
Switzerland	1.0163	1.2892	0.0120	1.5603	...	0.9546
Britain	0.6513	0.8262	0.0077	...	0.6409	0.6118
Japan	84.454	107.13	...	129.66	83.102	79.330
Euro area	0.7883	...	0.0093	1.2103	0.7757	0.7405
United States	...	1.2686	0.0118	1.5354	0.9840	0.9393

cross rate
Exchange rate calculated using two other exchange rates.

dollar, we calculate what is called a **cross rate**—an exchange rate calculated using two other exchange rates.

Cross rates between two currencies can be calculated using both currencies' indirect or direct exchange rates with a third currency. For example, suppose we want to know the cross rate between the currencies of the Netherlands and Japan. Looking at Table 9.1 again, we see that the direct quote on the euro is € 0.7883/$. The direct quote on the Japanese yen is ¥ 84.3770/$. To find the cross rate between the euro and the yen, with the yen as the base currency, we simply divide € 0.7883/$ by ¥ 84.3770/$:

$$€ \ 0.7883/\$ \div ¥ \ 84.3770/\$ = € \ 0.0093/¥$$

Thus, it costs 0.0093 euros to buy 1 *yen*.

Table 9.2 shows the cross rates for major world currencies. When finding cross rates using direct quotes, currencies down the left-hand side represent quoted currencies; those across the top represent base currencies. Conversely, when finding cross rates using indirect quotes, currencies down the left side represent base currencies; those across the top represent quoted currencies. Look at the intersection of the "Euro area" row (the quoted currency in our example) and the "*Yen*" column (our base currency). Note that the solution we calculated above for the cross rate between euro and *yen* match the listed rate of 0.0093 euros to the *yen*.

Naturally, the exchange rate between the euro and the *yen* is quite important to both the Japanese supplier and Dutch retailer we mentioned earlier. If the value of the euro falls relative to the *yen*, the Dutch company must pay more in euros for its Japanese products. This situation will force the Dutch company to take one of two steps: either increase the price at which it resells the Japanese product (perhaps reducing sales) or keep prices at current levels (thus reducing its profit margin).

Ironically, the Japanese supplier will suffer if the *yen* rises too much. Why? Under such circumstances, the Japanese supplier can do one of two things: allow the exchange rate to force its euro prices higher (thus maintaining profits) or reduce its *yen* prices to offset the decline of the euro (thus reducing its profit margin).

Both the Japanese supplier and the Dutch buyer can absorb exchange rate changes by squeezing profits—but only to a point. After that point is passed, they will no longer be able to trade. The Dutch buyer will be forced to look for a supplier in a country with a more favorable exchange rate or for a supplier in its own country (or another European country that uses the euro).

Spot Rates

spot rate
Exchange rate requiring delivery of the traded currency within two business days.

spot market
Market for currency transactions at spot rates.

All the exchange rates we've discussed so far are called **spot rates**—exchange rates that require delivery of the traded currency within two business days. Exchange of the two currencies is said to occur "on the spot," and the **spot market** is the market for currency transactions at spot rates. The spot market assists companies in performing any one of three functions:

1. Converting income generated from sales abroad into their home-country currency
2. Converting funds into the currency of an international supplier
3. Converting funds into the currency of a country in which they wish to invest

BUY AND SELL RATES The spot rate is available only for trades worth millions of dollars. That is why it is available only to banks and foreign exchange brokers. If you are traveling to another country and want to exchange currencies at your local bank before departing, you will not be quoted the spot rate. Rather, you will receive a quote that includes a markup to cover the costs your bank incurs when performing this transaction for you.

Suppose you are taking a business trip to Spain and need to buy some euros. The bank will quote you exchange-rate terms, such as $1.268/78 per €, which means that the bank will buy U.S. dollars at the rate of $1.268/€ and sell them at the rate of $1.278/€.

Forward Rates

When a company knows that it will need a certain amount of foreign currency on a certain future date, it can exchange currencies using a **forward rate**—an exchange rate at which two parties agree to exchange currencies on a specified future date. Forward rates represent the expectations of currency traders and bankers regarding a currency's future spot rate. Reflected in these expectations are a country's present and future economic conditions (including inflation rate, national debt, taxes, trade balance, and economic growth rate) as well as its social and political situation. The **forward market** is the market for currency transactions at forward rates.

To insure themselves against unfavorable exchange-rate changes, companies commonly turn to the forward market. It can be used for all types of transactions that require future payment in other currencies, including credit sales or purchases, interest receipts or payments on investments or loans, and dividend payments to stockholders in other countries. But not all nations' currencies trade in the forward market, such as countries experiencing high inflation or currencies not in demand on international financial markets.

forward rate
Exchange rate at which two parties agree to exchange currencies on a specified future date.

forward market
Market for currency transactions at forward rates.

FORWARD CONTRACTS Suppose a Brazilian bicycle maker imports parts from a Japanese supplier. Under the terms of their contract, the Brazilian importer must pay 100 million Japanese *yen* in 90 days. The Brazilian firm can wait until one or two days before payment is due, buy *yen* in the spot market, and pay the Japanese supplier. But in the 90 days between the contract date and the due date, the exchange rate will likely change. What if the value of the Brazilian *real* goes down? In that case, the Brazilian importer will have to pay more *reais* (plural of *real*) to get the same 100 million Japanese *yen*. Therefore, our importer may want to pay off the debt before the 90-day term. But what if it does not have the cash on hand? What if it needs those 90 days to collect accounts receivable from its own customers?

To decrease its exchange-rate risk, our Brazilian importer can enter into a **forward contract**—a contract that requires the exchange of an agreed-on amount of a currency on an agreed-on date at a specified exchange rate. Forward contracts are commonly signed for 30, 90, and 180 days into the future, but customized contracts (say, for 76 days) are possible. Note that a forward contract *requires* the exchange to occur: The bank must deliver the *yen,* and the Brazilian importer must buy them at the prearranged price. Forward contracts belong to a family of financial instruments called **derivatives**—instruments whose values *derive* from other commodities or financial instruments. These include not only forward contracts but also currency swaps, options, and futures (presented next in this chapter).

In our example, the Brazilian importer can use a forward contract to pay *yen* to its Japanese supplier in 90 days. It is always possible, of course, that in 90 days, the value of the *real* will be lower than its current value. But by locking in at the forward rate, the Brazilian firm protects itself against the less favorable spot rate at which it would have to buy *yen* in 90 days. In this case, the Brazilian company protects itself from paying more to the supplier at the end of 90 days than if it were to pay at the spot rate in 90 days. Thus, it protects its profit from further erosion if the spot rate becomes even more unfavorable over the next three months. Remember, too, that such a contract prevents the Brazilian importer from taking advantage of any increase in the value of the *real* in 90 days that would reduce what the company owed its Japanese supplier.

forward contract
Contract that requires the exchange of an agreed-on amount of a currency on an agreed-on date at a specified exchange rate.

derivative
Financial instrument whose value derives from other commodities or financial instruments.

Swaps, Options, and Futures

In addition to forward contracts, three other types of currency instruments are used in the forward market: currency swaps, options, and futures.

currency swap
Simultaneous purchase and sale of foreign exchange for two different dates.

CURRENCY SWAPS A **currency swap** is the simultaneous purchase and sale of foreign exchange for two different dates. Currency swaps are an increasingly important component of the foreign exchange market. Suppose a Swedish automaker imports parts from a subsidiary in Turkey. The Swedish company must pay the Turkish subsidiary in Turkish *lira* for the parts when they are delivered today. The company also expects to receive Turkish *liras* for automobiles sold in Turkey in 90 days. Our Swedish company exchanges *kronor* for *lira* in the spot market today to pay its subsidiary. At the same time, it agrees to a forward contract to sell Turkish *lira* (and buy Swedish *kronor*) in 90 days at the quoted 90-day forward rate for *lira*. In this way, the Swedish company uses a swap both to reduce its exchange-rate risk and to lock in the future exchange rate. In this sense, we can think of a currency swap as a more complex forward contract.

currency option
Right, or option, to exchange a specified amount of a currency on a specified date at a specified rate.

CURRENCY OPTIONS Recall that, once it is entered into, a forward contract *requires* an exchange of currencies. By contrast, a **currency option** is a right, or *option,* to exchange a specified amount of a currency on a specified date at a specified rate.

Suppose a company buys an option to purchase Swiss *francs* at SF 1.02/$ in 30 days. If, at the end of the 30 days, the exchange rate is SF 1.05/$, the company would *not* exercise its currency option. Why? It could get SF 0.03 more for every dollar by exchanging at the spot rate in the currency market rather than at the stated rate of the option. Companies often use currency options to hedge against exchange-rate risk or to obtain foreign currency.

currency futures contract
Contract requiring the exchange of a specified amount of currency on a specified date at a specified exchange rate, with all conditions fixed and not adjustable.

CURRENCY FUTURES CONTRACTS Similar to a currency forward contract is a **currency futures contract**—a contract requiring the exchange of a specified amount of currency on a specified date at a specified exchange rate, with all conditions fixed and not adjustable.

QUICK STUDY 3

1. Why is *exchange-rate risk* important to companies?
2. What is meant by the term *cross rate*? Explain how it is useful to businesses.
3. Explain how a *spot rate* and *forward rate* are used in the foreign exchange market.
4. What are the main differences between *currency swaps, options,* and *futures*?

Foreign Exchange Market Today

The foreign exchange market is actually an electronic network that connects the world's major financial centers. In turn, each of these centers is a network of foreign exchange traders, currency trading banks, and investment firms. The daily trading volume on the foreign exchange market (comprising currency swaps and spot and forward contracts) amount to around $4 trillion—an amount greater than the yearly gross domestic product of many small nations.[5] Several major trading centers and several currencies dominate the foreign exchange market.

Trading Centers

Most of the world's major cities participate in trading on the foreign exchange market. But in recent years, just three countries have come to account for more than half of all global currency trading: the United Kingdom, the United States, and Japan. Accordingly, most of this trading takes place in the financial capitals of London, New York, and Tokyo.

London dominates the foreign exchange market for historic and geographic reasons. The United Kingdom was once the world's largest trading nation. British merchants needed to exchange currencies of different nations, and London naturally assumed the role of financial trading center. London quickly came to dominate the market and still does so because of its location halfway between North America and Asia. A key factor is its time zone. Because of differences in time zones, London is opening for business as markets in Asia close trading for the day. When New York opens for trading in the morning, trading is beginning to wind down in London. Also, most large banks active in foreign exchange employ overnight traders to ensure continuous trading (see Figure 9.1).

FIGURE 9.1

Financial Trading Centers by Time Zone

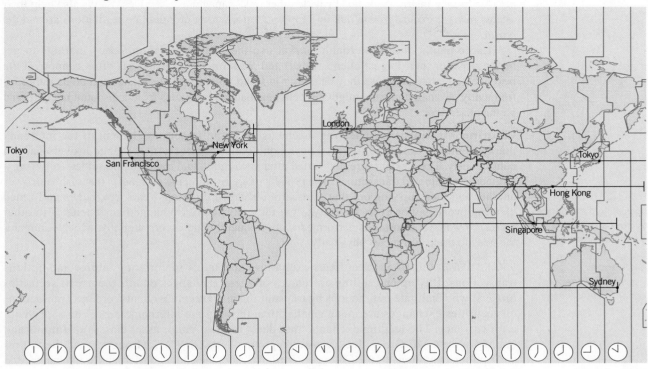

Important Currencies

Although the United Kingdom is the major location of foreign exchange trading, the U.S. dollar is the currency that dominates the foreign exchange market. Because the U.S. dollar is so widely used in world trade, it is considered a **vehicle currency**—a currency used as an intermediary to convert funds between two other currencies. The currencies most often involved in currency transactions are the U.S. dollar, European Union euro, Japanese *yen*, and British pound.

     One reason the U.S. dollar is a vehicle currency is because the United States is the world's largest trading nation. The United States is so heavily involved in international trade that many companies and banks maintain dollar deposits, making it easy to exchange other currencies with dollars. Another reason is that, following the Second World War, all of the world's major currencies were tied indirectly to the dollar because it was the most stable currency. In turn, the dollar's value was tied to a specific value of gold—a policy that held wild currency swings in check. Although world currencies are no longer linked to the value of gold (see Chapter 10), the stability of the dollar, along with its resistance to inflation, helps people and organizations maintain their purchasing power better than their own national currencies.

vehicle currency
Currency used as an intermediary to convert funds between two other currencies.

Institutions of the Foreign Exchange Market

So far, we have discussed the foreign exchange market only in general terms. We now look at the three main components of the foreign exchange market: the *interbank market, securities exchanges,* and the *over-the-counter market.*

INTERBANK MARKET It is in the **interbank market** that the world's largest banks exchange currencies at spot and forward rates. Companies tend to obtain foreign exchange services from the bank where they do most of their business. Banks satisfy client requests for exchange quotes by obtaining quotes from other banks in the interbank market. For transactions that involve commonly exchanged currencies, the largest banks often have sufficient currency on hand. Yet, rarely exchanged currencies are not typically kept on hand and may not even be easily obtainable from another bank. In such cases, banks turn to *foreign exchange brokers,* who maintain vast networks of banks through which they obtain seldom-traded currencies.

interbank market
Market in which the world's largest banks exchange currencies at spot and forward rates.

In the interbank market, then, banks act as agents for client companies. In addition to locating and exchanging currencies, banks commonly offer advice on trading strategy, supply a variety of currency instruments, and provide other risk-management services. Banks also help their clients manage exchange-rate risk by supplying information on rules and regulations around the world.

Large banks in the interbank market use their influence in currency markets to get better rates for their largest clients. Small and medium-sized businesses often cannot get the best exchange rates because they deal only in small volumes of currencies and do so rather infrequently. A small company might get better exchange rate quotes from a discount international payment service.

Clearing Mechanisms Clearing mechanisms are an important element of the interbank market. Foreign exchange transactions among banks and foreign exchange brokers happen continuously. The accounts are not settled after each individual trade but are settled following a number of completed transactions. The process of aggregating the currencies that one bank owes another and then carrying out that transaction is called **clearing**. Years ago, banks performed clearing every day or every two days, and they physically exchanged currencies with other banks. Nowadays, clearing is performed more frequently and occurs digitally, which eliminates the need to trade currencies physically.

clearing
Process of aggregating the currencies that one bank owes another and then carrying out the transaction.

securities exchange
Exchange specializing in currency futures and options transactions.

SECURITIES EXCHANGES **Securities exchanges** specialize in currency futures and options transactions. Buying and selling currencies on these exchanges entails the use of securities *brokers,* who facilitate transactions by transmitting and executing clients' orders. Transactions on securities exchanges are much smaller than those in the interbank market and vary with each currency. The leading exchange that deals in most major asset classes of futures and options is the CME Group, Inc. (www.cmegroup.com). The CME Group merged the futures and options operations of the Chicago Board of Trade, the Chicago Mercantile Exchange, and the New York Mercantile Exchange. The CME Group's foreign exchange marketplace is the world's second largest electronic foreign exchange marketplace, with more than $80 billion in daily liquidity.[6]

Another exchange is the London International Financial Futures Exchange (www.euronext.com), which trades futures and options for major currencies. In the United States, trading in currency *options* occurs only on the Philadelphia Stock Exchange (www.nasdaqtrader.com). It deals in both standardized options and customized options, allowing investors flexibility in designing currency option contracts.[7]

MANAGER'S BRIEFCASE   Managing Foreign Exchange

- *Match Needs to Providers.* Analyze your foreign exchange needs and the range of service providers available. Find a provider that offers the transactions you undertake in the currencies you need, and consolidate repetitive transfers. Many businesspeople naturally look to local bankers when they need to transfer funds abroad, but this may not be the cheapest or best choice. A mix of service providers sometimes offers the best solution.

- *Work with the Majors.* Money-center banks (those located in financial centers) that participate directly in the foreign exchange market can have cost and service advantages over local banks. Dealing directly with a large trading institution is often more cost effective than dealing with a local bank because it avoids the additional markup that the local bank charges for its services.

- *Consolidate to Save.* Save money by timing your international payments to consolidate multiple transfers into one large transaction. Open a local currency account abroad against which you

can write drafts if your company makes multiple smaller payments in the same currency. Consider allowing foreign receivables to accumulate in an interest-bearing account locally until you repatriate them in a lump sum to reduce service fees.

- *Get the Best Deal Possible.* If your foreign exchange activity is substantial, develop relationships with two or more money-center banks to get the best rates. Also, monitor the rates your company gets over time, as some banks raise rates if you're not shopping around. Obtain real-time market rates provided by firms like Reuters and Bloomberg.

- *Embrace Information Technology.* Every time an employee phones, e-mails, or faxes in a transaction, human error could delay getting funds where and when your company needs them. Embrace information technology in your business's international wire transfers and drafts. Automated software programs available from specialized service providers reduce the potential for errors while speeding the execution of transfers.

OVER-THE-COUNTER MARKET   The **over-the-counter (OTC) market** is a decentralized exchange encompassing a global computer network of foreign exchange traders and other market participants. All foreign exchange transactions can be performed in the OTC market, where the major players are large financial institutions.

The over-the-counter market has grown rapidly because it offers distinct benefits for business. It allows businesspeople to search freely for the institution that provides the best (lowest) price for conducting a transaction. It also offers opportunities for designing customized transactions. For additional ways companies can become more adept in their foreign exchange activities, see this chapter's Manager's Briefcase, titled "Managing Foreign Exchange."

over-the-counter (OTC) market
Decentralized exchange encompassing a global computer network of foreign exchange traders and other market participants.

Currency Convertibility

Our discussion of the foreign exchange market so far assumes that all currencies can be readily converted to another in the foreign exchange market. A **convertible (hard) currency** is traded freely in the foreign exchange market, with its price determined by the forces of supply and demand. Countries that allow full convertibility are those that are in strong financial positions and that have adequate reserves of foreign currencies. Such countries have no reason to fear that people will sell their own currency for that of another. Still, many newly industrialized and developing countries do not permit the free convertibility of their currencies. Let's take a look at why governments place restrictions on the convertibility of currencies and how they do it.

convertible (hard) currency
Currency that trades freely in the foreign exchange market, with its price determined by the forces of supply and demand.

Goals of Currency Restriction

Governments impose currency restrictions to achieve several goals. One goal is to preserve a country's reserve of hard currencies with which to repay debts owed to other nations. Developed nations, emerging markets, and some countries that export natural resources tend to have the greatest amounts of foreign exchange. Without sufficient reserves (liquidity), a country could default on its loans and thereby discourage future investment flows. This is precisely what happened to Argentina several years ago when the country defaulted on its international public debt.

A second goal of currency restriction is to preserve hard currencies in order to pay for imports and to finance trade deficits. Recall from Chapter 5 that a country runs a trade deficit when the value of its imports exceeds the value of its exports. Currency restrictions help governments maintain inventories of foreign currencies with which to pay for such trade imbalances. They also make importing more difficult because local companies cannot obtain foreign currency to pay for imports. The resulting reduction in imports directly improves the country's trade balance.

A third goal is to protect a currency from speculators. For example, in the wake of the Asian financial crisis years ago, some Southeast Asian nations considered controlling their currencies to limit the damage done by economic downturns. Malaysia stemmed the outflow of foreign money by preventing local investors from converting their Malaysian holdings into other currencies. Although the move also curtailed currency speculation, it effectively cut off Malaysia from investors elsewhere in the world.

A fourth (less common) goal is to keep resident individuals and businesses from investing in other nations. These policies can generate more rapid economic growth in a country by forcing investment to remain at home. Unfortunately, although this might work in the short term, it normally slows long-term economic growth. The reason is that there is no guarantee that domestic funds held in the home country will be invested there. Instead, they might be saved or even spent on consumption. Ironically, increased consumption can mean further increases in imports, making a trade deficit even worse.

Policies for Restricting Currencies

Certain government policies are frequently used to restrict currency convertibility. Governments can require that all foreign exchange transactions be performed at or approved by the country's central bank. They can also require import licenses for some or all import transactions. These licenses help the government control the amount of foreign currency leaving the country.

Some governments implement systems of *multiple exchange rates,* specifying a higher exchange rate on the importation of certain goods or on imports from certain countries. The government can thus reduce importation while ensuring that important goods still enter the country. It also can use such a policy to target the goods of countries with which it is running a trade deficit.

Other governments issue *import deposit requirements* that require businesses to deposit certain percentages of their foreign exchange funds in special accounts before being granted import licenses. In addition, *quantity restrictions* limit the amount of foreign currency that residents can take out of the home country when traveling to other countries as tourists, students, or medical patients.

countertrade

Practice of selling goods or services that are paid for, in whole or in part, with other goods or services.

COUNTERTRADE One way to get around national restrictions on currency convertibility is **countertrade**—the practice of selling goods or services that are paid for, in whole or in part, with other goods or services. One simple form of countertrade is a *barter* transaction, in which goods are exchanged for others of equal value. Parties exchange goods and then sell them in world markets for hard currency. For example, Cuba once exchanged $60 million worth of sugar for cereals, pasta, and vegetable oils from the Italian firm Italgrani. And Boeing (www.boeing.com) has sold aircraft to Saudi Arabia in return for oil. We detail the many different forms of countertrade in Chapter 13.

QUICK STUDY 4

1. What are the world's main foreign exchange trading centers? Identify the currencies most used in the foreign exchange market.
2. Describe the three main institutions of the foreign exchange market.
3. What are the reasons for restrictions on currency conversion? Identify policies governments use to restrict currency conversion.

BOTTOM LINE FOR BUSINESS

Well-functioning financial markets are essential to conducting international business. International financial markets supply companies with the mechanism they require to exchange currencies, and more. Here we focus on the main implications of these markets for international companies.

International Capital Market and Businesses

The international capital market joins borrowers and lenders from different national capital markets. A company unable to obtain funds in its own nation may use the international capital market to obtain financing elsewhere and allow the firm to undertake an otherwise impossible project. This option can be especially important for firms in countries with small or emerging capital markets.

Similar to the prices of any other commodity, the "price" of money is determined by supply and demand. If the supply increases, the price (in the form of interest rates) falls. The international capital market opens up additional sources of financing for companies, possibly financing projects previously regarded as not feasible. The international capital market also expands lending opportunities, which reduces risk for lenders by allowing them to spread their money over a greater number of debt and equity instruments and to benefit from the fact that securities markets do not move up and down in tandem.

International Financial Market and Businesses

Companies must convert to local currencies when they undertake foreign direct investment. Later, when a firm's international subsidiary earns a profit and the company wishes to return profits to the home country, it must convert the local money into the home currency. The prevailing exchange rate at the time profits are exchanged influences the amount of the ultimate profit or loss.

This raises an important aspect of international financial markets—fluctuation. International companies can use hedging in foreign exchange markets to lessen the risk associated with international transfers of funds and to protect themselves in credit transactions in which there is a time lag between billing and receipt of payment. Some firms take part in currency arbitrage when they have large sums of cash on hand. Companies can also use interest arbitrage to find better interest rates abroad than those available in their home countries.

Businesspeople are also interested in tracking currency values over time because changes in currency values affect their international transactions. Profits earned by companies that import products for resale are influenced by the exchange rate between their currency and that of the nation from which they import. Managers who understand that changes in these currencies' values affect the profitability of their international business activities can develop strategies to minimize risk.

In the next chapter, we extend our coverage of the international financial system to see how market forces (including interest rates and inflation) have an impact on exchange rates. We also conclude our study of the international financial system by looking at the roles of government and international institutions in managing movements in exchange rates.

Chapter Summary

MyManagementLab
Go to **mymanagementlab.com** to complete the problems marked with this icon .

1. **Discuss the purposes, development, and financial centers of the international capital market.**
   - The international capital market is meant to (1) expand the supply of capital for borrowers, (2) lower interest rates for borrowers, and (3) lower risk for lenders.
   - Growth in the international capital market is due mainly to (1) advances in *information technology,* (2) *deregulation* of capital markets, and (3) innovation in *financial instruments*.
   - London (UK), New York (U.S.), and Tokyo (Japan) are the world's most important financial centers.
   - *Offshore financial centers* handle less business than the world's most important financial centers but have few regulations and few, if any, taxes.

2. **Describe the international bond, international equity, and Eurocurrency markets.**
   - The *international bond market* consists of all bonds sold by issuers outside their own countries.
   - It is growing as investors in developed markets search for higher rates from borrowers in emerging markets, and vice versa.
   - The *international equity market* consists of all stocks bought and sold outside the home country of the issuing company.
   - Four factors driving growth in international equity are (1) privatization, (2) greater issuance of stock by companies in emerging and developing nations, (3) greater international reach of investment banks, and (4) global electronic trading.
   - The *Eurocurrency market* consists of all the world's currencies banked outside their countries of origin; its appeal is the lack of government regulation and the lower cost of borrowing.

3. **Discuss the four primary functions of the foreign exchange market.**
   - The *foreign exchange market* is the market in which currencies are bought and sold and in which currency prices are determined.
   - One function of the foreign exchange market is that individuals, companies, and governments use it, directly or indirectly, to *convert* one currency into another.
   - Second, it is used as a hedging device to *insure against* adverse changes in exchange rates.
   - Third, it is used to *earn a profit* from the instantaneous purchase and sale of a currency (arbitrage) or other interest-paying security in different markets.
   - Fourth, it is used to *speculate* about a change in the value of a currency and thereby earn a profit.

4. **Explain how currencies are quoted and the different rates that are given.**
   - An *exchange-rate quote* between currency A and currency B (A/B) of 10/1 means that it takes 10 units of currency A to buy 1 unit of currency B (this is a *direct quote* of currency A and an *indirect quote* of currency B).
   - Exchange rates between two currencies can also be found using their respective exchange rates with a common currency; the resulting rate is called a *cross rate*.
   - An exchange rate that requires delivery of the traded currency within two business days is called a *spot rate*.
   - The *forward rate* is the rate at which two parties agree to exchange currencies on a specified future date; it represents the market's expectation of a currency's future value.

5. **Identify the main instruments and institutions of the foreign exchange market.**
   - A *forward contract* requires the exchange of an agreed-on amount of a currency on an agreed-on date at a specified exchange rate.
   - A *currency swap* is the simultaneous purchase and sale of foreign exchange for two different dates.
   - A *currency option* is the right to exchange a specified amount of a currency on a specified date at a specified rate; it is sometimes used to acquire a needed currency.

- A *currency futures contract* requires the exchange of a specified amount of currency on a specified date at a specified exchange rate (no terms are negotiable).
- The *interbank market* is where the world's largest banks locate and exchange currencies for companies.
- *Securities exchanges* are physical locations at which currency futures and options are bought and sold (in smaller amounts than those traded in the interbank market).
- The *over-the-counter (OTC) market* is an exchange that exists in the form of a global computer network linking traders to one another.

6. Explain why and how governments restrict currency convertibility.
- One main goal of currency restriction is that a government may be attempting to preserve the country's hard currency reserves for repaying debts owed to other nations.
- Second, convertibility might be restricted in order to preserve hard currency to pay for needed imports or to finance a trade deficit.
- Third, restrictions might be used to protect a currency from speculators.
- Fourth, restrictions can be an attempt to keep badly needed currency from being invested abroad.
- Policies used to enforce currency restrictions include (1) government approval for currency exchange, (2) imposed import licenses, (3) a system of multiple exchange rates, and (4) imposed quantity restrictions.

Talk It Over

⭐1. What factors do you think are holding back the creation of a truly *global* capital market? How might a global capital market function differently from the present-day international market? (*Hint*: Some factors to consider are interest rates, currencies, regulations, and financial crises for some countries.)

2. The use of different national currencies creates a barrier to further growth in international business activity. What are the pros and cons, among companies *and* governments, of replacing national currencies with regional currencies? Do you think a global currency would be possible someday? Why or why not?

⭐3. Governments dislike the fact that offshore financial centers facilitate money laundering. Do you think that electronic commerce makes it easier or harder to launder money and camouflage other illegal activities? Do you think offshore financial centers should be allowed to operate as freely as they do now, or do you favor regulation? Explain your answers.

Teaming Up

1. **Research Project.** Form a team with several of your classmates. Suppose you work for a firm that has $10 million in excess cash to invest for one month. Your group's task is to invest this money in the foreign exchange market to earn a profit—holding dollars is not an option. Select the currencies you wish to buy at today's spot rate, but do not buy less than $2.5 million of any single currency. Track the spot rate for each currency over the next month in the business press. On the last day of the month, exchange your currencies at the day's spot rate. Calculate your team's gain or loss over the one-month period. (Your instructor will determine whether, and how often, currencies may be traded throughout the month.)

⭐2. **Market Entry Strategy Project.** This exercise corresponds to the *MESP* online simulation. For the country your team is researching, does it have a city that is an important financial center? What volume of bonds is traded on the country's bond market? How has its stock market(s) performed over the past year? What is the exchange rate between its currency and that of your own country? What factors are responsible for the stability or volatility in that exchange rate? Are there any restrictions on the exchange of the nation's currency? How is the forecast for the country's currency likely to influence business activity in its major industries? Integrate your findings into your completed *MESP* report. (*Hint*: Good sources are the monthly *International Financial Statistics* and the annual *Exchange Arrangements and Exchange Restrictions,* both published by the International Monetary Fund.)

Key Terms

base currency (p. 234)
bond (p. 227)
capital market (p. 226)
clearing (p. 240)
convertible (hard) currency (p. 240)
countertrade (p. 242)
cross rate (p. 236)
currency arbitrage (p. 233)
currency futures contract (p. 238)
currency hedging (p. 233)
currency option (p. 238)
currency speculation (p. 233)
currency swap (p. 238)
debt (p. 227)

derivative (p. 237)
equity (p. 227)
Eurobond (p. 230)
Eurocurrency market (p. 231)
exchange rate (p. 232)
exchange-rate risk (foreign exchange risk) (p. 235)
foreign bond (p. 230)
foreign exchange market (p. 235)
forward contract (p. 237)
forward market (p. 237)
forward rate (p. 237)
interbank interest rates (p. 231)
interbank market (p. 239)

interest arbitrage (p. 233)
international bond market (p. 229)
international capital market (p. 227)
international equity market (p. 230)
liquidity (p. 227)
offshore financial center (p. 229)
over-the-counter (OTC) market (p. 240)
quoted currency (p. 234)
securities exchange (p. 240)
securitization (p. 228)
spot market (p. 236)
spot rate (p. 236)
stock (p. 227)
vehicle currency (p. 239)

Take It to the Web

1. **Video Report.** Visit this book's channel on YouTube (www.YouTube.com/MyIBvideos). Click on "Videos" near the top of the page, and click on the set of videos labeled "Ch 09: International Financial Markets." Watch one video from the list, and then summarize it in a half-page report. Reflecting on the contents of this chapter, which aspects of international financial markets can you identify in the video? How might a company engaged in international business act on the information contained in the video?

2. **Website Report.** Visit the website of a financial institution or business periodical that publishes exchange rates among the world's currencies. Compare the exchange rate of the U.S. dollar against the European Union euro you find to that contained in Table 9.1.

   Has the dollar fallen or risen in value over time against the euro? What is the exchange rate between the dollar and euro using (a) an indirect quote on the dollar and (b) a direct quote on the dollar? What percent change has occurred in the *value of the dollar* against the euro? (Remember to mind your quoted and base currencies!) *The appendix to this chapter shows how to calculate percent change in exchange rates.*

   Conducting web-based research, what reasons lie behind the exchange-rate movement between the dollar and euro? Is the shift in the exchange rate due more to movement in the value of the dollar or the euro? Explain your answer. How has the exchange-rate change affected international business activity between the United States and European nations using the euro? Be specific.

Ethical Challenges

1. You are a U.S. senator serving on a subcommittee with the task of developing new regulations for U.S. firms doing business through offshore financial centers. Bank deposits in offshore financial centers grew from the tens of billions of dollars a few decades ago to more than $1 trillion today. "Dirty money" obtained through drug trafficking, gambling, and other illicit activities use offshore financial centers to escape the same things as respectable "clean capital": national taxation and government regulations. Some experts argue that institutions such as international currency markets and offshore tax havens reduce stability and are hostile to the public interest. They say that people use such institutions to get beyond the reach of the law and undermine what they consider to be inefficient and bureaucratic attempts to impose a certain morality on people. As senator, what type of regulations do you support? What rationale do you give business leaders in your constituency who do business with offshore financial centers? Do you think corporate use of offshore financial centers to avoid home-country bureaucracies and taxes is ethical? Why or why not?

2. You are a member of the board of directors for one of the nation's largest banks. Although recent banking deregulation is fostering greater competition in the industry, you are concerned about the direction in which banking is headed. The top management team of your bank is to meet soon with government officials to discuss the situation. The goal of government *regulation* of financial-services industries is to maintain the integrity and stability of financial systems, thereby protecting both depositors and investors. Regulations include prohibitions against insider trading, against lending by management to itself or to closely related entities (a practice called "self-dealing"), and against other transactions in which there is a conflict of interest. Yet in less than two decades, *deregulation* has transformed the world's financial markets. It has spurred competition and growth in financial sectors and has allowed capital to flow freely across borders, which has boosted the economies of developing countries. What advice do you give your bank's executives prior to meeting with the government? What do you see as the "dark side" of deregulation, in terms of business ethics? What do you think Adam Smith, one of the first philosophers of capitalism, meant when he warned against the dangers of "colluding producers"? Do you think this warning applies to the financial-services sector today?

MyManagementLab

Go to **mymanagementlab.com** for Auto-graded writing questions as well as the following Assisted-graded writing question:

9-1. Mymanagementlab Only – comprehensive writing assignment for this chapter.

Practicing International Management Case

Should We Cry for Argentina?

Argentina's past President Eduardo Duhalde had summed it up perfectly: "Argentina is bust. It's bankrupt. Business is halted, the chain of payments is broken, there is no currency to get the economy moving and we don't have a *peso* to pay Christmas bonuses, wages, or pensions," he said in a speech to Argentina's Congress.

Although it was the star of Latin America in the 1990s, Argentina defaulted on its $155 billion of public debt in early 2002, the largest default by any country ever. After taking office in January 2002, President Duhalde implemented many measures to keep the country's fragile economy from complete collapse after four years of recession. For 10 years, the Argentine *peso* was fixed at parity to the dollar through a currency board. The president cut those strings immediately. But when it was allowed to float freely on currency markets, Argentina's *peso* quickly lost two-thirds of its value and was trading at 3 *pesos* to the dollar. Then, strapped for cash, the government seized the savings accounts of its citizens and restricted how much they could withdraw at one time. Street protesters turned violent, beating up several politicians and attacking dozens of banks.

Local companies were having a difficult time, too. Many companies blamed their defaults on the requirement that they get authorization from the central bank to send money abroad. Stiff restrictions on foreign currency exchange forced importers to wait several months or more while the government authorized payments in dollars. Companies also struggled with new rules that raised taxes on exporters and other cash-rich firms to help the government pay for social services. Local firms also had a hard time obtaining funds to pay their debts to foreign suppliers. But the loss of confidence among non-Argentine businesses was more difficult to quantify. Many entered Argentina during a wave of free-market changes and privatizations in the 1990s. "If the government can just arbitrarily change contracts," said a foreign diplomat in Buenos Aires, "how can you feel safe about any business relationship here in the coming months?"

The declining *peso* intensified problems for U.S. companies that fought to manage soaring debts and mounting losses from their Argentine operations. Argentine units of U.S. companies, which tend to collect revenues in *pesos,* had an increasingly difficult time repaying their dollar-denominated debts as the *peso*'s value fell. The government decreed that electricity and gas companies switch their contracts from dollars to less valuable *pesos* and then froze utility rates to protect consumers. But parent companies were unlikely to rescue their ailing operations in Argentina because the parents generally were not required to support the cash flow or debt service obligations of these independent subsidiaries.

The government, trying to lighten its debt load and restore credibility with the International Monetary Fund (www.imf.org), ordered $50 billion in dollar-denominated government debt (mostly domestic) swapped into *pesos*. The swap was aimed at unlocking $10 billion in IMF loans that were frozen when Argentina failed to meet certain economic targets. U.S. and European investors owned another $46 billion in government bonds, which were to be restructured in a separate transaction. Argentina's government spent the previous decade amassing debts in dollars and other foreign currencies. But when the government cut loose the *peso* from the dollar in January 2002, the weak *peso* made the debt far more expensive to repay.

Argentina's economic collapse was devastating. From 2001 through 2002, the economy shrank by 15 percent, unemployment shot up to 21 percent, and poverty engulfed 56 percent of its citizens. The government's plan of stimulating demand by raising wages, imposing price controls, keeping the *peso* low, and spending public funds worked for a time. But inflation reached 26 percent and higher in 2012, cutting consumers' purchasing power and increasing poverty.

Thinking Globally

1. Update the economic situation in Argentina to reflect recent events. How is the value of the *peso* faring? Do you think it was wise to cut the ties between the *peso* and the dollar? Why did Argentina peg its currency to the dollar in the first place? Do you think that the link between the *peso* and the dollar contributed to Argentina's problems? Explain.
2. How did local and international companies adapt to the business environment at the height of Argentina's crisis? Did they pursue similar courses of action or design distinct strategies to deal with its effects? Be specific in your answer, and give examples.
3. What was the impact on ordinary citizens immediately after the default and later as the economy recovered? What do the aftereffects of the crisis mean long term for ordinary citizens' spending power? What has it done to the value of their savings? In your opinion, has international aid helped or hurt the ordinary people of Argentina? Explain your answer.

Source: "Economic and Financial Indicators," *The Economist*, October 6, 2012, p. 108; Roben Farzad, "Don't Cry for Argentina," *Bloomberg Businessweek*, May 24–May 30, 2010, pp. 9–10; "Clouds Gather Again over the Pampas," *The Economist*, August 23, 2008, pp. 30–31; "Who Needs Credit?" *The Economist* (www.economist.com), May 8, 2008.

Appendix Calculating Percent Change in Exchange Rates

Businesspeople and foreign exchange traders track currency values over time as measured by exchange rates because changes in currency values can benefit or harm current and future international transactions. Managers develop strategies to minimize exchange-rate risk (foreign exchange risk) by tracking percent changes in exchange rates.

For example, take P_N as the exchange rate at the end of a period (the currency's *new* price) and P_O as the exchange rate at the beginning of that period (the currency's *old* price). We now can calculate percent change in the value of a currency with the following formula:

$$\text{Percent change (\%)} = \frac{P_n - P_o}{P_o} \times 100$$

Note: This equation yields the percent change in the base currency, not in the quoted currency.

Let's illustrate the usefulness of this calculation with a simple example. Suppose that on February 1 of the current year, the exchange rate between the Norwegian *krone* (NOK) and the U.S. dollar was NOK 5/$. On March 1 of the current year, suppose the exchange rate stood at NOK 4/$. What is the change in the value of the base currency, the dollar? If we plug these numbers into our formula, we arrive at the following change in the value of the dollar:

$$\text{Percent change (\%)} = \frac{4 - 5}{5} \times 100 = -20\%$$

Thus, the value of the dollar has fallen 20 percent. In other words, one U.S. dollar buys 20 percent fewer Norwegian *krone* on March 1 than it did on February 1.

To calculate the change in the value of the Norwegian *krone,* we must first calculate the indirect exchange rate on the *krone*. This step is necessary because we want to make the *krone* our base currency. Using the formula presented earlier, we obtain an exchange rate of $.20/NOK ($1 \div$ NOK 5) on February 1 and an exchange rate of $.25/NOK ($1 \div$ NOK 4) on March 1. Plugging these rates into our percent-change formula, we get:

$$\text{Percent change (\%)} = \frac{.25 - .20}{.20} \times 100 = 25\%$$

Thus the value of the Norwegian *krone* has risen 25 percent. One Norwegian *krone* buys 25 percent more U.S. dollars on March 1 than it did on February 1.

How important is this difference to businesspeople and exchange traders? Consider that the typical trading unit in the foreign exchange market (called a *round lot*) is $5 million. Therefore, a $5 million purchase of *krone* on February 1 would yield NOK 25 million. But because the dollar has lost 20 percent of its buying power by March 1, a $5 million purchase would fetch only NOK 20 million—5 million fewer *krone* than a month earlier.

International Monetary System

LEARNING OBJECTIVES

After studying this chapter, you should be able to

1. Explain how exchange rates influence the activities of domestic and international companies.

2. Identify the factors that help determine exchange rates and their impact on business.

3. Describe the primary methods of forecasting exchange rates.

4. Discuss the evolution of the current international monetary system and explain how it operates.

A Look Back

Chapter 9 examined how the international capital market and foreign exchange market operate. We also learned how exchange rates are calculated and how different rates are used in international business.

A Look at This Chapter

This chapter extends our knowledge of exchange rates and international financial markets. We examine factors that help determine exchange rates and explore rate-forecasting techniques. We discuss international attempts to manage exchange rates and review recent currency problems in Russia, Argentina, and other emerging markets.

A Look Ahead

Chapter 11 introduces the topic of the last part of this book—international business management. We will explore the specific strategies and organizational structures that companies use in accomplishing their international business objectives.

EURO ROLLERCOASTER

BRUSSELS, Belgium—"Europe's Big Idea," "Ready, Set, Euros!" cried the headlines that greeted the launch of Europe's new currency, the euro. Not since the time of the Roman Empire has a currency circulated so widely in Europe. Greece even gave up its drachma, a currency it had used for nearly 3,000 years. The euro is the official currency for 17 European countries and is accepted as legal tender in a number of other European nations.

The euro initially traded at around one-for-one against the dollar. Its value began to rise significantly, and a euro soon could buy around $1.57. The rise of the euro demonstrated confidence in the future expected growth and development of nations in the euro zone. It also boosted the status of the euro as a global currency, one that could perhaps rival the U.S. dollar.

But the global credit crisis and subsequent recession exposed Europe's economies that were carrying too much national debt. By 2012, the euro could buy only around $1.25. In fact, speculation grew that Greece would exit the euro and return to its drachma, however unlikely that seemed. The euro rollercoaster rose and fell with each new revelation about the economic health of nations including Portugal, Ireland, Greece, and Spain. Shown here, a woman changes the digits on a display board at a currency exchange office in Bucharest, Romania.

The euro holds long-term benefits for European companies. Using a common currency in business transactions eliminates exchange-rate risk for companies in the euro zone and improves financial planning. It boosts competitiveness as synergies and economies of scale arise from mergers and acquisitions. Europe's exporters benefit from a weak euro because it lowers their prices on world markets. Some European companies who lost market share abroad when their currency was strong could perhaps win back some of those customers. As you read this chapter, consider how the international monetary system affects managerial decisions and firm performance.[1]

Source: ROBERT GHEMENT/Newscom

I n Chapter 9, we explained the fundamentals of how exchange rates are calculated and how different types of exchange rates are used. This chapter extends our understanding of the international financial system by exploring factors that determine exchange rates and various international attempts to manage them. We begin by learning how exchange-rate movements affect a company's activities. We then examine the factors that help determine currency values and, in turn, exchange rates. Next, we learn about different methods of forecasting exchange rates. We conclude this chapter by exploring the international monetary system and its performance.

How Exchange Rates Influence Business Activities

Movement in a currency's exchange rate affects the activities of both domestic and international companies. For example, exchange rates influence demand for a company's products in the global marketplace. A country with a currency that is *weak* (valued low relative to other currencies) will see a decline in the price of its exports and an increase in the price of its imports. Lower prices for the country's exports on world markets can give companies the opportunity to take market share away from companies whose products are priced high in comparison.

Furthermore, a company improves profits if it sells its products in a country with a *strong* currency (one that is valued high relative to other currencies) while sourcing from a country with a weak currency. For example, if a company pays its workers and suppliers in a falling local currency and sells its products in a rising currency, the company benefits by generating revenue in the strong currency while paying expenses in the weak currency. Yet, managers must take care not to view this type of price advantage as permanent because doing so can jeopardize a company's long-term competitiveness.

Exchange rates also affect the amount of profit a company earns from its international subsidiaries. The earnings of international subsidiaries are typically integrated into the parent company's financial statements *in the home currency*. Translating subsidiary earnings from a weak *host* country currency into a strong *home* currency *reduces* the amount of these earnings when stated in the home currency. Likewise, translating earnings into a weak home currency increases stated earnings in the home currency. Figure 10.1 shows exchange rates between the U.S. dollar and several major currencies.

The intentional lowering of the value of a currency by the nation's government is called **devaluation**. The reverse, the intentional raising of the value of a currency by the nation's government, is called **revaluation**. These concepts are not to be confused with the terms *weak currency* and *strong currency,* although their effects are similar.

devaluation
Intentionally lowering the value of a nation's currency.

revaluation
Intentionally raising the value of a nation's currency.

FIGURE 10.1

Exchange Rates of Major World Currencies

Source: Based on *Economic Report of the President*, Table B110, multiple years.

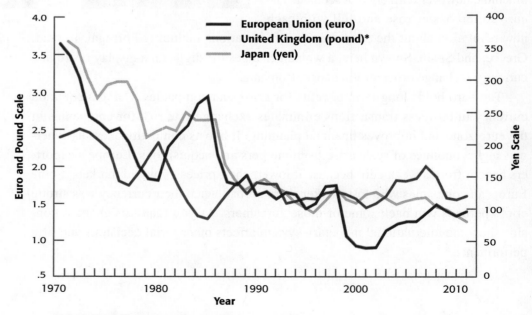

*Value is U.S. dollars per pound.
Prior to 1999, data for the Euro represents the German mark.

Devaluation lowers the price of a country's exports on world markets and increases the price of its imports because the value of the country's currency is now lower on world markets. Thus, a government might devalue its currency to give its domestic companies an edge over competition from other countries. But devaluation reduces the buying power of consumers in the nation. It can also allow inefficiencies to persist in domestic companies because there would then be less pressure to be concerned with production costs. Revaluation has the opposite effects: It increases the price of exports and reduces the price of imports.

Desire for Stability and Predictability

Unfavorable movements in exchange rates can be costly for domestic and international companies alike. Although methods do exist for insuring against potentially adverse movements in exchange rates, most of these are too expensive for small and medium-sized businesses. Moreover, as the unpredictability of exchange rates increases, so too does the cost of insuring against the accompanying risk. By contrast, *stable* exchange rates improve the accuracy of financial planning and make cash-flow forecasts more precise.

Managers also prefer that movements in exchange rates be *predictable*. Predictable exchange rates reduce the likelihood that companies will be caught off guard by sudden and unexpected rate changes. They also reduce the need for costly insurance (usually by currency hedging) against possible adverse movements in exchange rates. Rather than purchasing insurance, companies would be better off spending their money on more productive activities, such as developing new products or designing more-efficient production methods.

Figure 10.2 shows how the value of the U.S. dollar has changed over time. The figure reveals the dollar's periods of instability, which challenged the financial management capabilities of international companies.

QUICK STUDY 1

1. Why are exchange rates important to managers' decisions?
2. Explain the difference between *devaluation* and *revaluation*.
3. Why is it desirable for exchange rates to be stable and predictable?

What Factors Determine Exchange Rates?

To improve our knowledge of the factors that help determine exchange rates, we must first understand two important concepts: the *law of one price* and *purchasing power parity*. Each of these concepts tells us the level at which an exchange rate *should* be. While discussing these concepts, we will examine some factors that affect *actual* levels of exchange rates.

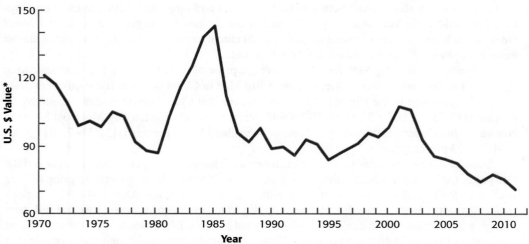

FIGURE 10.2

Value of the U.S. Dollar over Time

Source: Based on *Economic Report of the President*, Table B110, multiple years.

* Multilateral trade-weighted value of the U.S. dollar. (March 1973 = 100)

Law of One Price

An exchange rate tells us how much of one currency we must pay to receive a certain amount of another. But it does not tell us whether a specific product will actually cost us more or less in a particular country (as measured in our own currency). When we travel to another country, we discover that our own currency buys more or less than it does at home. In other words, we quickly learn that exchange rates do not guarantee or stabilize the buying power of our currency. Thus, we can lose purchasing power in some countries while gaining it in others. For example, a restaurant meal for you and a friend that costs $60 in New York might cost you 7,000 *yen* (about $80) in Japan and 400 *pesos* (about $30) in Mexico. Compared with your meal in New York, you've suffered a loss of purchasing power in Japan but benefited from increased purchasing power in Mexico.

law of one price
Principle that an identical item must have an identical price in all countries when the price is expressed in a common currency.

The **law of one price** stipulates that an identical product must have an identical price in all countries when the price is expressed in a common currency. For this principle to apply, products must be identical in quality and content in each country and be entirely produced within each country.

For example, suppose coal mined within the United States and Germany is of similar quality in each country. Suppose further that a kilogram of coal costs €1.5 in Germany and $1 in the United States. Therefore, the law of one price calculates the *expected* exchange rate between the euro and dollar to be €1.5/$. However, suppose the *actual* euro/dollar exchange rate as witnessed on currency markets is €1.2/$. A kilogram of coal still costs $1 in the United States and €1.5 in Germany. But to pay for German coal *with dollars denominated after the change in the exchange rate,* one must convert not just $1 into euros, but $1.25 (the expected exchange rate divided by the actual exchange rate, or €1.5 ÷ $1.2). Thus, the price of coal is higher in Germany than in the United States.

Moreover, because the law of one price is being violated in our example, an *arbitrage* opportunity arises—that is, an opportunity to buy a product in one country and sell it in a country where it has a higher value. For example, one could earn a profit by buying coal at $1 per kilogram in the United States and selling it at $1.25 (€1.5) per kilogram in Germany. But note that as traders begin buying in the United States and selling in Germany, greater demand drives *up* the price of U.S. coal, whereas greater supply drives *down* the price of German coal. Eventually, the price of coal in both countries will settle somewhere between the previously low U.S. price and the previously high German price.

If it seems that the arbitrage opportunity would disappear for the same reason that it arose, that is essentially the case. Some companies constantly seek new opportunities as they themselves arbitrage old ones out of existence. In other words, it is the nature of arbitrage to even out excessive fluctuation by destroying its own profitability.

MCCURRENCY The usefulness of the law of one price is that it helps us determine whether a currency is overvalued or undervalued. *The Economist* magazine publishes what it calls its "Big Mac Index" of exchange rates. This index uses the law of one price to determine the exchange rate that *should* exist between the U.S. dollar and other major currencies. It employs the McDonald's Big Mac as its single product to test the law of one price. Why the Big Mac? Because each one is fairly identical in quality and content across national markets and is almost entirely produced within the nation in which it is sold.

According to the Big Mac Index, the average price of a McDonald's Big Mac sandwich was $3.73 in the United States. Meanwhile, a Big Mac in China cost a dollar-equivalent price of $1.95. According to the Big Mac Index, this means that China's *yuan* is undervalued by 48 percent ([{3.73 − 1.95} / 3.73] × −100 = −48 percent). By contrast, a Big Mac cost $7.20 in Norway, which means that Norway's *krone* is overvalued by 93 percent ([{3.73 − 7.20} / 3.73] × −100 = 93 percent).[2]

Such large discrepancies between a currency's exchange rate on currency markets and the rate predicted by the Big Mac Index are not surprising. For one thing, the selling price of food is affected by subsidies for agricultural products in most countries. Also, a Big Mac is not a "traded" product in the sense that one can buy Big Macs in low-priced countries and sell them in high-priced countries. Prices can also be affected because Big Macs are subject to different marketing strategies in different countries. Finally, countries impose different levels of sales tax on restaurant meals.

The drawbacks of the Big Mac Index reflect the fact that applying the law of one price to a single product is too simplistic a method for estimating exchange rates. Nonetheless, academic studies find that currency values tend to change in the direction suggested by the Big Mac Index.

Purchasing Power Parity

We introduced the concept of purchasing power parity in Chapter 4 when we discussed economic development. The concept is also useful in determining at what level an exchange rate should be. Recall that *purchasing power parity (PPP)* is the relative ability of two countries' currencies to buy the same "basket" of goods in those two countries. Thus, although the law of one price holds for single products, PPP is meaningful only when applied to a *basket* of goods. Let's look at an example to see why this is so.

Suppose 650 *baht* in Thailand will buy a bag of groceries that costs $30 in the United States. What do these two numbers tell us about the economic conditions of people in Thailand as compared with people in the United States? First, they help us compare the *purchasing power* of a Thai consumer with that of a consumer in the United States. But the question is, Are Thai consumers better off or worse off than their counterparts in the United States? To address this question, suppose the *gross national product (GNP) per capita* of each country is as follows:

Thai GNP/capita = 122,277 *baht*
U.S. GNP/capita = 26,980 dollars

Suppose also that the *exchange rate* between the two currencies is 41.45 *baht* = 1 dollar. With this figure, we can translate 122,277 *baht* into dollars: 122,277 ÷ 41.45 = $2,950. We can now restate our question: Do prices in Thailand enable a Thai consumer with $2,950 to buy more or less than a consumer in the United States with $26,980?

We already know that 650 *baht* will buy in Thailand what $30 will buy in the United States. Thus we calculate 650 ÷ 30 = 21.67 *baht* per dollar. Note that, whereas the exchange rate on currency markets is 41.45 *baht*/$, the *purchasing power parity rate* of the *baht* is 21.67/$. Let's now use this figure to calculate a different comparative rate between the two currencies. We can now recalculate Thailand's GNP per capita at PPP as follows: 122,277 ÷ 21.67 = 5,643. Thai consumers on average are not nearly as affluent as their counterparts in the United States. But when we consider the *goods and services that they can purchase with their baht*—not the amount of U.S. dollars that they can buy—we see that a GNP per capita at PPP of $5,643 more accurately portrays the real purchasing power of Thai consumers.

Our new calculation considers *price levels* in adjusting the relative values of the two currencies. In the context of exchange rates, *the principle of purchasing power parity can be interpreted as the exchange rate between two nations' currencies that is equal to the ratio of their price levels*. In other words, PPP tells us that a consumer in Thailand needs 21.67 units (not 41.45) of Thai currency to buy the same amount of products as a consumer in the United States can buy with one dollar.

As we can see in this example, the exchange rate at PPP (21.67/$) is normally different from the actual exchange rate in financial markets (41.45/$). Economic forces, says PPP theory, will push the actual market exchange rate toward that determined by PPP. If they do not, arbitrage opportunities will arise. PPP holds for internationally traded products that are not restricted by trade barriers and that entail few or no transportation costs. To earn a profit, arbitrageurs must be certain that the basket of goods purchased in the low-cost country would still be lower-priced in the high-cost country *after adding transportation costs, tariffs, taxes, and so forth*. Let's now see what impact inflation and interest rates have on exchange rates and purchasing power parity.

ROLE OF INFLATION Inflation is the result of the supply and demand for a currency. If additional money is injected into an economy that is not producing greater output, people will have more money to spend on the same amount of products as before. As growing demand for products outstrips stagnant supply, prices will rise and devour any increase in the amount of money that consumers have to spend. Therefore, inflation erodes people's purchasing power.

Impact of Money-Supply Decisions Because of the damaging effects of inflation, governments try to manage the supply of and demand for their currencies. They do this through the use of two types of policies designed to influence a nation's money supply. *Monetary*

A resident of Harare, Zimbabwe, holds a new 100 billion Zimbabwe dollar (ZWD) note he just withdrew from a local bank. A loaf of bread at that time cost about 6 million ZWD. Zimbabwe's rate of inflation rocketed to over 100,000 percent shortly before the government abandoned its currency in 2009. The Reserve Bank of Zimbabwe declared that transactions could instead legally use foreign currencies, including the South African rand, Botswana *pula*, British pound, and the U.S. dollar. Zimbabwe faces a falling gross domestic product per capita, crumbling infrastructure, and shortages of food, fuel, and other necessities due to poor economic policies.

Source: DESMOND KWANDE/Getty Images/Newscom

policy refers to activities that directly affect a nation's interest rates or money supply. Selling government securities reduces a nation's money supply because investors pay money to the government's treasury to acquire the securities. Conversely, when the government buys its own securities on the open market, cash is infused into the economy and the money supply increases.

Fiscal policy involves using taxes and government spending to influence the money supply indirectly. For example, to reduce the amount of money in the hands of consumers, governments increase taxes—people are forced to pay money to the government coffers. Conversely, lowering taxes increases the amount of money in the hands of consumers. Governments can also step up their own spending activities in order to increase the amount of money circulating in the economy or can cut government spending to reduce it.

Impact of Unemployment and Interest Rates Key factors in the inflation equation are a country's unemployment and interest rates. When unemployment rates are low, there is a shortage of labor and employers pay higher wages to attract employees. To maintain reasonable profit margins with higher labor costs, companies then usually raise the prices of their products, passing the cost of higher wages on to the consumer and causing inflation.

Interest rates (discussed in detail later in this chapter) affect inflation because they affect the cost of borrowing money. Low interest rates encourage people to take out loans to buy items such as homes and cars and to run up debt on credit cards. High interest rates prompt people to cut down on the amount of debt they carry because higher rates mean larger monthly payments on debt. Thus, one way to cool off an inflationary economy is to raise interest rates. Raising the cost of debt reduces consumer spending and makes business expansion more costly.

How Exchange Rates Adjust to Inflation An important component of the concept of PPP is that exchange rates adjust to different rates of inflation in different countries. Such adjustment is necessary to maintain PPP between nations. Suppose that at the beginning of the year the exchange rate between the Mexican *peso* and the U.S. dollar is 8 *pesos/*\$ (or \$0.125/*peso*). Also suppose that inflation is pushing consumer prices higher in Mexico at an annual rate of 20 percent, whereas prices are rising just 3 percent per year in the United States. To find the new exchange rate (E_e) at the end of the year, we use the following formula:

$$E_e = E_b(1 + i_1)/(1 + i_2)$$

where E_b is the exchange rate at the beginning of the period, i_1 is the inflation rate in Country 1, and i_2 is the inflation rate in Country 2. Plugging the numbers for this example into the formula, we get the following:

$$E_e = 8_{pesos/\$}[(1 + 0.20)/(1 + 0.03)] = 9.3_{pesos/\$}$$

It is important to remember that *because the numerator of the exchange rate is in pesos, the inflation rate for Mexico must also be placed in the numerator for the ratio of inflation rates.* Thus, we see that the exchange rate adjusts from 8 *pesos*/$ to 9.3 *pesos*/$ because of the higher inflation rate in Mexico and the corresponding change in currency values. Higher inflation in Mexico reduces the number of U.S. dollars that a *peso* will buy and increases the number of *pesos* that a dollar will buy. In other words, whereas it had cost only 8 *pesos* to buy a dollar at the beginning of the year, it now costs 9.3 *pesos*.

In our example, companies based in Mexico must pay more in *pesos* for any supplies bought from the United States. But U.S. companies will pay less, in dollar terms, for supplies bought from Mexico. Also, tourists from the United States will be delighted, as vacationing in Mexico will be less expensive, but Mexicans will find the cost of visiting the United States is more expensive.

This discussion illustrates at least one of the difficulties facing countries with high rates of inflation. Both consumers and companies in countries experiencing rapidly increasing prices see their purchasing power eroded. Developing countries and countries in transition are those most often plagued by rapidly increasing prices.

ROLE OF INTEREST RATES To see how interest rates affect exchange rates between two currencies, we must first review the connection between inflation and interest rates within a single economy. We distinguish between two types of interest rates: *real interest rates* and *nominal interest rates*. Let's say that your local bank quotes you an interest rate on a new car loan. That rate is the nominal interest rate, which consists of the real interest rate plus an additional charge for inflation. The reasoning behind this principle is simple: The lender must be compensated for the erosion of its purchasing power during the loan period caused by inflation.

Fisher Effect Suppose your bank lends you money to buy a delivery van for your home-based business. Let's say that, given your credit-risk rating, the bank would normally charge you 5 percent annual interest. But if inflation is expected to be 2 percent over the next year, your annual rate of interest will be 7 percent: 5 percent real interest plus 2 percent to cover inflation. The principle that relates inflation to interest rates is called the **Fisher effect**—the principle that the nominal interest rate is the sum of the real interest rate and the expected rate of inflation over a specific period. We write this relation between inflation and interest rates as follows:

Fisher effect
Principle that the nominal interest rate is the sum of the real interest rate and the expected rate of inflation over a specific period.

$$\text{Nominal Interest Rate} = \text{Real Interest Rate} + \text{Inflation Rate}$$

If money were free from all controls when transferred internationally, the real rate of interest should be the same in all countries. To see why this is true, suppose that real interest rates are 4 percent in Canada and 6 percent in the United States. This situation creates an arbitrage opportunity: Investors could borrow money in Canada at 4 percent, lend it in the United States at 6 percent, and earn a profit on the 2 percent spread in interest rates. If enough people took advantage of this opportunity, interest rates would go up in Canada, where demand for money would become heavier, and down in the United States, where the money supply was growing. Again, the arbitrage opportunity would disappear because of the same activities that made it a reality. That is why real interest rates must theoretically remain equal across countries.

We saw earlier the relation between inflation and exchange rates. The Fisher effect clarifies the relation between inflation and interest rates. Now, let's investigate the relation between exchange rates and interest rates. To illustrate this relation, we refer to the **international Fisher effect**—the principle that a difference in nominal interest rates supported by two countries' currencies will cause an equal but opposite change in their *spot exchange rates*. Recall from Chapter 9 that the spot rate is the rate quoted for delivery of the traded currency within two business days.

international Fisher effect
Principle that a difference in nominal interest rates supported by two countries' currencies will cause an equal but opposite change in their spot exchange rates.

Because real interest rates are theoretically equal across countries, any difference in interest rates in two countries must be due to different expected rates of inflation. A country that is experiencing inflation higher than that of another country should see the value of its currency fall. If so, the exchange rate must be adjusted to reflect this change in value. For example, suppose nominal interest rates are 5 percent in Australia and 3 percent in Canada. Expected inflation in Australia, then, is 2 percent higher than in Canada. The international Fisher effect predicts that the value of the Australian dollar will fall by 2 percent against the Canadian dollar.

EVALUATING PPP   PPP is better at predicting long-term exchange rates (more than 10 years), but accurate forecasts of short-term rates are more beneficial to international managers. Even short-term plans must assume certain things about future economic and political conditions in different countries, including added costs, trade barriers, and investor psychology.

Impact of Added Costs   There are many possible reasons for the failure of PPP to predict exchange rates accurately. For example, PPP assumes no transportation costs. Suppose that the same basket of goods costs $100 in the United States and 950 *krone*r ($150) in Norway. Seemingly, one could make a profit through arbitrage by purchasing these goods in the United States and selling them in Norway. However, if it costs another $60 to transport the goods to Norway, the total cost of the goods once they arrive in Norway will be $160. Thus, no shipment will occur. Because no arbitrage opportunity exists after transportation costs are added, there will be no leveling of prices between the two markets and the price discrepancy will persist. Thus, even if PPP predicts that the Norwegian *krone* is overvalued, the effect of transportation costs will keep the dollar/*krone* exchange rate from adjusting. In a world in which transportation costs exist, PPP does not always correctly predict shifts in exchange rates.

Impact of Trade Barriers   PPP also assumes that there are no barriers to international trade. However, such barriers certainly do exist. Governments establish trade barriers for many reasons, including helping domestic companies remain competitive and preserving jobs for their citizens. Suppose the Norwegian government in our earlier example imposes a 60 percent tariff on the $100 basket of imported goods or makes its importation illegal. Because no leveling of prices or exchange-rate adjustment will occur, PPP will fail to predict exchange rates accurately.

Impact of Business Confidence and Psychology   Finally, PPP overlooks the human aspect of exchange rates—the role of people's confidence and beliefs about a nation's economy and the value of its currency. Many countries gauge confidence in their economies by conducting a *business confidence survey*. The largest survey of its kind in Japan is called the *tankan* survey. It gauges business confidence four times each year among 10,000 companies.

Investor confidence in the value of a currency plays an important role in determining its exchange rate. Suppose several currency traders believe that the Indian *rupee* will increase in value. They will buy Indian *rupees* at the current price, sell them if the value increases, and earn a profit. However, suppose that all traders share the same belief and all follow the same course of action. The activity of the traders themselves will be sufficient to push the value of the Indian *rupee* higher. It does not matter why traders believed the price would increase. As long as enough people act on a similar belief regarding the future value of a currency, its value will change accordingly.

That is why nations try to maintain the confidence of investors, businesspeople, and consumers in their economies. Lost confidence causes companies to put off investing in new products and technologies and to delay the hiring of additional employees. Consumers tend to increase their savings and not increase their debts if they have lost confidence in an economy. These kinds of behaviors act to weaken a nation's currency.

QUICK STUDY 2

1. Define the *law of one price,* and explain its limitations.
2. What is *purchasing power parity* in the context of exchange rates?
3. Briefly explain how both inflation and interest rates influence exchange rates.
4. What are the limitations of PPP in predicting exchange rates?

Forecasting Exchange Rates

Before undertaking any international business activity, managers should estimate future exchange rates and consider the impact of currency values on earnings. This section explores two distinct views regarding how accurately future exchange rates can be predicted by forward exchange rates—the rate agreed on for foreign exchange payment at a future date. We also take a brief look at different techniques for forecasting exchange rates.

Efficient Market View

A great deal of debate revolves around the issue of whether markets themselves are efficient or inefficient in forecasting exchange rates. A market is *efficient* if prices of financial instruments quickly reflect new public information made available to traders. The **efficient market view** thus holds that prices of financial instruments reflect all publicly available information at any given time. As applied to exchange rates, this means that forward exchange rates are accurate forecasts of future exchange rates.

Recall from Chapter 9 that a *forward exchange rate* reflects a market's expectations about the future values of two currencies. In an efficient currency market, forward exchange rates reflect all relevant publicly available information at any given time; they are considered the best possible predictors of exchange rates. Proponents of this view hold that there is no other publicly available information that could improve the forecast of exchange rates over that provided by forward rates. To accept this view is to believe that companies waste time and money collecting and examining information thought to affect future exchange rates. But there is always a certain amount of deviation between forward and actual exchange rates. The fact that forward exchange rates are less than perfect inspires companies to search for more-accurate forecasting techniques.

efficient market view
View that prices of financial instruments reflect all publicly available information at any given time.

Inefficient Market View

The **inefficient market view** holds that prices of financial instruments do not reflect all publicly available information. Proponents of this view believe that companies can search for new pieces of information to improve forecasting. But the cost of searching for further information must not outweigh the benefits of its discovery.

Naturally, the inefficient market view is more compelling when the existence of private information is considered. Suppose that a single currency trader holds privileged information regarding a future change in a nation's economic policy—information that she believes will affect that nation's exchange rate. Because the market is unaware of this information, it is not reflected in forward exchange rates. Our trader will no doubt earn a profit by acting on her store of private information.

Now that we understand the two basic views related to market efficiency, let's look at the specific methods that companies use to forecast exchange rates.

inefficient market view
View that prices of financial instruments do not reflect all publicly available information.

Forecasting Techniques

The issue of whether markets are efficient or inefficient forecasters of exchange rates leads to the question of whether experts can improve on the forecasts of forward exchange rates in *either* an efficient or inefficient market. As we have already seen, some analysts believe that forecasts of exchange rates can be improved by uncovering information not reflected in forward exchange rates. In fact, companies exist to provide exactly this type of service. There are two main forecasting techniques based on this belief in the value of added information—fundamental analysis and technical analysis.

FUNDAMENTAL ANALYSIS **Fundamental analysis** uses statistical models based on fundamental economic indicators to forecast exchange rates. These models are often quite complex, with many variations reflecting different possible economic conditions. These models include economic variables such as inflation, interest rates, money supply, tax rates, and government spending. Such analyses also often consider a country's balance-of-payments situation (see Chapter 7) and its tendency to intervene in markets to influence the value of its currency.

fundamental analysis
Technique that uses statistical models based on fundamental economic indicators to forecast exchange rates.

TECHNICAL ANALYSIS Another method of forecasting exchange rates is **technical analysis**—a technique that uses charts of past trends in currency prices and other factors to forecast exchange rates. Using highly statistical models and charts of past data trends, analysts examine conditions that prevailed during changes in exchange rates, and they try to estimate the timing, magnitude, and direction of future changes. Many forecasters combine the techniques of both fundamental and technical analyses to arrive at potentially more-accurate forecasts.

technical analysis
Technique that uses charts of past trends in currency prices and other factors to forecast exchange rates.

Difficulties of Forecasting

The business of forecasting exchange rates is a rapidly growing industry. This trend seems to provide evidence that a growing number of people believe that improving on the forecasts of

CULTURE MATTERS   The Long Arm of the Law

Culture can affect the degree of oversight that a government imposes on its business environment. Here are several U.S. agencies that monitor business activity:

- **U.S. Patent and Trademark Office (USPTO).** The USPTO is a noncommercial federal bureau within the Department of Commerce. By issuing patents, it provides incentives to invent, invest in, and disclose new technologies worldwide. By registering trademarks, it protects business investment and safeguards consumers against confusion and deception. By disseminating patent and trademark information, it facilitates the development and sharing of new technologies worldwide.
- **U.S. International Trade Commission (USITC).** The USITC is an independent, quasi-judicial federal agency. It provides trade expertise to both the legislative and executive branches of government, determines the impact of imports on U.S. industries, and directs actions against certain unfair trade practices such as patent, trademark, and copyright infringement. The agency has broad investigative powers on matters of trade and is a national resource where trade data are gathered and analyzed.
- **Federal Trade Commission (FTC).** The FTC enforces a variety of federal antitrust and consumer protection laws. It seeks to ensure that the nation's markets function competitively and are vigorous, efficient, and free of undue restrictions. The commission also works to enhance the smooth operation of the marketplace by eliminating acts or practices that are unfair or deceptive. In general, the commission's efforts are directed toward stopping actions that threaten consumers' opportunities to exercise informed choice.
- **U.S. Consumer Product Safety Commission (CPSC).** The CPSC is an independent federal regulatory agency created to protect the public from injury and death associated with some 15,000 types of consumer products, including car seats, bicycles and bike helmets, lawnmowers, toys, and walkers. It also provides information for businesses regarding the export of non-compliant, misbranded, or banned products.
- **Want to Know More?** Visit the websites of the following government agencies: USPTO (www.uspto.gov), USITC (www.usitc.gov), FTC (www.ftc.gov), and CPSC (www.cpsc.gov).

Source: Federal Trade Commission website (www.ftc.gov); U.S. Consumer Product Safety Commission website (www.cpsc.gov); U.S. Patent and Trademark Office website (www.uspto.gov); U.S. International Trade Commission website (www.usitc.gov).

exchange rates embodied in forward rates is possible. Difficulties of forecasting remain, however. Despite the existence of highly sophisticated statistical techniques in the hands of well-trained analysts, forecasting is not a pure science. Few, if any, forecasts are ever completely accurate because of unexpected events that occur throughout the forecast period.

Beyond the problems associated with the data used by these techniques, failings can be traced to the human element involved in forecasting. For example, people might miscalculate the importance of economic news becoming available to the market, placing too much emphasis on some elements and ignoring others.

Another factor that adds to the difficulty of forecasting exchange rates is changes in government regulation of business. Regulatory changes can improve or detract from the economic outlook for a nation's economy. As forecasts predict economic improvement or worsening, the exchange rate between a nation's currency and that of other nations also changes. Furthermore, a nation's culture tends to influence the emphasis its people place on regulation of private business. To read about several agencies responsible for the enforcement of U.S. business laws, see this chapter's Culture Matters box, titled "The Long Arm of the Law."

QUICK STUDY 3

1. What are the two market views regarding exchange-rate forecasting? Explain each briefly.
2. Identify the two main methods of forecasting exchange rates. What are the difficulties of forecasting?

Evolution of the International Monetary System

So far in this chapter, we have discussed how companies are affected by changes in exchange rates and why managers prefer exchange rates to be stable and predictable. We have seen how inflation and interest rates affect currency values, and in turn exchange rates, in different countries. We have also learned that, despite attempts to forecast exchange rates accurately, difficulties remain.

For all these reasons, governments develop systems designed to manage exchange rates among their currencies. Groups of nations have created both formal and informal agreements to control exchange rates among their currencies. The present-day **international monetary system** is the collection of agreements and institutions that govern exchange rates. In this section, we briefly trace the evolution of the current international monetary system and examine its performance.

international monetary system
Collection of agreements and institutions that govern exchange rates.

Early Years: The Gold Standard

In the earliest days of international trade, gold was the internationally accepted currency for payment of goods and services. Using gold as a medium of exchange in international trade had several advantages. First, the limited supply of gold made it a commodity in high demand. Second, because gold is highly resistant to corrosion, it was able to be traded and stored for hundreds of years. Third, because it could be melted into either small coins or large bars, gold was a good medium of exchange for both small and large purchases.

But gold also had its disadvantages. First, the weight of gold made transporting it expensive. Second, when a transport ship sank at sea, the gold also sank to the ocean floor and was lost. Thus, merchants wanted a new way to make their international payments without the need to haul large amounts of gold around the world. The solution was found in the **gold standard**—an international monetary system in which nations linked the value of their paper currencies to specific values of gold. Britain was the first nation to implement the gold standard in the early 1700s.

gold standard
International monetary system in which nations link the value of their paper currencies to specific values of gold.

PAR VALUE The gold standard required a nation to fix the value (price) of its currency to an ounce of gold. The value of a currency expressed in terms of gold is called its *par value*. Each nation then guaranteed to convert its paper currency into gold for anyone demanding it at its par value. The calculation of each currency's par value was based on the concept of purchasing power parity. This provision made the purchasing power of gold the same everywhere and maintained the purchasing power of currencies across nations.

All nations fixing their currencies to gold also indirectly linked their currencies to one another. Because the gold standard *fixed* nations' currencies to the value of gold, it is called a **fixed exchange-rate system**—one in which the exchange rate for converting one currency into another is fixed by international governmental agreement. This system and the use of par values made calculating exchange rates between any two currencies a very simple matter. For example, under the gold standard, the U.S. dollar was originally fixed at $20.67/oz of gold and the British pound at £4.2474/oz. The exchange rate between the dollar and pound was $4.87/£ (which is $20.67 ÷ £4.2474).

fixed exchange-rate system
System in which the exchange rate for converting one currency into another is fixed by international agreement.

ADVANTAGES OF THE GOLD STANDARD The gold standard was quite successful in its early years of operation. In fact, this early record of success is causing some economists and policy makers to call for its rebirth today. Three main advantages of the gold standard underlie its early success.

First, the gold standard drastically *reduced the risk in exchange rates* because it maintains highly fixed exchange rates between currencies. Deviations that did arise were much smaller than they are under a system of freely floating currencies. The more stable exchange rates are, the less companies are affected by actual or potential adverse changes in them. Because the gold standard significantly reduced the risk in exchange rates and, therefore, the risks and costs of trade, international trade grew rapidly following its introduction.

Second, the gold standard *imposed strict monetary policies* on all countries that participated in the system. Recall that the gold standard required governments to convert paper currency into gold if demanded by holders of the currency. If all holders of a nation's paper currency decided to trade it for gold, the government must have had an equal amount of gold reserves to pay them. That is why a government could not allow the volume of its paper currency to grow faster than the growth in its reserves of gold. By limiting the growth of a nation's money supply, the gold standard also was effective in controlling inflation.

Third, the gold standard could *help correct a nation's trade imbalance*. Suppose Australia was importing more than it was exporting (experiencing a trade deficit). As gold flowed out of Australia to pay for imports, its government had to decrease the supply of paper currency in the domestic economy because it could not have paper currency in excess of its gold reserves. As the money supply fell, so did prices of goods and services in Australia because demand was falling (consumers had less to spend)—whereas the supply of goods was unchanged. Meanwhile, falling prices of Australian-made goods caused Australian exports to become cheaper on world markets. Exports rose until Australia's international trade was once again in balance. The exact opposite occurred in the case of a trade surplus: The inflow of gold supported an increase in the supply of paper currency, which increased demand for, and therefore the cost of, goods and services. Thus, exports fell in reaction to their higher price until trade was once again in balance.

COLLAPSE OF THE GOLD STANDARD Nations involved in the First World War needed to finance their enormous war expenses, and they did so by printing more paper currency. This certainly violated the fundamental principle of the gold standard and forced nations to abandon the standard. The aggressive printing of paper currency caused rapid inflation for these nations. When the United States returned to the gold standard in 1934, it adjusted its par value from $20.67/oz of gold to $35.00/oz to reflect the lower value of the dollar that resulted from inflation. Thus, the U.S. dollar had undergone devaluation. Yet Britain returned to the gold standard several years earlier at its previous level, which did not reflect the effect inflation had on its currency.

Because the gold standard links currencies to one another, devaluation of one currency in terms of gold affects the exchange rates between currencies. The decision of the United States to devalue its currency and Britain's decision not to do so lowered the price of U.S. exports on world markets and increased the price of British goods imported into the United States. For example, whereas it had previously required $4.87 to purchase one British pound, it now required $8.24 (which is $35.00 ÷ £4.2474). This forced the cost of a £10 tea set exported from Britain to the United States to go from $48.70 before devaluation to $82.40 after devaluation. This drastically increased the price of imports from Britain (and other countries), lowering its export earnings. As countries devalued their currencies in retaliation, a period of "competitive devaluation" resulted. To improve their trade balances, nations chose arbitrary par values to which they devalued their currencies. People quickly lost faith in the gold standard because it was no longer an accurate indicator of a currency's true value. By 1939, the gold standard was effectively dead.

Bretton Woods Agreement

Bretton Woods Agreement
Agreement (1944) among nations to create a new international monetary system based on the value of the U.S. dollar.

In 1944, representatives from 44 nations met in the New Hampshire resort town of Bretton Woods to lay the foundation for a new international monetary system. The resulting **Bretton Woods Agreement** was an accord among nations to create a new international monetary system based on the value of the U.S. dollar. The new system was designed to balance the strict discipline of the gold standard with the flexibility that countries needed in order to deal with temporary domestic monetary difficulties. Let's take a brief look at the most important features of this system.

FIXED EXCHANGE RATES The Bretton Woods Agreement incorporated fixed exchange rates by tying the value of the U.S. dollar directly to gold and the value of other currencies to the value of the dollar. The par value of the U.S. dollar was fixed at $35/oz of gold. Other currencies were then given par values against the U.S. dollar instead of gold. For example, the par value of the British pound was established as $2.40/£. Member nations were expected to keep their currencies from deviating more than 1 percent above or below their par values. The Bretton Woods Agreement also improved on the gold standard by extending the right to exchange gold for dollars only to national governments, rather than to anyone who demanded it.

fundamental disequilibrium
Economic condition in which a trade deficit causes a permanent negative shift in a country's balance of payments.

BUILT-IN FLEXIBILITY The new system also incorporated a degree of built-in flexibility. For example, although competitive currency devaluation was ruled out, large devaluation was allowed under the extreme set of circumstances called **fundamental disequilibrium**—an economic condition in which a trade deficit causes a permanent negative shift in a country's balance of payments. In this situation, a nation can devalue its currency more than 10 percent. Yet devaluation under these circumstances should accurately reflect a permanent economic change for the country in question, not temporary misalignments.

WORLD BANK To provide funding for countries' efforts toward economic development, the Bretton Woods Agreement created the *World Bank*—officially called the International Bank for Reconstruction and Development (IBRD). The immediate purpose of the World Bank (www.worldbank.org) was to finance European reconstruction following the Second World War. It later shifted its focus to the general financial needs of developing countries. The World Bank finances many types of economic development projects in Africa, South America, and Southeast Asia.

The World Bank also offers funds to countries that are unable to obtain capital from commercial sources for some projects that are considered too risky. The bank often undertakes projects to develop transportation networks, power facilities, and agricultural and educational programs.

INTERNATIONAL MONETARY FUND In addition, the Bretton Woods Agreement established the *International Monetary Fund (IMF)* as the agency to regulate the fixed exchange rates and to enforce the rules of the international monetary system. At the time of its formation, the IMF (www.imf.org) had just 29 members—185 countries belong today. Included among the main purposes of the IMF are:[3]

- Promoting international monetary cooperation.
- Facilitating expansion and balanced growth of international trade.
- Promoting exchange stability, maintaining orderly exchange arrangements, and avoiding competitive exchange devaluation.
- Making the resources of the fund temporarily available to members.
- Shortening the duration and lessening the degree of disequilibrium in the international balance of payments of member nations.

Special Drawing Right (SDR) World financial reserves of dollars and gold grew scarce in the 1960s, at a time when the activities of the IMF demanded greater amounts of dollars and gold. The IMF reacted by creating what is called a **special drawing right (SDR)**—an IMF asset whose value is based on a weighted "basket" of four currencies, including the U.S. dollar, European Union (EU) euro, Japanese *yen*, and British pound. Figure 10.3 shows the "weight" each currency contributes to the overall value of the SDR. The value of the SDR is set daily and changes with increases and declines in the values of its underlying currencies. Today there are more than 204 billion SDRs in existence worth slightly less than $300 billion (1 SDR equals about $1.47).[4] The significance of the SDR is that it is the unit of account for the IMF. Each nation is assigned a quota based on the size of its economy when it enters the IMF. Payment of this quota by each nation provides the IMF with the funds it needs to make short-term loans to members.

special drawing right (SDR)
IMF asset whose value is based on a "weighted basket" of four currencies.

COLLAPSE OF THE BRETTON WOODS AGREEMENT The system developed at Bretton Woods worked quite well for about 20 years—an era that boasted unparalleled stability in exchange rates. But in the 1960s, the Bretton Woods system began to falter. The main problem was that the United States was experiencing a trade deficit (imports were exceeding exports) and a budget deficit (expenses were outstripping revenues). Governments that were holding dollars began to doubt that the U.S. government had an adequate amount of gold reserves to redeem all its paper currency held outside the country. When they began demanding gold in exchange for dollars, a large sell-off of dollars on world financial markets followed.

Smithsonian Agreement In August 1971, the U.S. government held less than one-fourth of the amount of gold needed to redeem all U.S. dollars in circulation. In late 1971, the United

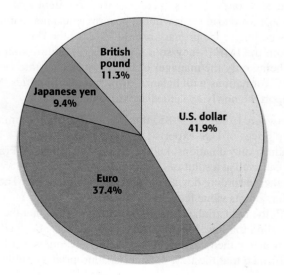

FIGURE 10.3

Valuation of the Special Drawing Right (SDR)

Source: Based on International Monetary Fund website (www.imf.org), Special Drawing Rights data section.

Smithsonian Agreement
Agreement (1971) among IMF members to restructure and strengthen the international monetary system created at Bretton Woods.

States and other countries reached the so-called **Smithsonian Agreement** to restructure and strengthen the international monetary system. The three main accomplishments of the Smithsonian Agreement were (1) to lower the value of the dollar in terms of gold to $38/oz, (2) to increase the values of other countries' currencies against the dollar, and (3) to increase to 2.25 percent from 1 percent the band within which currencies were allowed to float.

Final Days The success of the Bretton Woods system relied on the U.S. dollar remaining a strong reserve currency. High inflation and a persistent trade deficit in the United States kept the dollar weak, however, which demonstrated a fundamental flaw in the system. The weak U.S. dollar strained the capabilities of central banks in Japan and most European countries to maintain exchange rates with the dollar. Because these nations' currencies were tied to the U.S. dollar, as the dollar continued to fall, so too did their currencies. Britain left the system in the middle of 1972 and allowed the pound to float freely against the dollar. The Swiss abandoned the system in early 1973. In January 1973, the dollar was again devalued, this time to around $42/oz of gold. But even this move was not enough. As nations began dumping their reserves of the dollar on a massive scale, currency markets were temporarily closed to prevent further selling of the dollar. When markets reopened, the values of most major currencies were floating against the U.S. dollar. The era of an international monetary system based on *fixed* exchange rates was over.

QUICK STUDY 4

1. How did the *gold standard* function? Briefly describe its evolution and collapse.
2. Describe the most important features of the *Bretton Woods Agreement*.
3. What factors led to the demise of the monetary system created at Bretton Woods?

A Managed Float System Emerges

The Bretton Woods system collapsed because of its heavy dependence on the stability of the dollar. As long as the dollar remained strong, it worked well. But when the dollar weakened, it failed to perform properly. Originally, the new system of *floating* exchange rates was viewed as a temporary solution to the shortcomings of the Bretton Woods and Smithsonian Agreements. But no new coordinated international monetary system was forthcoming. Rather, there emerged several independent efforts to manage exchange rates.

Jamaica Agreement
Agreement (1976) among IMF members to formalize the existing system of floating exchange rates as the new international monetary system.

managed float system
Exchange-rate system in which currencies float against one another, with governments intervening to stabilize their currencies at particular target exchange rates.

free float system
Exchange-rate system in which currencies float freely against one another, without governments intervening in currency markets.

JAMAICA AGREEMENT By January 1976, returning to a system of fixed exchange rates seemed unlikely. Therefore, world leaders met to draft the so-called **Jamaica Agreement**—an accord among members of the IMF to formalize the existing system of floating exchange rates as the new international monetary system. The Jamaica Agreement contained several main provisions. First, it endorsed a **managed float system** of exchange rates—that is, a system in which currencies float against one another, with governments intervening to stabilize their currencies at particular target exchange rates. This is in contrast to a **free float system**—a system in which currencies float freely against one another without governments intervening in currency markets.

Second, gold was no longer the primary reserve asset of the IMF. Member countries could retrieve their gold from the IMF if they so desired. Third, the mission of the IMF was augmented: Rather than being only the manager of a fixed exchange-rate system, it was now also a "lender of last resort" for nations with balance-of-payment difficulties. Member contributions were increased to support the newly expanded activities of the IMF.

LATER ACCORDS Between 1980 and 1985, the U.S. dollar rose dramatically against other currencies, pushing up prices of U.S. exports and adding once again to a U.S. trade deficit. The world's five largest industrialized nations, known as the "G5" (Britain, France, Germany, Japan, and the United States), arrived at a solution. The *Plaza Accord* was a 1985 agreement among the G5 nations to act together in forcing down the value of the U.S. dollar. The Plaza Accord caused traders to sell the dollar, and its value fell.

By February 1987, the industrialized nations were concerned that the value of the U.S. dollar was in danger of falling too low. Meeting in Paris, leaders of the "G7" nations (the G5 plus Italy and Canada) drew up another agreement. The *Louvre Accord* was a 1987 agreement among the G7 nations that affirmed that the U.S. dollar was appropriately valued and that they would intervene in currency markets to maintain its current market value. Once again, currency markets responded, and the dollar stabilized.

Today's Exchange-Rate Arrangements

Today's international monetary system remains in large part a managed float system, whereby most nations' currencies float against one another and governments engage in limited intervention to realign exchange rates. Within the larger monetary system, however, certain countries try to maintain more-stable exchange rates by tying their currencies to other currencies. Let's take a brief look at two ways nations attempt to do this.

PEGGED EXCHANGE-RATE ARRANGEMENT   Think of one country as a small lifeboat tethered to a giant cruise ship as it navigates choppy monetary waters. Many economists argue that rather than let their currencies face the tides of global currency markets alone, developing economies should tie them to other, more stable currencies. Pegged exchange-rate arrangements "peg" a country's currency to a more stable and widely used currency in international trade. Countries then allow the exchange rate to fluctuate within a specified margin (usually 1 percent) around a central rate.

Many small countries peg their currencies to the U.S. dollar, the EU euro, the special drawing right (SDR) of the IMF, or another individual currency. Belonging to this first category are the Bahamas, El Salvador, Iran, Malaysia, Netherlands Antilles, and Saudi Arabia. Other nations peg their currencies to groups, or "baskets," of currencies. For example, Bangladesh and Burundi tie their currencies (the *taka* and Burundi *franc,* respectively) to those of their major trading partners. Other members of this second group are Botswana, Fiji, Kuwait, Latvia, Malta, and Morocco.

CURRENCY BOARD   A **currency board** is a monetary regime that is based on an explicit commitment to exchange domestic currency for a specified foreign currency at a fixed exchange rate. The government with a currency board is legally bound to hold an amount of foreign currency that is at least equal to the amount of domestic currency. Because a currency board restricts a government from issuing additional domestic currency unless it has the foreign reserves to back it, it helps cap inflation. Thus, survival of a currency board depends on wise budget policies.

Thanks to a currency board, the country of Bosnia-Herzegovina built itself a strong and stable currency. Argentina had a currency board from 1991 until it was abandoned in early 2002, when the *peso* was allowed to float freely on currency markets. Other nations with currency boards include Brunei Darussalam, Bulgaria, Djibouti, and Lithuania.

Doing business in an era of a managed float international monetary system means that companies need to monitor currency values. For a look at several approaches companies can use to counter the effects of a strong currency and of a weak currency, see this chapter's Manager's Briefcase, titled "Adjusting to Currency Swings."

currency board
Monetary regime based on an explicit commitment to exchange domestic currency for a specified foreign currency at a fixed exchange rate.

European Monetary System

Following the collapse of the Bretton Woods system, leaders of many EU nations did not give up hope for a system that could stabilize currencies and reduce exchange-rate risk. Their efforts became increasingly important as trade between EU nations continued to expand. In 1979, these nations created the *European monetary system (EMS)*. The EMS was established to stabilize exchange rates, promote trade among nations, and keep inflation low through monetary discipline. The system was phased out when the EU adopted a single currency.

HOW THE SYSTEM WORKED   The mechanism that limited the fluctuations of EU members' currencies within a specified trading range (or *target zone*) was called the *exchange rate mechanism (ERM)*. Members were required to keep their currencies within 2.25 percent of the highest- and lowest-valued currencies. To illustrate, suppose that a weakening French *franc* was about to reach the 2.25 percent variation in its exchange rate with the German *mark*. The central banks of both France and Germany were to drive the value of the French *franc* higher—forcing the exchange rate away from the 2.25 percent fluctuation limit. How did they do so? By buying up French *francs* on currency markets, thereby increasing demand for the *franc* and forcing its value higher.

MANAGER'S BRIEFCASE Adjusting to Currency Swings

A *strong and rising currency* makes a nation's exports more expensive. Here's how companies can export successfully despite a strong currency:

- *Prune Operations.* Cut costs and boost efficiency by downsizing staff and reworking factories at home to maintain production levels, and pursue customers abroad when export earnings decline.
- *Adapt Products.* Win customer business and loyalty by tailoring your products to the needs of global customers, and your company may retain its business despite your higher prices.
- *Source Abroad.* Source abroad for raw materials and other inputs to the production process—your supplier will likely earn an extra profit, and you'll get a better deal than is available domestically.
- *Freeze Prices.* A last resort may be to freeze prices of goods in foreign markets—this might boost overall profits if sales improve.

A *weak and falling currency* makes a nation's imports more expensive. Here's how companies can adjust to a weak currency:

- *Source Domestically.* Source domestically for raw materials and components to lower the cost of production inputs, to avoid exchange-rate risk, and to shorten the supply chain.
- *Grow at Home.* Fight for the business of domestic customers now that imported products of foreign competitors are priced high because of their relatively strong currencies.
- *Push Exports.* Exploit the price advantage you get from your country's weak currency by expanding your reach and depth abroad—people love a good bargain in all countries.
- *Reduce Expenses.* Counteract the rising cost of imported energy by using the latest communication and transportation technologies to reduce air travel, cut utility bills, and slash shipping costs.

The EMS was quite successful in its early years. Currency realignments were infrequent, and inflation was fairly well controlled. But in late 1992, both the British pound and the Italian *lira* had been on the lower fringe of the allowable 2.25 percent fluctuation range with the German *mark* for some time. Currency speculators began unloading their pounds and *lira*. The central banks of neither Britain nor Italy had enough money to buy their currencies on the open market. As their currencies' values plummeted, they were forced to leave the ERM. The EMS was revised in late 1993 to allow currencies to fluctuate 15 percent up or down from the midpoint of the target zone. Although the Italian *lira* returned to the ERM in November 1996, the British pound remained outside the ERM. Many European nations moved to the euro as their currency (see Chapter 8), which eliminated the need for the ERM.

Of the three nations (Britain, Denmark, and Sweden) that qualify to use the euro but have opted out, only Denmark participates in what is called the *exchange rate mechanism II (ERM II)*. The ERM II was introduced January 1, 1999, and continues to function today. The aim of ERM II is to support nations that seek future membership in the European monetary union (see Chapter 8) by linking their currencies to the euro. As such, Latvia and Lithuania also currently participate in ERM II. The euro acts as the center of a *hub and spokes* model, to which each currency is linked on a bilateral basis. The currencies of participating countries have a central rate against the euro with acceptable fluctuation margins of 15 percent, although narrower margins can be arranged. Future accession countries to the EU are obliged to join the single currency once they satisfy the criteria of the Maastricht Treaty.

Recent Financial Crises

Despite the best efforts of nations to head off financial crises within the international monetary system, the world has experienced several wrenching crises in recent years. Let's examine the most prominent of these.

DEVELOPING NATIONS' DEBT CRISIS By the early 1980s, certain developing countries (especially in Latin America) had amassed huge debts payable not only to large international commercial banks but also to the IMF and the World Bank. In 1982, Mexico, Brazil, and Argentina announced that they would be unable to pay interest on their loans. At the same time, many of these countries were also experiencing runaway inflation. Many countries in Africa were facing similar problems.

To prevent a meltdown of the entire financial system, international agencies stepped in with a number of temporary solutions to the crisis. Repayment schedules were revised to put off repayment further into the future. Then, in 1989, U.S. Treasury Secretary Nicholas Brady unveiled the Brady Plan. The Brady Plan called for large-scale reduction of the debt owed by poorer nations, the exchange of old loans for new low-interest loans, and the making of debt instruments (based on these loans) that would be tradable on world financial markets. This last feature allowed a debtor country to receive a loan from an institution and then use it to buy special securities (called "Brady Bonds") on financial markets. Funds for these new loans came from private commercial banks and were backed by the IMF and the World Bank.

MEXICO'S *PESO* CRISIS Armed rebellion in the poor Mexican state of Chiapas and the assassination of a presidential candidate shook investors' faith in Mexico's financial system in 1993 and 1994. Capital flowing into Mexico was mostly in the form of stocks and bonds (portfolio investment) rather than factories and equipment (foreign direct investment). Portfolio investment fled Mexico for the United States as the Mexican *peso* grew weak and U.S. interest rates rose. A lending spree by Mexican banks, coupled with weak banking regulations, also played a role in delaying the government's response to the crisis. In late 1994, the Mexican *peso* was devalued, forcing a loss of purchasing power on the Mexican people.

In response to the crisis, the IMF and private commercial banks in the United States stepped in with about $50 billion in loans to shore up the Mexican economy. Thus, Mexico's *peso* crisis contributed to an additional boost in the level of IMF loans. Mexico repaid the loans ahead of schedule and once again has a sizable reserve of foreign exchange.

SOUTHEAST ASIA'S CURRENCY CRISIS The roar of the "four tiger" economies and those of other high-growth Asian nations suddenly fell silent in the summer of 1997. For 25 years, the economies of five Southeast Asian countries—Indonesia, Malaysia, the Philippines, Singapore, and Thailand—had wowed the world with growth rates twice those of most other countries. Even though many analysts projected continued growth for the region, and even though billions of dollars in investment flooded in from the West, savvy speculators were pessimistic.

On July 11, 1997, the speculators struck, selling off Thailand's *baht* on world currency markets. The selling forced an 18 percent drop in the value of the *baht* before speculators moved on to the Philippines and Malaysia. By November, the *baht* had plunged another 22 percent, and every other economy in the region was in a slump. The shock waves of Asia's crisis could be felt throughout the global economy.

Suddenly, countries thought to be strong emerging market economies—"tigers" to be emulated by other developing countries—were in need of billions of dollars to keep their economies from crumbling. When the dust settled, Indonesia, South Korea, and Thailand all needed IMF and World Bank funding. As incentives for these countries to begin the long process of economic restructuring, IMF loan packages came with a number of strings attached. For example, the Indonesian loan package involved three long-term goals to help put the Indonesian economy on a stronger footing: (1) to restore the confidence of international financial markets, (2) to restructure the domestic financial sector, and (3) to support domestic deregulation and trade reforms.

What caused the crisis in the first place? Well, it depends on whom you ask. Some believe it was caused by an Asian style of capitalism. They say that blame lies with poor regulation, the practice of extending loans to friends and relatives who are poor credit risks, and a lack of transparency regarding the financial health of banks and companies. Others point to poor management of these nations' short-term debt obligations. Still others argue that persistent current account deficits in these countries are what caused the large dumping of these nations' currencies. What really caused the crisis is probably a combination of all these forces.[5]

RUSSIA'S *RUBLE* CRISIS Russia had a whole host of problems throughout the 1990s—some were constant, others were intermittent. For starters, Russia was not immune to the events unfolding across Southeast Asia in the late 1990s. As investors became wary of potential problems in other emerging markets worldwide, stock market values in Russia plummeted. Another problem contributing to Russia's issues was depressed oil prices. Because Russia depends on oil production for a large portion of its gross domestic product (GDP), the low price of oil on world markets cut into the government's reserves of hard currency. Also cutting into the government's coffers was an unworkable tax-collection system and a large underground economy—meaning that most taxes went uncollected.

There also was the problem of inflation. We learned earlier in this chapter how an expanded amount of money chasing the same amount of goods forces prices higher. This is exactly what happened when Russia released prices in 1992. As prices skyrocketed, people dug beneath their mattresses where they had stashed their *rubles* during times when there were no goods to purchase. We also saw earlier how inflation eats away at the value of a nation's currency. Russia saw inflation take its exchange rate from less than 200 *rubles* to the dollar in early 1992 to more than 5,000 to the dollar in 1995.

Then in early 1996, as currency traders dumped the *ruble,* the Russian government found itself attempting to defend the ruble on currency markets. As its foreign exchange reserves dwindled in a hopeless effort, the government asked for, and received, a $10 billion aid package from the IMF. In return, Russia promised to reduce its debt (which was averaging about 7 percent of GDP), collect taxes owed it, cease printing inflation-stoking sums of currency, and peg its currency to the dollar.

Things seemed to improve for a while, but then in mid-1998 the government found itself once again trying to defend the ruble against speculative pressure on currency markets. In a single day, the government spent $1 billion trying to prop up the *ruble*'s value, forcing its hard currency reserves to shrivel to $14 billion. As it grew obvious that the government would soon be bankrupt, the IMF stepped in and promised Russia another $11 billion. But when it was alleged that some of the IMF loan had been funneled into offshore bank accounts, the IMF held up distribution of the money. On August 17, 1998, badly strapped for cash, the government announced that it would allow the *ruble* to devalue by 34 percent by the end of the year. It also declared a 90-day foreign-debt moratorium and announced a de facto default on the government's domestic bond obligations. On August 26, the Russian Central Bank announced that it would no longer be able to support the *ruble* on currency markets. In less than one month, its value fell 300 percent. Inflation shot up to 15 percent a month in August from 0.2 percent in July and reached 30 percent in the first week of September. By the time it was all over in late 1998, the IMF had lent Russia more than $22 billion.

ARGENTINA'S *PESO* CRISIS Argentina was the star of Latin America in the early and mid-1990s. Yet by late 2001, Argentina had been in recession for nearly four years, mainly because of Brazil's devaluation of its own currency in 1999—making Brazil's exports cheaper on world markets. Meanwhile, Argentina's goods remained relatively expensive because its own currency was linked to a very strong U.S. dollar through a currency board. As a result, Argentina saw much of its export business dry up and its economy slow significantly. By late 2001, the IMF had already promised $48 billion to rescue Argentina.

Things came to a head when the country began running out of money to service its debt obligations. The country finally defaulted on its $155 billion of public debt in early 2002, the largest default ever by any country. The government scrapped its currency board that linked the *peso*

Demonstrators shout slogans during a protest march marking a 24-hour general strike in central Athens. People were enraged by the tough fiscal measures the Greek government imposed in order to obtain vital loans from the European Union. The fiscal plan was a tough reminder for Greece that belonging to the group of countries that use the euro means abiding by the rules of the Stability and Growth Pact, which demands fiscal discipline. Demonstrators participating in this march carried banners, one of which read "Stability pact? No thank you."

Source: SIMELA PANTZARTZI/Newscom

to the U.S. dollar, and the *peso* quickly lost around 70 percent of its value on currency markets. The government, strapped for cash, seized the savings accounts of its citizens and restricted how much they could withdraw at a time.

Argentina has seen its economy ride a roller coaster of sorts since its 2001–2002 collapse. From 2001 through 2002, the economy shrank by 15 percent, unemployment shot up to 21 percent, and poverty engulfed 56 percent of its citizens. The government's plan of stimulating demand by raising wages, imposing price controls, keeping the *peso* low, and spending public funds worked for a time. But inflation reached 26 percent in 2012, cutting consumers' purchasing power and increasing poverty.

Future of the International Monetary System

As this textbook goes to print, there is great consternation in Europe over what will become of their single currency, the euro. Most experts agree that it will survive but at less value than it had during its first decade of life. Many European politicians blame speculators and others for their woes, echoing arguments heard in Southeast Asia during its currency crisis.[6]

But the sad fact is that nations in Europe have let their debt-to-GDP levels spiral completely out of control. For example, the EU and the IMF put together a series of rescue packages for one EU member, Greece. But it is likely that Greece will continue to have a debt level that is greater than its national GDP. Other nations such as Portugal, Ireland, Italy, and Spain will likely face similar, if less dire, austerity plans if they are to straighten out their finances. And at the time of this writing, there is still no guarantee that Greece, or Spain even, will not default on its debt obligations.[7]

Meanwhile, recurring crises in the international monetary system are raising calls for a new system that is designed to meet the challenges of a global economy. Many believe that the vestiges of the IMF created by the Bretton Woods Agreement are no longer adequate to insulate the world's economies from disruptions in a single country or a small group of countries.

Meanwhile, leaders of many developing and newly industrialized countries are bemoaning what global capital has done to their economies. Although some call for the elimination of the IMF and its replacement by institutions not yet clearly defined, more likely will be revision of the IMF and its policy prescriptions. Efforts have already been made to develop internationally accepted codes of good practice to allow comparisons of countries' fiscal and monetary practices. Countries have also been encouraged to be more open and clear regarding their financial policies. Transparency on the part of the IMF is also being increased to instill greater accountability on the part of its leadership. The IMF also is increasing its efforts at surveillance of member nations' macroeconomic policies and is increasing its abilities in the area of financial-sector analysis.

Yet, orderly ways must still be found to integrate international financial markets so that risks are better managed. Moreover, the private sector must become involved in the prevention and resolution of financial crises. Policy makers are concerned with the way money floods into developing economies when growth is strong and then just as quickly heads for the exits at the first sign of trouble. Furthermore, some argue that because the IMF bails out debtor countries, private-sector banks do not exercise adequate caution when loaning money in risky situations—after all, the IMF will be there to pay off the loans of debtor countries. Greater cooperation and understanding among the IMF, private-sector banks, and debtor nations are needed.

QUICK STUDY 5

1. Why did the world shift to a *managed float system* of exchange rates? Briefly describe the performance of this system.
2. What was the purpose of the European monetary system? Describe how it functioned and performed.
3. What role did the International Monetary Fund have in assisting nations during recent financial crises?

BOTTOM LINE FOR BUSINESS

Recent financial crises underscore the need for managers to fully understand the complexities of the international financial system. But this knowledge must be paired with vigilance of financial market conditions in order to manage businesses effectively. Here we focus on the main implications for business strategy and forecasting earnings and cash flows.

Implications for Business Strategy

Exchange rates influence all sorts of business activities for domestic and international companies. A *weak* currency (valued low relative to other currencies) lowers the price of a nation's exports on world markets and raises the price of imports. Lower prices make the country's exports more appealing on world markets. This gives companies the opportunity to take market share away from companies whose products are priced higher in comparison.

Although a government might devalue its currency to give domestic companies an edge over competition from other countries, devaluation reduces the buying power of the home country consumers. Devaluation might also allow inefficiencies to persist in domestic companies because it can lessen concern for production costs. A company improves its profits if it is selling in a country with a strong currency (one that is valued high relative to other currencies) while paying workers in a country with a weak currency. But companies that benefit from a temporary price advantage caused by exchange rates must not grow complacent about their own long-term competitiveness.

Forecasting Earnings and Cash Flows

Exchange rates also affect the amount of profit a company earns from its international subsidiaries. The earnings of international subsidiaries are typically integrated into the parent company's financial statements in the home currency. Translating subsidiary earnings from a weak host country currency into a strong home currency reduces the amount of these earnings when stated in the home currency. Likewise, translating earnings into a weak home currency increases stated earnings in the home currency.

Sudden, unfavorable movements in exchange rates can be costly for both domestic and international companies. On the other hand, stable exchange rates improve the accuracy of financial planning, including cash flow forecasts. Although companies can insure (usually by currency hedging) against potentially adverse movements in exchange rates, most available methods are too expensive for small and medium-sized businesses. Moreover, as the unpredictability of exchange rates increases, so too does the cost of insuring against the accompanying risk.

Managers also prefer movements in exchange rates to be predictable. Predictable exchange rates reduce the likelihood that companies will be caught off guard by sudden and unexpected rate changes. They also reduce the need for costly insurance against possible adverse movements in exchange rates. Rather than purchasing insurance, companies would be better off spending their money on more productive activities, such as developing new products or designing more-efficient production methods.

As we saw in this chapter, not only are a company's financial decisions affected by events in international financial markets, so too are production and marketing decisions. The next chapter begins our in-depth look at the main aspects of managing an international business. Our understanding of national business environments, international trade and investment, and the international financial system will serve us well as we embark on our tour of the nuances of international business management.

Chapter Summary

MyManagementLab
Go to **mymanagementlab.com** to complete the problems marked with this icon .

1. Explain how exchange rates influence the activities of domestic and international companies.
   - When a country's currency is *weak* (valued low relative to other currencies), the price of its exports on world markets declines (making exports more appealing on world markets) and the price of imports rises. A *strong* currency has the opposite effects.
   - A company can improve profits if it sells in a country with a *strong* currency (one that is valued high relative to other currencies) while paying workers at home in its own weak currency.
   - The intentional lowering of a currency's value by a nation's government is called *devaluation*; this lowers the price of a country's exports on world markets and increases the price of imports.
   - The intentional raising of a currency's value by a nation's government is called *revaluation*; this increases the price of exports and reduces the price of imports.
   - Translating subsidiary earnings from a weak *host* country currency into a strong *home* currency *reduces* the amount of these earnings when stated in the home currency, and vice versa.

2. Identify the factors that help determine exchange rates and their impact on business.
   - The *law of one price* says that when price is expressed in a common currency, an identical product must have an identical price in all countries.
   - The concept of *purchasing power parity (PPP)* can be interpreted as the exchange rate between two nations' currencies that is equal to the ratio of their price levels.
   - Inflation occurs when money is injected into a static economy or when employers raise wages to attract employees and then pass increased labor costs on to consumers.
   - Interest rates affect inflation by affecting the cost of borrowing money: Low interest rates encourage spending and higher debt, whereas high rates prompt savings and lower debt.
   - Because real interest rates are theoretically equal across countries, a rate difference between two countries must be due to different expected rates of inflation.
   - A country experiencing inflation higher than that of another country should see the relative value of its currency fall.

3. Describe the primary methods of forecasting exchange rates.
   - A *forward exchange rate* is the rate agreed on for foreign exchange payment at a future date.
   - The *efficient market view* says that prices of financial instruments reflect all publicly available information at any given time, meaning that forward exchange rates accurately forecast future exchange rates.
   - The *inefficient market view* says that prices of financial instruments do not reflect all publicly available information, meaning that forecasts can be improved by information not reflected in forward exchange rates.
   - One forecasting technique based on a belief in the value of added information is *fundamental analysis,* which uses statistical models based on fundamental economic indicators to forecast exchange rates.
   - A second forecasting technique is *technical analysis,* which employs charts of past trends in currency prices and other factors to forecast exchange rates.

4. Discuss the evolution of the current international monetary system and explain how it operates.
   - The *Bretton Woods Agreement* (1944) created an international monetary system based on the value of the U.S. dollar and used the *gold standard* to link paper currencies to specific values of gold.
   - The most important features of the Bretton Woods system were fixed exchange rates, built-in flexibility, funds for economic development, and an enforcement mechanism.

- The *World Bank* funds poor nations' economic development projects such as the development of transportation networks, building of power facilities, and agricultural and educational programs.
- The *International Monetary Fund (IMF)* regulates fixed exchange rates and enforces the rules of the international monetary system.
- The *Jamaica Agreement* (1976) endorsed a *managed float system* of exchange rates in which currencies float against one another with limited government intervention in order to stabilize currencies at a target exchange rate.
- In a *free float system* currencies float freely without government intervention.
- Within today's managed float system, certain countries try to maintain more stable exchange rates by tying their currencies to another country's stronger currency.

Talk It Over

1. Do you think an international monetary system with currencies valued on the basis of gold would work today? Why or why not? Do you think implementing a global version of the old European monetary system would work today? Why or why not?
2. The activities of the IMF and the World Bank largely overlap each other. Devise a plan that reduces this duplication of services and assigns distinct responsibilities. Would you have them assume a greater role on the environment and corruption? Describe and justify your proposed solution.

Teaming Up

1. **Research Project.** Suppose you and several classmates are a marketing team assembled by your Brazil-based firm to estimate demand in the U.S. market for its newly developed product. The market research firm your team hired requires $150,000 to perform a thorough study. But your group is informed that the total research budget for the year is 3 million Brazilian *real* and that no more than 20 percent of the budget can be spent on any one project.
   a. If the current exchange rate is 5 *real*/$, will your group have the market study conducted? Why or why not?
   b. If the exchange rate changes to 3 *real*/$, will your group have the study conducted? Why or why not?
   c. At what exchange rate do you change your group's decision from rejecting the proposed research project to accepting the project?
⭐2. **Market Entry Strategy Project.** This exercise corresponds to the *MESP* online simulation. For the country your team is researching, is it a member of the IMF? Does it participate in a regional monetary system to manage exchange rates? How have inflation and interest rates affected the nation's exchange rate with other currencies? What impact has the country's exchange rate had on its imports and exports? How has the exchange rate recently affected (a) the activities of companies operating in the country and (b) the purchasing power of consumers? What is the forecasted exchange rate for the coming weeks, months, and year? (*Hint*: Good sources are the IMF's monthly *International Financial Statistics* and annual *Exchange Arrangements and Exchange Restrictions*.) Integrate your findings into your completed *MESP* report.

Key Terms

Bretton Woods Agreement (p. 262)
currency board (p. 265)
devaluation (p. 252)
efficient market view (p. 259)
Fisher effect (p. 257)
fixed exchange-rate system (p. 261)
free float system (p. 264)

fundamental analysis (p. 259)
fundamental disequilibrium (p. 262)
gold standard (p. 261)
inefficient market view (p. 259)
international Fisher effect (p. 257)
international monetary system (p. 261)
Jamaica Agreement (p. 267)

law of one price (p. 254)
managed float system (p. 264)
revaluation (p. 252)
Smithsonian Agreement (p. 264)
special drawing right (SDR) (p. 263)
technical analysis (p. 259)

Take It to the Web

1. **Video Report.** Visit this book's channel on YouTube (www.YouTube.com/MyIBvideos). Click on "Videos" near the top of the page, and click on the set of videos labeled "Ch 10: International Monetary System." Watch one video from the list, and then summarize it in a half-page report. Reflecting on the contents of this chapter, which aspects of the international monetary system can you identify in the video? How might a company engaged in international business act on the information contained in the video?

2. **Website Report.** Use the Internet to research the economic crisis that struck Argentina in recent years. Identify as many potential contributing factors to the crisis as you can. What are current conditions of Argentina's exchange rate, inflation, and debt load? What effect has the crisis had on Brazil and other South American economies? Do you think Argentina's involvement in the trading bloc MERCOSUR had anything to do with its problems?

   Update how Argentina's companies, investors, and citizens are faring. How did the crisis affect companies' earnings and future projects? Are investors gaining renewed confidence and returning to Argentina? Are Argentines seeing the rebound of their currency's purchasing power? What is the IMF currently doing to aid Argentina's economy?

Ethical Challenges

1. You are the senior economic advisor for currency analysis with the United Nations (UN). The president of Malaysia has accused currency speculators of conspiring to devalue the Malaysian *ringgit* and wants the UN to create a formal policy designed to prevent similar financial crises in the future. Some years ago, when currency speculators turned their backs on Malaysia and forced a devaluation of the *ringgit,* then prime minister Mahathir Mohamad denounced currency speculators as "immoral" and argued that currency trading should take place only to facilitate deals between countries. Although most observers dismissed these comments as coming from a man known for his outspoken tirades against Western investors, others contend that the prime minister's rhetoric voices a genuine concern. Do you think an international policy that restricts currency trading can prevent future problems? What other implications might stem from such a policy? Is it ethical for global currency speculators to bet against national currencies, perhaps sending whole economies into a tailspin while they profit? Or do you think that currency speculators perform a valuable service by correcting overvalued or undervalued currencies?

2. You are the chair of an IMF task force. Your job is to reevaluate the policy of bailing out national governments that suffer major losses in the private sector. Current policy is to enlist the help of industrialized countries in bailing out emerging nations in the midst of financial crises. Taxpayers in industrial countries typically foot the bill for IMF activities, with total loans running into the many billions of dollars. Recent examples are the bailouts of Mexico, Indonesia, and Thailand. Some critics call this system a kind of "remnant socialism" that rescues financial institutions and investors from their own mistakes with money from taxpayers. For instance, the financial crisis in Thailand was largely a private-sector affair. Thai banks and insurance companies were heavily in debt, and the central bank had recklessly pledged its foreign exchange reserves to shore up the currency. As chair of the task force, what is your position on this dilemma? Do you believe that the current system *socializes* losses (the government bails them out) and *privatizes* profits? Explain exactly who benefits from such bailouts. What is an alternative to an IMF bailout?

MyManagementLab

Go to **mymanagementlab.com** for Auto-graded writing questions as well as the following Assisted-graded writing questions:

10-1. Describe briefly the advantages and disadvantages of both floating and fixed exchange-rate systems. Do you think the world will move toward an international monetary system more characteristic of floating or fixed exchange rates in the future? Explain your answer.

10-2. At the time the HIPC initiative was being developed, some critics argued that it fell short and that the need for debt relief was obvious 10 years earlier. They believed that the situation for some countries was so grim that entire external indebtedness, not just half, should be written off. Do you think the World Bank and the IMF should write off the entire debt of countries? What are the pros and cons of this approach for debt relief?

10-3. Mymanagementlab Only – comprehensive writing assignment for this chapter.

Practicing International Management Case

Banking on Forgiveness

When James Wolfensohn became head of the World Bank, he bluntly admitted the bank had "screwed up" in Africa. Decades of loans had erected a vast modern infrastructure (dams, roads, and power plants) for Africa's poor, but the gap between rich and poor did not narrow. In fact, the policies of the bank and global financial regulators had created a new crisis in sub-Saharan Africa: These nations were now mired in debt they could not possibly repay. Africa's total debt at the time almost equaled the annual gross national product of the entire continent. For instance, in Mozambique, where 25 percent of all children die from infectious disease before the age of five, the government was spending twice as much paying off debt as it was spending on health care and education.

But just when many countries were receiving debt relief, the debate over aid versus loans arose again. Groups debated how to prevent economic collapses and debt problems in the developing world and how to use dwindling aid more efficiently. Some countries wanted to give more foreign aid but wanted the money to be given as grants to financially and politically stable nations. They also wanted World Bank funds to be given to poor nations as grants and not loans that nations would need to repay.

Other nations feared that giving the money away as grants would drain the World Bank's coffers, as well as their own. They acknowledged that they may not be able to do as much for the least-developed countries, but that the role of the World Bank, after all, is to act as a bank and not a donor. Support for this view was World Bank data that showed more than 95 percent of all loans are repaid and that poor nations are more careful with loans than they are with handouts.

For years, nongovernmental organizations (NGOs), such as advocacy group Oxfam International, had lobbied the Bank and the International Monetary Fund (IMF) to write off loans to their poorest borrowers, calling for "debt forgiveness" or "debt relief." Fortunately for the African people and their advocates, the new head of the bank put debt forgiveness at the top of his agenda. In the fall of 1996, the World Bank and the IMF announced a plan to reduce the external debt of the world's poorest, most heavily indebted countries. The purpose of the plan, called the Heavily Indebted Poor Countries (HIPC) Debt Initiative, is to slash overall *debt stocks* by 50 percent, lower poor nations' *debt service,* and boost social spending in poor nations. The HIPC initiative has identified countries in Africa, Latin America, Asia, and the Middle East that may qualify for debt reduction. But debt relief is not automatic. The international banking community is using debt as both a carrot and a stick: Whereas nations with good reform records will get relief, those without reforms will not.

Then, in 2006, the world's largest international lending institutions launched the Multilateral Debt Relief Initiative (MDRI) to work alongside the HIPC initiative to help countries reach their debt-relief goals. As of 2010, 35 countries identified for assistance have had their *debt stocks* reduced by 80 percent. For those countries, *debt service* as a percentage of exports fell from 18 percent in 1999 to 6 percent by 2010. And those nations have seen their debt service as a percentage of GDP drop from 114 percent to 35 percent over the same period.

One success story is Uganda. Uganda was the first country declared eligible for assistance in 1997 and was the first to receive debt relief under the HIPC initiative in 1998. The decision to begin the program with Uganda was not an arbitrary one. While under the brutal dictatorship of Idi Amin, Uganda was treated as a pariah by creditors. But then President Yoweri Museveni led the country through a decade-long process of economic reform. Uganda became a model country, boasting a steady growth rate of around 5 percent, with coffee as its main export. By offering debt relief to Uganda, the World Bank and the IMF rewarded Uganda's exemplary track record by reducing its debt to the lowest possible level—about twice the value of its exports. Savings from the debt-relief program are pledged to improve health care and to make primary education available to all Ugandan families.

Thinking Globally

1. In negotiating the HIPC Debt Initiative, the World Bank and the IMF worked closely together. At one point, however, the plan came to a standstill when the two organizations produced different figures for Uganda's coffee exports, with the IMF giving a more optimistic forecast and so arguing against the need for debt relief. In your opinion, is there any benefit to these organizations working together? Explain. Which organization do you think should play a greater role in aiding economic development? Why?

2. The World Bank and the IMF had once argued that the leniency of debt forgiveness would make it more difficult for the lenders themselves to borrow cheaply on the world's capital markets. If you were a World Bank donor, would you support the HIPC Debt Initiative or argue against it? Explain your answer.

Source: Heavily Indebted Poor Countries (HIPC) Initiative and Multilateral Debt Relief Initiative (MDRI)—Status of Implementation, World Bank website (www.worldbank.org), May 19, 2010; *HIPC at-a-Glance*, World Bank website (www.worldbank.org), Fall 2007.

International Strategy and Organization

LEARNING OBJECTIVES

After studying this chapter, you should be able to

1. Explain the stages of identification and analysis that precede strategy selection.

2. Identify the two international strategies and the corporate-level strategies that companies use.

3. Identify the business-level strategies of companies and the role of department-level strategies.

4. Discuss the important issues that influence the choice of organizational structure.

5. Describe each type of international organizational structure, and explain the importance of work teams.

A Look Back

Chapter 10 explored the international monetary system. We examined the factors that affect the determination of exchange rates and discussed international attempts to create a system of stable and predictable exchange rates.

A Look at This Chapter

This chapter introduces us to the strategies used by international companies. We explore the different types of strategies available to international companies and important factors in their selection. We also examine the organizational structures that companies devise to suit their international operations.

A Look Ahead

Chapter 12 explains how managers screen and research potential markets and sites for operations. We identify the information required in the screening process and explain where managers can go to obtain such information.

FLYING HIGH WITH LOW FARES

DUBLIN, Ireland—No one is as successful as Ryanair (www.ryanair.com) at offering no-frills flying, shuttling nearly 80 million passengers a year across Europe. Ryanair's fares are around 50 percent lower than Europe's big national carriers, and sometimes even one-tenth as much. In 25 years, Ryanair has grown from offering one flight a day between Ireland and England to more than 1,100 routes between 28 nations that connect 168 destinations.

Ryanair has successfully carved out a niche among the flying public. Describing his company's approach, CEO Michael O'Leary (pictured here) said, "It's very simple. We're like Walmart in the United States—we pile it high and sell it cheap." Ryanair's strategy is to use less-congested, secondary airports just outside Europe's biggest cities. Instead of serving London's Heathrow or Gatwick airport, Ryanair flies into Stansted. And rather than fly to Germany's Frankfurt Main airport, Ryanair services Hahn, a former U.S. fighter base 60 miles west of Frankfurt. With the flying public trying to save money during the recent global recession, Ryanair's low-cost strategy helped it take even more market share away from the national carriers.

Source: ZUMA Press/Newscom

Ryanair's strategy lets it negotiate airport fees as low as $1.50 per passenger as opposed to the $15 to $22 per passenger charged by Europe's major airports. Ryanair also slashes other expenses to achieve its mission: For example, not serving ice with drinks saves Ryanair $50,000 a year. Charging passengers for checked baggage means fewer bags, which saves fuel and cuts the cost of ground services. And rather than serve free water on flights, Ryanair charges several dollars a bottle.

Ryanair is hot on the heels of big national carriers, such as British Airways, Lufthansa in Germany, and Alitalia in Italy. Ryanair once painted "Arrivederci Alitalia" on one of its planes to anger its Italian competitor. O'Leary is confident his strategy will succeed. "Ryanair is going to be a monster in Europe within the next 10 to 12 years," he says. As you read this chapter, consider the creative strategies companies use to out-compete rivals and serve their customers.[1]

planning
Process of identifying and selecting an organization's objectives and deciding how the organization will achieve those objectives

strategy
Set of planned actions taken by managers to help a company meet its objectives.

Planning is the process of identifying and selecting an organization's objectives and deciding how the organization will achieve those objectives. In turn, **strategy** is the set of planned actions taken by managers to help a company meet its objectives. The key to developing an effective strategy, then, is to define a company's objectives (or goals) clearly and to plan carefully how it will achieve those goals. This requires a company to undertake an analysis of its own capabilities and strengths in order to identify what it can do better than the competition. It also means that a company must carefully assess the competitive environment and the national and international business environments in which it operates.

A well-defined strategy helps a company compete effectively in increasingly competitive international markets. It serves to coordinate a company's various divisions and departments so that the company reaches its overall goals in the most effective and efficient manner possible. A clear, appropriate strategy focuses a company on the activities that it performs best and on the industries for which it is best suited. It keeps an organization away from a future of mediocre performance or total failure. An inappropriate strategy can lead a manager to take actions that pull a company in opposite directions or take it into industries it knows little about.

We begin this chapter by exploring important factors that managers consider when analyzing their companies' strengths and weaknesses. We examine the different international strategies and the corporate-, business-, and department-level strategies that companies implement. Finally, we explore the different types of organizational structures that companies use to coordinate their international activities.

International Strategy

Managers confront similar concerns whether formulating a strategy for a domestic or an international company. Both types of firms must determine what products to produce, where to produce them, and where and how to market them. The biggest difference lies in complexity. Companies considering international production need to select from many potential countries, each likely having more than one possible location. Depending on its product line, a company that wants to market internationally might have an equally large number of markets to consider. Whether it is being considered as a site for operations or as a potential market, each international location has a rich mixture of cultural, political, legal, and economic traditions and processes. All these factors add to the complexity of planning and formulating strategy for international managers.

Strategy Formulation

The strategy-formulation process involves both planning and strategy. Strategy formulation permits managers to step back from day-to-day activities and get a fresh perspective on the current and future direction of the company and its industry. As shown in Figure 11.1, the strategy-formulation procedure can be regarded as a three-stage process. Let's examine several important factors that should be considered in each stage of this process.

Identify Company Mission and Goals

mission statement
Written statement of why a company exists and what it plans to accomplish.

Most companies have a general purpose for why they exist, which they express in a **mission statement**—a written statement of why a company exists and what it plans to accomplish. For example, one company might set out to supply the highest level of service in a *market segment*—a clearly identifiable group of potential buyers. Another might strive to be the lowest-cost supplier in its segment worldwide. The mission statement often guides decisions such as which industries to enter or exit and how to compete in chosen segments.

stakeholders
All parties, ranging from suppliers and employees to stockholders and consumers, who are affected by a company's activities.

TYPES OF MISSION STATEMENTS Mission statements often spell out how a company's operations affect its **stakeholders**—all parties, ranging from suppliers and employees to stockholders and consumers, who are affected by a company's activities. Some companies place corporate brands center stage and place the mission of creating well-liked brands above all else. The mission statements of other businesses focus on other issues, including superior shareholder returns, profitability, market share, and corporate social responsibility. Still other companies make their mission to be the interests of consumers. For example, the mission

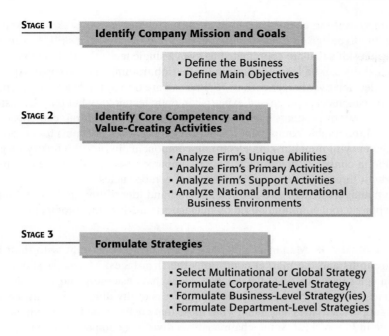

FIGURE 11.1

Strategy-Formulation Process

statement of global eye-care company Bausch & Lomb (www.bausch.com) focuses on the customer and reads as follows:

> Bausch & Lomb is the eye health company, dedicated to perfecting vision and enhancing life for consumers around the world®.[2]

The mission statement of an international business depends on (among other things) the type of business it is in, the stakeholders it is trying most to satisfy, and the aspect of business most important to achieving its goals. Yet companies must be sensitive to the needs of its different stakeholders in different nations. A company might need to balance the needs of stockholders for financial returns in the home nation, the needs of buyers for good value in a consumer market, and the needs of the public at large where it has a production facility.

Managers must also define the *objectives* they wish to achieve in the global marketplace. Objectives at the highest level in a company tend to be stated in the most general terms. An example of this type of objective is the following:

> To be the largest global company in each industry in which we compete.

Objectives of individual business units in an organization tend to be more specific. They are normally stated in more concrete terms and sometimes even contain numerical targets. For example, such a mission statement could be stated as follows:

> To mass-produce a zero-pollution-emissions automobile by 2020.

Objectives usually become even more precise at the level of individual departments and almost always contain numerical targets of performance. For example, the following could be the objective of a marketing and sales department:

> To increase global market share by 5 percent in each of the next three years.

Identify Core Competency and Value-Creating Activities

Before managers formulate effective strategies, they must analyze the company, its industry (or industries), and the national business environments in which it is involved. They should also examine industries and countries being targeted for potential future entry. We address the company and its industries in this section and examine the business environment in the next.

UNIQUE ABILITIES OF COMPANIES Although large multinational companies are often involved in multiple industries, most perform one activity (or a few activities) better than any competitor does. A **core competency** is a special ability of a company that competitors find extremely

core competency
Special ability of a company that competitors find extremely difficult or impossible to equal.

difficult or impossible to equal. It is not a skill; individuals possess skills. For example, an architect's ability to design an office building in the Victorian style is a skill. A core competency refers to multiple skills that are coordinated to form a single technological outcome.

Although skills can be learned through on-the-job training and personal experience, core competencies develop over longer periods of time and are difficult to teach. At one point, Canon of Japan (www.canon.com) purchased expertise in optic technology but only later succeeded in developing a variety of products based on optic technology—including cameras, copiers, and semiconductor lithographic equipment. Likewise, Sony (www.sony.com) for decades relied on its core competency in miniaturizing electronic components in order to fortify its global leadership position in consumer electronics. These companies possessed unique abilities to create superior products through development of their core competencies.

How do managers actually go about analyzing and identifying their firms' unique abilities? Let's explore a tool commonly used by managers to analyze their companies—*value-chain analysis*.

VALUE-CHAIN ANALYSIS Managers must select strategies consistent with their company's particular strengths and the market conditions the firm faces. Managers should also select company strategies based on what the company does that customers find valuable. This is why managers conduct a **value-chain analysis**—the process of dividing a company's activities into primary and support activities and identifying those that create value for customers.[3]

As we see in Figure 11.2, value-chain analysis divides a company's activities into primary activities and support activities that are central to creating customer value. *Primary activities* include inbound and outbound logistics, production (goods and services), marketing and sales, and customer service. Primary activities involve the creation of the product, its marketing and delivery to buyers, and its after-sales support and service. *Support activities* include business infrastructure, human resource management, technology development, and procurement (sourcing). Each of these activities provides the inputs and infrastructure required by the primary activities.

Each primary and support activity is a source of strength or weakness for a company. Managers determine whether each activity enhances or detracts from customer value, and they incorporate this knowledge into the strategy-formulation process. Analysis of primary and support activities often involves finding activities in which improvements can be made with large benefits. Let's take a look at how managers determine whether an activity enhances customer value.

Primary Activities When analyzing primary activities, managers often look for areas in which the company can increase the value provided to its customers. For example, managers might examine production processes and discover new, more-efficient manufacturing methods in order to reduce production costs and improve quality. Customer satisfaction might be increased by improving logistics management to shorten the time it takes to get a product to the buyer or by providing better customer service.

Companies might also lower costs by introducing greater automation into the production process. Computer maker Acer (www.acer.com) applied a fast-food production model to

value-chain analysis
Process of dividing a company's activities into primary and support activities and identifying those that create value for customers.

FIGURE 11.2

Company Value Chain

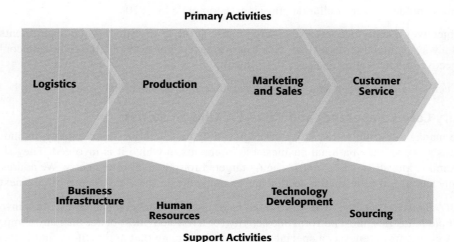

personal computer manufacturing. Rather than manufacture complete computers in Asia and ship them around the world, Acer builds components at plants scattered throughout the world. Those components are then shipped to assembly plants, where computers are built according to customer specifications. Acer adopted this approach because there was no longer any value added in simply assembling computers. By altering its production and logistics processes, Acer developed a business model that created value for customers.

Support Activities Support activities assist companies in performing their primary activities. For example, the actions of any company's employees are crucial to its success. Production, logistics, marketing, sales, and customer service all benefit when employees are qualified and well trained. International companies can often improve the quality of their products by investing in worker training and management development. In turn, ensuring quality can increase the efficiency of a firm's manufacturing, marketing and sales, and customer service activities. Effective procurement (or sourcing) can locate low-cost, high-quality raw materials or intermediate products and ensure on-time delivery to production facilities. Finally, a sophisticated infrastructure not only improves internal communication but also supports organizational culture and each primary activity.

The in-depth analysis of a company that is inherent in the strategy-formulation process helps managers to discover their company's unique core competency and abilities and to identify the activities that create customer value. For a checklist of issues companies should consider in a self-analysis of whether it is ready to go global, see this chapter's Manager's Briefcase, titled "Ask Questions before Going Global."

A company cannot identify its unique abilities in a vacuum, separate from the environment in which it operates. The external business environment consists of all the elements outside a company that can affect its performance, such as cultural, political, legal, and economic forces; workers' unions; consumers; and financial institutions. Let's look at several environmental forces that affect strategy formulation.

NATIONAL AND INTERNATIONAL BUSINESS ENVIRONMENTS National differences in language, religious beliefs, customs, traditions, and climate complicate strategy formulation. Language differences can increase the cost of operations and administration. Manufacturing processes must sometimes be adapted to the supply of local workers and to local customs, traditions, and practices. Marketing activities sometimes can result in costly mistakes if they do not incorporate cultural differences. For example, a company once decided to sell its laundry detergent in Japan but did not adjust the size of the box in which it was sold. The company spent millions of dollars developing a detailed marketing campaign and was shocked when it experienced disappointing sales. It turned out that the company should have packaged the detergent in smaller containers

---

MANAGER'S BRIEFCASE   Ask Questions before Going Global

It seems everywhere a business turns for advice these days it hears the mantra, "Go global." But a company needs a solid grasp of its capabilities and its product if it is going to be successful in global markets. Here is a brief checklist of issues for a business to consider:

- **Are You Ready?** Do you or your key personnel speak other languages? Have you or they lived in other cultures for extended periods? How long has your company been in business? What markets might need what your company sells? Can your business withstand the rough seas of global trade? What specific sales numbers are forecasted? Can you map your global business journey?

- **Is Your Product Ready?** Can your business capitalize on its strengths? Will you need to modify your product or your marketing approach? Will modifying the product or its marketing weaken your offering? Does your product satisfy all local safety

standards and other regulations? Can your product stand up to the competition and to the scrutiny of customers?

- **Is Each Department Ready?** Is your company's infrastructure capable of going global? Does each department (logistics, operations, marketing, sales, service, human resources, collections, etc.) have the resources to handle its international responsibilities? What is your company's financial strategy for international expansion? Can domestic sales support an initial period of money-losing international operations? Is everyone in the company committed to the international effort?

- **Is Your Strategy Ready?** Will your company's international effort conflict with or complement your overall business strategy? Will your company's foreignness be a hindrance, or can it be exploited profitably? Is your business capable of sustaining a lengthy international endeavor? How will your company break into long-established family networks and business relationships?

for the Japanese market. Japanese shoppers prefer smaller quantities because they tend to walk home from the store and have smaller storage areas in tight living quarters.

Differences in political and legal systems also complicate international strategies. Legal and political processes often differ in target countries to such an extent that firms must hire outside consultants to teach them about the local system. Such knowledge is important to international companies because the approval of the host government is almost always necessary for making direct investments. Companies need to know which ministry or department has the authority to grant approval for a big business deal—a process that can become extremely cumbersome. For example, non-Chinese companies in China must often get approval to conduct business from several separate agencies. The process is further complicated by the tendency of local government officials to interpret laws differently than do bureaucrats in Beijing (the nation's capital).

Different national economic systems further complicate strategy formulation. Negative attitudes of local people toward the impact of direct investment can generate political unrest. Economic philosophy affects the tax rates that governments impose. Whereas socialist economic systems normally levy high taxes on business profits, free-market economies tend to levy lower taxes. The need to work in more than one currency also complicates international strategy. To minimize losses from currency fluctuations, companies must develop strategies to deal with exchange-rate risk.

Finally, apart from complicating strategy, the national business environment can affect the location in which a company chooses to perform an activity. For example, a nation that spends a high portion of its GDP on research and development (R&D) attracts high-tech industries and high-wage jobs and, as a result, prospers. By contrast, countries that spend relatively little in the way of R&D tend to have lower levels of prosperity.

QUICK STUDY 1

1. What are the three stages of the strategy-formulation process? Describe what is involved at each stage.
2. Define what is meant by the term *core competency*. How does it differ from a skill?
3. What is *value-chain analysis*? Explain the difference between primary and secondary activities.
4. How do national and international business environments influence strategy formulation?

Formulate Strategies

As we have seen, the strengths and special capabilities of an international company, along with the environmental forces it faces, strongly influence its strategy. Let's examine this final stage in the planning and strategy-formulation process.

TWO INTERNATIONAL STRATEGIES Companies engaged in international business activities can approach the market using either a *multinational* or a *global* strategy. It is important to note that these two strategies do not include companies that export. Exporters do not have foreign direct investments in other national markets and should instead devise an appropriate export strategy (see Chapter 13). Let's now examine what it means for a company to follow a multinational or a global strategy.

multinational (multidomestic) strategy
Adapting products and their marketing strategies in each national market to suit local preferences.

Multinational Strategy Some international companies choose to follow a **multinational (multidomestic) strategy**—a strategy of adapting products and their marketing strategies in each national market to suit local preferences. In other words, a multinational strategy is just what its name implies—a separate strategy for each of the multiple nations in which a company markets its products. To implement a multinational strategy, companies often establish largely independent, self-contained units (or subsidiaries) in each national market. Each subsidiary typically undertakes its own product research and development, production, and marketing. In many ways, each unit functions largely as an independent company. Multinational strategies are often appropriate for companies in industries in which buyer preferences do not converge across national borders, such as certain food products and some print media.

The main benefit of a multinational strategy is that it allows companies to monitor buyer preferences closely in each local market and to respond quickly and effectively to emerging buyer preferences. Companies hope that customers will perceive a tailored product as delivering greater value than do competitors' products. A multinational strategy, then, should allow a company to charge higher prices and/or gain market share.

The main drawback of a multinational strategy is that companies cannot exploit scale economies in product development, manufacturing, or marketing. The multinational strategy typically increases the cost structure for international companies and forces them to charge higher prices to recover such costs. As such, a multinational strategy is usually poorly suited to industries in which price competitiveness is a key success factor. The high degree of independence with which each unit operates also may reduce opportunities to share knowledge among units within a company.

Global Strategy Other companies decide that what suits their operations is a **global strategy**—a strategy of offering the same products using the same marketing strategy in all national markets. Companies that follow a global strategy often take advantage of scale and location economies by producing entire inventories of products or components in a few optimal locations. They also tend to perform product research and development in one or a few locations and typically design promotional campaigns and advertising strategies at headquarters. So-called global products are most common in industries characterized by price competition and, therefore, pressure to contain costs. They include certain electronic components, a wide variety of industrial goods such as steel, and some consumer goods such as paper and writing instruments.

global strategy
Offering the same products using the same marketing strategy in all national markets.

The main benefit of a global strategy is cost savings due to product and marketing standardization. These cost savings can then be passed on to consumers to help the company gain market share in its market segment. A global strategy also allows managers to share lessons learned in one market with managers at other locations.

The main problem with a global strategy is it can cause a company to overlook important differences in buyer preferences from one market to another. A global strategy does not allow a company to modify its products except for the most superficial features, such as the color of paint applied to a finished product or a small add-on feature. This can present a competitor with an opportunity to step in and satisfy any unmet needs of local buyers, thereby creating a niche market.

In addition to deciding whether the company will follow a multinational or a global strategy, managers must formulate strategies for the corporation, each business unit, and each department. Let's look closely at the three different levels of company strategy: *corporate-, business-, and department-level* strategies (see Figure 11.3).

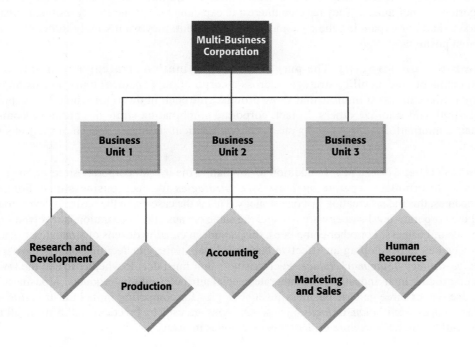

FIGURE 11.3

Three Levels of Company Strategy

CORPORATE-LEVEL STRATEGIES Companies involved in more than one line of business must first formulate a *corporate-level strategy*. This means, in part, identifying the national markets and industries in which the company will operate. It also involves developing overall objectives for the company's different business units and specifying the role that each unit will play in reaching those objectives. The four key approaches to corporate strategy are *growth, retrenchment, stability,* and *combination*.

growth strategy
Strategy designed to increase the scale (size of activities) or scope (kinds of activities) of a corporation's operations.

Growth Strategy A **growth strategy** is designed to increase the scale or scope of a corporation's operations. *Scale* refers to the *size* of a corporation's activities, *scope* to the *kinds* of activities it performs. Yardsticks commonly used to measure growth include geographic coverage, number of business units, market share, sales revenue, and number of employees. *Organic growth* refers to a corporate strategy of relying on internally generated growth. For example, management at 3M (www.3m.com) strongly encourages entrepreneurial activity, often spinning off business units to nurture the best ideas and carry them to completion.

Other methods of growth include mergers and acquisitions, joint ventures, and strategic alliances (see Chapter 13). Companies use these tactics when they do not wish to invest in developing certain skills internally or when other companies already do what managers are trying to achieve. Common partners in implementing these strategies include competitors, suppliers, and buyers. Corporations typically join forces with competitors to reduce competition, expand product lines, or expand geographically. A common motivation for joining forces with suppliers is to increase control over the quality, cost, and timing of inputs.

retrenchment strategy
Strategy designed to reduce the scale or scope of a corporation's businesses.

Retrenchment Strategy The exact opposite of a growth strategy is a **retrenchment strategy**—a strategy designed to reduce the scale or scope of a corporation's businesses. Corporations often cut back the *scale* of their operations when economic conditions worsen or competition increases. They may do so by closing factories with unused capacity and by laying off workers. Corporations can also reduce the scale of their operations by laying off managers and salespeople in national markets that are not generating adequate sales revenue. Corporations reduce the *scope* of their activities by selling unprofitable business units or those that are no longer directly related to their overall aims. Weaker competitors often resort to retrenchment when national business environments grow more competitive.

stability strategy
Strategy designed to guard against change and used by corporations to avoid either growth or retrenchment.

Stability Strategy A **stability strategy** is designed to guard against change. Corporations often use a stability strategy when trying to avoid either growth or retrenchment. Such corporations have typically met their stated objectives or are satisfied with what they have already accomplished. They believe that their strengths are being fully exploited and their weaknesses fully protected against. They also see the business environment as posing neither profitable opportunities nor threats. They have no interest in expanding sales, increasing profits, increasing market share, or expanding the customer base; at present, they want simply to maintain their current positions.

combination strategy
Strategy designed to mix growth, retrenchment, and stability strategies across a corporation's business units.

Combination Strategy The purpose of a **combination strategy** is to mix growth, retrenchment, and stability strategies across a corporation's business units. For example, a corporation can invest in units that show promise, retrench in those for which less exposure is desired, and stabilize others. In fact, corporate combination strategies are quite common because international corporations rarely follow identical strategies in each of their business units.

BUSINESS-LEVEL STRATEGIES In addition to stipulating the overall corporate strategy, managers must also formulate separate *business-level strategies* for each business unit. For some companies, this means creating just one strategy. This is the case when the business-level strategy and the corporate-level strategy are one and the same because the corporation is involved in just one line of business. For other companies, this can mean creating dozens of strategies.

The key to developing an effective business-level strategy is deciding on a *general competitive strategy in the marketplace*. Each business unit must decide whether to sell the lowest-priced product in an industry or to integrate special attributes into its products. A business unit can use one of three generic business-level strategies for competing in its industry—*low-cost leadership, differentiation,* or *focus*.[4] These strategies are used by practically all firms in all markets worldwide. Let's explore each of these strategies in detail.

Low-Cost Leadership Strategy A strategy in which a company exploits economies of scale to have the lowest cost structure of any competitor in its industry is called a **low-cost leadership strategy**. Companies that pursue the low-cost leadership position also try to contain administrative costs and the costs of their various primary activities, including marketing, advertising, and distribution. We saw in this chapter's opening company profile how Ryanair engages in aggressive cost cutting in order to be Europe's leading low-cost airline. Although cutting costs is the mantra for firms that pursue a low-cost leadership position, other important competitive factors such as product quality and customer service cannot be ignored. Factors underlying the low-cost leadership position (efficient production in large quantities) help guard against attack by competitors because of the large upfront cost of getting started. The strategy typically requires a company to have a large market share because achieving low-cost leadership tends to rely on large-scale production to contain costs. One negative aspect of the low-cost leadership strategy is low customer loyalty—all else being equal, buyers will purchase from any low-cost leader.

A low-cost leadership strategy works best with mass-marketed products aimed at price-sensitive buyers. This strategy is often well suited to companies with standardized product and marketing promotions. Two global companies vying for the low-cost leadership position in their respective industries include Casio (www.casio.com) in sports watches and Texas Instruments (www.ti.com) in calculators and other electronic devices.

low-cost leadership strategy
Strategy in which a company exploits economies of scale to have the lowest cost structure of any competitor in its industry.

Differentiation Strategy A **differentiation strategy** is one in which a company designs its products to be perceived as unique by buyers throughout its industry. The perception of uniqueness can allow a company to charge a higher price and enjoy greater customer loyalty than it could as a low-cost leader. But a perception of exclusivity, or meeting the needs of a small group of buyers, tends to force a company into a lower market-share position. A company using this strategy must develop a loyal customer base to offset its smaller market share and higher costs of producing and marketing a unique product.

One way products can be differentiated is by improving their reputation for *quality*. Ceramic tableware for everyday use is found at department stores in almost every country. But Japanese producer Noritake differentiates the ceramic tableware it makes (www.noritake.com) from common tableware by emphasizing its superior quality. The perception of higher quality allows manufacturers to charge higher prices for their products worldwide.

Other products are differentiated by distinctive *brand images*. Armani (www.armani.com) and DKNY (www.dkny.com), for example, are relatively pricey global clothiers appealing to a young, fashionable clientele. Each is continually introducing new textures and colors that are at once stylish and functional. Another example is Italian carmaker Alfa Romeo (www.alfaromeo.com), which does not compete in the fiercely competitive mass-consumer segment of the global automobile industry. If it were to do so, it would have to be price-competitive and offer a wider selection of cars. Instead, Alfa Romeo offers a high-quality product with a brand image that rewards the Alfa Romeo owner with status and prestige.

Another differentiating factor is *product design*—the sum of the features by which a product looks and functions according to customer requirements. Special features differentiate both goods and services in the minds of consumers who value those features. Manufacturers can also combine several differentiation factors in formulating their strategies. For example, the designs of Casio (www.casio.com) and other makers of mass-market sports watches stress functionality. The sports watches of TAG Heuer (www.tagheuer.com) of Switzerland, on the other hand, offer class and style in addition to performance.

differentiation strategy
Strategy in which a company designs its products to be perceived as unique by buyers throughout its industry.

Focus Strategy A **focus strategy** is one in which a company focuses on serving the needs of a narrowly defined market segment by being the low-cost leader, by differentiating its product, or both. Increasing competition often means more products distinguished by price or differentiated by quality, design, and so forth. In turn, a greater product range leads to the continuous refinement of market segments. Today, many industries consist of large numbers of market segments and even smaller subsegments. For example, some firms try to serve the needs of one ethnic or racial group, whereas others, often entrepreneurs and small businesses, focus on a single geographic area.

Johnson & Johnson (J&J; www.jnj.com) is commonly thought of as being a single, large consumer-products company. In fact, it is a conglomerate of more than 250 operating companies

focus strategy
Strategy in which a company focuses on serving the needs of a narrowly defined market segment by being the low-cost leader, by differentiating its product, or both.

Employees of China's largest home appliances maker, Haier, work on the refrigerator production line in Qingdao, Shandong province. By analyzing its industry and assets, a company based in an emerging market can determine whether its competitive edge is germane to the local market, or if it is transferable to other markets. Haier is taking the battle for market share to highly industrialized nations and is now the world's fourth largest home appliances manufacturer—employing more than 50,000 people globally.

Source: Peng Neng/Newscom

that market an enormous variety of products to a wide array of market segments. Many individual J&J companies try to dominate their segments by producing specialty goods and services. In so doing, they focus on narrow segments by using either low-cost leadership or differentiation techniques.[5]

A focus strategy often means designing products and promotions aimed at consumers who are either dissatisfied with existing choices or who want something distinctive. Consider the highly fragmented gourmet coffee market. One extremely unusual brand of coffee called Luwak sells for up to *$300 per pound*! Apparently, luwaks (weasels on the Indonesian island of Java) eat coffee berries containing coffee beans. The beans "naturally ferment" as they pass through the luwaks and are later recovered. The beans are then washed, roasted, and sold around the world as a specialty coffee.[6]

DEPARTMENT-LEVEL STRATEGIES Achieving corporate- and business-level objectives depends on effective departmental strategies that focus on the specific activities that transform resources into products. Formulation of *department-level strategies* brings us back to where we began our analysis of a company's capabilities that support its strategy: to the primary and support activities that create value for customers. After managers analyze these activities, they must develop strategies that exploit their firm's value-creating strengths.

Primary and Support Activities Each department is instrumental in creating customer value through lower costs or differentiated products. This is especially true of departments that conduct *primary activities*. Manufacturing strategies are obviously important in cutting the production costs of both standardized and differentiated products. They are also crucial to improving product quality. Effective marketing strategies allow companies to promote the differences in their products. A strong sales force and good customer service contribute to favorable images among consumers or industrial buyers and generate loyal customers of both kinds. Efficient logistics in bringing raw materials and components into the factory and getting the finished product out the factory door can result in substantial cost savings.

Support activities also create customer value. For example, R&D identifies market segments with unsatisfied needs and designs products to meet them. Human resource managers can improve efficiency and cut costs by hiring well-trained employees and conducting worker training and management development programs. Procurement tasks provide operations with quality resources at a reasonable cost. Accounting and finance (elements of a firm's infrastructure) must develop efficient information systems to assist managers in making decisions and maintaining financial control, thus having an impact on costs and quality in general.

There are important elements that drive the decisions of world-class companies with regard to strategy formulation. For example, the important *production* issues to consider are the number and dispersion of production facilities and whether to standardize production processes for all markets. The important *marketing* issue is whether to standardize either the physical features of products or their marketing strategies across markets. We present the strategic considerations of production and marketing activities in later chapters.

QUICK STUDY 2

1. Compare and contrast *multinational strategy* and *global strategy*. When is each appropriate?
2. What are the four corporate-level strategies? Identify the main characteristics of each.
3. Identify the three business-level strategies. Describe how they differ from one another.
4. Explain the importance of department-level strategies. How do primary and support activities help a firm achieve its goals?

International Organizational Structure

Organizational structure is the way in which a company divides its activities among separate units and coordinates activities among those units. If a company's organizational structure is appropriate for its strategic plans, it will be more effective in working toward its goals. In this section, we explore several important issues related to organizational structures and will examine several alternative forms of organization.

organizational structure
Way in which a company divides its activities among separate units and coordinates activities among those units.

Centralization versus Decentralization

A vital issue for top managers is determining the degree to which decision making in the organization will be centralized or decentralized. *Centralized decision making* concentrates decision making at a high organizational level in one location, such as at headquarters. *Decentralized decision making* disperses decisions to lower organizational levels, such as to international subsidiaries.

Should managers at the parent company be actively involved in the decisions made by international subsidiaries? Or should they intervene relatively little, perhaps only in the most crucial decisions? Some decisions, of course, must be decentralized. If top managers involve themselves in the day-to-day decisions of every subsidiary, they are likely to be overwhelmed. For example, managers cannot get directly involved in every hiring decision or assignment of people to specific tasks at each facility. On the other hand, overall corporate strategy cannot be delegated to subsidiary managers because only top management is likely to have the appropriate perspective needed to formulate corporate strategy.

In our discussion of centralization versus decentralization of decision making, it is important to remember two points:

1. Companies rarely centralize or decentralize all decision making. Rather, they seek an approach that will result in the greatest efficiency and effectiveness.
2. International companies may centralize decision making in certain geographic markets while decentralizing it in others. Numerous factors influence this decision, including the need for product modification and the abilities of managers at each location.

With these points in mind, let's take a look at some specific factors that determine whether centralized or decentralized decision making is most appropriate.

WHEN TO CENTRALIZE Centralized decision making helps coordinate the operations of international subsidiaries. This is important for companies that operate in multiple lines of business or in many international markets. It is also important when one subsidiary's output is another's input. In such situations, coordinating operations from a single, high-level vantage point is more efficient. Purchasing is often centralized if all subsidiaries use the same inputs in production. For example, a company that manufactures steel filing cabinets and desks will need a great deal of sheet steel. A central purchasing department will get a better bulk price on sheet steel than would subsidiaries negotiating their own agreements. Each subsidiary would then benefit by purchasing sheet steel from the company's central purchasing department at a lower cost than it would pay in the open market.

Some companies maintain strong central control over financial resources by channeling all subsidiary profits back to the parent for redistribution to subsidiaries based on their needs. This practice reduces the likelihood that certain subsidiaries will undertake investment projects when more promising projects at other locations go without funding. Other companies centrally design policies, procedures, and standards to encourage a single global organizational culture. This policy makes it more likely that all subsidiaries will enforce company rules uniformly. The policy also helps when companies transfer managers from one location to another because uniform policies can smooth transitions for managers and subordinates alike.

WHEN TO DECENTRALIZE Decentralized decision making is beneficial when fast-changing national business environments put a premium on local responsiveness. Decentralized decisions can result in products that are better suited to the needs and preferences of local buyers because subsidiary managers are in closer contact with the local business environment. Local managers are more likely to perceive environmental changes that managers at headquarters might not notice. By contrast, central managers may not perceive such changes or would likely get a secondhand account of local events. Delayed response and misinterpreted events could then result in lost orders, stalled production, and weakened competitiveness.

Participative Management and Accountability Decentralization can also help foster participative management practices. The morale of employees is likely to be higher if subsidiary managers and subordinates are involved in decision making. Subsidiary managers and workers can grow more dedicated to the organization when they are involved in decisions related to production, promotion, distribution, and pricing strategies.

Decentralization also can increase personal accountability for business decisions. When local managers are rewarded (or punished) for their decisions, they are likely to invest more effort in making and executing them. Conversely, if local managers must do nothing but implement policies dictated from above, they can attribute poor performance to decisions that were ill-suited to the local environment. When managers are held accountable for decision making and implementation, they typically delve more deeply into research and consider all available options. The results are often better decisions and improved performance.

Coordination and Flexibility

When designing the organizational structure, managers seek answers to certain key questions: What is the most efficient method of linking divisions to each other? Who should coordinate the activities of different divisions in order to achieve overall strategies? How should information be processed and delivered to managers when it is required? What sorts of monitoring mechanisms and reward structures should be established? How should the company introduce corrective measures, and whose responsibility should it be to execute them? To answer these types of questions, we must look at the issues of coordination and flexibility.

STRUCTURE AND COORDINATION As we have seen, some companies have a presence in several or more national business environments—they manufacture and market products practically everywhere. Others operate primarily in one country and export to, or import from, other markets. Each type of company must design an appropriate organizational structure. Each needs a structure that clearly defines areas of responsibility and **chains of command**—the lines of authority that run from top management to individual employees and that specify internal reporting relationships. Finally, every firm needs a structure that brings together areas that require close cooperation. For example, to avoid product designs that make manufacturing more difficult and costly than necessary, most firms ensure that R&D and manufacturing remain in close contact.

STRUCTURE AND FLEXIBILITY Organizational structure is not permanent but is often modified to suit changes both within a company and in its external environment. Because companies usually base organizational structures on strategies, changes in strategy usually require adjustments in structure. Similarly, because changes in national business environments can force changes in strategy, the same changes will influence company structure. It is especially important to monitor closely the conditions in countries characterized by rapidly shifting cultural, political,

chains of command
Lines of authority that run from top management to individual employees and that specify internal reporting relationships.

and economic environments. Let's now explore four organizational structures that have been developed to improve the responsiveness and effectiveness of companies conducting international business activities.

QUICK STUDY 3

1. Explain what is meant by *organizational structure*. What is the difference between centralized and decentralized decision making?
2. Why are coordination and flexibility important when designing organizational structure?
3. Describe what is meant by the term *chains of command*.

Types of Organizational Structure

There are many different ways in which a company can organize itself to carry out its international business activities. But four organizational structures tend to be most common for the vast majority of international companies: division structure, area structure, product structure, and matrix structure.

INTERNATIONAL DIVISION STRUCTURE An **international division structure** separates domestic from international business activities by creating a separate international division with its own manager (see Figure 11.4). In turn, the international division is typically divided into units corresponding to the countries in which a company is active—say, Brazil, China, and France. Within each country, a general manager controls the manufacture and marketing of the firm's products. Each country unit typically carries out all of its own activities with its own departments, such as marketing and sales, finance, and production.

Because the international division structure concentrates international expertise in one division, divisional managers become specialists in a wide variety of activities such as foreign exchange, export documentation, and host government relations. By consigning international activities to a single division, a firm can reduce costs, increase efficiency, and prevent international activities from disrupting domestic operations. These are important criteria for firms new to international business and whose international operations account for a small percentage of their total business.

An international division structure can, however, create two problems for companies. First, international managers must often rely on home-country managers for the financial resources and technical know-how that give the company its international competitive edge. Poor coordination between managers can hurt the performance not only of the international division but also of the entire company. Second, the general manager of the international division typically is responsible for operations in all countries. Although this policy facilitates coordination across countries, it reduces the authority of each country manager. Rivalries and poor cooperation between the general manager and country managers can be damaging to the company's overall performance.

international division structure
Organizational structure that separates domestic from international business activities by creating a separate international division with its own manager.

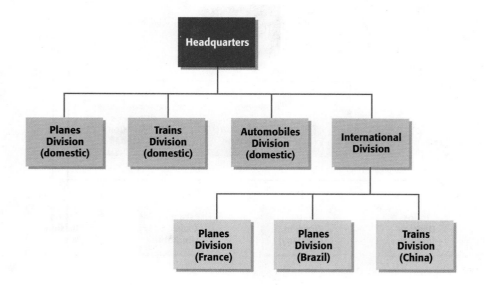

FIGURE 11.4

International Division Structure

FIGURE 11.5

International Area Structure

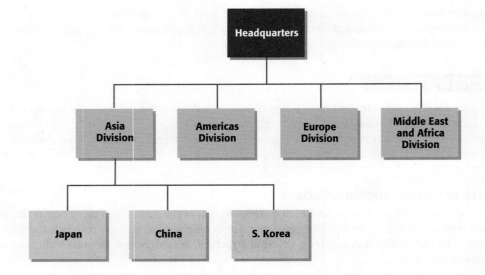

international area structure
Organizational structure that organizes a company's entire global operations into countries or geographic regions.

INTERNATIONAL AREA STRUCTURE An **international area structure** organizes a company's entire global operations into countries or geographic regions (see Figure 11.5). The greater the number of countries in which a company operates, the greater the likelihood it will organize into regions—say, Asia, Europe, and the Americas—instead of countries. Typically, a general manager is assigned to each country or region. Under this structure, each geographic division operates as a self-contained unit, with most decision making decentralized in the hands of the country or regional managers. Each unit has its own set of departments—purchasing, production, marketing and sales, R&D, and accounting. Each unit also tends to handle much of its own strategic planning. Management at the parent-company headquarters makes decisions regarding overall corporate strategy and coordinates the activities of various units.

The international area structure is best suited to companies that treat each national or regional market as unique. It is particularly useful when there are vast cultural, political, or economic differences between nations or regions. When they enjoy a great deal of control over activities in their own environments, general managers become experts on the unique needs of their buyers. On the other hand, because units act independently, allocated resources may overlap, and cross-fertilization of knowledge from one unit to another may be less than desirable.

global product structure
Organizational structure that divides worldwide operations according to a company's product areas.

GLOBAL PRODUCT STRUCTURE A **global product structure** divides worldwide operations according to a company's product areas. Figure 11.6 shows how a simplistic and fictional transportation company might be divided into planes, trains, and automobiles divisions.

FIGURE 11.6

Global Product Structure

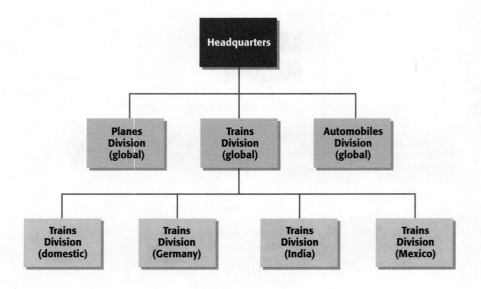

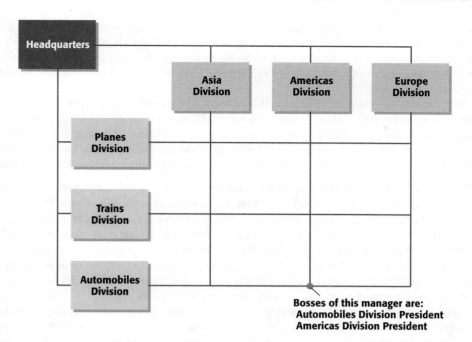

FIGURE 11.7
Global Matrix Structure

A computer company might be separated into divisions of Internet and Communications, Software Development, and New Technologies, for example. Each product division is then divided into domestic and international units. Each function—R&D, marketing, and so forth—is thus duplicated in both the domestic and international units of each product division.

The global product structure is suitable for companies that offer diverse sets of products or services because it overcomes some coordination problems of the international division structure. Because the primary focus is on the product, activities must be coordinated among a product division's domestic and international managers so they do not conflict.

GLOBAL MATRIX STRUCTURE A **global matrix structure** splits the chain of command between product and area divisions (see Figure 11.7). Each manager reports to two bosses—the president of the product division and the president of the geographic area. A main goal of the matrix structure is to bring together *geographic* area managers and *product* area managers in joint decision making. In fact, bringing together specialists from different parts of the organization creates a sort of team organization. The popularity of the matrix structure has grown among companies trying to increase local responsiveness, reduce costs, and coordinate worldwide operations.

global matrix structure
Organizational structure that splits the chain of command between product and area divisions.

The matrix structure resolves some of the shortcomings of other organizational structures, especially by improving communication among divisions and increasing the efficiency of highly specialized employees. At its best, the matrix structure can increase coordination while simultaneously improving agility and local responsiveness.

However, the global matrix structure suffers from two major shortcomings. First, the matrix form can be quite cumbersome. Numerous meetings are required simply to coordinate the actions of the various division heads, let alone the activities within divisions. In turn, the need for complex coordination tends to make decision making time consuming and slows the reaction time of the organization. Second, individual responsibility and accountability can become foggy in the matrix organization structure. Because responsibility is shared, managers can attribute poor performance to the actions of the other manager. Moreover, the source of problems in the matrix structure can be hard to detect and corrective action difficult to take.

There are other ways international companies can improve responsiveness and effectiveness. An increasingly popular method among international companies is the implementation of work teams to accomplish goals and solve problems. Let's explore in detail the use of work teams.

Work Teams

Globalization is forcing companies to respond more quickly to changes in the business environment. The formation of teams can be highly useful in improving responsiveness by cutting across functional boundaries—such as that between production and marketing—that slow decision making in an organization. Although a matrix organization accomplishes this by establishing cross-functional cooperation, companies do not always want to change their entire organizational structure in order to reap the benefits that cross-functional cooperation provides. In such cases, companies can implement several different types of teams without changing the overall company structure.

Work teams are assigned the tasks of coordinating their efforts to arrive at solutions and implementing corrective action. Today, international companies are turning to work teams on an unprecedented scale to increase direct contact between different operating units. Companies are even forming teams to design and implement their competitive strategies. Let's take a look at several different types of teams—self-managed teams, cross-functional teams, and global teams.

self-managed team
Team in which the employees from a single department take on the responsibilities of their former supervisors.

SELF-MANAGED TEAMS A **self-managed team** is one in which the employees from a single department take on the responsibilities of their former supervisors. When used in production, such teams often reorganize the methods and flow of production processes. Because they are "self-managed," they reduce the need for managers to watch over their every activity. The benefits of self-managed teams typically include increased productivity, product quality, customer satisfaction, employee morale, and company loyalty. In fact, the most common self-managed teams in many manufacturing companies are *quality-improvement teams,* which help reduce waste in the production process and, therefore, lower costs.

The global trend toward "downsizing" internal operations to make them more flexible and productive has increased the popularity of teams because they reduce the need for direct supervision. Companies around the world now employ self-managed teams in international operations. Yet, research indicates that cultural differences can influence resistance to the concept of self-management and the practice of using teams. Among other things, experts suggest that international managers follow some basic guidelines:[7]

- Use selection tests to identify the employees most likely to perform well in a team environment.
- Adapt the self-managed work-team concept to the national culture of each subsidiary.
- Adapt the process of integrating self-managed work teams to the national culture of each subsidiary.
- Train local managers at the parent company and allow them to introduce teams at a time they feel is most appropriate.

Similarly, the cultural differences discussed in Chapter 2 are important to managers who design teams in international operations. For example, certain cultures are more collectivist in nature. Some cultures harbor greater respect for differences in people's status. In some cultures, people believe the future is largely beyond their personal control. And some cultures display a so-called work-to-live mentality. Researchers say that in these cases conventional management should retain fairly tight authority over teams. But teams are likely to be productive if given greater autonomy in a culture where people are very hardworking.[8]

cross-functional team
Team composed of employees who work at similar levels in different functional departments.

CROSS-FUNCTIONAL TEAMS A **cross-functional team** is one composed of employees who work at similar levels in different functional departments. These teams work to develop changes in operations and are well suited to projects that require coordination across functions, such as reducing the time needed to get a product from the idea stage to the marketplace. International companies also use cross-functional teams to improve quality by having employees from purchasing, manufacturing, and distribution (among other functions) work together to address specific quality issues. For the same reason, cross-functional teams can help break down barriers between departments and reorganize operations around processes rather than by functional departments.

global team
Team of top managers from both headquarters and international subsidiaries who meet to develop solutions to company-wide problems.

GLOBAL TEAMS Finally, large international corporations are creating so-called **global teams**— groups of top managers from both headquarters and international subsidiaries who meet to develop solutions to company-wide problems. For example, Nortel Networks (www.nortel.com) of Canada created a global team of top executives from Britain, Canada, France, and the United States that traveled to Asia, Europe, and North America looking for ways to improve product-development practices.

Depending on the issue at hand, team members can be drawn from a single business unit or assembled from several different units. Whereas some teams are disbanded after resolving specific issues, others move on to new problems. The performance of global teams can be impaired by matters such as large distances between team members, lengthy travel times to meetings, and the inconvenience of working across time zones. Companies can sometimes overcome these difficulties, although doing so can be rather costly.

> ### QUICK STUDY 4
>
> 1. What four main types of organizational structure are used in international business?
> 2. Explain how each type of organizational structure differs from the other three.
> 3. Identify the three different types of work teams. How does each improve responsiveness and effectiveness?

A Final Word

Managers have the important and complicated task of formulating international strategies at the corporation, business unit, and individual department levels. Managers often analyze their companies' operations by viewing them as a chain of activities that create customer value (value-chain analysis). It is through this process that managers can identify and implement strategies suited to their companies' unique capabilities. The strategies that managers select then determine the firm's organizational structure. National business environments also affect managers' strategy and structure decisions, including whether to alter their products (standardization versus adaptation), where to locate facilities (centralized versus decentralized production), and what type of decision making to implement (centralized versus decentralized decision making).

The role of managers in formulating strategies and creating the overall organizational structure cannot be overstated. The strategies they choose determine the market segments in which their firms will compete and whether their firms will pursue low-cost leadership in their industry or will differentiate their products and charge a higher price. These decisions are crucial to all later activities of firms that are going international. They also influence how a company (1) enters international markets, (2) employs its human resources, and (3) manages its day-to-day production, marketing, and other operations.

Chapter Summary

MyManagementLab
Go to **mymanagementlab.com** to complete the problem marked with this icon .

1. **Explain the stages of identification and analysis that precede strategy selection.**
   - *Planning* means identifying and selecting an organization's objectives and deciding how the organization will achieve them.
   - *Strategy* is the set of planned actions taken by managers to help a company meet its objectives.
   - Prior to formulating strategy, managers must first *identify* the company's mission, goals, core competency, and value-creating activities.
   - Managers can identify a company's abilities that create customer value using *value-chain analysis,* which divides a company's activities into *primary* activities and *support* activities that are central to creating value for customers.
   - Managers must also analyze the cultural, political, legal, and economic environments.
2. **Identify the two international strategies and the corporate-level strategies that companies use.**
   - A *multinational (multidomestic) strategy* means adapting products and their marketing strategies in each national market to suit local preferences.
   - A *global strategy* means offering the same products using the same marketing strategy in all national markets.
   - Companies in more than one line of business must formulate a *corporate-level strategy* that encompasses all of the company's different business units.

- A *growth strategy* increases the scale (size of activities) or scope (kinds of activities) of a corporation's operations.
- A *retrenchment strategy* reduces the scale or scope of a corporation's businesses.
- A *stability strategy* guards against change and is used to avoid a corporation's growth or retrenchment.
- A *combination strategy* mixes growth, retrenchment, and stability strategies across a corporation's business units.

3. Identify the business-level strategies of companies and the role of department-level strategies.
   - A *low-cost leadership strategy* means exploiting economies of scale to have the lowest cost structure of any competitor in an industry.
   - A *differentiation strategy* involves designing products to be perceived as unique by buyers throughout an industry.
   - A *focus strategy* means serving the needs of a narrowly defined market segment by being the low-cost leader, by differentiating the product, or both.
   - Achieving corporate- and business-level objectives depends on effective *department-level strategies* that focus on the specific activities that create customer value—whether a department conducts *primary* or *support activities.*

4. Discuss the important issues that influence the choice of organizational structure.
   - *Organizational structure* is the way in which a company divides its activities among separate units and coordinates activities among those units.
   - Important to organizational structure is the degree to which decision making in an organization will be centralized (made at a high level) or decentralized (made at a subsidiary level).
   - *Centralized decision making* helps coordinate operations of international subsidiaries, whereas *decentralized decision making* places a premium on local responsiveness.
   - When designing organizational structure, managers must consider the issues of *coordination* and *flexibility.*
   - Organizational structure must define areas of responsibility and *chains of command*—lines of authority that specify internal reporting relationships.

5. Describe each type of international organizational structure, and explain the importance of work teams.
   - An *international division structure* separates domestic from international activities by creating a separate division with its own manager.
   - An *international area structure* organizes a company's entire global operations into countries or geographic regions, with each division operating as a self-contained unit.
   - A *global product structure* divides worldwide operations into product divisions, which are then divided into domestic and international units.
   - A *global matrix structure* splits the chain of command and forces each manager and employee to report to two bosses—the general manager of the product division and the general manager of the geographic area.
   - *Work teams* are assigned the tasks of coordinating their efforts to arrive at solutions and implementing corrective action; different types are *self-managed teams, cross-functional teams,* and *global teams.*

Talk It Over

★1. "Cultures around the world are becoming increasingly similar, so companies should standardize both their products and global marketing efforts." Do you agree or disagree with this reasoning? Are there certain industries for which it might be more or less true?

Teaming Up

1. **Ideas Project.** As a team, list five products that you consumed (breakfast, chewing gum, etc.) or used (Wi-Fi Internet service, radio program, etc.) within the past 24 hours. What strategy does the company behind each good or service employ: low-cost, differentiation, or focus? For each company, write one or two paragraphs on how you arrived at your answer.

2. **Research Project.** As a group, select an international company that interests you and locate its annual report from its investor relations department on the Internet. What is the company's mission statement or overriding objective? What are its corporate- and business-level strategies? In which nations does it produce and market its products? Are its production facilities centralized or decentralized? Does it standardize products or adapt them for different markets? What type of organizational structure does it have? Which of the two types of international strategy does it seem to follow? Does the company make use of work teams? Present your group's findings to the class.

3. **Debate Project.** In this project, two groups of four students each will debate the merits of adopting either a multinational or a global strategy (each side will advocate one strategy). After the first student from each side has spoken, the second student will question the opposing side's arguments, looking for holes and inconsistencies. The third student will attempt to answer these arguments. The fourth student will present a summary of each side's arguments. Finally, the class will vote to determine which team has offered the more compelling argument.

Key Terms

chains of command (p. 288)
combination strategy (p. 284)
core competency (p. 279)
cross-functional team (p. 292)
differentiation strategy (p. 285)
focus strategy (p. 285)
global matrix structure (p. 291)
global product structure (p. 290)
global strategy (p. 283)

global team (p. 292)
growth strategy (p. 284)
international area structure (p. 290)
international division structure (p. 289)
low-cost leadership strategy (p. 285)
mission statement (p. 278)
multinational (multidomestic) strategy (p. 282)

organizational structure (p. 287)
planning (p. 278)
retrenchment strategy (p. 284)
self-managed team (p. 292)
stability strategy (p. 284)
stakeholders (p. 278)
strategy (p. 278)
value-chain analysis (p. 280)

Take It to the Web

1. **Video Report.** Visit this book's channel on YouTube (www.YouTube.com/MyIBvideos). Click on "Videos" near the top of the page, and click on the set of videos labeled "Ch 11: International Strategy and Organization." Watch one video from the list, and then summarize it in a half-page report. Reflecting on the contents of this chapter, which components of international strategy and organization can you identify in the video? How might a company engaged in international business act on the information contained in the video?

2. **Website Report.** Before the spin-off of Kraft Foods in 2007, Altria Group was the parent company of both Kraft and Philip Morris. Visit the Web site of the Altria Group (www. altria.com). What corporate-level strategies do you think Altria was pursuing in its different businesses prior to the spin-off?

   Visit the websites of Kraft Foods (www.kraft.com) and Philip Morris (www. philipmorrisusa.com)—both their domestic and international operations. What business-level strategies are being pursued by (a) Kraft and (b) Philip Morris?

   Why do you think the Altria Group made Kraft its own company? Do you think it had anything to do with the mix of businesses in which then-parent Altria Group was involved? Why or why not? Identify as many stakeholders of Altria, Philip Morris, and Kraft Foods as you can. Aside from past smoking-related lawsuits, are there any trends that encouraged Kraft's independence?

Ethical Challenges

1. You are the CEO of a multinational corporation that operates in more than 100 nations worldwide. Recent changes in the global economy are redrawing many geographical and political borders. The growing interdependence of socially, politically, economically, and legally diverse countries is causing firms to revise operating policies and strategies. You are personally involved in developing a code of ethics for your firm that reflects today's legal and moral atmosphere. You want your firm's code to be effective across all markets in which it operates. Given the complexity of the issues involved, what sort of policy do you think is appropriate for a firm involved in dissimilar nations? Do you think that it is possible to create a uniform code of ethics that is applicable to any business operating in any culture? What issues should such a code address?

2. You are a member of an international ethics commission assembled by the World Trade Organization (WTO). Your team has been asked to assess the global tactics of Microsoft in recent years. A primary issue is whether Microsoft took unfair advantage of its powerful position in the computer industry by using "strong-arm tactics" on software customers and by crushing weaker rivals. Regardless of whether or not Microsoft is guilty of anticompetitive acts in a legal sense, do you believe that Microsoft has conducted itself ethically in its business dealings? Do you argue that Microsoft has abused its power in the industry, or is it simply a tough competitor? Do you think the WTO should develop a policy on the competitive tactics of global powerhouses such as Microsoft? Why or why not?

3. You are the new president of Star Manufacturing, an international subsidiary of a large multinational firm that makes automotive parts. Since you arrived at Star three months ago, you are finding it difficult to get your firm's materials and finished products through customs quickly. Local legal counsel suggests a payment to local officials to eliminate your problem with customs, an apparently common local practice. The bribe would expedite the entire shipping process, which will help improve profits. What do you do? Is there a specific policy your firm could develop that all Star employees could follow? What other issues must you consider? If additional information would be helpful to you, what would it be?

MyManagementLab

Go to **mymanagementlab.com** for Auto-graded writing questions as well as the following Assisted-graded writing questions:

11-1. "The elements that affect strategy formulation are the same whether a company is domestic or international." Do you agree or disagree with this statement? Why? Support your argument with examples.

11-2. Continuous advancements in technology are deeply affecting the way international businesses are managed. Do you think technology (the Internet, for example) should radically alter the fundamental strategies and organizational structures of international companies? Or do you think companies can simply graft new strategies and structures onto existing ones? Explain your answers.

11-3. Mymanagementlab Only – comprehensive writing assignment for this chapter.

Practicing International Management Case

IKEA's Global Strategy

IKEA (www.ikea.com) is a nearly $30 billion global furniture powerhouse based in Sweden. With more than 301 stores in 37 countries, the company's success reflects founder Ingvar Kamprad's "social ambition" of selling a wide range of stylish, functional home furnishings at prices so low that the majority of people can afford to buy them. The story of Kamprad's success is detailed in a book titled *IKEA: The Entrepreneur, the Business Concept, the Culture*. The store exteriors are painted with Sweden's national colors, bright blue and yellow. Shoppers view furniture in scores of realistic settings arranged throughout the cavernous showrooms.

In a departure from standard industry practice, IKEA's furniture bears names such as "Ivar" and "Sten" as well as model numbers. At IKEA, shopping is very much a self-service activity—after browsing and writing down the names of desired items in the showroom, shoppers pick their furniture off shelves, where they find boxes containing the furniture in kit form. One of the cornerstones of IKEA's strategy is having customers take their purchases home and assemble the furniture themselves. The typical IKEA store also contains a Swedish-cuisine restaurant, a grocery store called the Swede Shop, a supervised play area for children, and a baby-care room.

IKEA's approach to the furniture business enables it to rack up impressive growth in an industry in which overall sales are flat. Sourcing furniture from more than 1,500 suppliers in 50 countries helps the company maintain its low-cost position. IKEA has also opened stores in emerging markets, such as in Central and Eastern Europe. Because many consumers in those regions have relatively low purchasing power, the stores offer a smaller selection of goods, and some of the furniture is designed specifically for the cramped living styles typical in former Soviet bloc countries. Throughout Europe, IKEA benefits from the perception that Sweden is the source of high-quality products. In fact, one of the company's key selling points is its "Swedishness." IKEA also operates in emerging markets like Russia, where its core strategy and anticorruption policies have been effective.

Industry observers predict that the United States will eventually be IKEA's largest market. The company opened its first U.S. store in Philadelphia in 1985 and today has dozens of outlets that generate billions of dollars in sales annually. IKEA's competitors take the company very seriously. Jeff Young, chief operating officer of Lexington Furniture Industries, says, "IKEA is on the way to becoming the Walmart Stores of the home-furnishing industry. If you're in this business, you'd better take a look." Some U.S. customers, however, are irked to find popular items sometimes out of stock. Another problem is the long lines resulting from the company's no-frills approach. Complained one shopper, "Great idea, poor execution. The quality of much of what they sell is good, but the hassles make you question whether it's worth it."

Goran Carstedt, president of IKEA North America, responds to such criticism by referring to the company's mission. He notes that IKEA's ability to keep prices low rests on the strategy of providing limited services. Customers return to IKEA despite having to make some small sacrifices because they value the company's low prices, he says. To keep them coming back, IKEA is spending millions on advertising to get its message across. Whereas common industry practice is to rely heavily on newspaper and radio advertising, two-thirds of IKEA's North American advertising budget is allocated for TV. John Sitnik, an executive at IKEA U.S. Inc., says, "We distanced ourselves from the other furniture stores. We decided TV is something we can own."

Incredibly, IKEA has also expanded into apartment building. The retail giant has 3,500 of its prefab homes throughout Sweden, Norway, Finland, and the United Kingdom. IKEA's BoKlok (meaning "smart living" in Swedish) apartments resemble IKEA's modern furniture. The apartments are designed with open-plan living spaces with high ceilings, windows on three sides, and, of course, pre-fitted IKEA kitchens.

Thinking Globally

1. Has IKEA taken a standardization approach or an adaptation approach in its markets around the world? Do you think the company's approach is the right one for the future? Explain.
2. Which retailers are IKEA's biggest competitors in the United States? Why?
3. When company founder Kamprad decided to expand into China, his decision was not based on market research but, rather, on his own intuition. How well is IKEA doing in China? Did Kamprad's decision pay off?
4. After failing in Japan two decades earlier, IKEA returned in 2006. Conduct some research into how IKEA fared the second time around in Japan. Was IKEA able to avoid the mistakes it made in its first failed attempt?

Source: "The Corruption Eruption," *The Economist*, May 1, 2010, p. 73; Dianna Dilworth, "Ikea Enters UK's Housing Market," *Bloomberg Businessweek* (www.businessweek.com), April 20, 2007; Kerry Capell, "Ikea's New Plan for Japan," *Bloomberg Businessweek* (www.businessweek.com), April 26, 2006; Ikea website (www.ikea.com), selected reports.

Analyzing International Opportunities

LEARNING OBJECTIVES

After studying this chapter, you should be able to

1. Explain each of the four steps in the market- and site-screening process.

2. Describe the three primary difficulties of conducting international market research.

3. Identify the main sources of secondary international data and explain their usefulness.

4. Describe the main methods used to conduct primary international research.

A Look Back

Chapter 11 showed us how companies plan and organize themselves for international operations. We explored the different types of strategies and organizational structures that international companies use to accomplish their strategic goals.

A Look at This Chapter

This chapter begins with an explanation of how managers screen potential new markets and new sites for operations. We then discuss the main difficulties of conducting international market research. We also identify the information required in the screening process and where managers can go to obtain such information.

A Look Ahead

Chapter 13 describes the selection and management issues surrounding the different entry modes available to companies going international. We examine the importance of an export strategy for exporters and the pros and cons of each entry mode.

STARBUCKS CAUSES GLOBAL JITTERS

SEATTLE, Washington—Starbucks (www.starbucks.com) began its global journey in 1996 with its first coffeehouse in Tokyo, Japan. Today, Starbucks has 17,000 retail stores in 55 markets outside North America. Pictured here is a busy Starbucks Café located in Bangkok, Thailand. Although it has closed some underperforming stores, Starbucks still causes jitters globally for customers and competitors.

Starbucks brought European-style coffee to the United States and then took its American-style coffeehouses to Europe. The coffee giant was right that paper-cupped lattes and nonsmoking venues could take on Europe's traditional cafés. Although in Britain since the late 1990s, Starbucks waited patiently before steaming into Zurich, Switzerland, in 2001 and into Paris, France, in 2004. Starbucks carefully researched Europe's markets before opening its first European café in Zurich and then branching out to other nations. With its multicultural and multilingual population, the Swiss market gave Starbucks a "tremendous opportunity to learn how to operate elsewhere in Europe," revealed Mark McKeon, president of Starbucks Europe, Middle East, and Africa.

Source: VINAI DITHAJOHN/Newscom

At the same time, Starbucks introduced a coffee culture to tea lovers in China. Starbucks is encouraged by the fact that one-third of all Chinese households keep a jar of instant coffee on hand. Starbucks is trying to make coffee the drink of choice for the average 18- to 45-year-old Chinese consumer. "Per capita consumption of coffee in China is very small," admitted Howard Behar, president of Starbucks Coffee International. "But what you have is a tremendous amount of people, so the market will grow."

Starbucks had struggled in recent years, but the company now has rebounded nicely as a leaner version of its former self. It has a renewed focus on its core product, coffee, and on its image as a socially responsible multinational with its "Shared Planet" commitment. As you read this chapter, consider how companies research, analyze, and select the international markets they enter.[1]

Companies traditionally become involved in international business by choosing to enter familiar, nearby countries first. Managers feel comfortable entering nearby markets because they likely have already interacted with the people of those cultures and have at least some understanding of them. Companies in Canada, Mexico, and the United States often gain their initial international experiences in one another's markets. Likewise, businesses in Asia often seek out opportunities in one another's markets before pursuing investment opportunities outside the region.

Yet, companies today find themselves bridging the gaps presented by space and culture far more often than in the past. For one thing, technological advances in communication and transportation continue to open markets around the globe. Some companies can realistically consider nearly every location on earth either as a potential market or as a site for business operations. The expansion of regional markets (such as the European Union) also causes companies to analyze opportunities farther from home. Businesses locate production facilities within regional markets because producing in one of a region's countries provides duty-free access to every consumer in the trade bloc.

The rapidly changing global marketplace forces companies to view business strategies from a global perspective. Businesses today formulate production, marketing, and other strategies as components of integrated plans. For example, to provide a continuous flow of timely information into the production process, more and more firms locate research and development (R&D) facilities near their production sites abroad. Managers also find themselves screening and analyzing locations as potential markets and as potential sites for operations simultaneously. When Mercedes (www.mercedes.com) introduced the M-class sport utility vehicle to the U.S. market, executives also decided to build the vehicle there. The company did not merely estimate the size of the potential market for the vehicle but simultaneously selected a suitable production site.

This chapter presents a systematic screening process for both markets and sites. After describing important cultural, political, legal, and economic forces affecting the screening process, we explain the difficulties of conducting international research. We then explore the central sources of existing market data and the prime methods for conducting international research firsthand.

Screening Potential Markets and Sites

Two important issues concern managers during the market- and site-screening process. First, they want to keep search costs as low as possible. Second, they want to examine every potential market and every possible location. To accomplish these two goals, managers can segment the screening of markets and sites into the following four-step process (see Figure 12.1):

1. Identify basic appeal.
2. Assess the national business environment.
3. Measure market or site potential.
4. Select the market or site.

This screening process involves spending more time, money, and effort on the markets and sites that remain in the later stages of screening. Expensive feasibility studies (conducted later in the process) are performed on a few markets and sites that hold the greatest promise. This approach creates a screening process that is cost effective yet does not overlook potential locations. Let's now discuss each of the four steps in detail.

Step 1: Identify Basic Appeal

We have already seen that companies go international either to increase sales (and thus profits) or to access resources. The first step in identifying potential markets is to assess the basic demand for a product. Similarly, the first step in selecting a site for a facility to undertake production, R&D, or some other activity is to explore the availability of the resources required.

DETERMINING BASIC DEMAND   The first step in searching for potential markets means finding out whether there is a basic demand for a company's product. Important in determining this basic appeal is a country's climate. For example, no company would try to market snowboards in Indonesia, Sri Lanka, or Central America because they receive no snowfall. The same

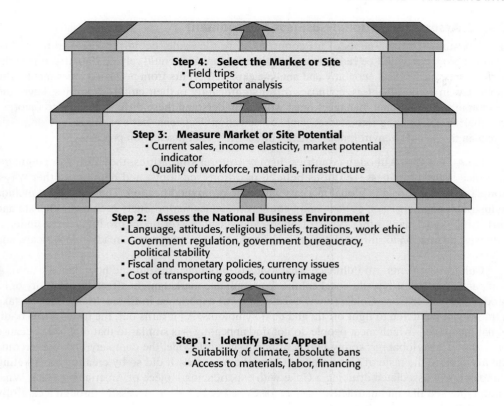

FIGURE 12.1

Screening Process for Potential Markets and Sites

product, on the other hand, is well suited for markets in the Canadian Rockies, northern Japan, and the Swiss Alps. Although this stage seems simple, it cannot be taken too lightly. A classic example is when, during its initial forays into international business, Walmart (www.walmart.com) found ice-fishing huts in its Puerto Rico inventory and no snowshoes at its stores in Ontario, Canada.

Certain countries also ban specific goods. Islamic countries, for instance, forbid the importation of alcoholic products, and the penalties for smuggling are stiff. Although alcohol is available on the planes of international airlines such as British Airways (www.ba.com) and KLM (www.klm.com), it cannot leave the airplane, and consumption cannot take place until the plane has left the airspace of the country operating under Islamic law.

DETERMINING AVAILABILITY OF RESOURCES Companies that require particular resources to carry out local business activities must be sure they are available. Raw materials needed for manufacturing either must be found in the national market or must be imported. Yet imports may encounter tariffs, quotas, or other government barriers. Managers must consider the additional costs of importing to ensure that total product cost does not rise to unacceptable levels.

The availability of labor is essential to production in any country. Many companies choose to relocate to countries where workers' wages are lower than they are in the home country. This practice is most common among makers of labor-intensive products—those for which labor accounts for a large portion of total cost. Companies considering local production must determine whether there is enough labor available locally for production operations.

Companies that hope to secure financing in a market abroad must determine the availability and cost of local capital. If local interest rates are too high, a company might be forced to obtain financing in its home country or in other markets in which it is active. On the other hand, access to low-cost financing may provide a powerful inducement to a company that is seeking to expand internationally. British entrepreneur Richard Branson opened several of his Virgin (www.virgin.com) Megastores in Japan despite its reputation as a tough market to crack. One reason for Branson's initial attraction to Japan was a local cost of capital that was roughly one-third the cost in Britain.

Markets and sites that fail to meet a company's requirements for basic demand or resource availability in Step 1 are removed from further consideration.

Step 2: Assess the National Business Environment

If the business environments of all countries were the same, deciding where to market or produce products would be rather straightforward. Managers could rely on data that report the performance of the local economy and analyze expected profits from proposed investments. But as we saw in earlier chapters, countries differ significantly in their cultures, politics, laws, and economies. International managers must work to understand these differences and to incorporate their understanding into market- and site-selection decisions. Let's examine how domestic forces in the business environment actually affect the location-selection process.

CULTURAL FORCES Although countries display cultural similarities, they differ in language, attitudes toward business, religious beliefs, traditions, customs, and countless other ways. Some products are sold in global markets with little or no modification. These products include industrial machinery such as packaging equipment, consumer products such as toothpaste and soft drinks, and many other types of goods and services. Yet many products must undergo extensive adaptation to suit local preferences, such as books, magazines, ready-to-eat meals, and others.

Cultural elements can influence what kinds of products are sold and how they are sold. A company must assess how the local culture in a candidate market might affect the salability of its product. Consider Coca-Cola's (www.coca-cola.com) experience in China. Many Chinese take a traditional medicine to fight off flu and cold symptoms. As it turns out, the taste of this traditional medicine—which most people do not find appealing—is similar to that of Coke. Because of Coca-Cola's global marketing policy of one taste worldwide, the company had to overcome the aversion to the taste of Coke among Chinese consumers. It did so by creating a marketing campaign that associated drinking a Coke with experiencing a piece of American culture. What initially looked like an unattractive market for Coke became very successful through a carefully tailored marketing campaign.

Cultural elements in the business environment can also affect site-selection decisions. When substantial product modifications are needed for cultural reasons, a company might choose to establish production facilities in the target market itself. Yet serving customers' special needs in a target market must be offset against any potential loss of economies of scale due to producing in several locations rather than just one. Today, companies can minimize such losses through the use of flexible manufacturing methods. Although cellular phone manufacturer Nokia (www. nokia.com) produces in locations worldwide, it ensures that each one of its facilities can start producing any one of its mobile phones for its different markets within 24 hours.

A qualified workforce is important to a company no matter what activity it is to undertake at a particular site. Also, a strong work ethic among the local workforce is essential to having productive operations. Managers must assess whether an appropriate work ethic exists in each potential country for the purposes of production, service, or any other business activity. An adequate level of educational attainment among the local workforce for the planned business activity is also very important. Although product-assembly operations may not require an advanced education, R&D, high-tech production, and certain services normally will require extensive higher education. If the people at a potential site do not display an appropriate work ethic or educational attainment, the site will be ruled out for further consideration.

POLITICAL AND LEGAL FORCES Political and legal forces also influence the market and site-location decision. Important factors include government regulation, government bureaucracy, and political stability. Let's take a brief look at each of these factors.

Government Regulation As we saw in earlier chapters, a nation's culture, history, and current events cause differences in attitudes toward trade and investment. Some governments take a strong nationalistic stance, whereas others are quite receptive to international trade and investment. A government's attitude toward trade and investment is reflected in the quantity and types of restrictions it places on imports, exports, and investment in its country.

Government regulations can quickly eliminate a market or site from further consideration. First of all, they can create investment barriers to ensure domestic control of a company or industry. One way in which a government can accomplish this is by imposing investment rules on matters such as business ownership—for example, forcing foreign companies into joint ventures. Governments can extend investment rules to bar international companies entirely from competing in certain sectors of the domestic economy. The practice is usually defended as a matter of national security. Economic sectors commonly declared off-limits include TV and radio broadcasting, automobile manufacturing, aircraft manufacturing, energy exploration, military-equipment manufacturing, and iron and steel production. Such industries are protected either because they are culturally important, are engines for economic growth, or are essential to any potential war effort. Host governments often fear that losing control in these economic sectors means placing their fate in the hands of international companies.

Second, governments can restrict international companies from freely removing prof-its earned in the nation. This policy can force a company to hold cash in the host country or to reinvest it in new projects there. Such policies are normally rooted in the inability of the host-country government to earn the foreign exchange needed to pay for badly needed imports. For instance, Chinese subsidiaries of multinational companies must convert the local currency (*renminbi*) to their home currency when remitting profits back to the parent company. Multina-tionals can satisfy this stipulation only as long as the Chinese government agrees to provide it with the needed home-country currency.

Third, governments can impose very strict environmental regulations. In most industrial countries, factories that produce industrial chemicals as their main output or as byproducts must adhere to strict pollution standards. Regulations typically demand the installation of expensive pollution-control devices and close monitoring of nearby air, water, and soil quality. While protecting the environment, such regulations also increase short-term production costs. Many developing and emerging markets have far less strict environmental regulations. Regrettably, some companies are alleged to have moved production of toxic materials to emerging markets in order to take advantage of lax environmental regulations and, in turn, of lower production costs. Although such behavior is roundly criticized as highly unethical, it will occur less often as nations continue cooperating to formulate common environmental protection policies.

Finally, governments can also require that companies divulge certain information. Coca-Cola actually left India when the government demanded that it disclose its secret Coke formula as a requirement for doing business there. Coca-Cola returned only after the Indian government dropped its demand.

Government Bureaucracy A lean and smoothly operating government bureaucracy can make a market or site more attractive. On the other hand, a bloated and cumbersome system of obtaining approvals and licenses from government agencies can make it less appealing. In many developing countries, what should be a relatively simple matter of obtaining a license to establish a retail outlet often means acquiring numerous documents from several agencies. The bureaucrats in charge of these agencies generally are little concerned with providing businesses with high-quality service. Managers must be prepared to deal with administrative delays and a maze of rules. For example, country managers for Millicom International Cellular (www.millicom.com) in Tanzania needed to wait 90 days to get customs clearance on the monthly import of roughly $1 million in cellular telephone equipment. Millicom endured this bureaucratic obstacle because of the local market's potential.

Companies will endure a cumbersome bureaucracy if the opportunity is sufficient to off-set any potential delays and expenses. Companies entering China cite the patience needed to navigate a maze of government regulations that often contradict one another, and they com-plain about the large number of permissions required from different agencies. The trouble stems from the fact that China is continually revising and developing its system of business law as its economy develops. But an unclear legal framework and inefficient bureaucracy are not deterring investment in China because the opportunities for both marketers and manufacturers are simply too great to ignore.

Political Stability Every nation's business environment is affected to some degree by political risk. As we saw in Chapter 3, political risk is the likelihood that a society will undergo political changes that negatively affect local business activity. Political risk can threaten the market of an exporter, the production facilities of a manufacturer, or the ability of a company to remove profits from the country in which they were earned.

The key element of political risk that concerns companies is *unforeseen political change*. Political risk tends to rise if a company cannot estimate the future political environment with a fair degree of accuracy. An event with a negative impact that is expected to occur in the future is

Stability can attract international business, but social unrest can severely disrupt operations and drive out international firms. Here, a man throws a rock at police during a riot in Paranaque City south of the capital Manila in the Philippines. Riots erupted as hundreds of families who claimed they were legally allowed to occupy land resisted demolition teams. Illegal demolition is frequent in these urban centers where many impoverished rural workers reside.

Source: imago stock&people/Newscom

not, in itself, bad for companies because the event can be planned for and necessary precautions taken. It is the unforeseen negative events that create political risk for companies.

Managers' perceptions of a market's political risk are often affected by their memories of past political unrest in the market. Yet managers cannot let past events blind them to future opportunities. International companies must try to monitor and predict political events that threaten operations and future profits. By investigating the political environment proactively, managers can focus on political risk and develop action plans for dealing with it.

But where do managers get the information to answer such questions? They may assign company personnel to gather information on the level of political risk in a country, or they may obtain it from independent agencies that specialize in providing political-risk services. The advice of country and regional specialists who are knowledgeable about the current political climate of a market can be especially helpful. Such specialists can include international bankers, political consultants, reporters, country-risk specialists, international relations scholars, political leaders, union leaders, embassy officials, and other local businesspeople currently working and living in the country in question.

ECONOMIC AND FINANCIAL FORCES Managers must carefully analyze a nation's economic policies before selecting it as a new market or site for operations. The poor fiscal and monetary policies of a nation's central bank can cause high rates of inflation, increasing budget deficits, a depreciating currency, falling productivity levels, and flagging innovation. Such consequences typically lower investor confidence and force international companies to scale back or cancel proposed investments. For instance, India's government finally reduced its restrictive trade and investment policies and introduced more-open policies. These new policies encouraged investment by multinationals in production facilities and R&D centers, especially in the computer software industry.

Currency and liquidity problems pose special challenges for international companies. Volatile currency values make it difficult for firms to predict future earnings accurately in terms of the home-country currency. Wildly fluctuating currency values also make it difficult to calculate how much capital a company needs for a planned investment. Unpredictable changes in currency values can also make liquidating assets more difficult because the greater uncertainty will likely reduce liquidity in capital markets—especially in countries with relatively small capital markets, such as Bangladesh and Slovakia.

In addition to their home government's resources, managers can obtain information about economic and financial conditions from institutions such as the World Bank, the International Monetary Fund, and the Asian Development Bank. Other sources of information include all types of business and economic publications and the many sources of free information on the Internet.

OTHER FORCES Transport costs and country image also play important roles in the assessment of national business environments. Let's take a brief look at each of these forces.

Cost of Transporting Materials and Goods The cost of transporting materials and finished goods affects any decision about where to locate manufacturing facilities. Some products cost very little to transport through the production and distribution process, whereas others cost a great deal. **Logistics** refers to management of the physical flow of products from the point of origin as raw materials to end users as finished products. Logistics weds production activities to the activities needed to deliver products to buyers. It includes all modes of transportation, storage, and distribution.

logistics
Management of the physical flow of products from the point of origin as raw materials to end users as finished products.

To realize the importance of efficient logistics, consider that global logistics is a $400 billion industry. We often think of the United States as an efficient logistics market because of its extensive interstate road system and rail lines that stretch from east to west. But because of overcrowded highways, 2 billion people-hours are lost to gridlock each year. That translates into $48 billion in lost productivity. Transport companies and cargo ports strenuously advertise their services precisely because of the high cost to businesses of inefficient logistics.

Country Image Because *country image* embodies every facet of a nation's business environment, it is highly relevant to the selection of sites for production, R&D, or any other activity. For example, country image affects the location of manufacturing or assembly operations because products must typically be stamped with labels identifying where they were made or assembled—such as "Made in China" or "Assembled in Brazil." Although such labels do not affect all products to the same degree, they can present important positive or negative images and boost or dampen sales.

Products made in relatively developed countries tend to be evaluated more positively than products from less-developed countries.[2] This relation is due to the perception among consumers that the workforces of certain nations have superior skills in making particular products. For example, consumer product giants Procter & Gamble (www.pg.com) and Unilever (www.unilever.com) have manufacturing facilities in Vietnam. But Vietnamese consumers tend to shun these companies' locally made Close-Up toothpaste and Tide detergent, instead seeking out identical products and brands produced in neighboring countries, such as Thailand. As one young Vietnamese shopper explained, "Tide from Thailand smells nicer." A general perception among Vietnamese consumers is that goods from Japan or Singapore are the best, followed by Thai goods. Unfortunately for Procter & Gamble and Unilever in Vietnam, many goods from other countries are smuggled in and sold on the black market, thereby denying the companies local sales revenue.

A country's image can be positive in one product class but negative in another. For example, the fact that Volkswagen's (www.volkswagen.com) new Beetle is made in Mexico for the U.S. market has not hurt the Beetle's sales. But would affluent consumers buy a hand-built Rolls-Royce (www.rolls-roycemotorcars.com) automobile if it were produced in Bolivia? Because Rolls-Royce buyers pay for the image of a brilliantly crafted luxury car, the Rolls-Royce image probably would not survive intact if the company were to produce its cars in Bolivia.

Finally, note that country image can and does change over time. For example, "Made in India" has traditionally been associated with low-technology products such as soccer balls and many types of textile products. But today, world-class computer software companies increasingly rely on the software-development skills of engineers located in and around Madras and Bangalore in southern India.

Throughout our discussion of Step 2 of the screening process (assessing the national business environment), we have presented many factors central to traditional business activities. To explore issues specific to entering international markets successfully over the Internet, see the Manager's Briefcase, titled "Conducting Global e-Business."

QUICK STUDY 1

1. What are the four steps in the screening process?
2. Identify the main factors to investigate when identifying the basic appeal of a market or site for operations.
3. What key forces should be examined when assessing a nation's business environment?
4. How do transport costs and country image affect the location decision?

MANAGER'S BRIEFCASE   Conducting Global e-Business

Generating sales in new geographic markets over the Internet is an increasingly popular method of expansion for large multinationals and entrepreneurs alike. Here are some issues managers should consider when entering new markets using the Internet.

Market Access

- **Infrastructure.** Before investing heavily in e-business, investigate whether your potential customers have easy access to the Internet. Determine whether their government is developing advanced digital networks.
- **Content.** Companies must be informed about the different policies of each country through which their information travels in order to avoid liability. Key topics are truth in advertising, fraud prevention, and violent, seditious, or graphic materials.
- **Standards.** It is not always entirely clear which country has the power to establish standards of operations for e-business. Standards might be set up as trade barriers to keep international companies out of a domestic market.

Legal Issues

- **Privacy.** One strength of e-business is that consumer data can be collected easily and used to generate sales. But consumer groups in some countries view the collection of such data as an invasion of privacy. Consumers are particularly vehement if they are unaware that this information is being collected and of how it is being used.
- **Security.** Companies must ensure their data communications are safe from unauthorized access or modification. Security technology, such as encryption, password controls, and firewalls, still needs support from a global infrastructure.
- **Intellectual Property.** International agreements govern and protect copyrights, databases, patents, and trademarks. Yet these issues will remain a global concern for e-business until a widely accepted legal framework is established for the Internet.

Financial Matters

- **Electronic Payments.** Online use of credit cards remains a security concern for many consumers. Global electronic payment systems such as stored-value, smart cards, and other systems are in various stages of development and will alleviate many security issues.
- **Tariffs and Taxation.** International policies regarding which party in an international e-business transaction owes taxes to which nation are not yet fully developed. Countries differ widely on how these matters should be treated.

Step 3: Measure Market or Site Potential

Markets and sites passing the first two steps in the screening process undergo further analysis in order for companies to arrive at a more manageable number of potential locations. Despite the presence of a basic need for a product and an adequately stable national business environment, potential customers might not be ready or able to buy a product for a variety of reasons. Despite the availability of resources, certain sites may be unable to supply a given company with the *level* of resources it needs. Let's explore the factors that further influence the potential suitability of markets and sites for operations.

MEASURING MARKET POTENTIAL As barriers to trade are reduced worldwide, companies are looking to increase sales in industrialized and emerging markets alike. But businesses can seldom create one marketing plan that will cover every market in which they sell their products. Nations enjoy different levels of economic development that affect what kinds of goods are sold, the manner in which they are sold, and their inherent features. Likewise, different levels of economic development require varying approaches to researching market potential. But how do managers estimate potential demand for particular products? Let's look at the factors managers consider when analyzing industrialized markets and then examine a special tool for analyzing emerging markets.

Industrialized Markets The information needed to estimate the market potential for a product in industrialized nations tends to be more readily available than for emerging markets. In fact, for the most-developed markets, research agencies exist for the sole purpose of supplying market data to companies. Euromonitor (www.euromonitor.com) is one such company with an extensive global reach in consumer goods. The company sells reports and does company-specific studies for many international corporations and entrepreneurs. Some of the information in a typical industry analysis includes the following:

- Names, production volumes, and market shares of the largest competitors
- Volume of exports and imports of the product
- Structure of the wholesale and retail distribution networks

- Background on the market, including population figures and key social trends
- Total expenditure on the product (and similar products) in the market
- Retail sales volume and market prices of the product
- Future outlook for the market and potential opportunities

The value of such information supplied by specialist agencies is readily apparent—these reports provide a quick overview of the size and structure of a nation's market for a product. Reports vary in their cost (depending on the market and product), but many can be had for around $750 to $1,500. The company also allows online purchase of reports in small segments for as little as $20 each. We discuss other sources for this type of market data later in this chapter.

Thus, companies that enter the market in industrialized countries often have a great deal of data available on that particular market. What becomes important then is the forecast for the growth or contraction of a potential market. One way of forecasting market demand is by determining a product's **income elasticity**—the sensitivity of demand for a product relative to changes in income. The income-elasticity *coefficient* for a product is calculated by dividing a percentage change in the quantity of a product demanded by a percentage change in income. A coefficient greater than 1.0 conveys an *income-elastic* product, or one for which demand increases more relative to an increase in income. These products tend to be discretionary purchases, such as computers, video games, jewelry, or expensive furniture—generally not considered essential items. A coefficient less than 1.0 conveys an *income-inelastic* product, or one for which demand increases less relative to an increase in income. These products are considered essential and include food, utilities, and beverages. To illustrate, if the income-elasticity coefficient for carbonated beverages is 0.7, the demand for carbonated beverages will increase 0.7 percent for every 1.0 percent increase in income. Conversely, if the income-elasticity coefficient for smartphones is 1.3, the demand for smartphones will increase 1.3 percent for every 1.0 percent increase in income.

income elasticity
Sensitivity of demand for a product relative to changes in income.

Emerging Markets The biggest emerging markets are more important today than ever. Nearly every large company engaged in international business is either already in or is considering entering the big emerging markets such as China and India. With their large consumer bases and rapid growth rates, they whet the appetite of marketers around the world. Although these markets are surely experiencing speed bumps along their paths of economic development, in the long term they cannot be ignored.

Companies considering entering emerging markets often face special problems related to a lack of information. Data on market size or potential may not be available, for example, because of undeveloped methods for collecting such data in a country. But there are ways companies can assess potential in emerging markets. One way is for them to rank different locations by developing a so-called *market-potential indicator* for each. This method, however, is only useful to companies considering exporting. Companies considering investing in an emerging market must look at other factors, which we examine next in the discussion of measuring site potential. The main variables commonly included in market-potential analyses are as follows:[3]

- **Market Size.** This variable provides a snapshot of the size of a market at any point in time. It does not estimate the size of a market for a particular product but rather the size of the overall economy. Market-size data allows managers to rank countries from largest to smallest, regardless of a particular product. Market size is typically estimated from a nation's total population or the amount of energy it produces and consumes.
- **Market Growth Rate.** This variable reflects the fact that, although the overall size of the market (economy) is important, so too is its rate of growth. It helps managers avoid markets that are large but shrinking and instead target those that are small but rapidly expanding. It is generally obtained through estimates of growth in gross domestic product (GDP) and energy consumption.
- **Market Intensity.** This variable estimates the wealth or buying power of a market from the expenditures of both individuals and businesses. It is estimated from per capita private consumption and/or per capita gross domestic product (GDP) at purchasing power parity (see Chapter 4).

- **Market Consumption Capacity.** The purpose of this variable is to estimate spending capacity. It is often estimated from the percentage of a market's population that is in the middle class, thereby concentrating on the core of an economy's buying power.
- **Commercial Infrastructure.** This factor attempts to assess channels of distribution and communication. Variables may include the number of telephones, TVs, fax machines, or personal computers per capita; the density of paved roads or number of vehicles per capita; and the population per retail outlet. An increasingly important variable for businesses relying on the Internet for sales is the number of Internet hosts per capita. But because these data become outdated quickly, care must be taken to ensure accurate information from the most current sources.
- **Economic Freedom.** This variable attempts to estimate the extent to which free-market principles predominate. It is typically a summary of government trade policies, government involvement in business, the enforcement of property rights, and the strength of the black market. A useful resource is the annual *Freedom in the World* report published by Freedom House (www.freedomhouse.org).
- **Market Receptivity.** This variable attempts to estimate market "openness." One way it can be estimated is by determining a nation's volume of international trade as a percentage of GDP. If a company wants to see how receptive a market is to goods from its home country, it can ascertain the amount of per capita imports entering the market from the home country. Managers can also examine the growth (or decline) in these imports.
- **Country Risk.** This variable attempts to estimate the total risk of doing business, including political, economic, and financial risks. Some market-potential estimation techniques include this variable in the market-receptivity variable. This factor is typically obtained from one of the many services that rate the risk of different countries, such as Political Risk Services Group (www.prsgroup.com).

After each of these factors is analyzed, they are assigned values according to their importance to the demand for a particular product. Potential locations are then ranked (assigned a market-potential indicator value) according to their appeal as a new market. As you may recall, we discussed several of these variables earlier in the book under the topics of national and international business environments. For example, *country risk* levels are shown in Map 3.1 (pages 82–83), *economic freedom* is shown in Map 4.1 (pages 114–115), and *market receptivity* (or openness) is shown in Map 5.1 (pages 134–135). Map 12.1 (pages 310–311) captures one other variable, *commercial infrastructure,* by showing the number of fixed-line and mobile phone subscribers per 1,000 people in each nation. This variable is an important indicator of a nation's overall economic development. Other variables that are also good proxies for this variable include the portion of a nation's roads that are paved or the number of personal computers, fax machines, and Internet hosts it has. One key cautionary note, however, is that emerging markets often either lack such statistics or, in the case of paved roads, international comparison is difficult.

MEASURING SITE POTENTIAL In this step of the site-screening process, managers must carefully assess the quality of the locally available resources. For many companies, the most important of these will be human resources—both labor and management. Wages are lower in certain markets because labor is abundant, relatively less skilled (though perhaps well educated), or both. Employees may or may not be adequately trained to manufacture a given product or to perform certain R&D activities. If workers are not adequately trained, the site-selection process must consider the additional money and time needed to train them.

Training local managers also requires a substantial investment of time and money. A lack of qualified local managers sometimes forces companies to send managers from the home market to the local market. This adds to costs because home-country managers must often receive significant bonuses for relocating to the local market. Companies must also assess the productivity of local labor and managers. After all, low wages tend to reflect low productivity levels of a workforce.

Managers should also examine the local infrastructure, including roads, bridges, airports, seaports, and telecommunications systems, when assessing site potential. Each of these systems can have a major impact on the efficiency with which a company transports materials and products. Of chief importance to many companies today is the state of a country's telecommunications infrastructure. Much business today is conducted through e-mail, and many businesses relay information electronically about matters such as sales orders, inventory levels, and production strategies, which must be coordinated among subsidiaries in different countries. Managers, therefore, must examine each potential site to determine how well it is prepared for contemporary communications.

Step 4: Select the Market or Site

This final step in the screening process involves the most intensive efforts to assess the remaining potential markets and sites—typically less than a dozen, sometimes just one or two. At this stage, managers normally want to visit each remaining location in order to confirm earlier expectations and to perform a competitor analysis. In the final analysis, managers normally evaluate each potential location's contribution to cash flows by undertaking a financial evaluation of a proposed investment. The specialized and technical nature of this analysis can be found in most textbooks on corporate finance.

FIELD TRIPS   The importance of top managers making a personal visit to each remaining potential market or site cannot be overstated. Such trips typically involve attending strings of meetings and engaging in tough negotiations. The trip represents an opportunity for managers to see firsthand what they have so far seen only on paper. It gives them an opportunity to experience the culture, observe in action the workforce that they might soon employ, or make personal contact with potential new customers and distributors. Any remaining issues tend to be thoroughly investigated during field trips so that the terms of any agreement are precisely known in the event that a particular market or site is chosen. Managers can then usually return to the chosen location to put the terms of the final agreement in writing.

COMPETITOR ANALYSIS   Because competitor analysis was covered in detail in Chapter 11, we offer only a few comments here. Intensely competitive markets typically put downward pressure on the prices that firms can charge their customers. In addition, intensely competitive sites for production and R&D activities often increase the costs of doing business. Naturally, lower prices and higher costs due to competitive forces must be balanced against the potential benefits offered by each market and site under consideration. At the very least, then, competitor analysis should address the following issues:

- Number of competitors in each market (domestic and international)
- Market share of each competitor
- Whether each competitor's product appeals to a small market segment or has mass appeal
- Whether each competitor focuses on high quality or low price
- Whether competitors tightly control channels of distribution
- Customer loyalty commanded by competitors
- Potential threat from substitute products
- Potential entry of new competitors into the market
- Competitors' control of key production inputs (such as labor, capital, and raw materials)

So far, we have examined a model that many companies follow when selecting new markets or sites for operations. We have seen what steps companies take in the screening process, but we have yet to learn how they undertake such a complex task. Let's now explore the types of situations companies encounter when conducting research in an international setting and the specific tools used in their research.

QUICK STUDY 2

1. What is the significance of *income elasticity* in measuring market potential?
2. Identify each component of a market-potential indicator. Why is each component useful in assessing emerging markets?
3. What are the most important factors to consider when measuring site potential?
4. Explain why a field trip and competitor analysis are useful in the final stage of the screening process.

MAP 12.1
Nations'
Commercial
Infrastructure

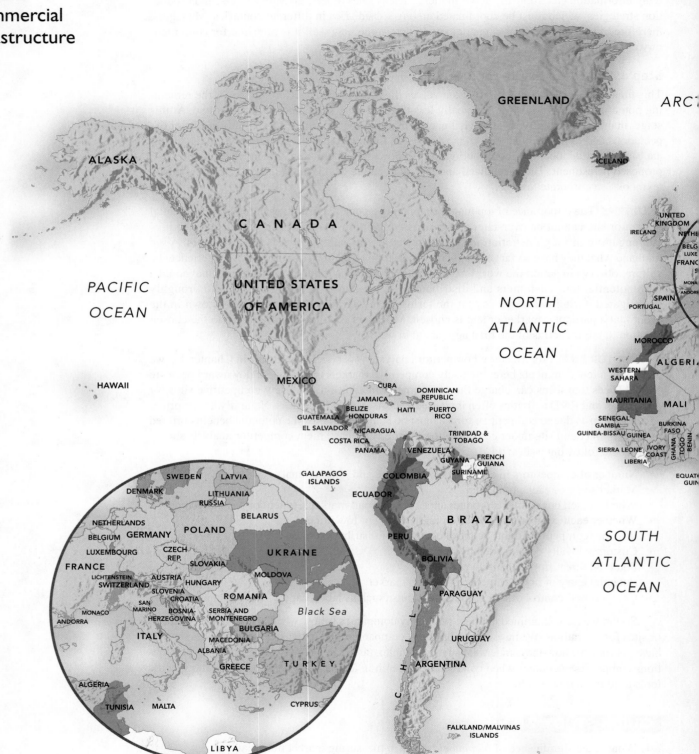

**Fixed lines and mobile phones
(per 1,000 people)**

- more than 1,500
- 1,000–1,499
- 500–999
- 300–499
- 100–299
- less than 100
- no data available

Conducting International Research

Increasing global competition forces companies to engage in high-quality research and analysis before selecting new markets and sites for operations. Companies are finding that such research helps them to better understand both buyer behavior and business environments abroad. **Market research** is the collection and analysis of information used to assist managers in making informed decisions. We define market research here to apply to the assessment of both potential markets and sites for operations. International market research provides information on national business environments, including cultural practices, politics, regulations, and the economy. It also informs managers about a market's potential size, buyer behavior, logistics, and distribution systems.

Conducting market research on new markets is helpful in designing all aspects of marketing strategy and understanding buyer preferences and attitudes. What works in France, for example, might not work in Singapore. Market research also lets managers learn about aspects of local business environments such as employment levels, wage rates, and the state of the local infrastructure before committing to the new location. It supplies managers with timely and relevant market information so that they can anticipate market shifts, changes in current regulations, and the potential entry of new competitors.

In this section, we first learn about several common problems that confront companies when conducting international research. We then explore some actual sources that managers use to assess potential new locations. We then examine some methods commonly used for conducting international research firsthand.

Difficulties of Conducting International Research

Market research serves essentially the same function in all nations. Unique conditions and circumstances, however, present certain difficulties that often force adjustments in the way research is performed in different nations. It is important for companies that are conducting market research themselves to be aware of potential obstacles so that their results are reliable. Companies that hire outside research agencies must also be aware of such difficulties. After all, they must evaluate the research results and assess their relevance to the location-selection decision. The following are three main difficulties associated with conducting international market research that we will examine:

1. Availability of data
2. Comparability of data
3. Cultural differences

AVAILABILITY OF DATA When trying to target specific population segments, marketing managers require highly detailed information. Fortunately, companies are often spared the time, money, and effort of collecting firsthand data for the simple reason that it has already been gathered. This is particularly true in highly industrialized countries, including Australia, Canada, Japan, those in Western Europe, and the United States, where both government agencies and private research firms supply information. Three of these information suppliers are ACNielsen (www.nielsen.com), SymphonyIRI Group (www.symphonyiri.com), and Survey Research Group (www.surveyresearchgroup.com). Table 12.1 lists the world's top market research firms.

In many emerging and developing countries, however, previously gathered quality information is hard to obtain. Even when market data is available, its reliability is questionable. For example, analysts sometimes charge the governments of certain emerging markets with trying to lure investors by overstating estimates of gross income and consumption levels. In addition to deliberate misrepresentation, tainted information can also result from improper local collection methods and analysis techniques. But research agencies in emerging and developing markets that specialize in gathering data for clients in industrialized countries are developing higher-quality techniques of collection and analysis. For example, information supplier and pollster Gallup (www.gallup.com) is aggressively expanding its operations throughout Southeast Asia in response to the need among Western companies for more accurate market research.

market research
Collection and analysis of information used to assist managers in making informed decisions.

TABLE 12.1 Top Global Market Research Firms

Rank	Company Name	Country
1	Nielsen Holdings N.V.	United States
2	The Kantar Group	United Kingdom
3	Ipsos-Synovate	France/United Kingdom
4	Westat, Inc.	United States
5	SymphonyIRI Group	United States
6	Arbitron Inc.	United States
7	GfK Group	Germany
8	IMS Health Inc.	United States
9	The NPD Group	United States
10	ICF International Inc.	United States

Source: Based on "Honomichl Top 50," *Marketing News*, June 30, 2012, pp. 25–26.

COMPARABILITY OF DATA Data obtained from other countries must be interpreted with great caution. Because terms such as *poverty, consumption,* and *literacy* differ greatly from one country to another, such data must be accompanied by precise definitions. In the United States, for example, a family of four is said to be below the poverty line if its annual income is $23,050.[4] The equivalent income for a Vietnamese family of four would place it in the upper class.

The different ways in which countries measure data also affect comparability across borders. For instance, some countries state the total quantity of foreign direct investment in their nations in terms of its *monetary value*. Others specify it in terms of the number of *investment projects* implemented during the year. But a single foreign direct investment into an industrialized nation can be worth many times what several or more projects are worth in a developing nation. To gather a complete picture of a nation's investments, researchers will often need to obtain both figures. Moreover, reported statistics may not distinguish between foreign direct investment (accompanied by managerial control) and portfolio investment (which is not accompanied by managerial control). Misinterpreting data because one does not know how they are compiled or measured can sabotage even the best marketing plans and production strategies.

CULTURAL DIFFERENCES Marketers who conduct research in unfamiliar markets must pay attention to the ways in which cultural variables influence information. Perhaps the single most important variable is language. For example, if researchers are unfamiliar with a language in the market they are investigating, they might be forced to rely on interpreters. Interpreters might unintentionally misrepresent certain comments or be unable to convey the sentiment with which statements are made.

Researchers might also need to survey potential buyers through questionnaires written in the local language. To avoid any misstatement of questions or results, questionnaires must be translated into the language of the target market and the responses then translated back into the researcher's language. Written expressions must be highly accurate so that results do not become meaningless or misleading. The potential to conduct written surveys is also affected by the illiteracy rates among the local population. A written survey is generally impossible to conduct in countries with high illiteracy rates such as Burkina Faso (71 percent), Morocco (44 percent), and Nigeria (39 percent).[5] Researchers would probably need to choose a different information-gathering technique, such as personal interviews or observation of retail purchases.

Companies that have little experience in an unfamiliar market often hire local agencies to perform some or all of their market research. Local researchers know the cultural terrain. They understand which practices are acceptable and which types of questions can be asked. And they typically know whom to approach for certain types of information. Perhaps most importantly, they know how to interpret the information they gather and are likely to understand its reliability. But a company that decides to conduct its own market research must, if necessary, adapt its research techniques to the local market. Many cultural elements that are taken for granted in the home market must be reassessed in the host business environment.

Sources of Secondary International Data

Companies can consult a variety of sources to obtain information on a nation's business environment and markets. The particular source that managers should consult depends on the company's industry, the national markets they are considering, and how far along they are in their location-screening process. The process of obtaining information that already exists within the company or that can be obtained from outside sources is called **secondary market research**. Managers often use information gathered from secondary research activities to broadly estimate market demand for a product or to form a general impression of a nation's business environment. Secondary data are relatively inexpensive because they have already been collected, analyzed, and summarized by another party. Let's take a look at the main sources of secondary data that help managers make more-informed location-selection decisions.

secondary market research
Process of obtaining information that already exists within the company or that can be obtained from outside sources.

INTERNATIONAL ORGANIZATIONS There are excellent sources of free and inexpensive information about product demand in particular countries. For example, the *International Trade Statistics Yearbook* published by the United Nations (www.un.org) lists the export and import volumes of different products for each country. It also furnishes information on the value of exports and imports on an annual basis for the most recent five-year period. The International Trade Center (www.intracen.org), based in Geneva, Switzerland, also provides current import and export figures for more than 100 countries.

International development agencies, such as the World Bank (www.worldbank.org), the International Monetary Fund (www.imf.org), and the Asian Development Bank (www.adb.org), also provide valuable secondary data. For example, the World Bank publishes annual data on each member nation's population and economic growth rate. Today, most secondary sources supply downloadable data through the Internet or through traditional printed media.

GOVERNMENT AGENCIES Commerce departments and international trade agencies of most countries typically supply information about import and export regulations, quality standards, and the size of various markets. This data is normally available directly from these departments, from agencies within each nation, and from the commercial attaché in each country's embassy abroad. In fact, visiting embassies and attending their social functions while visiting a potential location are excellent ways of making contact with prospective future business partners.

Granted, the attractively packaged information supplied by host nations often ignores many potential hazards in a nation's commercial environment—governments typically try to present their countries in the best possible light. By the same token, such sources are prone to paint

Initial analyses of foreign market potential do not involve sending researchers to distant markets. Instead, companies acquire secondary market research. Obtaining secondary data is a cost-effective way to begin exploring potential markets. From its home base, a company can get an initial feel for buyer behavior in an unfamiliar market. Here, a woman browses clothing displayed at a newly opened store of Spanish clothing retailer Zara in Johannesburg, South Africa. The Spanish retail chain hopes to target the country's increasingly diverse middle class.

Source: ALEXANDER JOE/Getty Images/ Newscom

incomplete or one-sided portraits of the home market. It is important for managers to seek additional sources that take a more objective view of a potential location.

One source that takes a fairly broad view of markets is the Central Intelligence Agency's *World Factbook* (www.cia.gov). This source can be a useful tool throughout the entire market- or site-screening process because of its wealth of facts on each nation's business environment. It identifies each nation's geography, climate, terrain, natural resources, land use, and important environmental issues in detail. It also examines each nation's culture, system of government, and economic conditions, including government debt and exchange-rate conditions. It also provides an overview of the quality of each country's transportation and communication systems.

The Trade Information Center (TIC; www.export.gov), operated by the U.S. Department of Commerce, is a first stop for many importers and exporters. The TIC details product standards in other countries and offers advice on opportunities and best prospects for U.S. companies in individual markets. It also offers information on federal export-assistance programs that can be essential for first-time exporters. Other TIC information includes the following:

- National trade laws and other regulations
- Trade shows, trade missions, and special events
- Export counseling for specific countries
- Import tariffs and customs procedures
- The value of exports to other countries

The Chilean Trade Commission within Chile's Ministry of Foreign Affairs has been particularly aggressive in recent years in promoting Chile to the rest of the world. ProChile (www.chileinfo.com) has 35 commercial offices worldwide. The organization assists in developing the export process, establishing international business relationships, fostering international trade, attracting investment, and forging strategic alliances. It offers a wealth of information on all of Chile's key industries and provides business environment information such as risk ratings. It also provides details on important trade regulations and standards of which exporters, importers, and investors must be aware.[6]

Commercial offices of the states and provinces of many countries also typically have offices in other countries to promote trade and investment. These offices usually encourage investment in the home market by companies from other countries and will sometimes even help companies in other countries export to the home market. For example, the Lorraine Development Corporation in Atlanta is the investment-promotion office of the Lorraine region of France. This corporation helps U.S. companies evaluate location opportunities in the Lorraine region—a popular area for industrial investment. It supplies information on sites, buildings, financing options, and conditions in the French and European Union business environment and conducts 10 to 20 site-selection studies per year for investors.

Finally, many governments open their research libraries to businesspeople from all countries. For example, the Japanese External Trade Organization (JETRO; www.jetro.go.jp) in central Tokyo has a large library full of trade data that is available to international companies already in Japan. In addition, the JETRO website is useful for companies screening the potential of the Japanese market for future business activities from any location. The organization is dedicated to serving companies interested in exporting to or investing in Japan in addition to assisting Japanese companies in going abroad.

INDUSTRY AND TRADE ASSOCIATIONS Companies often join associations composed of firms within their own industry or trade. In particular, companies trying to break into new markets join such associations in order to make contact with others in their field. The publications of these organizations keep members informed about current events and help managers to keep abreast of important issues and opportunities. Many associations publish special volumes of import and export data for domestic markets. They frequently compile directories that list each member's top executives, geographic scope, and contact information such as phone numbers and addresses. Today, many associations also maintain informative websites. Two interesting examples are the websites of the National Pasta Association (www.ilovepasta.org) and the National Onion Association (www.onions-usa.org).

Sometimes industry and trade associations commission specialized studies of their industries, the results of which are then offered to their members at subsidized prices. These types of studies typically address particularly important issues or explore new opportunities for international growth. The National Confectioners Association (www.candyusa.com) of the United States, together with the state of Washington's Washington Apple Commission (www.bestapples.com), once hired a research firm to study the sweet tooth of Chinese consumers. The findings of the study were then made available to each organization's members to act on as they saw fit.

SERVICE ORGANIZATIONS Many international service organizations in fields such as banking, insurance, management consulting, and accounting offer information to their clients on cultural, regulatory, and financial conditions in a market. For example, the accounting firm of Ernst & Young (www.ey.com) publishes a "Doing Business In" series for most countries. Each booklet contains information on a nation's business environment, regulations regarding foreign investment, legal forms of businesses, labor force, taxes, and culture. Other companies provide specific and overall information on world markets. Managers can consult such organizations for specialized reports on market demographics, lifestyles, consumer data, buyer behavior, and advertising.

INTERNET Companies engaged in international business are quickly realizing the wealth of secondary research information available on the Internet and the World Wide Web. These electronic resources are usually user friendly and have vast amounts of information.

LEXIS-NEXIS (www.lexisnexis.com) is a leading online provider of market information. This database of full-text news reports from around the world is updated continually. It also offers special services such as profiles of executives and products and information on the financial conditions, marketing strategies, and public relations of many international companies. Other popular online providers of global information include DIALOG (www.dialog.com) and Dow Jones (www.dowjones.com). Internet search engines such as Google (www.google.com) and Yahoo! (www.yahoo.com) are also helpful in narrowing down the plethora of information available electronically.

The Internet can be especially useful in seeking information about potential production sites. Because field trips to the most likely candidates are expensive, online information can be enormously helpful in saving both time and money. For example, you can begin a search for information on a particular country or region with most large online information providers. Narrowing your search to a more manageable list of subjects—say, culture, economic conditions, or perhaps a specific industry—can yield clues about sites that are promising and those that are not.

QUICK STUDY 3

1. Identify the benefits associated with conducting international *secondary market research*.
2. What are the three main difficulties of conducting research in international markets? Explain each briefly.
3. Identify some of the main sources of *secondary market research* data.

Methods of Conducting Primary International Research

primary market research
Process of collecting and analyzing original data and applying the results to current research needs.

Although secondary information is very useful in the early stages of the screening process, sometimes more-tailored data on a location is needed. Under such circumstances, it might be necessary to conduct **primary market research**—the process of collecting and analyzing original data and applying the results to current research needs. This type of information is very helpful in filling in the blanks left by secondary research. Yet, it is often more expensive to obtain than secondary research data because studies must be conducted in their entirety. Let's explore some of the more common methods of primary research used by companies in the location-screening process.

trade show
Exhibition at which members of an industry or group of industries showcase their latest products, study activities of rivals, and examine recent trends and opportunities.

TRADE SHOWS AND TRADE MISSIONS An exhibition at which members of an industry or group of industries showcase their latest products, study activities of rivals, and examine recent trends and opportunities is called a **trade show**. Trade shows are held on a continuing basis in virtually all markets and normally attract companies from around the globe. They are typically held by national or global industry trade associations or by government agencies. An excellent source of information about trade shows and exhibitions worldwide is Expo Central (www.expocentral.com).

CULTURE MATTERS   Is the World Your Oyster?

The business culture of every nation supports the international expansion efforts of its businesses to some degree. But what kinds of actions and information are useful to companies? Here are a few helpful pointers followed by two company examples:

- Small companies must first do lots of homework before jumping into the global marketplace. Going international is a long-term investment, and preparedness is a critical success factor. Companies must plan on investing a good deal of cash. A typical small business can expect to pay anywhere from $10,000 to $20,000 to perform basic market research, to attend a trade show, and to visit one or two countries.
- Lucille Farms, Inc., of Montville, New Jersey, produces and markets cheese products. Alfonso Falivene, Lucille's chief executive, is taking a cautious approach to going international. He recently joined the U.S. Dairy Export Council, which offers members,

among other things, international trips to study new business opportunities and the competition. The council also offers its members a great deal of free information on international markets. Falivene says the council supplied market information that would have cost him thousands of dollars to obtain on his own.

- Meter-Man, Inc., of Winnebago, Minnesota, manufactures agricultural measuring devices. When Meter-Man decided to go international, it saw trade shows as a great way to gain market intelligence and establish contacts. At a five-day agricultural fair in Paris, company executives held 21 meetings with potential customers and sealed an agreement with a major distributor that covers the Parisian market for Meter-Man's products. Meter-Man's sales and marketing director was on a flight to a trade show in Barcelona, Spain, and struck up a conversation with the man next to him. The man wound up ordering $200,000 of Meter-Man's products and is today a major South American distributor for the company.

Not surprisingly, the format and scope of trade shows differ from country to country. For example, because of its large domestic market, shows in the United States tend to be oriented toward business opportunities within the U.S. market. In line with U.S. culture, the atmosphere tends to be fairly informal. Conversely, because of the relatively smaller market of Germany and its participation in the European Union, trade shows there tend to showcase business opportunities in markets all across Europe and tend to be quite formal.

National culture plays a role in the extent to which companies take advantage of trade shows and other tools to become successful abroad. The entrepreneurial culture of the United States ensures that trade groups actively encourage small businesses to pursue international opportunities. To see how two small U.S. companies pursued opportunities to go international, read this chapter's Culture Matters feature, titled "Is the World Your Oyster?"

A **trade mission** is an international trip by government officials and businesspeople that is organized by agencies of national or provincial governments for the purpose of exploring international business opportunities. Businesspeople who attend trade missions are typically introduced both to important business contacts and to well-placed government officials.

Small and medium-sized companies often find trade missions very appealing for two reasons. First, the support of government officials gives them additional clout in the target country as well as access to officials and executives whom they would otherwise have little opportunity to meet. Second, although such trips can sometimes be expensive for the smallest of businesses, they are generally worth the money because they almost always reap cost-effective rewards. Trade missions to faraway places sometimes involve visits to several countries in order to maximize the return for the time and money invested. For instance, a trade mission for European businesspeople to Latin America may include stops in Argentina, Brazil, Chile, and Mexico. A trade mission to Asia for North American or European companies might include stops in China, Hong Kong, Japan, South Korea, and Thailand.

INTERVIEWS AND FOCUS GROUPS Although industry data are useful to companies early in the screening process for potential markets, subsequent steps must assess buyers' emotions, attitudes, and cultural beliefs. Industry data cannot tell us how individuals feel about a company or its product. This type of buyer information is required when deciding whether to enter a market and when developing an effective marketing plan. Therefore, many companies supplement the large-scale collection of country data with other types of research such as interviews with prospective customers. Interviews, of course, must be conducted carefully if they are to yield reliable and unbiased information. Respondents in some cultures might be unwilling to answer certain questions or may intentionally give vague or misleading answers in order to avoid getting too personal. For example, although individuals in the United States are renowned for their willingness to divulge all sorts of information about their shopping habits and even their personal lives, this is very much the exception among other countries.

trade mission
International trip by government officials and businesspeople that is organized by agencies of national or provincial governments for the purpose of exploring international business opportunities.

focus group
Unstructured but in-depth interview of a small group of individuals (8 to 12 people) by a moderator in order to learn the group's attitudes about a company or its product.

consumer panel
Research in which people record in personal diaries information on their attitudes, behaviors, or purchasing habits.

survey
Research in which an interviewer asks current or potential buyers to answer written or verbal questions in order to obtain facts, opinions, or attitudes.

An unstructured but in-depth interview of a small group of individuals (8 to 12 people) by a moderator in order to learn the group's attitudes about a company or its product is called a **focus group**. Moderators guide a discussion on a topic and interfere as little as possible with the free flow of ideas. The interview is recorded for later evaluation to identify recurring or prominent themes among the participants. This type of research helps marketers to uncover negative perceptions among buyers and to design corrective marketing strategies. Because subtle differences in verbal and body language could go unnoticed, focus group interviews tend to work best when moderators are natives of the countries in which the interview is held. Ironically, it is sometimes difficult to conduct focus groups in collectivist cultures (see Chapter 2) because people have a tendency to agree with others in the group. In such instances, it might be advisable to conduct a **consumer panel**—research in which people record in personal diaries information on their attitudes, behaviors, or purchasing habits.

SURVEYS Research in which an interviewer asks current or potential buyers to answer written or verbal questions in order to obtain facts, opinions, or attitudes is called a **survey**. For example, if Saucony (www.saucony.com) wants to learn about consumer attitudes toward its latest women's running shoe, it could ask a sample of women about their attitudes toward the shoe. Verbal questioning could be done in person or over the telephone, whereas written questioning could be done in person, through the mail, or through forms completed at Saucony's website. The results would then be tabulated, analyzed, and applied to the development of a marketing plan.

The single greatest advantage of survey research is the ability to collect vast amounts of data in a single sweep. But as a rule, survey methods must be adapted to local markets. For example, survey research can be conducted by any technological means in industrialized markets, such as over the telephone or the Internet. But telephone interviewing would yield poor results in Bangladesh because only a small percentage of the general population has telephones. Also, although a survey at a website is an easy way to gather data, it must be remembered that even in some industrialized nations users still represent mostly middle- to upper-income households.

Written surveys can also be hampered by other problems. Some countries' postal services are unreliable to the point that parcels are delivered weeks or months after arriving at post offices, or they never arrive at all because they are stolen or simply lost. Naturally, written surveys are impractical to conduct in countries with high rates of illiteracy, although this problem can perhaps be overcome by obtaining verbal responses to spoken questions.

environmental scanning
Ongoing process of gathering, analyzing, and dispensing information for tactical or strategic purposes.

ENVIRONMENTAL SCANNING An ongoing process of gathering, analyzing, and dispensing information for tactical or strategic purposes is called **environmental scanning**. The environmental scanning process entails obtaining both factual and subjective information on the business environments in which a company is operating or considering entering. The continuous monitoring of events in other locations keeps managers aware of potential business opportunities and threats. Environmental scanning contributes to making well-informed decisions and to the development of effective strategies. It also helps companies develop contingency plans for a particularly volatile environment.

QUICK STUDY 4

1. How does *primary market research* differ from secondary market research?
2. Describe each main method used to conduct primary market research.
3. What are some of the difficulties of conducting international market research?

A Final Word

To keep pace with an increasingly hectic and competitive global business environment, companies should follow a systematic screening process that incorporates high-quality research methods. This chapter provides a systematic way to screen potential locations as new markets or sites for business operations. But these issues constitute only the *first step* in the process of "going international." The next step involves actually accomplishing the task of entering selected markets and establishing operations abroad. In the following chapters, we survey the types of entry modes available to companies, how they acquire the resources needed to carry out their activities, and how they manage their sometimes far-flung international business operations.

Chapter Summary

MyManagementLab
Go to **mymanagementlab.com** to complete the problem marked with this icon .

1. **Explain each of the four steps in the market- and site-screening process.**
   - Step 1 involves identifying basic appeal for potential markets (e.g., basic product demand) and/or assessing availability of resources for production (e.g., raw materials, labor, capital).
   - Step 2 involves examining the local culture, political and legal forces (e.g., government bureaucracy, political stability), and economic variables (e.g., fiscal and monetary policies).
   - Step 3 is to measure the potential of each market (e.g., market size and growth, *market-potential indicator*) and/or suitability of a site for operations (e.g., availability of workers, managers, raw materials, infrastructure).
   - Step 4 involves visiting each remaining location to make a final decision (e.g., competitor analysis, financial evaluation).

2. **Describe the three primary difficulties of conducting international market research.**
   - Unique conditions and circumstances often force adjustments in the *way* market research is performed in different nations.
   - *Availability of data:* In addition to the problem of deliberate misrepresentation, obtaining high-quality, untainted, and reliable information can be difficult because of improper collection methods and analysis techniques.
   - *Comparability of data:* Definitions of terms such as *poverty, consumption, and literacy* differ across markets and so do ways of measuring variables.
   - *Cultural differences:* Companies entering unfamiliar markets often hire local agencies to do their market research for them because locals understand acceptable practices, types of questions to ask, and how to interpret information and its reliability.

3. **Identify the main sources of secondary international data and explain their usefulness.**
   - *Secondary market research* is the process of obtaining information that already exists within the company or that can be obtained from outside sources.
   - *International organizations* that offer free or inexpensive information about product demand in a particular country include international development agencies, such as the World Bank and the International Monetary Fund.
   - *Government agencies* such as commerce departments and international trade agencies have information on import–export regulations, quality standards, and the sizes of markets.
   - *Industry and trade associations* of firms within an industry or trade often publish reports to keep managers abreast of important issues and opportunities.
   - International *service organizations* in fields such as banking, insurance, management consulting, and accounting offer clients information on a market's cultural, regulatory, and financial conditions.

4. **Describe the main methods used to conduct primary international research.**
   - *Primary market research* is the process of collecting and analyzing original data and applying the results to current research needs.
   - A *trade show* is an exhibition where members of an industry or group of industries showcase their latest products, see what rivals are doing, and learn about recent trends and opportunities.
   - A *trade mission* is an international trip by government officials and businesspeople that is organized by agencies of national or provincial governments for the purpose of exploring international business opportunities.
   - Companies can use *interviews* to assess potential buyers' emotions, attitudes, and cultural beliefs.
   - A *focus group* is an unstructured but in-depth interview of a small group of individuals by a moderator in order to learn the group's attitudes about a company or its product.
   - In *surveys,* interviewers obtain facts, opinions, or attitudes by asking current or potential buyers to answer written or verbal questions.
   - Ongoing gathering, analyzing, and dispensing of information for tactical or strategic purposes is called *environmental scanning.*

Talk It Over

1. Although Sony's (www.sony.com) MiniDisc recorder/player was a huge hit in Japan, initial response to the MiniDisc in the U.S. market was lukewarm. When Sony mounted its third official attempt to launch its MiniDisc in the United States, it thought it finally had the right formula. A Sony executive noted, "This time around, we've done our homework, and we've found out what's in consumers' heads." What type of research do you think Sony used to "get inside the heads" of its target market? Do you think different cultures prefer to conduct certain types of market research? Explain.

Teaming Up

1. **Research Project.** As a group, visit your college's library and consult the *Encyclopedia of Associations* or a similar organization on the web. Select one or two industry associations of interest to your group. Write or call the association(s) and request an information packet, and then compile a summary of the information you received. Compare the information your group receives with information sent by trade associations researched by the other student groups. Rank the trade associations in terms of the usefulness of their information.

⭐2. **Emerging Markets Project.** Select an emerging market that your team would like to learn more about. Start by compiling fundamental country data, and then do additional research, following the steps in this chapter, to flesh out the nature of the market opportunity offered by this country or its suitability as a manufacturing site. Make a list of the international companies pursuing market opportunities in the country, and identify the products or brands that the companies are marketing. Are their reasons for doing business in the country consistent with the market opportunity as you have researched it? Determine whether these companies have established facilities for manufacturing, sales, or both.

Key Terms

consumer panel (p. 318)	logistics (p. 305)	secondary market research (p. 314)
environmental scanning (p. 318)	market research (p. 312)	survey (p. 318)
focus group (p. 318)	primary market research	trade mission (p. 317)
income elasticity (p. 307)	(p. 316)	trade show (p. 316)

Take It to the Web

1. **Video Report.** Visit this book's channel on YouTube (www.YouTube.com/MyIBvideos). Click on "Videos" near the top of the page, and click on the set of videos labeled "Ch 12: Analyzing International Opportunities." Watch one video from the list, and then summarize it in a half-page report. Reflecting on the contents of this chapter, which aspects of international-opportunity analysis can you identify in the video? How might a company engaged in international business act on the information contained in the video?

2. **Website Report.** Because the U.S. market absorbs the vast majority of Mexico's exports, the fact that the fates of the two economies are closely related is no surprise. Yet, the relatively high cost of Mexico's economy means that some Western companies are heading instead to Asia.

   Research Mexico's economy on the Internet (both Mexican and U.S. publications if possible) and update its performance using the business press and statistical databases. (*Hint*: You may begin your Internet research by visiting some of the many websites listed in this chapter.) If wages are rising, why are companies still investing in Mexico? If wages are rising, is it across the board or just in specific sectors? From what sectors are investments flowing into Mexico, and from where are they coming?

   Select a country that competes with Mexico for foreign direct investment. What characteristics make Mexico a better production base? What makes it a worse production base? Compare the two countries in terms of their long-term market potential.

Ethical Challenges

1. You are a member of the Council of Economic Advisors to the U.S. president. The council is asked to assess the moral basis for outsourcing to low-wage countries. Some people opposed to globalization argue that multinational corporations from wealthy countries endanger the global economic system by investing capital in developing countries and by laying off workers at home. They say globalization pits the interests of more prosperous workers in wealthy countries against the interests of lower-paid workers in developing countries. It is also claimed that the practice pits nations against one another as companies move from one developing country to another in search of lower wages or bigger market opportunities. Do multinational corporations have an ethical obligation to try to preserve jobs for workers in their home-country markets? How do you believe the council should advise the president on this issue? Justify your advice.

2. You are the CEO of a large multinational company that has become highly profitable by investing in a Latin American country. As a catalyst in mobilizing the nation's low-cost labor force, your company has helped the nation achieve double-digit economic growth. Following a political upheaval, however, a military government takes control. Workers' rights are being violated, as are those of individual citizens. As CEO, it is up to you to decide on a course of action. Do you pull out of the country, effectively abandoning your employees? Do you publicly and directly confront the leaders of the new government and insist that they respect workers' rights? Do you proceed more discreetly and pursue diplomacy out of the public's eye? Or do you advise a different course of action? Can you make an ethical decision that is also a good business decision?

3. You are the executive director of Qualitative Research Consultants Association (QRCA), an organization designed to assist market research practitioners. As part of their membership agreement, QRCA members agree to abide by a ten-point code of ethics that forbids practices such as discriminating in respondent recruitment and offering kickbacks or other favors in exchange for business. The code also calls for research to be conducted for legitimate research purposes and not as a front for product promotion. Why do you think the QRCA and other market research organizations create such codes? Do you believe such codes are helpful in reducing unethical research practices? As QRCA director, what other areas of marketing research do you believe should be covered by ethical codes of conduct?

MyManagementLab

Go to **mymanagementlab.com** for Auto-graded writing questions as well as the following Assisted-graded writing questions:

12-1. For many global companies, China represents a highly attractive market in terms of size and growth rate. Yet China ranks lower in terms of economic freedom and higher in political risk than do some other countries. Despite these risks, hundreds of companies have established manufacturing operations in China. In large part, this is because the Chinese government makes selling in China contingent on a company's willingness to locate production there. The government wants Chinese companies to learn modern management skills from non-Chinese companies and to acquire technology. Some believe that Western companies are bargaining away important industry know-how in exchange for sales today by agreeing to such conditions. Should companies go along with China's terms, or should they risk losing sales by refusing to transfer technology? What do you think might be the long-term results of either solution?

12-2. What are some of the benefits of "soft" market research data gathered using techniques such as focus groups and observation? What are the benefits of using "hard" data such as statistics on consumers' buying habits and figures on market size? When might each kind of data be preferred and why?

12-3. Mymanagementlab Only – comprehensive writing assignment for this chapter.

Practicing International Management Case

Vietnam's Emerging Market Potential

Around 25 years ago, Vietnam's government first introduced *doi moi*. This "renewal" policy initiated free-market reforms while preserving a communist political system. In 1990, Vietnam's communist government announced that non-Vietnamese manufacturers were welcome to set up shop in the Southeast Asian country. South Korea's Daewoo (www.dm.co.kr) quickly established itself as the number-one investor in Vietnam. Other well-known companies, including Toshiba (www.toshiba.co.jp), Peugeot (www.peugeot.com), and British Petroleum (www.bp.com) also took Hanoi up on its invitation.

The absence of trade and diplomatic relations between the United States and Vietnam, however, meant that U.S. companies had to sit on the sidelines. Nearly four years later, the U.S. government lifted the trade embargo with Vietnam, paving the way for a host of U.S. companies to pursue opportunities there. Vietnam's location in the heart of Asia and the presence of a literate, low-wage workforce are powerful magnets for international companies.

Today, there are many challenges for investors in Vietnam. The population of around 82 million is very poor, with an annual per capita income (at purchasing power parity) of only about $2,900. The infrastructure is undeveloped: Only 25 percent of roads are paved, electricity sources are somewhat unreliable, and the banking system is undeveloped. And although Vietnam holds tremendous long-term potential, it may be two decades before Vietnam reaches the level of economic development found even in Thailand today.

In addition, the Communist Party of Vietnam is struggling to adapt to the principles of a market economy, and the layers of bureaucracy built up over decades of communist rule slow the pace of change. Despite the efforts of the State Committee for Cooperation and Investment, the government sometimes still conducts itself in a way that leaves international investors scratching their heads. In one incident, Hanoi embarked on a "social evils crackdown" that included pulling down or painting over any sign or billboard printed in a language other than Vietnamese. And laws concerning taxes and foreign exchange are in constant flux.

Yet an emerging entrepreneurial class in Vietnam has developed a taste for expensive products such as Nikon (www.nikon.co.jp) cameras and Ray-Ban (www.ray-ban.com) sunglasses—both of which are available in stores. But if official economic statistics tell us that many Vietnamese are poor, where does the money come from to afford such luxury items? The answer is found in the large unofficial economy. It is typical for a person to live only 5 or 10 days a month on their official salary, with the majority of their purchasing power coming from moonlighting activities and business conducted in the informal economy.

In late 2001, Vietnam and the United States signed a trade deal that gave Vietnam normal trade status with the United States. This meant that Vietnam could ship goods to the U.S. market at the lowest possible tariff rates. Meanwhile, U.S. companies are gaining continually greater access to Vietnam. As a result, Vietnam's export activity (worth around $90 billion in 2012) is booming, due largely to its cheap, efficient workforce and growing foreign investment. Vietnam's exports to the United States are doubling each year. The diversified nature of the country's exports—including commodities, agricultural products, and manufactured goods—means it is somewhat immune to large swings in the price of any one export. Vietnam is now the world's largest exporter of pepper, it may soon overtake Thailand in rice exports, and it even exports tea to India.

Vietnam has become one of Asia's best-performing economies. Over the past decade, Vietnam grew nearly 8 percent a year. In fact, throughout the currency crisis that gripped Southeast Asia in the late 1990s, Vietnam's economic growth rate never dipped below 4.8 percent. The recent global slowdown, however, did tug down on Vietnam's upward trajectory. Still, the nation's trade-driven economy has lifted many Vietnamese out of poverty. Whereas the World Bank labeled as much as 70 percent of the population poor in the 1980s, that number was around 18 percent in 2012.

Thinking Globally

1. Update the political, legal, and economic situation in Vietnam; then select a product of your choosing and evaluate Vietnam's potential both as a market and as a manufacturing site.
2. What, if anything, can Western countries do to help improve the political climate for doing business in Vietnam? Give specific examples.
3. What problems might a company encounter while conducting market research in Vietnam? Explain your answer.
4. What is your perception of products labeled "Made in Vietnam"? Do you think the type of product would play a role in forming your perception? If so, why?

Sources: "Touchable after All," *The Economist*, August 25, 2012, p. 32; "V Not Yet for Victory," *The Economist* (www.economist.com), September 24, 2009; "Half-Way from Rags to Riches," *The Economist*, Special Report, April 26, 2008, pp. 1–16; "Good Morning at Last," *The Economist*, August 5, 2006, pp. 37–38; "Vietnam's Export Worth $22.3 Billion," Vietnam Ministry of Trade press release, July 25, 2006.

Selecting and Managing Entry Modes

LEARNING OBJECTIVES

After studying this chapter, you should be able to

1. Explain how companies use exporting, importing, and countertrade.

2. Explain the various means of financing export and import activities.

3. Describe the different contractual entry modes that are available to companies.

4. Explain the various types of investment entry modes.

5. Discuss the important strategic factors in selecting an entry mode.

A Look Back

Chapter 12 explained how companies analyze international business opportunities. We learned how managers screen and research both potential markets and sites for operations.

A Look at This Chapter

This chapter introduces the different entry modes companies use to "go international." We discuss the important issues surrounding the selection and management of (1) exporting, importing, and countertrade; (2) contractual entry modes; and (3) investment entry modes.

A Look Ahead

Chapter 14 explains the international marketing efforts of companies. We identify the key elements that influence how companies promote, price, and distribute their products.

LICENSE TO THRILL

LONDON, England—Marvel Enterprises (www.marvel.com) is a global character-based entertainment licensing company that over a span of 70 years developed a library of more than 5,000 characters. Shown here is Stan Lee, creator of Spiderman and a comic book writer, an editor, an actor, a producer, a publisher, and the former president and chairman of Marvel Comics.

Marvel initially pursued licensing as a means to become more than just a comics and toy company, and it has already brought top comic-book characters—including Iron Man, Spider-Man, Blade, X-Men, and the Hulk—to the big screen with enormous success. The films do generate revenue for Marvel, but their main function is to popularize the company's comic-book characters.

Driving Marvel's earnings in recent years are its character-based licensing agreements for products such as lunchboxes, toys, and video games. Marvel's licensing business includes a deal with Hasbro (www.hasbro.com) to distribute action figures based on Marvel characters through the year 2017. Marvel earns royalties on all its toys sold worldwide (except Japan) through Hasbro. And Marvel's

Source: ZUMA Press/Newscom

recent sale to Disney (www.disney.com) for $4.3 billion means that its characters are sure to take their adventures to even more movies, theme parks, and stores worldwide.

Marvel's 50/50 joint venture with Sony (www.sony.com) oversees all licensing and merchandising activities for the film *Spider-Man,* as well as Sony's animated TV series titled *Spider-Man*. Marvel went solo with *Iron Man,* taking the film to the big screen on its own.

But the company is not resting easy, marveling at its past success. Marvel International, based in England, is developing the firm's licensing business in strategic international markets. Marvel's former CEO Allen Lipson said, "This is a major strategic initiative for the company. Marvel's international growth is largely untapped." As you read this chapter, consider why companies go international, what the market entry modes available to them are, and when each mode is appropriate.[1]

entry mode
Institutional arrangement by which a firm gets its products, technologies, human skills, or other resources into a market.

The decision of how to enter a new market abroad must take into account many factors, including the local business environment and a company's own core competency. An **entry mode** is the institutional arrangement by which a firm gets its products, technologies, human skills, or other resources into a market. Companies seeking entry into new markets for manufacturing and/or marketing purposes have many potential entry modes at their disposal. The specific mode chosen depends on many factors, including experience in a market, the amount of control managers desire, and the potential size of the market. In this chapter, we explore the following three categories of entry modes:

1. Exporting, importing, and countertrade
2. Contractual entry
3. Investment entry

Exporting, Importing, and Countertrade

The most common method of buying and selling goods internationally is exporting and importing. Companies often import products in order to obtain less expensive goods or those that are simply unavailable in the domestic market. Companies export products when the international marketplace offers opportunities to increase sales and, in turn, profits. Companies worldwide (from both developed and developing countries) often see the United States as a great export opportunity because of the size of the market and the strong buying power of its citizens. Figure 13.1 showcases the top 10 exporters to the United States in terms of the value of goods sold.

Because this chapter focuses on how companies take their goods and services to the global marketplace, this first section concentrates on exporting. We then explain how companies use *countertrade* when cash transactions are not possible and discuss the main export/import financing methods. Because importing is a sourcing decision for most firms, it is covered in Chapter 15.

Why Companies Export

In the global economy, companies increasingly sell goods and services to wholesalers, retailers, industrial buyers, and consumers in other nations. Generally speaking, there are three main reasons why companies begin exporting:

1. *Expand sales.* Most large companies use exporting as a means of expanding total sales when the domestic market has become saturated. A greater sales volume allows them to spread the fixed costs of production over a greater number of manufactured products, thereby lowering the cost of producing each unit of output. In short, going international is one way to achieve economies of scale.
2. *Diversify sales.* Exporting permits companies to diversify their sales. In other words, they can offset slow sales in one national market (perhaps due to a recession) with increased sales in another. Diversified sales can level off a company's cash flow, making it easier to coordinate payments to creditors with receipts from customers.

FIGURE 13.1

Top Exporters to the United States

Source: Based on data contained in *International Trade Statistics 2011* (Geneva, Switzerland: World Trade Organization, November 2011), Table II.30, pp. 81–82.

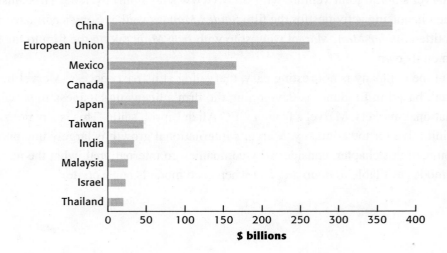

3. *Gain experience.* Companies often use exporting as a low-cost, low-risk way of getting started in international business. Owners and managers of small companies, which typically have little or no knowledge of how to conduct business in other cultures, use exporting to gain valuable international experience.

Developing an Export Strategy: A Four-Step Model

Companies are often drawn into exporting when customers in other countries solicit their goods. In this way, companies become aware of their products' international potential and get their first taste of international business.

Yet, a company should not fall into the habit of simply responding to random international requests for its products. A more logical approach is to research and analyze international opportunities and to develop a coherent export strategy. A business with such a strategy actively pursues export markets rather than sitting back and waiting for international orders to come in. Let's take a look at the four steps in developing a successful export strategy.

STEP 1: IDENTIFY A POTENTIAL MARKET To identify whether demand exists in a particular target market, a company should perform market research and interpret the results (see Chapter 12). Novice exporters should focus on one or only a few markets. For example, a first-time Brazilian exporter might not want to export simultaneously to Argentina, Britain, and Greece. A better strategy would likely be to focus on Argentina because of its cultural similarities with Brazil (despite having a different, though related, language). The company could then expand into more diverse markets after it gains initial international experience in a nearby country. The would-be exporter should also seek expert advice on the regulations and general process of exporting and on any special issues related to a selected target market.

STEP 2: MATCH NEEDS TO ABILITIES The next step is to determine whether the company is capable of satisfying the needs of the market. Suppose a market located in a region with a warm, humid climate for much of the year displays the need for home air-conditioning equipment. If a company recognizes this need but makes only industrial-sized air-conditioning equipment, it might not be able to satisfy demand with its current product. But if the company is able to use its smallest industrial air-conditioning unit to satisfy the needs of several homes, it might have a market opportunity. If there are no other options or if consumers want their own individual units, the company will likely need to design a smaller air-conditioning unit or rule out entry into that market.

STEP 3: INITIATE MEETINGS Holding meetings early in the process with potential local distributors, buyers, and others is a must. Initial contact focuses on building trust and developing a cooperative climate among all parties. The cultural differences between the parties will come into play already at this stage. Beyond building trust, successive meetings are designed to estimate the potential success of any agreement if interest is shown on both sides. At the most advanced stage, negotiations take place and details of agreements are finalized.

For example, a group of environmental technology companies in Arizona was searching for markets abroad. A delegation from Taiwan soon arrived in the Arizona desert to survey the group's products. Although days were busy with company visits, formal meetings, and negotiations, evenings were used for building relationships. There were outdoor barbecues, hayrides, line dancing, and frontier-town visits that gave the visitors a feel for local culture and history. To make their counterparts from Taiwan feel comfortable, nighttime schedules included visits to karaoke spots and Chinese restaurants where a good deal of singing took place. Follow-up meetings resulted in several successful deals.

STEP 4: COMMIT RESOURCES After all the meetings, negotiations, and contract signings, it is time to put the company's human, financial, and physical resources to work. First, the objectives of the export program must be clearly stated and should extend out at least three to five years. For small firms, it may be sufficient to assign one individual the responsibility for drawing up objectives and estimating resources. Yet, as companies expand their activities to include more products and/or markets, many firms discover the need for an export department or division. The head of this department usually has the responsibility (and authority) to formulate, implement, and evaluate the company's export strategy. See Chapter 11 for a detailed discussion of organizational design issues to consider at this stage.

Degree of Export Involvement

Companies of all sizes engage in exporting, but not all companies become involved in exporting to the same extent. Some exporting companies (usually entrepreneurs and small and medium-sized firms) perform few or none of the activities necessary to get their products into a market abroad. Instead, they use intermediaries that specialize in getting products from one market into another. Other exporting companies (usually only the largest companies) perform all of their export activities themselves, with an infrastructure that bridges the gap between the two markets. Let's take a closer look at the two basic forms of export involvement—direct exporting and indirect exporting.

DIRECT EXPORTING   Some companies become deeply involved in the export of their products. **Direct exporting** occurs when a company sells its products directly to buyers in a target market. Direct exporters operate in many industries, including aircraft (Boeing; www.boeing.com), industrial equipment (John Deere; www.deere.com), apparel (Lands' End; www.landsend.com), and bottled beverages (Evian; www.evian.com). Bear in mind that "direct exporters" need not sell directly to *end users*. Rather, they take full responsibility for getting their goods into the target market by selling directly to local buyers and not going through intermediary companies. Typically, they rely on either local *sales representatives* or *distributors*.

Sales Representatives   A *sales representative* (whether an individual or an organization) represents only its own company's products, not those of other companies. Sales representatives promote those products in many ways, such as by attending trade fairs and by making personal visits to local retailers and wholesalers. They do not take title to the merchandise. Rather, they are hired by a company and normally are compensated with a fixed salary plus commissions based on the value of their sales.

Distributors   Alternatively, a direct exporter can sell in the target market through *distributors,* who take ownership of the merchandise when it enters their country. As owners of the products, distributors accept all the risks associated with generating local sales. They sell either to retailers and wholesalers or to end users through their own channels of distribution. Typically, distributors earn a profit equal to the difference between the price they pay and the price they receive for the exporter's goods. Although using a distributor reduces an exporter's risk, it also weakens an exporter's control over the price buyers are charged. A distributor who charges very high prices can stunt the growth of an exporter's market share. Exporters should choose, if possible, distributors who are willing to invest in the promotion of their products and who do not sell directly competing products.

INDIRECT EXPORTING   Some companies have few resources available to commit to exporting activities. Others simply find exporting a daunting task because of a lack of contacts and experience. Fortunately, there is an option for such firms. **Indirect exporting** occurs when a company sells its products to intermediaries who then resell to buyers in a target market. The choice of an intermediary depends on many factors, including the ratio of the exporter's international sales to its total sales, the company's available resources, and the growth rate of the target market. Let's take a closer look at several different types of intermediaries: *agents, export management companies,* and *export trading companies.*

Agents   Individuals or organizations that represent one or more indirect exporters in a target market are called **agents**. Agents typically receive compensation in the form of commissions on the value of sales. Because establishing a relationship with an agent is relatively easy and inexpensive, it is a fairly common approach to indirect exporting. Agents should be chosen very carefully because terminating an agency relationship if problems arise can be costly and difficult. Careful selection is also essential because agents often represent several indirect exporters simultaneously. Agents might focus their promotional efforts on the products of the company paying the highest commission rather than on the company with the better products.

Export Management Companies   A company that exports products on behalf of an indirect exporter is called an **export management company (EMC)**. An EMC operates contractually, either as an agent (being paid through commissions based on the value of sales) or as a distributor (taking ownership of the merchandise and earning a profit from its resale).

direct exporting
Practice by which a company sells its products directly to buyers in a target market.

indirect exporting
Practice by which a company sells its products to intermediaries who then resell to buyers in a target market.

agents
Individuals or organizations that represent one or more indirect exporters in a target market.

export management company (EMC)
Company that exports products on behalf of indirect exporters.

An EMC will usually provide additional services on a retainer basis, charging set fees against funds deposited on account. Typical EMC services include gathering market information, formulating promotional strategies, performing specific promotional duties (such as attending trade fairs), researching customer credit, making shipping arrangements, and coordinating export documents. It is common for an EMC to exploit contacts predominantly in one industry (say, agricultural goods or consumer products) or in one geographic area (such as Latin America or the Middle East). Indeed, the biggest advantage of an EMC is usually a deep understanding of the cultural, political, legal, and economic conditions of the target market. Its staff works comfortably and effectively in the cultures of both the exporting and the target nation. The average EMC tends to deploy a wide array of commercial and political contacts in order to facilitate business activities on behalf of its clients.

Perhaps the only disadvantage of hiring an EMC is that the breadth and depth of its service can potentially hinder the development of the exporter's own international expertise. But an exporter and its EMC typically have such a close relationship that an exporter often considers its EMC as a virtual exporting division. When this is the case, exporters learn a great deal about the intricacies of exporting from their EMC. Then, after the EMC contract expires, it is common for a company to go it alone in exporting its products.

Export Trading Companies A company that provides services to indirect exporters in addition to activities directly related to clients' exporting activities is called an **export trading company (ETC)**. Whereas an EMC is restricted to export-related activities, an ETC assists its clients by providing import, export, and countertrade services; developing and expanding distribution channels; providing storage facilities; financing trading and investment projects; and even manufacturing products.

European trading nations first developed the ETC concept centuries ago. More recently, the Japanese have refined the concept, which they call *sogo shosha*. The Japanese ETC can range in size from small, family-run businesses to enormous conglomerates such as Mitsubishi (www.mitsubishi.com), Mitsui (www.mitsui.com), and ITOCHU (www.itochu.co.jp). An ETC in South Korea is called a *chaebol* and includes well-known companies such as Samsung (www.samsung.com) and Hyundai (www.hyundaigroup.com).

Japanese and South Korean ETCs have become formidable competitors because of their enormous success in gaining global market share. These Asian companies quickly came to rival the dominance of the largest U.S. multinational corporations, which lobbied U.S. lawmakers for assistance in challenging Asian ETCs in global markets. The result was the Export Trading Company Act passed in 1982. Despite this effort, the ETC concept never really caught on in the United States. Operations of the typical ETC in the United States remain small and are dwarfed by those of their Asian counterparts. One reason for the lack of interest in the ETC concept in the United States relative to that in Asia is that governments, financial institutions, and companies have much closer working relationships in Asia. The formation of huge conglomerates that engage in activities ranging from providing financing to manufacturing to distribution is easier to accomplish there. By contrast, the regulatory environment in the United States is wary of such cozy business arrangements, and the lines between companies and industries are more clearly drawn.

Avoiding Export and Import Blunders

There are several errors common to companies new to exporting. First, many businesses fail to conduct adequate market research before exporting. In fact, many companies begin exporting by responding to unsolicited requests for their products. If a company enters a market in this manner, it should quickly devise an export strategy to manage its export activities effectively and not strain its resources.

Second, many companies fail to obtain adequate export advice. National and regional governments are often willing and able to help managers and small-business owners understand and cope with the vast amounts of paperwork required by each country's export and import laws. Naturally, more experienced exporters can be extremely helpful as well. They can help novice exporters avoid embarrassing mistakes by guiding them through unfamiliar cultural, political, and economic environments.

To better ensure that it will not make embarrassing blunders, an inexperienced exporter might also want to engage the services of a **freight forwarder**—a specialist in export-related

export trading company (ETC)
Company that provides services to indirect exporters in addition to activities related directly to clients' exporting activities.

freight forwarder
Specialist in export-related activities such as customs clearing, tariff schedules, and shipping and insurance fees.

activities such as customs clearing, tariff schedules, and shipping and insurance fees. Freight forwarders also can pack shipments for export and take responsibility for getting a shipment from the port of export to the port of import.

QUICK STUDY 1

1. Briefly describe each of the four steps involved in building an export strategy.
2. How does *direct exporting* differ from *indirect exporting*?
3. Compare and contrast *export management companies* and *export trading companies*.

Countertrade

Companies are sometimes unable to import merchandise in exchange for financial payment. The reason is either that the government of the importer's nation lacks the hard currency to pay for imports or that it intentionally restricts the convertibility of its currency. Fortunately, there is a way for firms to trade by using either a small amount of hard currency or even none at all. Selling goods or services that are paid for, in whole or in part, with other goods or services is called **countertrade**. Although countertrade often requires an extensive network of international contacts, even smaller companies can take advantage of its benefits.

Nations that have long used countertrade are found mostly in Africa, Asia, Eastern Europe, and the Middle East. A lack of adequate hard currency often forced those nations to use countertrade to exchange oil for passenger aircraft and military equipment. Today, because of insufficient hard currency, developing and emerging markets frequently rely on countertrade to import goods. The greater involvement of firms from industrialized nations in those markets is expanding the use of countertrade.

TYPES OF COUNTERTRADE There are several different types of countertrade: *barter, counterpurchase, offset, switch trading,* and *buyback.* Let's take a brief look at each of these.

- **Barter** is the exchange of goods or services directly for other goods or services without the use of money. It is the oldest known form of countertrade.
- **Counterpurchase** is the sale of goods or services to a country by a company that promises to make a future purchase of a specific product from that country. This type of agreement is designed to allow the country to earn back some of the currency that it paid for the original imports.

---

countertrade
Practice of selling goods or services that are paid for, in whole or in part, with other goods or services.

barter
Exchange of goods or services directly for other goods or services without the use of money.

counterpurchase
Sale of goods or services to a country by a company that promises to make a future purchase of a specific product from the country.

Barter, or *trueque*, became a way of life in Argentina when the nation's economy was mired in a seemingly endless recession. Residents of Buenos Aires, Argentina, bartered goods using *Ticket Trueque*, or "Barter Vouchers." In markets near Buenos Aires, you can swap CDs, DVDs, clothing, fruit, plumbing supplies, vegetables, and much more. Local newspapers run ads for such things as apartments, cars, and washing machines, all offered on a barter basis. Shown here, a man pays for fresh vegetables using *trueque.*

Source: Agencia el Universal/El Universal de Mexico/Newscom

- **Offset** is an agreement that a company will offset a hard-currency sale to a nation by making a hard-currency purchase of an unspecified product from that nation in the future. It differs from a counterpurchase in that this type of agreement does not specify the type of product that must be purchased, just the amount that will be spent. Such an arrangement gives a business greater freedom in fulfilling its end of a countertrade deal.
- **Switch trading** is countertrade whereby one company sells to another its obligation to make a purchase in a given country. For example, in return for market access, a firm that wants to enter a target market might promise to buy a product for which it has no use. The company then sells this purchase obligation to a large trading company that makes the purchase itself because it has a use for the merchandise. If the trading company has no use for the merchandise, it can arrange for yet another buyer who needs the product to make the purchase.
- **Buyback** is the export of industrial equipment in return for products produced by that equipment. This practice usually typifies long-term relationships between the companies involved.

Countertrade can provide access to markets that are otherwise off-limits because of a lack of hard currency. It can also cause headaches. Much countertrade involves commodity and agricultural products such as oil, wheat, or corn—products whose prices on world markets tend to fluctuate a good deal. A problem arises when the price of a bartered product falls on world markets between the time that a deal is arranged and the time at which one party tries to sell the product. Fluctuating prices generate the same type of risk encountered in currency markets. Managers might be able to hedge some of this risk on commodity futures markets similar to how they hedge against currency fluctuations in currency markets (see Chapter 9).

Export/Import Financing

International trade poses risks for both exporters and importers. Exporters run the risk of not receiving payment after their products are delivered. Importers fear that delivery might not occur once payment is made for a shipment. Export/import financing methods designed to reduce these risks include *advance payment, documentary collection, letter of credit,* and *open account* (see Figure 13.2). Let's explore each of these methods.

ADVANCE PAYMENT Export/import financing in which an importer pays an exporter for merchandise before it is shipped is called **advance payment**. This method of payment is common when two parties are unfamiliar with each other, the transaction is relatively small, or the buyer is unable to obtain credit because of a poor credit rating at banks. Payment normally takes the form of a wire transfer of money from the bank account of the importer directly to that of the exporter. Although prior payment eliminates the risk of nonpayment for exporters, it creates the complementary risk of nonshipment for importers—importers might pay for goods but never receive them. Thus, advance payment is the most favorable method for exporters but the least favorable for importers.

offset
Agreement that a company will offset a hard-currency sale to a nation by making a hard-currency purchase of an unspecified product from that nation in the future.

switch trading
Practice in which one company sells to another its obligation to make a purchase in a given country.

buyback
Export of industrial equipment in return for products produced by that equipment.

advance payment
Export/import financing in which an importer pays an exporter for merchandise before it is shipped.

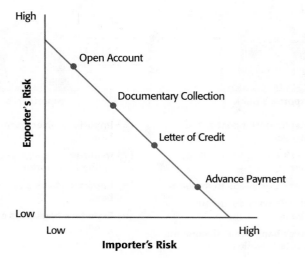

FIGURE 13.2

Risk of Alternative Export/ Import Financing Methods

documentary collection
Export/import financing in which a bank acts as an intermediary without accepting financial risk.

draft (bill of exchange)
Document ordering an importer to pay an exporter a specified sum of money at a specified time.

bill of lading
Contract between an exporter and a shipper that specifies merchandise destination and shipping costs.

DOCUMENTARY COLLECTION Export/import financing in which a bank acts as an intermediary without accepting financial risk is called **documentary collection**. This payment method is commonly used when there is an ongoing business relationship between two parties. The documentary collection process can be broken into three main stages and nine smaller steps (see Figure 13.3).

1. Before shipping merchandise, the exporter (with its banker's assistance) draws up a **draft (bill of exchange)**—a document ordering the importer to pay the exporter a specified sum of money at a specified time. A *sight draft* requires the importer to pay when goods are delivered. A *time draft* extends the period of time (typically 30, 60, or 90 days) following delivery by which the importer must pay for the goods. (When inscribed "accepted" by an importer, a time draft becomes a negotiable instrument that can be traded among financial institutions.) This stage includes Steps 1 and 2 in Figure 13.3.
2. Following creation of the draft, the exporter delivers the merchandise to a transportation company for shipment to the importer. The exporter then delivers to its banker a set of documents that includes the draft, a *packing list* of items shipped, and a **bill of lading**—a contract between the exporter and shipper that specifies merchandise destination and shipping costs. The bill of lading is proof that the exporter has shipped the merchandise. An international ocean shipment requires an *inland bill of lading* to get the shipment to the exporter's border and an *ocean bill of lading* for water transport to the importer nation. An international air shipment requires an *air way bill* that covers the entire international journey. This stage includes Steps 3 and 4 in Figure 13.3.
3. After receiving appropriate documents from the exporter, the exporter's bank sends the documents to the importer's bank. After the importer fulfills the terms stated on the draft and pays its own bank, the bank issues the bill of lading (which becomes title to the merchandise) to the importer. This stage includes Steps 5 through 9 in Figure 13.3.

Documentary collection reduces the importer's risk of nonshipment because the packing list details the contents of the shipment and the bill of lading is proof that the merchandise has been shipped. The exporter's risk of nonpayment is increased because, although the exporter retains title to the goods until the merchandise is accepted, the importer does not pay until all necessary

FIGURE 13.3

Documentary Collection Process

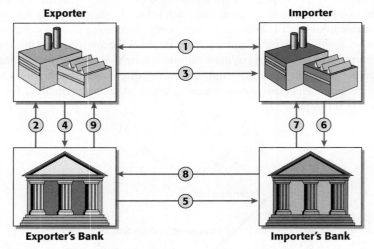

1. Exporter/importer contract to sell/buy goods
2. Exporter's bank gives draft to exporter
3. Exporter ships goods to importer
4. Exporter delivers documents to its bank
5. Exporter's bank sends documents to importer's bank
6. Importer delivers payment to its bank
7. Importer's bank gives bill of lading to importer
8. Importer's bank pays exporter's bank
9. Exporter's bank pays exporter for goods

documents have been received. Although importers have the option of refusing the draft (and, therefore, the merchandise), this action is unlikely. Refusing the draft—despite all terms of the agreement being fulfilled—would make the importer's bank unlikely to do business with the importer in the future.

LETTER OF CREDIT Export/import financing in which the importer's bank issues a document stating that the bank will pay the exporter when the exporter fulfills the terms of the document is called **letter of credit**. A letter of credit is typically used when an importer's credit rating is questionable, when the exporter needs a letter of credit to obtain financing, and when a market's regulations require it. Before a bank issues a letter of credit, it checks on the importer's financial condition. This stage includes Steps 1 and 2 in Figure 13.4.

Banks normally issue letters of credit only after an importer has deposited on account a sum equal in value to that of the imported merchandise. The bank is still required to pay the exporter, but the deposit protects the bank if the importer fails to pay for the merchandise. Banks will sometimes waive this requirement for their most reputable clients.

There are several types of letters of credit:

- An *irrevocable letter of credit* allows the bank issuing the letter to modify its terms only after obtaining the approval of both exporter and importer.
- A *revocable letter of credit* can be modified by the issuing bank without obtaining approval from either the exporter or the importer.
- A *confirmed letter of credit* is guaranteed by both the exporter's bank in the country of export and the importer's bank in the country of import.

After the issuance of a letter of credit, the importer's bank informs the exporter (through the exporter's bank) that a letter of credit exists and that it may now ship the merchandise. The exporter then delivers a set of documents (according to the terms of the letter) to its own bank. These documents typically include an invoice, customs forms, a packing list, and a bill of lading. The exporter's bank ensures that the documents are in order and pays the exporter. This stage includes Steps 3 through 7 in Figure 13.4.

letter of credit
Export/import financing in which the importer's bank issues a document stating that the bank will pay the exporter when the exporter fulfills the terms of the document.

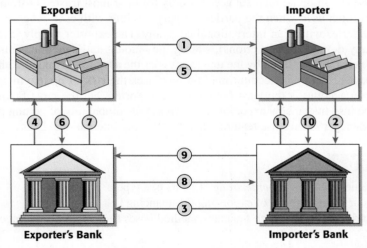

FIGURE 13.4
Letter of Credit Process

(1) **Exporter/importer contract to sell/buy goods**

(2) **Importer applies for letter of credit**

(3) **Importer's bank issues letter of credit to exporter's bank on importer's behalf**

(4) **Exporter's bank informs exporter of letter of credit**

(5) **Exporter ships goods to importer**

(6) **Exporter delivers documents to its bank**

(7) **Exporter's bank checks documents and pays exporter**

(8) **Exporter's bank delivers documents to importer's bank**

(9) **Importer's bank sends payment to exporter's bank**

(10) **Importer pays its bank for value of goods**

(11) **Importer's bank delivers documents to importer**

MANAGER'S BRIEFCASE   Collecting International Debts

What is the point of working hard to make an international sale if the buyer does not pay? There are seldom easy answers when an exporter is stuck without payment. Here are several pointers on what businesses can do to reduce the likelihood of not receiving payment:

- Knowledge of the market you are exporting to is your first and best defense. Understanding its culture, the language spoken, and its legal system is ideal. You should also understand if there is typically a payment lag for business debts and customary debt-collection procedures.
- Be aware of countries that commonly cause problems when it comes to debt collection. Regularly consult the many free sources of information available on the Internet to learn which

countries are problems. Avoid doing business with them and seek markets elsewhere.
- Both parties clearly understanding the payment terms in your export sales agreement is essential to preventing later collection problems. Also, be sure the buyer knows precisely when payment is to be issued.
- Do not wait too long to begin collecting a past-due account. Exporters who delay will likely never receive payment. Begin with firmly worded communications via phone, fax, e-mail, and letter.
- Consult an international trade attorney or hire an international debt-collection agency if necessary. If you are encouraged to accept arbitration as a way to resolve the issue, do so, as this often poses your best chance of seeing at least partial payment.

When the importer's bank is satisfied that the terms of the letter have been met, it pays the exporter's bank. At that point, the importer's bank is responsible for collecting payment from the importer. Letters of credit are popular among traders because banks assume most of the risks. This stage includes Steps 8 through 11 in Figure 13.4.

The letter of credit reduces the importer's risk of nonshipment (as compared with advance payment) because the importer receives proof of shipment before making payment. Although the exporter's risk of nonpayment is slightly increased, it is a more secure form of payment for exporters because the nonpayment risk is accepted by the importer's bank when it issues payment to the exporter's bank.

open account
Export/import financing in which an exporter ships merchandise and later bills the importer for its value.

OPEN ACCOUNT   Export/import financing in which an exporter ships merchandise and later bills the importer for its value is called **open account**. Because some receivables may not be collected, exporters should reserve shipping on open account only for their most trusted customers. This payment method is often used when the parties are very familiar with each other or for sales between two subsidiaries within an international company. The exporter simply invoices the importer (as in many domestic transactions), stating the amount and date due. This method reduces the risk of nonshipment faced by the importer under the advance payment method.

By the same token, the open account method increases the risk of nonpayment for the exporter. Thus, open account is the least favorable for exporters but the most favorable for importers. For some insights on how exporters can increase the probability of getting paid for a shipment, see the Manager's Briefcase feature, titled "Collecting International Debts."

QUICK STUDY 2

1. Why do companies engage in *countertrade*? List its five types.
2. What are the four main methods of export/import financing?
3. Describe the various risks that each financing method poses for exporters and importers.

Contractual Entry Modes

The products of some companies simply cannot be traded in open markets because they are *intangible*. Thus, a company cannot use importing, exporting, or countertrade to exploit opportunities in a target market. Fortunately, there are other options for this type of company. A company can use a variety of contracts—*licensing, franchising, management contracts,* and *turnkey projects*—to market highly specialized assets and skills in markets beyond its nations' borders.

Licensing

licensing
Practice by which one company owning intangible property (the licensor) grants another firm (the licensee) the right to use that property for a specified period of time.

Companies sometimes grant other firms the right to use an asset that is essential to the production of a finished product. **Licensing** is a contractual entry mode in which a company that owns intangible property (the *licensor*) grants another firm (the *licensee*) the right to use that property for a specified period of time. Licensors typically receive royalty payments based on a percentage of the licensee's sales revenue generated by the licensed property. The licensors might also receive a one-time fee to cover the cost of transferring the property to the licensee. Commonly licensed intangible property includes patents, copyrights, special formulas and designs, trademarks, and brand names. Thus, licensing often involves granting companies the right to use *process technologies* inherent to the production of a particular good.

Here are a few examples of successful licensing agreements:

- Novell (United States) licensed its software to three Hong Kong universities that installed it as the campus-wide standard.
- Hitachi (Japan) licensed from Duales System Deutschland (Germany) technology to be used in the recycling of plastics in Japan.
- Hewlett-Packard (United States) licensed from Canon (Japan) a printer engine for use in its monochrome laser printers.

An *exclusive license* grants a company the exclusive rights to produce and market a property, or products made from that property, in a specific geographic region. The region can be the licensee's home country or can extend to worldwide markets. A *nonexclusive license* grants a company the right to use a property but does not grant it sole access to a market. A licensor can grant several or more companies the right to use a property in the same region.

Cross licensing occurs when companies use licensing agreements to exchange intangible property with one another. For example, Fujitsu (www.fujitsu.com) of Japan signed a five-year cross-licensing agreement with Texas Instruments (www.ti.com) of the United States. The agreement allowed each company to use the other's technology in the production of its own goods—thus lowering research and development (R&D) costs. The very extensive arrangement covered all but a few semiconductor patents owned by each company. Because asset values are seldom exactly equal, cross licensing also typically involves royalty payments from one party to the other.

cross licensing
Practice by which companies use licensing agreements to exchange intangible property with one another.

ADVANTAGES OF LICENSING There are several advantages to using licensing as an entry mode into new markets. First, licensors can use licensing to finance their international expansion. Most licensing agreements require licensees to contribute equipment and investment financing, whether by building special production facilities or by using existing excess capacity. Access to such resources can be a great advantage to a licensor who wants to expand but lacks the capital and managerial resources to do so. And because it need not spend time constructing and starting up its own new facilities, the licensor earns revenues sooner than it would otherwise.

Second, licensing can be a less risky method of international expansion for a licensor than other entry modes. Whereas some markets are risky because of social or political unrest, others defy accurate market research for a variety of reasons. Licensing helps shield the licensor from the increased risk of operating its own local production facilities in markets that are unstable or hard to assess accurately.

Third, licensing can help reduce the likelihood that a licensor's product will appear on the black market. The side streets of large cities in many emerging markets are dotted with tabletop vendors eager to sell bootleg versions of computer software, Hollywood films, and recordings of internationally popular musicians. Producers can, to some extent, foil bootleggers by licensing local companies to market their products at locally competitive prices. Royalties will be lower than the profits generated by sales at higher international prices, but lower profits are better than no profits at all—which is what owners get from bootleg versions of their products.

Finally, licensees can benefit by using licensing as a method of upgrading existing production technologies. For example, manufacturers of plastics and other synthetic materials in the Philippines attempted to meet the high standards demanded by the local subsidiaries of Japanese electronics and office equipment producers. To do this, D&L Industries of the Philippines upgraded its manufacturing process by licensing materials technology from Nippon Pigment of Japan.

DISADVANTAGES OF LICENSING There also are important disadvantages to using licensing. First, it can restrict a licensor's future activities. Suppose a licensee is granted the exclusive right to use an asset but fails to produce the sort of results that a licensor expected. Because the license agreement is exclusive, the licensor cannot simply begin selling directly in that particular market in order to meet demand itself nor can it contract with another licensee. A good product and lucrative market, therefore, do not guarantee success for a producer entering a market through licensing.

Second, licensing might reduce the global consistency of the quality and marketing of a licensor's product in different national markets. A licensor might find the development of a coherent global brand image an elusive goal if each of its national licensees can operate in any manner it chooses. Promoting a global image might later require considerable amounts of time and money in order to change the misconceptions of buyers in the various licensed markets.

Third, licensing might amount to a company "lending" strategically important property to its future competitors. This is an especially dangerous situation when a company licenses assets on which its competitive advantage is based. Licensing agreements are often made for several years and perhaps even a decade or more. During this time, licensees often become highly competent at producing and marketing the licensor's product. When the agreement expires, the licensor might find that its former licensee is capable of producing and marketing a better version of its own product. Licensing contracts can (and should) restrict licensees from competing in the future with products based strictly on licensed property. But enforcement of such provisions works only for identical or nearly identical products, not when substantial improvements are made.

Franchising

franchising
Practice by which one company (the franchiser) supplies another (the franchisee) with intangible property and other assistance over an extended period.

Franchising is a contractual entry mode in which one company (the *franchiser*) supplies another (the *franchisee*) with intangible property and other assistance over an extended period. Franchisers typically receive compensation as flat fees, royalty payments, or both. The most popular franchises are those with widely recognized brand names, such as Mercedes (www.mercedes.com), McDonald's (www.mcdonalds.com), and Starbucks (www.starbucks.com). In fact, the brand name or trademark of a company is normally the single most important item desired by the franchisee. This is why smaller companies with lesser-known brand names and trademarks have greater difficulty locating interested franchisees.

Franchising differs from licensing in several ways. First, franchising gives a company greater control over the sale of its product in a target market. Franchisees must often meet strict guidelines on product quality, day-to-day management duties, and marketing promotions. Second, although licensing is fairly common in manufacturing industries, franchising is primarily used in service industries such as auto dealerships, entertainment, lodging, restaurants, and business services. Third, although licensing normally involves a one-time transfer of property, franchising requires ongoing assistance from the franchiser. In addition to the initial transfer of

Tesco is the largest British-based international grocery and general merchandising retail chain as ranked by global sales. Originally specializing in food and drink, it has diversified into areas such as consumer electronics, financial services, movies and music, Internet service, and health insurance. Franchising helps Tesco ensure that individual stores meet company guidelines on matters such as company policies, product offerings, and service. Can you think of other industries that employ franchising?

Source: DIEGO AZUBEL/Newscom

property, franchisers typically offer start-up capital, management training, location advice, and advertising assistance to their franchisees.

The following are examples of the kinds of companies involved in international franchising:

- Ozemail (Australia) awarded Magictel (Hong Kong) a franchise to operate its Internet phone and fax service in Hong Kong.
- Jean-Louis David (France) awarded franchises to more than 200 hairdressing salons in Italy.
- Brooks Brothers (United States) awarded Dickson Concepts (Hong Kong) a franchise to operate Brooks Brothers stores across Southeast Asia.

Companies based in the United States dominate the world of international franchising. U.S. companies perfected the practice of franchising in their large, homogeneous domestic market with low barriers to interstate trade and investment. Yet franchising is growing in the European Union, with the advent of a single currency and a unified set of franchise laws. Many European managers with comfortable early-retirement packages have discovered franchising to be an appealing second career.

Despite projections for robust growth, European franchise managers often misunderstand the franchising concept. One example is when Holiday Inn's franchise expansion in Spain was moving more slowly than expected. According to the company's development director in Spain, Holiday Inn found that it needed to convince local managers that Holiday Inn did not want to "take control" of their hotels.[2] In some Eastern European countries, local managers do not understand why they must continue to pay royalties to brand and trademark owners. Franchise expansion in Eastern European markets also suffers from a lack of local capital, high interest rates, high taxes, bureaucratic obstacles, restrictive laws, and corruption.[3]

ADVANTAGES OF FRANCHISING There are several important advantages of franchising. First, franchisers can use franchising as a low-cost, low-risk entry mode into new markets. Companies following global strategies rely on consistent products and common themes in worldwide markets. Franchising allows them to maintain consistency by replicating the processes for standardized products in each target market. Many franchisers, however, will make small modifications in products and promotional messages when marketing specifically to local buyers.

Second, franchising is an entry mode that allows for rapid geographic expansion. Firms often gain a competitive advantage by being first in seizing a market opportunity. For example, Microtel Inns & Suites (www.microtelinn.com) of Atlanta, Georgia, is using franchising to fuel its international expansion. Microtel is boldly entering Argentina and Uruguay and eyeing opportunities in Brazil and Western Europe. Rooms cost around $75 per night and target business travelers who cannot afford $200 per night.[4]

Finally, franchisers can benefit from the cultural knowledge and know-how of local managers. This helps lower the risk of business failure in unfamiliar markets and can create a competitive advantage.

DISADVANTAGES OF FRANCHISING Franchising can also pose problems for both franchisers and franchisees. First, franchisers may find it cumbersome to manage a large number of franchisees in a variety of national markets. A major concern is that product quality and promotional messages among franchisees will not be consistent from one market to another. One way to ensure greater control is by establishing in each market a so-called *master franchisee,* which is responsible for monitoring the operations of individual franchisees.

Second, franchisees can experience a loss of organizational flexibility in franchising agreements. Franchise contracts can restrict their strategic and tactical options, and they may even be forced to promote products owned by the franchiser's other divisions. For years PepsiCo (www. pepsico.com) owned the well-known restaurant chains Pizza Hut, Taco Bell, and KFC. As part of their franchise agreements with PepsiCo, restaurant owners were required to sell only PepsiCo beverages to their customers. Many franchisees worldwide were displeased with such restrictions on their product offerings and were relieved when PepsiCo spun off the restaurant chains.

Management Contracts

Under the stipulations of a **management contract**, one company supplies another with managerial expertise for a specific period of time. The supplier of expertise is normally compensated with either a lump-sum payment or a continuing fee based on sales volume. Such contracts are

management contract
Practice by which one company supplies another with managerial expertise for a specific period of time.

commonly found in the public utilities sectors of developed and emerging markets. Two types of knowledge can be transferred through management contracts—the specialized knowledge of technical managers and the business-management skills of general managers.

The following are two examples of management contracts:

- DBS Asia (Thailand) awarded a management contract to Favorlangh Communication (Taiwan) to set up and run a company supplying digital television programming in Taiwan.
- Lyonnaise des Eaux (France) and RWE Aqua (Germany) agreed to manage drinking-water quality and client billing and to maintain the water infrastructure for the city of Budapest, Hungary, for 25 years.

ADVANTAGES OF MANAGEMENT CONTRACTS Management contracts can benefit organizations and countries. First, a firm can award a management contract to another company and thereby exploit an international business opportunity without having to place a great deal of its own physical assets at risk. Financial capital can then be reserved for other promising investment projects that would otherwise not be funded.

Second, governments can award companies management contracts to operate and upgrade public utilities, particularly when a nation is short of investment financing. That is why the government of Kazakhstan contracted with a group of international companies called ABB Power Grid Consortium to manage its national electricity-grid system for 25 years. Under the terms of the contract, the consortium paid past wages owed to workers by the government and invested more than $200 million during the first three years of the agreement. The Kazakhstan government had neither the cash flow to pay the workers nor the funds to make badly needed improvements.

Third, governments use management contracts to develop the skills of local workers and managers. ESB International (www.esb.ie) of Ireland signed a three-year contract not only to manage and operate a power plant in Ghana, but also to train local personnel in the skills needed to manage it at some point in the future.

DISADVANTAGES OF MANAGEMENT CONTRACTS Unfortunately, management contracts also pose two disadvantages for suppliers of expertise. First, although management contracts reduce the exposure of physical assets in another country, the same is not true for the supplier's personnel: Political or social turmoil can threaten managers' lives.

Second, suppliers of expertise may end up nurturing a formidable new competitor in the local market. After learning how to conduct certain operations, the party that had originally needed assistance may be capable of competing on its own. Firms must weigh the financial returns from a management contract against the potential future problems caused by a newly launched competitor.

Turnkey Projects

turnkey (build–operate–transfer) project
Practice by which one company designs, constructs, and tests a production facility for a client firm.

When one company designs, constructs, and tests a production facility for a client, the agreement is called a **turnkey (build–operate–transfer) project**. The term *turnkey project* is derived from the understanding that the client, who normally pays a flat fee for the project, is expected to do nothing more than simply "turn a key" to get the facility operating. The company awarded a turnkey project completely prepares the facility for its client.

Similar to management contracts, turnkey projects tend to be large-scale and often involve government agencies. But unlike management contracts, turnkey projects transfer special process technologies or production-facility designs to the client. They typically involve the construction of power plants, airports, seaports, telecommunication systems, and petrochemical facilities that are then turned over to the client. Under a management contract, the supplier of a service retains the asset—the managerial expertise.

The following are two examples of international turnkey projects:

- Telecommunications Consultants India constructed telecom networks in both Madagascar and Ghana—two turnkey projects worth a combined total of $28 million.
- Lubei Group (China) agreed with the government of Belarus to join in the construction of a facility for processing a fertilizer byproduct into cement.

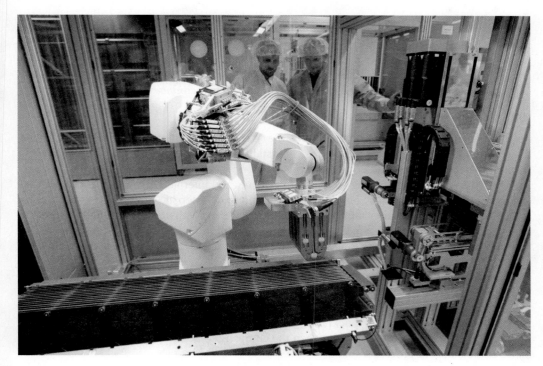

A turnkey project is a venture in which one organization designs, builds, and tests a facility for another, which then merely "turns the key" to get things underway. Here, employees of Solar World monitor the automated refinement process of silicon wafers at the company plant in Freiberg, Germany. The wafers are then integrated into modules at Solar World subsidiaries, which fabricate turnkey-ready solar power plants. What other types of operations are appropriate for a turnkey project?

Source: Agentur/Newscom

ADVANTAGES OF TURNKEY PROJECTS Turnkey projects provide benefits to providers and recipients. First, turnkey projects permit firms to specialize in their core competencies and to exploit opportunities that they could not undertake alone. Exxon Mobil (www.exxonmobil.com) awarded a turnkey project to PT McDermott Indonesia (www.mcdermott.com) and Toyo Engineering (www.toyo-eng.co.jp) of Japan to build a liquid natural gas plant on the Indonesian island of Sumatra. The providers are responsible for constructing an offshore production platform, laying a 100-kilometer underwater pipeline, and building an on-land liquid natural gas refinery. The $316 million project is feasible only because each company contributes unique expertise to the design, construction, and testing of the facilities.

Second, turnkey projects allow governments to obtain designs for infrastructure projects from the world's leading companies. For instance, Turkey's government enlisted two separate consortiums of international firms to build four hydroelectric dams on its Coruh River. The dams combine the design and technological expertise of each company in the two consortiums. The Turkish government also awarded a turnkey project to Ericsson (www.ericsson.com) of Sweden to expand the country's mobile telecommunication system.

DISADVANTAGES OF TURNKEY PROJECTS Among the disadvantages of turnkey projects is the fact that a company may be awarded a project for political reasons rather than for technological know-how. Because turnkey projects are often of high monetary value and awarded by government agencies, the process of awarding them can be highly politicized. When the selection process is not entirely open, companies with the best political connections often win contracts, usually at inflated prices—the costs of which are typically passed on to local taxpayers.

Second, like management contracts, turnkey projects can create future competitors. A newly created local competitor could become a major supplier in its own domestic market and perhaps even in other markets where the supplier operates. Therefore, companies try to avoid projects in which there is danger of transferring their core competencies to others.

QUICK STUDY 3

1. Identify the advantages and disadvantages of *licensing* for the licensor and the licensee.
2. Describe how *franchising* differs from licensing. What are its main benefits and drawbacks?
3. When is a *management contract* useful? Identify two types of knowledge it is used to transfer.
4. What is a *turnkey project*? Describe its main advantages and disadvantages.

Investment Entry Modes

Investment entry modes entail direct investment in plant and equipment in a country coupled with ongoing involvement in the local operation. Entry modes in this category take a company's commitment in a market to a higher level. Let's explore three common forms of investment entry: *wholly owned subsidiaries, joint ventures,* and *strategic alliances.*

Wholly Owned Subsidiaries

wholly owned subsidiary
Facility entirely owned and controlled by a single parent company.

As the term suggests, a **wholly owned subsidiary** is a facility entirely owned and controlled by a single parent company. Companies can establish a wholly owned subsidiary either by forming a new company and constructing entirely new facilities (such as factories, offices, and equipment) or by purchasing an existing company and internalizing its facilities. Whether an international subsidiary is purchased or newly created depends to a large extent on its proposed operations. When a parent company designs a subsidiary to manufacture the latest high-tech products, it typically must build new facilities. The major drawback of creation from the ground up is the time it takes to construct new facilities, hire and train employees, and launch production.

Conversely, finding an existing local company capable of performing marketing and sales will be easier because special technologies are typically not needed. By purchasing the existing marketing and sales operations of an existing firm in the target market, the parent can have the subsidiary operating relatively quickly. Buying an existing company's operations in the target market is a particularly good strategy when the company to be acquired has a valuable trademark, brand name, or process technology.

ADVANTAGES OF WHOLLY OWNED SUBSIDIARIES There are two main advantages to entering a market using a wholly owned subsidiary. First, managers have complete control over day-to-day operations in the target market and access to valuable technologies, processes, and other intangible properties within the subsidiary. Complete control also decreases the chance that competitors will gain access to a company's competitive advantage, which is particularly important if it is technology-based. Managers also retain complete control over the subsidiary's output and prices. Unlike licensors and franchisers, the parent company also receives all profits generated by the subsidiary.

Second, a wholly owned subsidiary is a good mode of entry when a company wants to coordinate the activities of all its national subsidiaries. Companies using global strategies view each of their national markets as one part of an interconnected global market. Thus, the ability to exercise complete control over a wholly owned subsidiary makes this entry mode attractive to companies that are pursuing global strategies.

DISADVANTAGES OF WHOLLY OWNED SUBSIDIARIES Wholly owned subsidiaries also present two primary disadvantages. First, they can be expensive undertakings because companies must typically finance investments internally or raise funds in financial markets. Obtaining the necessary funds can be difficult for small and medium-sized companies but relatively easy for the largest companies.

Second, risk exposure is high because a wholly owned subsidiary requires substantial company resources. One source of risk is political or social uncertainty or outright instability in the target market. Such risks can place both physical assets and personnel in serious jeopardy. The sole owner of a wholly owned subsidiary also accepts the risk that buyers will reject the company's product. Parent companies can reduce this risk by gaining a better understanding of consumers prior to entering the target market.

Joint Ventures

joint venture
Separate company that is created and jointly owned by two or more independent entities to achieve a common business objective.

Under certain circumstances, companies prefer to share ownership of an operation rather than take complete ownership. A separate company that is created and jointly owned by two or more independent entities to achieve a common business objective is called a **joint venture**. Joint venture partners can be privately owned companies, government agencies, or government-owned companies. Each party may contribute anything valued by its partners, including managerial talent, marketing expertise, market access, production technologies, financial capital, and superior knowledge or techniques of R&D.

Examples of joint ventures include the following:

- A joint venture between Suzuki Motor Corporation (Japan) and the government of India to manufacture a small-engine car specifically for the Indian market
- A joint venture between a group of Indian companies and a Russian partner to produce television sets in Russia for the local market
- A joint venture between Biltrite Corporation (United States) and Shenzhen Petrochemical (China) to create a shoe-soling factory in China to supply global shoe manufacturers located in China

JOINT VENTURE CONFIGURATIONS   As we see in Figure 13.5, there are four main joint venture configurations.[5] Although we illustrate each of these as consisting of just two partners, each configuration can also apply to ventures of several or more partners.

Forward Integration Joint Venture   Figure 13.5(a) outlines a joint venture characterized by *forward integration*. In this type of joint venture, the parties choose to invest together in *downstream* business activities—activities further along in the "value system" that are normally performed by others. For instance, two household appliance manufacturers opening a retail outlet in a developing country would be a joint venture characterized by forward integration. The two companies now perform activities normally performed by retailers further along in the product's journey to buyers.

Backward Integration Joint Venture   Figure 13.5(b) outlines a joint venture characterized by *backward integration*. In other words, the joint venture signals a move by each company into *upstream* business activities—activities earlier in the value system that are normally performed by others. Such a configuration would result if two steel manufacturers formed a joint venture to mine iron ore. The companies now engage in an activity that is normally performed by mining companies.

Buyback Joint Venture   Figure 13.5(c) outlines a joint venture whose input is provided by, and whose output is absorbed by, each of its partners. A *buyback joint venture* is formed when each partner requires the same component in its production process. It might be formed when a production facility of a certain minimum size is needed to achieve economies of scale but neither partner alone enjoys enough demand to warrant building it. However, by combining resources, the partners can construct a facility that serves their needs while achieving savings from economies of scale production. For instance, this was one reason behind the $500 million joint venture between Chrysler (www.chrysler.com) and BMW (www.bmw.com) to build small-car engines in Latin America. Each party benefited from the economies of scale offered by the plant's annual production capacity of 400,000 engines—a volume that neither company could absorb alone.

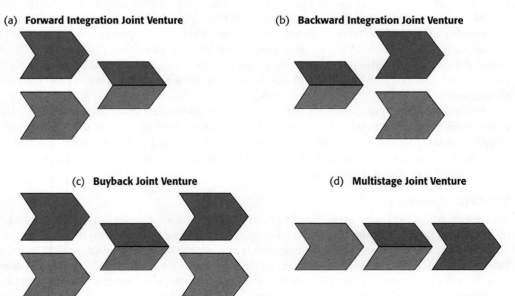

(a) **Forward Integration Joint Venture**

(b) **Backward Integration Joint Venture**

(c) **Buyback Joint Venture**

(d) **Multistage Joint Venture**

FIGURE 13.5

Alternative Joint Venture Configurations

Source: Based on Peter Buckley and Mark Casson, "A Theory of Cooperation in International Business," in Farok J. Contractor and Peter Lorange (eds.), *Cooperative Strategies in International Business* (Lexington, MA: Lexington Books, 1988), pp. 31–53.

Multistage Joint Venture Figure 13.5(d) outlines a joint venture that features downstream integration by one partner and upstream integration by another. A *multistage joint venture* often results when one company produces a good or service required by another. For example, a sporting goods manufacturer might join with a sporting goods retailer to establish a distribution company designed to bypass inefficient local distributors in a developing country.

ADVANTAGES OF JOINT VENTURES Joint ventures offer several important advantages to companies going international. Above all, companies rely on joint ventures to reduce risk. Generally, a joint venture exposes fewer of a partner's assets to risk than would a wholly owned subsidiary—each partner risks only its own contribution. That is why a joint venture entry might be a wise choice when market entry requires a large investment or when there is significant political or social instability in the target market. Similarly, a company can use a joint venture to learn about a local business environment prior to launching a wholly owned subsidiary. In fact, many joint ventures are ultimately bought outright by one of the partners after it gains sufficient expertise in the local market.

Second, companies can use joint ventures to penetrate international markets that are otherwise off-limits. Some governments either require nondomestic companies to share ownership with local companies or provide incentives for them to do so. Such requirements are most common among governments of developing countries. The goal is to improve the competitiveness of local companies by having them team up with and learn from international partner(s).

Third, a company can gain access to another company's international distribution network through the use of a joint venture. The joint venture between Caterpillar (www.caterpillar.com) of the United States and Mitsubishi Heavy Industries (www.mitsubishi.com) of Japan was designed to improve the competitiveness of each against a common rival, Komatsu (www.komatsu.com) of Japan. While Caterpillar gained access to Mitsubishi's distribution system in Japan, Mitsubishi got access to Caterpillar's global distribution network—helping it to compete more effectively internationally.

Finally, companies form international joint ventures for defensive reasons. Entering a joint venture with a local government or government-controlled company gives the government a direct stake in the venture's success. In turn, the local government will be less likely to interfere if it means that the venture's performance will suffer. This strategy can also be used to create a more "local" image when feelings of nationalism are running strong in a target country.

DISADVANTAGES OF JOINT VENTURES Among its disadvantages, joint venture ownership can result in conflict between partners. Conflict is perhaps most common when management is shared equally—that is, when each partner supplies top managers in what is commonly known as a "50–50 joint venture." Because neither partner's managers have the final say on decisions, managerial paralysis can result, causing problems such as delays in responding to changing market conditions. Conflict can also arise from disagreements over how future investments and profits are to be shared. Parties can reduce the likelihood of conflict and indecision by establishing unequal ownership, whereby one partner maintains 51 percent ownership of the voting stock and has the final say on decisions. A multiparty joint venture (commonly referred to as a *consortium*) can also feature unequal ownership. For example, ownership of a four-party joint venture could be distributed 20–20–20–40, with the 40-percent owner having the final say on decisions.

Second, loss of control over a joint venture's operations can also result when the local government is a partner in the joint venture. This situation occurs most often in industries considered culturally sensitive or important to national security, such as broadcasting, infrastructure, and defense. Thus, a joint venture's profitability could suffer because of local government motives based on cultural preservation or security.

Strategic Alliances

Sometimes companies who are willing to cooperate with one another do not want to go so far as to create a separate, jointly owned company. A relationship whereby two or more entities cooperate (but do not form a separate company) to achieve the strategic goals of each is called a **strategic alliance**. Similar to joint ventures, strategic alliances can be formed for relatively short periods or for many years, depending on the goals of the participants. Strategic alliances can be established between a company and its suppliers, its buyers, and even its competitors. In forming

strategic alliance
Relationship whereby two or more entities cooperate (but do not form a separate company) to achieve the strategic goals of each.

such alliances, sometimes each partner purchases a portion of the other's stock. In this way, each company has a direct stake in its partner's future performance. This decreases the likelihood that one partner will try to take advantage of the other.

The following are examples of strategic alliances:

- An alliance between Siemens (Germany) and Hewlett-Packard (United States) to create and market devices used to control telecommunications systems
- A strategic alliance between Nippon Life Group (Japan) and Putnam Investments (United States) to permit Putnam to develop investment products and manage assets for Nippon

ADVANTAGES OF STRATEGIC ALLIANCES Strategic alliances offer several important advantages to companies. First, companies use strategic alliances to share the cost of an international investment project. For example, many firms are developing new products that not only integrate the latest technologies but also shorten the life spans of existing products. In turn, the shorter life span is reducing the number of years during which a company can recoup its investment. Thus, many companies are cooperating to share the costs of developing new products. For example, Toshiba (www.toshiba.com) of Japan, Siemens (www.siemens.com) of Germany, and IBM (www.ibm.com) of the United States shared the $1 billion cost of developing a facility near Nagoya, Japan, to manufacture small, efficient computer memory chips.

Second, companies use strategic alliances to tap into competitors' specific strengths. Some alliances formed between Internet portals and technology companies are designed to do just that. For example, an Internet portal provides access to a large, global audience through its website, while the technology company supplies its know-how in delivering, say, music over the Internet. Meeting the goal of the alliance—marketing music over the Web—requires the competencies of both partners.

Finally, companies turn to strategic alliances for many of the same reasons that they turn to joint ventures. Some businesses use strategic alliances to gain access to a partner's channels of distribution in a target market. Other firms use them to reduce exposure to the same kinds of risks from which joint ventures provide protection.

DISADVANTAGES OF STRATEGIC ALLIANCES Perhaps the most important disadvantage of a strategic alliance is that it can create a future local or even global competitor. For example, one partner might be using the alliance to test a market and prepare the launch of a wholly owned subsidiary. By declining to cooperate with others in the area of its core competency, a company can reduce the likelihood of creating a competitor that would threaten its main area of business. Likewise, a company can insist on contractual clauses that constrain partners from competing against it with certain products or in certain geographic regions. Companies are also careful to protect special research programs, production techniques, and marketing practices that are not committed to the alliance. Naturally, managers must weigh the potential for encouraging new competition against the benefits of international cooperation.

As in the case of joint ventures, conflict can arise and eventually undermine cooperation. Alliance contracts are drawn up to cover as many contingencies as possible, but communication and cultural differences can still arise. When serious problems crop up, dissolution of the alliance may be the only option.

Selecting Partners for Cooperation

Every company's goals and strategies are influenced by both its competitive strengths and the challenges it faces in the marketplace. Because the goals and strategies of any two companies are never exactly alike, cooperation can be difficult. Moreover, ventures and alliances often last many years, perhaps even indefinitely. Therefore, partner selection is a crucial ingredient for success. The following discussion focuses on partner selection in joint ventures and strategic alliances. Yet many of the same points also apply to contractual entry modes such as licensing and franchising, for which choosing the right partner is also important.

Every partner must be firmly committed to the goals of the cooperative arrangement. Many companies engage in cooperative forms of business, but the reasons behind each party's participation are never identical. Sometimes, a company stops contributing to a cooperative arrangement once it achieves its own objectives. Detailing the precise duties and contributions of each party to an international cooperative arrangement through prior negotiations can go a long way toward ensuring continued cooperation.

CULTURE MATTERS   Negotiating Market Entry

Global business managers negotiate the terms of many deals. A cooperative atmosphere between potential partners depends on both parties viewing contract negotiations as a success. Managers should be aware of the negotiation process and the roles played by culture and other influential factors:

- *Stage 1: Preparation.* Negotiators must have a clear vision of what the company wants to achieve. Negotiation will vary depending on whether the proposed business arrangement is a one-time deal or just the first phase of a lengthy partnership.
- *Stage 2: Opening Positions.* Discussions begin as each side states its opening position, which is each side's most favorable terms. Positions might emerge gradually to leave negotiators room to maneuver.
- *Stage 3: Hard Bargaining.* The relative power of each party is key in the outcome of negotiations. Direct conflict is likely at this stage, and culture plays a role. For example, Chinese negotiators will likely try to avoid conflict and may call off talks if conflict erupts.

- *Stage 4: Agreement and Follow-Up.* Negotiations reaching this stage are a success. Whereas Western negotiators view signing contracts as the end of negotiations, most Asian negotiators see contracts as the start of a flexible relationship.

Two key elements influence international business negotiations:

- *Cultural Elements.* Negotiating styles differ from culture to culture. Successful negotiations in Asian cultures mean protecting the other party from losing face (being embarrassed or shamed) and meeting the other party halfway. Yet, negotiators in Western cultures typically hope to gain many concessions with little concern for embarrassing the other party.
- *Political and Legal Elements.* Negotiators may have political motives. A rigid public position might be taken to show the company or government officials back home that they are working in the company's or nation's interest. Also, consumer groups and labor unions might lobby government officials to ensure that a proposed agreement benefits them.

Although the importance of locating a trustworthy partner seems obvious, cooperation should be approached with caution. Companies can have hidden reasons for cooperating. Sometimes they try to acquire more from cooperation than their partners realize. If a hidden agenda is discovered during the course of cooperation, trust can break down—in which case the cooperative arrangement is virtually destroyed. Because trust is so important, firms naturally prefer partners with whom they have had a favorable working relationship in the past. However, such arrangements are much easier for large multinational corporations than for small and medium-sized companies with little international experience and few international contacts.

Each party's managers must be comfortable working with people of other cultures and with traveling to (even perhaps living in) other cultures. As a result, cooperation will go more smoothly and the transition—both in work life and in personal life—will be easier for managers who are sent to work for a joint venture. Each partner's managers should also be comfortable working with, and within, one another's *corporate* culture. For example, although some companies encourage the participation of subordinates in decision making, others do not. Such differences often reflect differences in national culture, and when managers possess cultural understanding, adjustment and cooperation are likely to run more smoothly.

Above all, a suitable partner must have something valuable to offer. Firms should avoid cooperation simply because they are approached by another company. Rather, managers must be certain that they are getting a fair return on their cooperative efforts. And they should evaluate the benefits of a potential international cooperative arrangement just as they would any other investment opportunity. For some key considerations in negotiating international agreements, see the Culture Matters feature, titled "Negotiating Market Entry."

Strategic Factors in Selecting an Entry Mode

The choice of entry mode has many important strategic implications for a company's future operations.[6] Because enormous investments in time and money can go into determining an entry mode, the choice must be made carefully. Several key factors that influence a company's international entry mode selection are the *cultural environment, political and legal environments, market size, production and shipping costs,* and *international experience.* Let's explore each of these factors.

Cultural Environment

As we saw in Chapter 2, the dimensions of culture—values, beliefs, customs, languages, religions—can differ greatly from one nation to another. In such cases, managers can be less confident in their ability to manage operations in the host country. They can be concerned about the potential not only for communication problems but also for interpersonal difficulties. As a result, managers may avoid investment entry modes in favor of exporting or a contractual mode. On the other hand, cultural similarity encourages confidence and thus the likelihood of investment. Likewise, the importance of cultural differences diminishes when managers are knowledgeable about the culture of the target market.

Political and Legal Environments

As mentioned earlier in this chapter, political instability in a target market increases the risk exposure of investments. Significant political differences and levels of instability cause companies to avoid large investments and to favor entry modes that shelter assets.

A target market's legal system also influences the choice of entry mode. Certain import regulations, such as high tariffs or low quota limits, can encourage investment. A company that produces locally avoids tariffs that increase product cost; it also does not have to worry about making it into the market below the quota (if there is one). But low tariffs and high quota limits discourage market entry by means of investment. Also, governments may enact laws that ban certain types of investment outright. For many years, China had banned wholly owned subsidiaries by non-Chinese companies and required that joint ventures be formed with local partners. Finally, if a market is lax in enforcing copyright and patent laws, a company may prefer to use investment entry to maintain control over its assets and marketing.

Market Size

The size of a potential market also influences the choice of entry mode. For example, rising incomes in a market encourage investment entry modes because investment allows a firm to prepare for expanding market demand and to increase its understanding of the target market. High domestic demand in China is attracting investment in joint ventures, strategic alliances, and wholly owned subsidiaries. On the other hand, if investors believe that a market is likely to remain relatively small, better options might include exporting or contractual entry.

Production and Shipping Costs

By helping to control total costs, low-cost production and shipping can give a company an advantage. Accordingly, setting up production in a market is desirable when the total cost of production there is lower than in the home market. Low-cost local production might also encourage contractual entry through licensing or franchising. If production costs are sufficiently low, the international production site might even begin supplying other markets, including the home country. An additional potential benefit of local production might be that managers could observe buyer behavior and modify products to better suit the needs of the local market. Lower production costs at home make it more appealing to export to international markets.

Companies that produce goods with high shipping costs naturally prefer local production. Contractual and investment entry modes are viable options in this case. Alternatively, exporting is feasible when products have relatively lower shipping costs. Finally, because they are subject to less price competition, products for which there are fewer substitutes or those that are discretionary items can more easily absorb higher shipping and production costs. In this case, exporting is a likely selection.

International Experience

Most companies enter the international marketplace through exporting. As companies gain international experience, they tend to select entry modes that require deeper involvement. But this means businesses must accept greater risk in return for greater control over operations and strategy. Eventually, they may explore the advantages of licensing, franchising, management contracts, and turnkey projects. After businesses become comfortable in a particular market, joint ventures, strategic alliances, and wholly owned subsidiaries become viable options.

This evolutionary path of accepting greater risk and control with experience does not hold for every company. Whereas some firms remain fixed at one point, others skip several entry modes altogether. Advances in technology and transportation are allowing small companies to leapfrog several stages at once. These relationships also vary for each company depending on its product and the characteristics of home and target markets.

QUICK STUDY 4

1. What is a *wholly owned subsidiary*? Identify its advantages and disadvantages.
2. What is meant by the term *joint venture*? Identify four joint venture configurations.
3. How does a *strategic alliance* differ from a joint venture? Explain the advantages and disadvantages of such alliances.
4. Discuss the strategic factors to consider when selecting an entry mode.

A Final Word

This chapter explained important factors in selecting entry modes and key aspects in their management. We studied the circumstances under which each entry mode is most appropriate and the advantages and disadvantages that each provides. The choice of which entry mode(s) to use in entering international markets matches a company's international strategy. Some companies will want to use entry modes that give them tight control over international activities because they are pursuing a global strategy. Meanwhile, other companies might not require an entry mode with central control because they are pursuing a multinational strategy. The entry mode must also align well with an organization's structure.

Chapter Summary

MyManagementLab

Go to **mymanagementlab.com** to complete the problem marked with this icon .

1. **Explain how companies use exporting, importing, and countertrade.**
   • Exporting helps a company to expand sales, diversify sales, or gain experience and represents a low-cost, low-risk way of getting started in international business.
   • A successful export strategy involves (1) identifying a potential market, (2) matching needs to abilities, (3) initiating meetings, and (4) committing resources.
   • *Direct exporting* occurs when a company sells its products directly to buyers in a target market through local *sales representatives* or *distributors*.
   • *Indirect exporting* occurs when a company sells its products to intermediaries (*agents, export management companies,* and *export trading companies*) who then resell to buyers in a target market.
   • *Countertrade* is selling goods or services that are paid for with other goods or services; it can take the form of (1) *barter*, (2) *counterpurchase*, (3) *offset*, (4) *switch trading,* and (5) *buyback*.

2. **Explain the various means of financing export and import activities.**
   • With *advance payment* an importer pays an exporter for merchandise before it is shipped.
   • *Documentary collection* calls for a bank to act as an intermediary without accepting financial risk.
   • Under a *letter of credit,* the importer's bank issues a document stating that the bank will pay the exporter when the exporter fulfills the terms of the document.
   • Several types of letters of credit are *irrevocable letter of credit, revocable letter of credit,* and *confirmed letter of credit.*
   • Under *open account,* an exporter ships merchandise and later bills the importer for its value.

3. Describe the different contractual entry modes that are available to companies.
   - *Licensing* is a contractual entry mode in which a company that owns intangible property (the *licensor*) grants another firm (the *licensee*) the right to use that property for a specified period of time.
   - *Franchising* is a contractual entry mode in which one company (the *franchiser*) supplies another (the *franchisee*) with intangible property and other assistance over an extended period.
   - A *management contract* is where one company supplies another with managerial expertise for a specific period of time; it is used to transfer two types of knowledge—the specialized knowledge of technical managers and the business-management skills of general managers.
   - A *turnkey (build–operate–transfer) project* is where one company designs, constructs, and tests a production facility for a client.
4. Explain the various types of investment entry modes.
   - *Investment entry modes* entail the direct investment in plant and equipment in a country coupled with ongoing involvement in the local operation.
   - A *wholly owned subsidiary* is a facility entirely owned and controlled by a single parent company.
   - A separate company created and jointly owned by two or more independent entities to achieve a common business objective is called a *joint venture*.
   - Joint ventures can involve *forward integration* (investing in downstream activities), *backward integration* (investing in upstream activities), a *buyback joint venture* (input is provided by and output is absorbed by each partner), and a *multistage joint venture* (downstream integration by one partner and upstream integration by another).
   - A *strategic alliance* is a relationship in which two or more entities cooperate (but do not form a separate company).
5. Discuss the important strategic factors in selecting an entry mode.
   - Managers are typically less confident in their ability to manage operations in unfamiliar cultures and may avoid investment entry modes in favor of exporting or a contractual mode.
   - Large political differences and high levels of instability cause companies to avoid large investments and favor entry modes that shelter assets.
   - Rising incomes encourage investment entry because investment allows a firm to prepare for expanding market demand and to increase its understanding of the target market.
   - Producing locally is desirable when the total cost of production in a market is lower than in the home market and when shipping costs are high.
   - Companies tend to make their initial foray into international markets using exporting and to select entry modes that require deeper involvement as they gain international experience.

Talk It Over

1. Not all companies "go international" by first exporting, then using contracts, and then investing in other markets. How does a company's product influence the process of going international? How (if at all) does technology, such as the Internet, affect the process of going international?
2. "Companies should use investment entry modes whenever possible because they offer the greatest control over business operations." Do you agree or disagree with this statement? Are there times when other types of market entry offer greater control? When is investment entry a poor option?

Teaming Up

1. **Research/Interview Project.** As a team of three or four students, interview a manager of a company involved in international business. What method did the company use initially to go international? Does the company export? If so, is it a direct or an indirect exporter? How does the company receive payment for its goods? Does the company use different entry modes in different markets? What factors influenced its choice of entry mode in each case? How do managers deal with cultural differences when negotiating across cultures? Provide any other information on the company your team believes is relevant to the discussion of market entry.

2. **Negotiation Project.** This project is designed to introduce you to the complexity of negotiations and to help develop your negotiating skills.

   Background: A Western European automobile manufacturer is considering entering markets in Southeast Asia. The company wants to construct an assembly plant outside Bangkok, Thailand, to assemble its lower-priced cars. Major components would come from manufacturing plants in Brazil, Poland, and China. The cars would then be sold in emerging markets throughout Southeast Asia and the Indian subcontinent. Managers are hoping to strike a $100 million joint venture deal with the Thai government. The company would supply technology and management for the venture, and the government would contribute a minority share of financing to the venture. The company considers the government's main contributions to be providing tax breaks (and other financial incentives) and a stable business environment in which to operate.

   Financial capital is flowing into Thailand at a fair pace. The currency is strong, and inflation remains low. As with other nations in the region, investors are generally wary of the nation's stability. The new auto assembly plant would boost the local economy, reduce unemployment, and increase local wages. But some local politicians fear the company might be interested only in exploiting the country's relatively low-cost labor.

   Activity: Break into an equal number of negotiating teams of three or four persons. Half the teams are to represent the company and the other half the government. As a group, meet for 15 minutes to develop the team's opening position and negotiating strategy. Meet with a team from the other side and undertake 20 minutes of negotiations. After the negotiating session, spend 15 minutes comparing the progress of your negotiations with that of the other pairs of teams.

Key Terms

Take It to the Web

1. **Video Report.** Visit this book's channel on YouTube (www.YouTube.com/MyIBvideos). Click on "Videos" near the top of the page, and click on the set of videos labeled "Ch 13: Selecting and Managing Entry Modes." Watch one video from the list, and then summarize it in a half-page report. Reflecting on the contents of this chapter, which aspects of selecting and managing entry modes can you identify in the video? How might a company engaged in international business act on the information contained in the video?

2. **Website Report.** This chapter's opening company profile discussed Marvel's 50/50 joint venture with Sony that oversees all licensing and merchandising for *Spider-Man,* as well as Sony's animated TV series titled *Spider-Man.* Not mentioned in the opener is that Marvel and Sony became embroiled in a series of lawsuits and countersuits. Perform an Internet search for the name of the joint venture, "Spider-Man Merchandising L.P.," and locate stories that discuss the lawsuits and their settlement.

    What reasons did Marvel give for its initial lawsuit against Sony over its activities? Do you think Marvel was justified in filing suit against Sony? Was it a ruse for Marvel to exact something out of Sony, as some believe? Do you think Sony was right to countersue as it did? What do you think was the main motivation to form the venture from the perspective of each partner?

    Do you think the 50/50 split had anything to do with the joint venture's difficulties? Why or why not? Do you think differences in organizational culture (perhaps rooted in national culture) played any role in the conflict? Do you think anything could have been done during the formation of the joint venture that would have reduced the chances of this dispute arising? Explain.

Ethical Challenges

1. You are the director of international operations for a leading clothing designer based in New York. Your firm recently formed a 50/50 joint venture with a top Latin American manufacturer. On a recent trip to the joint venture's factory in Latin America, you uncovered discrepancies between the financial results sent to the U.S. parent company and those sent to the local parent firm. Further investigation has convinced you that the local venture's top management is keeping two sets of accounting records to facilitate the diversion of funds to personal bank accounts. This scenario is not surprising to you, however, because it is rather common in the local country. What do you do? Do you confront your local joint venture partner directly or find another solution? Might you devise a policy that encourages the local partner to be honest in its financial reporting? If so, how do you go about doing this?

2. You own a small manufacturing firm in California and are considering entering either Australia or Hong Kong. You are unsure which country you should target, and you are unclear about which entry mode is most appropriate. A recent study investigated the differences between ethical perceptions of business managers from Australia and Hong Kong. The researchers determined two factors that affect the perception of ethical problems: (a) culture and (b) the particular mode of market entry (e.g., exporting, contractual, investment in subsidiaries, or joint ventures). What ethical issues do you think might arise in conjunction with the various market entry modes discussed in this chapter? How might these issues influence your entry-mode selection?

3. You are chief operating officer of a Germany-based telecommunications firm considering a joint venture inside China with a Chinese firm. The consultant you've hired to help you through the negotiations has just informed you that ethical concerns can arise when international companies consider a cooperative form of market entry (such as a joint venture) with a local partner. This is especially true when each partner contributes personnel to the venture because cultural perspectives cause people to see ethical decisions differently. This is of special concern to you because the venture plans to employ people from both China and Germany—which have very different cultural backgrounds. Is there anything that your two companies can do to establish ethical principles in such a situation—either before or after formation of the cooperative arrangement? Can you think of a company that succeeded in the face of such difficulties?

MyManagementLab

Go to **mymanagementlab.com** for Auto-graded writing questions as well as the following Assisted-graded writing questions:

13-1. In earlier chapters, we learned how governments get involved in the international flow of trade and foreign direct investment. We also learned how regional economic integration is influencing international business. Identify two market entry modes, and describe how each might be affected by the actions of governments and by increasing regional integration.

13-2. Mymanagementlab Only – comprehensive writing assignment for this chapter.

Practicing International Management Case

Telecom Ventures Unite the World

The world of telecommunications is changing. The era of global e-commerce is here, driven by new technologies such as broadband and wireless Internet access that make possible video telephone connections and high-speed data transmission. Annual worldwide revenues for telecommunications services total $600 billion, with international companies accounting for 20 percent of the business.

Market opportunities are opening around the world as post, telephone, and telegraph (PTT) monopolies are undergoing privatization. Since 1998, telecom deregulation has been taking place in earnest in Europe. Meanwhile, governments in developing countries are boosting investments in infrastructure improvements to increase the number of available telephone lines. The demand for telephone service is growing at a sharp pace; international telephone-call volume more than doubled over a recent six-year period. The net result of these changes is the globalization of the telecommunications industry. As William Donovan, a vice president at Sea-Land Service, said recently, "I don't want to have to talk to a bunch of different PTTs around the world. I don't want to have to go to one carrier in one country and a second in another just because it doesn't have a presence there."

Several alliances and joint venture partnerships formed between companies hoping to capitalize on the changed market and business environment. France Telecom, Deutsche Telekom, and Sprint created Global One to bring international telecommunications services to multinational companies. As part of the deal, Sprint sold 10 percent of its stock to each of its French and German partners. One hurdle for the company was how to integrate the three partners' communication networks into a unified whole. Also, start-up costs were high, and the need to communicate in three different languages created some friction among personnel. Early on, lengthy negotiations were required to reach agreement about the value each partner brought to the venture. A former Global One executive noted, "There is no trust among the partners." Other problems included equipment and billing incompatibilities resulting from distribution agreements with telephone monopolies in individual countries. And then there were the financial losses that prompted Sprint chairman William T. Esrey to install Sprint executive Gary Forsee as CEO and president of Global One.

AT&T also depends on various partnership strategies as entry modes. WorldPartners began as an alliance of AT&T, Kokusai Denshin Denwa (KDD) of Japan, and Telecom of Singapore. The goal was to provide improved telecommunications services for companies conducting business globally. Today, WorldPartners is composed of 10 companies, including Telecom New Zealand, Telstra (Australia), Hong Kong Telecom, and Unisource.

Unisource is itself a joint venture that originally included Sweden's Telia AB, Swiss Telecom PTT, and PTT Telecom Netherlands. Later, Telefonica de España became an equal equity partner in Unisource. Unisource and AT&T then agreed to form a 60–40 joint venture known as AT&T–Unisource Communications to offer voice, data, and messaging services to businesses with European operations. AT&T would have preferred to form a joint venture with the French or German telephone companies. Yet European regulators, concerned about AT&T's strong brand name and enormous size, refused to approve such a deal.

There was strong logic for the deal. AT&T–Unisource CEO James Cosgrove explained from headquarters near Amsterdam in Hoofddorp that to be competitive in Europe a telecom company needs to have a base there and offer global solutions. Despite the fact that there are five corporate parents, a sense of equality and congeniality has developed. CEO Cosgrove explained that after working together for two years, the parent companies realized that their own success is tied to the success of the shared venture. The presence of Telefonica de España in the alliance was especially significant for AT&T because of the Spanish company's strong influence in Latin America. Unfortunately, the alliance was weakened when Telefonica decided to ally itself with Concert Communications. To fill the void, AT&T and Italy's Stet announced a new alliance that would expand communication services to Latin America as well as Europe.

The third major telecommunications alliance, Concert Communications, was formed when British Telecommunications PLC bought a 20-percent stake in MCI Communications. Again, the goal of the alliance was to offer global voice and data network services to global corporations.

Thinking Globally

⭐ 1. What strengths did AT&T bring to its joint venture with Unisource?

2. Can you think of any potential complications that could arise in the AT&T–Unisource joint venture?

3. Assess the formation of Global One, Unisource, and other partnerships discussed in this case in terms of the strategic factors for selecting entry modes identified in the chapter.

Source: Barbara Martinez, "Sprint Names Its Long-distance Chief to Run Loss-Beset Global One Venture," *Wall Street Journal,* February 17, 1998, p. B20; Jennifer L. Schenker and James Pressley, "European Telecom Venture with Sprint Hasn't Become the Bully Some Feared," *Wall Street Journal,* December 23, 1997, p. A11; Alan Cane, "Unisource Partners to Strengthen Ties," *Financial Times,* June 4, 1997, p. 13; Gautam Naik, "Unisource Expected to Merge Operations," *Wall Street Journal,* June 4, 1997, p. B6.

Developing and Marketing Products

LEARNING OBJECTIVES

After studying this chapter, you should be able to

1. Explain the impact globalization is having on international marketing activities.

2. Describe the types of things managers must consider when developing international product strategies.

3. Discuss the factors that influence international promotional strategies and the blending of product and promotional strategies.

4. Explain the elements that managers must take into account when designing international distribution strategies.

5. Discuss the elements that influence international pricing strategies.

A Look Back

Chapter 13 explained the pros and cons of international entry modes and when each one is most appropriately used. We also described management issues with regard to each entry mode and the important strategic factors in their selection.

A Look at This Chapter

This chapter explores how globalization and differences in national business environments impact the development and marketing of products internationally. We examine the many variables that must be considered when creating product, promotional, distribution, and pricing strategies.

A Look Ahead

Chapter 15 explains how companies launch and manage their international production efforts. Again, an emphasis is placed on how environmental variables affect production strategies.

WINGS FOR LIFE

VIENNA, Austria—When Dietrich Mateschitz traveled to Asia on business, he got a taste of some popular energy drinks. Sensing opportunity, he brought a sample of the drinks back to Austria and in 1987 started Red Bull (www.redbull.com). Red Bull Energy Drink is now available in more than 164 countries, and sales are in excess of 4.6 billion cans of the raging stuff each year.

Red Bull is identical in every market in which it is sold. Each slender red, blue, and silver can contains caffeine, carbohydrates, vitamins, and the amino acid taurine. That is music to the ears of club goers, who swear by the drink's ability to keep them going till dawn. Sales are soaring among this crowd partly due to the word-of-mouth advertising the company gets from loyal customers. Around the world, Red Bull recruits "brand ambassadors," who hand out free samples at events, and hires "student managers," who spread the word about the beverage and drink it on campuses.

Source: JOERG MITTER/Getty Images/Newscom

Red Bull is also racking up double-digit revenue growth with creative TV ads. The ads display the company's "Red Bull Gives You Wings" tagline as cartoon characters float into the air after downing a can of the sweet drink. Red Bull also sponsors top athletes in racing and sporting events, including snowboarding, hang-gliding, skateboarding, and daredevil stunts. Shown here, freestyle motocross rider Mat Rebeaud of Switzerland performs a jump near the Hagia Sofia Mosque in Istanbul, Turkey.

The company does not seem to mind that some people complain about Red Bull's extreme sweetness. "It's not meant to be a taste drink; you either love us or you hate us," says a spokesperson. Although Denmark, Norway, and Uruguay ban the drink because of its contents, it seems that many other people are happily running with the bull. As you read this chapter, think about the many ways in which products are marketed around the world.[1]

In earlier chapters, we emphasized the greater complexity of managing an international business as compared with a purely domestic one. Myriad differences in all aspects of a nation's business environment complicate management. Managing marketing activities that span time zones and cultures can test the most seasoned marketing managers.

We first introduced the concept of globalization and how it affects international business activities in Chapter 1 and returned to this theme in subsequent chapters. We have seen that globalization's impact is not uniform: It affects industries and products in different ways and to varying degrees. Some companies can take advantage of globalization's effects and create a single product that is marketed identically around the world. As we saw in this chapter's opening company profile, Red Bull markets an identical energy drink in the same manner in more than 160 countries around the world. Other companies realize that differences in national business environments are too great to ignore. This group then must create new products, modify promotional campaigns, or adjust their marketing strategies in some other way.

We begin this chapter by taking a brief look at the debate over the extent to which globalization *should* affect marketing strategies. We then describe how marketing internationally differs in terms of how companies create their product strategies, promote and advertise a product, decide on a pricing strategy, and design distribution channels. Throughout the chapter, we examine how globalization on one hand and national differences on the other are having an impact on international marketing activities.

Globalization and Marketing

Globalization is transforming the way in which some products are marketed internationally, but not all. Some companies implement a global strategy that uses similar promotional messages and themes to market the same product around the world. Others find that their products require physical changes to suit the tastes of consumers in markets abroad. Other firms' products need different marketing campaigns to reflect the unique circumstances of local markets. How do managers decide when their marketing strategies need modifying? In this section, we explain the impact of globalization on the standardization-versus-adaptation decision.

Standardization versus Adaptation

In a well-known article, U.S. researcher Theodore Levitt argued that because the world is becoming standardized and homogeneous, companies should market the same products in the same way in all countries.[2] Technology, claimed Levitt, was already causing people's needs and preferences to converge throughout the world. He urged companies to reduce production and marketing costs by standardizing both the physical features of their products and their strategies for marketing them.

Yet, standardization is just one of a number of strategies with which firms successfully enter the international marketplace today and it may not always be the most appropriate strategy. A company may be better off adapting to local cultures and exploiting their international image in order to gain market share locally. In addition to the product itself, managers should also consider the benefits of adapting the company's website to national markets. To read about how a business can tailor a website to suit local culture, see this chapter's Culture Matters feature, titled "Localizing Websites."

INFLUENCE OF NATIONAL BUSINESS ENVIRONMENTS Consumers in different national markets often demand products that reflect their unique tastes and preferences. Cultural, political, legal, and economic environments have a great deal to do with the preferences of both consumers and industrial buyers worldwide. Recall from Chapter 2 that a culture's aesthetics involves, among other things, preferences for certain colors. Ohio-based Rubbermaid (www.rubbermaid.com) discovered the role of aesthetics as it attempted to increase its international sales. Consumers in the United States prefer household products in neutral blues or almond; in southern Europe, red is the preferred color. The Dutch want white. In addition, many European cultures perceive plastic products as inferior and want tight lids on metal wastebaskets as opposed to U.S.-style plastic versions with open tops.

But certain products do appeal to practically all cultures. Although it is not a traditional Asian drink, red wine is sweeping Asian markets such as Hong Kong, Singapore, Taiwan, and

CULTURE MATTERS   Localizing Websites

When going global with an Internet presence, the best strategy may be to localize as much as possible. Online customers often want an experience that corresponds to their cultural context offline. Here are a few tips for perfecting an online presence:

- *Choosing Colors.* A black-and-white website is fine for many countries, but in Asia visitors may think you are inviting them to a funeral. In Japan and across Europe, websites in pastel color schemes often work best.
- *Selecting Numbers.* Many Chinese-speaking cultures consider the number *4* unlucky, although *8* and *9* symbolize prosperity. Be careful that your web address and phone numbers do not send the wrong signal.
- *Watching the Clock.* If marketing to countries that use the 24-hour clock, adjust times stated on the site so it reads, "Call between 9:00 and 17:00" instead of "Call between 9 a.m. and 5 p.m."
- *Avoiding Slang.* English in Britain is different from that in the United States, Spanish in Spain is different from that

in Mexico, and French in France is different from that in Quebec. Avoid slang to lessen the potential negative impact of such differences.

- *Waving the Flag.* Using national flags as symbols for buttons that access different language versions of your site should be done carefully. Mexican visitors to your site may be put off by a Spanish flag to signify the site's Spanish-language version, for example.
- *Doing the Math.* Provide conversions into local currencies for buyer convenience. For online ordering, be sure your site calculates any shipping costs, tax rates, tariffs, and so on. Also allow enough blanks on the order form to accommodate longer international addresses.
- *Getting Feedback.* Finally, talk with customers to learn what they want to accomplish on your website. Then, thoroughly test the site to ensure that it functions properly.

Thailand. Driving demand are medical studies reporting the health benefits of red wine (the king of Thailand has publicly proclaimed its healthy properties). But other factors—including the fact that red is considered good luck in many Asian cultures—are also at work. Many Asians choose red wine at restaurants because of its image as the beverage of choice for people who are sophisticated and successful. (The same is not true of white wine because from a distance it may resemble water.) Today in Beijing, fashionable young people often give red wine as a housewarming present instead of the traditional favorites of their parents and grandparents.

Product standardization is more likely when nations share the same level of economic development. In years past, consumers in India faced limited options when it came to purchasing automobiles. Most automobiles available were made in India, were expensive, and were not fuel-efficient. Thanks to steady economic progress over the past two decades, Indian consumers have a better standard of living and more discretionary income. Being able to afford an imported brand-name automobile with a global reputation, such as Suzuki (www.suzuki.co.jp) or Ford (www.ford.com), is more commonplace in Indian cities than it was years ago.

With this brief introduction to some of the issues relevant to international marketing strategy, let's take an in-depth look at the elements that influence a company's *product, promotional, distribution,* and *pricing strategies.*

Developing Product Strategies

Companies can standardize or adapt their products in many alternative ways when they decide to "go international." Let's look at some of the factors that influence the standardize-versus-adapt decision as well as at several other international product strategy issues.

Laws and Regulations

Companies must often adapt their products to satisfy laws and regulations in a target market. People's tastes also vary across markets, and taste in chocolate is no exception to the rule. A so-called Chocolate War has erupted in the European Union (EU) as it tries to standardize member countries' product content regulations. On one side stand the so-called cocoa purists, including Belgium, France, Germany, Spain, Italy, the Netherlands, Luxembourg, and Greece. Opposite stand Britain, Denmark, Portugal, Austria, Finland, and Sweden—nations who permit manufacturers to add vegetable fats to chocolate products. The purists argue not only that European advertising should be restricted to using the word *chocolate* for 100-percent cocoa products but also that the term *milk chocolate* be outlawed altogether. They want nonpure products labeled something like "chocolate with milk and noncocoa vegetable fats."

The fact that many developing countries have fewer consumer protection laws creates an ethical issue for some companies. Ironically, lower levels of education and less buying experience mean that consumers in developing countries are more likely to need protection. However, many governments impose fewer regulations in order to hold down production costs and consumer prices. Unfortunately, this can be an invitation for international distributors to withhold full information about products and their potential dangers.

Cultural Differences

Companies also adapt their products to suit local buyers' product preferences, which are rooted in culture. Häagen-Dazs (www.haagendazs.com) is an international company that prides itself on its ability to identify the taste preferences of consumers in target markets. It then modifies its base product with just the right flavor to make a product that satisfies consumers' needs. Following years of trial and error developing secret formulas and conducting taste tests, Häagen-Dazs finally launched its green-tea flavor ice cream throughout Japan. The taste is that of *macha* tea— an elite strain of green tea that has been used in elaborate Japanese ceremonies for centuries. Green-tea ice cream was an instant hit and one day may even surpass Häagen-Dazs' perennial flavor champion in Japan—vanilla.

Not all companies need to modify their product to the culture; instead, they may need to identify a different cultural need that it satisfies. Altoids (www.altoids.com), for example, is a British product that has been used for 200 years to soothe upset stomachs. But the company identified a different use for its product in the United States. Because of its strong flavor, Altoids is sold in the U.S. market as a breath mint and has pushed aside weaker-flavored candies.

Brand and Product Names

brand name
Name of one or more items in a product line that identifies the source or character of the items.

Several issues related to a company's brand name are important concerns for the day-to-day activities of international managers. A **brand name** is the name of one or more items in a product line that identifies the source or character of the items. When we see a product labeled with a particular brand name, we assign to that product a certain value based on our past experiences with that brand. That is why a brand name is central to a product's personality and the image that it presents to buyers. It informs buyers about a product's source and protects both customer and producer from copycat products. Brand names help consumers to select, recommend, or reject products. They also function as legal property that owners can protect from trespass by competitors.

A brand name is central to a product's personality and to how buyers perceive it. The brands of all types of global companies blend into the urban surroundings in almost every nation. Shown here are the logos of Starbucks and McDonald's in the center of Beijing, China. A strong brand is essential for a global company whether its industry is fast food, delivery services, mobile phones, financial services, or computer software. What are some of the reasons why having a global brand image is so important today?

Source: ADRIAN BRADSHAW/Newscom

Indeed, a strong brand can become a company's most valuable asset and primary source of competitive advantage. A consistent worldwide brand image is increasingly important as more consumers and businesspeople travel internationally than ever before. An inconsistent brand name can confuse existing and potential customers. Although companies normally keep their brand names consistent across markets, they can create new product names or modify existing ones to suit local preferences.

Companies also need to review the image of their brand from time to time and update it if it seems old-fashioned. One classic example is that of Lipton (www.lipton.com). The company wanted people to think of Lipton tea as an alternative to colas and other soft drinks. Since the 1890s, Lipton had as its mascot Sir Thomas J. Lipton, the tea maker's founder. But in a major overhaul of the brand, all references to Mr. Lipton were removed because he gave the product a dated image—young people thought of Lipton tea as a drink for their parents' generation. To breathe new life into the brand, Lipton booted the founder in favor of "Tom," a sassy young Briton.

SELECTING INTERNATIONAL BRAND AND PRODUCT NAMES Whether they are standardized or adapted locally, products in international markets need carefully selected names. All company and product brand names (like all nouns) are made up of *morphemes*—semantic elements, or language building blocks, such as the *van* in *advantage*. NameLab (www.namelab.com) is an identity-consulting firm that uses more than 6,000 morphemes to develop new product names. NameLab points out that because most Western languages stem from the same linguistic source—Indo-European—companies can create brand names having similar meanings in these nations. *Accu,* for example, connotes *accuracy* in both Western and Japanese cultures. Thus Honda (www.honda.com) named its upscale car division Acura. Other names that are constructed to have similar connotations in many languages or to embody no cultural bias include Compaq (www.compaq.com), Kodak (www.kodak.com), and Sony (www.sony.co.jp).[3] After they choose a name, companies can survey local native speakers about their reactions to it. These techniques help companies reduce the likelihood of committing potential marketing blunders.

Brand names seldom offend people in international markets, but product names can be highly offensive if they are not carefully researched and selected. Clarks Shoes (www.clarks.com), a British shoe company, once gave a name to a line of shoes that was offensive to the Hindu religious community in Britain. Consequently, the company issued a statement in the British press apologizing for naming some of its products with the names of the Hindu Gods Vishnu and Krishna and for offending the British Hindu community. In the future, Clarks Shoes promised to carry out more extensive marketing research before naming its products.

Other times, product names must be changed, not because they are offensive, but because they mislead consumers. Consider the problem faced by the British beverage and chocolate producer Cadbury Schweppes (www.cadburyschweppes.com). When Swiss chocolate manufacturers sued on the grounds that the public was being misled into thinking that Cadbury's Swiss Chalet bar was genuine Swiss chocolate, the company was forced to withdraw the product from the marketplace. A British court confirmed that the name and packaging of the product—the "Swiss" part of the name and the image of a snow-capped Swiss Alp—were likely to mislead consumers.

National Image

The value customers obtain from a product is heavily influenced by the image of the country in which it is designed, manufactured, or assembled. We consider the influence of a country's name when thinking of Italian shoes, German luxury cars, and Japanese electronics. This image can be positive for some products but negative for others. For example, the best Russian caviar and vodkas have reputations of quality around the world. But how do you feel about Russian automobiles or computers? Attaching "Russia" to certain products is beneficial, whereas attaching it to others could be detrimental.

Because it affects buyers' perceptions of quality and reliability, national image is an important element of product policy. Yet national image can and does change slowly over long periods of time. Decades ago, Japanese products were considered to be of poor quality and rather unreliable. A national effort toward quality improvement and the installation of quality-control procedures by companies has earned Japan a national image for precision and quality products. Once vehicles for budget-conscious consumers, Japanese cars now include some of the finest-built luxury automobiles in the world.

Likewise, years ago Taiwan was known for basic, no-frills items such as toys and industrial products of all sorts. But today, many of Taiwan's industries possess a reputation for innovation—designing products that reflect decades of investing in people's research and engineering skills. One company that benefited from an intense devotion to research and development (R&D) is Taiwanese bicycle manufacturer Giant (www.giant-bicycles.com). The company began in Taichung, Taiwan, nearly three decades ago producing bikes under the brand names of other companies. But when the company began to manufacture under its own brand name, it carved itself a solid niche in the mountain bike market. Giant's innovation in using lightweight materials and creating groundbreaking designs even earned it sponsorship of Spain's world-champion racing team. Today, high-tech products—and even those not traditionally thought of as high tech (such as bikes)—stamped "Made in Taiwan" command respect in global markets.

Counterfeit Goods and Black Markets

In Chapter 3 we discussed how companies are trying to protect their intellectual property and trademarks from counterfeit goods. Recall that *counterfeit goods* are imitation products passed off as legitimate trademarks, patents, or copyrighted works—products that normally enjoy legal protection. Because developing nations often are weakest in enforcing such legal protections, they normally have the most active counterfeiting markets. Countries that top the list for the portion of their markets comprised of counterfeits include China, India, Russia, Thailand, and Turkey.

Counterfeiting is common among highly visible brand-name consumer goods, including watches, perfumes, clothing, movies, music, and computer software. Counterfeit products are typically sold to consumers on what is called the black market—a marketplace of underground transactions that typically appears because a product is either illegal (such as counterfeits) or tightly regulated. Tabletop vendors working the back streets of the world's largest cities represent the retail side of the black market. For example, in Sofia, the capital of Bulgaria, you can buy one CD-ROM that contains 50 software applications for $10; buying all the official versions of these products would cost about $5,000. In Estonia's Kadaka flea market, you can find the full Microsoft Office (www.microsoft.com) software bundle for around $18—about one-fiftieth of its official selling price. Increasingly, engineered industrial components such as aircraft parts, medicines, and other pharmaceutical products are also becoming targets of counterfeiters.

Counterfeit goods can damage buyers' image of a brand when the counterfeits are of inferior quality—which is nearly always the case. Buyers who purchase an item bearing a company's brand name expect a certain level of craftsmanship and, therefore, satisfaction. But when the product fails to deliver on the expectations, the buyers are dissatisfied, and the company's reputation is tarnished. Japanese motorcycle manufacturers recently saw their sales in China fall sharply, because people were buying near-replicas of their products at discounts of up to 40 percent of the originals. But the counterfeiting problem is more serious today because the Chinese producers are now exporting their cycles to other Asian nations. Yamaha (www.yamaha-motor.com), Japan's second-largest motorcycle producer, is considering legal action against one Chinese company. Yamaha officials say that the Chinese company's products resemble its own models right down to the Yamaha name stamped on the side.

Shortened Product Life Cycles

Companies traditionally managed to extend a product's life by introducing it into different markets consecutively. They did this by introducing products in industrialized countries and only later marketing them in developing and emerging markets. Thus, while a product's sales are declining in one market, they might be growing in another.

Advances in telecommunications, however, have alerted consumers around the world to the latest product introductions. Consequently, consumers in developing and emerging markets also demand the latest products and are not happy with receiving what is yesterday's fad in the highly developed nations. Also, the rapid pace with which technological innovation occurs today is shortening the life cycles of products. The actions of international companies themselves actually helped to create this situation. Companies are undertaking new-product development at an increasingly rapid pace and are thus shortening the life cycles of their products.

QUICK STUDY 1

1. How is globalization affecting international marketing activities?
2. List elements of the national business environment that influence the standardization-versus-adaptation decision.
3. What is the link between *brand names* and competitive advantage?
4. Explain the potential impact of national image and counterfeit products on international product strategy.

Creating Promotional Strategies

Promotion mix comprises a company's efforts to reach distribution channels and target customers through communications, such as personal selling, advertising, public relations, and direct marketing. (For more on distribution channels, see "Designing Distribution Strategies" on pages 364–366.) Not surprisingly, promotional activities often receive the greatest attention among marketers because many people, even professionals, tend to equate *marketing* with *promotion*. After we examine two general promotional strategies, we discuss the complications that can arise in international advertising and communications.

Push and Pull Strategies

There are two general promotional strategies that companies can use to get their marketing message across to buyers. Companies can rely completely on just one of these strategies or use them in combination. A promotional strategy designed to create buyer demand that will encourage distribution channel members to stock a company's product is called a **pull strategy**. In other words, buyer demand is generated in order to "pull" products through distribution channels to end users. Creating consumer demand through direct marketing techniques is a common example of a pull strategy. For example, when Procter & Gamble (www.pg.com) encountered distribution difficulties when trying to introduce Rejoice hair-care products into Asia, the company opted to generate grassroots consumer demand. The company hired a fleet of trucks to drive through village squares and hand out free trial packages to potential end users.

By contrast, a **push strategy** is a promotional strategy designed to pressure distribution channel members to carry a product and promote it to final users. Manufacturers of products commonly sold through department and grocery stores often use a push strategy. For example, manufacturer's sales representatives are constantly calling on Walmart (www.walmart.com) to encourage it to stock the manufacturer's product and give it good visibility. Push strategies are also used for office products, including computers and office furniture. A company's international sales force is the key to successfully implementing a push strategy abroad. For insights into how companies can better manage their salespeople in other cultures, see the Manager's Briefcase, titled "Managing an International Sales Force."

Whether the push or pull strategy is most appropriate in a given marketing environment depends on several factors:

- **Distribution System.** Implementing a push strategy can be difficult when distribution channel members (such as distributors) wield a great deal of power relative to that of producers. It can also be ineffective when distribution channels are lengthy: The more levels of intermediaries that there are, the more distribution channel members there are who must be convinced to carry a product. In such cases, it might be easier to create buyer demand using a pull strategy than to persuade distributors to stock a particular product.
- **Access to Mass Media.** Developing and emerging markets typically have fewer available forms of mass media for use in implementing a pull strategy. Accordingly, it is difficult to increase consumer awareness of a product and to generate product demand. Many consumers in these markets cannot afford cable or satellite TV, or perhaps even glossy magazines.
  In such cases, advertisers might turn to billboards and radio. At other times, gaining wide exposure can be difficult because existing media have only local, as opposed to national, reach. For example, Indonesia did not launch its first nationwide TV station until 1994. Yet in other situations, advertising certain products on certain media is unlawful. For example, companies that enter Canada or the United States cannot use TV or radio to advertise tobacco products.

promotion mix
Efforts by a company to reach distribution channels and to target customers through communications, such as personal selling, advertising, public relations, and direct marketing.

pull strategy
Promotional strategy designed to create buyer demand that will encourage distribution channel members to stock a company's product.

push strategy
Promotional strategy designed to pressure distribution channel members to carry a product and to promote it to final users of the product.

MANAGER'S BRIEFCASE   Managing an International Sales Force

Today, companies reap a greater portion of their revenues from international sales. How can you become a better global manager of your company's international sales force? Here are some helpful hints on improving the effectiveness of your company's representatives abroad:

- **Know the Sales Scene.** Your company should conduct research before hiring and managing an international sales force, then should formulate a targeted sales strategy and empower your sales force to meet their performance targets. The amount of compensation, as well as the way in which it is delivered, varies from country to country. For example, in the United States a greater portion of salary is based on commission than it is in Europe. Know the salary structure and incentive plans of salespeople with similar jobs at local companies.
- **Research the Customer.** Do not assume that customers abroad have the same needs and preferences as customers at home. Investigate what potential buyers want and how much they are willing to pay. When ECA International (a market information provider) tried to expand into Asia, it was unsuccessful time and again. The company learned through its sales force that potential customers wanted to buy research piece by piece rather than buy a membership in the company. ECA was able to sell its memberships in Asia after it adapted its methods to suit local buyers.

- **Work with the Culture.** "In order to motivate individuals, you need to set realistic objectives for salespeople, and much of that is culturally bound," says John Wada, sales and marketing director for IOR, a cross-cultural management company. Your company should seek answers to a host of questions: Do people in the local culture feel differently about work teams and competition than your sales force at home? How about schedules and deadlines? Are you moving into a culture where "time is of the essence" or one where time is less important? Your company and its local sales force must understand what is expected of one another.
- **Learn from Your Representatives.** If your salespeople believe they are pushing products that bear no relationship to the local market, their performance will suffer. "I'd do a great job," so the story goes, "but the product just won't sell here." Salespeople may begin focusing on critiquing products rather than selling them. Involve your sales reps in the R&D process so that they have a better sense of what is going on with the product. Perhaps bring your sales force to the home office to learn about your business so they understand their vital link in your company's chain of business activities. Finally, top managers should visit the local office to better comprehend the needs of local customers.

Source: Based on Charlene Marmer Solomon, "Managing an Overseas Sales Force," *World Trade*, Global Sales and Technology Special Section, pp. S4–S6.

- **Type of Product.** A pull strategy is most appropriate when buyers display a great deal of brand loyalty toward one particular brand name. In other words, brand-loyal buyers know what brand of a product they want before they go shopping. On the other hand, push strategies tend to be appropriate for inexpensive consumer goods characterized by buyers who are not brand loyal. Low brand loyalty means that a buyer will go shopping for a product not knowing which brand is best, and simply will buy one of those carried by the retailer or wholesaler. A push strategy is also suited to industrial products because potential buyers usually need to be informed about a product's special features and benefits.

International Advertising

International advertising differs a great deal from advertising in domestic markets. Managers must rely on their knowledge of a market to decide whether an ad is suitable for the company's international promotional efforts. Cultural similarities can mean that ads need only slight modification for different nations, whereas cultural differences may mean that entirely new ads must be created.

Coca-Cola's (www.cocacola.com) classic experience in creating an ad to appeal to the people of China illustrates the problems that can arise when developing specialized ads. Coca-Cola's desire to create a Coke ad that looked authentically Chinese drew a commercial crew to Harbin, a city in northeast China. But during the journey to Harbin the bus carrying the crew that was filming the commercial stalled. When the driver lit a fire under the gas tank to thaw the fuel, the horrified crew scrambled off the bus, thinking it might explode. The crew stood in biting, subzero temperatures until the bus was once again running—the director's frostbitten nose bears the scars of the adventure. Then, when a local older man hired to be in the ad had trouble following the director's instructions, local villagers pointed out why—he was deaf. Finally, the crew had to trudge around in knee-deep snow first to get a field of frozen red pinwheels to spin and then to reorient the whole set so that the wind (which was blowing in an unfavorable direction) could spin the pinwheels. But it appears that Coke's efforts at creating an ad depicting people celebrating Chinese New Year in the traditional manner in a picturesque village paid off—"It made me feel very emotional," said Fang Chuanbao, an office worker in Shanghai who saw the ad. The localized ads exemplify Coke's "think local, act local" mantra, which was pioneered by Chairman Douglas Daft as part of an effort to remake Coke into the nimble marketer it once was.[4]

Let's now explore some of the factors involved in the decision of whether to standardize or adapt advertisements.

STANDARDIZING OR ADAPTING ADVERTISEMENTS The vast majority of advertising that occurs in any one nation is produced solely for that domestic audience. But companies that advertise in multiple markets must determine the aspects of the advertising campaign that can be standardized across markets and those that cannot. Companies that do market their products across national boundaries try to contain costs by standardizing as many aspects of their campaigns as possible. However, companies seldom standardize all aspects of their international promotions for a variety of reasons, including differences in culture and laws.

Firms that standardize advertising often control campaigns from the home office. This policy helps them to project consistent brand images and promotional messages across all markets—the aim of a global strategy (see Chapter 11). Companies can achieve consistency by standardizing their basic promotional message, creative concepts, graphics, and information content. After a company decides to pursue a global marketing strategy, it naturally tries to get the most for its advertising expenditure.

One way companies can reach a global audience is to sponsor global sporting events, such as the Olympics, World Cup Soccer, and Formula One automobile racing. These types of events receive heavy media coverage and are often telecast simultaneously in multiple nations. Even posting banners around the venues of such events can boost recognition of a company's brand name by exposing it to perhaps millions of viewers around the world. Viewers in 102 countries see the banners of companies that sponsor Formula One automobile racing.

CASE: THE ELUSIVE EURO-CONSUMER The continuing integration of nations belonging to the European Union is causing many marketers to dream of a day when they can standardize their advertising to appeal to a so-called Euro-consumer. But the Euro-consumer remains a rare, mythical creature that eludes even the world's most clever advertisers.

Michael Bradley scores the United States' second goal against Slovenia in the FIFA World Cup in Johannesburg, South Africa. The global broadcast of the World Cup every four years offers companies a chance to put their messages before an audience totaling 30 billion cumulative viewings. The brands of global companies are plastered on signs around the perimeters of playing fields and are seen worldwide during matches. Advertising by each individual sporting goods company can total hundreds of millions of dollars during the World Cup.

Source: ZUMA Press/Newscom

Some well-known international advertising agencies have tried a pan-European advertising approach only to fail because of national differences. Consider the experience of the acclaimed Leo Burnett Company (www.leoburnett.com) when it took on the goal of creating a single European campaign for United Distillers' Johnnie Walker (www.johnniewalker.com) whiskey. It took many painful tests and revisions before the ad could be rolled out. In the original ad, the tag line read "The Water of Life" and showed a man attending "the running of the bulls" in Pamplona, Spain. After narrowly escaping being trampled by the bull, the man celebrates with a glass of Johnnie Walker Red Label. But in many countries, the Pamplona setting raised hackles because people said, "The Spanish don't know anything about making good whiskey." Tests of the ad in Germany showed it would not work because to Germans it seemed simply reckless—not a widely admired trait there. Says Jenny Vaughn, worldwide brand director for Johnnie Walker, "Also, because of the German animal rights campaigners, you can't show a goldfish in a goldfish bowl on German television, so a bull run was just not [acceptable]." The tagline "The Water of Life" was baffling in many languages. "People thought it meant watered-down whiskey," said Vaughn, so the line was changed to "Taste Life." Then a voice-over in the ad was incorrectly translated in one language as "when your life flashes in front of you, make sure it's worth watching." In every market, either the words didn't make sense or the meaning was lost. In Italy, the line was totally discarded. In Germany, attempts at translation proved so maddening that the line was replaced with "Live every day as if it were your last."

Europe's many languages certainly create thorny translation issues for marketers. Thus, the most successful pan-European ads are those that contain a great deal of visuals, have few written or spoken words, and focus on the product and consumer. One such ad is that for TAG Heuer (www.tagheuer.com) watches, which positions the company's product as competitive and a winner. In the ad, a swimmer is shown racing a shark and a hurdler is shown leaping an oversize razor blade. The highly visual ad gets across the company's message that it is a winner.

Blending Product and Promotional Strategies

When companies extend their marketing efforts internationally, they develop communication strategies that blend product and promotional strategies.[5] A company's communication strategy for a particular market takes into account the nature of the product being marketed and the promotion mix to market it. After we discuss the marketing communication process, we examine five product/promotional methods companies use and the appropriate situation for each.

COMMUNICATING PROMOTIONAL MESSAGES The process of sending promotional messages about products to target markets is called **marketing communication**. Communicating the benefits of a product can be more difficult in international business than in domestic business for several reasons. Marketing internationally usually means translating promotional messages from one language into another. Marketers must be knowledgeable of the many cultural nuances that can affect how buyers interpret a promotional message. A nation's laws that govern the promotion of products in another country can also force changes in marketing communication.

Marketing communication is typically considered a circular process, as shown in Figure 14.1. The company with an idea it wishes to communicate is the source of the communication. The idea is *encoded* (translated into images, words, and symbols) into a *promotional message* that the company is trying to get across. The promotional message is then sent to the *audience* (potential buyers) through various *media*. Media commonly used by companies to communicate their promotional messages include radio, TV, newspapers, magazines, billboards, and direct mailings. After the audience receives the message, they decode the message and interpret its meaning. Information in the form of *feedback* (purchase or nonpurchase) then flows back to the source of the message. The decoding process by the audience can be disrupted by the presence of *noise*—anything that disrupts the audience's ability to receive and interpret the promotional message. By ignoring important cultural nuances, companies can inadvertently increase the potential for noise that can cloud the audience's understanding of their promotional message. For example, language barriers between the company and potential buyers can create noise if a company's promotional message is translated incorrectly into the local language.

PRODUCT/COMMUNICATIONS EXTENSION (DUAL EXTENSION) This method extends the same home-market product and marketing promotion into target markets. Under certain conditions, it can be the simplest and most profitable strategy. For example, because of a common language

marketing communication
Process of sending promotional messages about products to target markets.

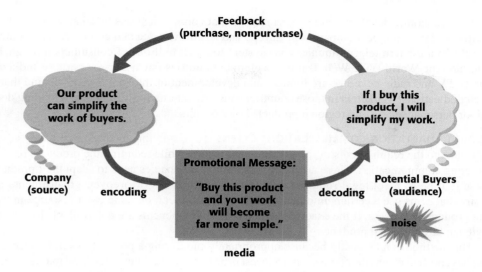

FIGURE 14.1

Marketing Communications Process

Source: Based on Courtland L. Bovee, John V. Thill, George P. Dovel, and Marian Burk Wood, *Advertising Excellence* (New York, NY: McGraw-Hill, 1995), p. 14.

and other cultural similarities, companies based in English-speaking Canadian provinces can sell the same product with packaging and advertising in the U.S. market—provided the product is not required by the U.S. government to carry any special statements or warnings. The Canadian companies contain costs by developing a single product and one promotional campaign for both markets. Yet it is important for Canadian companies not to ignore any subtle cultural differences that could cause confusion in interpreting the promotional message.

As the information age continues to knit the world more tightly together, this dual extension method will probably grow more popular. Today, consumers in seemingly remote parts of the world are rapidly becoming aware of the latest worldwide fads and fashions. But this strategy appears to be better suited for certain groups of buyers, including brand-conscious teenagers, business executives, and wealthy individuals. The strategy also tends to be better suited for companies that use a global strategy with their products, such as upscale personal items with global brand names—examples include Rolex (www.rolex.com) watches, Hermes (www.hermes.com) scarves and ties, and Chanel (www.chanel.com) perfumes. It can also be appropriate for global brands that have mass appeal and that cut across all age groups and social classes—such as Canon (www.canon.com), Mars (www.mars.com), and Samsung (www.samsung.com). The strategy also is useful to companies that are the low-cost leaders in their industries: One product and one promotional message keep costs down.

PRODUCT EXTENSION/COMMUNICATIONS ADAPTATION   Under this method, a company extends the same product into target markets but alters its promotion. Communications require adaptation because the product satisfies a different need, serves a different function, or appeals to a different type of buyer. Companies can adjust their marketing communication to inform potential buyers that the product either satisfies their needs or serves a distinct function. This approach helps companies contain costs because the good itself requires no alteration. Altering communications can be expensive, however, especially when cultural differences among target markets are significant. Filming altered ads with local actors and on location can add significantly to promotional costs.

One company that changes its promotional message for international markets is the Japanese retailer Muji (www.muji.net). Muji offers a wide variety of goods, including writing materials, clothing, and home furnishings inspired by a central theme rooted in centuries of Japanese culture—the simplicity of everyday life. Muji's philosophy is one of selling unbranded quality goods, and company promotions boast the motto "Functional Japanese minimalism for everyone." Its target market in Japan is the average school-aged child and young adult. But Muji's European stores use a different promotional message. Muji's European customers tend to be older and see themselves as sophisticated and stylish buyers of the company's products. In Europe, Muji's promotional message is "shop at a business that has a very respectable brand name"—clearly different from its message in Japan. Also, the company's European customers are not simply buying a product (as do its Japanese customers); they are buying into the traditional Japanese concept of simplicity.[6]

Low economic development also can require that communications be adapted to suit local conditions. For example, companies in Europe and North America and certain Asian countries can rely on a modern telecommunications system to reach millions of consumers through TV, radio, and the World Wide Web. But in developing countries (such as rural parts of India and China), TV and radio coverage are limited, and development of the Web is years behind that of developed nations. Marketers in those countries must use alternative techniques, including door-to-door personal selling and regional product shows or fairs.

PRODUCT ADAPTATION/COMMUNICATIONS EXTENSION Using this method, a company adapts its product to the requirements of the international market while retaining the product's original marketing communication. There are many reasons why companies need to adapt their products. One might be to meet legal requirements in the local market. Moreover, governments can require that firms use a certain amount of local materials, labor, or some other resource in their local production process. If the exact same materials or components are not available locally, the result can be a modified product.

This method can be costly because appropriately modifying a product to suit the needs of local buyers often means the company must invest in production facilities in the local market. If each national market requires its own production facility, cost savings provided by economies of scale in production can be elusive. Still, a company can implement this strategy successfully if it sells a differentiated product for which it can charge a higher price to offset the greater production costs.

PRODUCT/COMMUNICATIONS ADAPTATION (DUAL ADAPTATION) This method adapts both the product and its marketing communication to suit the target market. The product itself is adapted to match the needs or preferences of local buyers. The promotional message is adapted to explain how the product meets those needs and preferences. Because both production and marketing efforts must be altered, this strategy can be expensive; therefore, it is not very common. It can be implemented successfully, however, if a sufficiently large and profitable market segment exists.

PRODUCT INVENTION This method requires that an entirely new product be developed for the target market. Product invention is often necessary when many important differences exist between the home and target markets. One reason for product invention is that local buyers cannot afford a company's current product because of low purchasing power. For example, Honda (www.honda.com) developed a car called the City for budget-conscious buyers in Southeast Asia and Europe.

Product inventions can also arise because of a lack of adequate infrastructure needed to operate certain products. One day, London inventor Trevor Baylis was watching a TV documentary on the difficulty of educating Africans about AIDS because much of the continent did not have the electricity infrastructure or batteries to operate radios. Baylis set to work and developed the Freeplay windup radio—30 seconds of cranking keeps it going for 40 minutes. Baylis and several South African businessmen then formed a company called Bay-Gen Power Corporation in Cape Town, South Africa. The radio was first sold only to relief agencies working in developing nations. But due mostly to word of mouth, it is now popular worldwide among hikers, environmentalists, and even hip shoppers looking for eco-friendly appliances.

QUICK STUDY 2

1. Identify several factors that influence the choice between a *push strategy* and a *pull strategy*.
2. What issues affect the decision of whether to standardize or adapt international advertising?
3. Identify each element in the *marketing communications* process, and describe how they interact.
4. What five generic methods are used to blend product and promotional strategies for international markets? Describe each briefly.

distribution
Planning, implementing, and controlling the physical flow of a product from its point of origin to its point of consumption.

Designing Distribution Strategies

Planning, implementing, and controlling the physical flow of a product from its point of origin to its point of consumption is called **distribution**. The physical path that a product follows on its way to customers is called a *distribution channel*. Companies along this channel that work together in delivering products to customers are called *channel members* or *intermediaries*. Bear in mind that manufacturers of goods are not the only producers who need distribution channels. Service providers, such as consulting companies, health-care organizations, and news services, also need distribution (or delivery) systems to reach their customers. In the business of delivering news services over the World Wide Web, channel members involved in getting news from the newsroom to the reader can include, among others, Internet service providers and search engine suppliers.

Companies develop their international distribution strategies based on two related decisions: (1) how to get goods *into* a country and (2) how to distribute goods *within* a country. We presented the different ways companies get their products into countries in Chapter 13. Here we focus on distribution strategies within countries.

Designing Distribution Channels

Managers consider two overriding concerns when establishing channels of distribution: (1) the amount of *market exposure* a product needs and (2) the *cost* of distributing a product. Let's take a look at each of these concerns.

DEGREE OF EXPOSURE   In promoting its product to the greatest number of potential customers, a marketer must determine the amount of exposure needed. An **exclusive channel** is one in which a manufacturer grants the right to sell its product to only one or a limited number of resellers. An exclusive channel gives producers a great deal of control over the sale of their product by wholesalers and retailers. It also helps a producer to constrain distributors from selling competing brands. In this way, an exclusive channel creates a barrier that makes it difficult or impossible for outsiders to penetrate the channel. For example, in most countries new-car dealerships reflect exclusive distribution—normally, Mitsubishi dealerships cannot sell Toyotas, and General Motors dealers cannot sell Fords.

When a producer wants its product to be made available through as many distribution outlets as possible, it prefers to use an **intensive channel**—one in which a producer grants the right to sell its product to many resellers. An intensive channel provides buyers with location convenience because of the large number of outlets through which a product is sold. It does not create strong barriers to channel entry for other producers, however. Nor does it provide much control over reseller decisions, such as what competing brands to sell.

Large companies whose products are sold through grocery stores and department stores typically take an intensive channel approach to distribution. The obstacle for small companies that choose an intensive channel approach is gaining shelf space—especially companies with lesser-known brands. The increasing global trend toward retailers developing their own *private-label brands* (brands created by retailers themselves) exacerbates this problem. In such cases, retailers tend to give their own brands prime shelf space and give lesser-known brands poorer shelf locations that are up high or near the floor.

CHANNEL LENGTH AND COST   *Channel length* refers to the number of intermediaries between the producer and the buyer. In a *zero-level channel*—which is also called direct marketing—producers sell directly to final buyers. A *one-level channel* places only one intermediary between the producer and the buyer. Two intermediaries make up a *two-level channel,* and so forth. In general, the greater the number of intermediaries in a channel, the more costly it becomes. This happens because each additional member adds a charge for its services onto the product's total cost. This is an important consideration for companies that sell price-sensitive consumer products, such as candy, food, and small household items, which usually compete on the basis of price. As we saw in Chapter 11, companies that sell highly differentiated products can charge higher prices because of their products' distinctiveness; therefore, they have fewer problems using a channel of several levels.

Influence of Product Characteristics

The value of a product relative to its weight and volume is called its **value density**. Value density is an important variable in formulating distribution strategies. As a rule, *the lower a product's value density, the more localized the distribution system*. Most commodities, including cement, iron ore, and crude oil, have low value-density ratios—they're heavy but not particularly

exclusive channel
Distribution channel in which a manufacturer grants the right to sell its product to only one or a limited number of resellers.

intensive channel
Distribution channel in which a producer grants the right to sell its product to many resellers.

value density
Value of a product relative to its weight and volume.

"valuable" if gauged in, say, shipping weight per cubic meter. Relative to their values, the cost of transporting these goods is high. Consequently, such products are processed or integrated into the manufacturing process at points close to their original locations. Products with high value-density ratios include emeralds, semiconductors, and premium perfumes. Because the cost of transporting these products is small relative to their value, they can be processed or manufactured in the optimal location and then shipped to market. Because Johnson & Johnson's (www .jnj.com) Vistakon contact lenses have high value density, the company produces and inventories its products in one U.S. location and serves the world market from there.

When products need to be modified for local markets, companies can design their distribution systems accordingly. Caterpillar (www.cat.com) redesigned its distribution system so that it doubles as the final component in the company's production system. Each national market carries a range of optional product components for Caterpillar's lift trucks. The company ships partially completed lift trucks, along with optional parts, to distribution warehouses in each target market. After a buyer decides what options it desires, final assembly takes place. Caterpillar's distribution warehouses now extend the company's assembly line—allowing the company to maintain or improve service at little cost.

Special Distribution Problems

A nation's distribution system develops over time and reflects its unique cultural, political, legal, and economic traditions. Although each nation's distribution system has its own unique pros and cons, it is the negative aspects of distribution that pose the greatest threat to the business activities of international companies. In some countries, risks arise mostly from the potential for theft and property damage. In others, it is simply the lack of understanding that creates uncertainty and risk. Let's take a look at two special problems that can affect a company's international distribution activities.

LACK OF MARKET UNDERSTANDING Companies can experience a great deal of frustration and financial loss simply by not fully understanding the local market in which they operate. In one now-classic case, Amway Asia Pacific Ltd., the Asian arm of U.S.-based Amway (www.amway. com), learned the hard way about the pitfalls of overestimating the knowledge of distributors in emerging markets. The company has a worldwide policy of giving distributors a full refund on its soaps and cosmetics if the distributor's customers are dissatisfied—even if the returned containers are empty. But the policy had some bizarre results shortly after Amway entered China. Word of the guarantee spread quickly. Some distributors repackaged the products in other containers, sold them, and took the original containers back to Amway for a refund. Others scoured garbage bins, gathering bags full of discarded bottles. In Shanghai, returns were beginning to total $100,000 a day. Amway's Shanghai chief Percy Chin admitted, "Perhaps we were too lenient." Amway soon changed its refund policy to allow a refund only for bottles at least half full.[7]

THEFT AND CORRUPTION A high incidence of theft and corruption can present obstacles to distribution. The distribution system in Russia reflects its roughly 75-year experiment with communism. When Acer Computers (www.acer.com) decided to sell its computers in Russia, it built production facilities in Russia's stable neighbor, Finland, because the company was leery of investing directly in Russia. Acer also considered it too risky to navigate Russia's archaic distribution system on its own. In three years' time, a highway that serves as a main route to get goods overland from Finland to Russia saw 50 Finnish truckers hijacked, 2 drivers killed, and another 2 go missing. Acer solved its distribution problem by selling its computers to Russian distributors outside its factory in Finland. The Russian distributors, who understood how to negotiate their way through Russia's distribution system, would then deal with any distribution problems in Russia.[8]

QUICK STUDY 3

1. How do *exclusive* and *intensive* channels of distribution differ? Give an example of each.
2. Explain the importance of *value density* to distribution strategy.
3. How might a lack of market understanding, theft, and corruption affect international distribution?

Developing Pricing Strategies

The pricing strategy that a company adopts must match its overall international strategy. The product of a company that is the low-cost leader in its industry usually cannot be sold at a premium price because it likely has few special features and stresses functionality rather than uniqueness. On the other hand, a company that follows a differentiation strategy usually can charge a premium price for its product because buyers value the product's uniqueness. Let's now examine two pricing policies (*worldwide pricing* and *dual pricing*) that companies use in international markets and then explore the important factors that influence managers' pricing decisions.

Worldwide Pricing

A pricing policy in which one selling price is established for all international markets is called **worldwide pricing**. In practice, a worldwide pricing policy is very difficult to achieve. First, production costs differ from one nation to another. Keeping production costs the same is not possible for a company that has production bases within each market it serves. As a result, selling prices often reflect these different costs of production.

Second, a company that produces in just one location (to maintain an equivalent cost of production for every product) cannot guarantee that selling prices will be the same in every target market. The cost of exporting to certain markets will likely be higher than the cost of exporting to other markets. In addition, distribution costs differ across markets. Where distribution is efficient, selling prices might well be lower than in locations where distribution systems are archaic and inefficient.

Third, the purchasing power of local buyers must be taken into account. Managers might decide to lower the sales price in a market so that buyers can afford the product and the company can gain market share.

Finally, fluctuating currency values also must be taken into account. When the value of the currency in a country where production takes place rises against a target market's currency, the product will become more expensive in the target market.

worldwide pricing
Policy in which one selling price is established for all international markets.

Dual Pricing

Because of the problems associated with worldwide pricing, another pricing policy is often used in international markets. A pricing policy in which a product has a different selling price in export markets than it has in the home market is called **dual pricing**. When a product has a higher selling price in the target market than it does in the home market (or the country where production takes place), it is called *price escalation*. It is commonly the result of the reasons just discussed—exporting costs and currency fluctuations.

But sometimes a product's export price is lower than the price in the home market. Under what circumstances does this occur? Some companies determine that domestic market sales are intended to cover all product costs (such as expenses related to R&D, administration, and overhead). They then require exports to cover only the *additional* costs associated with exporting and selling in a target market (such as tariffs). In this sense, exports are considered a sort of "bonus."

To apply dual pricing successfully in international marketing, a company must be able to keep its domestic buyers and international buyers separate. Buyers in one market might cancel orders if they discover that they are paying a higher price than are buyers in another market. If a company cannot keep its buyers separate when using dual pricing, buyers could potentially undermine the policy through *arbitrage*—buying products where they are sold at lower prices and reselling them where they command higher prices. As is often the case, however, the higher selling price of a product in an export market often reflects the additional costs of transportation to the local market and any trade barriers of the target market, such as tariffs. For arbitrageurs to be successful, the profits they earn must be enough to outweigh these additional costs.

dual pricing
Policy in which a product has a different selling price (typically higher) in export markets than it has in the home market.

Factors That Affect Pricing Decisions

Many factors have an important influence on managers' pricing decisions. We devote the following discussion to four of the most important—transfer prices, arm's length pricing, price controls, and dumping.

TRANSFER PRICES Prices charged for goods or services transferred among a company and its subsidiaries are called **transfer prices**. It is common for parent companies and their subsidiaries to buy from one another. For example, the parent company often licenses technologies to its

transfer price
Price charged for a good or service transferred among a company and its subsidiaries.

subsidiaries in return for royalties or licensing fees. Subsidiaries prefer this route to buying on the open market because they typically receive lower prices. Parent companies then buy finished products from subsidiaries at the stated transfer price.

At one time, companies enjoyed a great deal of freedom in setting their transfer prices. Subsidiaries in countries with high corporate tax rates would reduce their tax burdens by charging a low price for their output to other subsidiaries. The subsidiary lowered the taxes that the parent company must pay by reducing its profits in the high-tax country. Likewise, subsidiaries in countries with low tax rates would charge relatively high prices for their output.

Transfer prices followed a similar pattern based on the tariffs of different nations. Subsidiaries in countries that charged relatively high tariffs were charged lower prices to lower the cost of the goods in the local market. This pattern of transfer prices helped large corporations with many subsidiaries to manage their global tax burden better and to become more price-competitive in certain markets.

arm's length price
Free-market price that unrelated parties charge one another for a specific product.

ARM'S LENGTH PRICING Increased regulation of transfer-pricing practices today is causing reduced freedom in manipulating transfer prices. Many governments now regulate internal company pricing practices by assigning products approximate transfer prices based on their free-market price. Therefore, most international transfers between subsidiaries now occur at a so-called **arm's length price**—the free-market price that unrelated parties charge one another for a specific product.

Another factor that is increasing the use of arm's length pricing is pressure on companies to be good corporate citizens in each of their target markets. Developing and emerging markets are hurt most by lost revenue when international companies manipulate prices to reduce tariffs and corporate taxes. They depend on the revenue for building things such as schools, hospitals, and infrastructure, including telecommunications systems and shipping ports. These items in turn benefit international companies by improving the productivity and efficiency of the local business environment. Indeed, some international companies have even developed codes of conduct specifying that transfer prices will follow the principle of arm's length pricing.

price controls
Upper or lower limits placed on the prices of products sold within a country.

PRICE CONTROLS Pricing strategies must also consider the potential for government **price controls**—upper or lower limits placed on the prices of products sold within a country. Upper-limit price controls are designed to provide price stability in an inflationary economy (one in which prices are rising). Companies that want to raise prices in a price-controlled economy must often apply to government authorities to request permission to do so. Companies with good contacts in the government of the target market might be more likely to get a price-control exemption. Those unable to obtain an exemption will typically try to lessen the impact of upper-limit price controls by reducing production costs.

By contrast, lower-limit price controls prohibit the lowering of prices below a certain level. Governments sometimes impose lower-limit price controls to help local companies compete against the less expensive imports of international companies. Other times, lower-limit price controls are designed to ward off price wars that could eliminate the competition and thereby give one company a monopoly in the domestic market.

DUMPING We detailed the practice of dumping in Chapter 6 when discussing government involvement in international trade. Recall that *dumping* occurs when the price of a good is lower in export markets than it is in the domestic market. Accusations of dumping are often made against competitors from other countries when inexpensive imports flood a nation's domestic market. Although charges of dumping normally result from deliberate efforts to undercut the prices of competitors in the domestic market, changes in exchange rates can cause unintentional dumping. When a country's government charges another nation's producers of dumping a good on its market, antidumping tariffs are typically imposed. Such tariffs are designed to punish producers in the offending nation by increasing the price of their products to a fairer level.

QUICK STUDY 4

1. What is the difference between *worldwide pricing* and *dual pricing*?
2. Explain what is meant by the terms *transfer pricing* and *arm's length pricing*.
3. How might price controls and dumping affect the pricing decisions of international companies?

A Final Word

Despite the academic debate over globalization and the extent to which companies should standardize their international marketing activities, many companies continue to adapt to local conditions. Sometimes this takes the form of only slightly modifying promotional campaigns; at other times it can require the creation of an entirely new product. The causes of alterations in promotional aspects of marketing strategy can be cultural, such as language differences. They can also be legal, such as requirements to produce locally so as to help ease local unemployment or to spur local industry around the production facility. Other companies are able to reap the rewards of standardization and centralized production that can result from the ability to sell one product worldwide. In the next chapter, we take an in-depth look at the factors that influence the development of production strategies and the types of decisions managers must make along the way.

Chapter Summary	MyManagementLab
	Go to **mymanagementlab.com** to complete the problem marked with this icon .

1. Explain the impact globalization is having on international marketing activities.
   - Companies may be able to reduce production and marketing costs by standardizing the physical features of their products and by standardizing their marketing strategies.
   - Other companies may find that standardization is just one of a number of strategies or that it is not always the best strategy to use.
   - Consumers worldwide appear content with a standardized product in *certain* product categories, but in others they demand products that reflect their unique tastes and preferences.
   - National business environments affect the preferences of both consumers and industrial buyers worldwide, with product standardization more likely when levels of economic development are similar.
2. Describe the types of things managers must consider when developing international product strategies.
   - Companies may need to undertake mandatory product adaptation in response to a target market's laws and regulations and to suit cultural differences.
   - Companies try to keep their brand names consistent across markets but will create new product names or modify existing ones to suit local preferences.
   - The image of a nation in which a company designs, manufactures, or assembles a product can influence buyer perception of quality and reliability.
   - Counterfeit goods can damage buyers' image of a brand when the counterfeits are of inferior quality.
   - Shortened product life cycles are affecting decisions of when to market internationally.
3. Discuss the factors that influence international promotional strategies and the blending of product and promotional strategies.
   - *Promotion mix* comprises company efforts to reach distribution channels and to target customers through communications, such as personal selling, advertising, public relations, and direct marketing.
   - A *pull strategy* creates buyer demand that will encourage distribution channel members to stock a company's product; a *push strategy* pressures distribution channel members to carry a product and promote it to final users of the product.
   - *Product/communications extension (dual extension)* extends the same home-market product and marketing promotion into target markets.
   - *Product extension/communications adaptation* extends the same product into new target markets but alters its promotion.
   - *Product adaptation/communications extension* adapts a product to the requirements of the international market while retaining the product's original marketing communication.

- *Product/communications adaptation (dual adaptation)* adapts both the product and its marketing communication to suit the target market.
- *Product invention* requires that an entirely new product be developed for the target market.

4. Explain the elements that managers must take into account when designing international distribution strategies.
   - *Distribution* involves the planning, implementation, and control of the physical flow of a product from its point of origin to its point of consumption; the physical path a product follows to customers is a *distribution channel*.
   - An *exclusive channel* is one in which a manufacturer grants the right to sell its product to only one or a limited number of resellers, which gives wholesalers and retailers significant control over a products' sale.
   - An *intensive channel* is one in which a producer grants the right to sell its product to many resellers, which offers less control over reseller decisions.
   - *Channel length* refers to the number of intermediaries between the producer and the buyer: In a *zero-level channel,* producers sell directly to final buyers; in a *one-level channel,* one intermediary is between producer and buyer, and so forth.

5. Discuss the elements that influence international pricing strategies.
   - *Worldwide pricing* is the strategy of using one selling price for all international markets—a difficult task to achieve in practice.
   - *Dual pricing* means having a different selling price in export markets than in the home market.
   - *Price escalation* occurs when a product has a higher selling price in the target market than it does in the home market (or the country where production takes place).
   - A *transfer price* is the price charged for products sold between a company's divisions or subsidiaries.
   - An *arm's length price* is the free-market price that unrelated parties charge one another for a specific product.

Talk It Over

⭐1. Suppose that the product preferences of cultures and people around the world continue to converge. Identify two products that will likely be affected and two products that will likely not be affected by this convergence. For each product, how will the changes influence the marketing manager's job?

Teaming Up

1. **Research Project.** With several of your classmates, choose a company in which you are interested. Consult recent annual reports and Internet sources to find out what new products that company has brought to market in the past year or two. Are those products truly new innovations, or are they simply extensions of existing products? What considerations likely guided the company in its product development efforts?

2. **Advertisement Project.** For this team project, ask each member of your group to select a magazine publication from a nation other than his or her own. Look through each of the magazines for ads from a single international firm or for advertisements featuring a particular product or brand. After you have identified three or four such ads, determine which of the five types of product and promotion policies is being used: dual extension, product extension/communications adaptation, product adaptation/communications extension, dual adaptation, or product invention. What explanation do you have for the particular method being used?

Key Terms

arm's length price (p. 368)
brand name (p. 356)
distribution (p. 364)
dual pricing (p. 367)
exclusive channel (p. 365)

intensive channel (p. 365)
marketing communication (p. 362)
price controls (p. 368)
promotion mix (p. 359)
pull strategy (p. 359)

push strategy (p. 359)
transfer price (p. 367)
value density (p. 365)
worldwide pricing (p. 367)

Take It to the Web

1. **Video Report.** Visit this book's channel on YouTube (YouTube.com/MyIBvideos). Click on "Videos" near the top of the page, and click on the set of videos labeled "Ch 14: Developing and Marketing Products." Watch one video from the list, and then summarize it in a half-page report. Reflecting on the contents of this chapter, which aspects of developing and marketing products can you identify in the video? How might a company engaged in international business act on the information contained in the video?

2. **Website Report.** Companies must carefully consider every facet of marketing, including product, promotional, distribution, and pricing strategies.

    The websites of both Adobe (www.adobe.com) and Amazon (www.amazon.com) are reputed to be excellent examples of marketing. Partner with another student, and visit the website of one of these companies while your partner visits the other firm's website. For the site you chose, what features do you think account for the favorable reputation? Note the different ads on the site, and rate their effectiveness. Compare your findings with those of your partner.

    Now select another international company of your choosing and visit as many of its national websites as you can locate. How much freedom do you think the company allows in each nation's website design? Why? If you were the CEO of the company, would you follow a similar approach, or would you centralize/decentralize authority over the website's design? How do Adobe and Amazon compare to the apparent freedom (or lack of freedom) that this company allows? Explain your answer.

Ethical Challenges

1. You are a lawyer working with the International Court of Justice in The Hague in the Netherlands. You have been asked to review a recent decision regarding extraterritoriality. The case: French survivors of the Holocaust sued Yahoo! U.S.A. because French citizens were purchasing Nazi memorabilia on Yahoo!'s U.S. website. The lawsuit also charged Yahoo! U.S.A. with hosting the websites of anti-Semitic groups. Although both these actions are illegal according to French law, they are permitted in the United States because of U.S. legislation protecting free speech. Because Yahoo!'s French website did not violate French law, the U.S. federal judge hearing the case threw it out. The judge ruled that French law does not have the right to dictate the behavior of U.S. firms operating inside the United States. Today, the Internet sometimes makes it difficult to determine where jurisdictions begin and end. If you had been the judge in this case, would you have ruled similarly? List the factors you considered in arriving at your decision. Can you think of any Internet controls that could stop such cases from happening in the future?

2. You are an independent consultant currently working for Philip Morris. Competitors are alleging that in important developing markets, such as Turkey, Philip Morris created special tobacco blends containing additives that give brands such as Marlboro an extra "kick." If true, practices such as this by tobacco companies put the "standardization-versus-adaptation" issue in an unusual perspective. If Philip Morris does, in fact, adapt its products this way, do you argue such policies are ethical? If summoned before the firm's board of directors, what advice would you give regarding the company's policy on this issue?

MyManagementLab

Go to **mymanagementlab.com** for Auto-graded writing questions as well as the following Assisted-graded writing questions:

14-1. Price escalation can present serious problems for companies wishing to export their products to other markets under a worldwide pricing policy. How might companies combat the effects of price escalation? List as many possibilities as you can.

14-2. Certain organizations regularly attack advertisers for their promotional methods. What could the advertising industry do to make themselves a smaller target for such criticisms? Be specific.

14-3. Mymanagementlab Only — comprehensive writing assignment for this chapter.

Practicing International Management Case

Psychology of Global Marketing

It's no secret that marketers use a good dose of psychology in both designing and implementing their promotional campaigns—or at least it should not be. But some people, including Gary Rushkin of Washington, DC–based Commercial Alert (www.commercialalert.org), argue that parents are being duped. "I don't think people understand the extent of psychological tools employed against their kids to whip up their desire to buy products," says Rushkin. "When they find out, they're horrified." Rushkin's organization was behind a recent letter signed by 60 U.S. psychologists that was sent to the American Psychological Association (www.apa.org) that complained of "the use of psychology to exploit and influence children for commercial purposes."

What was the cause of their fury? Apparently, it was an article by Dr. James McNeal appearing in *Marketing Tools* magazine that described what is called a projective completion test. Suppose a children's TV program is a hit and boys are buying the company's toy that is tied to the program but girls aren't. To find out why, a company assembles a group of girls. They are given a picture of a boy and girl watching the program in which the boy is asking the girl, "Why do you like watching this program?" The girls' answers help provide clues to how the company can modify its marketing strategy to appeal to girls. Dr. McNeal refers to the method as "good sense and good science." Rushkin counters, "Psychologists are going to have to decide whether psychology is a tool for healing or for exploitation." The American Psychological Association admits that there are currently no guidelines for psychologists working in advertising.

Advertising executives are not just busy creating TV ads. Over a recent one-year period, the number of children's websites with no advertising dropped from 10 percent down to 2 percent. In what forms do the promotions appear? One tool is *games*. Roughly 55 percent of all children and teens' websites feature games. Ellen Neuborne told her six-year-old that he could choose a candy at the supermarket checkout. With a pack of Sweet Tarts in hand, he broke into a little song-and-dance about the sweets. When asked if that was from the TV commercial, he replied, "No. It's from the Sweet Tarts Internet game." With the use of such games, companies get to spend an extended period of time with kids—far more than they get from a TV ad.

Another tool is *e-mail*. The U.S. Children's Online Privacy Act forbids companies from using e-mail to sell to kids under age 13 without parental permission. But companies get around the problem by having kids e-mail each other. For example, children can go to the website (www.sesameworkshop.org) and e-mail a greeting card to a friend that features a Sesame Street character. And then there are the *chat rooms*. Brian Rubash is manager for technical marketing at Tiger electronics (www.tigertoys.com), a division of toy-maker Hasbro (www.hasbro.com). He says that he regularly signed on to a newsgroup he found on Yahoo! (www.yahoo.com) to offer product news and to answer questions about the i-Cybie robotic dog the company was launching.

European nations have some of the strictest regulations covering marketing to children. However, nations belonging to the European Union (EU) have widely varying rules. For example, Greece bans all TV ads for war toys and bans ads for all other toys between 7 a.m. and 10 p.m. The Dutch-speaking part of Belgium bans TV advertising within five minutes of the start and end of children's programs. Sweden bans all ads aimed at children under age 12. This means that when kids in Sweden watch the Pokémon cartoon series, they do not hear the closing jingle "Gotta catch'em all" that plays elsewhere.

But the problem for the Swedes (and others with more restrictive bans) is that they can only enforce their laws on programs originating from within the country. They have no power of enforcement over programs broadcast from other nations or from satellite transmissions. That is why the Swedes are pushing for a common restrictive policy toward advertising aimed at children. "They're gradually trying to forge a consensus among the member states," says Stephan Loerke, a lobbyist for the World Federation of Advertisers (www.wfanet.org) in Brussels, Belgium. Although an outright ban like Sweden's is unlikely, partial bans such as that in place in Belgium could be implemented. To forestall stricter EU–wide legislation, advertisers could initiate "voluntary" limits themselves.

Yet some marketers are defending their actions. Advertising executive Geoffrey Roche of Toronto, Canada, dismissed the influence of psychologists, saying, "They don't have mind-altering powers, and kids are a lot smarter than we give them credit for. I don't think there is any way that we, as advertisers, can convince children of anything." But Dr. Allen Kanner asks, "If advertising is so ineffective, then why do they spend billions of dollars on it each year?" Dr. Curtis Haugtvedt, president of the Society for Consumer Psychology, says that although evidence of the negative aspects of advertising does exist, ads can also benefit kids. "Even Barbie has pluses and minuses," says Haugtvedt. "Barbie helps kids imagine and play with one another, but Barbie also portrays the image of a certain body shape." Haugtvedt also stresses the role of guidance in helping kids become responsible consumers, saying, "The child hopefully is not making choices about purchasing things in a vacuum."

Thinking Globally

1. Put yourself in the position of Stephan Loerke of the World Federation of Advertisers. First, make an argument for why the EU should not enact more strict advertising laws. Second, make a case for why advertisers operating in the EU should initiate "voluntary" limits. Third, make a case for why current laws need no modification whatsoever. Which case do you agree with? Which case do you think is the strongest?

2. Some critics charge advertisers with creating wants among consumers rather than helping them satisfy needs. Select a product and describe how, if it were marketed in a developing economy, it could create wants and not satisfy needs. Explain the ethical issues surrounding the decision of whether to market the product in developing nations.

Source: Ellen Neuborne, "For Kids on the Web, It's an Ad, Ad, Ad, Ad World," *Bloomberg Businessweek* (www.businessweek.com), August 12, 2001; Brandon Mitchener, "Banning Ads on Kids' TV," *Wall Street Journal Europe*, May 22, 2001, p. 25; James MacKinnon, "Psychologists Act against Ad Doctors," *Adbusters* website (www.adbusters.org).

Managing International Operations

LEARNING OBJECTIVES

After studying this chapter, you should be able to

1. Identify the elements that are important to consider when formulating production strategies.

2. Identify key considerations when acquiring physical resources.

3. Identify several production matters that are of special concern to managers.

4. Describe the three potential sources of financing and the main financial instruments of each.

A Look Back

Chapter 14 explored the influence of globalization on international marketing activities. We also examined how differences in national business environments impact the development of marketing strategies.

A Look at This Chapter

This chapter examines how companies launch and manage their international production efforts. We analyze how companies acquire the materials and products they need and how aspects of the business environment affect production strategies. We also look briefly at how companies finance their activities.

A Look Ahead

Chapter 16 examines how international companies manage their human resources. Topics include international staffing policies, recruitment, training, compensation, labor relations, and culture shock.

TOYOTA RACES AHEAD

KOLIN, Czech Republic—Toyota Motor Corporation (www.toyota-global.com) controls more than 14 percent of the world car market. Toyota is the fifth-largest company in the world, with annual sales of around $250 billion and 317,000 employees.

Toyota has spread its activities across the globe by operating 50 production facilities in 26 countries and selling in more than 170 countries. It has 14 design and research and development (R&D) centers worldwide in countries as dissimilar as Australia, Belgium, Japan, Thailand, and the United States. Toyota also owns Lexus (luxury automobiles), Hino (commercial vehicles), and Daihatsu (compact cars).

Shown here, a worker assembles a Lexus at Toyota's plant in Fukuoka prefecture, Japan. Most of Toyota's worldwide production operations are wholly owned factories, but some are cooperative ventures. For example, Toyota has a joint venture with Peugeot-Citroën in the Czech Republic called TPCA that produces 300,000 cars a year. Production at TPCA is devoted equally to each of the three cars made there—the Toyota Aygo, the Peugeot 107, and the Citroën C1.

Naturally, Toyota undertakes a great deal of planning for production capacity, where to locate facilities, the technology used in production, and the layout of facilities.

Source: KEN SHIMIZU/Getty Images/Newscom

As you can imagine, building an automobile plant requires a great deal of money. For part of its funding, Toyota looks to capital markets in Japan and abroad. To access investors in the U.S. capital markets as a non–U.S. company, however, Toyota must issue what are called *American Depository Receipts (ADRs)*. These ADRs are certificates that trade in the United States and that represent a specific number of shares of Toyota's stock. Of course, Toyota also finances its activities with profits earned on vehicle sales. As you read this chapter, consider how companies structure their global production facilities and how they finance all of their business activities.[1]

Whether an international company's production activity involves manufacturing a product or providing a service, it must acquire many resources before beginning operations. Where will it get the raw materials or components it needs to perform its production activities? How much production capacity is needed? Will the company construct or buy new facilities? How large must its service centers be? Where will it get the financial capital it needs? The answers to these questions are complex and interrelated.

This chapter begins by examining important issues to consider when formulating international production strategies. The topics covered include decisions about whether to centralize or decentralize production and whether production will be standardized or adapted to national markets. In the process, we draw linkages to earlier discussions, including overall corporate strategy and marketing strategy. We then describe how companies acquire the resources they need to accomplish their production goals. We explain how firms acquire fixed (or tangible) assets, including production facilities, offices, equipment, and materials. We also consider several key production concerns, such as international logistics and total quality management. We then explain important factors influencing managers' decisions about whether to expand or reduce operations abroad. We close by taking a brief look at how companies finance their international production operations and other activities.

Production Strategy

Production operations are important to achieving a company's strategy. Careful planning of all aspects of production helps companies cut costs (to become low-cost leaders) or design new products and product features necessary for a differentiation strategy. Among the important strategic issues that managers must consider are planning for production capacity, the location of facilities, production processes to be used, and the layout of facilities.

Capacity Planning

capacity planning
Process of assessing a company's ability to produce enough output to satisfy market demand.

The process of assessing a company's ability to produce enough output to satisfy market demand is called **capacity planning**. Companies must estimate global demand for their products as accurately as possible. If the capacity being used is greater than the expected market demand, a company may need to scale back production by perhaps reducing the number of employees or work shifts at some facilities. Yet, countries have different laws regulating the ability of employers to eliminate jobs. So, depending on the country, a firm may or may not need to give advance notice of layoffs or plant closings. On the other hand, if market demand is growing, managers must determine in which facilities to expand production or whether additional facilities are needed to expand capacity. Rather than miss out on potential sales, a company might contract with other producers to meet the excess demand until new facilities are up and running.

Capacity planning is also extremely important for service companies. For example, a hotel chain moving into a new geographic market must estimate the number of rooms that its facilities should contain. It must also determine whether a facility will be used for conventions and the like and the number of meeting rooms it must build. Videoconferencing facilities might be added if local firms require them to keep in touch with geographically dispersed operations.

Facilities Location Planning

facilities location planning
Selecting the location for production facilities.

Selecting the location for production facilities is called **facilities location planning**. Companies often have many potential locations around the world from which to choose a site for production, R&D, or some other activity. Aspects of the business environment that are important to facilities location planning include the cost and availability of labor and management, raw materials, component parts, and energy. Other key factors include political stability, the extent of regulation and bureaucracy, economic development, and the local culture, including beliefs about work and important traditions.

Reducing production costs by taking advantage of lower wages in another country is often essential to keeping a company's products competitively priced. This is especially important when the cost of labor contributes greatly to total production costs. But the lower wages of a nation's workforce must be balanced against its potentially lower productivity. Worker productivity tends to be lower in most developing nations and some emerging markets as compared with developed nations.

Companies do an enormous amount of planning for operations when undertaking international business. As business grows increasingly global, supply chains grow longer and more complex. Shown here, trucks queue at the port of Rio de Janeiro in Brazil, which is the world's sixth-largest economy. Sourcing components from abroad and sending finished goods to other nations means examining the ports through which goods will flow.

Source: VANDERLEI ALMEIDA/Getty Images/Newscom

Although most service companies must locate near their customers, they must still consider a wide variety of customers' needs when locating facilities. Are convenience and being located in a high-traffic area important to customers? Such a location is clearly important for some companies, including restaurants, banks, and cinemas. For other service businesses, such as consulting companies or public utilities, a convenient location is less important.

Supply issues are also important in location planning. For any one mode of transportation, the greater the distance between production facilities and target markets the longer it takes for customers to receive shipments. In turn, companies must compensate for delays by maintaining larger inventories in target markets—adding to storage and insurance costs. Shipping costs are also greater when production occurs away from target markets. Transportation costs are one of the driving forces behind the globalization of the steel industry. Shipping costs for steel can run $40 to $50 per ton—a significant amount when steel sells for $400 to $500 per ton. By building steel mills in countries where their customers are located, steel producers significantly reduce their transportation costs.

Automobile makers from Japan and Germany invested in production facilities inside the United States for some of the reasons just identified. For example, Toyota (www.toyota.com) and other Japanese automobile companies manufacture cars in the United States to offset the risks from currency fluctuations, to defuse political concerns about the United States' trade deficit with Japan, and to be closer to customers. BMW (www.bmw.com) of Germany assembles automobiles in the United States for similar reasons. For one, the past strength of Germany's currency made German products more expensive on world markets. Another reason is that Germany is home to the world's highest paid workers—the average hourly income is approximately $32. Finally, German companies were attracted by the lower cost of land and concessions, including tax breaks offered by state governments eager to attract industry.

LOCATION ECONOMIES Selecting highly favorable locations often allows a company to achieve **location economies**—economic benefits derived from locating production activities in optimal locations. Location economies result from the right mix of the kinds of elements previously described. To take advantage of location economies, companies either undertake business activities themselves in a particular location or obtain products and services from other companies located there. Location economies involve almost any business activity that companies in a particular location perform very well, such as R&D or providing advertising services.

location economies
Economic benefits derived from locating production activities in optimal locations.

The following examples illustrate the extent to which service and manufacturing companies exploit location economies. One company designed its precision ice hockey equipment in Sweden, obtained financing from Canada, assembled it in Cleveland and Denmark, and marketed it in North America and Europe. This equipment incorporated alloys whose molecular structure was researched and patented in Delaware and fabricated in Japan. Airplane manufacturer Boeing (www.boeing.com) designed aircraft in the state of Washington and Japan, assembled it in Seattle with tail cones made in Canada, special tail sections made in China and Italy, and engines made in Great Britain. As a final example, one company's advertising campaign was conceived in Great Britain, filmed in Canada, dubbed in Great Britain, and edited in New York.[2]

The key fact to remember is that *each production activity generates more value in a particular location than it could generate elsewhere.* Productivity is a very important (although not the only) factor in determining the value that a location adds to a certain economic activity. Two resources—labor and capital—heavily influence the productivity of a location.

Granted, to take advantage of location economies, managers might need to familiarize themselves with vastly different customs and traditions. Political and legal differences can force firms to retain outside consultants or to train corporate lawyers in local traditions. Language differences might mean translating important documents on an ongoing basis. For these reasons, companies sometimes hire other companies in a location to perform an activity for them.

CENTRALIZATION VERSUS DECENTRALIZATION An important consideration for production managers is whether to centralize or decentralize production facilities. *Centralized production* refers to the concentration of production facilities in one location. With *decentralized production,* facilities are spread over several locations and could even mean having one facility for each national business environment in which the company markets its products—a common policy for companies that follow a multinational strategy. Companies often centralize production facilities in pursuit of low-cost strategies and to take advantage of economies of scale—a typical policy for companies that follow a global strategy. By producing large quantities of identical products in one location, the companies cut costs by reducing the per-unit cost of production.

Transportation costs and the physical landscape also affect the centralization-versus-decentralization decision. Because they usually sell undifferentiated products in all their markets, low-cost competitors generally do not need to locate near their markets in order to stay on top of changes in buyer preferences. That is why low-cost producers often choose locations with the lowest combined production and transportation costs. But even these firms must balance the cost of getting inputs into the production process and the cost of getting products to markets. Key factors in the physical environment that affect the transport of goods are the availability of seaports, airports, or other transportation hubs.

Conversely, companies that sell differentiated products may find decentralized production the better option. By locating separate facilities near different markets, they remain in close contact with customers and can respond quickly to changing buyer preferences. Closer contact with customers also helps firms develop a deeper understanding of buyer behavior in local cultures.

When close cooperation between R&D and manufacturing is essential for effective differentiation, both activities are usually conducted in the same place. Yet, new technologies are giving companies more freedom to separate these activities. Today's rapid speed of communications allows a subsidiary and its home office to be large distances from each other.

Process Planning

process planning
Deciding the process that a company will use to create its product.

Deciding on the process that a company will use to create its product is called **process planning**. The particular process to be used is typically determined by a firm's business-level strategy. For example, low-cost strategies normally require large-scale production because producers want the cost savings generated by economies of scale. A company that mass-produces snowboards for average skiers will typically use a highly automated production process that integrates advanced computer technology. Differentiation strategies, however, demand that producers provide extra value by offering customers something unique, such as superior quality, added features, or special brand images. Companies that handcraft snowboards for professionals will rely not on automated production but on skilled craftspeople. The company will design and produce each snowboard to suit the habits and special needs of each individual snowboarder. For such a company, service is a major component of the production process.

Availability and cost of labor in the local market is crucial to process planning. If labor in the host country is relatively cheap, an international company will likely opt for less technology and for more labor-intensive methods in the production process—depending on its particular product and strategy. But again, the availability of labor and the level of wages in the local market must be balanced against the productivity of the local workforce.

STANDARDIZATION VERSUS ADAPTATION Another important issue in production strategy is deciding whether the production process will be standardized for all markets or adapted to manufacture products modified for different markets. For example, low-cost leadership often dictates automated, standardized production in large batches. Large production batches reduce the cost of producing each unit, thus offsetting the higher initial investment in automation. And production costs are reduced further as employees improve performance by repeating their activities and learning new procedures that would, for example, help minimize errors and waste.

But differentiation often demands decentralized facilities designed to improve local responsiveness. Because decentralized production facilities produce for one national market or for a regional market, they tend to be smaller. This tends to eliminate the potential to take advantage of economies of scale and therefore increases per-unit production costs. Similarly, the smaller market share that a differentiation strategy targets normally requires relatively smaller-scale production. Differentiating a product by incorporating certain features desired by customers requires more costly manufacturing processes. R&D costs also tend to be higher for products with special product designs, styles, and features.

Facilities Layout Planning

Deciding the spatial arrangement of production processes within production facilities is called **facilities layout planning**. Consider the fact that in Japan, Singapore, and Hong Kong, the supply of land is limited and its cost is high. Companies that locate in these markets must use the available space wisely by designing compact facilities. Conversely, in countries such as Canada, China, and the United States, an abundance of space reduces the cost of building facilities in many locations. Because land is cheaper, companies have more flexibility in designing facilities.

facilities layout planning
Deciding the spatial arrangement of production processes within production facilities.

More importantly, facility layout depends on the type of production process a company uses, which in turn depends on a company's business-level strategy. For instance, rather than producing mass quantities of computers to be stored in inventory, Compaq (www.compaq.com) competes by manufacturing computers as it receives orders from individual customers. To implement this business strategy, Compaq executives decided to replace mass-assembly lines with three-person work cells. In production trials at a plant in Scotland, output increased 23 percent as compared with the previous best assembly line. In addition, output per square foot went up 16 percent—a significant increase in the efficiency within the facility.

QUICK STUDY 1

1. Explain why *capacity planning* is important when formulating production strategy.
2. How is *facilities location planning* affected by (a) *location economies* and (b) centralized versus decentralized production?
3. Explain how *process planning* is affected by the standardization-versus-adaptation decision.
4. How is *facilities layout planning* relevant to the formulation of production strategies?

Acquiring Physical Resources

Before an international company begins operations, it must acquire a number of physical resources. For example, managers must answer questions that include, Will the company make or buy the components it needs in the production process? What will be the sources of any required raw materials? Will the company acquire facilities and production equipment or build its own? In this section, we present the main elements that managers need to consider when answering these types of questions.

Dell Computer Corporation perfected the art of outsourcing. The company designs and builds computing systems for consumers and companies, but it does not build the computer components itself. This production strategy made Dell a model of efficiency in the personal computer (PC) industry. Dell can deliver custom-made PCs in just three days, whereas most of its rivals measure their delivery times in weeks. Do you think outsourcing will continue to gain acceptance in the future?

Source: FRANCK ROBICHON/Newscom

make-or-buy decision
Deciding whether to make a component or to buy it from another company.

vertical integration
Extension of company activities into stages of production that provide a firm's inputs (backward integration) or absorb its output (forward integration).

Make-or-Buy Decision

The typical manufacturing company requires a wide range of inputs into its production process. These inputs typically enter the production line either as raw materials that require processing or as components needing only assembly. Bear in mind, too, that a component may require minor adjustments or other minor processing before it goes into production. Deciding whether to make a component or to buy it from another company is called the **make-or-buy decision**. Each option has its own set of advantages and disadvantages.

REASONS TO MAKE **Vertical integration** is the process by which a company extends its control over additional stages of production—either inputs or outputs. When a company decides to make a product rather than buy it, it engages in "upstream" activities (production activities that come before a company's current business operations). For example, an automobile manufacturer that decides to manufacture its own window glass is engaging in a new upstream activity.

Lower Costs Above all, companies make products rather than buy them in order to reduce total costs. Generally speaking, the manufacturer's profit is the difference between the product's selling price and its production cost. When a company buys a product, it rewards the manufacturer by contributing to the latter's profit margin. Yet, a company often undertakes in-house production when it can manufacture a product for less than it must pay another business to produce it. Thus, in-house production allows a company to lower its own production costs.

For example, a computer motherboard is the physical foundation of a personal computer to which the microprocessor, memory chips, and other components are attached. This critical component accounts for about 40 percent of a personal computer's total cost. Compaq (www.compaq.com) discovered that it could produce motherboards itself for $25 less than its Asian suppliers and save two weeks' shipping time in the process.

Small companies are less likely than large ones to make rather than buy, especially when a product requires a large financial investment in equipment and facilities. But this rule of thumb might not necessarily hold if the company possesses a proprietary technology or some other competitive advantage that is not easily copied.

Greater Control Companies that depend on others for key ingredients or components give up a degree of control. Making rather than buying can give managers greater control over raw materials, product design, and the production process itself—all of which are important factors in product quality. In turn, quality control is especially important when customers are highly sensitive to even slight declines in quality or company reputation.

In addition, persuading an outside supplier to make significant modifications to quality or features can be difficult. This is especially true if modifications entail investment in costly equipment or if they promise to be time-consuming. If just one buyer requests costly product adaptations or if there is reason to suspect that a buyer will eventually take its business elsewhere, a supplier may be reluctant to undertake a costly investment. Unless that buyer purchases in large volumes, the cost of the modifications may be too great for the supplier to absorb. In such a case, the buyer simply may be unable to obtain the product it wants without manufacturing it in-house. Thus, companies maintain greater control over product design and product features if they manufacture components themselves.

Finally, making a product can be a good idea when buying from a supplier means providing the supplier with a firm's key technology. Through licensing agreements (see Chapter 13), companies often provide suppliers in low-wage countries with the technologies needed to make their products. But if a company's competitive advantage depends on that technology, the licensor could inadvertently be creating a future competitor. When controlling a key technology is paramount, it is often better to manufacture in-house.

REASONS TO BUY The practice of buying from another company a good or service that is part of a company's value-added activities is called **outsourcing**. Outsourcing results from continuous specialization and technological advancement. For each successive specialization of its operations process, a manufacturer requires greater skill and knowledge than it did before. By outsourcing, a company can reduce the degree to which it is vertically integrated and the overall amount of specialized skills and knowledge that it must possess.

outsourcing
Practice of buying from another company a good or service that is part of a company's value-added activities.

Outsourcing has become extremely popular in the business of computer manufacturing. Component makers—including Intel (www.intel.com) in microprocessors, Seagate (www.seagate.com) in hard drives, U.S. Robotics (www.usr.com) in modems, and Mitsumi (www.mitsumi.com) in DVD drives—supply big and small manufacturers worldwide. Computer companies buy components from these manufacturers, assemble them in their own facilities, and sell completed systems to consumers and businesses. A related practice in the computer industry is known as "stealth manufacturing," which calls for outsourcing the actual assembly of the computers themselves, plus the job of shipping them to distributors and other intermediaries.

A new and interesting type of outsourcing seems to be increasingly popular. The online forum called InnoCentive (www.innocentive.com) connects companies and institutions seeking solutions to difficult problems using a global network of more than 145,000 creative thinkers. These engineers, scientists, inventors, and businesspeople with expertise in life sciences, engineering, chemistry, math, computer science, and entrepreneurship compete to solve some of the world's toughest problems in return for significant financial awards. InnoCentive is open to anyone, is available in seven languages, and pays cash awards that range from as little as $2,000 to as much as $1 million.[3]

Many companies buy when buying is the lower-cost option. When a firm cannot integrate vertically by manufacturing a product for less than a supplier can, it will typically outsource. Let's explore some other reasons why companies prefer to buy rather than make.

Lower Risk In earlier chapters, we described many types of risks faced by companies that construct and staff facilities in other countries. For example, recall that political risk is quite high in certain markets. Social unrest or open conflict can threaten physical facilities, equipment, and employee safety.

One way a company can eliminate the exposure of assets to political risk in other countries is simply by refusing to invest in plants and equipment abroad. It can instead purchase products from international suppliers. This policy also eliminates the need to purchase expensive insurance coverage that is needed when a company undertakes production in an unstable country. Yet, this policy will not completely shield the buyer from all potential disruptions—political instability can cause delays in the timely receipt of needed parts. Indeed, even under normal circumstances, the longer delivery times involved in international outsourcing can increase the risk that the buyer will not meet its own production schedule.

Greater Flexibility Maintaining sufficient flexibility to respond to market conditions is increasingly important for companies everywhere. Making an in-house product that requires large investments in equipment and buildings often reduces flexibility. By contrast, companies that source products from one or more outside suppliers gain flexibility. In fact, added flexibility is the key factor in a fundamental change in attitude toward outsourcing, which many managers now regard as a full-fledged strategy for change rather than a limited tactical tool for solving immediate problems.

Maintaining flexibility is important when the national business environments of suppliers are volatile. Buying from several suppliers, or establishing production facilities in more than one country, allows a company to outsource products from one location if instability erupts in another. The same is true during periods of great volatility in exchange rates. Exchange-rate movements can increase or decrease the cost of importing a product from a given country. By buying from multiple suppliers located in several countries, a company can maintain the flexibility needed to change sources and reduce the risk associated with sudden swings in exchange rates.

Companies also maintain operational flexibility simply by not having to invest in production facilities. Unencumbered by investment in costly production equipment and facilities, a firm can alter its product line very quickly. This capability is especially important for products with small production runs or those with highly uncertain potential. Furthermore, a company can obtain financial flexibility if its capital is not locked up in plants and equipment. It can then use excess financial capital to pursue other domestic or international opportunities. Outsourcing can also free a company from having to invest in R&D and then to earn a return on that investment.

Market Power Companies can gain a great deal of power in their relationships with suppliers simply by becoming important customers. In fact, sometimes a supplier can become a sort of hostage to one particular customer. This situation occurs when a supplier becomes heavily dependent on a company that it serves with nearly all of its production capacity. If the main buyer suddenly begins outsourcing elsewhere, the supplier will have few other customers to whom it can turn. This situation gives the buyer significant control in dictating quality improvements, forcing cost reductions, and making special modifications.

Barriers to Buying For various reasons, companies sometimes face obstacles when buying products from international suppliers. First, the government of the buyer's country may impose import tariffs designed to improve the nation's balance of trade. Tariffs can add anywhere from 15 to 50 percent to the cost of a component that a manufacturer needs from abroad.

Second, the services provided by intermediaries increase the cost of buying abroad. Obtaining letters of credit, arranging physical transportation, and obtaining insurance all add to the final cost that a manufacturer pays for a product supplied from abroad. Although these expenses are currently lower than they have ever been, they can significantly increase total product cost. If high enough, they can negate any advantage of buying from an international supplier.

Raw Materials

Decisions about the selection and acquisition of raw materials are important to many different types of manufacturers. The twin issues of quantity and quality drive many of these decisions. First, some industries and companies rely almost exclusively on the quantity of locally available raw materials. This is most true for companies involved in mining, forestry, and fishing. There must be an adequate supply of iron ore, oil, lumber, or fish to justify the large financial investment required to build processing facilities.

Second, the quality of raw material has a huge influence on the quality of a company's end product. For instance, food-processing companies must examine the quality of the locally grown fruit, vegetables, grains, and any other ingredients. Beverage companies must assess the quality of the local water supply. Some markets may require large financial investments to build water-purifying facilities. Elsewhere (such as much of the Middle East), the only local water source may be seawater that must be desalinized.

fixed (tangible) assets
Company assets such as production facilities, inventory warehouses, retail outlets, and production and office equipment.

Fixed Assets

Most companies must acquire **fixed (tangible) assets**—such as production facilities, inventory warehouses, retail outlets, and production and office equipment—in the host country. Many companies have the option of either (1) acquiring or modifying existing factories or (2) building entirely new facilities—called a *greenfield* investment. Considering either option involves many individuals within the company. For example, production managers must verify that an existing facility (or an empty lot) is large enough and will suit the company's facility layout needs. Site-acquisition experts and legal staff must guarantee that the proposed business activity abides by local laws. Public relations staff must work with community leaders to ensure that the company does not jeopardize the rights, values, and customs of the local population.

Finally, managers must make sure that the local infrastructure can support the firm's proposed on-site business operations. Also, factory and office equipment is likely to be available locally in most newly industrialized and developed markets, but not in developing markets. Thus, managers must assess both the cost in tariffs that will be imposed on imported equipment and the cost in time and effort that will be required to import it.

QUICK STUDY 2

1. List the main reasons why a company might decide to either *make or buy* a component.
2. Explain the roles of *vertical integration* and *outsourcing* in the make-or-buy decision.
3. What are the main factors involved in acquiring (a) *raw materials* and (b) *fixed assets*?

Key Production Concerns

In Chapter 11, we presented how the number and location of manufacturing facilities can affect company strategy and organizational structure. At this point, there remain just several issues to discuss related to manufacturing operations. In this section, we first examine how companies maximize quality and minimize shipping and inventory costs. Then we take a brief look at the important reinvestment-versus-divestment decision.

Quality Improvement Efforts

Companies strive toward quality improvement for two reasons: costs and customer value. First, quality products help keep production costs low because they reduce waste in valuable inputs, reduce the cost of retrieving defective products from buyers, and reduce the disposal costs that result from defective products. Second, some minimum level of acceptable quality is an aspect of nearly every product today. Even companies that produce low-cost products try to maintain or improve quality, as long as it does not erode their position in what is typically a price-competitive market or market segment. A company that succeeds in combining a low-cost position with a high-quality product can gain a tremendous competitive advantage in its market.

Improving quality is also important for a company that provides services—whether as its only product or in conjunction with the goods it manufactures and markets. Managing quality in services is complicated by the fact that a service is created and consumed at the same time. For this reason, the human interaction between the employee who delivers the service and the buyer is important to service quality. Still, activities that must be conducted prior to the actual delivery of a service are also important. For example, it is important that a restaurant be clean and have on hand the ingredients it needs to prepare the meals on its menu. Likewise, a bank can provide high-quality service only if employees arrive for work on time and interact professionally with customers.

Let's take a brief look at two movements that inspire the drive toward quality: total quality management and International Standards Organization (ISO) 9000 certification.

TOTAL QUALITY MANAGEMENT Company-wide commitment to meet or exceed customer expectations through continuous quality improvement efforts and processes is called **total quality management (TQM)**. TQM also places a great deal of responsibility on each individual to be focused on the quality of his or her own output—regardless of whether the employee's activities are based in the factory, in administration, or in management.

By continuously improving the quality of its products, a company can differentiate itself from rivals and attract loyal customers. The TQM philosophy initially took hold in Japan, where electronics and automobile firms applied TQM techniques to reduce costs and thereby gain significant market share around the world through price competitiveness and a reputation for quality. It was not until U.S. and European companies lost a great deal of market share to their Japanese rivals that they embraced TQM principles.

total quality management (TQM)
Company-wide commitment to meet or exceed customer expectations through continuous quality improvement efforts and processes.

MANAGER'S BRIEFCASE   World-Class Standards

In today's competitive environment, many companies are applying TQM principles. For companies doing business internationally, ISO 9000 certification is becoming increasingly important. But the ISO 9000 standards do not specify how a company should develop its quality processes. Rather, ISO requires each company to define and document its own quality processes and show evidence of implementing them. The following is a framework describing how TQM and ISO 9000 principles can be linked to enhance a company's capability for delivering quality products or services.

The main principles of TQM include the following:

- *Delight the Customer.* Companies must strive to be the best at what customers consider most important. This can change over time, so business owners must be in close touch with customers.
- *Use People-Based Management.* Systems, standards, and technology cannot, in and of themselves, guarantee quality. The key is to provide employees with the knowledge of what to do and how to do it and to provide feedback on performance.
- *Provide Continuous Improvement.* TQM is not a short-term quick fix but is a continual process. Achieving major breakthroughs is less important than smaller, incremental improvements.

- *Create Management by Fact.* Quality management and improvement requires that managers clearly understand how consumers perceive the performance of a company's goods and services. Rather than trusting "gut feelings," obtain factual information, and share it with employees.

Companies can link these TQM principles to ISO 9000 standards in three ways:

- *Process Definition.* The existing business process must be defined. Once defined, it must be satisfying to key stakeholders, and it must "delight the customer."
- *Process Improvement.* To achieve positive results, everyone within the organization should use the defined process properly; otherwise, a company may need to adjust its policies.
- *Process Management.* Management and employees must possess factual knowledge about process details in order to manage them properly.

Source: Based on G.K. Kanji, "An Innovative Approach to Make ISO 9000 Standards More Effective." *Total Quality Management*, February 1998, pp. 67–79.

ISO 9000   The ISO 9000 is an international certification that companies get when they meet the highest quality standards in their industries. Firms in the European Union are leading the way in quality certification. But both European and non-European companies alike are working toward certification in order to ensure access to the European marketplace. To become certified, companies must demonstrate the reliability and soundness of all business processes that affect the quality of their products. Many companies also seek ISO 9000 certification because of the message of quality that certification sends to prospective customers. For information on how companies can blend TQM principles and the drive toward ISO 9000 certification, see the Manager's Briefcase, titled "World-Class Standards."

Shipping and Inventory Costs

Shipping costs can have a dramatic effect on the cost of getting materials and components to the location of production facilities. When the cost of getting inputs into the production process is a large portion of the product's total cost, producers tend to locate close to the source of those inputs. Shipping costs are affected by many elements of a nation's business environment, such as its general level of economic development, including the condition of seaports, airports, roads, and rail networks.

It used to be that producers would buy vast quantities of materials or components and store them in large warehouses until they were needed in the production process. Storing great amounts of inventory for production, however, is costly in terms of insuring them against damage or theft and the rent or purchase price of the warehouse needed to store them.

Because companies have far better uses for the money tied up in such inventory, they developed better inventory management techniques. A production technique in which inventory is kept to a minimum and inputs to the production process arrive exactly when they are needed (or *just in time*) is called **just-in-time (JIT) manufacturing**. Although the technique was originally developed in Japan, it quickly spread throughout manufacturing operations worldwide. JIT manufacturing drastically reduces the costs associated with large inventories. It also helps reduce wasteful expenses because defective materials and components are spotted quickly during production. Under traditional systems, defective materials or components were sometimes discovered only after being built into finished products.

just-in-time (JIT) manufacturing
Production technique in which inventory is kept to a minimum and inputs to the production process arrive exactly when they are needed.

Reinvestment versus Divestment

Companies maintain the current level of operations when no new opportunities are foreseen. Yet, changing conditions in the competitive global marketplace often force managers to choose between *reinvesting* in operations and *divesting* them.

Companies often reinvest profits in markets that require long payback periods as long as the long-term outlook is good. This is often the case in developing countries and large emerging markets. For example, corruption, red tape, distribution problems, and a vague legal system present challenges for non-Chinese companies. But because long-term returns on their investments are expected, Western companies reinvest heavily in China despite what are sometimes uncertain short-term profits. Most of these companies invest in production facilities to take advantage of a low-cost labor pool and low-cost energy.[4]

Companies scale back their international operations when it becomes apparent that making operations profitable will take longer than expected. Again, China serves as a good example. Some companies were lured to China by the possibilities for growth offered by 1.2 billion consumers; however, some had to scale back ambitions that had been based on overly optimistic marketing plans.

Companies usually decide to reinvest when a market is experiencing rapid growth. Reinvestment can mean either expanding in the market itself or expanding in a location that serves the growing market. Investing in expanding markets is often an attractive option because potential new customers usually have not yet become loyal to the products of any one company or brand. It can be easier and less costly to attract customers in such markets than it is to gain a share of markets that are stagnant or contracting.

Yet, problems in the political, social, or economic sphere can force a company either to reduce or to eliminate operations altogether. Such problems are usually intertwined with one another. For example, in recent years some Western companies pulled their personnel out of Indonesia because of intense social unrest stemming directly from a combination of political problems (discontent with the nation's political leadership), economic difficulties, and terrorist attacks.

Finally, companies invest in the operations that offer the best return on their investments. That policy often means reducing or divesting operations in some markets, even though they may be profitable, in order to invest in more profitable opportunities elsewhere.

QUICK STUDY 3

1. How do *TQM* and ISO 9000 help companies improve quality and control costs?
2. Explain how shipping and inventory costs influence a firm's international logistics decisions. What is *just-in-time manufacturing*?
3. What are several considerations that underlie the reinvest-versus-divest decision?

Financing Business Operations

Companies need financial resources to pay for a variety of operating expenses and new projects. They must buy raw materials and component products for manufacturing and assembly activities. At certain times, they need large sums of capital, whether for expanding production capacity or entering new geographic markets. But companies also need financing to pay for all sorts of activities in addition to those related to production. They must pay for training and development programs and compensate workers and managers. Businesses must pay advertising agencies for helping the company promote its goods and services. They must also make periodic interest payments to lenders and perhaps reward stockholders with dividends.

But all companies have a limited supply of resources at their disposal to invest in current operations or new endeavors. So where do companies obtain needed funds? Generally speaking, organizations obtain financial resources through one of three sources:

1. Borrowing (debt)
2. Issuing equity (stock ownership)
3. Internal funding

Borrowing

International companies (like domestic companies) try to get the lowest interest rates possible on borrowed funds. However, this objective is more complex on a global scale. Difficulties include exchange-rate risk, restrictions on currency convertibility, and restrictions on the international flow of capital.

Borrowing locally can be advantageous, especially when the value of the local currency has fallen against that of the home country. Suppose a Japanese company borrows from U.S. banks for investment in the United States. Let's say that one year later the U.S. dollar has fallen against the Japanese *yen*—in other words, fewer *yen* are now needed to buy one dollar. In that case, the Japanese company can repay the loan with fewer *yen* than would have been required if the value of the dollar had not fallen.

But companies are not always able to borrow funds locally. Often they are forced to seek international sources of capital. This is sometimes the case when a subsidiary is new to the market and has not yet built a reputation with local lenders. In such cases, a parent firm can help a subsidiary acquire financing through a so-called **back-to-back loan**—a loan in which a parent company deposits money with a host-country bank, which then lends the money to a subsidiary located in the host country.

For example, suppose that a Mexican company forms a new subsidiary in the United States but that this subsidiary cannot obtain a U.S. bank loan. The Mexican parent company can deposit Mexican *pesos* in the branch of a U.S. bank in Mexico (see Figure 15.1). The U.S. bank's home office then lends dollars to the subsidiary in the United States. The amount of money lent in dollars will be equivalent to the amount of *pesos* on deposit with the U.S. bank's Mexican branch. When the U.S. subsidiary repays the loan in full, the parent company withdraws its deposit (plus any interest earned) from the U.S. bank's Mexican branch.

Issuing Equity

Recall from Chapter 9 that the *international equity market* consists of all stocks bought and sold outside the home country of the issuing company. Companies issue such stock primarily to access pools of investors with funds that are unavailable domestically. Yet, getting shares

back-to-back loan
Loan in which a parent company deposits money with a host-country bank, which then lends the money to a subsidiary located in the host country.

FIGURE 15.1

Mexico–United States Back-to-Back Loan

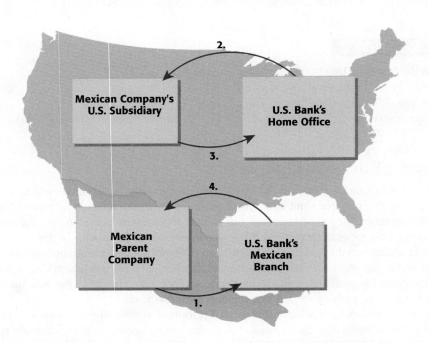

1. Mexican parent company deposits pesos in U.S. bank's branch in Mexico.
2. U.S. bank's home office lends dollars to Mexican company's subsidiary in the United States.
3. Mexican subsidiary repays the dollar loan.
4. Mexican parent company withdraws peso deposit plus interest.

listed on another country's stock exchange can be a complex process. For one thing, complying with all the rules and regulations governing the operation of a particular stock exchange costs a great deal of time and money. Only large companies, therefore, tend to list shares on multiple exchanges.

ISSUING AMERICAN DEPOSITORY RECEIPTS   To maximize international exposure (and to access funds), non–U.S. companies often list themselves on U.S. stock exchanges. Non–U.S. companies can list shares directly in the United States by issuing **American Depository Receipts (ADRs)**—certificates that trade in the United States and that represent a specific number of shares in a non–U.S. company. Large U.S. banks, such as Citibank (www.citibank.com), issue ADRs that then trade on the New York Stock Exchange (www.nyse.com), the computerized National Association of Securities Dealers Automated Quotation system (www.nasdaq.com), and the over-the-counter (OTC) market. As we saw in the company profile at the start of this chapter, Japan-based Toyota (www.toyota.co.jp) accesses U.S. investors by issuing ADRs.

International companies also make use of Global Depository Receipts (GDRs). These are similar in principle to ADRs but are listed and traded in London and Luxembourg. Companies from India aggressively issue GDRs to circumvent stringent listing requirements in their home market.[5]

Advantages of ADRs   Companies gain several important advantages through ADRs. First, investors who buy ADRs pay no currency-conversion fees. By contrast, if a U.S. investor were to purchase the shares of a non–U.S. company on another country's stock exchange, he or she would incur the expense of converting currencies. Avoiding such expenses, plus the added convenience of paying in dollars, encourages U.S. investors to buy ADRs. Second, there are no minimum purchase requirements for ADRs, as there sometimes are for shares of a company's stock.

Third, companies offer ADRs in the United States to appeal to mutual funds. Investment laws in the United States limit the amount of money that a mutual fund can invest in the shares of companies not registered on U.S. exchanges. U.S. mutual fund managers were forced to sell shares of German software producer SAP (www.sap.com) when they appreciated in price. Says Kevin McKay, chief operating officer of SAP America, "Some of these guys were telling us, 'We hate to sell, but we have to. Please get some ADRs.'" SAP complied. Listing ADRs in the United States also allowed the company to reward employees with discounted shares of company stock—something that it could not have done otherwise because companies are barred from awarding shares in unregistered companies to employees in the United States.[6]

VENTURE CAPITAL   Another source of equity financing for entrepreneurial start-ups and small businesses is **venture capital**—financing obtained from investors who believe that the borrower will experience rapid growth and who receive equity (part ownership) in return. Those who supply the venture with the capital it needs are called *venture capitalists*. Although there is often substantial risk associated with new, rapidly expanding enterprises, venture capitalists invest in them because they can also generate very large returns on investment.

Venture capitalists with deep pockets now have a global reach. Nevertheless, many small companies around the world confront real obstacles when trying to obtaining financing. Entrepreneurs in the United States, however, tend to have a relatively easier time financing activities and expansion because of a culture that values entrepreneurship. The culture of the United States is individual-oriented and rewards individual business risk-taking with financial rewards. For some key strategies that entrepreneurs use to find international investors, see the Culture Matters feature, titled "Financing Business from Abroad."

EMERGING STOCK MARKETS   Naturally, companies from countries with emerging stock markets face certain problems. First, emerging stock markets commonly experience extreme volatility. An important contributing factor is that investments into emerging stock markets are often so-called *hot money*—money that can be quickly withdrawn in times of crisis. By contrast, *patient money*—foreign direct investment in factories, equipment, and land—cannot be pulled out as readily. Large and sudden sell-offs of equity are signs of market volatility that characterize many emerging stock markets. Such large sell-offs occur because of uncertainty regarding the nation's future economic growth.

American Depository Receipt (ADR)
Certificate that trades in the United States and that represents a specific number of shares in a non–U.S. company.

venture capital
Financing obtained from investors who believe that the borrower will experience rapid growth and who receive equity (part ownership) in return.

CULTURE MATTERS   Financing Business from Abroad

Small-business financing is becoming more global as national economies become interwoven and as technology eases communication. To simply gain a position in the relatively safe U.S. market, for example, an international investor may accept a lower rate of return. Here are some tips from entrepreneurs who found international capital for their companies:

- **Business School International Programs.** Instructors of international business courses often have contacts in both education and industry abroad. To break into this network, perhaps visit your local college and take an executive education course or join a program in which you can work closely with entrepreneurial advisers.
- **Your Country's Commerce Department.** Ask about potential international markets to which your product might be appealing. Developing, emerging, and highly developed countries all have needs in practically every economic sector. Your nation's

commerce department can help in your preliminary scouting of opportunities, as can your country's embassies.

- **Leverage Your Contacts.** Tap the professionals with whom you work—especially attorneys and accountants with international ties. Long before you start pursuing overseas investors, consider asking a respected executive with international experience to serve on your board of directors.
- **Industry Events in Other Countries.** Do this to increase your contacts and exposure. Your specific trade association should be able to provide you with a schedule of shows taking place in other countries.
- **Hire an Intermediary to Find Capital.** These types of intermediaries can help locate funding from international venture-capital firms, banks, and other lending institutions. They also can help expanding businesses get capital from financial institutions in other parts of the world.

Second, companies that issue equity on their countries' emerging stock markets are often plagued by poor market regulation. This can allow large local companies to wield a great deal of influence over their domestic stock markets. As long as powerful domestic shareholders dominate such exchanges, international investors will likely hesitate to enter. The root of the problem often lies in regulation that favors insiders over international investors.

Internal Funding

Ongoing international business activities and new investments can also be financed internally, whether with funds supplied by the parent company or by its international subsidiaries.

INTERNAL EQUITY, DEBT, AND FEES Spin-off companies and new subsidiaries typically require a period of time before they become financially independent. During this period, they often obtain internal financing from parent companies.

Many international subsidiaries obtain financial capital by issuing equity, which as a rule is not publicly traded. In fact, equity is often purchased solely by the parent company, which obviously enjoys great influence over the subsidiary's decisions. If the subsidiary performs well, the parent earns a return from the appreciating share price that reflects the increased valuation of the company. If the subsidiary decides to pay stock dividends, the parent company can also earn a return in this way. Parent companies commonly lend money to international subsidiaries during the start-up phase and when subsidiaries undertake large new investments. Conversely, subsidiaries with excess cash often lend money to parent or sister companies that need capital.

revenue
Money earned from the sale of goods and services.

REVENUE FROM OPERATIONS Money earned from the sale of goods and services is called **revenue**. This source of capital is the lifeblood of international companies and their subsidiaries. If a company is to succeed in the long term, it must at some point generate sufficient internal revenue to sustain day-to-day operations. At that point, outside financing is required only to expand operations or to survive lean periods—say, during seasonal sales fluctuations.

As we saw in earlier chapters, international companies and their subsidiaries also internally generate revenues through so-called *transfer prices*—prices charged for goods or services transferred among a company and its subsidiaries. Companies set subsidiaries' transfer prices high or low, according to their own goals. For instance, often companies pursue transfer pricing aggressively when they wish to minimize taxes in a high-taxation country. Transfer pricing can be used if there are no national restrictions on the use of foreign exchange or on the repatriation of profits to home countries. Figure 15.2 summarizes the internal sources of capital for international companies and their subsidiaries.

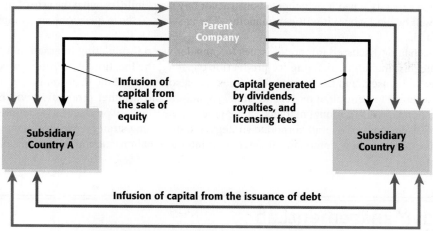

FIGURE 15.2

Internal Sources of Capital for International Companies

Capital Structure

The **capital structure** of a company is the mix of equity, debt, and internally generated funds that it uses to finance its activities. Firms try to strike the right balance among financing methods to minimize risk and the cost of capital.

Debt requires periodic interest payments to creditors such as banks and bondholders. If the company defaults on interest payments, creditors can take the company to court to force it to pay—even forcing it into bankruptcy. On the other hand, in the case of equity, only holders of certain types of preferred stock (which companies issue sparingly) can force bankruptcy because of default. As a rule, then, companies do not want to carry too much debt in relation to equity that can increase their risk of insolvency. Debt still appeals to companies in many countries, however, because interest payments can be deducted from taxable earnings—thus lowering the amount of taxes the firm must pay.

The basic principles of capital structure do not vary from domestic to international companies. But research indicates that multinational firms have lower ratios of debt to equity than domestic firms. Why is this so? Some observers cite increased political risk, exchange-rate risk, and the number of opportunities available to multinational companies as possible explanations for the difference. Others suggest that the debt-versus-equity option depends on a company's national culture. But this suggestion has come under fire because companies from all cultures want to reduce their cost of capital. Moreover, many large international companies generate revenue from a large number of countries. How does one determine the "national culture" of these companies?

National restrictions can influence the choice of capital structure. These restrictions include limits on the international flows of capital, the cost of local financing versus the cost of international financing, access to international financial markets, and controls imposed on the exchange of currencies. The choice of capital structure for each of a company's international subsidiaries—and, therefore, its own capital structure—is a highly complex decision.

capital structure
Mix of equity, debt, and internally generated funds used to finance a company's activities.

QUICK STUDY 4

1. Explain when a *back-to-back loan* might be useful to a company.
2. Why might a firm list its stock in the international capital market? Explain the advantages of an *American Depository Receipt (ADR)*.
3. Identify several difficulties facing companies that issue equity on emerging stock markets.
4. What is meant by the term *capital structure*? Explain its significance.

A Final Word

Whether an international company's production activity involves manufacturing a product or providing a service, it must acquire many resources before beginning operations. It needs to resolve issues such as where it will get raw materials or components, how much production capacity it needs, whether to construct or buy new facilities, what the size of its service centers will be, and where it will get financing. The answers to these questions are complex and interrelated.

This chapter discussed important issues to consider when formulating international production strategies, including planning for production capacity, the location of facilities, production processes to be used, and the layout of facilities. We also discussed the decision that companies face of whether to centralize or decentralize production and whether production will be standardized or adapted to national markets. In the process, we saw how production issues are linked to earlier discussions of overall corporate strategy and marketing strategy. We closed the chapter with a discussion of how companies finance their international production operations and other activities.

Chapter Summary

MyManagementLab

Go to **mymanagementlab.com** to complete the problem marked with this icon .

1. Identify the elements that are important to consider when formulating production strategies.
   - Assessing a company's ability to produce enough output to satisfy market demand is called *capacity planning.*
   - *Facilities location planning* that selects a highly favorable location can allow a company to achieve *location economies*—economic benefits derived from locating production activities in optimal locations.
   - Essential to facilities location planning is whether to *centralize* or *decentralize* production.
   - Deciding the process that a company will use to create its product is called *process planning.*
   - A key production issue is whether to *standardize* the manufacture of products or *adapt* it for different markets.
   - Deciding the spatial arrangement of production processes within facilities, called *facilities layout planning,* depends on the type of production process a company employs.

2. Identify key considerations when acquiring physical resources.
   - The *make-or-buy* decision is a choice for or against greater *vertical integration*—the process of extending control over additional stages of production.
   - A firm that chooses to *make* a particular product or component often does so to take advantage of lower costs or to achieve greater control.
   - *Outsourcing* can provide greater flexibility while reducing exposure to exchange-rate fluctuations and other risks.
   - Key issues facing firms producing locally are the *quantity* and *quality* of locally available raw materials.
   - Companies can either (1) acquire or modify existing factories (*fixed assets*) or (2) build entirely new facilities.

3. Identify several production matters that are of special concern to managers.
   - *Total quality management (TQM)* is a company-wide commitment to meet or exceed customer expectations through continuous quality improvement efforts and processes.
   - International Standards Organization (ISO) 9000 certification is awarded to firms that meet the highest quality standards in their industries.
   - *Shipping costs* can have a dramatic effect on the cost of getting materials and components to production facilities.
   - *Just-in-time (JIT) manufacturing* is a technique in which inventory and its cost are minimized and inputs to the production process arrive exactly when needed.
   - Companies often *reinvest* in operations when (1) a market is expected to provide a large return or (2) a market is growing rapidly.
   - Companies often *divest* when (1) profitability is delayed; (2) problems arise in the political, social, or economic sphere; or (3) other, more profitable opportunities arise.

4. Describe the three potential sources of financing and the main financial instruments of each.

- In *back-to-back loans,* parent firms loan money to subsidiaries by depositing money in host-country banks.
- Non–U.S. companies can access the U.S. capital market by issuing *American Depository Receipts (ADRs)*—certificates that trade in the United States and that represent a specific number of shares in a non–U.S. company.
- *Venture capital* is a source of equity for entrepreneurial start-ups and small businesses.
- Parent companies and their subsidiaries can obtain *internal funding* through (1) a swapping of debt or equity and (2) charging one another royalties and licensing fees.
- *Revenue* from ongoing operations can help finance company expansion.
- *Transfer prices* are prices charged between companies and their subsidiaries for goods and services purchased internally.

Talk It Over

1. Companies around the world are increasingly committing themselves to attaining ISO certification in a variety of areas, including quality and pollution minimization. Do you think this is just the beginning of a trend toward worldwide homogenization of product and process standards? Do you think that someday all companies and their products will need certification in order to conduct international business? Explain your answers.

Teaming Up

1. **Research Project.** The United States is home to some of the world's leading computer software companies, most of which commonly outsource software development to other countries, including Egypt, India, Ireland, Israel, Malaysia, Hungary, and the Philippines. As a group, select one of these countries, and explain why it has become a supplier to the computer software industry. Do you think that development of the industry in your chosen country is a threat to companies in the United States? Why or why not?
2. **Interview Project.** With several classmates, contact a manager at a local company that does business internationally. Talk to the manager about TQM and ISO standards. Find out whether the company has a formal TQM program and whether it has obtained any type of ISO certification. Compile your findings, and present them to the class in a short talk. Compare and contrast the findings obtained for each company the class studied.
3. **Financing Project.** Suppose you and several classmates are a team assembled by the chief financial officer of a consumer-goods company based in Mexico. Your company wishes to expand internationally but lacks the necessary financial capital. Describe all the financing options that are available to your company. Explain why each option is feasible, taking into account the prevailing situation in the Mexican and international capital markets. Develop a short presentation to be delivered to your board of directors (the rest of your classmates).

Key Terms

American Depository Receipt (ADR) (p. 387)	facilities location planning (p. 376)	outsourcing (p. 381)
back-to-back loan (p. 386)	fixed (tangible) assets (p. 382)	process planning (p. 378)
capacity planning (p. 376)	just-in-time (JIT) manufacturing (p. 384)	revenue (p. 388)
capital structure (p. 389)	location economies (p. 377)	total quality management (TQM) (p. 383)
facilities layout planning (p. 379)	make-or-buy decision (p. 380)	venture capital (p. 387)
		vertical integration (p. 380)

Take It to the Web

1. **Video Report.** Visit this book's channel on YouTube (www.YouTube.com/MyIBvideos). Click on "Videos" near the top of the page, and click on the set of videos labeled "Ch 15: Managing International Operations." Watch one video from the list, and then summarize it in a half-page report. Reflecting on the contents of this chapter, which aspects of managing international operations can you identify in the video? How might a company engaged in international business act on the information contained in the video?

2. **Website Report.** Visit the website of Netherlands-based Philips NV (www.philips.com), and research the company on the Internet. As best you can, identify Philips' production and assembly locations. What types of products does Philips, one of the world's top three consumer-electronics companies, produce? Do you think Philips is following a centralized or a decentralized production strategy? Explain your answer. Where does Philips conduct much of its R&D, and why is it performed there?

   Visit the website of LG Philips LCD (www.lgphilips-lcd.com) and Philips' joint venture with South Korean firm LG (www.lg.co.kr). What do you think Philips had to gain by cooperating with LG? Why do you think Philips did not simply build its own facilities in South Korea to produce LCD displays? How can the LG and Philips joint venture be explained using the criteria of a make-or-buy decision? Explain your answers.

Ethical Challenges

1. You are the senior vice president of human resources for a major multinational company. Your firm recently "reengineered" and fired a number of longtime workers. Your firm then rehired many of the same workers, but this time as consultants with no benefits paid by your firm. Critics charge that your firm's practice of reengineering is synonymous with "downsizing"—laying off employees or reducing employment ranks through early retirement and other means. Is it ethical for your company to behave in this manner? As the head of human resources, is there an alternative to the current practice of your firm?

2. You are special assistant to the governor of a southeastern U.S. state in which unemployment (especially in rural areas) is well above the national average. After nearly three years in office and elected on a pledge to attract industry and create jobs, the governor is concerned. Because he respects your moral stance on issues, the governor has come seeking your insights. A European automobile maker has just told the governor that your state is on its short list of potential sites for a new manufacturing facility. The facility is expected to employ about 1,500 people, with plenty of spillover effects on the wider economy. The governor informs you that the European automaker expects significant incentives and concessions. The governor would like to offer some $300 million in tax breaks and subsidies in an effort to bring the new plant to the state. How do you advise the governor? Would the outlay be proper use of taxpayer money? Why or why not? Would you feel comfortable defending your advice if it were to become public?

MyManagementLab

Go to **mymanagementlab.com** for Auto-graded writing questions as well as the following Assisted-graded writing questions:

15-1. Despite the difficulties many technology companies experienced in the early 2000s, e-business is here to stay. What resources does an Internet retailer need other than merely a storefront on the Internet? Does it require fewer physical, financial, and human resources than a traditional retailer or just as many? Explain your answer.

15-2. Many companies seek to cut costs and improve quality by introducing techniques such as just-in-time and quality circles. The results, however, often fall short of those achieved at Toyota. Why do you think this is the case?

15-3. Mymanagementlab Only – comprehensive writing assignment for this chapter.

Practicing International Management Case

Toyota's Strategy for Production Efficiency

Toyota Motor Corporation (www.toyota-global.com) commonly appears in most rankings of the world's most respected companies. One reason for Toyota's strong showing in such rankings is that the company always seems to maintain profitability in the face of economic downturns and slack demand. Another reason is that leaders in a wide range of industries have high regard for Toyota's management and production practices.

Toyota first began producing cars in 1937. In the mid-1950s, a machinist named Taiichi Ohno began developing a new concept of automobile production. Today, the approach known as the Toyota Production System (TPS) has been intensely studied and widely copied throughout the automobile industry. Ohno, who is addressed by fellow employees as *sensei* ("teacher and master"), followed the lead of the family that founded Toyota (spelled Toyoda) by exhibiting high regard for company employees. Ohno also believed that mass production of automobiles was obsolete and that a flexible production system that produced cars according to specific customer requests would be superior.

It was at Toyota that the well-known just-in-time approach to inventory management was developed and perfected. Implementing just-in-time required *kanban,* a simple system of colored paper cards that accompanied the parts as they progressed down the assembly line. *Kanban* eliminates inventory buildup by quickly telling the production personnel which parts are being used and which are not. The third pillar of the TPS was quality circles, groups of workers who discussed ways to improve the work process and make better cars. Finally, the entire system was based on *jidoka,* which literally means "automation." As used at Toyota, however, the word expresses management's faith in the worker as a human being and a thinker.

A simple example illustrates the benefits of Toyota's system. Toyota dealerships found that customers kept returning their vehicles with leaking radiator hoses. When a team of workers at the U.S. plant where the vehicle was made was asked to help find a solution, they found the problem was the clamp on the radiator hose. In assembly, the clamp is put over the hose, a pin on the side is pulled out, and the hose is secured. But sometimes the operator would forget to pull out the pin. The hose would remain loose and would leak. So the team installed a device next to the line that contains a funnel and electric eye. If a pin is not tossed into the funnel (passing the electric eye) every 60 seconds, the device senses that the operator must have forgotten to pull the pin and stops the line. As a result, a warranty problem at the dealerships was eliminated, customer dissatisfaction was reduced, and productivity was increased.

Nearly 50 years after the groundwork for the TPS was first laid, the results speak for themselves. Toyota's superior approach to manufacturing has been estimated to yield a cost advantage of $600 to $700 per car due to more efficient production, plus another $300 savings per car because fewer defects mean less warranty repair work. Ohno's belief in flexible production can also be seen in the fact that Toyota's Sienna minivan is produced on the same assembly line in Georgetown, Kentucky, as the company's Camry models. The Sienna and Camry share the same basic chassis and 50 percent of their parts. Out of 300 different stations on the assembly line, Sienna models require different parts at only 26 stations. Toyota expects to build one Sienna for every three Camrys that come off the assembly line.

Thinking Globally

1. Chrysler engineers helped Toyota develop its Sienna minivan. In return, Toyota provided input on automobile production techniques to Chrysler. Why do you think Chrysler was willing to share its minivan know-how with a key competitor?
2. What other benefits do you think Toyota obtains from its production system? Think in broader terms than just production, and consider financial, marketing, and human resource management issues.

Source: Hirotaka Takeuchi, Emi Osono, and Norihiko Shimizu, "The Contradictions That Drive Toyota's Success," *Harvard Business Review*, June 2008, pp. 96–104; David Welch, "What Could Dull Toyota's Edge," *Bloomberg Businessweek*, April 28, 2008, p. 38; "Q&A: Pushing Carmakers to Rev Up Factories," *Bloomberg Businessweek* (www.businessweek.com), February 17, 2002.

Hiring and Managing Employees

LEARNING OBJECTIVES

After studying this chapter, you should be able to

1. Explain the three different types of staffing policies used by international companies.

2. Describe the recruitment and selection issues facing international companies.

3. Discuss the importance of training and development programs, especially cultural training.

4. Explain how companies compensate managers and workers in international markets.

5. Describe the importance of labor–management relations and how they differ around the world.

A Look Back

Chapter 15 examined how companies launch and manage their international production efforts. We also explored briefly how companies finance their various international business operations.

A Look at This Chapter

This final chapter examines how a company acquires and manages its most important resource—its employees. The topics we explore include international staffing policies, recruitment and selection, training and development, compensation, and labor–management relations. We also learn about culture shock and how employees can deal with its effects.

LEAPING CULTURES

HO CHI MIN CITY, Vietnam—Intel (www.intel.com) created the world's first microprocessor in 1971. Today, annual revenue is $54 billion, around 75 percent of which is earned outside the United States. Intel is the world's largest maker of computer chips and is a leading manufacturer of computer, networking, and communications products. Shown here, Intel employees pose for a photo at the grand opening of Intel's assembly and test facilities at Saigon Hi-Tech Park in Ho Chi Minh City, Vietnam.

With nearly 83,000 employees worldwide, Intel must deal with many issues when managing people. The company must answer some important questions when selecting people to manage each local facility in 45 countries. Can a qualified manager be found locally? If so, what salary should Intel pay the local manager? Or will a manager need to be sent from the United States or from a facility in another nation? If so, what should Intel pay that individual? Intel's compensation and benefits packages vary greatly from one country to another because of different practices around the world.

There is also the issue of culture. Al-though the depth of cultural knowledge re-

Source: LiPo Ching/MCT/Newscom

quired of various employees differs, Intel wants all its employees to be culturally astute. Its culture-specific training courses teach its employees how business differs across cultures. Intel says its training is designed "to develop the knowledge, aware-ness, and skills to ensure effectiveness and productivity and to identify strategies for successfully doing business in other countries and with people from other countries."

From tech-support reps working long distance with customers abroad to globe-trotting executives, many Intel employees regularly rely on their cross-cultural communication skills. As you read this chapter, consider all the human resource issues that arise when international companies manage their employees around the world.[1]

Perhaps the most important resource of any successful business is the people who comprise it. If a company gives its human resource management practices the importance they deserve, it can have a profound impact on performance. Highly trained and productive employees who are proficient in their duties allow a company to achieve its business goals both domestically and internationally. **Human resource management (HRM)** is the process of staffing a company and ensuring that employees are as productive as possible. It requires managers to be effective in recruiting, selecting, training, developing, evaluating, and compensating employees and in forming good relationships with them.

International HRM differs considerably from HRM in a domestic setting because of differences in national business environments. There are concerns over the employment of **expatriates**—citizens of one country who are living and working in another. Companies must deal with many issues when they have expatriate employees on job assignments that could last several years. Some of these issues are related to the inconvenience and stress of living in an unfamiliar culture. In the company profile at the start of this chapter, we saw how Intel (www.intel.com) enrolls its employees in culture-specific training courses to prepare them for doing business internationally.

Training and development programs must often be tailored to local practices. Some countries, such as Germany and Japan, have extensive vocational-training schools that turn out graduates ready to perform their jobs proficiently. Finding well-qualified nonmanagerial workers in those markets is relatively easy. By contrast, developing a production facility in many emerging markets requires far more basic training of workers. For example, workers in China work hard and tend to be well educated. But because China lacks an advanced vocational training system like those in Germany and Japan, Chinese workers tend to require more intensive on-the-job training. Recruitment and selection practices must also be adapted to the host nation's hiring laws. Hiring practices regarding nondiscrimination among job candidates must be carefully monitored so that the company does not violate such laws. And companies that go abroad to lower labor expenses must adjust pay scales and advancement criteria to suit local customs.

Because culture is so important to international business, we studied culture early (Chapter 2) and returned repeatedly to the topic throughout this book. Culture is also central to this final chapter's discussion of how international companies manage their employees. We begin by discussing the different types of human resource staffing policies that international companies use. Then, we learn about the important factors that affect recruitment and selection practices internationally. We explore the many different types of training and development programs companies can use to improve the effectiveness of their employees. We also examine the compensation policies of international companies. We close the chapter with a discussion of the importance of labor–management relations around the world.

human resource management (HRM)
Process of staffing a company and ensuring that employees are as productive as possible.

expatriates
Citizens of one country who are living and working in another.

International Staffing Policy

staffing policy
Customary means by which a company staffs its offices.

The customary means by which a company staffs its offices is called its **staffing policy**. Staffing policy is greatly influenced by the extent of a firm's international involvement. There are three main approaches to the staffing of international business operation: *ethnocentric, polycentric*, and *geocentric*. Although we discuss each of these approaches as being distinct from one another, companies often blend different aspects of each staffing policy in practice. The result is an almost infinite variety of international staffing policies among international companies.

Ethnocentric Staffing

ethnocentric staffing
Staffing policy in which individuals from the home country manage operations abroad.

In **ethnocentric staffing**, individuals from the home country manage operations abroad. This policy tends to appeal to companies that want to maintain tight control over decision making in branch offices abroad. Accordingly, those companies try to formulate policies designed to work in every country in which they operate. But note that firms generally pursue this policy in their international operations for top managerial posts—implementing it at lower levels is often impractical.

ADVANTAGES OF ETHNOCENTRIC STAFFING Firms pursue this policy for several reasons. First, locally qualified people are not always available. In developing and newly industrialized countries, there is often a shortage of qualified personnel that creates a highly competitive local labor market.

Second, companies use ethnocentric staffing to re-create local operations in the image of home-country operations. Especially if they have climbed the corporate ladder in the home office, expatriate managers tend to infuse branch offices with the corporate culture. This policy is important for companies that need a strong set of shared values among the people in each international office—such as firms implementing global strategies. For example, Mihir Doshi was born in Bombay, but his family moved to the United States in 1978. Doshi graduated from New York University and became a naturalized U.S. citizen in 1988. In 1995 he became executive director of Morgan Stanley's (www.morganstanley.com) operations in India. "Mentally," he reports, "I'm very American. Here, I can be Indian. What the firm gets is somebody to indoctrinate Morgan Stanley culture. I provide the link."[2]

By the same token, a system of shared values is important when a company's international units are highly interdependent. For instance, fashioning branch operations in the image of home-office operations can also ease the transfer of special know-how. This advantage is particularly valuable when that know-how is rooted in the expertise and experience of home-country managers.

Finally, some companies feel that managers sent from the home country will look out for the company's interests more earnestly than will host-country natives. Japanese companies are notorious for their reluctance to place non-Japanese managers at the helm of international offices. And when they do appoint a foreigner, they often place a Japanese manager in the office to monitor important decisions and report back to the home office. Companies that operate in highly nationalistic markets and those worried about industrial espionage also typically find an ethnocentric approach appealing.

DISADVANTAGES OF ETHNOCENTRIC STAFFING Despite its advantages, ethnocentric staffing has its negative aspects. First, relocating managers from the home country is expensive. The bonuses that managers often receive for relocating plus relocation expenses for entire families can increase the cost of a manager several times over. Likewise, the pressure of cultural differences and long periods away from relatives and friends can contribute to the failure of managers on international assignments.

Second, an ethnocentric policy can create barriers for the host-country office. The presence of home-country managers in the host country might encourage a "foreign" image of the business. Lower-level employees might feel that managers do not really understand their needs because they come from another culture. Occasionally they are right: Expatriate managers

Sending an expatriate manager to another country to run things can send the wrong message to local employees. eBay (www.ebay.com) hired Mr. Muralikrishnan, shown here, to be its country manager in India. eBay is trying to boost its share of the Indian market, which is dominated by domestic players such as Flipkart (www.flipkart.com). eBay believed that Muralikrishnan had the local cultural knowledge and business acumen to achieve the company's goals.

Source: REUTERS/Vivek Prakash

sometimes fail to integrate themselves into the local culture. And if they fail to overcome cultural barriers, they typically fail to understand the needs of their local employees and those of their local customers.

Polycentric Staffing

polycentric staffing
Staffing policy in which individuals from the host country manage operations abroad.

In **polycentric staffing**, individuals from the host country manage operations abroad. Companies can implement a polycentric approach for top- and mid-level managers, for lower-level staff, or for nonmanagerial workers. It is well suited to companies who want to give national units a degree of autonomy in decision making. This policy does not mean that host-country managers are left to run operations in any way they see fit. Large international companies usually conduct extensive training programs in which host-country managers visit home offices for extended periods. This exposes them to the company's culture and specific business practices. Small and medium-sized companies can find this policy expensive, but being able to depend on local managers who fully understand what is expected of them can far outweigh any costs.

ADVANTAGES AND DISADVANTAGES OF POLYCENTRIC STAFFING Polycentric staffing places managerial responsibility in the hands of people intimately familiar with the local business environment. Managers with deep cultural understanding of the local market can be an enormous advantage. They are familiar with local business practices and can read the subtle cues of both verbal and nonverbal language. They need not overcome any cultural barriers created by an image of being an outsider, and they tend to have a better feel for the needs of employees, customers, and suppliers.

Another important advantage of polycentric staffing is elimination of the high cost of relocating expatriate managers and families. This benefit can be extremely helpful for small and medium-sized businesses that cannot afford the expenses associated with expatriate employees.

The major drawback of polycentric staffing is the potential for losing control of the host-country operation. When a company employs natives of each country to manage local operations, it runs the risk of becoming a collection of discrete national businesses. This situation might not be a problem when a firm's strategy calls for treating each national market differently. It is not a good policy, however, for companies that are following global strategies. If these companies lack integration, knowledge sharing, and a common image, performance will surely suffer.

Geocentric Staffing

geocentric staffing
Staffing policy in which the best-qualified individuals, regardless of nationality, manage operations abroad.

In **geocentric staffing**, the best-qualified individuals, regardless of nationality, manage operations abroad. The local operation may choose managers from the host country, from the home country, or from a third country. The choice depends on the operation's specific needs. This policy is typically reserved for top-level managers.

ADVANTAGES AND DISADVANTAGES OF GEOCENTRIC STAFFING Geocentric staffing helps a company develop global managers who can adjust easily to any business environment—particularly to cultural differences. This advantage is especially useful for global companies trying to break down nationalistic barriers, whether between managers in a single office or between different offices. One hope of companies using this policy is that a global perspective among its managers will help them seize opportunities that may otherwise be overlooked.

The downside of geocentric staffing is the expense. Understandably, top managers who are capable both of fitting into different cultures and being effective at their jobs are highly prized among international companies. The combination of high demand for their skills and their short supply inflates their salaries. Moreover, there is the expense of relocating managers and their families—sometimes every year or two.

QUICK STUDY 1

1. List several ways in which *human resource management* differs in the international versus domestic environment.
2. What are the three different types of international *staffing policies* that companies can implement?
3. Identify the advantages and disadvantages of each type of international staffing policy.

Recruiting and Selecting Human Resources

Naturally, companies try to recruit and select qualified managers and nonmanagerial workers who are well suited to their tasks and responsibilities. But how does a company know the number of managers and workers it needs? How does it recruit the best available individuals? How does it select from the pool of available candidates? In this section, we explore some answers to these and other important questions about recruiting and selecting employees.

Human Resource Planning

Recruiting and selecting managers and workers requires **human resource (HR) planning**—the process of forecasting a company's human resource needs and its supply. The first phase of HR planning involves taking an inventory of a company's current human resources—that is, collecting data on every employee, including educational background, special job skills, previous jobs, language skills, and experience living abroad.

The second phase of HR planning is estimating the company's future HR needs. For example, consider a firm that plans to sell its products directly to buyers in a new market abroad. Will it create a new operation abroad and staff it with managers from the home office, or will it train local managers? Will it hire its own local sales force, or will it hire a distributor? Likewise, manufacturing or assembling products in an international market requires factory workers. A company must decide whether to hire these people itself or to subcontract production to other producers—thus eliminating the need for it to hire the workers. For additional issues that companies should consider when staffing internationally, see the Manager's Briefcase feature, titled "Growing Global."

As we noted in previous chapters, this decision frequently raises ethical questions. The general public is becoming increasingly well informed about the fact that global companies make extensive use of subcontractors in low-wage nations. Of particular concern is the question of whether subcontractors are taking advantage of "sweatshop" labor. But publicity generated by allegations of workplace abuse caused many firms to establish codes of conduct, and they stepped up efforts to ensure compliance. For example, Apple (www.apple.com) sent a team of investigators to China to look into charges of sweatshop-like conditions at a company manufacturing Apple's iPod. The company that Apple investigated was a division of the world's largest contract electronics manufacturer, Hon Hai Precision Industry.[3]

Another example on this topic involves Levi Strauss (www.levistrauss.com). When apparel contractors in Bangladesh admitted that they hired children, Levi Strauss demanded that they comply with local regulations. Unfortunately, it turned out that many of the underage

human resource planning
Process of forecasting a company's human resource needs and its supply.

MANAGER'S BRIEFCASE   Growing Global

Going global successfully requires experience and business acumen. It can also strain a company's resources of time, money, and people. Here is some advice on human resource issues to consider when expanding internationally:

- ***Don't Rely Solely on Home-Country Expatriates.*** Sending employees from the home country to manage host-country operations is not always best, according to Joseph Monti, a partner at Grant Thornton (www.grantthornton.com). Although they know the company and its products, home-country employees often lack experience and contacts in the local culture. Monti says a better strategy may be to "Have a local general manager with a support staff that could be seeded with U.S. expatriates."

- ***Contacts Do Not Guarantee Contracts.*** "Relationships matter more than mere contacts," said Virginia Kamsky, CEO of Kamsky Associates, Inc. (www.kamsky.com). "Don't assume that hiring the son of a government official will automatically get you business. It's more important to hire a person with

a good attitude and strong relationship-building skills," she added.

- ***Treat Your Employees Abroad as You Want to Be Treated.*** "People are basically the same worldwide; it doesn't matter where you are," notes Jeff Dzuira, director of international sales at Ferris Manufacturing (www.polymem.com). "Awareness and respect of cultural protocol demonstrates honesty and goodwill, and this leads to trust, which in turn leads to mutually profitable relationships."

- ***Employ the Web in Your Search.*** One of the largest employment websites is Monster (www.monster.com). It has branches in 22 countries and literally millions of résumés and is larger than ever since its merger with HotJobs. Employers can also post job announcements on the website at Overseas Jobs (www.overseasjobs.com). Of course, there are many more websites out there, and undertaking an aggressive job search or recruitment drive on the Internet is becoming increasingly common.

workers were their families' sole sources of support. So Levi's struck a deal: Contractors agreed to continue paying wages to the youngsters while they went to school, and then they would be rehired when they reached age 14. Levi's paid for them to attend school until they came of age.

In the third phase of HR planning, managers develop a plan for recruiting and selecting people to fill vacant and anticipated new positions, both managerial and nonmanagerial. Sometimes, a firm must also make plans for reducing its workforce—a process called *decruitment*—when current HR levels are greater than anticipated needs. Planning for decruitment normally occurs when a company decides to discontinue manufacturing or selling in a market. Unfortunately, the decision by global companies to shift the location of manufacturing from one country to another can also result in lost jobs. Let's now take a closer look at the recruitment and selection processes.

Recruiting Human Resources

recruitment
Process of identifying and attracting a qualified pool of applicants for vacant positions.

The process of identifying and attracting a qualified pool of applicants for vacant positions is called **recruitment**. Companies can recruit internally from among their current employees or look to external sources.

CURRENT EMPLOYEES Finding an international manager among current employees is easiest for a large company with an abundance of internal managers. Likely candidates within the company are managers who were involved in previous stages of an international project—say, in *identifying* the new production site or potential market. It is likely that these individuals have already made important contacts inside the host country and that they have already been exposed to its culture.

RECENT COLLEGE GRADUATES Companies also recruit from among recent college graduates who have come from other countries to attend college in the firm's home country. This is a particularly common practice among companies in the United States. Over a one-year period, these new hires receive general and specialized training and then are given positions in their native countries. As a rule, they learn about the organization's culture and the way in which it conducts business. Most important, perhaps, is their familiarity with the culture of the target market, including its customs, traditions, and language.

LOCAL MANAGERIAL TALENT Companies can also recruit local managerial talent. Hiring local managers is common when cultural understanding is a key job requirement. Hiring local managers with government contacts can speed the process of getting approvals for local operations. In some cases, governments force companies to recruit local managers so that they can develop their own internal pools of managerial talent. Governments sometimes also restrict the number of international managers that can work in the host country.

NONMANAGERIAL WORKERS Companies typically recruit locally for nonmanagerial positions because there is often little need for highly specialized skills or training. However, a specialist from the home country is typically brought in to train people chosen for more demanding positions.

Firms also turn to the local labor market when governments restrict the number of people allowed into the host country for work purposes. Such efforts are usually designed to reduce unemployment among the local population. On the other hand, countries sometimes permit the importation of nonmanagerial workers. Kuwait, a wealthy oil-producing country in the Middle East, has brought in large numbers of nonmanagerial workers for its blue-collar and technical jobs. Many of these workers come from Egypt, India, Lebanon, Pakistan, and the Philippines in search of jobs or higher wages.

Selecting Human Resources

selection
Process of screening and hiring the best-qualified applicants with the greatest performance potential.

The process of screening and hiring the best-qualified applicants with the greatest performance potential is called **selection**. The process for international assignments includes measuring a person's ability to bridge cultural differences. Expatriate managers must be able to adapt to a new way of life in the host country. Conversely, native host-country managers must be able to work effectively with superiors who have different cultural backgrounds.

In the case of expatriate managers, cultural differences between home country and host country are important factors in their potential success. Culturally sensitive managers increase the likelihood that a company will achieve its international business goals. Recruiters can assess cultural sensitivity by asking candidates questions about their receptiveness to new ways of doing things and questions about racial and ethnic issues. They can also use global aptitude tests to assess an employee's readiness for an international assignment.

It is also important to examine the cultural sensitivity of each family member who will be going to the host country. The ability of a family member (particularly a spouse) to adapt to a new culture can be a key factor in the success or failure of an expatriate manager.

Culture Shock

Successful international managers typically do not mind, and often enjoy, living and working outside their native lands. In extreme cases, they might even be required to relocate every year or so. These individuals are capable of adapting quickly to local conditions and business practices. Such managers are becoming increasingly valuable with the emergence of markets in Asia, Central and Eastern Europe, and Latin America. They are also helping to create a global pool of managers who are ready and willing to go practically anywhere on short notice. The size of this pool, however, remains limited because of the difficulties that many people experience in relocating to unfamiliar cultures.

Living in another culture can be a stressful experience. Selecting managers comfortable traveling to and living in unfamiliar cultures, therefore, is an extremely important factor when recruiting for international posts. Set down in the midst of new cultures, many expatriates experience **culture shock**—a psychological process affecting people living abroad that is characterized by homesickness, irritability, confusion, aggravation, and depression. In other words, they have trouble adjusting to the new environment in which they find themselves. *Expatriate failure*—the early return by an employee from an international assignment because of inadequate

culture shock
Psychological process affecting people living abroad that is characterized by homesickness, irritability, confusion, aggravation, and depression.

CULTURE MATTERS   A Shocking Ordeal

Culture shock typically occurs during stays of a few months or longer in an unfamiliar culture. It begins on arrival and normally occurs in four stages (although not all people go through every stage):

- *Stage I:* The "honeymoon" typically lasts from a few days to a few weeks. New arrivals are fascinated by local sights, pleasant hospitality, and interesting habits. They are thrilled about their opportunity and are optimistic about prospects for success. Yet this sense of security is often false because, so far, interactions with locals are similar to those of a tourist.
- *Stage II:* This stage lasts from a few weeks to a few months; in fact, some people never move on to Stage 3. Unpredictable quirks of the culture become annoying, even maddening. Visitors begin mocking the locals and regarding the ways of their native cultures as superior. Relationships with spouses and children suffer, and depression, perhaps even despair, sets in.
- *Stage III:* Emotions hit bottom and recovery begins. Cynical remarks cease as visitors begin to learn more about the local culture, interact more with locals, and form friendships.
- *Stage IV:* Visitors not only better understand local customs and behavior but actually appreciate many of them. They now treat differences as "unique" solutions to familiar problems in different cultural contexts. Reaching this stage is a sign that the expatriate has adapted well and that success in his or her international assignment is likely.

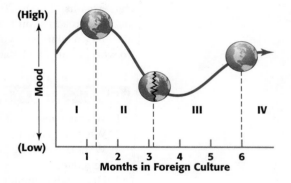

Here are some steps that prospective expatriates can take to reduce the burden of culture shock during an international assignment:

- Undergo extensive psychological assessment to ensure that both you and your family members are emotionally able to handle the assignment.
- Obtain knowledge of the local culture (especially its language) and critically examine your own culture biases before leaving home.
- If possible, visit the assigned country, mingling with local people and getting a feel for your future assignment. Ask about local educational, financial, and health-care services.
- After you are inside a culture, meet with others—both natives and expatriates—to discuss your negative and positive experiences.
- Most important: Relax, be adventurous, take a worldly perspective, and keep your sense of humor.

job performance—often results from cultural stress. The higher cost of expatriate failure is convincing many companies to invest in cultural-training programs for employees sent abroad. For a detailed look at the culture-shock process and how to reduce its effects, see the Culture Matters feature, titled "A Shocking Ordeal."

Reverse Culture Shock

Ironically, expatriates who successfully adapt to new cultures often undergo an experience called **reverse culture shock**—the psychological process of readapting to one's home culture. Because values and behavior that once seemed so natural now seem so strange, reverse culture shock may be even more disturbing than culture shock. Returning managers often find that either no position or merely a "standby" position awaits them in the home office. Companies often do not know how to take full advantage of the cross-cultural abilities developed by managers who have spent several potentially valuable years abroad. It is not uncommon for expatriates to leave their companies within a year of returning home because of difficulties blending back into the company culture.

Moreover, spouses and children often have difficulty leaving the adopted culture and returning home. For many Japanese employees and their families, reentry into Japanese culture after a work assignment in the United States can be particularly difficult. The fast pace of business and social life in the United States, plus the relatively high degree of freedom and independence for women, contrasts with life in Japan. Returning Japanese expatriates can find it difficult to adjust back to life in Japan after years of living in the United States.

DEALING WITH REVERSE CULTURE SHOCK   The effects of reverse culture shock can be reduced. Home-culture reorientation programs and career-counseling sessions for returning managers and their families can be highly effective. For example, the employer might bring the entire family home for a short stay several weeks before the official return. This kind of trip allows returnees to prepare for at least some of the reverse culture shock that may await them.

Good career development programs can help companies retain valuable managers. Ideally, the career development plan is worked out before the employee goes abroad and is revised before his or her return. Some companies work with employees before they go abroad to plan career paths of up to 20 years within the company. Mentors who have previously gone abroad and had to adjust on returning home can also be assigned to returning managers. The mentor becomes a confidant with whom the expatriate manager can discuss particular problems related to work, family, and readjusting to the home culture.

QUICK STUDY 2

1. Why is *human resources planning* important? Identify its three phases.
2. What are the main sources from which companies *recruit* their international managers?
3. What is meant by the term *culture shock*? Describe its four stages and how its effects can be reduced.
4. Under what circumstances might someone experience *reverse culture shock*?

Training and Development

After a company recruits and selects its managers and other employees, it normally identifies the skills and knowledge that employees have and those that they need in order to perform their duties. Employees who lack the necessary skills or knowledge can then be directed into specific training or development programs.

Approximately 300,000 U.S. citizens live outside the United States on international assignments, in addition to hundreds of thousands more who travel abroad on business for stays of up to several weeks. Some of the many costs of relocating an employee for a long-term international assignment include moving expenses and ongoing costs for things such as housing, education, and cost-of-living adjustments. That is why many companies realize the need for in-depth training and development programs if they are to get the maximum productivity from managers posted abroad.

As companies increasingly reach out to the world to obtain services, they are turning to online training (eTraining) programs that teach skills immediately relevant to employees' jobs. These programs include administrative training, human resources training, compliance training, and training in frontline issues such as the consumer benefits of a new product. The appeal of eTraining to international companies is its consistency: eTraining delivers a consistent message in the same way to an infinite number of employees. By contrast, employees receiving other types of training in diverse settings worldwide can go away with many different perceptions or biases. Workplace eTraining is not perfect: It can be difficult to engage people online and to teach soft skills, such as appropriate facial expressions and tone of voice. But its ability to flexibly train large groups cost-effectively makes it a viable alternative to traditional training methods.[4]

Methods of Cultural Training

Ideally, everyone involved in business should be culturally literate and prepared to go anywhere in the world at a moment's notice. Realistically, many employees and many companies do not need or cannot afford to be entirely literate in another culture. The extent of a company's international involvement demands a corresponding level of cultural knowledge from its employees. Companies whose activities are highly international need employees with language fluency and in-depth experience in other countries. Meanwhile, small companies or those new to international business can begin with some basic cultural training. As a company increases its international involvement and cross-cultural contact, employees' cultural knowledge must keep pace.

As we see in Figure 16.1, companies use many methods to prepare managers for an international assignment. These methods tend to reflect a manager's level of international involvement. The goal is to create informed, open-minded, flexible managers with a level of cultural training appropriate to the duties required of them.

ENVIRONMENTAL BRIEFINGS AND CULTURAL ORIENTATIONS *Environmental (area) briefings* constitute the most basic level of training—often the starting point for studying other cultures. Briefings include information on local housing, health care, transportation, schools, and climate. Such knowledge is normally obtained from books, films, and lectures. *Cultural orientations* offer insight into social, political, legal, and economic institutions. Their purpose is to add depth and substance to environmental briefings.

CULTURAL ASSIMILATION AND SENSITIVITY TRAINING *Cultural assimilation* teaches the culture's values, attitudes, manners, and customs. So-called guerrilla linguistics, which involves learning some phrases in the local language, is often used at this stage. It also typically includes

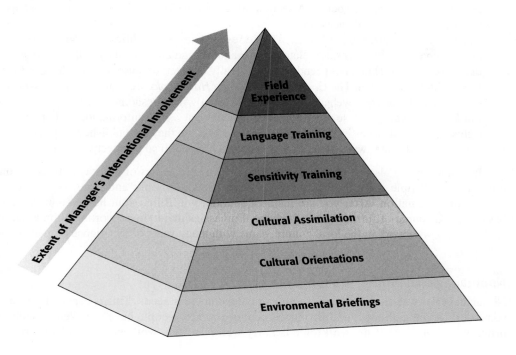

FIGURE 16.1

International Assignment Preparation Methods

role-play exercises: The trainee responds to a specific situation and is evaluated by a team of judges. This method is often used when someone is given little notice of a short stay abroad and wishes to take a crash course in social and business etiquette and communication. *Sensitivity training* teaches people to be considerate and understanding of other people's feelings and emotions. It gets the trainee "under the skin" of the local people.

LANGUAGE TRAINING The need for more-thorough cultural preparedness brings us to intensive *language training*. This level of training entails more than memorizing phrases for ordering dinner or asking directions. It gets a trainee "into the mind" of local people. The trainee learns more about why local people behave as they do. This is perhaps the most critical part of cultural training for long-term assignments.

A survey of top executives found that foreign-language skills topped the list of skills needed to maintain a competitive edge. According to the survey, 31 percent of male employees and 27 percent of female employees lacked foreign-language skills. To remedy this situation, many companies either employ outside agencies that specialize in language training, or they develop their own programs. Employees at 3M Corporation (www.3m.com) developed a third way. They created an all-volunteer "Language Society" composed of current and retired employees and family members. About 1,000 people are members, and the group offers classes in 17 languages taught by 70 volunteer employee teachers. The society meets 45 minutes per week and charges a nominal $5 membership fee. Officials at 3M say that the society nicely complements the company's formal language education program.[5]

FIELD EXPERIENCE *Field experience* means visiting the culture, walking the streets of its cities and villages, and becoming absorbed by it for a short time. The trainee gets to enjoy some of the unique cultural traits and to feel some of the stresses inherent in living in the culture.

Finally, remember that spouses and children also need cultural training. Training for them is a good investment because the alternatives—an international "commuter marriage" or an expatriate failure—are both psychologically and financially expensive options.

Compiling a Cultural Profile

Cultural profiles can be quite helpful in deciding whether to accept an international assignment. The following are some excellent sources for constructing a cultural profile:

- *CultureGrams.* Published by ProQuest, this guide can be found in the reference section of many libraries. Frequent updates make *CultureGrams* (www.culturegrams.com) a timely source of information. Individual sections profile each culture's background and its people, customs, courtesies, and society. A section titled "For the Traveler" covers details such as required entry visas and vaccinations.
- *Country Studies Area Handbooks.* This series explains how politics, economics, society, and national security issues are related to one another and are shaped by culture in more than 70 countries. Handbooks tend to be politically oriented because they are designed for U.S. military personnel. The *Country Studies Area Handbooks* are available on the Web at the Library of Congress website (http://lcweb2.loc.gov/frd/cs/cshome.html).
- *Background Notes.* These notes contain much relevant factual information on human rights and related issues in various countries. Yet because they are published by the U.S. Department of State (www.state.gov), they take a U.S. political perspective.

Information can also be obtained by contacting the embassies of other countries in your home nation. People with firsthand knowledge and specific books and films are also good sources of information. After you are inside a country, you'll find your home country's embassy a good source of further cultural advice. Embassies maintain networks of home-nation professionals who work in the local culture, some with many years of experience on which you can draw.

Nonmanagerial Worker Training

Nonmanagerial workers also have training and development needs. This is especially true in some developing and newly industrialized countries where people have not even completed primary school. Even if the workforce is fairly well educated, workers may lack experience working in industry. In such cases, companies that do business abroad can train local workers in how to work on an assembly line or to cultivate business leads to make sales. The need for such basic-skills training continues to grow as companies increasingly explore opportunities in emerging markets.

In many countries, national governments cooperate with businesses to train nonmanagerial workers. Japan and Germany lead the world in vocational training and apprenticeship programs for nonmanagerial workers. Students who are unable or unwilling to enter college can enter programs paid for by the government and private industry. They undergo extensive practical training that exposes them to the cutting-edge technologies used by the country's leading companies. For example, Germany's Mittelstand is a network of three million small and medium-sized companies that account for about two-thirds of the country's jobs. Mittelstand companies provide 80 percent of Germany's apprenticeships. Although they typically employ fewer than 100 people, many Mittelstand companies are export powerhouses.

Employee Compensation

Essential to good international HRM is a fair and effective compensation (reward) system. Such a system is designed to attract and retain the best and brightest employees and to reward them for their performance. Because a country's compensation practices are rooted in its culture and legal and economic systems, determining compensation can be complicated. For example, base pay accounts for nearly all employee compensation in some countries. In others, bonuses and fringe benefits account for more than half of a person's compensation.

Managerial Employees

Naturally, compensation packages for managers differ from company to company and from country to country. Good packages are fairly complicated to design, for several reasons. Consider the effect of *cost of living,* which includes factors such as the cost of groceries, dining out, clothing, housing, schooling, health care, transportation, and utilities. Quite simply, it costs more to live in some countries than in others. Moreover, within a given country, the cost of living typically varies from large cities to rural towns and villages. Most companies add a certain amount to an expatriate manager's pay to cover greater cost-of-living expenses. On the other hand, managers who are relocating to lower cost-of-living countries are typically paid the same amount that they were receiving at the home office—otherwise, they would be financially penalized for accepting an international job assignment.

Companies must cover other costs incurred by expatriate managers even when the cost of living abroad is lower than at home. One important concern for relocating managers is the quality of local education. In many cases, children cannot immediately enter local classes because they do not speak the local language. In such instances, most companies pay for private-school education.

BONUS AND TAX INCENTIVES Companies commonly offer managers inducements to accept international postings. The most common is a financial bonus. This bonus can be in the form of a one-time payment or an add-on to regular pay—generally 15 to 20 percent. Bonuses for managers who are asked to go into a particularly unstable country or one with a very low standard of living often receive *hardship pay.*

Managers can also be attracted by another income-related factor. For example, the U.S. government permits citizens working abroad to exclude $95,100 of "foreign-earned income" from their taxable income in the United States—even if it was earned in a country with no income tax. But earnings over that amount are subject to income tax, as are employee benefits such as free housing.[6]

CULTURAL AND SOCIAL CONTRIBUTORS TO COST Culture also plays an important role in the compensation of expatriate managers. Some nations offer more paid holidays than others. Many offer free medical care to everyone living and working there. Granted, the quality of locally available medical care is not always good. Many companies, therefore, have plans to take seriously ill expatriates and family members home or to nearby countries where medical care is equal to that available in the home country.

Companies that hire managers in the local market might encounter additional costs engendered by social attitudes. For instance, in some countries employers are expected to provide free or subsidized housing. In others, the government obliges employers to provide paid maternity leaves of up to one-and-a-half years. Government-mandated maternity leaves vary significantly across European countries. Although not all such costs need to be absorbed by companies, they do tend to raise a country's cost of doing business.

Managers recruited from within the host country generally receive the same pay as managers who work for local companies. Yet they often receive perks not offered by local firms. And some managers are required to visit the home office at least several times per year. If time allows, many managers will make these into short vacations by taking along their families and adding a few extra days onto the length of the trip.

Nonmanagerial Workers

Two main factors influence the wages of nonmanagerial workers. First, their compensation is strongly influenced by increased cross-border business investment. Employers can relocate fairly easily to nations where wages are lower. In the home country, meanwhile, workers must often accept lower wages when an employer gives them a choice of accepting the reduction or watching their jobs move abroad. This situation is causing a trend toward greater equality in workers' pay around the world. This equalizing effect encourages economic development and improvement in workers' lives in some nations at the expense of workers in other nations.

The freedom with which an employer can relocate differs from country to country, however. Although firms in some countries are allowed to move with little notice, in others they are highly restricted. Some countries force companies to compensate workers who lose their jobs because of relocation. This policy is common in European countries that have erected extensive social safety nets for unemployed workers.

Second, the greater mobility of labor today affects wages. Although labor laws in Europe are still more stringent than in the United States, the countries of the European Union (EU) are abolishing the requirement that workers from one EU nation must obtain visas to work in another. If workers in Spain cannot find work at home or if they feel that their current pay is inadequate, they are free to move to another EU country where unemployment is lower (say, Great Britain). A problem that plagues some European countries today is that they seem to be creating a group of people who are permanently unemployed.

QUICK STUDY 3

1. Identify the types of training and development used for (a) international managers and (b) nonmanagerial workers.
2. Describe each type of cultural training used to prepare managers for international assignments.
3. What variables are involved in decisions regarding employee compensation for (a) managers and (b) nonmanagerial workers?

Labor–Management Relations

labor–management relations
Positive or negative condition of relations between a company's management and its workers.

The positive or negative condition of relations between a company's management and its workers (labor) is referred to as **labor–management relations**. Cooperative relations between labor and management can give a firm a tremendous competitive advantage. When management and workers realize they depend on one another, the company is often better prepared to meet its goals and to surmount unexpected obstacles that may crop up. Giving workers a greater stake in the company—say, through profit-sharing plans—is one way to increase morale and generate commitment to improved quality and customer service.

Because relations between laborers and managers are human relations, they are rooted in culture and are often affected by political movements in a market. Large international companies tend to make high-level labor decisions at the home office because it gives them greater control over their network of production operations around the world—yet lower-level decisions are often left to managers in each country. In effect, this policy places decisions that have

Workers in Germany and France are typically protected by very powerful labor unions. In fact, German workers have a direct influence on company decisions through a plan called *codetermination*. Here, employees of EasyJet strike at the airport in Schoenefeld, Germany. Why do you think countries around the world differ in the amount of influence they give labor unions?

Source: Z1015/_Bernd Settnik/Newscom

a direct impact on workers' lives in the hands of experts in the local market. Such decisions might include the number of annual paid holidays, the length of maternity leave, and the provision of day-care facilities. Localizing such management decisions tends to contribute to better labor–management relations because managers familiar with local practices are better equipped to handle matters that affect workers personally.

Importance of Labor Unions

The strength of labor unions in a country where a company has operations is important to its performance and can even affect the selection of a location. Developing and emerging markets in Asia are a popular location for international companies. Some Asian governments appeal to international companies to locate facilities in their nations by promising to keep labor unions in check. But companies also find developed nations attractive if, for whatever reason, a cooperative atmosphere exists between company management and labor unions. In some Asian countries, especially Japan, a cultural emphasis on harmony and balanced interests discourages confrontation between labor and management.

Ireland became a favorite location for a toehold in the European Union (EU). The main attractions are productive labor, lower wages, and a reduced likelihood of disruptive strikes. Labor unions are not as strong there as they are on the continent, particularly in France and Germany. Nevertheless, Germany has not been immune to the trend of falling union membership. Union membership has dropped off in Germany over the past decade from about 12 million to about 8 million workers. The main reason for the decline is the lack of interest in union membership in the former East German territories. In addition, labor unions comprise only about 9 percent of the labor force in the United States today, compared with 36 percent 50 years ago.

Despite declines in union membership, labor in Germany exercises a good deal of power over management decisions. In fact, under a plan called *codetermination*, German workers enjoy a direct say in the strategies and policies of their employers. This plan allows labor representatives to participate in high-level company meetings by actually voting on proposed actions.

INTERNATIONAL LABOR MOVEMENTS The global activities of unions are making progress in areas such as improving the treatment of workers and reducing incidents involving child labor. But the efforts of separate national unions to increase their cooperation are somewhat less successful. Although unions in one nation might want to support their counterparts in another country, generating grassroots support is difficult for two reasons. First, events taking place in another country are difficult for many people to comprehend. Distance and cultural difference make it hard for people to understand others who live and work elsewhere.

Second, whether they realize it or not, workers in different countries sometimes compete against one another. For example, today firms can relocate internationally rather easily. Thus, labor unions in one country might offer concessions to attract the jobs that will be created by a new production facility. In this way, unions in different nations can wind up competing against one another. Some observers argue that this phenomenon creates downward pressure on both wages and union power worldwide.

QUICK STUDY 4

1. What is meant by the term *labor–management relations*?
2. Explain how labor–management relations differ around the world.

A Final Word

This chapter has concluded our survey of international business. We studied how firms, ranging from small and medium-sized businesses to large global companies, hire and manage their most important resource—their employees. We covered a great deal of territory in our tour of international business. We hope we piqued your interest in the global marketplace and in the activities of all types of international companies. Yet our learning does not end here. Each of us will continue to be exposed to international business in our daily lives—whether as consumers or as current or future business managers. We will continue to expand our knowledge of other national cultures, the international business environment, and how companies manage their international operations. We wish you well on your continued journey through this fascinating and dynamic subject!

Chapter Summary

MyManagementLab
Go to **mymanagementlab.com** to complete the problems marked with this icon .

1. Explain the three different types of staffing policies used by international companies.
   - *Ethnocentric staffing* means staffing operations outside the home country with home-country nationals; it can give a company tight control over subsidiary decision making.
   - *Polycentric staffing* means staffing operations with host-country natives; it can give subsidiaries some autonomy in decision making.
   - *Geocentric staffing* means staffing operations with the best-qualified individuals, regardless of nationality; it is typically reserved for top-level managers.
2. Describe the recruitment and selection issues facing international companies.
   - Large companies often recruit international managers from within the ranks of existing employees, but smaller companies may need to hire outside managers.
   - International students who have graduated from colleges abroad can be hired, trained locally, and posted in their home countries.
   - Local managerial talent may be recruited in the host country to obtain people with an understanding of the local culture and political system; this is often required when a company engages extensively in manufacturing or marketing abroad.
3. Discuss the importance of training and development programs, especially cultural training.
   - *Culture shock* refers to the psychological difficulties experienced when living in an unfamiliar culture; it is characterized by homesickness, irritability, confusion, aggravation, and depression.
   - *Reverse culture shock* is the psychological process of readapting to one's home culture.
   - *Cultural training* can reduce the effects of culture shock and reverse culture shock.
   - *Environmental briefings* and *cultural orientations* provide insight on local housing, health care, and political, economic, and social institutions.

- *Cultural assimilation* and *sensitivity training* explain the local values, attitudes, and customs, and they stress understanding local feelings and emotions.
- *Language training* provides specific, practical skills that allow employees to communicate in the local language.
- *Field experience* means visiting the culture for a brief period to begin growing accustomed to it.

4. Explain how companies compensate managers and workers in international markets.
   - An effective compensation policy takes into account local cultures, laws, and practices; key issues are base pay, bonuses, and fringe benefits.
   - Managerial compensation packages may need adjustment to reflect the local cost of living and, perhaps, the cost of education.
   - *Bonus payments* or hardship pay may be needed to entice managers to accept international assignments.
   - Nonmanagerial compensation levels can be influenced by wage rates in other countries.

5. Describe the importance of labor–management relations and how they differ around the world.
   - *Labor–management relations* are the positive or negative condition of relations between company management and its workers.
   - Good labor–management relations can help a company meet its goals and surmount unexpected obstacles.
   - Labor–management relations are rooted in culture and are often affected by political movements in the local market.
   - The strength of labor unions where a company operates can affect its performance and can affect site-selection decisions.

Talk It Over

✪1. Many Japanese companies use ethnocentric staffing policies in international operations. Why do you think Japanese companies prefer to have Japanese in top management positions? Would you recommend a change in this policy?

2. Did you ever experience culture shock? If so, in which country did it occur? What, if anything, did you do to overcome it? Did your methods work? Did you experience reverse culture shock on returning home?

Teaming Up

1. **Labor-Relations Project.** Suppose you and several of your classmates are the senior management team for a major automobile manufacturer. Among your company's worldwide operations are plants in Spain and Germany. Your company is considering closing these two plants and moving production to Poland in order to take advantage of lower wages. As a group, write a short report explaining how easy (or difficult) it will be for your company to close the plant and lay off workers in both Spain and Germany.

2. **Research Project.** Small and medium-sized businesses sometimes face significant obstacles when expanding operations abroad. Write a group report on the obstacles they face in the area of recruiting and selecting employees when first venturing internationally. Address specific issues such as financial constraints, a lack of contacts, cultural differences, legal issues, geographical distance, and so on.

Key Terms

culture shock (p. 401)
ethnocentric staffing (p. 396)
expatriates (p. 396)
geocentric staffing (p. 398)
human resource management (HRM) (p. 396)

human resource planning (p. 399)
labor–management relations (p. 406)
polycentric staffing (p. 398)
recruitment (p. 400)

reverse culture shock (p. 402)
selection (p. 400)
staffing policy (p. 396)

Take It to the Web

1. **Video Report.** Visit this book's channel on YouTube (www.YouTube.com/MyIBvideos). Click on "Videos" near the top of the page, and click on the set of videos labeled "Ch 16: Hiring and Managing Employees." Watch one video from the list, and then summarize it in a half-page report. Reflecting on the contents of this chapter, which aspects of hiring and managing employees can you identify in the video? How might a company engaged in international business act on the information contained in the video?

2. **Website Report.** Visit the website of the Intercultural Business Center (www.ib-c.com) and read about the cultural training services of this top-ranked company. One evaluative technique the firm offers is called the Global Business Competency Test that measures a person's aptitude for doing business globally.

   A British company recently found that the top three reasons people quit or under-perform are rooted in personality rather than skill, knowledge, or qualification. What do you think are the aspects of a person's personality that cause this to occur? Explain your answer. What advantages do you think global aptitude tests might offer companies doing business internationally?

   Personality testing in the workplace is widespread in Australia, Europe, and the United States, but it is just starting to catch on in Asia. Why do you think this is? Do you think the reason could be rooted in Asian societies and culture? Explain your answer.

   What personal characteristics do you think make someone better suited to doing business globally? Be specific. Do you think these characteristics are innate, or can they be learned?

Ethical Challenges

1. You are an expatriate manager at a manufacturing facility in Asia on your first assignment abroad. You are aware of increasing concern among your employees (mostly young women) about wages that barely permit them to live at subsistence level. The plant is not unionized, and you know that your superiors in your home country are not particularly supportive of efforts to organize workers. You also know that if workers vote to form a union and then demand higher wages, headquarters is likely to shift production elsewhere. If the plant were shut down, your employees would lose their jobs, and you would be transferred. Should you encourage or discourage your workers in their efforts to unionize? Explain your decision.

2. You are an assistant marketing manager for a financial services firm expanding operations in Latin America. You were sent to Mexico City, Mexico, in part because you double-majored in Spanish and marketing and spent a semester abroad there. Your company's policy is to provide you and your expatriate colleagues with hardship pay, a generous housing allowance, a company car, and a fund of several thousand dollars to be used at your discretion. You are quite comfortable living abroad, but you have some expatriate friends who have not adjusted so well. Every two months or so, they fly back home to visit friends and get a change of scenery. You are not homesick at all, but your friends want you to go with them on an upcoming holiday. What would you do? Would you dip into your discretionary funds and go along? Or would you remain in the community and do volunteer work with a local charity?

MyManagementLab

Go to **mymanagementlab.com** for Auto-graded writing questions as well as the following Assisted-graded writing questions:

16-1. What are some key reasons for keeping expatriate managers in top positions?

16-2. Suppose a company decides that it has made a mistake by hiring local personnel in a key Asian country. What are some potential problems that it will face if it decides to install or reinstate expatriate managers in these positions?

16-3. Mymanagementlab Only – comprehensive writing assignment for this chapter.

Practicing International Management Case

Expatriation or Discrimination?

One issue faced by companies with international operations is determining the right time to bring expatriate managers home, or "repatriate" them. Promoting host-country personnel into key managerial positions can boost morale and provide a sense of equal opportunity. Also, local managers often have keen insights into local business conditions and, therefore, a potential advantage when it comes to decision making. Moreover, by bringing expatriate managers home, firms can often save considerable amounts of money. In China, for example, compensation for an expatriate can cost between $200,000 and $300,000 per year; the total package includes both cost-of-living and hardship allowances of 15 to 20 percent each. By comparison, total compensation for a top-notch Chinese manager would be only about $50,000 per year.

Despite the benefits to be gained from turning over control to local managers, some industry experts warn that "localizing" too quickly can be a mistake. For example, as one expatriate manager in China put it, "Doing business the Chinese way is much less well-documented and can be dangerous. There is a serious risk when you give up financial control." Another problem is the fact that many expatriate managers are evaluated according to operating results rather than according to their efforts to train local managers.

The issue of expatriate assignments is not limited to emerging markets such as China. In developed countries, laying off employees or replacing local managers with persons from the home country can be controversial moves. For example, Japanese-owned Ricoh Corporation (www.ricoh.com) replaced a U.S. manager with a Japanese manager in charge of optical computer disc sales at its California File Products Division (FPD). After being laid off as a result of the move, Chet Mackentire sued his former employer for discrimination under Title VII of the Civil Rights Act of 1964. But Ricoh argued that Mackentire was laid off for business reasons, not because he was a Caucasian-American.

Mackentire lost his case. The court said that it found "no evidence to support Mackentire's theory that the layoff was discriminatory" and ruled that there was "substantial evidence that it was due to business necessity." Mackentire appealed the ruling but lost again. The appellate court wrote that Ricoh "offered affidavits stating that FPD was losing money, running into the millions of dollars annually. It also offered evidence that it reorganized the division to de-emphasize the product for which Mackentire was most responsible."

Thinking Globally

1. In addition to those mentioned in the case, what are some other advantages associated with the hiring of local managers in emerging markets?

2. What steps should a company take to ensure that, if taken to court, it can demonstrate that staffing cuts have not been discriminatory?

Source: "Staffing Globalization," *The Economist* (www.economist.com), June 24, 2006, pp. 77–80; James Harding, "When Expats Should Pack Their Bags," *Financial Times*, September 1, 1998, p. 10; C. K. Prahalad and Kenneth Lieberthal, "The End of Corporate Imperialism," *Harvard Business Review*, July–August 1998, pp. 68–79.

Endnotes

Chapter 1

1. Brent Schlender, "Apple's Not-so-Secret Weapon," *Fast Company*, September 2012, pp. 31–32; Kirsten Chang, "iPad Mini Should Drive Apple to $1001: Top Analyst," CNBC website (www.cnbc.com), July 5, 2012; Peter Burrows, "The First Five Years of Mass Obsession," *Bloomberg Businessweek*, June 25–July 1, 2012, pp. 34, 36; "When the Jobs Inspector Calls," *The Economist* (www.economist.com), March 31, 2012; Fred Vogelstein, "Mastering the Art of Disruption," *Fortune*, February 6, 2006, pp. 23–24.
2. Peter Burrows, "The First Five Years of Mass Obsession," *Bloomberg Businessweek*, June 25–July 1, 2012, pp. 34, 36.
3. Source: "Fortune Global 500: The World's Largest Corporations," *Fortune*, July 23, 2012, pp. F1–F7; *International Trade Statistics 2011* (Geneva, Switzerland: World Trade Organization, November 2011), Tables I.8 and I.10 (www.wto.org).
4. Innocentive website (www.innocentive.com).
5. "Fortune Global 500: The World's Largest Corporations," *Fortune*, July 23, 2012, pp. F1–F7.
6. Vellus Products Company website (www.vellus.com).
7. Weekend in Italy website (en.firenze.waf.it), select articles.
8. Moisés Naim, "Post-Terror Surprises," *Foreign Policy* (www.foreignpolicy.com), September 1, 2002.
9. Melanie Lee, "China's Internet Users Breach Half Billion Mark," *Reuters* (www.reuters.com), January 11, 2012.
10. Brundtland Commission, *Our Common Future* (New York: Oxford University Press, 1997).
11. Yvo de Boer et al., *Expect the Unexpected: Building Business Value in a Changing World* (Amstelveen, Netherlands: KPMG International Cooperative, 2012).
12. *The Simpsons* website (www.thesimpsons.com).
13. "The Doha Round: Dead Man Talking," *The Economist* (www.economist.com), April 28, 2011.
14. Peter Burrows, "A Videoconference on the Cheap," *Bloomberg Businessweek*, October 6, 2008, p. 56.
15. iMeet website (www.imeet.com).
16. For a discussion of each item of data contained in this index, see the detailed explanation of the KOF Index (http://globalization.kof.ethz.ch/static/pdf/method_2012.pdf).
17. This comparison between the first and second ages of globalization is drawn from Thomas L. Friedman, *The Lexus and the Olive Tree* (New York: Anchor Books, 2000), pp. xvi–xix.
18. "Economics A-Z," *The Economist* (www.economist.com).
19. Naomi Klein, "Outsourcing the Friedman," Naomi Klein's website (www.naomiklein.org), March 6, 2004.
20. "At the Front of the Back Office," *The Economist*, June 23, 2012, p. 68.

21. The results of these two studies are reported in Daniel W. Drezner, "Bottom Feeders," *Foreign Policy* (www.foreignpolicy.com), November 1, 2000.
22. M. Lundberg and L. Squire, *The Simultaneous Evolution of Growth and Inequality* (Washington, DC: World Bank, 1999).
23. David Dollar and Aart Kraay, *Growth Is Good for the Poor* (Washington, DC: World Bank, 2001), available at www.worldbank.org.
24. Studies cited in *Poverty in an Age of Globalization* (Washington, DC: World Bank, 2000).
25. As reported in "A Wealth of Data," *The Economist*, July 31, 2010, p. 62.
26. *World Economic Outlook* (Washington, DC: International Monetary Fund, April 2008), Figure in Box 5.1, "Financial Openness and GDP Growth," available at www.imf.org.
27. Xavier Sala-i-Martin, "The World Distribution of Income: Falling Poverty and … Convergence, Period," working paper, Columbia University website (www.columbia.edu), October 9, 2005.
28. Shaohua Chen and Martin Ravallion, "How Well Did the World's Poorest Fare in the 1990s?" *Review of Income and Wealth*, vol. 47, September 2003, pp. 283–300.
29. "Debt Relief under the Heavily Indebted Poor Countries (HIPC) Initiative," International Monetary Fund website (www.imf.org), March 2008.
30. "Undermining Sovereignty and Democracy," *The Ten Year Track Record of the North American Free Trade Agreement* (Washington, DC: Public Citizen's Global Trade Watch, 2004).
31. Stephen Krasner, "Sovereignty," *Foreign Policy*, January/February 2001, pp. 20–29.

Chapter 2

1. Lorraine Mirabella, "German Gummi Bear Maker Aims for Bigger Share of U.S. Market," *Baltimore Sun* (www.baltimoresun.com), April 7, 2012; Hans Greimel, "Gummi Bears Solve a Sticky Problem," *International Herald Tribune*, April 17, 2001, p. 14; Haribo website (www.haribo.com).
2. "Lady Gaga's Indonesia Concert Permit Denied," ABC News (www.abc.go.com), May 16, 2012.
3. Jack Ewing, "From Reality TV to Big-Screen Dreams," *Bloomberg Businessweek*, February 11, 2008, pp. 64–65.
4. Alibaba website (www.alibaba.com), various company reports.
5. "Tight-Pants Ban Begins in Indonesia District," *AZ Central* (www.azcentral.com), May 27, 2010.
6. Greg Burke, "Catholics Push Hyundai to Cancel Commercial," Fox News *Liveshots* Blog (http://liveshots.blogs.foxnews.com), June 14, 2010.
7. Susan Fenton, "Wanted: Manager, Chinese-Speaking Only," *Yahoo News* (www.yahoo.com), April 28, 2008.

8. "Habbo's Second Global Youth Survey Reveals the Digital Profiles of Teens Online," Habbo Press Release (www.habbo.com), March 4, 2008.

9. "Top Spanish Translation Blunders," SDL Blog (http://blog.sdl.com), January 4, 2010.

10. "Rakuten to Make English Official In-House Language by the End of 2012," *Japan Today* (www.japantoday.com), July 1, 2010.

11. Adam Aston, "Reading, Writing, and Rankings: America and the World," *Bloomberg Businessweek*, March 24, 2008, p. 15.

12. Susan Fenton, "Wanted: Manager, Chinese-Speaking Only," *Yahoo News* (www.yahoo.com), April 28, 2008.

13. Florence Kluckhohn and F. L. Strodtbeck, *Variations in Value Orientations* (Evanston, IL: Harper & Row, 1961).

14. Hofstede's original study has been criticized as having a Western bias, ignoring subcultures, and being outdated, as it was conducted in the 1960s and 1970s. See R. Mead, *International Management: Cross-Cultural Dimensions* (Oxford: Basil Blackwell, 1994), pp. 73–75.

15. Geert Hofstede, "The Cultural Relativity of Organizational Practices and Theories," *Journal of International Business Studies*, Fall 1983, pp. 75–89; Geert Hofstede's website (www.geert-hofstede.com).

Chapter 3

1. "Cola Wars, Continued: Good for You, Not for Shareholders," *The Economist* (www.economist.com), March 15, 2012; Nanette Byrnes, "Pepsi Brings in the Health Police," *Bloomberg Businessweek*, January 25, 2010, pp. 50–51; Bibhudatta Pradhan and Pooja Thakur, "PepsiCo to Invest $200 Million More in India," *Bloomberg Businessweek* (www.businessweek.com), January 9, 2010; PepsiCo website (www.pepsico.com), various reports.

2. Annette Weisbach, "Why Germans Want out of Google's Street View," CNBC website (www.cnbc.com), August 14, 2010.

3. "The PRI's Qualified Comeback," *The Economist*, July 7, 2012, pp. 36–37.

4. E. N. Hester, "Kidnap and Ransom Insurance to the Rescue," Insure.com website (www.insure.com), January 9, 2010.

5. "Corporate Stakes in Cuba," *Fortune*, May 5, 2008, p. 40.

6. "Argentina's Expropriation of Energy Company Only Isolates Country," *Globe and Mail* (www.theglobeandmail.com), April 18, 2012.

7. Shell website (www.shell.com).

8. *Eighth Annual BSA and IDC Global Software Piracy Study* (Washington, DC: Business Software Alliance, May 2011), pp. 8–9, available at www.bsa.org/globalstudy.

9. Peter Burrows, "Why China Is Finally Tackling Video Piracy," *Bloomberg Businessweek*, June 9, 2008, p. 73.

10. Ron Nurwisah, "Indonesian Smoking Toddler Cuts Back to 15 Cigarettes Daily," *National Post* (www.nationalpost.com), June 9, 2010.

11. Daniel Franklin, "Just Good Business," *The Economist*, Special Report on Corporate Social Responsibility, January 19, 2008, pp. 3–6.

12. Milton Friedman, "The Social Responsibility of Business Is to Increase Its Profits," *New York Times Magazine*, September 13, 1970, pp. 32–33, 122, 126.

13. Sarah Johnson, "You Complete My Audit," *CFO Magazine*, May 2010, p. 17; Nanette Byrnes, "Sarbanes-Oxley Lifts Some Directors' Pay Higher than $1 Million," *Bloomberg Businessweek* (www.businessweek.com), February 12, 2010.

14. Levi-Strauss website (www.levistrauss.com).

15. Daniel Franklin, "A Stitch in Time," *The Economist*, Special Report on Corporate Social Responsibility, January 19, 2008, pp. 12–14.

16. Starbucks website (www.starbucks.com).

17. Fair Trade USA website (www.fairtrade.org).

18. Carbon Footprint website (www.carbonfootprint.com).

19. Heather Green and Kerry Capell, "Carbon Confusion," *Bloomberg Businessweek* (www.businessweek.com), March 6, 2008.

20. Michelle Conlin, "Sorry, I Composted Your Memorandum," *Bloomberg Businessweek*, February 18, 2008, p. 60.

21. Alissa Walker, "Spin the Bottle," *Fast Company*, June 2008, pp. 54–55.

22. Jack Ewing, "The Wind at Germany's Back," *Bloomberg Businessweek*, February 11, 2008, p. 68.

Chapter 4

1. "Grow, Grow, Grow," *The Economist*, April 17, 2010, pp. 10–12; Reena Jana, "India's Next Global Export: Innovation," *Bloomberg Businessweek* (www.businessweek.com), December 2, 2009; Steve Hamm, "Outsourcing the Offshore Operations," *Bloomberg Businessweek* (www.businessweek.com), July 16, 2008; Infosys website (www.infosys.com), select reports.

2. "Not Waving. Perhaps Drowning," *The Economist*, May 29, 2010, pp. 23–25.

3. Martin Fackler, "A Capitalist Enclave in North Korea Survives," *New York Times* (www.nytimes.com), July 6, 2010.

4. "The World Turned Upside Down," *The Economist*, April 17, 2010, pp. 3–6.

5. "Economics Focus: Socialist Workers," *The Economist* (www.economist.com), June 10, 2010.

6. "First Break All the Rules," *The Economist*, April 17, 2010, pp. 6–8.

7. "Hong Kong: Democracy Denied," *The Economist* (www.economist.com), January 3, 2008.

8. "Economic and Financial Indicators," *The Economist*, July 14, 2012, p. 84.

9. Chris Prentice, "Shadow Economies on the Rise around the World," *Bloomberg Businessweek* (www.businessweek.com), July 29, 2010.

10. Daniel S. Levine, "Got a Spare Destroyer Lying Around? Make a Trade: Embracing Counter Trade as a Viable Option," *World Trade*, June 1997, pp. 34–35.

11. "Teachers Paid in Vodka," BBC website (www.bbc.co.uk).

12. Data obtained from Organisation for Cooperation and Development (OECD), "Statistics" section (www.oecd.org).

13. "Another BRIC in the Wall," *The Economist* (www.economist.com), April 21, 2008.
14. "Deadly Business in Moscow," *Bloomberg Businessweek*, March 1, 2010, pp. 22–23.
15. "Another Great Leap Forward?" *The Economist*, March 13, 2010, pp. 27–28.

Chapter 5

1. Stephanie Clifford and Stephanie Rosenbloom, "With Backdrop of Glamour, Wal-Mart Stresses Global Growth," *New York Times* (www.nytimes.com), June 4, 2010; Andrew Winston, "Wal-Mart's New Sustainability Mandate in China," *Bloomberg Businessweek* (www.businessweek.com), October 28, 2008; Walmart website (www.walmart.com), select fact sheets.
2. "Getting on the Fast Track: Small Business and International Trade," Small Business Survival Committee website (www.sbsc.org).
3. *International Trade Statistics 2011* (Geneva: World Trade Organization, November 2011), Tables I.8 and I.10, available at www.wto.org.
4. "Business in China: High Seas, High Prices," *The Economist* (www.economist.com), August 7, 2008.
5. Adam Smith, *The Wealth of Nations*, first published in 1776.
6. David Ricardo, *The Principles of Political Economy and Taxation*, first published in 1817.
7. Bertil Ohlin, *Interregional and International Trade* (Cambridge, MA: Harvard University Press, 1933).
8. Wassily Leontief, "Domestic Production and Foreign Trade: The American Capital Position Re-Examined," *Economia Internationale*, February 1954, pp. 3–32.
9. Raymond Vernon and Louis T. Wells Jr., *Economic Environment of International Business*, 7th ed. (Upper Saddle River, NJ: Prentice Hall, 1991).
10. Sébastien Miroudot and Norihiko Yamano, "Towards Measuring Trade in Value-Added and Other Indicators of Global Value Chains," Presentation at the World Bank, June 9–10, 2011.
11. Ingenico website (www.ingenico.com), select reports and press releases.
12. Elhanan Helpman and Paul Krugman, *Market Structure and Foreign Trade* (Cambridge, MA: MIT Press, 1985).
13. For a detailed discussion of the first-mover advantage and its process, see Alfred D. Chandler, *Scale and Scope* (New York: Free Press, 1990).
14. Michael E. Porter, *The Competitive Advantage of Nations* (New York: Free Press, 1990).
15. Michael E. Porter, "Clusters and the New Economics of Competition," *Harvard Business Review* (November–December 1998), pp. 77–90.

Chapter 6

1. Tom Lowry, "At Time Warner, Local Content, Global Profits," *Bloomberg Businessweek* (www.businessweek.com), February 3, 2010; Brooks Barnes, "Warner Shifts Web Course, Shouldering Video Costs," *New York Times* (www.nytimes.com), September 10, 2007; Time Warner website (www.timewarner.com), select reports.
2. David Leonhardt, "The Politics of Trade in Ohio," *New York Times* (www.nytimes.com), February 27, 2008.
3. "What You Don't Know About NAFTA," *Bloomberg Businessweek* (www.businessweek.com), March 18, 2008.
4. Arun Kumar, "Indian American Admits to Selling Dual-Use Items to India," *The Indian Star* (www.twocircles.net/node/55572), March 14, 2008.
5. "U.S. Is $500 Million Supermarket to Cuba," CNBC website (www.cnbc.com), May 28, 2010; "Big Brother's Shadow," *The Economist*, August 2, 2008, p. 42.
6. "The Chaebol Conundrum," *The Economist*, April 3, 2010, pp. 14–15.
7. Tariq Hussain, "What's a Chaebol to Do?" *Strategy & Business* (www.strategy-business.com), April 3, 2007.
8. "Signs of the Zeitgeist," *The Economist*, May 29, 2010, p. 52.
9. Julio Godoy, *Europe: Subsidies Feed Food Scarcity*, Global Policy Forum (www.globalpolicy.org), April 25, 2008.
10. Keith Bradsher, "Fuel Subsidies Overseas Take a Toll on U.S.," *New York Times* (www.nytimes.com), July 28, 2008.
11. These facts on the WTO are drawn from the WTO website (www.wto.org).
12. Daniel Ten Kate and Barry Porter, "Asean Sees Little Optimism on Doha Round Accord, Mustapa Says," *Bloomberg Businessweek* (www.businessweek.com), February 27, 2010.

Chapter 7

1. Alex Taylor III, "Das Auto Giant," *Fortune*, July 23, 2012, pp. 150–155; Mike Gavin, "Volkswagen Aims to Double China Capacity by 2013/14, CEO Says," *Bloomberg Businessweek* (www.businessweek.com), June 9, 2010; Nikki Tait, Bertrand Benoit, and Richard Milne, "Brussels Legal Threat to VW Law," *Financial Times* (www.ft.com), June 4, 2008; Volkswagen website (www.vw.com), select reports.
2. This section draws on information contained in the *World Investment Report 2012* (Geneva, Switzerland: UNCTAD, June 2012), Overview.
3. Raymond Vernon and Louis T. Wells Jr., *Economic Environment of International Business*, 7th ed. (Upper Saddle River, NJ: Prentice Hall, 1991).
4. John H. Dunning, "Toward an Eclectic Theory of International Production," *Journal of International Business Studies*, Spring–Summer 1980, pp. 9–31.
5. For an excellent discussion of the economic benefits provided by particular geographic locations, see Paul Krugman, "Increasing Returns and Economic Geography," *Journal of Political Economy*, June 1991, pp. 483–499.
6. *World Investment Report 2012* (Geneva, Switzerland: UNCTAD, June 2012), Overview, Table 5, p. 18.

Chapter 8

1. Toby Webb, "Nestlé + Greenpeace: A Model for Sustainable Sourcing of Palm Oil?" Triple Pundit website (www.triplepundit.com), May 19, 2012; Tom

Mulier, "Nestlé Targets Malnutrition to Fight Danone's Gains," *Bloomberg Businessweek* (www.businessweek .com), January 18, 2010; Thomas Mulier, "Nestlé Seeks Emerging Market Acquisitions, Spurning Cadbury," *Bloomberg Businessweek* (www.businessweek.com), January 7, 2010; Nestlé website (www.nestle.com), select reports and fact sheets.

2. *NAFTA after Five: The Impact of the North American Free Trade Agreement on Australia's Trade and Investment*, Australian Department of Foreign Affairs and Trade (www.dfat.gov.au/geo/americas/nafta).

3. Data obtained from the Office of the United States Trade Representative website (www.ustr.gov).

4. "The Dark Side of Globalization," *The Economist*, May 31, 2008, pp. 5–7.

5. "The ECB's Bond-Buying Plan," *The Economist*, September 15, 2012, p. 68.

6. Data obtained from United States–Mexico Chamber of Commerce website (www.usmcoc.org); *North American Free Trade Agreement (NAFTA)*, Office of the United States Trade Representative website (www.ustr.gov/trade-agreements/free-trade-agreements /north-american-free-trade-agreement-nafta).

7. Data obtained from Industry of Canada Strategis website (www.strategis.ic.gc.ca); *North American Free Trade Agreement (NAFTA)*, Office of the United States Trade Representative website (www .ustr.gov/trade-agreements/free-trade-agreements /north-american-free-trade-agreement-nafta).

8. Data obtained from Office of the United States Trade Representative website (www.ustr.gov).

9. Data obtained from the AFL-CIO website (www.aflcio.org).

10. *NAFTA: Myth vs. Facts*, Office of the United States Trade Representative (www.ustr.gov), March 2008.

11. Office of the United States Trade Representative (www.ustr.gov), select reports; U.S. Government Export Portal (www.export.gov), select reports.

Chapter 9

1. Kyo Sasaki, "Analyst: Nintendo Will Ship 4 Million Wii U Consoles to Retail," Wii U Daily website (www.wiiudaily.com), July 26, 2012; Martyn Williams, "Nintendo Records a Loss as DS Sales Plummet," *Bloomberg Businessweek* (www.businessweek.com), July 29, 2010; Matt Vella, "Wii Fit Puts the Fun in Fitness," *Bloomberg Businessweek* (www.businessweek.com), May 21, 2008; Nintendo website (www.nintendo.com), various articles and annual reports.

2. "Maul Street," *The Economist*, May 15, 2010, pp. 84–85.

3. "Shine A Light," *The Economist*, March 27, 2010, pp. 16–18.

4. "Assessing the Damage," *Euromoney* (www .euromoney.com).

5. Bank for International Settlements website (www.bis .org), Foreign Exchange Statistics section.

6. CME Group website (www.cmegroup.com).

7. Philadelphia Securities Exchange website (www.phlx.com).

Chapter 10

1. "The Euro: The Flight from Spain," *The Economist*, July 28, 2012, p. 10; Bradley Davis, "Euro Weakens as Debt Jitters Outweigh Data," *Wall Street Journal* (www.wsj.com), June 17, 2010; "Emergency Repairs," *The Economist*, May 15, 2010, pp. 77–79; "The Euro in the World," European Commission website (www.ec.europa.eu).

2. "The Big Mac Index: Calories and Currencies," *The Economist*, July 28, 2012, p. 66; "When the Chips Are Down," *The Economist*, July 24, 2010, p. 72.

3. International Monetary Fund website (www.imf.org), select reports.

4. *SDR Valuation*, International Monetary Fund website (www.imf.org).

5. Robert N. McCauley and Jens Zukunft, "The Asian Financial Crisis: International Liquidity Lessons," *BIS Quarterly Review* (www.bis.org), June 9, 2008.

6. "That Sinking Feeling," *The Economist*, May 22, 2010, pp. 75–76.

7. Antonia Oprita, "Double-Dip Risk Is Rising in the Euro Zone: Roubini," CNBC website (www.cnbc.com), June 15, 2010.

Chapter 11

1. "Malev Stops Flying: Survival of the Fittest," *The Economist* (www.economist.com), February 3, 2012; "Sackcloth and Ashes," *The Economist*, May 22, 2010, pp. 60–61; "Damp Squid," *The Economist* (www .economist.com), August 6, 2009; Phil Stewart, "Ryanair Gives Alitalia the Finger," *International Herald Tribune* (www.iht.com), July 25, 2008; Ryanair website (www.ryanair.com), select reports.

2. Bausch & Lomb website (www.bausch.com).

3. For an excellent discussion of this approach, see Michael E. Porter, *On Competition* (Boston: Harvard Business School Press, 2008).

4. The discussion of these strategies is based on Michael E. Porter, *Competitive Strategy* (New York: Free Press, 1980), pp. 34–46.

5. Johnson & Johnson website (www.jnj.com).

6. Norimitsu Onishi, "From Dung to Coffee Brew with No Aftertaste," *New York Times* (www.nytimes.com), April 17, 2010.

7. Bradley L. Kirkman and Debra L. Shapiro, "The Impact of Cultural Values on Employee Resistance to Teams," *Academy of Management Review*, vol. 22 (no. 3), 1997, pp. 730–757.

8. Ibid.

Chapter 12

1. Alistair Dawber, "British Rebound Gave Starbucks a Lift," *Bloomberg Businessweek* (www.businessweek .com), January 22, 2010; "Starbucks Fact Sheet" (www .starbucks.com), February 2008; Maria Bartiromo, "Howard Schultz on Reinventing Starbucks," *Bloomberg Businessweek* (www.businessweek.com), April 8, 2008; Starbucks website (www.starbucks.com), select reports.

2. Johny K. Johansson, Ilkka A. Ronkainen, and Michael R. Czinkota, "Negative Country-of-Origin Effects: The Case of the New Russia," *Journal of International Business Studies*, vol. 25 (no. 1), pp. 157–176.
3. This discussion is based on S. Tamer Cavusgil, "Measuring the Potential of Emerging Markets: An Indexing Approach," *Business Horizons*, January–February 1997, pp. 87–91; "Market Potential Indicators for Emerging Markets," Michigan State University CIBER (http://ciber.bus.msu.edu).
4. "The Future of Medicaid: Run for Cover," *The Economist* (www.economist.com), July 7, 2012.
5. Data obtained from *World Development Indicators Database* (www.worldbank.org).
6. Information obtained from the ProChile website (www.chileinfo.com).

Chapter 13

1. Erik Larson, "Marvel Sues over Copyright Claims by Artist's Heirs," *Bloomberg Businessweek* (www.businessweek.com), January 8, 2010; Ronald Grover, "Iron Man Spawns a Marvel of a Movie Studio," *Bloomberg Businessweek* (www.businessweek.com), April 29, 2008; Ronald Grover, "Spider-Man's Guardian Angels," *Bloomberg Businessweek* (www.businessweek.com), June 26, 2005; Marvel website (www.marvel.com), select reports.
2. David Ing, "Spain Proves Tough to Crack," *Hotel & Motel Management*, vol. 212 (no. 15), p. 8.
3. Laura Gatland, "Eastern Europe Eagerly Accepts U.S. Franchisors," *Franchise Times*, vol. 3 (no. 9), p. 17.
4. Frank H. Andorka Jr., "Microtel Introduces New-Construction Plan," *Hotel & Motel Management*, vol. 212 (no. 13), p. 1.
5. This classification is made in Peter Buckley and Mark Casson, "A Theory of Cooperation in International Business," in Farok J. Contractor and Peter Lorange (eds.), *Cooperative Strategies in International Business* (Lexington, MA: Lexington Books, 1988), pp. 31–53.
6. This section is based in part on Franklin R. Root, *Entry Strategies for International Markets* (Lexington, MA: Lexington Books, 1987), pp. 8–21.

Chapter 14

1. Alex Duff, "Red Bull's Mark Webber Wins Spanish Formula One Race," *Bloomberg Businessweek* (www.businessweek.com), May 9, 2010; Rob Taylor, "Red Bull Drink Lifts Stroke Risk: Australian Study," *Reuters* (www.reuters.com), August 14, 2008; "Skydiver in Record Channel Flight," *BBC News* (www.bbc.co.uk), July 31, 2003; Red Bull website (www.redbull.com), select reports.
2. To read the original, classic article, see Theodore Levitt, "The Globalization of Markets," *Harvard Business Review*, May–June 1983, pp. 92–102.

3. NameLab, Inc., website (www.namelab.com).
4. Alessandra Galloni, "Coca-Cola Tests the Waters with Localized Ads in Europe," *Wall Street Journal* (www.wsj.com), July 18, 2001.
5. This section draws on the classic discussion of these strategies in Warren J. Keegan, *Global Marketing Management*, 5th ed. (Upper Saddle River, NJ: Prentice Hall, 1995), pp. 489–494.
6. Muji website (www.muji.com), select reports.
7. Craig S. Smith, "In China, Some Distributors Have Really Cleaned Up with Amway," *Wall Street Journal*, August 4, 1997, p. B1.
8. "Laptops from Lapland," *The Economist*, September 6, 1997, pp. 67–68.

Chapter 15

1. *Auto Sales: Overview Charts*, *Wall Street Journal* website (www.wsj.com), August 1, 2012; "Global 500," *Fortune*, July 21, 2008, pp. 156–182; Toyota Peugeot Citroën Automobile website (www.tpca.cz); Toyota Motor Corporation website (www.toyota.co.jp), select reports.
2. This classic example is found in Robert B. Reich, *The Work of Nations* (New York: Vintage Books, 1992), p. 112.
3. InnoCentive website (www.innocentive.com).
4. Stefanie Olsen, "Venture Money Flows in India and China," *Bloomberg Businessweek* (www.businessweek.com), August 22, 2008.
5. "Depository Receipts Hit Record Trading Volume in First Half of 2008," *Reuters* (www.reuters.com), July 14, 2008.
6. Andy Serwer, "It's Big. It's German. It's SAP," *Fortune*, September 7, 1998, p. 191.

Chapter 16

1. "Global 500," *Fortune*, July 21, 2008, pp. 156–182; Peter Burrows, "High-Tech's 'Sweatshop' Wakeup Call," *Bloomberg Businessweek* (www.businessweek.com), June 14, 2006; Intel website (www.intel.com), select reports.
2. Barry Newman, "Expat Archipelago: The New Yank Abroad Is the 'Can-Do' Player in the Global Village," *Wall Street Journal*, December 12, 1995, p. A12.
3. Arik Hesseldahl, "Fixing Apple's 'Sweatshop' Woes," *Bloomberg Businessweek* (www.businessweek.com), June 28, 2006.
4. Mathew Simond, "Can Online Learning Be Cost-Effective?" *EzineArticles* (www.ezinearticles.com), March 3, 2008; Nina Silberstein, "On-the-Job Training Goes Online," *Online Degrees*, Fall/Winter 2007, pp. 30–32.
5. Stephen Dolainski, "Are Expats Getting Lost in the Translation?" *Workforce*, February 1997, pp. 32–39.
6. "Taxing Americans Abroad: Costing More over There," *The Economist* (www.economist.com), June 22, 2006, p. 78.

Glossary

Absolute advantage. Ability of a nation to produce a good more efficiently than any other nation.

Ad valorem tariff. Tariff levied as a percentage of the stated price of an imported product.

Administrative delays. Regulatory controls or bureaucratic rules designed to impair the flow of imports into a country.

Advance payment. Export/import financing in which an importer pays an exporter for merchandise before it is shipped.

Aesthetics. What a culture considers "good taste" in the arts, the imagery evoked by certain expressions, and the symbolism of certain colors.

Agents. Individuals or organizations that represent one or more indirect exporters in a target market.

American Depository Receipt (ADR). Certificate that trades in the United States and that represents a specific number of shares in a non–U.S. company.

Antidumping duty. Additional tariff placed on an imported product that a nation believes is being dumped on its market.

Antitrust (antimonopoly) laws. Laws designed to prevent companies from fixing prices, sharing markets, and gaining unfair monopoly advantages.

Arm's length price. Free-market price that unrelated parties charge one another for a specific product.

Attitudes. Positive or negative evaluations, feelings, and tendencies that individuals harbor toward objects or concepts.

Back-to-back loan. Loan in which a parent company deposits money with a host-country bank, which then lends the money to a subsidiary located in the host country.

Balance of payments. National accounting system that records all receipts coming into the nation and all payments to entities in other countries.

Barter. Exchange of goods or services directly for other goods or services without the use of money.

Base currency. The denominator in a quoted exchange rate, or the currency that is to be purchased with another currency.

Berne Convention. International treaty that protects copyrights.

Bill of lading. Contract between an exporter and a shipper that specifies merchandise destination and shipping costs.

Body language. Language communicated through unspoken cues, including hand gestures, facial expressions, physical greetings, eye contact, and the manipulation of personal space.

Bond. Debt instrument that specifies the timing of principal and interest payments.

Born global firm. Company that adopts a global perspective and engages in international business from or near its inception.

Brain drain. Departure of highly educated people from one profession, geographic region, or nation to another.

Brand name. Name of one or more items in a product line that identifies the source or character of the items.

Bretton Woods Agreement. Agreement (1944) among nations to create a new international monetary system based on the value of the U.S. dollar.

Buyback. Export of industrial equipment in return for products produced by that equipment.

Capacity planning. Process of assessing a company's ability to produce enough output to satisfy market demand.

Capital account. National account that records transactions involving the purchase and sale of assets.

Capital market. System that allocates financial resources in the form of debt and equity according to their most efficient uses.

Capital structure. Mix of equity, debt, and internally generated funds used to finance a company's activities.

Capitalism. Belief that ownership of the means of production belongs in the hands of individuals and private businesses.

Carbon footprint. Environmental impact of greenhouse gases (measured in units of carbon dioxide) that results from human activity.

Caste system. System of social stratification in which people are born into a social ranking, or caste, with no opportunity for social mobility.

Centrally planned economy. Economic system in which a nation's land, factories, and other economic resources are owned by the government, which plans nearly all economic activity.

Chains of command. Lines of authority that run from top management to individual employees and that specify internal reporting relationships.

Civil law. Legal system based on a detailed set of written rules and statutes that constitute a legal code.

Class system. System of social stratification in which personal ability and actions determine social status and mobility.

Clearing. Process of aggregating the currencies that one bank owes another and then carrying out the transaction.

Combination strategy. Strategy designed to mix growth, retrenchment, and stability strategies across a corporation's business units.

Common law. Legal system based on a country's legal history (tradition), past cases that have come before its courts (precedent), and how laws are applied in specific situations (usage).

Common market. Economic integration whereby countries remove all barriers to trade and to the movement of labor and capital among themselves and set a common trade policy against nonmembers.

Communication. System of conveying thoughts, feelings, knowledge, and information through speech, writing, and actions.

Communism. Belief that social and economic equality can be obtained only by establishing an all-powerful Communist Party and by granting the government ownership and control over all types of economic activity.

Comparative advantage. Inability of a nation to produce a good more efficiently than other nations but an ability to produce that good more efficiently than it does any other good.

Compound tariff. Tariff levied on an imported product and calculated partly as a percentage of its stated price and partly as a specific fee for each unit.

Confiscation. Forced transfer of assets from a company to the government without compensation.

Consumer panel. Research in which people record in personal diaries information on their attitudes, behaviors, or purchasing habits.

Convertible (hard) currency. Currency that trades freely in the foreign exchange market, with its price determined by the forces of supply and demand.

Copyright. Property right giving creators of original works the freedom to publish or dispose of them as they choose.

Core competency. Special ability of a company that competitors find extremely difficult or impossible to equal.

Corporate social responsibility. Practice of companies going beyond legal obligations to actively balance commitments to investors, customers, other companies, and communities.

Counterpurchase. Sale of goods or services to a country by a company that promises to make a future purchase of a specific product from the country.

Countertrade. Practice of selling goods or services that are paid for, in whole or in part, with other goods or services.

Countervailing duty. Additional tariff placed on an imported product that a nation believes is receiving an unfair subsidy.

Cross licensing. Practice by which companies use licensing agreements to exchange intangible property with one another.

Cross rate. Exchange rate calculated using two other exchange rates.

Cross-functional team. Team composed of employees who work at similar levels in different functional departments.

Cultural diffusion. Process whereby cultural traits spread from one culture to another.

Cultural imperialism. Replacement of one culture's traditions, folk heroes, and artifacts with substitutes from another.

Cultural literacy. Detailed knowledge about a culture that enables a person to work happily and effectively within it.

Cultural trait. Anything that represents a culture's way of life, including gestures, material objects, traditions, and concepts.

Culture. Set of values, beliefs, rules, and institutions held by a specific group of people.

Culture shock. Psychological process affecting people living abroad that is characterized by homesickness, irritability, confusion, aggravation, and depression.

Currency arbitrage. Instantaneous purchase and sale of a currency in different markets for profit.

Currency board. Monetary regime based on an explicit commitment to exchange domestic currency for a specified foreign currency at a fixed exchange rate.

Currency controls. Restrictions on the convertibility of a currency into other currencies.

Currency futures contract. Contract requiring the exchange of a specified amount of currency on a specified date at a specified exchange rate, with all conditions fixed and not adjustable.

Currency hedging. Practice of insuring against potential losses that result from adverse changes in exchange rates.

Currency option. Right, or option, to exchange a specified amount of a currency on a specified date at a specified rate.

Currency speculation. Purchase or sale of a currency with the expectation that its value will change and generate a profit.

Currency swap. Simultaneous purchase and sale of foreign exchange for two different dates.

Current account. National account that records transactions involving the export and import of goods and services, income receipts on assets abroad, and income payments on foreign assets inside the country.

Current account deficit. When a country imports more goods and services and pays more abroad than it exports and receives from abroad.

Current account surplus. When a country exports more goods and services and receives more income from abroad than it imports and pays abroad.

Customs. Habits or ways of behaving in specific circumstances that are passed down through generations in a culture.

Customs union. Economic integration whereby countries remove all barriers to trade among themselves and set a common trade policy against nonmembers.

Debt. Loan in which the borrower promises to repay the borrowed amount (the principal) plus a predetermined rate of interest.

Demand. Quantity of a good or service that buyers are willing to purchase at a specific selling price.

Democracy. Political system in which government leaders are elected directly by the wide participation of the people or by their representatives.

Derivative. Financial instrument whose value derives from other commodities or financial instruments.

Devaluation. Intentionally lowering the value of a nation's currency.

Developed country. Country that is highly industrialized and highly efficient, and whose people enjoy a high quality of life.

Developing country. Nation that has a poor infrastructure and extremely low personal incomes. Also called less-developed countries.

Differentiation strategy. Strategy in which a company designs its products to be perceived as unique by buyers throughout its industry.

Direct exporting. Practice by which a company sells its products directly to buyers in a target market.

Distribution. Planning, implementing, and controlling the physical flow of a product from its point of origin to its point of consumption.

Documentary collection. Export/import financing in which a bank acts as an intermediary without accepting financial risk.

Draft (bill of exchange). Document ordering an importer to pay an exporter a specified sum of money at a specified time.

Dual pricing. Policy in which a product has a different selling price (typically higher) in export markets than it has in the home market.

Dumping. Exporting a product at a price either lower than the price that the product normally commands in its domestic market or lower than the cost of production.

E-business (e-commerce). Use of computer networks to purchase, sell, or exchange products; to service customers; and to collaborate with partners.

Eclectic theory. Theory stating that firms undertake foreign direct investment when the features of a particular location combine with ownership and internalization advantages to make a location appealing for investment.

Economic development. Measure for gauging the economic well-being of one nation's people as compared with that of another nation's people.

Economic system. Structure and processes that a country uses to allocate its resources and conduct its commercial activities.

Economic transition. Process by which a nation changes its fundamental economic organization and creates new free-market institutions.

Economic union. Economic integration whereby countries remove barriers to trade and the movement of labor and capital among members, set a common trade policy against nonmembers, and coordinate their economic policies.

Efficient market view. View that prices of financial instruments reflect all publicly available information at any given time.

Embargo. Complete ban on trade (imports and exports) in one or more products with a particular country.

Emerging markets. Newly industrialized countries plus those with the potential to become newly industrialized.

Entry mode. Institutional arrangement by which a firm gets its products, technologies, human skills, or other resources into a market.

Environmental scanning. Ongoing process of gathering, analyzing, and dispensing information for tactical or strategic purposes.

Equity. Part ownership of a company in which the equity holder participates with other part owners in the company's financial gains and losses.

Ethical behavior. Personal behavior in accordance with guidelines for good conduct or morality.

Ethnocentric staffing. Staffing policy in which individuals from the home country manage operations abroad.

Ethnocentricity. Belief that one's own ethnic group or culture is superior to that of others.

Eurobond. Bond issued outside the country in whose currency it is denominated.

Eurocurrency market. Market consisting of all the world's currencies (referred to as "Eurocurrency") that are banked outside their countries of origin.

European monetary union. European Union plan that established its own central bank and currency.

Exchange rate. Rate at which one currency is exchanged for another.

Exchange-rate risk (foreign exchange risk). Risk of adverse changes in exchange rates.

Exclusive channel. Distribution channel in which a manufacturer grants the right to sell its product to only one or a limited number of resellers.

Expatriates. Citizens of one country who are living and working in another.

Export management company (EMC). Company that exports products on behalf of indirect exporters.

Export trading company (ETC). Company that provides services to indirect exporters in addition to activities related directly to clients' exporting activities.

Exports. Goods and services sold abroad and sent out of a country.

Expropriation. Forced transfer of assets from a company to the government with compensation.

Facilities layout planning. Deciding the spatial arrangement of production processes within production facilities.

Facilities location planning. Selecting the location for production facilities.

Factor proportions theory. Trade theory stating that countries produce and export goods that require resources (factors) that are abundant and import goods that require resources in short supply.

First-mover advantage. Economic and strategic advantage gained by being the first company to enter an industry.

Fisher effect. Principle that the nominal interest rate is the sum of the real interest rate and the expected rate of inflation over a specific period.

Fixed (tangible) assets. Company assets such as production facilities, inventory warehouses, retail outlets, and production and office equipment.

Fixed exchange-rate system. System in which the exchange rate for converting one currency into another is fixed by international agreement.

Focus group. Unstructured but in-depth interview of a small group of individuals (8–12 people) by a moderator in order to learn the group's attitudes about a company or its product.

Focus strategy. Strategy in which a company focuses on serving the needs of a narrowly defined market segment by being the low-cost leader, by differentiating its product, or both.

Folk custom. Behavior, often dating back several generations, that is practiced by a homogeneous group of people.

Foreign bond. Bond sold outside the borrower's country and denominated in the currency of the country in which it is sold.

Foreign Corrupt Practices Act. A 1977 statute that forbids U.S. companies from bribing government officials or political candidates in other nations.

Foreign direct investment. Purchase of physical assets or a significant amount of the ownership (stock) of a company in another country to gain a measure of management control.

Foreign exchange market. Market in which currencies are bought and sold and their prices determined.

Foreign trade zone (FTZ). Designated geographic region through which merchandise is allowed to pass with lower customs duties (taxes) and/or fewer customs procedures.

Forward contract. Contract that requires the exchange of an agreed-on amount of a currency on an agreed-on date at a specified exchange rate.

Forward market. Market for currency transactions at forward rates.

Forward rate. Exchange rate at which two parties agree to exchange currencies on a specified future date.

Franchising. Practice by which one company (the franchiser) supplies another (the franchisee) with intangible property and other assistance over an extended period.

Free float system. Exchange-rate system in which currencies float freely against one another, without governments intervening in currency markets.

Free trade. Pattern of imports and exports that occurs in the absence of trade barriers.

Free trade area. Economic integration whereby countries seek to remove all barriers to trade among themselves but where each country determines its own barriers against nonmembers.

Freight forwarder. Specialist in export-related activities such as customs clearing, tariff schedules, and shipping and insurance fees.

Fundamental analysis. Technique that uses statistical models based on fundamental economic indicators to forecast exchange rates.

Fundamental disequilibrium. Economic condition in which a trade deficit causes a permanent negative shift in a country's balance of payments.

GDP or GNP per capita. Nation's GDP or GNP divided by its population.

General Agreement on Tariffs and Trade (GATT). Treaty designed to promote free trade by reducing both tariffs and nontariff barriers to international trade.

Geocentric staffing. Staffing policy in which the best-qualified individuals, regardless of nationality, manage operations abroad.

Global matrix structure. Organizational structure that splits the chain of command between product and area divisions.

Global product structure. Organizational structure that divides worldwide operations according to a company's product areas.

Global strategy. Offering the same products using the same marketing strategy in all national markets.

Global team. Team of top managers from both headquarters and international subsidiaries who meet to develop solutions to company-wide problems.

Globalization. Trend toward greater economic, cultural, political, and technological interdependence among national institutions and economies.

Gold standard. International monetary system in which nations link the value of their paper currencies to specific values of gold.

Gross domestic product (GDP). Value of all goods and services produced by a domestic economy over a one-year period.

Gross national product (GNP). Value of all goods and services produced by a country's domestic and international activities over a one-year period.

Growth strategy. Strategy designed to increase the scale (size of activities) or scope (kinds of activities) of a corporation's operations.

Hofstede framework. Framework for studying cultural differences along five dimensions, such as individualism versus collectivism and equality versus inequality.

Human development index (HDI). Measure of the extent to which a government equitably provides its people with a long and healthy life, an education, and a decent standard of living.

Human resource management (HRM). Process of staffing a company and ensuring that employees are as productive as possible.

Human resource planning. Process of forecasting a company's human resource needs and its supply.

Imports. Goods and services purchased abroad and brought into a country.

Income elasticity. Sensitivity of demand for a product relative to changes in income.

Indirect exporting. Practice by which a company sells its products to intermediaries who then resell to buyers in a target market.

Industrial property. Patents and trademarks.

Inefficient market view. View that prices of financial instruments do not reflect all publicly available information.

Intellectual property. Property that results from people's intellectual talent and abilities.

Intensive channel. Distribution channel in which a producer grants the right to sell its product to many resellers.

Interbank interest rates. Interest rates that the world's largest banks charge one another for loans.

Interbank market. Market in which the world's largest banks exchange currencies at spot and forward rates.

Interest arbitrage. Profit-motivated purchase and sale of interest-paying securities denominated in different currencies.

International area structure. Organizational structure that organizes a company's entire global operations into countries or geographic regions.

International bond market. Market consisting of all bonds sold by issuing companies, governments, or other organizations outside their own countries.

International business. Commercial transaction that crosses the borders of two or more nations.

International capital market. Network of individuals, companies, financial institutions, and governments that invest and borrow across national boundaries.

International division structure. Organizational structure that separates domestic from international business activities by creating a separate international division with its own manager.

International equity market. Market consisting of all stocks bought and sold outside the issuer's home country.

International Fisher effect. Principle that a difference in nominal interest rates supported by two countries' currencies will cause an equal but opposite change in their spot exchange rates.

International Monetary Fund. Agency created to regulate fixed exchange rates and to enforce the rules of the international monetary system.

International monetary system. Collection of agreements and institutions that govern exchange rates.

International product life cycle. Theory stating that a company begins by exporting its product and then later undertakes foreign direct investment as the product moves through its life cycle.

International trade. Purchase, sale, or exchange of goods and services across national borders.

Jamaica Agreement. Agreement (1976) among IMF members to formalize the existing system of floating exchange rates as the new international monetary system.

Joint venture. Separate company that is created and jointly owned by two or more independent entities to achieve a common business objective.

Just-in-time (JIT) manufacturing. Production technique in which inventory is kept to a minimum and inputs to the production process arrive exactly when they are needed.

Kluckhohn–Strodtbeck framework. Framework for studying cultural differences along six dimensions, such as focus on past or future events and belief in individual or group responsibility for personal well-being.

Labor–management relations. Positive or negative condition of relations between a company's management and its workers.

Law of one price. Principle that an identical item must have an identical price in all countries when the price is expressed in a common currency.

Legal system. Set of laws and regulations, including the processes by which a country's laws are enacted and enforced and the ways in which its courts hold parties accountable for their actions.

Letter of credit. Export/import financing in which the importer's bank issues a document stating that the bank will pay the exporter when the exporter fulfills the terms of the document.

Licensing. Practice by which one company owning intangible property (the licensor) grants another firm (the licensee) the right to use that property for a specified period of time.

Lingua franca. Third or "link" language understood by two parties who speak different native languages.

Liquidity. Ease with which bondholders and shareholders may convert their investments into cash.

Lobbying. Policy of hiring people to represent a company's views on political matters.

Local content requirements. Laws stipulating that a specified amount of a good or service be supplied by producers in the domestic market.

Location economies. Economic benefits derived from locating production activities in optimal locations.

Logistics. Management of the physical flow of products from the point of origin as raw materials to end users as finished products.

Low-cost leadership strategy. Strategy in which a company exploits economies of scale to have the lowest cost structure of any competitor in its industry.

Make-or-buy decision. Deciding whether to make a component or to buy it from another company.

Managed float system. Exchange-rate system in which currencies float against one another, with governments intervening to stabilize their currencies at particular target exchange rates.

Management contract. Practice by which one company supplies another with managerial expertise for a specific period of time.

Manners. Appropriate ways of behaving, speaking, and dressing in a culture.

Market economy. Economic system in which the majority of a nation's land, factories, and other economic resources are privately owned, either by individuals or businesses.

Market imperfections. Theory stating that when an imperfection in the market makes a transaction less efficient than it could be, a company will undertake foreign direct investment to internalize the transaction and thereby remove the imperfection.

Market power. Theory stating that a firm tries to establish a dominant market presence in an industry by undertaking foreign direct investment.

Market research. Collection and analysis of information used to assist managers in making informed decisions.

Marketing communication. Process of sending promotional messages about products to target markets.

Material culture. All the technology used in a culture to manufacture goods and provide services.

Mercantilism. Trade theory that nations should accumulate financial wealth, usually in the form of gold, by encouraging exports and discouraging imports.

Mission statement. Written statement of why a company exists and what it plans to accomplish.

Mixed economy. Economic system in which land, factories, and other economic resources are rather equally split between private and government ownership.

Multinational corporation (MNC). Business that has direct investments abroad in multiple countries.

Multinational (multidomestic) strategy. Adapting products and their marketing strategies in each national market to suit local preferences.

National competitive advantage theory. Trade theory stating that a nation's competitiveness in an industry depends on the capacity of the industry to innovate and upgrade.

Nationalism. Devotion of a people to their nation's interests and advancement.

Nationalization. Government takeover of an entire industry.

New trade theory. Trade theory stating that (1) there are gains to be made from specialization and increasing economies of scale, (2) the companies first to market can create barriers to entry, and (3) government may play a role in assisting its home companies.

Newly industrialized country (NIC). Country that has recently increased the portion of its national production and exports derived from industrial operations.

Normal trade relations (formerly "most favored nation status"). Requirement that WTO members extend the same favorable terms of trade to all members that they extend to any single member.

Offset. Agreement that a company will offset a hard-currency sale to a nation by making a hard-currency purchase of an unspecified product from that nation in the future.

Offshore financial center. Country or territory whose financial sector features very few regulations and few, if any, taxes.

Open account. Export/import financing in which an exporter ships merchandise and later bills the importer for its value.

Organizational structure. Way in which a company divides its activities among separate units and coordinates activities among those units.

Outsourcing. Practice of buying from another company a good or service that is part of a company's value-added activities.

Over-the-counter (OTC) market. Decentralized exchange encompassing a global computer network of foreign exchange traders and other market participants.

Patent. Property right granted to the inventor of a product or process that excludes others from making, using, or selling the invention.

Planning. Process of identifying and selecting an organization's objectives and deciding how the organization will achieve those objectives.

Political risk. Likelihood that a society will undergo political changes that negatively affect local business activity.

Political system. Structures, processes, and activities by which a nation governs itself.

Political union. Economic and political integration whereby countries coordinate aspects of their economic *and* political systems.

Polycentric staffing. Staffing policy in which individuals from the host country manage operations abroad.

Popular custom. Behavior shared by a heterogeneous group or by several groups.

Portfolio investment. Investment that does not involve obtaining a degree of control in a company.

Price controls. Upper or lower limits placed on the prices of products sold within a country.

Primary market research. Process of collecting and analyzing original data and applying the results to current research needs.

Private sector. Segment of the economic environment comprising independently owned firms that seek to earn profits.

Privatization. Policy of selling government-owned economic resources to private operators.

Process planning. Deciding the process that a company will use to create its product.

Product liability. Responsibility of manufacturers, sellers, individuals, and others for damage, injury, or death caused by defective products.

Promotion mix. Efforts by a company to reach distribution channels and to target customers through communications, such as personal selling, advertising, public relations, and direct marketing.

Property rights. Legal rights to resources and any income they generate.

Pull strategy. Promotional strategy designed to create buyer demand that will encourage distribution channel members to stock a company's product.

Purchasing power. Value of goods and services that can be purchased with one unit of a country's currency.

Purchasing power parity (PPP). Relative ability of two countries' currencies to buy the same "basket" of goods in those two countries.

Push strategy. Promotional strategy designed to pressure distribution channel members to carry a product and to promote it to final users of the product.

Quota. Restriction on the amount (measured in units or weight) of a good that can enter or leave a country during a certain period of time.

Quoted currency. The numerator in a quoted exchange rate, or the currency with which another currency is to be purchased.

Rationalized production. System of production in which each of a product's components is produced where the cost of producing that component is lowest.

Recruitment. Process of identifying and attracting a qualified pool of applicants for vacant positions.

Regional economic integration (regionalism). Process whereby countries in a geographic region cooperate to reduce or eliminate barriers to the international flow of products, people, or capital.

Representative democracy. Democracy in which citizens elect individuals from their groups to represent their political views.

Retrenchment strategy. Strategy designed to reduce the scale or scope of a corporation's businesses.

Revaluation. Intentionally raising the value of a nation's currency.

Revenue. Money earned from the sale of goods and services.

Reverse culture shock. Psychological process of readapting to one's home culture.

Secondary market research. Process of obtaining information that already exists within the company or that can be obtained from outside sources.

Secular totalitarianism. Political system in which leaders rely on military and bureaucratic power.

Securities exchange. Exchange specializing in currency futures and options transactions.

Securitization. Unbundling and repackaging of hard-to-trade financial assets into more liquid, negotiable, and marketable financial instruments (or *securities*).

Selection. Process of screening and hiring the best-qualified applicants with the greatest performance potential.

Self-managed team. Team in which the employees from a single department take on the responsibilities of their former supervisors.

Smithsonian Agreement. Agreement (1971) among IMF members to restructure and strengthen the international monetary system created at Bretton Woods.

Social group. Collection of two or more people who identify and interact with each other.

Social mobility. Ease with which individuals can move up or down a culture's "social ladder."

Social stratification. Process of ranking people into social layers or classes.

Social structure. A culture's fundamental organization, including its groups and institutions, its system of social positions and their relationships, and the process by which its resources are distributed.

Socialism. Belief that social and economic equality is obtained through government ownership and regulation of the means of production.

Special drawing right (SDR). IMF asset whose value is based on a "weighted basket" of four currencies.

Specific tariff. Tariff levied as a specific fee for each unit (measured by number, weight, etc.) of an imported product.

Spot market. Market for currency transactions at spot rates.

Spot rate. Exchange rate requiring delivery of the traded currency within two business days.

Stability strategy. Strategy designed to guard against change and used by corporations to avoid either growth or retrenchment.

Staffing policy. Customary means by which a company staffs its offices.

Stakeholders. All parties, ranging from suppliers and employees to stockholders and consumers, who are affected by a company's activities.

Stock. Shares of ownership in a company's assets that give shareholders a claim on the company's future cash flows.

Strategic alliance. Relationship whereby two or more entities cooperate (but do not form a separate company) to achieve the strategic goals of each.

Strategy. Set of planned actions taken by managers to help a company meet its objectives.

Subculture. A group of people who share a unique way of life within a larger, dominant culture.

Subsidy. Financial assistance to domestic producers in the form of cash payments, low-interest loans, tax breaks, product price supports, or other forms.

Supply. Quantity of a good or service that producers are willing to provide at a specific selling price.

Survey. Research in which an interviewer asks current or potential buyers to answer written or verbal questions in order to obtain facts, opinions, or attitudes.

Sustainability. Development that meets the needs of the present without compromising the ability of future generations to meet their own needs.

Switch trading. Practice in which one company sells to another its obligation to make a purchase in a given country.

Tariff. Government tax levied on a product as it enters or leaves a country.

Tariff-quota. Lower tariff rate for a certain quantity of imports and a higher rate for quantities that exceed the quota.

Technical analysis. Technique that uses charts of past trends in currency prices and other factors to forecast exchange rates.

Technological dualism. Use of the latest technologies in some sectors of the economy coupled with the use of outdated technologies in other sectors.

Theocracy. Political system in which a country's religious leaders are also its political leaders.

Theocratic law. Legal system based on religious teachings.

Theocratic totalitarianism. Political system under the control of totalitarian religious leaders.

Topography. All the physical features that characterize the surface of a geographic region.

Total quality management (TQM). Company-wide commitment to meet or exceed customer expectations through continuous quality improvement efforts and processes.

Totalitarian system. Political system in which individuals govern without the support of the people, tightly control people's lives, and do not tolerate opposing viewpoints.

Trade creation. Increase in the level of trade between nations that results from regional economic integration.

Trade deficit. Condition that results when the value of a country's imports is greater than the value of its exports.

Trade diversion. Diversion of trade away from nations not belonging to a trading bloc and toward member nations.

Trade mission. International trip by government officials and businesspeople that is organized by agencies of national or provincial governments for the purpose of exploring international business opportunities.

Trade show. Exhibition at which members of an industry or group of industries showcase their latest products, study activities of rivals, and examine recent trends and opportunities.

Trade surplus. Condition that results when the value of a nation's exports is greater than the value of its imports.

Trademark. Property right in the form of words or symbols that distinguish a product and its manufacturer.

Transfer price. Price charged for a good or service transferred among a company and its subsidiaries.

Turnkey (build–operate–transfer) project. Practice by which one company designs, constructs, and tests a production facility for a client firm.

United Nations (UN). International organization formed after World War II to provide leadership in fostering peace and stability around the world.

Value added tax (VAT). Tax levied on each party that adds value to a product throughout its production and distribution.

Value-chain analysis. Process of dividing a company's activities into primary and support activities and identifying those that create value for customers.

Value density. Value of a product relative to its weight and volume.

Values. Ideas, beliefs, and customs to which people are emotionally attached.

Vehicle currency. Currency used as an intermediary to convert funds between two other currencies.

Venture capital. Financing obtained from investors who believe that the borrower will experience rapid growth and who receive equity (part ownership) in return.

Vertical integration. Extension of company activities into stages of production that provide a firm's inputs (backward integration) or absorb its output (forward integration).

Voluntary export restraint (VER). Unique version of export quota that a nation imposes on its exports, usually at the request of an importing nation.

Wholly owned subsidiary. Facility entirely owned and controlled by a single parent company.

World Bank. Agency created to provide financing for national economic development efforts.

World Trade Organization (WTO). International organization that enforces the rules of international trade.

Worldwide pricing. Policy in which one selling price is established for all international markets.

Name/Company Index

Subject Index

This index contains concepts, countries, organizations, and agencies. Page numbers in **bold** indicate maps.